ALL the BOOKS and CHAPTERS
of the BIBLE

ALL the BOOKS and CHAPTERS of the BIBLE

COMBINATION OF BIBLE STUDY AND DAILY MEDITATION PLAN

by
DR. HERBERT LOCKYER, F.R.G.S.

Read a Bible chapter a day,
To keep all doubt away.

ZONDERVAN PUBLISHING HOUSE
GRAND RAPIDS   MICHIGAN

Dedicated to

My Gifted Literary Typist
E. R. JENNINGS
whose ability to transform
my almost unreadable notebooks
into attractive manuscript form
is deeply appreciated.

CONTENTS

INTRODUCTION

The Bible, as we all know, is made up of 1189 chapters, 773,746 words. The Old Testament has 929 chapters and the New Testament 260 chapters. We know that the longest chapter is Psalm 119, and the shortest, Psalm 117, which is also the middle chapter of the Bible. These chapters vary considerably in length, and the relative size of a book is indicated by the number of pages rather than by the number of chapters. For instance, *Ecclesiastes* has 12 chapters but only nine pages, whereas *Daniel* has 12 chapters and twice the number of pages – 18 in the English Bible.

Accustomed as we are in following the chapters and verses making up the books of the Bible, it is hard for us to realize that the original Scriptures had no such division. The first five books of the Bible, from Genesis to Deuteronomy, comprised one roll, scroll or book, and are thus referred to as *The Book of Moses*. Isaiah, given as 66 chapters, was one scroll or unbroken narrative. When, then, did this breaking up of the books of the Bible begin? Up until A.D. 1200 no translated copies of Scripture contained any of these somewhat tantalizing and far from happily arranged chapters and verses.

Their commencement is traced to Cardinal Hugo who was the first to divide the Old Testament into chapters for the purpose of a Latin concordance he prepared. The New Testament was similarly divided by Hugo de St. Cher about 1240. The Septuagint arranges and titles the Old Testament books the same as is found in our Bible. The division of Old Testament chapters into verses came about 300 years later by Rabbi Mordecai Nathan in order to assist in the study of the Hebrew Bible and thereby simplify his work. These divisions were adopted by Robert Stephens, a renowned French printer and Bible publisher in his edition of the Vulgate Version in A.D. 1555 and were transferred to the Authorized or King James Version in 1611. Stephens supplied the verses for the New Testament which were transferred to the English Version in Geneva in A.D. 1560. Until the end of the 16th century the whole Bible was divided into chapters, but only the Old Testament into verses.

While the thousand or more chapters provide a convenient arrangement for reference they have serious drawbacks. In many instances carelessness characterizes the division of the chapters of a book. Ellicott remarks, "In the division of our Bible into chapters, with a carelessness only equalled by that perversity which has formed the ninth chapter of Isaiah out of the end and the beginning of two incongruous prophecies, the seventh day's rest is separated from the account of six working days, thus the very purpose of the narrative is concealed." Thus the main thought is broken by these divisions and one often fails to grasp the writer's message.

The two Books of Samuel, and of Kings, and of Chronicles were originally one book each with no chapters or verses. Often the separation of these books in pairs is forced, and tends to destroy the connection. It would have been better if the original arrangement had been adhered to. Several years ago, the Oxford University Press issued the King James Version of the Bible in eight volumes so that it could be read without any chapters, verses or references whatever.

A danger to guard against in studying a chapter is that of dealing with it as being a complete embodiment in itself. It is but part of the whole book, and must be dealt with as a part of the whole. Very seldom do you find a theme exhausted in a single chapter. While, for devotional purposes, we have separated the chapters and commented upon them, in Bible study work any chapter considered must be dealt with what precedes and follows it, and also in the light of the Bible as a whole. It is only thus that we can rightly divide the entire Word of Truth.

A word of explanation is necessary as to the presence of the writer's comments alongside of indicated chapters. One of the most reliable of American prophetic magazines, which, in its days enjoyed a wide circulation, was *Our Hope* which was owned and edited by Dr. Arno C. Gaebelein. When this renowned expositor was called home, his gifted son, Dr. Frank E. Gaebelein inherited the journal and Dr. E. Schuyler English became its editor. Ultimately the magazine was incorporated with *Eternity*, during the time the late Dr. Donald G. Barnhouse was its editor.

In 1948, my good friend, Schuyler English, asked me to write a series of daily devotional readings for *Our Hope,* and consenting, we chose the general title of *Daily Bible Treasury* and decided on a chapter-by-chapter commentary on all the chapters of the Bible — a task taking almost three years to cover. These comments have been revived and revised, and given the addition of a brief synopsis of each book of the Bible. A footnote to the original readings ran — "As a stimulus to the knowledge of the Word of God and consequent spiritual growth, the reader is urged to turn to the assigned portion in the Bible and to read it before making use of these Comments" — which counsel is herewith reiterated.

Actually, this present volume presents a double-barreled design. Not only does it provide a brief summary of every chapter of the Bible which the preacher and student can enlarge upon for Bible study purposes, but also a daily devotional book with a daily message for every day of the year, for almost *three years.* For family worship then, it is suggested that the plan followed in this volume be adopted. First, read the assigned chapter, then follow with the comments given. By this means, worship and prayer will be stimulated. The worshipers will also discover that by going from chapter to chapter, from Genesis to Revelation, that "the golden cord of revelation and redemption" binds the 1189 chapters of the 66 books together, fashioning them into what Jerome called *The Divine Library.*

It is but fitting to remark that when I originally prepared the *Daily Bible Treasury,* some 16 years ago, while I had on hand various commentaries and also reference books on each Bible book, I did not have by me the monumental work of Dr. G. Campbell Morgan, *An Exposition Of The Whole Bible,* which appeared in 1950. This is a remarkable chapter by chapter study of the Bible in one volume. Had I possessed this treasure of a book at the time, I would never have dared to present my *Readings,* similar in concept. Dr. Morgan, who knew the Bible better than almost any man of his generation, bound together "the central thoughts of all the chapters as a road-building engineer might bind together main and tributary avenues into a cross-country highway." The reader is urged to secure this wonderful compilation and compare with my humble effort. There is also Dr. Morgan's companion volume on *Great Chapters Of The Bible,* in which in greatly extended form, he deals with 100 chapters of the Bible, voted the favorites by his wonderful Friday night Bible Class at Westminster Chapel, London.

When published in their original magazine form there was no thought whatever of these daily readings being revised and expanded into book form. Then, with the passage of many years, the exact source of some quotations used have been forgotten. Nevertheless, deep gratitude is expressed to all who provided grist for my mill whether named or otherwise. The Lord continue to bless and use their precious thoughts!

ALL the BOOKS and CHAPTERS
of the BIBLE

GENESIS

Genesis, meaning, "beginning" or "origin," is the most remarkable and indispensable small book in the world. As its name suggests, it is a book of beginnings – of creation, the human race, marriage, the family, the state, nations, civilization, history – of law, government, penalty – of worship, covenant, the call to God, the elect people – of promise and prophecy – of language, literature, mechanic arts, fine arts, science and poetry. The Bible, as a whole, is the complete revelation of God, and of His love, will and purpose. *Genesis* is the foundation upon which this divine revelation rests; the root out of which the branches grow. Final revelation is not to be found here. *Genesis* is the beginning and the anticipated explanation of all that follows in the rest of the 65 books of the Bible. Thus, as one writer puts it, "The roots of all subsequent revelation are planted deep in *Genesis* and whoever would truly comprehend that revelation must begin here." You can usually test a man's orthodoxy by the way he treats this initial book of the Bible, especially its first eleven chapters. If he is wrong here, his outlook on the whole Word of God is warped. *Genesis* covers a period of over 2,300 years.

revelation given to Moses by God. In our limited space, we cannot go into detail of the six days' work brought before us in Genesis 1. Suffice it to say that no honest mind can fail to be impressed with the orderly manner in which God wrought out His creative plan, the ease with which He accomplished His task, the excellency of His work, and the simplicity of the narrative recording His creative acts. Let the young read Ecclesiastes 12:1.

The word "was" in Genesis 1:2, should be translated, "became," indicating that between verses 1 and 2, ruin overtook God's original creation. What we have after verse 2 refers, not to a perfect creation, but to a restoration of that which is recounted in verse 1. It may be that such chaos was connected with the apostasy of Satan and the rebellion of some of the heavenly host (Isaiah 24:1; 45:18; Jeremiah 4:23,26; Ezekiel 28:12-15). There is, of course, no conflict between true science and the Bible. Between verses 1 and 2 may be placed all the millions of years science claims for the prehistoric ages. From Genesis 1:3 and on, we have the record of some 6,000 years of human history. Praise God, the New Creation is not far away!

Chapter 1

The opening book of the Bible is a book of beginnings. In it, we have the beginning of all things, apart from God, who had no beginning. Several writers speak of it as "the seed plot of the Bible." All great themes, fully developed in succeeding books, can be found in Genesis in germ form. We discount the contention of the modernist who declares that this chapter can be treated merely as an allegory. We hold it to contain a literal, historical statement of divine

Chapter 2

What a beautiful description the opening verses of this chapter give us of the Sabbath rest of God! Note the two words, "created" and "made," referring, it would seem, to creation and restoration. We have before us a summary of the creative acts of God as given in chapter 1, with the addition of the habitation enjoyed by our first parents. Enlargement on the method of the creation of Adam and Eve is likewise stated. Have you ever compared the "tree" of verse

9 with the "tree" of the cross? (Acts 5:30; I Peter 2:24). The first tree was planted by God; the second tree by man. The tree that Eve saw was pleasant to the eyes; the tree of the cross was an ugly, vulgar sight. Man was forbidden to eat of the tree in the garden; the tree at Calvary is for all to appropriate. Having eaten of the first tree, Adam was cast out of paradise; having eaten of the second tree, the dying thief entered paradise.

In I Thessalonians 5:23; Hebrews 4:12 we see that man is considered to be a trinity in unity. He is a tripartite being, made up of body, soul and spirit. The body, formed of the dust, possesses the five senses: seeing, smelling, tasting, hearing and feeling. The body connects us with the world, without and around, and stands for world-consciousness. The soul is the central part of man and is equivalent to what we call personality. My soul is myself, and represents self-consciousness. The spirit is the deepest part of man. God breathed into Adam the breath, or spirit, of life. With this act, something from God Himself entered Adam. And this part of our being is related to worship, adoration and prayer, and speaks of God-consciousness. Paul reminds us that it is God's desire that we should be sanctified wholly, that is, having our whole being, spirit and soul and body, dominated by the Holy Spirit.

Chapter 3

This chapter is one of the most vital in all the Bible. The fall of man and God's gracious provision to meet the sinner's need are herewith presented. Man, at heart, is a fallen creature and desperately wicked. It is here that we meet, for the first time, the devil, who is introduced with no word of explanation. Later Scripture unfolds his past glory, and presents his diabolical designs. In Satan's approach to Eve we have a sample of his cunning methods. His first work is to substitute his lies for God's truth. He endeavored to cast doubt upon divine declarations: "Yes, hath God said?" (verse 1). Of course He had, and Satan knew it, but Eve was deceived. Listening to the seductive serpent, she disobeyed God, and thus commenced the terrible trail of sin. Conscious of their sin, Adam and Eve tried to cover their nakedness and hide themselves from God. "Where art thou?" cried God. Have you been discovered as a fallen sinner, and naked, have you come to Christ for dress?

How good is the God we adore! With the occasion of man's sin, there came the announcement of a divine remedy, for, in verse 15, we have the first promise of redemption. And it must be noted that Satan, the one responsible for sin was the first to receive intimation of the cross. By woman came sin. By woman came also the Saviour from sin. In verse 21, we have the first picture of Calvary. The self-made covering for nakedness was rejected by God (verse 7). He made coats of skins and clothed them. Our first parents were entirely passive. Provision was of God, and God alone. Skins imply sacrifice. Life had to be surrendered and blood shed, ere the first sinners could be clothed. At Calvary, through the shed blood of the Redeemer, a perfect covering was provided for "a world of sinners lost, and ruined by the fall." Be sure that you are clothed with divine righteousness.

Chapter 4

In chapter 3, we have sin against God. Here, in chapter 4, we have sin against man. Several firsts can be discerned in this chapter: first children, first offerings, first murder, first civilization and first spiritual seed. As a whole, the chapter is taken up with Cain and Abel, who can be considered historically, typically and dispensationally. In his valuable exposition of this chapter, Dr. Alexander Maclaren observes: "The first recorded act of worship occasions the first murder. Is not that only too correct a forecast of the oceans of blood which have been shed in the name of religion, and a striking proof of the subtle power of sin to corrupt the best, and out of it to make the worst? What a lesson against the bitter hatred which has too often sprung up on so-called religious grounds!" Cain's offering was rejected. It represented self-effort and was bloodless. Abel's sacrificial offering was pleasing to God and typifies Christ's work on our behalf (Hebrews 11:4).

Chapter 5

A key to the outline of Genesis is found in the word "generations," used ten times in the book. It is profitable to compare verse 1 with Matthew 1:1. Before us is "the book of the generations of Adam," a record of the fallen descendants of the first Adam. "The book of the generations of Jesus Christ," speaks of the redeemed. Adam and Christ are the two federal heads. In Adam we die; in Christ we are made alive. Who is your head? A sinner by ancestry and birth, are you still a sinner by practice? If so, by grace your name can be blotted out of the book of death and will then be found in the Lamb's Book of Life. A somewhat monotonous narrative of death is broken into by Enoch's translation, "who was not, for God took him" (verse 24). Accustomed as he was to a daily walk with God, Jehovah said to him on one occasion: "Better come all the way today!" And so up Enoch went. Oh, to be thus ready for such a blessed rapture!

Chapter 6

In this narrative, describing as it does, the rapid progress of sin, Noah stands out as a saint among sinners. He was the only light in his crooked and perverse generation. Among the faithless, he alone was faithful. As a Christian, are you, too, living as a lily among thorns? How beautifully grace is mingled with judgment! Sentence of destruction was pronounced upon the guilty, but the ark provided for Noah and his own. For universal apostasy, there came universal death. What was the exact corruption and wickedness occasioning the flood? Our conviction is that sin reached its climax in the illicit intercourse between fallen angels and women, as indicated in verses 1 and 2 (see II Peter 2:4; Jude 6). We must place Matthew 24:37 alongside of this chapter. How ripe the earth is for another divine visitation in judgment!

Chapter 7

Of the typical significance of the ark we could write at length. Suffice it to say that it fully illustrates the work of Christ, providing as it does, a perfect shelter from the storm of God's wrath. Obeying the divine command, Noah went into the ark and was delivered from judgment: "Come thou and all thy house into the ark" (verse 1). In the next chapter God says: "Go forth of the ark" (8:16). Noah had to *come* before he could *go*. And unless we know what it is to respond to the royal invitation: "Come unto me, and I will give you rest" (Matthew 11:28), we are not qualified to "go into all the world and preach the gospel" (Mark 16:15). The tragedy is that far too many are trying to *go* without having *come*. They are endeavoring to serve the Lord without being saved. "Examine yourselves whether ye be in the faith" (II Corinthians 13:5). Why, the very carpenters who helped build the ark perished in the waters of judgment! How sad it will be if, after all one's *mental* familiarity with the faith, the Lord should have to say: "Depart from me, for I never knew you!"

Chapter 8

After the flood, God made, as it were, a fresh beginning, and so entered into a covenant with Noah. Altogether, there are seven covenants to be traced in the Scriptures. Here we have the second, related as it is to the earth and its seasons. The occasion of this covenant was the beginning of a new world. Saved from the destruction overtaking all human beings and the lower creation, Noah emerges from the ark to start afresh the human race. Have you come across Scofield's marginal note on the raven and the dove, typifying the two natures in the believer? What is uppermost in your experience, the raven (the old nature), or the dove (the new nature)? Some scholars affirm that the last three verses of this chapter rightly belong to chapter 9. Be this as it may, the first act of Noah on leaving the ark was to build an altar and offer a sacrifice, well-pleasing to the Lord. All the blessings of the covenant were related to sacrifice. And all blessings, both spiritual and temporal, are ours today as the result of the cross.

Chapter 9

The terms of the Noahic Covenant, beginning in chapter 8:20 and completed in the chapter before us, prove that all natural laws are governed by nature's Lord. Even though man is trying, in these scientific days, to produce rain and snow, he has never been able to control natural elements. Man was not able to prevent the deluge. Because of divine grace, the earth has been spared another deserved flood. Look at 9:11, and whenever you see a rainbow praise God for His faithfulness. Among the conditions of the covenant, it will be noted that blood was not to be eaten, the principle of retributive judgment had to be enforced, and the human race, destroyed by the flood, had to be multiplied. The sin and shame of Noah and his son, Ham, prove how soon the human heart can forget a merciful deliverance. From Noah's fall we learn how faithful the Bible is in recording human nature. The sins of its saints and heroes are not concealed. And, realizing that here are men of like passions as ourselves, our hearts are revealed and also encouraged.

Chapter 10

Genealogies, while they may appear dry and uninteresting to us, provide valuable historical links. This is why the Jews were meticulously careful in the keeping of such records. In the portion we are considering we have the ways of men in a new world, and what a sad story of revolt we encounter! Man, by his own effort, wanted to climb up to God. Nimrod and Babel cannot be neglected by the careful student of the Word. In Nimrod, we have a foreshadowing of the Antichrist. "Nimrod," meaning *the rebel*, is a type of the "lawless one." "Babel," the name given to the world empire that man endeavored to establish, reappears often as Babylon. In Revelation 17 it is spoken of as "Mystery, Babylon," which represents man's last effort to organize a universal imperial government. What happened to Babel will likewise befall Babylon when Christ appears as the King of kings, to inaugurate His world empire! And think of it! We are to reign with Him. Then He will divide His inheritance with us.

Chapter 11

We unite these portions, seeing that both of them indicate incomplete obe-

dience. Terah should have gone all the way into Canaan, but, reaching Haran, dwelt and died there. "Terah died in Haran" (verse 32); he only got half way in his obedience to a divine revelation. Do not be among the number who leave the Ur of the Chaldees, but never enter Canaan. Have we stopped halfway – saved, but not separated? For their partial conversion, Ananias and Sapphira were smitten with sudden death (Acts 5:1-11). What gaps in the ranks of saints there would be if God acted in this way today! Abram should not have yielded to Terah, his father, and tarried five years in Haran. Ultimately obeying, Abram went all the way. Have you noticed that, when Abram is mentioned in the New Testament roll of saints, nothing is said of his disobedience? "He . . . obeyed; and he went out, not knowing whither he went" (Hebrews 11:8). How like God this is, who is ever willing to blot out our sins!

Chapter 12

Abram's call was a distinct call to separate himself from all natural ties. As Arthur W. Pink expresses it, in his volume on Genesis: "Abram called upon to separate himself from his home and kindred and bidden to go into a place which afterwards God would give him for an inheritance, typifies the one whose citizenship is in Heaven but who is still in the world, and in consequence, called upon to walk by faith and live as a stranger and pilgrim on the earth. In a word, Abram illustrates the *heavenly calling* of those who are members of the body of Christ." You will, of course, bear in mind that Abram, the first Hebrew or Jew, was a Gentile. Without doubt Abram, whose name was changed to Abraham, the father of all them that believe, is the most renowned figure in Old Testament history. Remember, will you, the principle enunciated in verse 2: "I will bless thee . . . thou shalt be a blessing"!

Verses 10-20 comprise a somewhat sad portion, introducing us, as they do, to Abram's second failure. True, famine was in the land, but Abram forgot that need could never throttle God, so he went down into Egypt. The famine was a test of Abram's faith, but he failed and sought the sustenance of Egypt. *He went down!* And it is ever a shameful descent when a Christian turns to Egypt for help. Sin is never alone. Loving company, one sin gives birth to another. Thus, Abram's failure in the hour of trial led to deception. With Sarai, his wife, he was guilty of lying, and endangered, thereby, the honor of his dearest partner. Are you losing time in Egypt? Are you out of touch with God? Do you feel, with the meal somewhat low in the faith-barrel, that the world has more to offer? Let Abram's failure serve as a warning signal. God was so good to His servant in preserving and restoring him.

Chapter 13

The opening verses of this chapter record Abram's restoration to full fellowship. In disobedience, he *went down* to Egypt. Now we read that he *"went up* out of Egypt . . . unto the altar, which he had made there at the first"* (verses 1,4). There was no altar in Eygpt, no communion there. It is time to *go up!* The strife between the herdsmen of Abram and Lot reveals that, although Abram's sin was forgiven, the effect of it remained. Increasing wealth ruptured the fellowship between relatives. One wonders what the Canaanites and Perizzites nearby thought of the quarrel between the servants of Abram and Lot. Earthly riches gathered in Egypt often bring with them a good deal of heartache. Abram and Lot stand out in sharp contrast. Abram walked by faith, Lot by sight. Abram was as generous as Lot was greedy. With true magnanimity, Abram told Lot to make his choice. And what a choice! Lust of the eyes conquered and ultimately brought ruin to Lot and his family.

The various steps in Lot's backsliding are as clearly marked as those in Peter's denial. Lot "lifted up his eyes and beheld" (verse 10), "chose him all the plains of Jordan" (verse 11), "dwelled in the cities of the plain and pitched his tent *toward* Sodom" (verse 12), "dwelt in Sodom" (14:12), and "sat in the gate of Sodom" (19:1). Lot's choice resulted in misery and loss. Sowing to the flesh, he reaped corruption. Graciously, Peter speaks of him as "just Lot, vexed with the filthy conversation of the wicked" (II Peter 2:7).

To look at him ending his days in a cave, with all he coveted taken from him, his wife turned into a pillar of salt, and the terrible sin of his daughters, confirms the saying that his chickens had come home to roost. How different were the results of Abram's choice! What a glorious and abiding heritage is his! Putting God first, he came to possess riches far beyond the temporary wealth Lot found in Sodom. Think of the covenant God made with Abram in the closing verses of this chapter, and know God's choice for those who honor Him is ever *choice!*

Chapter 14

In this chapter is recorded the first war in the Bible. Learning of Lot's captivity, Abram hastened to his rescue. He carried no root of bitterness. He might have said: "It serves him right. Let him suffer." But God-like, Abram returned good for evil. Although Lot was his nephew, he is here called his "brother." It is good to know what it is to restore a sinning brother in the spirit of meekness. What we would not give to know the feelings of Lot as he realized how his uncle had delivered him from captivity! Do you never wonder what they had to say to each other as they left Hobah? Whatever repentance there might have been on Lot's part for going down to Sodom, it was short-lived, for he deliberately returned to Sodom, and like a sow, wallowed again in the mire of ungodliness. Sodom was in his heart, and back he went.

We are here introduced to the mysterious personage of Melchizedek, fitting type of Christ as the King-Priest. "After the order of Melchizedek" signifies "the royal authority and unending duration of Christ's high priesthood" (Hebrews 6:20; 7:23,24). The fact that Melchizedek is spoken of as being "without father, without mother, without descendent, having neither beginning nor end of life" (Hebrews 7:3), does not mean that he was a supernatural or divine being. It simply denotes that Scripture is silent regarding his parentage, which, as a human being, he must have had. His priestly benediction of Abram for his victory is noteworthy, for it introduces us to a very rare, divine title: "God most high." God is Supreme, and as such was Abram's "exceeding great reward." Others might take the spoils of victory, but not Abram, who had God's promise of the land and numerous blessings. Rather than *take* anything, he *gave* tithes of all. We ought to be as disinterested in earthly riches and honor as Abram was.

Chapter 15

The opening phrase of this chapter, "after these things," should be thoughtfully considered. If Abram was tempted to think of a possible return of the kings from the north, then it must have been comforting to have God as his shield. Remembering how he had refused to receive even a thread for his conquest, it was most suitable for God to speak of Himself as Abram's reward. Note the requests of the chapter. Was Abram humble or presumptuous in their presentation? A progressive revelation is discernible in this fifth recorded divine revelation given to Abram. What definite and impressive dealings he had with God! This is the right and privilege of every child of God. Is yours a clearer understanding of the secret of the Lord as the days go by?

Chapter 16

That Abram, in spite of his past exalted spiritual experiences, was still human and prone to wander, is evident by the record of his false step with Hagar. Palestine, today, with all its strife and bloodshed between Jews and Arabs, is the aftermath of Abram's use of Hagar. The sorrowful results of Abram's action are clearly evident: pride, misery, jealousy and injustice. Yet how gracious God was in His provision for Hagar and her child! When she was cast out, the angel found her. Thirsty, she discovered the well of Beer-la-hai-roi, meaning, "the well of the living one who sees me." There are many solemn lessons to be gathered from this chapter. After believing God, Abram acted in the energy of the flesh. And, must we not confess such a sad inconsistency? Then there is the far-reaching effect of sin. Like the ever-widening ripples that are caused by a stone thrown into a pool, our sin never ends with ourselves. Our only avenue of protection against failure is the constant remembrance of our high and holy calling.

Chapter 17

We come to the sixth recorded divine appearance to Abram, a revelation of the character of God adapted to the patriarch's need. In connection with this further covenant, look at its content (verses 10,12,13), continuance (verse 7), token (verse 11), and promise (verses 6,7,8). Thinking of a crisis that Abram reached in this chapter, we realize that thirteen years had elapsed since God's last appearance. The interval seems to be a blank. Turning aside from faith and following the flesh, Abram entered a period of barrenness. Now at 99 years of age, he receives another divine visitation. The circumcision enforced speaks of surrender, separation, purity and possession. Let us ask ourselves if *we* are thus fully given to God. The Covenant of Grace calls for the requirements of which circumcision speaks.

The changing of names is significant. Abram (father) is now Abraham (father of nations), and Sarai becomes Sarah (princess), mother of the promised seed. Of the laughter, Dr. Griffith Thomas says: "The laugh is evidently not the laugh of unbelief, but of a faith which, while taking God at His Word, considers the news almost too good to be true. God's revelations to His people often seem to be too good to be true, and yet they are true!" Abraham's concern for Ishmael is touching, and he is assured that he (Ishmael) will not be forgotten. God's everlasting covenant, however, is to be realized through Isaac, to which declaration Abraham was willingly submissive. To Isaac there came a fresh realization of the divine character, a clearer vision of the divine purpose, a deeper insight into the divine will, and a fuller understanding of divine grace. To walk before the Lord is to know the avenue of purity, power and provision.

Chapter 18

This chapter presents a beautiful picture of oriental life. Reading it as a whole, we are impressed with Abraham's character, hospitality, civility and humility. We have here God's first communication to Sarah concerning Isaac. Do you feel that she was less developed in faith than her husband, or that Abraham had not informed his wife

of God's promise as to Isaac (verses 13,15,17)?
Abraham's maturity of spirituality is evidenced by the fact that God could not
keep anything back from him, as His "friend."
Oh, that we could know more of the sacred
intimacy Abraham enjoyed! Such unclouded
fellowship found response in earnest, effective intercession. How Abraham poured
out his heart for a doomed city! How audacious was his approach to God! Why did
Abraham stop at ten when pleading for the
Sodomites? Did he think there was a limit
to divine forbearance? In the light of Calvary,
there is no limit.

Chapter 19

What a dark and disastrous chapter this
is! Its key words are: degradation, deliverance and destruction. A sad feature of the
record is that when Lot, the backslider,
reached his peril, and endeavored to warn
his relatives, that "he seemed as one that
mocked" (verse 14). His testimony had gone.
He had lived too long as a Sodomite, and
with a life Sodom-like; his warning was
without conviction and avail. His life and
lips contradicted each other; thus his warning fell on deaf ears. When judgment fell
upon Sodom, and Lot with his family departed, it would seem as if his wife was
loath to leave the city. She looked back,
and that look cost her her life. The last
part of the chapter is a record of unutterable shame, showing how drunkenness and
degradation go together. What a terrible end
for one who is called "righteous"! Abraham
is ever remembered, but Lot passes into oblivion. May this chapter remind us of the
shameful results of backsliding! The Lord
keep us near Himself.

Chapter 20

Abraham, by his lapse at Gerar, became
his own foe! Making all allowance for the
times in which Abraham lived – times God
overlooked (Acts 17:30) – the repetition of an
old sin cannot be excused (Genesis 12:13).
It was exceedingly low of Abraham to try
to protect himself at the expense of his wife.
God graciously intervened, and Sarah was
restored to her husband. How often God
saves us from ourselves! Abimelech was most
commendable in his conduct. Abraham cer-

grace

tainly deserved Abimelech's just reproof.
While not having Abraham's sublime revelation of God, Abimelech yet manifested moral
superiority. Too often, men of the world
seem to put to shame, by their integrity
of life, those who profess to be Christians.
In spite of his deception, God still looked
upon His erring friend as a "prophet."
What matchless grace is His!

Chapter 21

After twenty-five years, the promise made
to Abraham is realized (12:2; 13:16), for with
the birth of Isaac we reach "a pivotal poinin the outworking of God's eternal purpose."
For a quarter of a century Abraham waited
for the fulfilment of God's plan, learning
that He is never before His time and never
after. The natural and physical impossibility
of Sarah bearing a child presented no difficulty to God, to whom "all things are possible." At the appointed time, Isaac came
as the child of promise, of whose birth more
is said than of any other, except the One
who came from Abraham's line. Isaac's birth,
like Christ's, was miraculous. Supernaturally,
Sarah was able to conceive seed, which was
one of God's ways of preparing Israel for
the Incarnation of our Lord. The brevity
and delicacy of the record of Isaac's conception and birth must not be overlooked.
Abraham's violation of the law of marriage
brought him much trouble. For the New
Testament application of Sarah and Hagar,
turn to Galatians 4 and 5. Abraham gave
Hagar a bottle of water; God gave her a
well. How bountiful He is!

Chapter 22

It is most difficult to condense the significance of this chapter. Here, for the first
time, God desired, seemingly, human sacrifice to expiate sin. Later on, beasts were
offered up. God, however, is intimating, in
the surrender of Isaac, that, as man has
sinned, it must be by man that His justice
is satisfied. This chapter presents a notable
foreshadowing of Calvary. There is this difference, though: Isaac was offered, but spared;
Christ was offered, and died. The question
of Isaac, "where is the lamb?" (verse 7)
remains unanswered all through the Old
Testament. Its answer is in the Baptist's

words: "Behold the Lamb of God, which taketh away the sin of the world" (John 1:29,36). The truth of substitution is taught in verse 13. The ram caught in the thicket was offered up "in the stead of Isaac." Isaac should have died, but the ram took his place. At the cross, Christ died for our sins. "In our place condemned He stood." Is this Saviour-Substitute yours? He bore your sin and died your death. Do you believe this?

Chapter 23

This touching narrative of the death and burial of Sarah reveals the impression that the personality of Abraham made upon his neighbors. Holding him in highest esteem, they wanted him to have the best of sepulchres for his dead. Women, generally, are touchy about their age. Sarah is the only woman whose age is recorded in Scripture. At the age of 127, she passed over the river of death. (Of her spiritual oneness with Abraham, see Hebrews 11:11-13; and I Peter 3:5,6.) One writer points out that this is "the first occasion in Scripture of the record of a man's tears, and they were neither idle, nor unmanly, nor morbid, but the genuine and rightful expression of Abraham's deep sorrow." Jesus wept over the death of one He loved, and His tears have forever sanctified ours. The funeral of Sarah brings us to "the first grave we have any record of in Holy Writ. The last offices of respect were paid, and the lonely old man went back home." That the patriarch believed in "the sure and certain hope" of a joyful resurrection is hinted at in Hebrews 11:14. Have you said good-by to some dear one? Well, is it not blessed to know that you do not sorrow as those who have no hope? (I Thessalonians 4:13-18).

Chapter 24

In this beautiful chapter, describing the securing of a bride for Isaac, we are given an insight into his character. Isaac was a man of prayer (verses 62,63). In contrast to his father, who was positive and aggressive, Isaac was of a quiet, retiring disposition. He was also a man of the well; Abraham was a man of the altar. In Abraham's command that his son should not take a wife from the daughters of the Canaan-

ites, he reveals his undiminished faith and persistence regarding the revelation of God concerning him and his seed. Now an old man, Abraham had a deep insight into God's purpose (verses 6,7), and the absolute assurance of His favor (verses 7-9). In the model servant seeking out a bride for Isaac, we have a fitting type of the Holy Spirit's ministry in this age. His is the sacred task of seeking out a Bride for the heavenly Isaac. "Wilt thou go with this Man, the Lord Jesus Christ?" "Yes, Lord, I will go!"

Chapter 25

What a crowded chapter this is, telling of Abraham's marriage to Keturah, his disposal of possessions and his death! Then the generations of both Ishmael and Isaac are set forth. The birth of Esau and Jacob is likewise recorded, along with the sale of the birthright. What other historian could have told so much in as few words? (For an understanding of the nature of the birthright that Esau sold, read Numbers 24:17-19.) How many there are who barter their present birthright away! Country, family, religion, education mean nothing to them. (Look at Hebrews 12:14,15.) Esau was destitute of spiritual insight and of appreciation of the blessings of the Abrahamic covenant. He, like many today, alas, lived only for the present and lost the birthright.

Chapter 26

The Bible, a biography of human life, is a faithful mirror of character. Isaac lived the longest of all the patriarchs, and although less is recorded of him than of others, his experiences, like ours, were marked by light and shade, sin and chastening, grace and mercy. In this chapter, exclusively devoted to Isaac, he comes before us as the ordinary son of a famous father, and in turn, the ordinary father of a famous son, Jacob. By going down to Gerar, Isaac walked by sight rather than by faith. "Go not down," he was told, but down he went like his father before him, and like his father, he lied about his wife. Abimelech, an upright man, rebuked Isaac, and preserved Rebekah and her lying husband from harm. As the well-digger, Isaac reopened the wells of Abraham, calling them by their old names. Modernism has closed a good many refreshing wells. May grace be ours to dig them again, and return to them their old evangelical names! Isaac was both impelled and compelled to leave the land of the Philistines, and as he did so, divine favor was his. "The Lord appeared unto him *the same night*" (verse 24). At last he was back in God's will and able to receive a divine revelation. Now, for the first time, we have the familiar title: "The God of Abraham." Have we become entangled with the Philistines, and thus not spiritually fit to know the secret of the Lord? Well, Isaac's experience teaches us that, for immediate restoration, there is immediate revelation. The four-fold evidence of Isaac's return can be clearly traced: the altar, representing consecration; prayer, with its recognition of need and God's ability to meet it; the tent, eloquent of witness to those around; and the well, answering to the supply of the Spirit. An obvious lesson to be gleaned from the latter half of the chapter is the necessity of separation from the world. Down in Gerar, Isaac had no joy, no peace and no influence. He found himself thwarted by the Philistines and the butt of their jealousy. My soul, take heed!

Chapter 27

In connection with the stolen blessing, it is essential to observe that while Esau was rejected because he first rejected the blessing, Jacob's selection was not due to his worthiness, of which he had little. "It was of God, who sheweth mercy that His purpose of grace might stand." How much Jacob owed to grace! And so do we! Hardly any of the persons mentioned in this chapter appear in a commendable light. Can you trace the failings of each? General Gordon, while at Khartoum, wrote in his diary: "I thank God that He has given me strength to avoid all tricks." The plot of Isaac had sad results. He feigned approaching death, but lived for 40 years after pronouncing the patriarchal blessing. His partiality and fleshly appetite led Isaac into grievous sin. Then we have Rebekah's counterplot, which, although inspired by a very high motive, cannot be excused. Tricks followed tricks, and so we have Jacob's deception. The victim of a mother's love,

he silenced his better nature and practiced a hideous deception. Truly, this is a chapter of desires and devices, with its warning never to realize desire by means of unworthy devices.

Chapter 28

One wonders how much of the significance of "the blessing of Abraham" Isaac and Jacob understood (Galatians 3:14,15). The opening verses prove how true it is that God has a plan for every life. He had one for Jacob's life, a plan unhindered by the action of Isaac or Esau, a plan uninfluenced by the cleverness and craft of Rebekah. We must learn the divine plan for our lives and realize it. At Bethel, God began to shape and mould Jacob. Because of his vision there, it stands out as one of the most important places in Scripture. Read thoughtfully the narrative, noting the *place*, the *time*, the *vision*, the *vow*, the *message*. Guilty, as Jacob had been, of cunning bargaining, we do not think his bargaining disposition was Godward, as his vow proves (verses 20-22). This was no ordinary vow. Jacob was pledging himself and his possessions in thankful recognition of God's favor. As one has said: "It is the grand and solemn expression of the soul's full, free and perpetual acceptance of the Lord to be its own God."

Chapter 29

Jacob, at Haran, emphasized the fact that God often permits His children to reap the shame and sorrow of a self-chosen way. Two bargain-makers meet, with Jacob being paid back in his own coin. He had deceived his father; now he was deceived by Laban. Further, Jacob's sojourn in his uncle's home proved how God not only *rules*, but *over-rules*. Says Arthur Pink: "What a showing forth of the fact that even in our smallest actions we are controlled by the most High!" All unconsciously to themselves, these wives of Jacob's, in naming their babies, and in stating the reasons for their names, were outlining the Gospel of God's grace, and were prophetically foreshadowing the early history of the nation which descended from their sons (Romans 11:36). Jacob learned many lessons in the discipline he tarried in for almost 40 years of his life. There was much to be corrected in his deceptive character, and many natural disadvantages to be overcome. Thus, Jacob profited by God's disciplinary methods. And so it should be with ourselves.

Chapter 30

Sad and sordid incidents make up this chapter. The possession of two wives brought much strife into the home. And that the friction and jealousy between Rachel and Leah exercised their pernicious influence over the temperaments of their children, can be traced in after days. At the birth of Joseph, Jacob had a desire to return to his own land. Laban was reluctant to let so valued a servant go, so we come to schemer meeting schemer, with Jacob proving to be the equal of his crafty uncle. Laban's deception does not surprise us, but with Jacob it is different. He was the man who had had a Bethel, met God, seen angels and made a solemn covenant. Yet here is one, spiritually privileged, trying to outwit Laban and match his own craftiness against his uncle's. When a believer falls, the descent is sometimes deplorable. Yet how patient and long-suffering God is! In spite of disappointment, surely, God waited until at last His erring child came to the end of himself. No wonder He is so often spoken of as "the God of Jacob."

Chapter 31

Jacob is homeward bound at long last. With his separation from Laban, Jacob gives witness to the fact that God has been his Helper and Preserver. (Compare 28:15 with the directions of verse 3 here.) During Jacob's twenty years in Haran, there is no reference to prayer, fellowship or the altar. There was nothing to distinguish Jacob from the worldlings around. But although he had forgotten God, God had not forgotten him. How like the Lord! Are you in some Haran, away from God, suffering as the result of a self-chosen way? Then listen to His voice – "Return . . . I will be with thee." Of course, we cannot condone Jacob's stealth in his departure from Haran, while Laban was absent (see Isaiah 52:12), yet God's time for Jacob to leave had come. Of Jacob's

flight and his dream, and of Laban's pursuit, much could be written. In the covenant made between them, we must understand properly the meaning of "Mizpah" (verse 49), the name Jacob gave to the heap of stones. Today this is used as a motto, to express union and trust, but God was invoked to watch between and to keep the two from harming each other. Neither trusted the other, so God was asked to act as Watchman!

Chapter 32

Jacob's contact with angels here and at other times (28:12; 31:11), brings us to the question of their ministry, so prominent in Scripture. What we are apt to forget is the fact that angels are the servants of saints, as well as of God (see Psalm 34:7; Daniel 6:22; Hebrews 1:14; I Peter 1:12). Jacob saw two hosts, as *Mahanaim* means. One camp was made up of his wives, children and helpless self; the other, the angelic bodyguard, to safeguard him as he journeyed on. "Vision," said Swift, "is the art of seeing the invisible." Is ours the eye of faith, able to see the great and glorious host surrounding us? Do we endure as seeing Him, who is invisible? Features of what happened at the brook are not hard to trace. Jacob sought solitude, and while in prayer the Wrestler appeared. In his struggle Jacob revealed one of his most prominent traits, namely, persistence. He persisted in resisting, until his thigh was touched, then persisted in clinging until blessing was bestowed. After confession and blessing, name and character were changed, and Jacob, thereafter, became a different man.

Chapter 33

There is no other book in the entire realm of literature so faithful in the portrayal of human character, as the Bible. What unvarnished records it presents! Sad and conspicuous inconsistencies of the noblest saints are not glossed over. Here is Jacob who, after his wondrous experience at Peniel, distrusts God and yields to the fear of man. Prostrating himself before Esau was surely a lack of faith on Jacob's part, for had he not been made the recipient of a divine manifestation? And had he not received a new name, Israel, meaning, a prince of, or with God? Yes, but he failed to live up to his princely name, and resorted to his old time deception. Jacob's fear of his brother was soon dispelled. The God who is able to turn the heart "whithersoever He will," changed the revengeful, fierce heart of Esau into a kindly one. Thus, seeing his brother, he "fell on his neck and kissed him" (verse 4). And Jacob-like, the patriarch depended upon his gifts, rather than upon God, to appease his brother Esau. Is there someone you are afraid to meet, someone you have wronged? Well, if you are willing to right what is wrong, trust God to prepare your way!

Chapter 34

The trouble overtaking Jacob at Shechem marks the harvest he was forced to reap of earlier years (Galatians 6:7,8). After his vow (28:22), Jacob should have gone directly to Bethel (35:1), but, as with Lot, surrounding country was very attractive to him, and so he extended his stay, with dire results in his family life. It is hard to imagine that this father, Jacob, whose children were guilty of dark deeds, was the man who had seen God face to face. Yet, here he is, swayed by material advantages and losing, thereby, the smile of God. How often we choose our surroundings, independent of their effect upon life and character! Schools are chosen, without any thought of their influence upon the impressionable young. Living near Shechem is very risky, as Jacob proved. It resulted in his daughter's shame, and the treacherous crime of his sons. Too late, Jacob sought to rebuke his sons for their cruel vindictiveness. The character of the rebuke is very noticeable. Jacob was only sorry for the crime of his sons because of his own reputation and possessions. There was no true repentance because of what the dark deeds meant to the reputation of Israel as a divinely privileged people. (Yet, see 49:6,7.)

Chapter 35

We now come to the Bethel life of Jacob, in which he breathed a purer air. The last chapter is as "God-less" as this one is "God-full." "The contrast between a believer's and an unbeliever's life is scarcely more marked than the contrast between a half-hearted and a whole-hearted believer's life." Humiliated by what had happened in Shechem, Jacob was forced to leave. His extremity was God's opportunity, so on he went to Bethel. Was there not a kindly rebuke when God said: "When thou fleddest from the face of Esau thy brother"? (verse 1). But almost 30 years, with their spiritual declension, intervened, and now God reminded Jacob of an unredeemed pledge. With a quickened conscience, Jacob strove to eliminate the corrupt family practices he had indulgently allowed. Can it be that our vows have been forgotten too? Once we were spiritual, but prosperity came our way and we settled down in Shechem. Sorrow and heartache have been ours, but God is saying: "Arise, go up to Bethel and dwell *there*." May the Lord enable us to put away our goods, and experience the full restoration to communion Jacob did, when once again he "set up a pillar," and talked with God (28:18; 35:14).

Chapter 36

Esau's character affords a study in contrasts. Compared with Jacob his brother, how different he was! Commendable and attractive in many ways, Esau was yet earthbound. Bethel and its altar were not for him. The New Testament speaks of him as "a profane person" (Hebrews 12:16). The word, "profane," has a different sense in the New Testament, from what we usually ascribe to it. Originally, it indicated an enclosure, outside the Tabernacle, that was not set apart for any sacred purpose. With Esau there was no sacred enclosure. Everything about him was related to the flesh. His entire life was lived on an earthly plane. Is it not thus with many around us? They have education, culture, charm and wealth, but the earthly and natural are supreme in their lives. Jacob, of course, inherited all the spiritual blessings of the covenant, but had Esau turned to God, he could have enjoyed divine favor. He elected, however, to live his life outside the will and promises of God. So here we have two brothers, but poles apart in spiritual awareness. How like life this is! The generations of Esau became associated with Edom, a country having remarkable prophetic significance.

Chapter 37

The household of Jacob had now become a nation in Egypt. In this chapter is told the early life of Joseph, whose story is full of charm for all Bible readers. Before us is Joseph's home life (verses 28-36). Dr. Griffith Thomas remarks that this narrative is worthy of consideration because of a four-fold value. It gives the explanation of the development of the Hebrews. It is a remarkable proof of the quiet operation of divine Providence, over-ruling evil, and leading at length to the complete victory of truth and righteousness. It affords a splendid example of personal character. Joseph's life is one of the finest of all those recorded in Scripture. It provides a striking series of typical illustrations of Christ. Without doubt, Joseph is one of the most perfect types of our Lord. Jacob, upon whom many sorrows had fallen, suffered the severest blow when Joseph, his favorite, was taken from him and mourned as dead. The patriarch, however, came to prove the "afterward" of peaceable fruit of righteousness. Ultimately, when he saw Joseph as a saviour in Egypt, he *knew* that all things had worked together for good.

Chapter 38

It has been asked why this parenthetical chapter, taken up with the shameful sin of Judah, is introduced at this point. While the chapter gives us a glimpse of the character of the heathenism under whose influence Judah came, there must be a reason for this interruption of the story of Jacob and Joseph. The unsavory account occurs in the book where the first step, that led Jacob's family to Egypt, is found. Joseph had been sold as a slave, who finally became the instrument of the transfer of his people into Egypt. This chapter reveals the need of such a removal. To stay in Canaan meant terrible contamination for the chosen family. "At this time Israel had neither family nor possessions in Canaan. They could soon have sought both; and the character already manifested by Jacob's sons augured ill for their preserving either purity

or piety among the Canaanites." Yet here is a chapter magnifying the grace of God. In spite of Judah's fearful story, God permitted Christ to come, not only from Judah, but Tamar (Matthew 1:3; Hebrews 7:14). How blessed are the transforming influences of God's love and grace!

Chapter 39

The many sided character of Joseph is revealed in the crises he had to face. When cast into the pit, and then sold by his jealous brothers, he manifested silent submission in the hour of such a wrong. True, twenty years later Joseph referred to "the anguish of his soul" (Genesis 42:21) at that time, but there was no sign of it as the foreign merchants took him away. Now we see him tested by adversity. Raised to a responsible position in Potiphar's household, there came that fierce temptation to surrender his virtue, but he refused to satisfy the sensual desires of his master's wife. With her passion thwarted and disappointed, she lied against Joseph, and brought about his captivity in prison. There is nothing finer in literature than this simple, yet dignified, narrative of a young man, attractive in every way, tested and yet triumphant. But with such treatment, Joseph's silence again stands out. No self-defense was his. No word of accusation escaped his lips. Submissively, he endured the wrong, even as the One whom he typifies, did. "The Lord was with Joseph," we read, and Joseph justified Him. May this be true of all of us.

Chapter 40

Viewing this chapter, we find it easy to believe that "stone walls do not a prison make." Adversity never caused Joseph to compromise. He was loyal to God under all circumstances. In prison, Joseph confessed his convictions, was sympathetic, and knew how to win and hold confidence. Thus, his captivity was the providential preparation for his magnificent future. To him was granted the interpretation of dreams. God was so real to His suffering servant, that it was easy for him to reveal to the butler and the baker the meaning of their respective dreams. All that Joseph received from the Lord, he relayed. Nothing was added or subtracted. And is this not our obligation with the Truth we have been given to declare? "Yet did not the chief butler remember Joseph but forgot him" (verse 23). Two years later, the butler *did* remember Joseph, but think of what those two years must have meant to the waiting prisoner!

Chapter 41

Humbled, Joseph now found himself exalted. God is able to bring all things to our remembrance, and it was thus that the butler, at the opportune moment, recalled his forgotten promise. Simply, he told of Joseph's ability to interpret dreams, and paved the way, thereby, for Joseph's liberation and exaltation. Egypt is a fitting type of the world, but how its wise men displayed their ignorance! How utterly inadequate their human wisdom was to interpret what God had caused Pharaoh to dream! Joseph, the man Spirit-possessed, was the only one who could unfold the prophetic significance of the dreams. As the result of this God-given ability, Joseph was given a position of superiority over the wise men of Egypt, and with wisdom from on high, guided the destiny of the nation. The new name he received is suggestive in meaning, "Saviour of the World" (verse 45), and speaks of Him who was exalted to be a Prince and a Saviour. A further type can be found in Joseph's age when he went on his mission (compare verse 46 and Luke 3:23). We could name this chapter: "From Pit to Palace."

Chapter 42

The record now returns to the family of Joseph, of whom nothing has been said since chapter 38. What a surprise awaited the brethren of Joseph! How little they knew that the one they were so jealous of, and had sold into slavery, would be the one they would have to plead with for bread! Unknown and unrecognized by his brothers, Joseph yet knew them, and disciplined them for their past dealing with him. Altogether, this is a fascinating chapter. As you read of Joseph making known a way of deliverance through substitution, provision for his

own in a strange land, and of his revealing himself to his brothers, see if you can work out striking types of Christ's association with Israel. For pathos, Jacob's wail is matchless (verses 36-38). He cried: "All these things are against me." But he came to learn that his dark clouds were big with mercy. As you view your present circumstances, does it seem as if all things are against you? Be patient, friend! Before long you will discover that behind your life the Weaver stands and works His wondrous plan.

Chapter 43

Observe in this chapter, *the naturalness of the address of the steward* (verses 19-22); *Judah's dignified and forceful appeal* (verses 8-10), and recall his part in selling Joseph; *the touching tenderness of Jacob* (verses 6, 7,11-14); and *the self-control and love of Joseph.* The guilt-stricken brothers of Joseph had no idea that he knew of their convicted consciences (42:21,22) years after they had sold him. Joseph, however, was about to return good for evil. Are we free from the shadow of unforgiven sin? Has our heavenly Joseph anything against us? One cannot read verse 30 and remain unmoved. How deeply stirred Joseph was! He carried no bitterness in his heart. Bountifully, he provided for his erring brothers. And in such treatment we have a striking type of Christ's compassion and forgiving grace, not only for Israel, His brethren according to the flesh, but for ourselves, as those whose sin was responsible for His anguish of soul.

Chapter 44

In order to catch the spirit of Judah's plea, one should be alone and read this literary gem aloud: "a more moving oration than oratory ever pronounced." Dr. W. W. White speaks of it as being "unstudiedly artful and unforcedly rhetorical. It is sustained, pathetic, simple, dramatic. The entire story of Joseph is a masterpiece of composition." Attention must be paid to the confession of guilt in verse 16: "God hath found out the iniquity of thy servants." Joseph did not reveal himself until such an acknowledgment had been made. And Israel will have to acknowledge their offense before the blessing of heaven can be theirs

(Ezekiel 20:42,43; Hosea 5:15; Acts 3:19,20). Grace alone can deal with guilt. Is it not wonderful to realize that, although it was our sins that caused Christ's death, now, as the Saviour, He can fully clear us by His blood?

Chapter 45

The simplicity and beauty of this section, in which Joseph reveals himself to his brothers, is worthy of a prolonged study. Note the prominence given to God by Joseph. "It was not you that sent me hither, BUT GOD" (verse 8). Yes, God turned the curse into a blessing. Behind the terrible experience of being sold as a slave, was God preparing a channel of deliverance for His own. Twice over Joseph confessed: "God sent me before you." But what a strange way it must have seemed – from a pit into a prison, before he became the saviour in Egypt! In and through our adversities, God is working out His purposes. The late Dr. Jowett writes of "the Ministry of the Bleeding Heart." Joseph, having bled, was now able to bless. Would that we had space to write of Joseph, acting in marvelous grace, revealing himself as the compassionate one, proclaiming his glory, a blessed type of Him, who, because of His cross, has reached His crown! What a day that will be when He reveals Himself!

It was a testimony to Joseph's integrity and ability that Pharaoh was well-pleased to learn of the advent of Joseph's family, and invited all who formed it to come and stay in Egypt and eat of the fat of the land. Poor Jacob! He found it hard to believe that Joseph was alive and that he was lord in Egypt. And, Jacob-like, the old patriarch could not get away from the visible and the temporal. "When he saw the wagons . . . the spirit of Jacob . . . revived" (verse 27). He was dubious of the declaration of his sons as to Joseph's prominence; yet all his life he had been impressed with the tangible and material, and, seeing the well-laden wagons, Jacob determined to arise and go to Joseph. Knowing our frailty, may God send us, as we need them, many "wagons" to revive our drooping spirits.

Chapter 46

As Jacob prepared to go to Egypt, God assured him of a glorious heritage. Of Joseph's making ready of his chariot to meet his father, Jacob, Dr. I. M. Haldeman remarks concerning him on this occasion: "This is really his epiphany. He reveals himself in splendor and kingliness to his people. He meets Judah in Goshen first and then meets his father, the household of Jacob. This is a representation of the truth as we have already seen it. It is the coming of Christ in His Glory to meet Judah first, and then all Israel. Our attention is especially drawn to his appearing to the people in chariots of glory. So of the greater Joseph we read, 'For, behold, the Lord will come with fire, and *with his chariots* like a whirlwind' (Isaiah 66:15)." We cannot but notice the tender love of Joseph for his father, and Jacob's complete satisfaction at seeing his dear son's face again. Long absence had made the heart grow fonder.

Chapters 47,48

The settlement and exaltation of Jacob and his descendants in Egypt, as well as Joseph's famine-policy, are before us in this portion. Professor Sayce reminds us that "the changes which the administration of Joseph is said to have made in the land-tenure of Egypt, find support in Egyptian history." How wisely and efficiently Joseph ruled as Food-Controller! For the crisis, God had His man. And these famine-stricken days of ours require another Joseph! What a suggestive confession that is in 47:25! Our blessed "Joseph" has saved us. Because of His grace, we have found grace in His sight. And, realizing that we owe all that we are and have to His redeeming and preserving mercy, what else can we say but, "We will be Thy servants forever"? Not only Jacob and his sons, but the whole of Egypt became utterly dependent upon Joseph. And God, although not universally recognized, is the Benefactor of all.

The last days of Jacob in Egypt are somewhat touching. After a varied career of 147 years, he could die triumphantly. His request about his burial in Canaan reveals his faith in the divine covenant. As he died, he worshiped (Hebrews 11:21). A grand way to die, was it not? As you read the portion for today, pause over Jacob's testimony to the goodness of God (48:3,15,16), his remarkable spiritual insight, although physical vision was gone, and his determination to return to Canaan in spite of the fact that for seventeen years he had had the very best in Egypt. If you are reaching the sunset of life, and you feel, somehow, that your departure is at hand, subscribe heartily to Jacob's sincere confession: "God, which hath fed me all my life long unto this day, the Angel which redeemed me from all evil" be praised. May your end be as blessed as Jacob's.

Chapter 49

The prophetic, dying blessing of Jacob deserves our closest study. We have not space to grasp the central thought in the blessing pronounced upon each son. Attention must be given to the detailed account of Judah's blessing. Judah was to be victorious (Psalm 18:40), supreme among his brethren (Psalm 60:7), among the Tribes, the royal one, qualified for leadership (Revelation 5:5). Do you own the *Sceptre* who came out of Judah? Has the Lion of the Tribe of Judah delivered you from the devil? Dwell upon verse 18 for a moment. It seems to be out of place, yet is in vital relation to the whole chapter. It is a key verse, having a backward and a forward look. What a vitality of faith it expresses! Because our Salvation is not something, but SOMEONE, we wait for Him to appear and usher us into the prepared Home above.

Chapter 50

What tender love Joseph manifested for his father! The scene depicted in the opening verse must have been a touching one. We cannot do better than quote Dr. Scofield's comment, as we conclude the story of Jacob. "His life, ending in serenity and blessing, testifies to the power of God to transform character. His spiritual progress has six notable phases: (1) The first exercise of faith, as shown in the purchase of the birthright (25:28-34; 27:10-12); (2) the vision at Bethel (28:10-19); (3) walking in the flesh (29:1; 31:55); (4) the transforming experience (32:24-31); (5) the return to Bethel,

idols put away (35:1-7); (6) the walk of faith (37:1; 49:33)." Thinking of Jacob we recall the lines:

Enough to know that through the winter's
    frost
And summer's heat, no seed of truth is lost
And every duty pays at last its cost.

With Jacob dead and buried, Joseph's brothers became afraid. Their fear was that their father's death might be followed by an outbreak of long-smothered revenge in the heart of Joseph. And, as Dr. Alexander Maclaren puts it: "They thought Joseph like themselves, and they knew themselves capable of nursing wrath to keep it warm through long years of apparent kindliness. They had no room in their hearts for frank, full forgiveness. So they had lived on through numberless signs of their brother's love and care, and still kept the old dread, and probably, not a little of the old envy. How much happiness they had lost by their slowness to believe in Joseph's love!" Joseph's tears ought to have silenced their fears; they were strong evidence of his forgiving heart. If only those cowering brothers had loved Joseph in return, he might have died happier.

How tragically Genesis ends! "A coffin in Egypt." The book begins with God, the Author of life, and ends with death. Such is the story of Genesis. Death has come upon all men, for all have sinned. As Joseph came to die, as the New Testament asserts, the ancestral spirit was strong within him (Hebrews 11:22). He believed God's promise, and earnestly longed for its fulfilment. Although so long in Egypt, he was not of it: "Carry up my bones from hence" (verse 25). Ever an Israelite in heart, he looked beyond all his Egyptian associations and honors to the land promised by God to his fathers. And what a blessed hope is ours! We are in the world, yet we are not of it. Death may overtake the body, and a coffin be ours in the Egypt of this world, but ours is the forward look. Our dust, glorified, will be carried up, out of the bondage of corruption, into that glorious City, whose Builder and Maker is God.

EXODUS

This second book of the Bible records the greatest migration ever witnessed on earth. Think of it – two million souls on the march! History has no spectacle equal to this. If *Genesis* is a record of the old creation of nature, *Exodus* is an account of the new creation of redeeming grace. Its title signifies "a going out," or "a departure," and prepares us for the departure or going forth of the Israelites out of Eygpt. The book proves that God is supreme in every realm and teaches that redemption is by blood and power. The story of *Exodus* is repeated in every redeemed soul. Instruction follows deliverance, so we have the Sinai laws given for the regulation of life and worship. The key chapter is the *twelfth*, where the angel of judgment passes over the dwellings of the Hebrews covered by the sprinkled blood. One of the most thrilling national epics of literature, *Exodus* can be looked upon as the original *Pilgrim's Progress* with the *pillar* of God's presence leading the way (12:21,22). A store of information for the scholar, and a source of inspiration for the believer this *redemption book* taken up with the fortunes of Israel prefigures the slavery of sin, backslidings, discipline and deliverance in Christian experience. If in *Genesis* the earth is born by the Spirit out of the water, in *Exodus* Israel is born anew by the Spirit out of the water.

Chapter 1

The Book of Exodus records the beginning of Israel's national existence, and contains the fulfilment of Genesis 50:24. Thus Exodus is a continuation of Genesis. The title in our English version means "The Way Out," and is found in the word "exit." Recording, then, the redemption out of Egyptian bondage, the book is typical of Christ as the ground of our redemption from sin. Broadly speaking, this first chapter describes how the people were prepared for deliverance. The new king, who knew not Joseph, made Israel to serve with rigor. Grievous was the lot of the people redeemed by the power of God. Had He forsaken His own? No! He was standing in the shadows and over-ruling their bondage for ultimate blessing. The more Pharaoh afflicted them, the more they grew. Is your affliction adding to your spiritual stature?

Chapter 2

A deliverer is now prepared for the people. Strange, was it not, that Moses was prepared by the one who had sought to kill him? His godly mother "hid him three months" (verse 2). Can it be that God has someone, presently hidden, who before long will stand out as another deliverer of the people – another D. L. Moody who rocked two continents nearer heaven? The name *Moses* means "to draw out." It commemorated his deliverance from the water. When he came of age he was not ashamed to identify himself with his brethren, an identification costing him a 40 year exile as a stranger in a strange land. But it took those 80 years, 40 in Egypt learning to be somebody, 40 in Midian learning to be nobody, to prepare God's man for the mighty task of delivering Israel lasting another 40 years.

Chapter 3

This remarkable chapter, containing the call of Moses, is full of spiritual import for our hearts. The opening verses give us *humiliation*–"Moses kept the flock" (later he had a different one to keep!); *separation* –"the backside of the desert" (deserts are good training grounds for God's leaders); *elevation*–"the mountain of God"; *revelation* –"the angel of the Lord appeared unto him." What profound reverence for the presence of God Moses manifested. He realized how unworthy he was to stand before the great "I AM that I am." Is this our constant attitude? The name Gòd uses for Himself (verse 14), speaks of Him as the same unchanging One who had made the promises to Abraham, and who was about to fulfil them. When Moses commanded the people to prepare for their deliverance, he urged them to *ask*, not borrow (verse 22) jewels and raiment which were their due, seeing they had been robbed for years.

Chapter 4

Moses tried to contend his unfitness for the leadership of Israel on two grounds, namely: the unbelief of the people whom he was called to deliver, and his own lack of eloquence to speak as a leader. He wanted God to find a better man. Are you in the process of shirking some tremendous responsibility God is thrusting upon you? If so, step out on the glorious fact that "faithful is he that calleth you, who also will do it" (I Thessalonians 5:24). His commands are His enablings. The "rod" and the "hand" are two signs, speaking of preparation for service: first, consecration – our capacity taken up for God; second, the hand that holds the rod of God's power must be a cleansed hand swayed by a new heart. Yet Moses failed, and a stern reminder that God must be obeyed was given (verse 24).

Chapter 5

The first contest with Pharaoh only accentuated Israel's plight. The king charged Moses and Aaron with hindering the people from doing their work, and so additional labors were imposed. Pharaoh determined to crush Israel. The same quantity of bricks was required without supplying the necessary straw. Perhaps it was this extra load that gave birth to the initiative and inventiveness so characteristic of the Jew. Such a severe demand proved a failure. The people found the task impossible and appealed to the king, only to be charged with laziness. No wonder the hard-driven Israelites heaped indignation upon Moses and Aaron, as being the cause of their anguish! The leaders carried the complaint to God and pleaded anew for the promised deliverance. Does God seem long in answering some of His promises on your behalf? Courage, friend, deliverance from your Pharaoh may be around the corner.

Chapter 6

God did not chide the leaders or the people for their complaint. Encouragement, based on His own character as the covenant-keeping One, was given. The promise of chapter 3:13-15 was confirmed, with added promises. Underline the seven "I wills." The awesome name *Jehovah* speaks of Him as the eternal, unchangeable, and ever dependable God of His people. Alas, Israel was too depressed and discouraged to be heartened by God's glorious assurances! Are you in such a condition of mind? Moses presented his second challenge, but without avail. The last section of this chapter is taken up with the genealogy of the tribes, and is doubtless inserted here as a prelude to their deliverance by Moses and Aaron. Dividing the chapter, we have *God in the past* (verses 4,5); *God in the present* (verses 2,3); and *God in the future* (verses 6-8).

Chapter 7

Moses became a "god" and Aaron a "prophet," meaning both were to function as God's representatives before Pharaoh. From now on, the two leaders manifested a fearlessness of faith in God. The word "harden" (verse 3) has troubled some minds. It is not to be interpreted as a divine action, but an attitude produced by Pharaoh's disobedience to divine appeals. God meant all the plagues to soften the king's heart, but Pharaoh failed to yield to the divine will, thereby hardening his heart. The first sign of the rod becoming a serpent seemed to be a failure, in that Egyptian magicians were able to imitate the miracle. Superiority, however, was seen in that Aaron's rod was able to swallow up the Egyptian rods. The first plague was directed against the sacred Nile, the pollution of which only added to Pharaoh's determination to keep Israel. How tragic self-will is, in the face of God's power!

Chapter 8

As we examine the second plague, it may be fitting to observe that in the ten plagues, God was judging Egypt for its ten-fold form of idolatry. There were ten gods worshiped by the people, and each plague was directed against a particular heathen deity. Frogs were held sacred and were, therefore, never killed. Pharaoh acknowledged the power of God, and begged Moses to entreat God on his behalf. The king, however, remained adamant and would not let the people go. How terrible is the wilful resistance of God! The plague of lice found the magicians unable to ape God any longer, and left Pharaoh still resisting God. With the fourth plague, with its swarm of flies or beetles, there came proof of the distinction between Israel and Egypt (verses 22,23). Compromises were proposed by Pharaoh, but they were rejected by Moses. Religious compromise is ever serious. It sacrifices truth.

Chapter 9

Previous plagues attacked persons, now the fifth plague descends on property. The severity of this judgment and its limitations to Egyptian cattle left Pharaoh unperturbed. The sixth plague came without warning, and fell upon all, even the magicians (verse 11). Even yet the king was unmoved. Pharaoh was solemnly warned beforehand, in a long, unique message (verses 13-19), of the seventh plague. The courage of Moses is in sharp contrast to his former hesitation. At length death comes! This seventh plague thoroughly arouses Pharaoh, who confesses his sin, and begs for the removal of the plague! But his penitence was quickly forgotten, for he hardened his heart against Israel. Too often the shallowness of repentance is apparent. There is a concern merely to escape the consequences of sin. We need to pray for a deep and thorough conviction of sin as being against God.

Chapter 10

The struggle with Pharaoh continued, but at last the Egyptian officers pleaded with the king to satisfy the demands of Moses. The effect of the locust plague was profound, compelling Pharaoh to offer a third compromise, which was equally rejected by Moses. To leave the young behind would mean the return of their parents, who would again be used as slaves. The disastrous effects of the locusts forced Pharaoh to call hastily for Moses who, in turn, looked to God for relief. But again Pharaoh refused to let Israel go. Then came the miracle of darkness overtaking Egypt without warning. Behind any natural causes of the dense darkness was the work of God's supernatural visitation. Deeply impressed, Pharaoh offered a fourth compromise. It was refused by Moses and Aaron with courage and scorn. In anger, the king dismissed Moses, whose departure meant that the limit of God's for-

bearance had been reached. Have you light in your dwelling (see verses 21-23), even Him who is the Light of the World? (John 14:6).

Chapter 11

While Pharaoh never saw Moses again, he did witness another, and dreadful, display of the power of God, whom Moses represented, and which was to be the instrument of divine judgment. A summary is given of the approaching plague and its fearful results. The plagues as a whole were intended to convince Egypt and the surrounding nations, of the might and majesty of Israel's God. And every phase of nature was covered by His judgments – mineral, animal, vegetable and human – proving that He is Lord over all. Contrasts also, are suggested by the plagues: contrast in character between consistency and changeableness; contrast between strength and weakness; contrast between God and idols; and contrast between the saved and the lost.

Chapter 12

A new festival, the Passover, was to mark a new beginning for Israel. The remarkable fulness of detail in the instructions prove that the Passover was to be far more than the occasion of deliverance from Egypt; it was to become an integral part of Israel's life. Continuance year by year was ordered (verses 14-20), indicating thereby the permanence and prominence of the festival. The absence of leaven, its want suggesting purity, was another reminder of God's requirements as the holy One. All instructions were received in an attitude of reverence and were immediately put into practice. With the terrible death plague, Pharaoh completely surrendered and allowed Israel to go. About two million left the land of bondage. For the saints, the Passover is luminous with spiritual significance. It speaks of perfect redemption from the bondage of sin. Are you secure 'neath the blood?

Chapter 13

At long last the new life begins. After deliverance came dedication. "Israel had been saved through the destruction of Egypt's first-born, and now they were required to dedicate their own first-born in a constant memorial of their deliverance." Leaven, a symbol of evil, is again absent. God claimed the best the people had. Guidance followed redemption (verses 17,18). Brought out, the people were now to be brought through. And how miraculous God's guidance was! Supernaturally, by the pillar of cloud and fire, God led His own. Manifestations of the cloud and fire were according to need. How wise God is in the leading of His inexperienced people (verses 17,18)! The perpetual presence of God is always the foundation, inspiration and the satisfaction of the redeemed (Matthew 28:20; Hebrews 13:5).

Chapter 14

Canaan-bound, Moses led the people within Egypt's fertile fields, preventing thereby, many hardships of the desert. Pharaoh, recovering from the effects of the plagues, pursued Israel, hoping to recapture the hosts. The sight of the dreaded king filled the people with dismay. Fear gripped the multitudes, and for Moses the test was severe. Memory was short-lived. Recent deliverance from Pharaoh was soon forgotten. Moses' courage, however, did not fail. Fearlessly he faced the situation and reminded the people of a supernatural power well able to deal with Pharaoh (verse 14). There comes a time when action, rather than prayer, is needed (verse 15). Force had to be met by faith. Go forward! At the Red Sea, the natural and the supernatural were blended (verse 21), and Pharaoh and his hordes were destroyed. The Red Sea, placed between Egypt and Israel, typifies Christ's Resurrection as marking the gulf between sin and salvation, peril and protection (Romans 5: 8-10).

Chapter 15

The wilderness was necessary as God's permissive discipline to test and train His people. Wandering in the wilderness was not of God. The Song of Moses is the first poem of the nation, and is made up of retrospect (verses 1-12) and prospect (verses 15-18). Past deliverances and anticipated results are clearly defined. Resuming their journey, the people came to Marah and to a further test. But again God displayed His power in making the bitter, sweet. The tree,

thrown into the bitter water, is surely a type of the cross, which is able to sweeten every bitter cup. At Marah a divine statute, promising exemption from disease on fulfilment of certain conditions, was given. The Song of Moses and Miriam should be compared with "The Songs of Moses and the Lamb" (Revelation 15). Our Song of redemption has the same notes – God is our salvation, then our strength and then our song. As saved ones, let us sing!

Chapter 16

At the seventh stage of the wilderness journey, hunger overtook Israel. The fleshpots of Egypt were desired. Slavery in Egypt and God's deliverances were forgotten. Spiritual deterioration had set in. But again the God of compassion comes to bless a wayward people. Bread from heaven is promised. *Manna* means "this is a gift" (verse 15), and is a wonderful type of Christ, expressing both man's need and God's love and provision (John 6:33). The manna had to be gathered daily and eaten. Christ, as the source, sustenance and satisfaction in our lives, must be constantly appropriated by faith (John 6:35).

> Thou bruised and broken Bread,
> My life-long wants supply;
> As living souls are fed,
> Oh, feed me, or I die.

Chapter 17

What murmurers the Israelites became, and how God hates grumbling! At Marah, the water was undrinkable. Here, at Rephidim, there was no water and the people murmured against Moses. Their chiding of Moses and constant reference to Egypt were unfair and bitter. What disappointment God had to endure! Again Moses took the trouble to God, and another divine intervention was experienced. God has unexpected ways of provision, even for His unworthy people. The smitten rock reminds us of Christ, the source of the water of life, ever fresh, pure, abundant, suitable, accessible and unfailing (I Corinthians 10:4; John 7:37-39). Conflict with Amalek resulted in a God-given victory. In fighting against God's people, Amalek was really fighting against God. Amalek symbolizes the flesh, our nearest and closest foe, as Amalek was Israel's. Victory, however, is ever certain in the might of God. The flesh is doomed to die in due course (Galatians 5:24).

Chapter 18

Jethro, who is spoken of as Moses' father-in-law, dominates this chapter. Willingly he recognized *God's power* (verses 1,9,10), *God's supremacy* (verse 11), *God's presence* (verse 12), *God's righteousness* (verse 21), and *God's will* (verses 19,23). Jethro's wise counsel is worthy of note. He saw the heavy strain on Moses who, as yet, had not delegated authority, and advised appointment of associates as judges. Moses accepted the advice, and selection was made of men of ability, piety and veracity. Too many leaders "wear away" simply because they try to carry all the load. Lesser details, delegated to competent aides, would save time, thought and energy. The blessed thing about our heavenly Moses is that His task is never too heavy for Him. Hard causes and small matters can be brought to Him, for His unerring judgment.

Chapter 19

This chapter opens with a summary of Israel's journey from Egypt to Sinai. Called to meet God on the mount, Moses received from Him the first covenant for the people. Verses 3-9 are important to observe. Israel's history, past (verse 4), present (verse 5), and prospective (verse 6) had to be rehearsed. Then God's purpose, in and through Israel, is indicated. The people were to be His special representatives. As the priest represented man to God (Hebrews 5:1), the people of Israel were to be "priests" for the world. Here we see also holy preparation for entrance into the covenant. The people had to be sanctified. This was followed by a divine manifestation, impressing Israel with the reality and majesty of God, with whom they were entering into covenant. As those who are embraced in a better covenant, are we showing the world who and what God is?

Chapter 20

After the special preparation of the people for the reception of the Ten Commandments, there came the delivery of "the Decalogue," or *ten words*. A study of the law proves it to be a perfect moral code, suited for all men, times and circumstances. Ten, being one of the perfect numbers of Scripture, signifies perfection of divine order – the whole cycle is complete, nothing wanting. In the Ten Commandments, then, we have the complete revelation of the mind of God to the mind of man. Five commandments express man's relationship Godward, and the other five, his relationship manward. And the law, it will be seen, is based on redemption (verse 2). The effect on the people was evident: they feared God. But to Moses God said: "Fear not." The distance of Israel and the nearness of Moses are contrasted in verse 21. Would that God's holiness and majesty could produce the same awe and dread today! No longer under the law, we are yet "in-lawed" to Christ.

Chapter 21

In this and the following two chapters, we are told of "The Book of the Covenant" (24:7), with its record of civil, social and religious enactments. These chapters give us a detailed account of Israel's duty to God and to neighbors. In the chapter before us, we have "the rights of persons." *Laws concerning slavery* occupy verses 1-11. Slavery was a recognized institution at that time, but the law modified it and lessened its severities. *Laws concerning injuries* take up the rest of the chapter. Murder, homicide, kidnapping, assaults by man and beast, are all dealt with alike. Compensation and property rights are also dispensed. Lessons learned from this chapter are precious in these days when life is held so cheaply. We have the sanctity of life, the freedom of human life (verse 5), the reverence for parental life, the Christian law of life (Matthew 5:38-42). What a peaceful world this would be if only dictators and warmongers could live in this chapter!

Chapter 22

Continuing the laws governing human rights, we have read of *theft* (verses 1-4), *trespass* (verses 5,6), *deposits* (verses 7-13), *borrowing* (verses 14,15), and *various laws* (verses 16-31). Flagrant sins are to be severely dealt with. Judgment on witchcraft (verse 18) reveals the solemn fact of man's association with evil powers against God. Excessive and exorbitant demands were prohibited. Thus the Jews were forbidden to lend on interest among themselves. All of this reveals the perfect discrimination of God in regard to offenses, blending tenderness and severity. Then it also emphasized that the law of love should dominate every phase of life (verses 7,8). Betrayal of confidence is all too common today. Taking this declaration of rights as a whole, we are led to bless God for His care of the weak and helpless. The secret of all His provision is wrapped up in the phrase, "I am gracious" (verse 27).

Chapter 23

Twelve *miscellaneous laws* open this chapter (verses 1-9); then comes the *law of the sabbatical year* (verses 10-13). Such a law was unique; it was associated only with Israel. The *law of the feasts* (verses 14-19) blended agricultural, historical and spiritual elements. The three special seasons were: the feast of unleavened bread, the feast of first fruits and the feast of harvest. General instructions, promises, and warnings form a fitting conclusion to such precise laws. In promising His provision, protection and power, God promised to send His angel before His people (verse 20). By this angel, we are not to understand a created angel but a divine manifestation. Without doubt this was a promised premanifestation of Christ, one of His theophanic appearances (verse 21). How much we can learn from God's call to His people to "be circumspect" (verse 13), "beware" (verse 21), and "obey" (verse 22)! Note the great "I wills" in this chapter.

Chapter 24

Moses came near, but the people worshiped afar off. The nearness of Israel's leader, and the distance of Israel, are again mentioned. As a nation, Israel now ratified the divinely-conceived book of the covenant. Blood is prominent in this chapter, and represents the surrender of life to God. First there is propitiation; then, consecration. How impressive is the portion dealing with the

vision of God and the sacrificial feast (verses 9-11)! As God cannot be seen by man, some divine appearance is meant by "they saw God." The personal and private interview with God, lasting for six weeks (Deuteronomy 9:9) reveals the intimate fellowship with God that Moses enjoyed. Such fellowship is our highest spiritual privilege. Moses came down from the mount bearing unconsciously the glory of the divine presence. "He wist not that his face shone" (Exodus 34:29). The moment we are conscious of having a shining face, it ceases to shine.

Chapter 25

Divine instructions as to the building of the tabernacle take up chapters 25-31. The people were urged to contribute material for its construction, and the whole structure was to be made, even down to minute details, according to the pattern given to Moses by God. Continuing in the divine will and way, Israel must regularly worship God in God's way. The most important feature, the ark, is mentioned first, seeing it was the symbol of approach to God. The shewbread, or "the bread of the face, or presence," was exhibited to God. The golden lampstand provided light for the holy place. How suggestive the tabernacle is of Christ! He is our ark, our only avenue of approach to God. He is our propitiation, sustenance and illumination. "There will I meet with thee" (verse 22). The meeting of the soul with God is a priceless privilege. Would that we could appropriate it more than we do!

Chapter 26

Details as to curtains, coverings and outer structure take up this chapter. We have, for example, *the inside curtains* (verses 1-6), *the outer covering of goatskin* (verses 7-13), *the outer covering of rams' skins* (verse 14), *boards and sockets* (verses 15-25), *stability bars* (verses 26-30), *the inner veil*, separating the holy place from the Holy of Holies (verses 31-35), and *the outer entrance veil* (verses 36,37). The epistle to the Hebrews gives the authority for pondering the spiritual meaning and message of these divine instructions (Hebrews 9:6-9). They form our picture book of Christ's redemptive work. The various divisions of the tabernacle suggest the separation of God from us, because of sin. Coming to the emphasis laid on the provision of the best possible materials, we glean the truth of God's holiness, and the necessity of giving to the utmost. It must ever be our "utmost for His highest."

Chapter 27

The brazen altar, which was to bear the sacrifices of the people, would serve to remind tnem of the one and only condition of approach to God. By a *brazen* altar, judgment is implied. Christ bore our judgment. Upon the cross He became the whole burnt-offering, offered without spot to God. The court (verses 9-18), was an oblong rectangle in front of the tabernacle, enclosed by curtains hung on pillars. This court, around 300 feet long and 75 feet broad, was deemed a sacred enclosure for worshipers only. Esau was "profane," meaning "before the temple," the place of general concourse. He was secular, having no sacred enclosure in his life. Of the vessels (verse 19) and oil (verses 20,21), much could be written. Oil is one of the symbols of the Holy Spirit (John 3:34; Acts 10:38; Hebrews 1:9). He it is who supplies the vessel of your life and mine with an unfailing source of illumination. As a lamp, do you always shine (verse 20)?

Chapter 28

We now come to the priesthood by which the services of the tabernacle were to be performed. The divinely appointed dress of the priest makes up this chapter, which opens with general directions as to attire. Then come instructions as to the ephod, a vest to carry the breastplate. Next in order is the breastplace. Mystery surrounds the purpose of Urim and Thummim, meaning "lights and perfections." In some way this part of the breastplate was used to ascertain God's will on special occasions (Ezra 2:63). The beautiful *robe of the ephod* is described in verses 31-35; the *holy crown* in verses 36-38, and the *priestly garments* of glory and beauty in verses 39-43. All believers are priests, representing man to God, and prophets, representing God to man. As priests, we have our garments for glory and beauty (verse 2). It is true, they are not material robes, ephods and crowns, but our attire is the whole armor of God. The detailed account of the garments suggests that everything in our approach to God must be perfect.

Chapter 29

The consecration of the priest meant entire dedication and devotion to his sacred office. We are told of *priestly offerings and worship* (verses 1-4), the *investiture of Aaron and his sons* (verses 5-9), *priestly offerings* (verses 10-25), *priestly food* (verses 26-34) and *priestly consecration* (verses 35-46). For the great priesthood of Christ, we turn to Hebrews 4:11-10:25. How comforting and inspiring is such a truth! From this chapter we learn that redemption is the basis and spring of service (verse 14). Purity is also emphasized as the necessary preliminary to, and continuous accompaniment of, the work of God (Isaiah 52:11). Indeed, we need a continual washing (I John 1:7). The continual burnt-offering suggests unceasing dedication to God (Romans 12:1). Blessings flowing from entire consecration are set forth (verses 43-46), and can be experienced by any believer to whom God is the center and circumference of all things in life.

Chapter 30

The altar of incense, spoken of in this chapter, is full of spiritual symbolism. Dividing the chapter, we have: *the altar and its location* (verses 1-10), *the ransom-money*, called "atonement-money," and likely used to cover the cost of the tabernacle worship (verses 11-16), *the laver* (verses 17-21), *the oil*, with full directions for its preparations and use (verses 22,23), and *the incense*, with detailed instructions as to its preparation (verses 34-38). The incense that we offer is prayer (Psalm 141:2; Revelation 8:3). How fragrant to God is Spirit-inspired prayer! In the ransom-money we see the necessity of the redeemed to surrender their substance for the maintenance of the work of the Lord. Coming to the laver, with its cleansing, we have the prerequisite for acceptable worship and work. Oil for the sanctuary typifies the Spirit's anointing which is never poured upon the flesh (verse 32). What a solemn truth to remember!

Chapter 31

Facts regarding the workmen who were to be responsible for the erection of the tabernacle are given in the first part of this chapter. Two men are named as having received divine appointment for this sacred work. Artistic beauty and skill of hand are as much the gifts of the Holy Spirit as His spiritual blessings. Would that we had more wise-hearted men, in whom the Spirit has implanted wisdom! Use of skill in the Lord's service is both a blessing to men and a glory to God. The rest of the chapter (verses 12-18) is taken up with the sabbath as a divine sign. New features are added to what had already been given. The observance of this day of rest and worship tended to keep the people true to God. Recognition of the sabbath is associated with God's consecration of the believer (verse 13). The sabbath was also to be a pledge of God's perpetual covenant with His people. The rest it brings is for our refreshment (verse 17).

Chapter 32

A parenthetical portion, covering chapters 32-34, describes happenings among the people during the absence of Moses. The impatience of the people was met by the weakness of Aaron, and so the golden calf appeared. Intended to represent God, the calf was a breach of the second commandment. How sinful were those who had been so signally blessed of God! Aaron's deplorable weakness was inexcusable. He should have known better and acted differently. Descending from the mount, Moses discovered what God had already known, and promptly interceded for a wilful people. Three pleas made up effectual intercession – Israel was God's people; Egypt would be exultant; divine promises were unfulfilled. Righteously indignant, Moses destroyed the tables of stone. The people were punished, and Moses pleaded again. How nobly he sacrificed himself for the sake of others (verse 32)! How powerful is intercession (Romans 8:34)!

Chapter 33

This chapter opens with God's concern for His own righteousness. His rebuke of the people bore results. Personal ornaments were discarded. Because of their sin, the Israelites were to be guided by an angel rather than by God Himself, a sad loss producing repentance. Moses' own tent became the temporary tabernacle wherein the Lord talked with Moses. God's acknowledgment of His servant's loyalty should be noted (verses 9-11), and also His answer to the prayer of Moses (verses 12-17). Moses desired a proof of the complete restoration of the people to divine favor, and a closer and fuller revelation than he had had in the past. While the full, unveiled sight of God could not be granted, a partial revelation was given. Graciously God answered Moses' prayer and His glory was seen in His "goodness" (verses 18,19). As we face unknown experiences, let us rest in the blessed promise of verses 14 and 15.

Chapter 34

Moses was commanded to ascend Mount Sinai, there to receive the God-written tables of stone. For tasks ahead, Moses was granted a fresh vision. The declaration of God's grace and truth brought Moses to adoration and prayer. A solemn reminder of divine righteousness can be found in the renewed covenant. Promises (verses 10-12) are to be met by obedience (verses 13-17) – a truth we often forget. The repetition of instructions as to feasts and sabbaths speaks of the necessity of loyalty to God. The feast of the first fruits had to be His. With what blessed results of fellowship with God the chapter closes! Those hallowed days in the presence of God left their mark, even on the face of Moses. Would that we could have a glory-face without knowing it! Others saw the reflection of glory, but Moses wist not that the skin of his face shone.

Chapter 35

Instructions as to the tabernacle are before us again. Commencing work on it, the people were reminded of the sabbath, the recognition of which would prove loyalty to God. This is why they were often reminded about the law of the sabbath. Its constant observance would be the best guarantee of unfailing devotion to God. Necessary gifts and labor were enumerated by

Moses, and the response of the people was remarkable. All willingly gave. None were forced to surrender their substance. With hearts stirred up, the result was surrendered treasures and time so that the tabernacle might be built. Giving to God is a "grace" (II Corinthians 8:7) and should always be "willing" and proportionate to ability (I Corinthians 16:2). To the workmen appointed to erect the structure divine wisdom was granted. Nothing was left to human ingenuity. The tabernacle had to be built in God's way by God's men.

Chapter 36

Such was the enthusiasm of the people that they had to be restrained from giving. Every morning freewill offerings were brought to Moses until he had more than sufficient for building the tabernacle. If only God's people gave as superabundantly today, there would be no church debts, and more than enough for the evangelization of the ends of the earth. What unity of action Moses witnessed among the people! There were no shirkers. The rest of the chapter records the progress of the work. Former details as to the various parts of the tabernacle are repeated, along with minute obedience as to the carrying out of the pattern given in the mount. Everything had to be fashioned as God had commanded Moses. Thus is it with the building and government of the Church. It is His Church and must be cared for in His way.

Chapter 37

Continued progress in the erection of the tabernacle occupies this chapter. Again we meet with the ark, the table of shewbread, the lampstand, the incense altar and the holy anointing oil. Gold, it will be seen, occupies a conspicuous place in the furnishings, telling us that nothing is too good for God and for His cause. Gold is symbolic of Deity, and as Christ is everywhere in the tabernacle, His Deity is emphasized. He is the substance of the shadow. He is our mercy seat, the One whose death and resurrection make possible acceptance with God. We can also see Him in the shewbread, food of God and man. As the lampstand, He is the light of the world. The incense

altar reminds us of His perpetual intercession on our behalf. How fragrant His daily ministry must be as He lives to make intercession for us!

Chapter 38

The work still goes on, with a colossal sum being spent on the erection of God's dwelling place. Details as to the brazen altar, the laver, the court and its gate, and the sum total of metal used, make up the chapter. Lessons to be gleaned from the chapter have been stated thus: "Self-sacrifice is based on piety. Motives make the man (verse 8). The court suggests separation, the great principle found all through the Bible, yet so sadly neglected by many Christians today (II Corinthians 6:17). The vast amount of money and labor given testifies to the greatness of the task and the liberality of God's people. The exact calculation teaches the necessity of thoroughness and accuracy in all things connected with money for God's work." There was no waste, no overlapping. God knew what would be needed and prompted the people to give accordingly.

Chapter 39

At last preparations were finished, and now we have here instructions as to Aaron's garments, which must have been magnificent to behold. How we would love to dwell upon the typical significance of all Aaron wore! The high priest's clothes were a symbol of "the beauty of holiness" (I Chronicles 16:29). There is one item we must draw attention to, namely, a bell and a pomegranate around the hem of the robe (verse 26). The bell stands for testimony and the pomegranate for the fruit; and the one ever goes with the other. The glory of completion can be found in the phrase, "thus was all the work . . . finished" (verse 32). Seven times over we have the statement: "as the Lord commanded Moses." May the same exactness of obedience be ours! No wonder Moses blessed the people for their faithfulness. (Compare verse 43 with Genesis 1:31; 2:1-3).

Chapter 40

What an impressive sight it must have been as the tabernacle was set up! Directions as to placing of furniture, consecration of the tabernacle by anointing, and actual erection occupy the bulk of the last chapter. Once it was reared up, there came divine recognition and the provision of divine guidance. How rich in typical teaching is the finished structure! It was the place where God localized His presence and was worshiped. Here God and His redeemed people met. The cloud was the sign and means of God's guidance. Christ is our tabernacle (John 1:14); and how the glory of the Lord filled the tabernacle! Such glory is promised to our lives. "The Lord will give . . . glory" (Psalm 84:11). In the Old Testament God had a tabernacle for His people; now His people are His tabernacle (I Corinthians 6:19).

LEVITICUS

Doubtless there are those who find this book a weariness to the flesh, or a book difficult to appreciate. Its intimate descriptions of the sacrifices seem to be without point. Yet no book of the Bible is so wonderfully profitable. The study of it intensifies our adoration of Christ who became our *Scapegoat*. To the Jewish fathers the ceremonies of this third pentateuchal book were signposts on the way, and if we read the book aright we shall discover the unsearchable riches of the Saviour in it. The central chapter is the sixteenth, and there is no more significant chapter in the whole of the Old Testament than this one introducing us, as it does, to *The Great Day of Atonement*. The name *Leviticus* itself means, "The Levitical Book," seeing it deals with the rites and ceremonies appointed in connection with the Levitical Priesthood. It was the guidebook for Priests (4:14; Hebrews 7:11). Arabic and Syriac Versions refer to it as *The Law Of The Priests*, or *The Law Of The Offerings* because of the prominence given to the sacrifices and services the Levitical Priesthood were responsible for. The Jews called it *Vayyikon*, being the equivalent of the first three words at the beginning of the book – "And he called" (1:1). *Leviticus* contains God's call to worship and fellowship, to holiness of heart and habit. We can call it *The Textbook On Holiness*. Because of His august holiness, God must have a holy people. Thus "holiness" and its cognates are found some 131 times in the book. Such "holiness" is made possible by atonement (16:34; 17:11). *Leviticus* naturally follows *Exodus*. The Tabernacle having been set up, the priests are now clearly defined.

Chapter 1

The keynote of the book is "holiness," in its primary meaning of separation *from* and separation *to* God. The references to Leviticus in the epistle to the Hebrews shows its importance and spiritual meaning. Leviticus carries two main divisions: *the way of approach to God*, chapters 1-16; and *the way of abiding with God*, chapters 17-27. The five offerings in the book teach that approach to God is ever by sacrifice. This opening chapter is occupied with the burnt offering, which suggests entire consecration. It can be applied to the relationship between Christ and His own. Christ, as the burnt offering, was fully surrendered to the Father, although such surrender involved the cross. As a burnt offering, the believer realizes that everything he is and has belongs to God, and must be used for His glory (Romans 12:1). When the burnt offering begins, the song of the Lord also begins. Sacrifice and song become one.

Chapter 2

The second offering is better known as "the meal offering." It was the only sacrifice without blood, and was called "a gift." This offering suggests man's homage to God, as shown by the presentation of the products of the earth, and can be traced in I Chronicles 29:14-16, where we have the idea of a gift pleasing to God. Although it accompanied the burnt offering, the meal offering was a separate offering. The former symbolized a life devoted to God; the latter, fruits of labor dedicated to Him. Note the features of this offering:

oil is a type of the Holy Spirit; frankincense means sacrifice accomplished by prayer; absence of leaven means purity; absence of honey, absence of everything impure or even doubtful; salt represents preservation and permanence as indications of God's government; fire represents divine acceptance; and sweet-savor, God's approval and pleasure.

Chapter 3

The distinctive feature of the peace offering was the feast after the sacrifice. This offering symbolizes reconciliation, as shown in the fellowship of eating. One portion was consumed by fire, indicating God's acceptance and participation. Another portion was eaten by the offerers, and as eating is always an element in a covenant, oneness between God and the offerer is here taught. A third portion was eaten by the priest, simply for his maintenance. As all the offerings reach their perfection in Christ, He is our peace offering, having made reconciliation for us. He is our Peace (Ephesians 2: 14-17). When we appropriate Him and are recipients in His finished work, peace becomes ours (Romans 5:1). Then we eat. Fellowship with Christ becomes the highest point of Christian privilege (Matthew 22: 1-14; Psalms 23:5; 36:8).

Chapter 4

By the sin offering we are taught the need of propitiation, expiation and atonement ere the sinner can approach God. And is there not constant need of expiation, even in the life of the believer? Until our dying breath, the blood will be needed. It will be found that this fourth offering is graded according to position: *priest* (verses 2-12); *people* (verses 13-21); *rulers* (verses 22-26); and *ordinary persons* (verses 27-35). The elaborate instructions teach the terribleness of sin in the sight of a holy God. No sin can be overlooked. Even for ignorance, or inadvertence, sacrifice was necessary. Christ became our sin offering. He was made sin, not a sinner, on our behalf. Now the sinner can be forgiven and made a son, because the innocent victim offered a sacrifice of expiation.

Chapter 5

It would seem as if the first part of this chapter continues the instruction concerning the sin offering, as related to ordinary people, offered according to capacity. The trespass offering, like the sin offering, was another new requirement for Israel. In the latter, the main thought was that of *guilt*, while in the trespass offering it was *injury* done to God and man. In the sin offering, it is expiation; in the trespass offering, it is satisfaction. Now the sinner is reinstated in the divine covenant. The application of this offering has been expressed thus: "Christ as our trespass offering means that God's rights must be upheld because sin is an offense against His position and character, and calls for reparation. The thought of satisfaction is a very important aspect of Christ's atoning work." Recognition of this truth leads to *reparation*, due from us, and to the acknowledgment that Christ made it on our behalf.

Chapter 6

The details about the laws of offerings continue in this chapter, and special reference is made to wrongs against man. Five cases are mentioned and, in each, restitution is required. Confession and reparation had to be made to the one wronged, and an offering presented to God. Verses 8-13 give the law of the burnt offering for the guidance of priests. Verses 24-30 tell us of the law of the sin offering. Here the priests were taught the special solemnity and sanctity of such offerings. How pointed is the message of this chapter for today! Sins against man must be met by confession and restitution. We further learn that "priestly life and service cannot be too particular in their care for the will of God to be done at every point. The best proof of life is faithfulness in little things."

Chapter 7

After outlining further facts concerning the trespass offering, Moses sets forth the law of the peace offering, which symbolizes the initial need of the sinner. Note the terms "leaven" (verse 13) and "unleavened wafers" (verse 12). It may be that the leaven offered after unleavened wafers suggests verse

12 as a type of the sinless Christ, and verse 13 as a type of our condition, notwithstanding our relation to God. The chapter concludes with a summary of the priests' portion and duties, in which the fact and meaning of sin are emphasized. And this assignment of priestly duties speaks of God's care for His own, the recognition of dependence upon Him. The heave offering (raised toward heaven) is an acknowledgment of God as the Lord of redemption; the wave offering (moved from left to right) shows that God is not only infinitely high, but infinitely nigh.

Chapter 8

This illuminating chapter, commencing the second section of the book, is taken up with the consecration of the priests, and is full of spiritual application for our hearts. Four main features of consecration can be traced: *cleansing* (verses 6,13); *clothing* (verses 7-9); *anointing* (verses 10-12); and *sacrifice* (verses 14-22). Every detail is symbolical. Note how all is from God and not man ("as the Lord commanded"). The application of the blood to ear, hand and foot speaks of the consecration of all faculties to God. What we hear, what we do, and where we go must indicate that we, too, are priests unto God. Christ is our high priest, fulfilling the two requirements of authority from God and oneness with man (Hebrews 5:5-8). His priesthood is also a safeguard against the believer sinning (Hebrews 4:14-16; 7:25). The seven days of separation can typify our entire dedication to Christian priesthood.

Chapter 9

After separation, service begins. After a week of consecration, Aaron and his sons commence this priestly service. Can we say that our service for our Lord is truly consecrated service? In the instructions regarding offerings for the priests, atonement is spoken of as being necessary for them ere they could render acceptable service (verses 8-14). The next section is taken up with offerings for the people. On the foundation of sacrifice, and through the channel of the mediating priesthood, the nation could not

approach God (*cf.* John 14:6). Compare the order of offerings with previous chapters. In the divine recognition and confirmation of all the ceremonies that Aaron presided over, "glory" refers to the manifestation of splendor, God's revelation of Himself. The fire alludes to acceptance and approval after obedience, and the people's attitude was one of awe. What a chapter to read on one's knees.

Chapter 10

It did not take long for the priestly influence to become stained. There is a parallel between the death of Nadab and Abihu, told in this chapter, and that of Ananias and Sapphira, written in Acts 5. The "strange fire" may suggest that the two sons of Aaron lit their censers from an ordinary fire instead of from the fire of the burnt offering. Whatever it was, it was not God-commanded; and thus it received His judgment. At the outset, Israel must know the real character of God. Marks of personal sorrow in the face of righteous judgment were not allowed (see Matthew 8:21 for the same principle). From the context, it would seem as if Nadab and Abihu were semi-intoxicated, thus preventing them from knowing the right and the wrong way of serving God. May we be saved from the sin of presumption! God's ways, not ours, must be followed at all costs. Spiritual worship and work can never be furthered by carnal means.

Chapter 11

Ceremonial and moral purity are now dealt with. A consideration of how impurity keeps man from God forms chapters 11 to 15. The first aspect of this purity is that of food. Some of the prohibitions are hard to understand. Extreme sanitation laws, however, were enforced to safeguard the health of the camp. Foul appearance and unclean habits are also symbolical of sin. Regulations as to quadrupeds, fish, birds, insects, creeping things and vermin, all carry the underlying principle of holiness. A holy people must have holiness stamped on every part of life. God took every precaution of emphasizing this truth. Too often, in this church age, we neglect the gospel of the body. Yet, the epistles lay stress on the body as a part of our redeemed being. If we are to glorify God in our body, then we must eat and drink to His glory, which surely means the exercise of care in the matter of diet.

Chapter 12

Bodily or ceremonial uncleanness as to childbirth comes as a natural sequence of the previous chapter. Laws of purification and of circumcision had to be scrupulously obeyed. For the law of circumcision, we must go back to Genesis 17:12, where both physical purity and moral purity are enjoined. The spiritual significance of this law is touched upon by Paul in his writings (see Colossians 2:10,11 and Philippians 3:3). For the law of the offerings (verses 6-8), compare Luke 2:22-24. Israel had to learn, as we must, that every phase of life must be holy unto the Lord. If only the deepest and most sacred elements of home-life were related to God, what a different nation ours would be. Let it never be forgotten that holiness involves atonement and purification (verse 7). Holiness also means wholeness in every phase of life.

Chapter 13

Leprosy in all its manifestations is now included in regulations governing the life of a holy people. Offensiveness of appearance and seriousness of condition are dealt with. The moral element is prominent, seeing that the leper required the priest rather than the doctor (verse 2). The chapter covers *doubtful cases* (verses 1-8), *actual cases* (verses 9-11), *real and apparent cases* (verses 12-17), *methods of examination* (verses 18-39), *head leprosy* (verses 40-44), *treatment* (verses 45,46), and *leprosy in garments* (verses 47-59). Compare the Bible records of lepers. Leprosy is one of the most striking types of sin: "insignificant and painless at the outset; gradual through slow development; serious results to the leper; repulsive to others; incurable by human means; the issue, death." Leprosy caused separation and required the ministry of a priest, who must insist on requirements being fulfilled. But what the priest could not cure, Christ can, for His blood can make the vilest clean.

Chapter 14

How striking are the eleborate instructions given of the cleansing of lepers! The first stage consisted of purification. Four features of restoration are typical of spiritual realities: sprinkling of blood, cedar wood, scarlet and hyssop. The two birds represent the double type of death and resurrection. It is important to note that not even the priest could cure. All healing is divine. The priest could only declare a person clean and enforce certain requirements. The second stage of purification (verses 9-32) was the restoration of the cleansed one to his home. Cleansing of the house came next (verses 33-53), suggesting for our hearts the need of a pure environment if we are to live aright. Personal cleansing and consecration must cover every phase of life. Would that multitudes of moral lepers could realize how helpless they are to cleanse and cure themselves!

Chapter 15

Five cases of ceremonial impurity, due to the physical defilement of leprosy, are touched upon in the imperatives of cleansing that make up this chapter. Men (verses 2-18) and women (verses 19-30) are reminded of the repulsiveness of leprosy as a disease, and that such repulsiveness is at once a physical peril and moral parable (verse 31). A holy God must have a holy people. This is why we have a solemn emphasis on sin as being ingrained in man's nature. Distinction must be drawn between sin (root) and sins (fruit); between unconscious sins and conscious sins. Unconscious sins are indicated in this chapter as requiring atonement and cleansing equally with all conscious sins. Thank God, He is able to deal with sin and sins! There is "the double cure" dealing with the guilt and power of sin. What do we know about deliverance from the government of sin, as well as its guilt?

Chapter 16

What a notable chapter this is! Expositor Kellogg says of it: "What the fifty-third of Isaiah is to the Messianic prophecies, the sixteenth of Leviticus is to the whole system of Mosaic types – the most consummate flower of the Messianic symbolism." All observances led to the annual day of atonement, the center and culmination of the Hebrew festivals. The key word of the chapter is "atonement" (verse 33), and it relates to *Aaron and his house* (verse 6), *the tabernacle* (verses 15,17), *the brazen altar* (verses 18,19), and *the whole congregation* (verses 20-22,33). Main features of this annual ceremony were sacrifices on the brazen altar, entrance of the high priest into the Holy of holies, the sprinkling of blood on and around the mercy seat, and the return of the high priest after the performance of duties – all of which speak of Christ's atonement, approach, appeal and advent.

Chapter 17

It is natural and fitting that, after instructions as to sacrifice, priesthood, purifications and atonement, the place where the people should gather is next in order. And, here again, nothing was left to human choice. The people were not to think that any place would do. For all observances, there was but one place, namely, the one of divine appointment (Deuteronomy 16:5,6). All ordinary places of worship at home were set aside for the tabernacle, where God localized His presence. As to the prohibition in regard to blood (verses 10-16), while the basis of such was doubtless hygienic, the prominent reason was religious, teaching the sacredness of the means of sacrifice. The divinely-chosen place speaks of Christ as the one and only way (John 14:6; Acts 4:12). God can only be approached in the place and means of His own appointing. Sacredness associated with common food, or "holiness in eating," emphasizes the principle of grace before meat (I Corinthians 10:31).

Chapter 18

Dr. C. I. Scofield names this chapter, "the relationship and walk of God's earthly people." Here God's commands against various forms of moral impurity are enforced. First, we have the *Hebrew law of marriage* (verses 1-5), and then, *details of this law and restraints against sin* (verses 6-18). *Further prohibitions* follow (verses 19-23). Idolatry and licentiousness went together (verse 21). The chapter concludes with solemn warnings. *Relationship between national life and individual life* are set forth (verses 24-30). A writer of keen insight says: "Dissolute morals are always a symptom which precedes the ruin of an empire, or the fall of a nation." For ourselves, as a heavenly people, there is much to learn from this chapter. God is the perfection of holiness. The basis of holiness (verses 2-4) should be studied. God's character and His claim on us form the foundation of true life. The principle of holiness is full separation (verse 3), and the evidence is seen in character and conduct (verses 4,5).

Chapter 19

Further laws on holiness are discussed by Moses, as he passes from licentiousness to deal with various kinds of unfaithfulness to God and man. While lack of system may characterize this presentation, a binding principle can be detected in verse 2, namely, every relationship is bound up with the truth of divine holiness. In unmistakable language, the will of God was communicated plainly to the people. God had separated them unto Himself and required them to be holy, seeing His character, laws and service were holy. The instructions as to divorce, cattle, mingled seed, mixture of garments, fittingly illustrate the New Testament exhortation of being separate from all that is alien to God's holy will. Other prohibitions impressed the minds of the Israelites with a sense of their duty, and God's claims to obedience. "The cause of God is holy, and useth holy things."

Chapter 20

Molech was the idol worshiped by the Ammonites. His devotees dedicated their children to him, which consisted in the infants being shaken over flames emanating from the idol. It was believed by the fire-worshipers that all children who did not undergo this purifying process would die in infancy. It is sad to realize that it was necessary to warn a redeemed people against this horrible form of idolatry. No wonder the severest penalties were enforced by Moses. The enumeration of incestuous and unnatural crimes reveal how Israel had been influenced by surrounding idolatrous nations.

Constantly the people forgot that God had separated them from the nations for the all-important end of preserving the knowledge and worship of Himself as the true God. Hence the repetition of laws regarding the difference between the clean and the unclean.

Chapter 21

From the people we come to priests. This chapter and the following deal with the defilement and defects of the priests. Special regulations are to be found in this section covering ceremonial and moral defilements and physical defects. *Family relations* are before us in verses 1 to 6; *moral blemishes*, in verses 7-9. The next section is taken up with the high priest. Even his private sorrows were not to interfere with his public work. Any *physical defect disqualified him* (verses 10-24). A perusal of this chapter makes it clear that God does not have two standards of holiness – one for priests, another for people. All who are His must be holy. "Be ye clean, that bear the vessels of the Lord" (Isaiah 52:11). Certainly those who are called to conspicuous service must so live that the ministry be not blamed. God, however, commands all his children to be holy.

Chapter 22

The separation of the priests is still before us. None who were ceremonially unclean were allowed to officiate or partake of sacrificial offerings. *Ministry ceased until all defilement was removed* (verses 1-4). *Members of a defiled priest's house, however, were permitted to eat of the offerings* (verses 10-13). All animals for sacrifice had to be physically perfect. If too young, they were counted as blemished (verses 17-27). How considerate God is, even over dumb creatures! Look at verse 28 for a suggestion of humanity and kindness (see also Exodus 23:19; Deuteronomy 14:21). The sacrifice of thanksgiving was doubtless some form of the peace offering (verses 29,30). The chapter concludes by summarizing Israel's solemn duty. Redemption is the basis of sanctification. Having been brought out of Egypt, the people had to be wholly given up to God.

Chapter 23

The contents of this chapter are highly instructive to the close student of the Word. How rich in typical teaching are these feasts! Stated times for approaching God were natural and inevitable for a people redeemed by blood and power. It will be seen that five of the feasts were related to the harvest, thus indicating their natural aspect. In order, we have *the weekly Sabbath* (verses 1-3), with the two main thoughts of rest and redemption; *the passover* (verses 4,5); *the feast of unleavened bread* (verses 6-8); *the first fruits* (verses 9-14); *Pentecost* (verses 15-22), *the trumpets* (verses 23-25), *the day of atonement* (verses 26-30), and *the tabernacles* (verses 33-38), appropriate after the removal of national sin on the day of atonement. All these festivals are typical of Christ, and likewise symbolize for us remembrance of redemption, joy in God, the worship of God and consecration.

Chapter 24

As the next chapter resumes and completes the teaching of chapter 23, the one before us may be parenthetical. Command as to the oil is repeated from Exodus 27:20. In the account of the shewbread, note how, in verse 6, God is a God of order. The act of blaspheming (verses 10-23), doubtless occurred at this time, and is so dealt with at this point. Pronounced judgment was a reminder of the holiness of God. "Holy and reverend is his name" (Psalm 111:9). God's fatherhood should always produce awe (I Peter 1:17). We have two types here: oil, the Holy Spirit (Psalm 43:3; Revelation 1:12-20) – there is our need of light, first in, and then through us (Matthew 5:14-16); the shewbread – Christ as the bread of God for our lives (John 6:32-51). Are we ready to be a blessing to others, the bread for their lives? Divinely fed, in turn we feed others.

Chapter 25

The instructions of chapter 23 are now resumed – the completion of the systems of festivals. The sacred seven is again evident. In connection with the law of the land, we have *the Sabbath feast* (verses 1-7); and *the jubilee feast* (verses 8-55), with its four-fold division, namely the ordinance itself (verses 8-12), law in relation to land (verses 13-28), to houses (verses 29-34), and to slaves (verses 35-55). Three aspects of God's character are emphasized: His claim, "Mine" (verse 23) – both the sabbatical and jubilee years reminded the people of God's right to their treasures and time; His bounty – God loves hilarious giving (II Corinthians 9:7), seeing He gives this way Himself; and His purpose – the years foreshadowed Christ as the Kingsman-Redeemer, and spoke of His final and complete redemption, and its permanent provision of liberty (Isaiah 61:1,2; Luke 4:18,19). Are we rejoicing in the glorious liberty of Christ secured for us by His cross?

Chapter 26

Some writers treat this chapter as the last of the book, with the next chapter as a mere appendix. Spiritual applications are herewith given. In introduction of the conditions of blessing and warnings of chastisement, we see a three-fold summary of duty (verses 1,2). Then come *the blessings of obedience* – plenty, peace, protection, power, prosperity and privilege (verses 3-13). *The results of disobedience* are equally emphasized. The recurring phrase, "seven times," refers to the *degree* of punishment not to *duration*. Persistence in disobedience meant

intensification of divine judgment (verses 14-39). *Repentance and restoration* conclude the chapter (verses 40-55). The same alternates face us today: blessing of obedience; bane of disobedience. These two phases are illustrated for us in the two men of Psalm 1. How full the Scripture is of Israel's history, past, present and future!

Chapter 27

In this appendix that deals with vows, some matters, once obligatory are now voluntary (Deuteronomy 23:22). We have *vows as to persons* (verses 2-8), *animals* (verses 9-13), *houses* (verses 14,15) and *lands* (verses 16-24). Then come *standards of calculation* (verse 25), *matters excluded from vows* (verses 26-33), and the *closing summary* of the book (verse 34). Old Testament vows form a fascinating study. Some were obligatory, others voluntary, and a few were foolish in nature. Faithfulness to the right kind of vows is enjoined (Ecclesiastes 5:5). In this Christian age vows are no longer a necessary part of our faith. God, however, loves and rejoices in every expression of our voluntary affection. Spontaneity of response proves the existence of power of love (Romans 12:1). "Love in the New Testament is not a feeling, but a fact; not a sentiment, but a sacrifice; not an emotion, but an energy." Because God loved, He gave.

NUMBERS

If the previous book instructs God's people how to be *worshipers*, this fourth book of Moses reminds them that they are likewise *warriors*. Numbers, so called, because of the numberings of the people is the book of pilgrimage and service. "Journeys" is its key word (33:1). Thus we are given the historical account of the 40 years wandering and training of the wilderness, and also of the equipping of the people for taking possession of the Promised Land. Are we not apt to forget that warfare is one of the necessary conditions of pilgrimage and possession (23:11)? The central chapters of the book are the 13th and 14th in which the

tribes, in response to the divine command, leave Sinai to possess Canaan some eleven days' march. Among camp regulations were those of sanctity and sanitary arrangements. The marching signals were both divine (the cloud moving) and human (sounding of trumpets).

Another characteristic feature of *Numbers* is that of its "murmurings," eight in all. Israel found it hard to learn that godliness with contentment is great gain. Alas, grace did not keep a redeemed people from grumbling! If you follow the downward course of Israel in *Numbers* you will find that they journeyed from discontent to lust to rebellion to idolatry. To be saved from the initial sin of murmuring is one step toward perfection (Philippians 2:14; I Thessalonians 5:18). A necessary lesson we must not forget to learn from this book is that while the wilderness is a part of the necessary discipline of a redeemed life, the long years of wandering, because of unbelief, are most unnecessary. What happened to Israel is for our warning, not imitation (I Corinthians 10:1-11; Hebrews 3:17-19).

Chapters 1,2

This book takes its name from the second verse of the first chapter, where Moses is told to take a census of the people. And, rest assured, that when God counts up His people, none are overlooked. This fourth book of the Pentateuch naturally follows Exodus, taking up the story of the wilderness journey where Exodus leaves it. Numbers reminds us of the service and walk of God's people. It brings them through the wilderness wanderings to the border of the land of promise. In the opening two chapters, we have the people numbered and arranged around the Tabernacle. In the setting up and setting forward of the camp, God was in the midst of the Tabernacle, surrounded by Levites, with all the tribes encamped around. As J. N. Darby expresses it: "It (the Tabernacle) was in the midst of them as of an army that was its guard, as the rallying point of worship and approach when the camp was at rest. They kept the charge of the Lord."

Chapter 3

We have here the setting apart of the Levites for service. And, as believers are priests unto God, we can find in this chapter fitting types of our privileged priesthood. In the choice of the tribe of Levi for the position of nearness to the Lord, we have an illustration of grace. The tribe did not have a commendable past (Genesis 49:5,6). It was the tribe pronouncing a curse upon Jacob and his descendants, causing Jacob and his family to remove. Apart from infinite grace there is no explanation for the Levites' becoming the most favored tribe, holding the distinct place of nearness, in contrast with other tribes. Thus is it with

the true Church. It is all of grace that she is gathered out of the world and brought nigh unto the Lord. The Levites were entirely given to Aaron, the high priest, and the service of believer-priests is of no avail unless it is linked with communion with Christ and likewise with His priesthood. Another typical aspect of the Levites is the fact that they accomplished, all equally or together, the ministry of the offering to God. And all believers are equal in access to God and relationship with Him; all are priests.

Chapter 4

The precise arrangements for the service of the Tabernacle, as given in this chapter, prove God to be of order, and not of confusion. Nothing was left to human choice or ingenuity. Down to the last detail, all was ordered of the Lord. Had we space we could show how all the divine arrangements are typical of the walk of the believer as he sojourns in the wilderness of this world. The ark of the covenant represents the holiness and justice of the throne of God. Badgers' skins typify the humanity of Christ. The covering of blue speaks of the heavenliness of His walk on earth. The table of shewbread speaks of Christ as satisfying food for both God and man. The Spirit's illumination and our personal witness can be gathered from the candlestick. Spiritual intercession is implied by the altar of incense. The brazen altar, with its purple covering, speaks of the cross and the crown of the Redeemer. You will find great delight in studying the Tabernacle in the light of Hebrews.

Chapter 5

If the thought of carefulness pervades the previous chapter, "holiness" certainly dominates this chapter. An orderly, careful people had to be a holy people. All orderly people are not as holy as they should be, and all holy people are not as orderly as they should be. We have met a few dear saints stressing holiness, but their homes are anything but clean and tidy. In connection with the purity of the camp as God's dwelling place, we note that defilement had to be purged out, all wrongs had to be amended, and jealousy had to be tested. In turn we have marital unfaithfulness manifested and judged. All concealed evil had to be brought to light. For the Church, the application is not far to seek. During our wilderness pilgrimage, all unfaithfulness must be judged and put away. As for the spirit of jealousy, how it permeates many relationships! Truly, jealousy is as cruel as the grave! There are, of course, two kinds of jealousy, heavenly and hellish. God is a jealous God. Paul speaks of a "godly jealousy" (II Corinthians 11:2). From the hellish kind, may the good Lord deliver us!

Chapter 6

The vow of the Nazarite presents a forceful lesson on service and the servant of the Lord. The Nazarite was one who was characterized by special separation and devotedness to God. Christ was the perfect Nazarite, and all who name His Name should follow His steps. We cannot do better than quote Scofield's comment here: "The Nazarite was a person of either sex separated wholly unto the Lord. Abstention from wine, the symbol of mere natural joy (Psalm 104:15), was the expression of a devotedness which found all its joy in the Lord . . . The long hair, naturally a reproach to man (I Corinthians 11:14), was at once the visible sign of the Nazarite's separation, and of his willingness to bear reproach for Jehovah's sake. The type found its perfect fulfilment in Jesus (Hebrews 7:26), who was utterly separated unto the Father (John 1:18; 6:38), who allowed no mere natural claim to hinder or divert Him (Matthew 12:46-50)." It is our blessed privilege to *enjoy* the lovely benediction of verses 24 to 27.

Chapter 7

Following cleansing and consecration come the united freewill offerings for the service of the sanctuary. Through the princes all the tribes participated, indicating united devotedness. All alike felt their responsibility. Would that it were so in the Church today! Doubtless you have noticed that this is the longest chapter of the book, and one of the longest in the Bible. In these days when churches have many different ways of providing money for their work, it is well to study the methods that are pleasing to God. What so many fail to remember is

that giving is a part of worship (Hebrews 13:15,16; II Corinthians 9:6-8). Are we willing, cheerful givers? The end of this chapter brings us to the anointing and dedication of the altar. And, "we have an Altar." It is not a church altar, but Calvary, where a sacrifice of nobler name and of richer blood than any beast offered on Jewish altars was offered up on our behalf.

Chapters 8,9

In continuation of the order of the host, we come to instructions regarding the pure golden candlestick, the cleansing of the Levites, and the passover. The lamps in question were made to diffuse light all around. So ought our personal testimony to be clear and consistent. Does our light so shine before men, as to compel them to glorify, not our works, but the God who makes them possible? Caring for lamps was a messy and menial task for a priest, but Aaron cared for the lamps daily as unto the Lord. This should transform the monotonous tasks of life for each of us. The purification and dedication of the Levites prefigures our consecration to God for His service (Romans 12:1,2). The Levites belonged to God, and had to dedicate themselves, *not* in order to *become* His, but *because* they *were* His. The observance of the passover, memorial of redemption, was obligatory during the wilderness journey. Such a feast reminded the people of a divine deliverance, and also acted as the symbol of the unity of a redeemed people. This is why, today, the Church values and observes the Lord's Supper.

Chapter 10

Coming to the beginning of the wilderness march, it is necessary to point out that the wilderness itself was ordered and necessary but not the wandering. Jesus had His wilderness, and there is one for each of us. Such an experience stands for testing and discipline. The wandering, however, is of the flesh. Israel could have gone from Egypt into Canaan inside of two weeks. Because of their waywardness, the journey took them 40 years. In the order of the march, we are reminded of how God orders our lives and labors. Everything had to be according to plan. The life of every child of God should be a God-planned life. The primary purpose of the silver trumpets was to gather the people in preparation for their journey. "The priests who, in communion with their Head, were to be in the intimacy of the thoughts of God, sounded the trumpets when needed." . In the closing verses, we are reminded that the Lord went a three days' journey to seek a resting place for the people. What a mighty, tender Leader He is! How precious is His grace as He provides for His own! Do you always wait for the guiding cloud?

Chapter 11

What a contrast this chapter provides! The previous chapter shows us how God wanted His people to go, but in this chapter we see how they went. Murmuring broke out in the camp. Numbers, it will be found, is a book of murmurings. There are some eight murmurs in all. Try to trace them. "The people complained" (verse 1). Do you? Alas, we all do! And such a spirit displeases the Lord. The first complaint was evidently over the resting place God had provided. Chastened by swift punishment, the people sought the prevailing intercession of Moses. Then came alienation of heart from the Lord, for the people allowed themselves to be seduced by the mixed multitude, that is, by those Egyptians who were impressed by the . display of divine power, but who had never experienced a change of heart. In the Church today unconverted, carnal-minded members are ever a source of defeat and division. They have no taste for heavenly manna. All things that are pleasing to the flesh are what they seek after. Full satisfaction may only be found with the Bread of God, however.

Chapter 12

This is another chastening chapter. Here is the story of a sister and brother jealous because of the kind of a wife their brother had chosen. What troubles arise over our criticism of partners other people take! Because of Moses' exalted position, Miriam and Aaron should have been afraid to speak against him. It is ever a serious offense to speak against one whom the Lord has blessed. "Touch not mine anointed, do my prophets no harm" (I Chronicles 16:22). Evidently Miriam was the instigator of the criticism of Moses, seeing she alone was smitten with leprosy. Aaron interceded for his jealous-minded sister, and in turn Moses cried unto the Lord for her restoration. How damnable and disastrous jealousy is! A point to note is that Miriam's action delayed the progress of Israel's journey for seven days (verse 15). The whole camp lost a week because of one sin of a woman. Is there anything in our lives, we ought to ask ourselves, that causes the chariot wheels of the Gospel to slow down? (Read Romans 10:1-15.)

Chapters 13,14

These chapters cover the murmurings of the host over Kadesh-barnea, the pleasant land Moses had brought them to, but which they despised. Twelve spies, sent out by Moses, brought in their report. Ten of them magnified the difficulties of taking the land, and thus discouraged the people. The other two spies, Joshua and Caleb, did not belittle the dangers of possession but declared that Israel was well able to conquer and possess. In this case, however, the minority report, although correct, was rejected. It is a reminder, surely, that majorities are not always right. Out of the original host leaving Egypt, Joshua and Caleb were the only persons privileged to enter the Land of Promise. All the rest perished in the wilderness. Brought out of Egypt, their unbelief and rejection of God made it impossible for Him to bring them into Canaan. Canaan, of course, is not a type of heaven, but of the fullness we have in Christ. Redeemed, do we yet fall short of the Highest (Hebrews 6:3-11)?

Chapter 15

In this anticipative chapter, divine instructions are given to guide the people once they are in the land. The ribband of blue (verse 38) reminded them that heavenliness must enter the minutest details of their life. It has been said that over chapters 13 and 14 we can write: "All flesh is grass"; for these are chapters of failure. Over the chapter before us, we can inscribe the words: "Beloved, I am the Lord, the God of all flesh"; for here we see what God can do for flesh, even when it is a failure. Instructions as to offerings make up the bulk of the chapter. Says a gifted expositor: "The introduction of the stranger in this chapter is of the highest interest, as a testimony to grace." How grateful all Gentiles should be that God ever had them in mind! Sins of ignorance, and sins of presumption, are likewise dealt with. May we be preserved from both. In conclusion, God said to His people: "Remember, and do . . . and be holy" (verse 40). Reflection, obedience, holiness – steps for all pilgrims to follow.

Chapter 16

We are up against failure again. A striking fact to observe, however, is that after every failure of Israel, God speaks of Canaan. Whatever the weakness and failure of His redeemed people,. God, according to His Word, will bring them through. In spite of all their murmurings and rebellion, they were still His people. The criticism of a one-man ministry on the part of a trinity of murmurers – Korah, Dathan and Abiram – gives us one of the saddest chapters in the Bible. "The gainsaying of Core" (Jude 11), was the denial of the authority of Moses as God's chosen spokesman, and intrusion into the priest's office. Korah's sin consisted in the attempt to create a priestly order without divine sanction (verse 10). There ought never to be jealousy of another worker the Lord has signally endowed. In effect Korah said: "Who is Moses anyway? I am as equally gifted, and can match his achievements." To Moses' credit, let it be said that, true to his meek character, he never answered back, but took it all to God.

Chapters 17,18

Levitical authority and service comprise these two chapters, heavy with typical significance. After the complaint of Miriam and Aaron against Moses' authority, and God's judgment of Miriam and His approval of Moses, rebellion against Aaron as God's high priest had to be dealt with. The blossoming, dry, dead stick – Aaron's rod – established his authority. All other rods remained dead. The budding of Aaron's rod is a fitting type of Christ raised from the dead, and thereby confirmed by God as our High Priest forever. In chapter 18 the position and privilege of Aaron and the Levites are clearly defined and confirmed. It will be noted that the priests alone ate the holy things, and had to eat them in holy places. Is there not a precious truth in the wave-breast and the right shoulder the priests could feast upon? The breast symbolizes *love,* and the shoulder *strength.* Do we in our priestly ministry, know what it is to rest upon our Lord's breast and shoulder? What love and strength are His!

Chapter 19

Defilements, gathered by the way, had to be removed, hence the provision of the red heifer. Why it had to be a *red* one is not stated. Red, of course, is the color of blood and suggests sacrifice. "Christ is presented as the red heifer as unspotted by sin, and as never having borne the yoke of it either; but He is led forth without the camp, as being wholly a sacrifice for sin." In the slaying of the sacrifice, the burning of it without the camp, the seven-fold sprinkling of blood, the cleansing operation, faith can discern how God deals with each defiled saint in this age of Grace (John 13:3-10; I John 1:7-10). It matters little whether we are clever, as long as we are clean. If we would be vessels unto honor, we must be purged from all that is alien to the mind of the Lord (II Timothy 2:21). Is daily cleansing mine, and being delivered from defilement, am I experiencing the joy of helping someone else out of sin? This, surely, is the lesson of the red heifer.

Chapter 20

The atmosphere of death pervades this chapter. It opens with the passing of Miriam, and closes with the death of her brother, Aaron. Other incidents are Moses' failure and the denial of his entrance into Canaan; further murmurs against God; and opposition from surrounding nations to Israel's progress. The notice of Miriam's death is somewhat meager. She died at Zin, and was buried there. Her record might have been different had she not sinned against God and Moses. Going over to Aaron's death, we have an indirect proof of immortality. It is not recorded that Aaron was about to leave his people but that he was to be "gathered unto his people" (verse 24). At his death he went home to join the shining host of godly souls who had preceded him. It is tragic to realize that losing his temper at the rock meant that Moses lost the joyful opportunity of entering the land of Canaan. Beloved, how careful we must be! One sin can rob us of so much.

Chapter 21

We can call this a "sandwich chapter," seeing we have victories at each end, but murmuring in between. Partially defeated by King Arad, the Israelites rallied, and in fulfilment of their vow, utterly destroyed all the Canaanites in the way. Then, in the march of Israel, we come to the brazen serpent episode, which is so full of spiritual import. Within the Pentateuch we have many striking figures of Christ, but this one of the serpent raised up on a pole is the type our Lord Himself used when He wanted to illustrate His death upon the tree (John 3:14). And, because there is still life for a look at the crucified One, it is to be hoped that all our readers have looked, and that they live. Calvary and Pentecost can be seen in this chapter. Following the upraised serpent, we have the upspringing well. "Spring up, O well" (verse 17). No more rock to smite or serpent to raise. Israel, delivered from death, is now refreshed and moves on to realize all the promises of God. How much do we know, in experience, of the Spirit springing up as a well of water?

Chapters 22-24

Three chapters are devoted to Balaam and his prophecies. This strange character, although he had partial knowledge, was a heathen and a diviner, or magician. Coming from the north country, he did not know very much about the Jews, but when Balaam was offered a reward by Balak, king of Moab, to curse the Jews, God marvelously circumvented the purpose of Satan, and used even a bad man to declare some of the great prophecies of Holy Writ. God's glorious plan for His people, as well as prophecies

of Christ, are in this section of Numbers. The rich lesson we gather from this portion is that none can curse those the Lord has blessed. Another lesson is that God always uses the best material at hand. Greedy Balaam was only after money, but God came upon him and possessed his mind and lips, making him, for the time being, a divine messenger. His prophecy, it will be found, was of a four-fold nature. Unhappy Balaam, whose heart was in the bond of iniquity, defeated in his purpose to curse Israel, endeavored to frustrate the blessing of God by leading the people into sin and idolatry.

Chapter 25

"The Doctrine of Balaam" is a fitting caption for this chapter. Scofield says: "The 'error' of Balaam must be distinguished from his 'way' (II Peter 2:15), and his doctrine (Revelation 2:14). The 'error' of Balaam was that, reasoning from natural morality and seeing the evil in Israel, he supposed a righteous God *must* curse them. He was blind to the higher morality of the Cross, through which God maintains and enforces the authority and awful sanctions of His Law, so that He can be just and the justifier of a believing sinner. The 'reward' of Jude 11, may not be money, but popularity or applause." Coming to the "doctrine" of Balaam the same expositor says that this "was his teaching Balak to corrupt the people who could not be cursed by tempting them to marry women of Moab, defile their separation, and abandon their pilgrim character. It is that union of the world and the church which is spiritual unchastity" (James 4:4). As for us, let us ask: "Are we in enjoyment of God's covenant of peace?" (verse 12).

Chapter 26

As the people are about to enter the land, God takes another census. Their pilgrimage is now over, and as heirs about to possess their inheritance, they are counted one by one. Bountifully, God had undertaken for the host. The multitude lacked nothing. Every need had been met. Now the details of their inheritance are settled. A leader is appointed to succeed Moses, and lead the people into Canaan. Such a long list of names may seem unnecessary, but, to sacred historians, genealogies were important, as we can see when we turn to Matthew 1 and Luke 3. These are days when people are proud of their pedigrees. Some time ago I met a lady who traced her descendants back to someone who crossed the ocean on *The Mayflower*. And how proud she was of her ancestry! Well, as sinners, we have nothing to be proud of, seeing our ancestry goes back to Adam and Eve, who, by their fall, brought such misery into the world. Praise God, we have a spiritual ancestry in Christ!

Chapter 27

Details of the order of the inheritance of the daughters of Zelophehad open this chapter. What a precious touch this is: "And Moses brought their cause before the Lord" (verse 5). Do you bring all your problems and difficulties before the Lord, whose wisdom is far greater than ours? The rest of the chapter is taken up with Moses' preparation for death. Graciously, God gave His honored servant a view of the land which the people were to possess under the leadership of Joshua. It must have been a pathetic moment, standing on the summit of Mount Abarim, viewing the landscape o'er, yet because of one sin, not permitted to go before the people whom he had guided through the wilderness. Wisely, Moses did not choose his successor. It would mean a lot for vacant pulpits if only pulpit committees kept in mind verses 15 and 16, in which Moses throws the responsibility of the choice of a shepherd for the flock upon the Lord. It thus came about that Joshua was appointed to lead Israel into the land.

Chapter 28

Chapters 28 and 29 are taken up with the worship of the people, once they are in Canaan. The order of the offerings speaks of the testimony of the worship rendered to God upon the earth. It is beyond the scope of these brief meditations to indicate the typical significance of all these offerings. This we have done in Leviticus. At this point we can observe that the emphasis is upon divine possession. Everything is the Lord's: "My offering, my bread, my sacrifice . . . ye shall offer unto me" (28:2).

God wanted all the sacrifice to be pleasing unto Him. Another precious aspect in connection with one of the offerings (28:3,4) is that there had to be two lambs offered day by day – one for the morning and the other for eventide. And how we need the Lamb, the Bleeding Lamb, not only morning and evening, but all the hours in between! Yes, and the day is coming when in all the universe praises unto the Lamb will be sung (Revelation 5:5-12; 7:14). Have you been washed in the blood of the Lamb? Are you, then, singing praises to the Lord?

Chapter 29

This chapter opens with a reference to the Feast of Trumpets. "A day of blowing the trumpet unto you" (verse 1). Such an act was associated with the gathering of the assembly. Two blasts brought the people together in orderly fashion to receive further instructions from the Lord, and, at the third blowing, the people marched forward, all of which is suggestive of I Thessalonians 4:16,17. As the redeemed of the Lord, are we not awaiting this feast of trumpets? When the trumpet of the Lord shall sound, what a gathering there will be unto the Lord. Emphasis in this chapter, and the previous one, is upon the present action of a sin-offering, which, of course, typifies the Lord Jesus Christ as the Sin-Bearer. And only those who know Him as such will discern the voice, the shout, and the trump – "they that are Christ's at his coming" (I Corinthians 15:23). Will you be among the first fruits to be gathered? All who are not sheltered by the blood at His Coming, must be left behind, to tribulation and remorse.

Chapter 30

We now come to the matter of vows, taken by men and women upon themselves in the presence of God, and which were not disannulled as He continued to govern the people. These vows offered no escape. All had to be realized to the full. Christ came from heaven, binding Himself to fulfill the Father's will, and at Calvary He carried out His vow to redeem. A man was under obligation until all was clear. He could never be delivered from his bond until everything had been worked out. Thus was it with Christ. He paid the debt and now we are free. Often we are guilty of taking useless, senseless vows upon ourselves. Many of the so-called vows of certain religious and Masonic orders are positively unchristian. If, however, we make a vow unto the Lord, we must fulfil it. "Pay me that thou owest" (Matthew 18:28). Think of the solemn covenants we take upon our lips in congregational hymn singing, which we have no intention of carrying out! May God forgive us for all broken or unrealized vows!

Chapter 31

We cannot read this chapter, containing, as it does, the last official act of Moses, without detecting the connection between idolatry and war. "They chose new gods, then was war in the gates" (Judges 5:8). The Midianites were ever a menace to Israel. They were not a war-like people. We are not told that they fought Israel, but they contrived to seduce the people. Fascinated by the wealth of Midian, God's people had traffic with them and inter-married against God's specific commands. And how many there are who scorn anything that is positively and outrageously sinful, but who yet succumb to the gold and glitter of the Midianites! It was so with Demas, who, loving this present world, forsook his friend Paul. Of the spoils brought back from war, Eleazar said: "Everything that may abide the fire, ye shall make it go through the fire" (verses 22,23). Does the language not suggest I Corinthians 3:12-14, where every man's work is to be tried by fire, of what sort it is?

Chapter 32

The children of Reuben, Gad and Manasseh chose their inheritance just outside the land. Recalling the contempt of the pleasant land at Kadesh-barnea, Moses severely rebuked Reuben and Gad, but their request was granted. So they stayed on this side of the land. And the curse of church-life and work today, is the presence of far too many border-line Christians. They are brought out, but are not willing to be brought in. Saved, and signally blessed of God, they are yet content with much the wilderness of this world offers. When they reach the border-line of the land of separation, their heart fails them. Embedded in the heart of our chapter is an oft' quoted verse: "Be sure your sin will find you out" (verse 23). What a persistent detective sin is! Has your sin found you out? Well, haste to the fountain opened for sin and uncleanness.

Chapter 33

In this retrospective chapter we have a summary of Israel's journeys from Egypt to Canaan. Moses, who wrote: "their goings out according to their journeys by the commandment of the Lord" (verse 2), now gives us a recapitulation of the wilderness experiences. Thinking of God's dealings with His people all through the Old Testament, we observe great insistence upon remembrance. Israel was forever being exhorted to remember all God had accomplished for and through her. The torment of hell will be that of remembrance: "Son, remember!" And, is it not a tonic to our faith to think back over the past? Of course, there is no need to drag out the guilty but forgiven past, when God Himself declared that He will remember our sins no more against us forever (Hebrews 10:17). Let us ever bless Him for Calvary, for our salvation, for all His unfailing goodness.

Chapter 34

Preparation to enter the land and the boundaries within, are enumerated in this chapter. Dry facts though these are, we cannot read them without realizing how God took care of His people in every way. He marked the limits of the country they were to enjoy. He settled the taking of possessions, and the portion of His servants, the Levites, who were not to have any inheritance. Presently, the Jews know little about these past inheritances. They do not even know where they belong in the twelve tribes. God alone knows who, and where, they are. But their division again into tribes is forecast by John (Revelation 7:4,5). And, the present passion of the Jew to return to the land, which is their inheritance by divine right and gift, indicates how near Israel is to the full realization of Scripture prophecies regarding her regathering and restoration to divine favor (Jeremiah 16:14-16), but not until they acknowledge Jesus as Messiah. The Jew, be it remembered, however, is ever God's index finger, when it comes to prophecy.

Chapter 35

As to the six cities of refuge, we have already noticed their significance in a previous daily portion. These particular cities were provided that every man might have a fair trial. All who unintentionally committed murder, could flee to one of these refuges for shelter from the avenger of blood. And there are Scriptures in abundance to prove that Christ is our City of Refuge, sheltering us from judgment. "The name of the Lord is a strong tower: the righteous runneth into it, and is safe" (Proverbs 18:10). Have you proved Him to be a refuge from sin, and a refuge in the time of storm? This chapter closes with a solemn injunction (verse 34). The people were exhorted to be holy, and to keep the land holy, for "I the Lord dwell among you" (Exodus 29:45,46). And the presence of Christ within a believer should sanctify every part of his life. What a thought! He dwells among us, and cannot tolerate anything alien to His holy mind and will.

Chapter 36

Inheritance is before us again in this last chapter of the book – the question of preserving a marred inheritance. Israel today has a marred inheritance, but all that God has given His ancient people will yet be possessed by them. "This last part of the book presents, not the passage itself through the desert," says Darby, "but the relationship between that position, and the possession of the promises and of the rest which follows. It is in the plain of Moab that Moses bore testimony . . . to the perverseness of the people; but where God justified them . . . without even their knowledge, and pursued all the designs of His grace and of His determinate purpose for the complete establishment of His people in the land He had promised them. Blessed be His Name! Happy are we in being allowed to study His ways!" And of this we are certain: the God who brought Israel into Canaan is desirous of each of us enjoying to the full all the spiritual blessings He has provided in Christ Jesus.

DEUTERONOMY

A special favorite with the prophets and our Lord, *Deuteronomy* contains no new laws. The old generation that had left Egypt died by the way, except the two faithful pilgrims, Joshua and Caleb, and a new generation must have the old-time laws rehearsed in their hearing. Thus *Deuteronomy* from "deuter," meaning "second," and "nomos," meaning "law" explains the purpose of the book, namely, the repetition of the laws of Sinai (17:18). It has thus been called, *The Book Of Reviews* – a review of the past with an eye to the future. "Remember," one of the key words of the book, occurs 18 times, and the remembrance of deliverance from Egypt is constantly urged as a motive to obedience (10:12,13). Now out of Egypt and through the wilderness and about to enter Canaan. Israel must be reminded that obedience to God is the condition of entrance into and continuity within the land. The central chapter of the book is the 29th, where Moses, dealing with the covenant of God, condenses the argument of the whole book. But it not only insists upon the full obedience of God's people: the book stoutly condemns *spiritism* (18:9-14) – declares the overthrow of Satan's power (34:2 with Matthew 17:3; Hebrews 2:14; Jude 9) – is effective in Satan's defeat (Matthew 4:4-10). *Deuteronomy* is a most integral part of the *pentateuch* seeing that it condenses and continues the great truths of the first four books of the Bible, namely –

Divine election of Israel, prominent in *Genesis;*

Divine deliverance of Israel, conspicuous in *Exodus;*

Divine holiness of Israel, pre-eminent in *Leviticus;*
Divine jealousy and determination, in *Numbers;*
and now
Divine love and bounty in *Deuteronomy.*

Chapter 1

The title of this book is rendered "copy" in 17:18, and means "duplicate." The book, then, contains a repetition, or duplication, of the law found in earlier books. Yet it embodies more than repetition. The Hebrew title comes from the opening phrase of the book: "These are the words." Deuteronomy records the preparation of the new generation for entering Canaan, and for their life there as the representatives of God. This chapter opens with a general introduction, author's name, contents and circumstances of place and time. Then we have God's call to His people to leave Sinai and the renewal of the promise concerning Canaan. The inability of Moses to deal with every question owing to the great increase of the people, the story of the spies, and presumption and its punishment make up the rest of the chapter. What a beautiful cameo of the loving and large heart of Moses, as well as the patience of God, this chapter affords!

Chapter 2

A review of the wilderness experience covers these two chapters. Narration, not exhortation, is before us. The "many days" (verse 1) means thirty-eight years. Kadesh to Seir, Moab, Zered, Ammon and Sihon were associated with Israel in the wanderings and conflicts of the wilderness. From chapter 2 we can learn much of *God's righteousness in protecting national rights* (verses 5,9,17), *God's insistence on obedience* (verses 3-37), *God's care for His own* (verse 7), and *God's blessing and protection* (verses 25,33). This chapter also records the conquest of Og, king of Bashan. All kinds of giants must fall before God-honored people. Distribution of territory among two and one-half tribes, conditions of possession, recognition of Joshua as leader, and the prayer of Moses complete a chapter so full of God. Note *His encouragement* (verses

2,22,28), *His relationship to His own* (verses 2,18,20,21), *His power* (verse 18), and *His will for His people* (verse 26). God always answers prayer, even when He says "No."

Chapters 3,4

A new generation must be taught the lessons of Sinai. So we have *exhortations* based on history, *two commands,* "hearken" and "do," and *three consequences,* "live," "go in," and "possess" making up the first eight verses. Then there are a *series of warnings* based on God's revelation of Himself (verses 15-20), on the divine nature (verses 21-24), and on the possibility of future disasters (verses 25-31). At the back of these warnings there is *God's special purpose* (verses 32-40). The cities of refuge, a pleasing picture of mercy and grace in the midst of insistence on obedience, and an introduction to the repetition of the Mosaic law, fill out the rest of chapter 3. Israel's loyalty to God (verse 4), her uniqueness in being God-chosen (verses 6-8, 32-35), her need of loyalty to God and His Word (verses 9,23,40), her suffering through disobedience (verses 25-30), and her safety through obedience (verses 1,2,36,40) are lessons to be noted in chapter 4.

Chapters 5,6

The second address of Moses, commencing here, extends to chapter 26. Moses recites the giving of the law, the basis of which was a covenant, one that was distinguishable from the Abrahamic covenant (Genesis 15). Differences between the Decalogue as written in Exodus 20, and the repetition here, will be observed. Special points in reference to the past are added (verses 6-21). The two narratives are, of course, complementary. Emphasis on "fire" as a symbol of God's holy presence is brought to Israel's notice (verses 22-27). (See Exodus 20:15-18.) Divine response and recognition, complete chapter 5. Chapter 6 continues the appeal, with the addition of warning about coming perils. The *purpose of the new life* (verses 1-3,24), the *principle of the new life* (verse 4), the *plan of the new life* (verses 6-10), and the *peril of the new life* (verse 12) are points to mark in your Bible. Do you know what is always good for you (verse 24)?

Chapter 7

The first half of this chapter is taken up with separation. The Israelites were chosen to be a special people unto God, and so Moses exhorted them to keep themselves from any alliances with those around them. In the Promised Land they were to live and act as God's redeemed children, separated wholly unto Him. Verses 7 and 8 give us an explanation of the unexplainable. God sets out to tell the people why He loved them. Negatively, the matter is explained all right, but coming to the positive side we read: "The Lord set his love upon you then . . . because the Lord loved you." Such is love's explanation. We sometimes say to a very dear friend, "I don't know why I love you, but I do." Obedience carries with it the promise of victory. Look at the manifold blessings in verses 13-26. There is no limit to what God is willing to do for the truly obedient heart. Disobedience robs Him of the joy of blessing us.

Chapter 8

Several chapters are devoted to warnings and exhortations. Moses calls the people to remember the past. The first five verses recall God's goodness in the wilderness. For forty years He bountifully maintained the people Moses was about to leave, and, what He had been He was willing to be if only they would observe to obey His commands. "Beware that thou forget not the Lord thy God" (verse 11). Surely the nations of today require such a solemn warning. How dependent the Israelites were upon God – "who led thee . . . who fed thee!" (verses 15,16). Why should we charge our souls with care when we have such a God to lead and feed us? Note the key words of the chapter: "Remember . . . forget." Failing to remember constituted hell for the man Jesus describes in Luke 16, "Son, remember." And the doomed one said: "I am tormented in this flame." His crown of sorrow was the remembrance of despised opportunities.

Chapters 9-11

Warnings continue. All we can do with these chapters is to indicate some of their conspicuous features. Great decisions were called for as the people faced a momentous day – "this day" (9:1,2). History is again provided as an incentive to obedience. Stiffnecked in the past, Israel must now act as being united and at one with God. In chapter 10, Moses relates further wilderness experiences, and then cites the character of God as being the basis of complete acquiescence with the plan and purpose of God. Because of all He had done, was, and would yet accomplish, Israel must strive to live as unto Him. As you read chapter 11, mark the key word, "therefore," meaning: "Here is what God has done and will yet do. Now let Him see what you are willing to do and be." Israel faced the alternatives of blessings and curses, and riches or ruin depended upon the way the people treated the divine commandments. Are we possessing our possessions (11:23-25)?

Chapter 12

Conditions of blessing in the Promised Land are herewith enumerated by Moses. What the people were to do is set forth under a number of "ye shalls." Count the times that this phrase occurs in the chapter. Instructions as to offerings, food and worship are clearly defined. Never must Israel forget her vow of separation. We know, of course, that once in the land, Israel degenerated and inquired after the gods of their neighbors. The people were not long in losing their distinctive feature as being God-chosen. Precise obedience was demanded. Nothing had to be added to or taken from the divine command. Man likes to whittle down divine requirements, or fit them to his own convenience. God, however, expects His people never to deviate one iota from what He has declared. When they were in the land, Joshua reminded the Israelites of this meticulous obedience (1:7). God will accept nothing less than implicit compliance.

Chapter 13

The test of false prophets fills up this chapter. Satanically inspired prophets and dreamers were able to perform miracles. This is also to be a characteristic feature of the great tribulation period yet to come (Matthew 24:24; II Thessalonians 2:9). As redeemed ones, the people were urged by Moses to follow the inner voice of the Lord and not the voice of any false prophet. "Blood is thicker than water," we say. But the tempting voice of even the dearest had to be spurned, even as Jesus rebuked Satan through Peter. For all who were exposed as deceivers, a deserved death was ordered. They were to be stoned with stones. What a day of false prophets this is! Why, the so-called ministry is full of them, and all of them are traitors to their trust. But we do not stone them in this apostate age. Instead, we give them the chief seats, and crown them with honored positions in the church!

Chapter 14

Further characteristics of the people of God are given by Moses. They must not practice physical lacerations or other heathen indications of mourning. As a holy people, sorrow had to be borne as befitting those who followed the Lord God. Then, there is written a recital of promises and prohibitions as to food, animals and birds. Two special prohibitions are in verse 21. Physical life would be greatly benefited today, if we would return to some of the dietary laws of Moses. The stranger, that is, the one not in the covenant relationship with God, was excused from these laws. The chapter concludes with instructions as to tithes and offerings, and their use. It is not hard to summarize the lessons of the chapter. We have *the attitude of the believer* – separation (verses 1-21); *the reason for such an attitude* – because of being God's children and holy (verses 1,21); and *the outcome of this attitude* – blessing (verse 29).

Chapter 15

The sabbatic year, as set forth in this chapter, begins with the release of debtors, "the Lord's release," as it is called (verse 2). Such a release does not seem to imply the entire remission of debt but only postponement of payment until the sabbatical year was over, because the land would not then be under cultivation. Foreigners, that is, those apart from Jews, were excluded (verse 3). A God, known for His bounty, urged upon His people a large-hearted unselfishness. Philanthropy toward the needy was enjoined. During this year slaves had to be emancipated and provision made for their property rights. The sanctification of first-born animals, taught earlier (Exodus 13), is again emphasized. Three great truths stand out as we review the chapter, namely: loyalty to God, love to man and liberality to the needy. Blessing is promised if the true life is practiced (verses 4,6,10).

Chapter 16

Three chief feasts occupy the chapter for today. Fuller instructions, as given in Leviticus 23, were for the priests. The briefer account here was specially suited for the people. Of the *passover* (verses 1-8) much could be written. Christ is the anti-type of this feast. As our passover, He was sacrificed for us (I Corinthians 5:7). The *feast of weeks* (verses 9-12) is a type of the resurrection and pentecost. Over against the "affliction" (verse 3) must be placed "joy" (verse 11). For the *feast of tabernacles* (verses 13-18) we go back to Exodus 23:17; 34:23 for other details. *Yearly gifts and proportionate giving* are not forgotten (verses 16,17). The chapter concludes with a warning regarding the peril of idolatry. Of the three feasts, the passover suggests pardon through the cross; the feast of weeks symbolizes provision through Christ's Resurrection; and the tabernacle foreshadows a glorious prospect through Christ's Second Advent. We have gratitude for the past, joy in the present and hope for the future.

Chapter 17

The chapter opens telling about the proper punishment for idolatry. A previous chapter (13) states the punishment for those who lead others into idolatry. Here it is those who are led who are judged. By the "gate" we understand the place of judicial proceedings. Today it would be the courthouse. Adequate evidence of evil had to be produced (verses 6,7). Judicial decisions were necessary and had to be just. The priests, who were of the Levitical tribe, formed the supreme tribunal (verses 8,13). Although Israel was a theocracy when Moses governed the people, the monarchy is here anticipated (verses 14-20). The people wanted to be like surrounding nations (verse 14), yet in many ways God told them to be unlike these nations. Outlining the necessities of the chapter we can trace: *all for God* (verse 1); *holiness of life* (verses 1-7); *justice in our dealings with others* (verses 8-13); *surrender to God* (verses 10-13); and *unswerving loyalty to God's Word* (verses 18,19). Can we say that these are our objectives?

Chapter 18

Priests and prophets dominate this portion. The maintenance of the Levitical order opens the chapter. The Lord was the inheritance of the priests (verses 1-8). Condemnation of idolatrous practices follows. Verse 11 condemns the spiritism of our time. Israel had to be in the land but not of it. The call and character of the true prophet occupies the closing section of the chapter. Dependence on diviners was unnecessary, seeing Israel had her good prophets. A succession of prophets was promised to combat idolatry. The use of the singular noun, "prophet," points to a pre-eminent prophet, and who could this be but Christ (Acts 3:22), who, like all true prophets, can be tested by fulfilment of predictions? He is the priest-prophet. Priests represented man to God, and Christ, our priest, represents us to God by sacrifice and intercession. Prophets represented God to man, and Christ, as our prophet, represents God to us by the revelation of His word and will.

Chapter 19

The cities of refuge appointed in Canaan offer a parable of our safety in Christ. Fullest instructions were given the people. Every facility was afforded those pursued by an avenger. As this provision was unknown outside of Israel, it presents a testimony of the justice and humaneness of the law. Conditions for using these three cities, besides, it would seem, the six cities Joshua mentions, are set forth. Because Israel's sin kept her from extending her boundaries, these extra cities were probably never used. Note the sanctity of blood (verse 10). It must be clearly understood that the refuge-cities were not for all offenders. Murderers were excluded. Modernists are guilty of

removing many an ancient landmark (verse 14). This is why a weary world is losing its way. The chapter concludes with a summary of adequate evidence and false witness. Three applications can be made: *refuge provided* (verses 1-10); *reality emphasized* (verses 11-14); and *righteousness demanded* (verses 15-21).

Chapter 20

The laws governing warfare are to be found in this book only. Would that modern conquerors could live by this chapter! We have encouragement in the face of foes with greater resources (verses 1-9). Priests were appointed to accompany the army. Certain men were exempted from military service. Kind treatment had to be given to the timid and fearful. When a city was under siege, certain factors had to be recognized. An invitation to surrender had to be given (verse 10). Then, we are told of the necessary action on refusal to surrender (verse 14). A gifted expositor indicates five lessons that can be learned from this chapter: (1) *God's promise in face of danger* (verses 1-4); (2) *God's provision in face of emergencies* (verses 6,7); (3) *God's peace in view of surrender* (verses 10,11); (4) *God's power in the midst of opposition* (verses 12-18); and (5) *God's principle in the presence of opportunity*, "that nothing be lost" (verses 19,20). As soldiers of Jesus Christ, are we fighting according to the rules of true *spiritual* warfare?

Chapter 21

Regulations as to unsolved murder and its expiation make up verses 1-9. The washing of hands was a symbolical declaration of innocence (verses 6,7). Regulations as to captive women were not for Canaanitish women, seeing no alliance with them was permitted. Shaving the head and paring the nails (verse 12) were the signs of symbolical purification, preparatory to severance from heathenism and entrance into God's covenant with Israel. Regulations as to justice to the first-born are found in verses 15-17, and as to a rebellious son, in verses 18-21. Here we have emphasis on obedience to parents as the foundation of social and national life. Compare the prodigal under the law with the prodigal son of Luke 15. The chapter closes with regulations regarding the exposure and burial of a corpse. "Accursed" means, *under God's ban or condemnation.* Man is in need of expiation, and Christ, who bore the curse, makes expiation possible.

Chapter 22

This chapter, made up of further regulations, does not lend itself to division. Duty of brotherhood in regard to loss is given attention (verses 1-4). Does modern woman look upon the wearing of male apparel as "an abomination" (verse 5)? Humanity and parental affection, protection of life, recognition of distinctions in nature, laws of personal purity with four distinguishing cases, the most terrible sin (verse 30; *cf.* Leviticus 18:7) are, in turn, given by Moses. Many little things are mentioned in this chapter. Michaelangelo remarked that "trifles go to make perfection, and perfection is no trifle." Little things play an important role in one's character. If we would be faithful in much, we must be faithful in that which is least. Before us there can be noted *brotherliness* (verses 1-4), *kindness to God's dumb creatures* (verse 4), *purity* (verses 5,13-30), *humaneness* (verses 6,7), *considerateness* (verse 8), *naturalness* (verses 9-11), and *sincerity* (verse 11).

Chapter 23

Regulations as to the exclusion of certain classes from membership in the Jewish community open this chapter. Make a list of the five *classes barred from the congregation* (verses 1-8). What spiritual churches we would have if only we were more careful regarding those admitted to membership! Rules as to physical impurity reveal that God forgets nothing. *Everything offensive had to be kept out of sight* (verses 9-14). The "paddle" or "spade" was included in military weapons used. Foreign slaves, when taken, were not to be surrendered but set free. Oppression, so common to communism, was condemned by God. *Sensuality had to be guarded against* (verses 17,18). *Personal rights and duties were enforced* (verses 24,25). As God's own people, holiness had to be written over every part of life. They had to walk as those

who were never out of God's sight. Is this how we live and labor?

Chapter 24

The Mosaic law of divorce was instituted, our Lord said, because of the hardness of Israel's heart. Passages like Matthew 19:8 and I Corinthians 7:12-15 should be studied alongside of verses 1-4. In these days, when Hollywood has helped to make marriage a mockery and divorce so cheap and easy, it is time to return to a Biblical understanding of divorce. Newly married men were exempted from military service for one year. How considerate God was in this! What not to pawn, regulations as to leprosy, pledges, justice to hired servants, personal responsibility, justice to the needy, positive kindness and not the mere avoidance of wrong and injustice are alike dealt with by Moses. Such regulations teach us the necessity of manifesting purity and kindness in every relationship of life. Surely God is not less particular now than He was in Israel's day!

Chapter 25

Regulations, somewhat monotonous to the casual reader to wade through, occupy this chapter also. First of all, we have two rules as to corporal punishment and its limits. Do you remember anything about the "forty stripes" in Paul's experience? Rights of animals in service had to be guarded (verse 4). Use is made of this in other ways (I Corinthians 9:9,10; I Timothy 5:17,18). Regulations as to levirate marriages were necessary to preserve families from extinction and their property from passing to strangers. Childlessness was considered a disgrace. Punishment for exceptional sin occupies the next two verses (verses 11,12). Businessmen had to practice strict justice. No dishonest transactions were permitted (verses 13-16). Amalek, Israel's inveterate foe, must be shown no quarter (verses 17-19). Israel had to show kindness one to the other, but no mercy toward Amalek. Summarizing the chapter, we see that there must be humanity in punishment, integrity in business and security against evil.

Chapter 26

The second address of Moses, commencing here, is akin to his first address in that it begins with a reference to the tabernacle, the central place of worship. As to the law of the offering of first fruits (Numbers 18:12) a joyous meal was to crown everything. Have we learned how to rejoice in every good thing which God has given us? Increase tithes (verses 12-15) must be carefully distinguished from the annual tithe mentioned elsewhere (Leviticus 27:30-33; Numbers 18:21-32). Every third year the tithe had to be given to the poor. Sincerity before God had to characterize living and giving. The chapter concludes with an earnest, solemn appeal for obedience. God owned and avouched Israel as His peculiar people. From the Latin, *peculiam,* "peculiar" means *a people for one's own possession.* Thus God's "peculiar" people are His possession. An exchange of solemn pledges can be noted – our pledges to God, and His to us (verses 17,18).

Chapter 27

Moses' third address carries us over to chapter 30. Israel had to bear witness to God in Canaan. Pillars had to be set up and God's law inscribed upon them. Several stones were necessary to record all the legislative laws. With a call to fresh obedience, Moses pronounced blessings and cursings. Twelve curses – twelve was the number of the tribes – answered to some particular sin against God's law, thus covering the entire law. Is it not blessed to know that Christ came to remove the curse (Galatians 3:13; Romans 8:1)? Within the chapter we have the elements of a godly life: *witness to God's law* (verses 1-3); *dedication of life* (verse 6); *fellowship with God* (verse 7); *obedience because of privilege* (verse 10); *divine favor* (verse 12); *judgment on sin* (verses 13-26); and *acceptance of position* (verse 26). "Amen" means a response of endorsement. Such an endorsement was general; for *all* the people said, "Amen." Those who have the gift of writing should strive to be plain (verse 8).

Chapter 28

What a contrast this chapter presents! In the previous one we had dreadful curses.

Here we have divine blessings. Yet curses make up this chapter also. How highly privileged Israel was, high above all nations of the earth. And this chapter must be read in the light of God's purpose for Israel. All blessings were based on obedience. Only if the people hearkened to the voice of the Lord would these blessings overtake them. Blessings related to personal life in eight aspects, and others associated with home and city, can be traced (verses 1-14). Curses, based on disobedience, likewise cover eight aspects of personal life (verses 15-68). These curses developed into predictions (verses 49-68) which Jewish history shows to have been fulfilled. Contrasts here cover the blessing of obedience and the blight of disobedience. Note two services (verses 47,48) and two joys (verse 63).

Chapter 29

The Palestinian covenant is embraced in this and the following chapter. It would seem as if this were a special covenant made with particular reference to Canaan, which the people were about to enter. As to the nature of this covenant, follow the notes given in the *Scofield Reference Bible.* Have you thought of the trinity of senses given in verse four? If we are disobedient, insight can never be ours (Isaiah 6:9,10). Obedience ever means a lightened understanding. An appeal that includes children and strangers will be found (verses 11,15). A strong warning as to the danger of apostasy concludes the chapter. Underline the word "lest" in the chapter: *lest* we forget (verse 18); *lest* we presume (verse 18); *lest* we forsake (verse 25). Under grace, God reveals His secrets to His own. "The secret of the Lord is with them that fear him" (Psalm 25:14). Are we intimate enough with the Lord as to receive and understand His secrets?

Chapter 30

Among God's "secret things" was the unfolding of His covenant, as herewith outlined. *Remembrance, repentance, restoration,* and *return* make up one-half of the chapter. Is it not thrilling today to see God's ancient people being established again in the land their fathers possessed? True, the Jews are now a nation, but, alas, they are back in unbelief. Not yet are they circumcising the heart. There is always something solemn about a dying message. In the last half of this chapter we have the dying charge of Moses. Alternatives are presented with emphasis on the power of choice. Some may disagree with the stern alternatives set forth in Scripture, but a sharp, emphatic division is given and a choice must be made: life or death; blessing or cursing; God or Satan; heaven or hell; and saved or lost. Character as well as destiny depends upon a personal choice.

Chapter 31

We have now reached the closing scenes in the honored life of Moses. His magnificent leadership was almost over. All that remained for him to do was the delivery of a few farewell counsels and warnings. In the first six verses we have Moses' last counsels to the people he had governed for so long. His had been a long life – 120 years, divided into three equal periods; forty years in Egypt, another forty in the backside of the desert, and the last forty in the wilderness as Israel's leader. In his exhortation to Joshua, Moses emphasized the necessity of courage. The promise of God's unfailing provision is carried over into the New Testament (*cf.* verse 6 with Hebrews 13:5). For the priests and elders Moses also had some final instructions, as to the feast of tabernacles. Then Moses warned the people of coming apostasy. Instructions for the Levites close the chapter. Go over it again and gather out an old man's counsels as to the essentials of spiritual success.

Chapter 32

What a wonderful song this is, composed by divine command (31:19), recited to Israel, and ultimately written (31:22)! The dominant theme of the song of Moses was the contrast between God and His own, between faithfulness and disloyalty, between love and rebellion. Much could be said regarding the message and magnificense of this God-inspired song, so full of His greatness, grace, faithfulness, justice, power, righteousness and mercy. Of course, the song belongs primarily to Israel and can only

be used by us with secondary spiritual application. On the basis of this stirring song, Moses called the people again to full obedience. At the close, Moses is told of his death. What deep feelings must have been his to know that he had brought the people to the border of the Promised Land but that, through losing his temper at Meribah, he himself could not take Israel into Canaan.

Chapter 33

Ere his lonely climb to the summit of Nebo, Moses blessed the tribes. Compare the blessings of this chapter with those of Jacob (Genesis 49). Moses is referred to as "the man of God," which is the title of Psalm 90 that he composed. God is declared to be the source of everything. Spiritual truths can be gathered from the characteristics and blessings of the tribes. Simeon, it will be seen, is omitted from the tribes, possibly because of his failure to help Levi (Exodus 32:26-29), or because he had the tendency to lose his tribal feature. In such a chapter of blessings there are so many things to gather out for one's own heart: *protection* (verse 12); what broad shoulders God has! Then there is *prosperity* (verses 13-17); how many precious things are ours in Christ! *Obedience* is here (verses 18,19). *Strength* can be learned from God (verses 20,21); *power* (verse 22); *satisfaction* (verse 23); and *sufficiency* (verses 24,25). How comforting is a verse like the twenty-seventh!

Chapter 34

The end is reached. Moses was allowed to see the land but not to enter it. His prayer to enter was answered at the transfiguration (Matthew 17)! Upon Mount Nebo, Moses was kissed to sleep by the angels, and God buried him. He is the only man in the Bible to have God as his undertaker. Why did Satan contend for the body of Moses (Jude 9)? Did he want to prevent his appearance with Elijah on another mount? A new leader arises. God buries His workmen but carries on His work. Moses' assistant, Joshua, succeeds to office. His qualifications and recognition by the people conclude this short, mournful chapter. The three-fold secret of the long and honored life of Moses can be gathered from the last three verses. There was his fellowship with God (verse 10), his service for God (verse 11), and his witness to God (verse 12). May such secrets be ours!

JOSHUA

As the successor of Moses, Joshua is the chief character in the history of Israel covered by this book, to which Joshua gave his name. The book as a whole, is the story of the military campaign led by Joshua by which Israel gained possession of Canaan. The book is an aggressive one, describing how Israel conquered Canaan, dispossessed its inhabitants and took over the land. Thus the key word, *possession* (1:3), summarizes the chief lesson of the book and instructs us in the necessity of possessing our spiritual possessions in and through Christ. Because of God's hatred of sin, His flaming sword of justice was unsheathed against the Canaanites whose terrible vices deserved judgment. The Canaanites can represent our besetting sins and spiritual foes. In our heavenly Joshua, however, there is One who can make us the recipients of the all-victorious life. Possession was, and is, by dispossession (Ephesians 6:10-18). Several writers point out that this book introduces us to a transition in the method of teaching. Hitherto, God had revealed His purpose by dreams, visions and by angelic ministry. Now we have the transition of teaching by the authoritative Word of God as written by Moses in the divine law, which is simply the word and will of God in written form. Joshua himself, who was 80 years old when he received his commission to possess the land and was 110 when he died, is one of the Bible characters who is portrayed as having a character without blemish. As the man of faith, fidelity, courage and consistency, he completed the redemption of Israel out of Egypt. Moses, representing the law, could only bring the people to the border of the Land of Promise. It took a Joshua, whose name is equivalent to *Jesus* to take the people into the land. The law may be able to point us to Christ, but cannot save us. Grace alone can enable us to possess all we have in Christ now, and in heaven hereafter. As there was a good

deal of conflict in Canaan it cannot be a perfect type of heaven. Canaan is more the type of the life of victory over the world, flesh and the devil here below. In the life of the believer conflict and conquest go together in the endeavor to possess his possessions.

(Read Exodus 17:8-15.) The first reference to Joshua in the Bible, along with succeeding references in *Exodus* and *Numbers*, indicates that Moses appointed Joshua to follow him in the peculiar and extraordinary office of general of Israel. He could not actually succeed Moses, since he was not a prophet. Joshua's task was to head the people in the war of invasion and the subsequent allocation of the tribes in the land of Canaan. And what abundant romance there is in the life and labors of Israel's military genius, who has been rightly called "the first soldier consecrated by sacred history." Tennyson's "Ode on the Death of the Duke of Wellington," is also true of Joshua:

> Great in council and great in war,
> Foremost captain of his time,
> Rich in saving common-sense,
> And, as the greatest only are,
> In his simplicity sublime.

(Read Numbers 27:15-23.) To evaluate the Book of *Joshua* aright, one must gather together the biographical sketches of Joshua himself. All the strategy he manifested as a military commander and statesman came as the result of a divine enduement (Deuteronomy 34:9). Would that all soldiers were silent, reverent worshipers (see Exodus 33:11)! He was ever the servant of God and man (Numbers 11:28; Joshua 24:13). To Joshua belonged the remarkable distinction of bearing the same name as Jesus (Acts 7:45). "It is not often either in sacred or common history that we are justified in passing on anything so outward and usually so accidental as a name." See what Scripture you can gather around Joshua as a son, slave, soldier, servant, spy, sojourner, saint, saviour and statesman. According to Jewish practice he was buried within the limits of his own inheritance. As a warrior, however, his soul goes marching on.

(Read Deuteronomy 34.) Scholars affirm this chapter formed at one time an introduction to the Book of *Joshua*, the first eight verses being written by Joshua, and the last four by Ezra. As a whole, the chapter is eloquent with the truth that although God buries His workmen, He carries on His work. How slow we are to realize that God does not exhaust Himself in any leader, no matter how conspicuous! He always has a Joshua to succeed a Moses. As a book, *Joshua* can be compared to *The Acts*. Moses lived again in Joshua, and the Lord Jesus lived again in the Holy Spirit, whom the ascended Lord sent to earth. Joshua carried forward the work of Moses and led Israel into the enjoyment of all Moses had made possible. Christ died for us, brought us to our Red Sea. After Calvary, the Spirit came to actualize the blessings of the cross. Try to work out other similarities.

Chapter 1

Joshua's immediate installation proves that no man is indispensable. The death of Moses was the call to action: "Therefore arise, go over this Jordan." Moses, representing the law, could only bring the people to the border of the land – it took a Joshua or Jesus to lead them in. What God gave, had to be possessed! Are you possessing your possessions? Is yours a personal appropriation of all you have in Christ? Entering the land, Israel had to observe the "curriculum of obedience" – observe to do! Courageously, Joshua went forth resting upon the covenant of God's presence. For the hard and perilous enterprise ahead, he had the promise: "The Lord thy God is with thee whithersoever thou goest" (verse 9). Without such an assurance any courage we may manifest will burst like a pricked balloon.

After listening to God, Joshua speaks to the people. Commissioned of God, he now commands. May we never be guilty of the folly of launching forth, unsent! And that the validity of a divine commission is immediately recognized is evident from the allegiance and obedience of the tribes addressed. Reuben, Gad and Manasseh testified to Joshua's authority, and expressed their readiness to redeem their pledge. Patriotic and pious feelings in verses 16 to 18 must have encouraged Joshua in such a time of crisis. Have we learned to reply to our heavenly Joshua: "All that thou commandest us we will do and whithersoever thou sendest us, we will go"? (verse 16). If we fail to obey the Lord and rebel against His commandments, what else but spiritual death can we expect? Let us enjoy our possessions (see verse 15).

Chapter 2

Divinely guided to Rahab's house, the spies quickly entered into a covenant to spare the harlot and her household, the scarlet line becoming the sign and pledge of safety, just as the bloody mark on the lintels of the houses of the Israelites in Egypt spoke of deliverance from death. That Rahab had come to a recognition of divine sovereignty is evident from her confession: "I know that . . . that . . . that . . ." She was cognizant of God's covenant. Then, conviction and confession as to God's supremacy are in the words: "Our hearts did melt . . . The Lord . . . he is God." Great honor became Rahab's, for she is mentioned as an ancestress of the Saviour (Matthew 1:5). The covenant of deliverance from death was respected by Joshua as he entered the land (Joshua 6:23-25; Hebrews 11:31). We, too, may look to God for tokens (see verse 12).

Chapter 3

It was certainly true that Joshua was about to lead the host over a way they had not passed heretofore. The path opening to them was through the oozy bed of the river, never seen by human eye before, never trodden by man's foot. But God makes no mistakes when He calls His own to step out upon some new and unknown path. There is always the guiding ark, the symbol of the divine Presence among men. For us, Christ is the true Ark of God, and He is ever with us to lead and guide our steps over untrodden paths. Do we know Him as the Director of our feet? Is He calling us to attempt a seemingly impossible task? Then we must never hesitate to follow, for we have His assured presence and protection until we have "passed clean over Jordan." In the directions for priests and people there are many lessons to be learned. How would you apply the responsibility and action of verses 3 and 4 to yourself?

It is delightful to note that God encourages Joshua, then Joshua in turn encourages the people. Tokens of divine favor were necessary for Joshua as he faced his monumental task, and in an unmistakable manner his mission and authority were attested to. The last verse summarizes the miracle of the passage through Jordan and anticipates what is still to follow. It must have been a wonderful scene as the priests stood on dry ground, and with a ring of grateful triumph, shouted: "What ailed thee, O thou sea, that thou fleddest? thou Jordan, that thou wast driven back?" (Psalm 114:5). For us, the dark flood of death was dried up as the pierced feet of Christ touched its cold waters. He went on before us, and shaking His hand over the river, caused His own to go over dry-shod. "When man acts in faith, God acts, too, often at the last moment when faith's action seems about to be proclaimed absurd."

Chapter 4

This chapter is one of "stones crying out." Two memorials are before us. "The twelve stones taken out of Jordan and erected by Joshua in Gilgal," says Dr. Scofield, "and the twelve stones left in Jordan to be overwhelmed by its waters are memorials marking the distinction between Christ's death under judgment in the believer's place (Psalms 42:7; 88:7; John 12:31-33), and the believer's perfect deliverance from judgment. The stones in Jordan stand, typically, for Psalm 22:1-18." Those gray stones set up on Gilgal testified at once the duty of remembering, and the danger of forgetting the past mercies of God. In an age when books were rare and monuments were relied upon to stir remembrance, those stones would proclaim to succeeding generations the guidance and government of God. And we have our remembrance stones, the most notable being the Lord's Supper, a constant reminder of His unspeakable love for a world of lost sinners.

Chapter 5

The Amorites and the Canaanites were paralyzed with fear as they witnessed the incontestable proof that God was on the side of Joshua. Doubtless they reckoned on the swollen river to protect them, but seeing it completely dried up, and the Israelites on their side of Jordan, their hearts were melted. The return of the separating sign of "circumcision," is full of spiritual import. Would that the reproach of Egypt could be rolled away from every blood-washed one! Since for a new sphere, new food was necessary, and the people did eat of "the old corn of the land." The portion taken up with the unseen Captain (13-15) proves how willing Joshua was to act as a subordinate. Without doubt, we have here a theophanic appearance of Christ, who, as the Commander-in-Chief with sword drawn, assumed the leadership in the crusade of possession. So ought we to own, and submit to, His generalship!

Chapter 6

The inescapable message of this dramatic chapter is "that spiritual victories are won by means and upon principles utterly foolish and inadequate in the view of human wisdom" (I Corinthians 1:17-29; II Corinthians 10:3-5). Reading the chapter, we are impressed with the fact that the Israelites were not told what was to be the end of this apparently useless and aimless promenade around the walls of Jericho. The announcement was left until the morning of the day of the miracle. Those six days with their impressive silence must have been a test of faith for Israel, and yet, a terrifying experience for the Jericho host. In obedience to a divine command the priests and men of war tramped around the walls; then on the seventh day the victory came, "the wall fell down flat," and obedience was vindicated. What a glorious event the trumpet and the shout of this chapter remind us of!

Chapter 7

This tragic chapter opens with a tragic *"but."* Pronouncing a curse upon any Israelite who might be guilty of looting Jericho, Joshua, flushed with victory, went forward to the occupancy of Ai, the name of which means "the ruin." This is a fitting name indeed when we think of Israel's humiliating defeat there. Achan's breach of trust, responsible for such a disgraceful defeat, was severely punished. The chastisement was too severe, some think, for why should his innocent family and beasts be included in the judgment that fell? One writer has it: "In Achan's case it was necessary to show plainly the need of corporate unity of heart. God's covenant was with the people, not individuals (Exodus 20:5). In choosing what was destined for destruction, Achan brought doom to his house." Look at verse 10! There are some prayers God does not want to listen to.

Chapter 8

The Valley of Achor became a door of hope (Hosea 2:15). With justice executed upon Achan, victory followed defeat. Ai forever remains a striking illustration of God's disciplinary government, in which chastisement for sin is often made to pave the way for a bestowment of those temporal benefits which, on account of sin, have been withdrawn or withheld for a time. If Moses had his rod, Joshua had his spear (verse 18). It is not our swords or spears, however, that secure victories, but the God behind them. "They got not the land in possession by their own sword, neither did their own arms save them: but thy right hand" (Psalm 44:3). Joshua's overthrow of Ai was certainly ingenious, but behind the military strategy of such a leader was the divine promise: "I will give it into thy hands." We can triumph where, in the past, we have failed. Our Valley of Achor may become a door of hope.

Chapter 9

If Joshua took Ai by guile, in an unguarded moment he found himself caught by the guile of the Gibeonite embassy. The Israelites fell into the mental ambush, and, against the mind of God, entered into a covenant of peace. This chapter seems to say: "Beware of mouldy-looking bread." Deceived by such, the Israelites manifested

excessive credulity and culpable negligence. Respecting the oath made, the Israelites degraded the Gibeonites to a servile condition, making them as menials to perform the drudgery of the sanctuary. How we need spiritual perception, causing us to discern the error lurking with the most plausible approach of Satan! What a tragic mistake verse 14 presents!

Chapter 10

What a dramatic chapter this is, with its record of five kings in a cave, and the miracle of the sun and moon standing still! Such a miracle has given rise to much discussion. Joshua fervently prayed that the day might not end until he had completely overthrown his enemies, and God responded by lengthening the day. Says Dr. W. S. Blackie: "Whatever allowance we may make for poetical license of speech, it is hardly possible not to perceive that the words as they stand imply a miracle of extraordinary sublimity." As the God of creation, the Sun obeyed His command. What a God we serve! He is One who is willing to hearken unto the voice of a man and fight for him against his spiritual enemies. He is ever on our side, marshalling all forces to our aid. The question is, "Are we fully on His side?"

Chapter 11

The defeat of the kings mentioned in this chapter proves the ability of Joshua to move swiftly and decisively against the occupants of the land. Coming upon the towns "whilst they were unprepared at a central rallying place unsuited to chariot warfare, he terrified the lines of horses," and pushed forward northward in his possession of the land. As Joshua is a fitting type of Christ in many ways, the Lord, like Joshua, has had a long war with the kings of earth. Through the generations they have set themselves against Him and His anointed, but Christ will yet take the whole earth, making its kingdom His own world-kingdom. And when He has subjugated all earthly rulers, and reigns as the King of kings, then the world will indeed rest from war.

Chapters 12,13

The twelfth chapter presents us with a detailed account of the previous chapters. Joshua recapitulates the conquests achieved, giving us a list of thirty-one of the chief towns occupied. On he went, possessing what God had given. Chapter 13 commences a new section of the book, for from here on, through chapter 19, we have a detailed account of the settlement of Israel in the land of Canaan. Joshua's advanced age was a special reason for the immediate discharge of his God-given task of distributing the land among the tribes of Israel. Though he was, probably, about 100 years old at this time, this notable military genius was urged to press on and subdue all the land. Some of us may be old and well-stricken in years and tempted to say: "Well, I can rest and let younger shoulders bear the burden." God's Word is: "There remaineth yet very much land to be possessed" (13:1).

Chapter 14

In the first five verses we are shown how nine and a half tribes chose the inheritance by lot, thereby fulfilling the divine promise to Moses (verse 5). Then follows the taking over of Hebron by faithful Caleb, who required and obtained this goodly part of the land. Facts to notice about Caleb are: his advanced age (verses 7,10); rare memories of youth, early promotion, great claim endorsed by Moses: "I wholly followed the Lord" (verses 9,14); a remarkable testimony to God's keeping power (verse 11); request for a hard task (verse 12) in fulfilment of a habitual conviction; his successful and lasting settlement (I Samuel 30:19). What do we know of abiding strength (verse 11)? Like the tribe of Caleb, let us follow the Lord, not by fits and starts, but continually and wholly.

Chapter 15

The bounds of Judah's settlement are given preeminence in token of the tribe's leadership among the tribes. Judah's destined superiority here receives the visible sanction of God. Caleb, who overcame the giant sons of Anak, consolidated his position by intermarriage. Such an alliance guaranteed a good water-supply for poor pastures. As our heavenly Caleb asks of us: "What wouldest thou"? may the language of Achsah, in verse 19, form our reply. The bounty of the Spirit is ever sufficient for the barrenness of earth. From verse 20 on, we have a list of cities Judah occupied, and such lists may make monotonous reading. They reveal, however, the exactness of sacred historians. Further, lists of names should always be read, for so often one can discover gems among stones. Look at the last verse, for example. Are there any Jebusites that we cannot drive out?

Chapter 16

The general borders allotted to the sons of Joseph stretched northwest from Gilgal. Turn back to Genesis 48:19,20, to see why Ephraim took precedence over Manasseh, the firstborn. Both tribes enjoyed a close relationship and were characterized by mutual aid (verses 8-10). What a tragic failure the last verse presents: "They drove not out the Canaanites"! This is the first mention of Israel's neglect of the divine command to purge the land of all its idolaters (Deuteronomy 20:16). Later those Canaanites brought grievous trouble to Israel. The spiritual application is obvious. Victorious in so many ways, there are yet those Canaanites we are unwilling to part with. "Destroy all," says God. Alas, however, we find it hard to slay some darling sins!

Chapter 17

"Ephraim had been mentioned first," says a renowned expositor, "as the more numerous and powerful branch of the family of Joseph (Genesis 48:19,20), but Manasseh still retained the right of primogeniture, and had a separate inheritance assigned." Commenting on the disobedience of verse 12, the same expositor remarks: "Indolence, a love of ease, perhaps a mistaken humanity, arising from a disregard or forgetfulness of the divine command, a decreasing principle of faith and zeal in the service of God, were the cause of their failure." My soul, beware! The subtle Canaanites may have iron chariots and much strength, but our heavenly Joshua declares we are able to drive them out. By faith we can clear the mountains and woods of deeply entrenched foes, and possess all God has for His own.

Chapter 18

Shiloh, where Joshua set up the tabernacle, remained its home for some 300 years (I Samuel 4:1-11). The name "Shiloh" means *rest*, and denotes the permanent station of the tabernacle. Joshua's report of the seven tribes who failed to take over their inheritance, conveys the impression that they were dilatory to a criminal extent. It is profitable to link verses 2 and 3 to II Peter 1:3-10, and to ask ourselves whether we are making our calling or election sure, or, in other words, possessing the land divinely given. Can it be that slackness is ours in possessing our possessions? Untold wealth is ours, but somehow we do not appropriate it; we are too content with the dross of earth. Ramoth-Gilead is ours, and we take it not!

Chapter 19

The territorial limits of Simeon, Zebulun, Asher, Issachar, Naphtali, Dan and Joshua, decided by lot, are described in this chapter. Joshua, retiring in honor to the place of his choice not far from Shiloh, was presented with his inheritance by the people (24:30), and it was an inheritance fitted to his dignity. But the gift, fitting as it was as a reward for his great work, was not merely the gift expressing the spontaneous feelings of a grateful people. It came to him "according to the Word of the Lord," evidence of an unrecorded praise similar to Caleb's (14:9). Ultimately, Joshua was buried in his inheritance (24:30). Israel's inheritance was, of course, of an earthly nature, while ours is a heavenly one. Turn over to Ephesians, the Joshua of the New Testament, and meditate upon Christ's inheritance in the saints, and theirs in Him.

Chapter 20

Provision for the right of asylum for any man guilty of unintentional homicide was foreshadowed by Moses, being included within the administration of the tribe of Levi (Exodus 21:13; Deuteronomy 19:1-12; Numbers 35:9-28). The number and locality of the six cities of refuge make them quickly accessible from all parts of the land. There were three on each side of Jordan, standing almost opposite each other. No matter where the fugitive was, he had no long distance between himself and safety. The difference between any Israelite and ourselves is that any one pursued had only the right of entry if his act had been inadvertent, but we have the right to hide ourselves in Christ, our strong City, just because we have sinned wilfully. "Thou blest Rock of Ages, I'm hiding in Thee."

Any man-slayer was safe as long as the high priest lived. His death released the fugitive, anointed with holy oil, from confinement. Thus, the death of the earthly high priest became a type of that of the heavenly One (Hebrews 9:14,15). We are safe as long as our Great High Priest lives. How long will He live? Why, He is alive forevermore, which means that we have eternal security. And so, the safety of the man-slayer in the city of refuge is a feeble shadow of the blessed immunity from condemnation that we experience as those who are sheltered by Christ's work on our behalf. "I give unto my sheep eternal life, and they shall never perish, neither shall any man pluck them out of my hand" (John 10:28). What a glorious truth! Do you believe it? If you have any doubt about it, remember the Master's word: "Because I live, ye shall live also" (John 14:19).

Chapter 21

While the Levites were prohibited from holding land like other tribes, they yet received certain townships within every tribal area. These were selected by Joshua's drawing lots, as he did for the rest of the tribes (18:10). Three sections are discernible: *Declaration of Levitical portions* (verses 1-8); *details of such* (verses 9-42); and *divine rest* (verses 43-45). The closing verses remind us that all the promises made to Moses, Joshua and the people had been, or were in the course of being, fulfilled. And such divine fulfilment offers a ground of hope and confidence to the people of God in every age, that all other promises made to His own will, in like manner, be accomplished. How blessedly true it is that God is never slack in the realization of any promise given!

Let us now meditate upon other evidences of the triumphant record of God's faithfulness. Turn to Joshua 23:14; Numbers 23:19; I Kings 8:56; I Corinthians 1:9; I Thessalonians 5:24; Titus 1:2; and with all these aspects before us, let us sing: "Great is Thy faithfulness." Dr. Alexander Maclaren's comment is worthy of notice: "The military genius and heroic constancy of Joshua, the eagerness for perilous honor that flamed, undimmed by age, in Caleb, the daring and strong arms of many a humble private in the ranks, have their due recognition and reward; but when the history that tells of these comes to sum up the whole, and to put the 'philosophy' of the conquest into a sentence, it has only one name to speak as the cause of Israel's victory, and that is – God." "The help that is done on earth, He doeth it all Himself."

Chapter 22

Joshua's benediction upon two and a half tribes, erection of an altar of testimony, contention and priestly satisfaction constitute this interesting chapter. With the campaign of settlement over, Joshua proclaimed the demobilization of the forces, urging them to possess their possessions and keep the law (verse 5). The dummy altar erected by the two and a half tribes almost resulted in a civil war. Balaam and Achan were remembered. To duplicate the worship of God implied the worship of another god. The tribes in question repented of their rash action, and ultimately all the tribes formed a united and obedient community of worshipers. God's presence and preventive goodness preserved the nation from the calamity of a fratricidal war. Would that it were so again among the professed saints of God!

Chapter 23

This and the following chapters contain Joshua's farewell speeches which should be compared with those of Moses (Deuteronomy 31; 33). The pathetic yet powerful last counsels in this chapter should be prayerfully read and applied to our own hearts and lives. We, too, must *possess what has been promised* (verse 5); *obey God's Word,* if we would avoid the snare of idolatry

(verses 6,7), and *cleave unto God,* if we would be victorious (verses 8-10). In the last half of Joshua's farewell speech, he declares that "God had kept his word" (verse 14); in that fact is the sweet evidence that a falling away in heart and conduct will bring a reversal of circumstances (verses 15,16). The appeal for full allegiance is based upon their experience, and on God's faithfulness also. Love toward God is inseparable from loyalty to "His law." Those of us who are facing extreme difficulties today may go out to claim verse 10.

Chapter 24

We come to Joshua's last charge and death. The theme before us is that of divine sovereignty – "God's initiative in choosing, guiding and preserving His people, His overruling providence in personal and political affairs, and His goodness in providing this land for a possession." Upon the basis of God's goodness, guidance and government, Israel must ever serve Him, and abandoning all other objects of worship serve only the Lord God. It has been pointed out that we have as a *Finale,* "three funerals, Joshua, Joseph's bones and Eleazar the priest – a great military leader, a great national statesman, and the religious head. The whole life of the people is summed up in the work and achievements of spiritual, historical and cultural leadership." What a heritage Israel had! Yet ours is greater.

As the book we have been considering is taken up with Joshua's exploits after he succeeded Moses, it is profitable to turn to Hebrews 11:23-31, the Bible's Westminster Abbey of the illustrious, and note how Moses and Joshua are brought together again. Moses, who occupies more attention than any other in God's honor roll, is pictured in all the daring of faith, leading Israel out of Egypt, and through the Red Sea. The next episode before us, in verse 30, is that of Joshua's victory at Jericho. For forty years Moses led the Israelites through the wilderness right up to the border of Canaan, but there is not a word about those forty years with all their sin and wandering. Why? God blots them out! "Your sins and iniquities will I remember no more against you forever." What grace!

JUDGES

What a sad book of sinning and repenting, sinning and repenting. Once settled in Canaan, Israel was not long in giving way to unbelief and ungodliness, and through all their departure from God one can hear the sob of divine disappointment from the divine heart. Yet over against the backsliding of the people is set God's amazing grace in restoring them to fellowship with Himself. The four key words summarize the 300 years covered by this book – *sin, sorrow, suffering, salvation*. Because of their *sin*, God permitted the people to go into *servitude*. Repentant, or *sorry* for their sin, and crying to Him for deliverance, He heard their cry and raised them up *saviours* or judges. The book is a record of seven apostasies, seven servitudes, seven cries to God and seven deliverances. *Judges*, as a whole, takes its name from the history of the 15 Judges raised up to rescue and rule Israel. Samson, one of the Judges selected to deliver Israel from the Philistines failed to do so completely. Although the Hercules of Scripture, Samson was too weak to rule his own passions. The double message of this sad and solemn book is clearly evident, namely, a manifestation of the perpetual proneness of the human heart to wander from God; and yet His unceasing desire to restore His backslidden people to fellowship with Himself. Have you need to cry, "Restore unto me the joy of thy salvation?" (Psalm 51:12).

Chapter 1

The mutilation of the hands and feet of Adoni-bezek illustrates the New Testament principle of reaping what we sow. Caleb, the veteran who urged the army on to fresh exploits, proves that old age need not dim one's zeal and fervor for the Lord. Achsah, Caleb's daughter, revealed quickness of discernment. She realized that land would be of little use without water, so received what she sought. As the year continues its course, situations will arise demanding immediate decisions. But only God, by His Spirit, can enable us to act wisely as well as promptly.

Judges is a book of failures. It records seven apostasies, and the root of such can be traced to the incompleted tasks of Benjamin and Manasseh. Is ours the tragedy of incompletion? God ordered the eradication of sin, for, if it was tolerated, Israel would yield to fleshly standards, as she did. The Canaanites were allowed to remain in the land, with dire results, as some of the dark passages of this book prove (Psalm 106:34). The land had become Israel's, and God was prepared to drive all the Canaanites out, but self-willed and persistent they remained. All of us know something of the curse of permitted evil. God, however, is able to conquer all our Canaanites, if we will but let Him.

Chapter 2

The opening part of this chapter reviews the invasion of Canaan to the death of Joshua, and is a record of wilful disobedience on the part of Israel. Convicted of their sin, however, "the people lifted up their voice, and wept" (verse 4). Has our own failure brought us to the valley of tears, as Bochim means (verse 5)? Responding to repentance, God raised them up judges to deliver them from the servitude their sin had produced. Israel should have had steady progression in spiritual and material prosperity, but infidelity robbed them of God's smile, and the Judges were necessary to bring the people temporary respites from bondage. For ourselves we have the King to reign over our lives.

Chapter 3

Here we have the account of the first three Judges raised up to deliver Israel from the servitude into which their apostasy had brought them. Sometimes deliverance comes from unexpected quarters. Ehud was left-handed, and having no sword on the accustomed side, was allowed to pass unchallenged into the king's presence. That the element of surprise sometimes works for good is shown by Nathan's rebuke of David. The call of Shamgar shows how God often finds His deliverers as they ply their daily task, and that He can use the most unlikely instruments. Shamgar's ox-goad demonstrates that God can take the foolish things to confound the wise.

Chapter 4

Sold again into captivity, Israel was in a sorry plight. The 900 chariots of Jabin caused the people to forget God, their Deliverer, and so for twenty years Jabin mightily oppressed them. But God in His graciousness had not forgotten His people, and so we have the call of Deborah and Barak. Deborah, although believing victory was of the Lord, yet wanted the help of Barak, and Barak although called, lacked courage and would do nothing unless Deborah was beside him. He is mentioned as one of the heroes of faith (Hebrews 11:32), but his faith lay in Deborah's influence with God rather than in his own. Nothing is so effective as direct dealings with God. May He save us from props!

What Israel had feared for twenty years, God destroyed in a day! Faith combined with works triumphed. God defeated the enemy, but Barak pressed the victory to the limit. Faith ever needs the cooperation of works, for without works it is dead. Sisera was guilty of a gross breach of Eastern custom when he entered the women's part of the tent. Thus Jael, in self-defense of her honor, and because of her sympathy with the cause of Israel, slew Sisera. True, Deborah and Jael did not have the standard of morals Christianity brought into being, yet they showed a faith and determination in a divine cause we would do well to imitate.

Chapter 5

The victorious song of Deborah and Barak is one of the most eloquent and expressive pieces of literature ever written. Rightly God was praised for the deliverance. Valiant though they were, the prophetess and her aide realized the majesty and might of God. Scathingly the apathy of the tribes, refusing to stir themselves in a time of desperate need, is condemned. On the other hand, the faithfulness and fearlessness of the few are commended. God's ultimate triumph is certain, but what sorrow and shame will be ours if we did nothing to bring it to pass. How many there are who fail to

realize their share in the fight of faith! The Reubenites are by no means dead.

Deborah knew how to say, "Thank you." All who had fought with her were gratefully remembered. The loyalty of co-workers should ever be fittingly acknowledged. After her praise to God and the tribes, Deborah concludes her song with prayer, and we may well take up her strain and make it our own. Have all the Lord's enemies perished in our lives? Loving Him, as we profess to do, are we as the sun going forth in his might? Says Dr. F. B. Meyer: "The world is sunless enough. Many are perishing for a bath of sunshine . . . Shine forth, ye righteous, in the kingdom of your Father, satellites of the greater central Sun of Righteousness!"

Chapter 6

This portion shows how Israel alternated between defeat and deliverance. Darkness and dawn tells the story of Judges. Utterly impoverished by the Midianites, and after seven years of travail, the people cried unto the Lord. Israel's extremity was God's opportunity. With ourselves He often allows us to go to the limit in suffering for sin before graciously delivering us. An unnamed prophet was sent to remind the people of all God had accomplished for them, and also of their persistent disobedience in the face of heaven's bounty. Such divine goodness only intensified the disobedience of Israel. As for ourselves, may we ever be found obeying GOD'S Word and will.

All who are called to serve the Lord can learn much from the call of Gideon to deliver Israel. Three good traits were his. First, he had a knowledge of God and His power, even though he wondered why the mighty One of the past was not Israel's Deliverer in the present. Second, Gideon had a deep sense of his own weakness and ability. His confession, verse 15, came quite naturally. But convinced that God was able to use the weak things of the world to confound the mighty, he laid hold of divine strength and never afterward faltered. Last of all, Gideon had a deep patriotic love for his nation and identified himself with it. Living in the dawn of divine revelation he needed outward signs to trust God, which signs God graciously gave.

The opening statement of this portion covering the obedience and enduement of Gideon, calls for comment. "It came to pass the *same* night." Have you ever thought of tracing this phrase through Scripture? Gideon's first mission to attack evil found him bold and thorough. The secret of his vitality and victory can be seen in the divine enduement of verse 34. Weak and insufficient in himself, Gideon, when mantled with the Holy Spirit, was more than a match for Baal's prophets, as well as the Midianites. How slow we are to learn that apart from the Spirit we are nothing and can do nothing! Gideon's trumpet sounded differently that night, as he rallied the host of Israel against a cruel foe. And it is ever so when our witness is Spirit-inspired.

Chapter 7

Gideon, like Napoleon and others also, had to learn that God is not always on the side of big battalions. He does not require numbers to achieve His victories. Thus Gideon's host had to be reduced from 32,000 to 300. The test of useableness and readiness affords a profitable lesson. Those who fell on their knees and thought only of water would have been helpless in an ambush, so God chose the men who, holding their weapons, took only sips of water. The dream of the cake of barley bread brought Gideon back to the simplicity and helplessness of his own resources. In victories already achieved there was much to inflate his pride, but God brought him back to the realization of his nothingness. Gideon was only a cake of barley bread at the best.

The chosen 300 were victorious over Midian in that they were united, obedient, cooperative and courageous. Dramatic indeed was the conquest of the foe, in which the divine and the human were linked together as one. "The sword of the Lord, and of Gideon." Not the Lord's exclusively, or Gideon's, but the one sword wielded by God and man. It is true that God alone can defeat the Midianites, but He does not always defeat them alone. He condescends to use human means. The Bible is a divine sword, yet the sword of the Lord *and of Gideon*. While God alone inspired the Scriptures, human hands wrote them and human lips must declare their glorious truths abroad.

Chapter 8

How many there are like Ephraim, who are waiting for a call! Surely, Israel's plight was an urgent enough call to action. What constitutes a call? Is it not a need, and our ability to meet it? There are one or two gems to ponder in this chapter. The valiant 300 were so faint and weary, yet never gave up the chase until victory was complete (verses 4,5). If we find ourselves weary in well-doing, may the grace of continuance be ours, until the battle is won. And then, what a magnificent tribute that was to the royal bearing of an illustrious family: "Each one resembled the children of a king"! (verse 18). As children of a nobler King, do we resemble Him in our walk?

Chapter 9

Abimelech prostituted a precious relationship: "Their hearts inclined to follow Abimelech, for they said, He is our brother" (verse 3). God has set us in families, and ties between brothers and sisters can be most sweet and sacred. Any person so utterly bereaved as to be destitute of some relative is to be pitied. Abimelech was rich in family associations, but took advantage of his favor with them to the undoing of all concerned. His wickedness was justly punished, and that in a simple way by an unknown woman who cast the stone that cracked Abimelech's skull. Have you noticed what an illustrious roll these "certain" people make? Hunt them out in your Bible, and mark the conquests of these unknown warriors.

Chapter 10

The record of Tola and Jair, the seventh and eighth Judges of Israel, makes drab reading. Between them there was a forty year reign, but nothing conspicuous was accomplished. Israel's sixth apostasy and servitude are true to pattern. In bondage, the people repented and cried unto the Lord. And how manifest is His compassion! Are we not amazed as we read: "His soul was grieved for the misery of Israel"? (verse 16). The nation's miseries were due to its sins with which its history is marked, but God's love brooded over His chosen, redeemed people and longed to deliver them. When Jesus beheld sinful Jerusalem, He could not withhold His tears. Do we share such compassion for them today?

Chapter 11

Jephthah, who by birth was a son of shame, yet became one of the most commendable of Israel's Judges. While a man is not responsible for the way he comes into the world, grace can be his to overcome any handicap as he commences the race of life. Dr. F. B. Meyer says that "Jephthah's action was admirable in his quiet expostulation, before resorting to force, in the defense of home and country against the aggression of Amalek . . . But there is no need to bribe God's help, as Jephthah did, by his rash promise. He will give gladly and freely out of His own heart of love the help and deliverance we need, if only our cause is rightly ordered before Him."

Much has been written about the vow of Jephthah, the Spirit-anointed ninth Judge of Israel. Whatever happened we cannot but admire his determination, having made it, to fulfil a solemn yet unnecessary vow: "I have opened my mouth unto the Lord, and I cannot go back" (verse 35). It is to her credit that Jephthah's daughter was zealous enough for her father to fulfil his vow. Her surrender as a burnt-offering does not necessarily prove that she was slain. Rather does the narrative indicate that her sacrifice involved perpetual virginity, as well as separation from her home. The latter was a tremendous sacrifice for a Jewish woman.

Chapter 12

The first part of this chapter is taken up with Ephraim's jealousy of Jephthah, and of his strong, yet subtle, treatment of the men of Ephraim. Do we have the right pronunciation when it comes to spiritual things (see verse 6)? Only the sound of "h" was missing, but it meant the death of the man who could not pronounce it. Of course, we should bless God that the reality of our regeneration is not tested by the accuracy with which we utter a creed. One may answer all the questions of a catechism, and yet die a lost soul. Follow-

ing Jephthah we have Ibzan, Elon and Abdon, of whom little is known, save that they had large families. These three judges are like so many of us who have position without power to produce results.

Chapter 13

Departing again from God, Israel was made to suffer bondage for forty years. But through these long years of suffering God was preparing His deliverer of the people. Would that the land had more godly homes like the one in which Samson was born! Manoah was somewhat pessimistic. His wife, like Hopeful of the *Pilgrim's Progress*, was able to pierce the gloom, and discern the silver lining to the cloud. Her faith was vital, and reminded her foreboding husband that, as God had accepted their sacrifice, they should not doubt His willingness to keep His Word.

Chapter 14

The stories of Samson's dramatic life never lose their popularity. This chapter illustrates the disastrous effects of intermarriage with an unbeliever. The way Samson dealt with his parents proves him to have been a spoiled child, which is ever the possibility with an only child. Strange, is it not, that a Spirit-anointed Judge, able to slay a lion, was as weak as water in the hands of a woman? Much can be learned from Samson's riddle. Sweetness is sometimes hidden in threatened disasters. Conquered temptations can yield both strength and sweetness.

Chapter 15

This chapter is a pitiful story of spiteful revenge. The woman Samson sought to defend was unworthy of his affection and the vengeance he heaped upon the Philistines for her sake. Perhaps you have noticed that the jawbone of the ass is one of the seven weak things mentioned in this book that God condescended to use. Samson was gracious enough to attribute the glory of his victory to God: "Thou hast given this great deliverance by my hand" (verse 18). We further see that God knows how to sustain those who fight His battles. Samson, the fighting warrior, came to prove that God's springs burst out where least expected. He can produce "streams in the desert."

Chapter 16

Samson failed to watch his vulnerable point, and so, once more, it was a woman who found out his weakness. After his bitter experience at Timnath, Samson should have been warned, but he fell again at Gaza. He played with sin, and at what cost both to himself and others. Samson's strength, of course, was not in his hair, but in his consecration to God, of which the Nazarite's long hair was the outward sign. His tragedy, however, was unperceived. "He wist not that the Lord was departed from him" (verse 20). How we need to be aware of unconscious spiritual decay! Gray hairs may be upon us without knowing it. We do not discover the termites until the house collapses.

Over Samson's prison house is written the warning, "Beware of playing with temptation." What a pathetic figure this one-time strong man is! Blind and bound, Samson gave the Philistines to believe that their god was superior to Jehovah. But as the Nazarite sign returned, Samson's strength was renewed. In darkness and bondage Samson prayed. If only he had done this before entering Delilah's house, he would have kept his strength and sight, and accomplished greater victories for Israel than the crowning one of his paradoxical career. While Samson wrought vengeance upon his foes, his premature death was a tragic end to usefulness.

Chapter 17

The story of Micah not only throws much light upon the religious practices of the Israelites in the days of the Judges, but also proves how man craves for a priest. "In every age of the world's history," says one expositor, "where there has been a tent indicating the presence of human life, there has been an altar indicating man's consciousness of God, and a priest suggesting his consciousness of unworthiness to enter into the divine presence. . . . Let us beware of the religion which ignores man's craving for a priest. Let us remember that all human priests must ultimately fail. God has put

them all aside, setting up the priesthood of the blessed Lord. . . No one has the right to pose as priest to others, except in the sense that all Christians are such."

Chapter 18

The grave and corrupting abuses unfolded in this chapter testify to the utter neglect of the law as given by Moses. Israel had allowed herself to be contaminated by contact with the religions of those around. Micah's wail was that he had lost his self-made gods and priest. Nothing or no one, however, can rob us of our great High Priest, for His is an unchangeable and undying priesthood. The Danites left Micah wailing. When he wanted the comfort of his priest most, low, he was gone. How different it is with the redeemed! We can never be separated from Him who ever liveth to make intercession for us (Hebrews 7:25).

Chapter 19

Dean Farrar says of this chapter that within it, "we see the unutterable depth of profligacy and shamelessness to which Israel had sunk. At the same time we see that the moral sense of the nation was still sufficiently keen to be aroused by the glare of unnatural illumination thus flung upon their consequences." The fourfold repetition of the phrase, "in those days when there was no king in Israel," gives us an insight into the reason for the total depravity recorded in this terrible chapter. The Book of Judges depicts the state of the heart refusing to acknowledge the Lordship of Christ. When He receives His proper dignity and honor from us, how different our lives are, both personal and national.

Chapter 20

Civil and religious confusion are still before us. The indignation of all Israel was roused against Benjamin, and so a battle was joined. Although God's chosen people included all the tribes, it is pathetic to see them fighting against each other. Alas, in these last days, when the Church should be standing together against a common foe, Satan has the saints actively fighting each other! Commendably, Israel promptly dealt with evil in the ranks. Knit together in a perfect unity of feeling and action, the people drastically dealt with that which they knew to be wrong. Each child of God should act in such a way.

Chapter 21

The men of Israel came to realize what the isolation of the Benjamites would lead to. They did not want one of the twelve tribes to face extinction; so we have their mourning for the lost tribe, and their planning to avoid the further isolation of Benjamin without going back on their vow. "Nowhere in this account does the writer tell us that in carrying out these plans the Israelites were doing the declared will of God, and there is no reason for us to try to defend their action. We have here merely an account of what took place. We must all agree that the crimes of murder and rape to which the Israelites resorted, in order to get around their foolish and rash vow, were much more serious than the breaking of the vow would have been."

Going over this concluding chapter again, our attention is claimed by two facts. First of all, while the people mourned over a lost tribe, they did not mourn over their sin. There was no sorrow because of national transgression, no effort to return to God. Secondly, the people were very tenacious as to the keeping of vows, ratified in the presence of God. Is ours the determination of the Psalmist when he said: "I will pay my vows unto the Lord now in the presence of all his people" (Psalm 116:14)? Vows conceived in self-will and with selfish ends in view have no right to be made. With Spirit-inspired and noble vows it is different.

Among the heroes of faith mentioned in Hebrews 11, four of the characters we have considered in our reading of the Book of Judges are conspicuous for their faith namely, Gideon, Barak, Samson and Jephthah. They are counted among those who obtained a good report through faith. Nothing is said about the failure of these deliverers of Israel. Grace forgives and forgets the failures and extols the faith. Here is Samson, for example, with no word whatever of his sensuality and miserable defeat. His sins and iniquities are not remembered, just as the 40 years of Israel's wandering are blotted out between verses 29 and 30. What amazing grace!

RUTH

This Hebrew and pastoral idyll is the most perfect, charming and touching narrative in Scripture; and one combining all the traits of human life and character. Of this rare, spiritual gem in the whole realm of literature, Dr. J. Vernon McGee says that it is "a love story without using the word love. The story of a prodigal family who went to the far country." While the small book portrays a striking picture of Christ and His Church, Ruth the Moabitess herself was the forerunner of the Gentiles incorporated within the Church. Boaz was a Jew, Ruth a Gentile, but both became one. Through Christ the middle wall of partition between Jew and Gentile was broken down (Ephesians 2:11-22). Two Bible books bear the name of women. *Ruth,* a Gentile who married a Jew: *Esther,* a Jewess who married a Gentile. While the chief message of the book is that of rest through redemption and union with the Redeemer, its outstanding purpose was to trace the genealogy of David, and of David's Greater Son, the Lord Jesus Christ. Because the blood of Ruth ran in His veins, she finds honorable mention in His human genealogy (Matthew 1:5). Notable because it is the only book in the Bible wholly devoted to the history of a woman, *Ruth* – which is an appendix to *Judges* – offers a contrast to the latter. After Israel's barren experiences in *Judges, Ruth* comes like an oasis in the desert.

Chapter 1

The charming and lovely story of Ruth should be read in connection with the first half of Judges, seeing that this sweet idyll describes the life of Israel at that time. The times of the Judges were stormy, but there were hidden nooks in the land where God was loved and His law honored. The Book of Ruth presents such a nook. Because of prevailing famine, Elimelech moved with his family across the hills to Moab, and in this removal stepped out of the will of God. His name means, "My God is King." But had he believed that God was King he would have stayed in Bethlehem, knowing that need could never throttle God. As a Jew, he had the promise: "In the days of famine thou shalt be satisfied." How careful we must be of a move to better ourselves! We have no right to change from one sphere to another without the clear guidance of heaven. Our path can only be directed aright as we fully acknowledge God.

Leaving three graves behind in Moab, Naomi returns to Bethlehem. When she entered the land it was the beginning of harvest time. It is ever thus when a soul returns to God. Naomi felt the misery of her separation from the Lord and His people, and wanted to get back home. Three widows stand together on the road to Bethlehem-Judah. A common grief made them one. But what a contrast Orpah and Ruth present. We cannot drift into grace with a companion or a church. There is no escape from a personal decision. Orpah made her decision, and going back to her gods, sank into oblivion. Ruth's decision was totally different. She reached a spiritual crisis and became, in turn, the ancestress of our blessed Lord. Ruth means "a closely drawn friend," and she was all that to her mother-in-law. How Calvary was enacted that day! From the cross one thief went out to perdition and the other thief to paradise.

Chapter 2

Boaz, courteous to his employees, stands out as a noble character. His name means, "strength" (I Kings 7:21), and he was strong in every way — in love, courage, grace and integrity. A somewhat elderly bachelor, he yet became deeply interested in the lovely Moabitess, for Ruth found grace in his sight. What a beautiful benediction he pronounced upon her (verse 12)! Under the law of Moses, gleaning was allowed for the widow as well as for strangers and the poor (Leviticus 19:9; Deuteronomy 24:19-22). The kindly heart of Boaz was eager to care for the maiden who had come to take refuge under the wings of the Lord God of Israel. We read it was "her hap to light on that part of the field belonging to Boaz" (verse 3), but there is no "hap" with God. If we are in His will, our steps, as well as our stops, are ordered by Him. He knows how to cause two souls to meet.

Boaz quickly extended to Ruth the privilege of a kinswoman. Returning to Naomi from the fields, Ruth was radiantly happy over what had befallen her. Quick to realize that Boaz was able to act as a redeemer, Naomi laid her plans for the redemption of Ruth's inheritance that was hers by her marriage to Mahlon. Our heavenly Boaz is here before us in type. He it is who blesses us, speaks kindly to us, bids us feast upon His bounty, causes handfuls to fall by the way on purpose, and redeems us unto Himself. Ruth herself is a fitting type of the Church in that Boaz redeemed her portion when she became the wife of her redeemer. Boaz was a Jew; Ruth, a Gentile — yet both were made one, and in the redeemed Church there is neither Jew nor Gentile. Christ, like Boaz, is likewise and indeed Lord of harvest, Dispenser of bread, Man of wealth, Advocate, Bridegroom, Lifegiver and Redeemer.

Chapter 3

Naomi's plan of bringing Boaz and Ruth together marks her out as a good matchmaker. Ruth deserved the fullest reward for her decision to serve God and her unselfish devotion to a widowed mother-in-law. How delicate and tender was that midnight meeting in the threshing floor! Discovering Ruth there, Boaz recognized the fear her womanly reserve prompted. Thoughts of purity and goodness alone passed between them. The "fear not" and "my daughter," constituted the tribute of Boaz to Ruth's virtue, and revealed his own nobility of character. As the summer night passed, Ruth left with a gift as a pledge that her desire was understood and that Boaz would do his part. Now Ruth could go home and rest, knowing that Boaz would not rest until he finished the thing. Has the Lord need to say to your worried, agitated mind: "Sit still my daughter"? "Be still, and know that I am God."

Chapter 4

Any one as next of kin, and having a claim on the land belonging to Ruth, had to be prepared to marry her. The nearest kinsman refused to do this, likely because he was already married. This left the way open for the deeds to be ceded to Boaz, who promptly bought back the inheritance and then married Ruth. The bargain was ratified according to the Mosaic law by the symbolic act of "handing over a shoe" (Deuteronomy 25:9), a custom surviving in the throwing of a shoe after a bride on her departure from her father's home. This may also explain the phrase: "Over Edom will I cast out my shoe" (Psalm 60:8). Some writers see in "the kinsman nearer than I," unable to redeem, the ancient law. What the law could not do, in that it was weak through the flesh, our heavenly Boaz accomplished. How willingly He paid the price, buying all that we are and have! Now, as His redeemed possession, we are His bride.

Boaz and Ruth became one, and such a blissful union brought joy to all. The fruit of such a union was a son Obed, by name signifying "a servant who worships." Are we true Obeds, servants who worship? Some serve but seldom worship. Others try to worship but forget to serve. Vision and vocation, however, should be happily blended. Thus, the romantic story ends. Opening in poverty, famine, exile and death, it leads up to David's throne. "Ruth was the Mary of the Old Testament." Her son was born in Bethlehem, and so was her illustrious Descendant, Mary's Child, who was born a Saviour. This is why Ruth finds honorable mention in our Lord's human genealogy (Matthew 1). In the veins of Jesus, both Gentile and Jewish blood flowed, a foreshadowing, surely, of the union of Jews and Gentiles in the Church He came to build.

I SAMUEL

While the Hebrews themselves treated I and II Samuel as one book, we are dealing with them separately as divided in our English Bible. Looking at them together we find that *I Samuel* opens with a prayer and that *II Samuel* closes with a prayer. In fact, the prominent message of *I Samuel* is the place for, and power of, prayer in all experiences of life. *Prayed* is a key word of the book (1:10-27; 7:5; 8:6; 12:19,23). The history of Samuel, Eli, Saul, David, Goliath, Nathan and Gad is given in the most attractive garb of biography. Because Samuel was the outstanding figure in the two books, they are given his name. The *prophet* now takes the place of the *priest*, and Samuel, who probably founded *the school of prophets* (10:5; 19:20), is the first of a noble line of writing prophets. As the conspicuous idea of the book is that of the organization of the Kingdom much space is given to its matter and manner, renewal and rending. The first occurrence of *Messiah* in Scripture—used by a woman—is found here (II Samuel 2:10; Hebrew). Of the character of *I Samuel*, Ellicott says, "It is more than a mere historic record of the fortunes of Israel during the momentous period of their rapid rise from semi-barbarism to a state of comparatively high civilization—more than a brilliant and vivid biography of the most gifted and famous children of Israel. . . . Because of *its deep religious spirit*, it takes the highest rank among the historical books of the Old Testament."

Chapter 1

The main theme in the two books of Samuel is the gradual change from theocracy, that is, a God-directed government through prophets, to a monarchy, that is, a government administered by kings. In successive stages, this delegation of authority from the divine to the human is clearly set forth. The story of Samuel has ever held charm for young and old alike. In this chapter, we have "an incomparable story of heart-rending anguish, prayer, misunderstanding, and the faith that was so assured of the favorable answer as to be no more sad." Hannah's prayer was answered and her son's name, Samuel, meaning "heard of God," commemorates her anguish and answer. From this godly Jewess we learn how to prevail in prayer. Hannah asked and received; sought and found. Many of us ask but receive not, simply because our prayers are only run-away knocks. We lack persistency in prayer.

Chapter 2

Hannah's magnificent ode is worthy of being placed alongside of Deborah's *Song of Triumph*, and Mary's *Magnificat*. Hannah's prayer is heavy with the misery of her people, yet reflects her lofty faith in restoration to holy privilege. Would that we had more women today of Hannah's piety and patriotism! Womanhood gives any age its keynote. The "horn" was the ornamental symbol of power, and should be remembered when we read of the Spirit having seven horns (Revelation 5:6). What a striking contrast there is between Hannah's son and the sons of Eli! Truly, a study in black and white! How weak Eli was! All who are priests unto God should meditate upon the terrible penalty his weakness produced. Divinely chosen and signally privileged, Eli was guilty of lightly esteeming the Lord, and consequently brought about the obscurity of his line.

Chapter 3

Sacrificially, Hannah gave her child up to the service of the tabernacle. Samuel was "a loan to Jehovah," and He paid back with great interest. As soon as Samuel's age permitted, simple duties were assigned him which he efficiently executed. The call of Samuel has been the basis of strong appeals for the young to make definite decisions for God. At first, Samuel mistook the voice of God for that of Eli. Surely this was thoughtfulness on God's part. He did not want to frighten the lad. Eli perceived the origin of the voice and through Samuel heard the doom awaiting his house. Eli's godless sons were the first to suffer

divine punishment. Samuel's natural modesty is characteristic of his strong character. He loved Eli and did not want to hurt or break his tender gentle spirit. At last, Israel rejoices that once again God has a direct and honorable messenger to proclaim His mind. Is ours the constant attitude: "Speak, Lord, for thy servant heareth"? When He speaks, do we obey?

Chapter 4

Samuel's growing importance as a prophet is indicated by the opening phrase of this chapter. Israel's ignoble defeat taught her that deliverance from formidable foes could not come simply by reliance upon the symbol of God's presence, the ark. Alone, it was a fetish. Accompanied by repentance and faith, it was the channel of victory. The news of Israel's defeat brought about Eli's death. Phinehas' wife, naming her child, died, as she bore him. "Ichabod," suggesting Israel's departing glory, has become the synonym of lost power. Carrying the ark into battle, an action similar to that of the Philistines, who likewise carried their gods to secure victory, suggests that outward symbols have their place. But of what avail are the accessories of worship, if the evidence of God's presence and power are lacking? It is the Spirit who gives it life.

Chapter 5

To carry off the gods of a nation was deemed equivalent to absolute victory. Thus, the ark was brought into the house of Dagon, the sea-god, half human and half like a fish, worshiped by the Philistines because of its supposed power to benefit science and arts. On the first morning the men of Ashdod found Dagon on its face before the ark, as if in reverent adoration. Set up again, the next day Dagon was found completely shattered. Manifold disasters overtook the Philistines as they retained the ark, and realizing that the heavy hand of God was upon them, they arose and returned the ark, at all hazards, to Israel. As the ark symbolizes the presence of God, what Dagon can stand before Him? God will brook no rival. The ark and Dagon cannot stand together. Have we any Dagons in our lives, needing, not only to be thrown down, but so broken that only stumps remain? Idols of the heart must yield to our heavenly ark.

Chapter 6

After seven months of disaster, the Philistines returned the ark to Israel; along with emblems of their sufferings. Thus, heathen though they were, they acknowledged the God of Israel as the source of their punishment. Contrary to natural instinct, the two milch cows went steadily forward bearing their precious burden. The five Philistine lords reverenced Jehovah, for we read they came with "a trespass offering unto the Lord." Of the lesson to be learned from the chapter, one expositor writes: "We are forcibly reminded of the repeated efforts of God to awaken the Jewish nation. Sometimes it was by the earthquake, at others by the fire or the mighty wind or the still small voice. He spoke to these people, whether in Philistine or Beth-shemesh in the only language they could understand." And this has always been the divine principle. When tribulation breaks loose on a godless world, there will be no mistaking of its divine source.

Chapter 7

The ark found a temporary home in the house of a Levite, Abinadab, whose son was consecrated to be its guardian until David claimed it. Amid the reverses Israel suffered, Samuel stands out as the conscience of the nation. Through twenty long years he labored for the spiritual reformation of the people. He never surrendered to despair. His untiring labors, burning patiotism, earnest resolve, and intense faith in God fired the people with new enthusiasm. As the result of his insistent appeal, Israel "lamented after the Lord," and idol worship was abandoned and a fresh start made. The terrific thunderstorm bringing defeat to the Philistines proves how God can employ natural forces for the deliverance of His own. As the people raised their "Ebenezer," have we erected ours? Do we ever remember what we vowed to be or do, what deliverances God hath wrought, that without His aid we could never have won? Bless Him, what He has

been He will be until traveling days are done.

Chapter 8

It must have been grievous to the prophet to know that his sons, although judges, were unworthy. Often the best of fathers have to sorrow over disappointing children. After all his consecrated ministry, Samuel's heart must have been saddened over Israel's clamor for a king. Neighboring nations had their titular heads, sovereigns with their palaces, and Israel wanted to be as her neighbors. The convention at Samuel's home in Ramah was most unwelcome to the prophet. His one and increasing purpose had been the restoration of the theocracy, and the desire for a monarchy was in conflict with Samuel's constant burden. He tried to show how unwise it would be to expose the nation to the caprice of one man, a thing that Israel came to learn. Yet Samuel was never so great as when, seeing it was the will of the people to have a king and that God sanctioned the change, he went along with the nation in the inauguration of the new form of government. How sensitive we must be to God's will, directive or permissive!

Chapter 9

The smallest tribe of Benjamin provided the first king. Thus, at forty years of age, as he was caring for his father's estate, Saul was called as king, and because of his towering height, noble features and deportment, seemed every inch a king. Little did he realize that, while searching for lost asses, he would come to a kingdom. Seeking God's direction is a fitting illustration of the Apostle Paul's exhortation about making requests known to God (Philippians 4:6). What a beautiful touch that is about God whispering in the ear of Samuel, the day before, what he should expect! Is ours the same intimate fellowship with the Father? No one was more surprised than Saul himself that he had been chosen as the desire of Israel. Saul, faithful over straying animals, was taken to be king. If faithful in a few things, the Lord will make us rulers over many things.

Chapter 10

Saul's anointing took place before the city was astir. We read that the newly anointed king was "turned into *another* man" (verse 6), but whether he became a *new* creature is another question. Certainly Saul awoke to a new consciousness of God, but his subsequent development would indicate that the crisis was not deep enough. With true reticence Saul said nothing of his honor to his own family until the secret call was endorsed by the nation. Once the assembly had been convened at Mizpah, Samuel presented Saul as God's choice, which choice was almost unanimously accepted. What an auspicious beginning he had; yet how ignominiously Saul ended his reign! Through grace ours is a greater privilege than that of Saul's, for we have been made "kings and priests unto God." Let us endeavor to be kingly in all our ways.

Chapter 11

The Ammonites, subdued by Jephthah some 150 years before, now pressed hard on some of the tribes, and Saul's soul was moved. Rising to the occasion as king of the people, he rallied all the tribes and fought the foe. Victory added to his prestige. Seizing upon the popular enthusiasm, Samuel summoned the people to Gilgal for a renewal of their covenant. As with Saul, so with ourselves, crisis meant conflict. Acclaimed king, there came the battle with the Ammonites. Satanic antagonism ever follows a spiritual crisis. After our Lord's experience at Jordan, there came the wilderness; after the dove, the devil. Victory in our wilderness, however, develops our character, and makes us still greater conquerors. Saul's first act as king was to deliver the oppressed. So we must ever use our sovereignty for the relief of others.

Chapter 12

Samuel's acclamation of the kingdom constitutes a great chapter. For himself, he wanted a clear verdict on his career, and the people enthusiastically supported the justice of his claim. Still smarting under the rejection of the theocracy, Samuel declared the people's choice of a king was wrong and unwise. Their popular desire for a visible head was a backward step, and one that would lead the people from God. A terrible thunderstorm seemed to give emphasis to Samuel's warning, and the people, convicted of their need, entreated the prophit's prayers. If he ceased to pray, Samuel said he would be guilty of sin. Do we realize that we sin if we fail to pray for our statesmen and rulers as they face the tremendous issues of our time? In spite of fierce opposition, Daniel could keep his windows open toward Jerusalem, and praying, prevailed. Because more things are wrought by prayer than this world dreams of, let us pray unceasingly for all men.

Chapter 13

Threatened by the Philistine armies which, at this epoch were at the zenith of their power, Saul endeavored to rally the men of Israel to battle, but behaved independently of Samuel's advice. Failing to act under divine instructions, Saul was guilty of self-will and self-assertion, and had to hear from the lips of Samuel the pronouncement of his disposition as king. How heavy with significance is this chapter for any of us to whom the Lord has entrusted any measure of leadership! Called to cooperate with God, we must not run before Him, but wait His time. Sometimes we are too anxious to push the hands of the divine clock forward. God, however, is never in a hurry. He alone knows when the right hour comes for His interposition to help us best. Philistines may surround us and we, impatient, may try to slay them before God says: "Strike!" If such a spirit of independence is ours, failure awaits us in the combat.

Chapter 14

There is something thrilling about the record of Jonathan's single-handed victory of Israel's foe. Daringly Saul's son and his armorbearer climbed the rocks and, at an agreed sign, surprised the Philistines, crying: "The Lord hath delivered them into our hands" (verse 12). When God begins to work, two dedicated souls are enough for Him to use. One, with God, is always a majority. Two are better than one, especially when one of the twain is God. And, as Jonathan declared, there is no restraint with Him to save by many or by few. What "a trembling of God" the whole host of the Philistines experienced!

Chapter 15

The story of Saul's incomplete obedience was a reflection of his nation's disobedience regarding the command never to mix with heathen nations, but utterly to destroy them. Again and again the Israelites lapsed into the customs of the Canaanites, earning thereby the displeasure and judgment of God. Because of his partial obedience, Saul was finally rejected, just as Ananias and Sapphira suffered instant death because of their partial consecration. Can it be that we have professed to destroy all, yet God hears the bleating of the sheep? Is there some darling sin we have spared? It is only when the complete sacrifice begins that the song of the Lord begins also. With Saul we, too, must learn that "no religious observance can compensate for disobedience to that inward voice which demands the sacrifice of all that is inconsistent with God's high claims." The chapter ends on a pathetic note. With the slaying of Agag, whom Saul had spared, prophet and king part, never to meet again.

Chapter 16

God, who setteth down one and raiseth up another, knew where to find Saul's successor. The failure of Israel's first king, who commenced his reign most auspiciously, must have grieved Samuel. He had built his hopes and affections on Saul, yet what a demoralizing influence the king had come to exert over the nation! Of the choice of David, much could be written. His name means, "the darling," or "the beloved." In the "cathedral of nature" he lived in communion with God. He was trained to become the sweet singer of Israel. Fearlessly he preserved his father's flocks, and all unconsciously was being prepared to serve as the nation's victorious leader. Thus, anointed with sacred oil from the tabernacle at Nob, David was ratified by a divine unction for kingship.

Chapter 17

From infancy we have been fascinated with the story of David and Goliath. What contrasts they present! Goliath, the proud hope of the Philistines, was about seven or eight feet in height, with a challenge that kept Israel in hopeless despair for forty days. Young David, learning of the giant's challenge, accepted it, relying not on his own skill, but upon God. He could not fight in ready-made armor. He had to have his shepherd's tunic and his slingshot and stones. Why did he take five stones from the dry river bed, if he knew that one would be sufficient to kill the giant? Well, it was an act of faith on David's part, for Goliath had four giant-like sons (II Samuel 21:22), making five in all; and with the five stones, with God behind the stones, each one could reach its target. But only one was needed. David went out with five stones, and he came back from his victory with five, not four. For the fifth was in Goliath's head which David carried back!

Chapter 18

Of David's greater Son we read that, beholding the rich young ruler, He loved him. And this was so in David's case, as soon as he saw Jonathan. Jealousy was foreign to his noble, loving character; and thus it was that, seeing Jonathan he loved him and came to love more than a man loves a woman (II Samuel 1:26). There is nothing more tender or beautiful in the famous love-stories of the world than the love covenant made between David and Jonathan in the wood. Such a love bond was to cover even their children. The conspicuous genius and courage of David made him the pride of the nation, and won for him an important command in Saul's army. David's popularity aroused Saul's jealousy and imperilled his own life. Yet Saul eyed David with awe as one divinely protected, and from his treatment of David we learn that jealousy is as cruel as the grave. Let us dread envy; it helped to crucify our Lord!

Chapter 19

Saul's determination to kill David made him resort to open violence, and, in this,

his third attempt, invite Jonathan and his servants to do away with David. But Jonathan did nothing else but plead for the man he loved. Fresh victories of David only aroused the worst passions in Saul, and in an outburst of mad jealousy he hurled his spear at his rival. David fled to his home, and was saved by his wife's clever device. Escaping to Ramah, to a school of prophets presided over by Samuel, David was followed closely by Saul, who found himself caught up in the high enthusiasm of gatherings tense with the overwhelming sense of God, and fell into a trance for twenty-four hours. David, who came to write so much about God as a Fortress and Deliverer, spoke out of a deep experience of God's ability to preserve His own. If we endeavor to live in the will of God, Satan will strive in many ways to bring about our end. But as those divinely guarded we are immortal until our work is finished.

Chapter 20

David's case was desperate, but his friend Jonathan nobly rose to the occasion, pledging his advocacy no matter what it cost. How touching is the love covenant in the wood! Once he was before Saul, Jonathan only brought upon his head avalanches of his father's hate. Back to the secluded spot Jonathan went, and a scheme was conceived whereby David could learn of Saul's final decision. Jonathan's pleading was in vain. The die was cast. David must die. Yet Jonathan knew that David would be Israel's next king, and that God would preserve him, although a fugitive. No weapon formed against him could prosper. Behind the circumstances driving him from home and palace, David could see the hand of God— "The Lord hath sent me away" (verse 22). When Chrysostom was being led out to exile, he exclaimed, "Glory to God for all events!"

Chapter 21

Fleeing from his native land, David found refuge with Achish, a renowned opponent. From Ahimelech, a grandson of Eli, he received food and also Goliath's sword. It is somewhat strange to read that Doeg, who recognized David and carried word to Saul of the whereabouts of his hated

foe, was "detained before the Lord" (verse 7). David feigned madness and his life was spared. He must have been a clever actor to impress King Achish with his madness, so much so that the king asked: "Have I need of mad men?" (verse 15). David thus escaped. Doubtless he was guilty of doubting God's power to preserve him when he became "sore afraid of Achish the king of Gath" (verse 12). He soon regained, however, the uplands of faith. His heart was finally fixed, trusting in the Lord. Subterfuges are usually a sign of doubt and fear.

Chapter 22

Forced to adopt an outlaw's life, David found shelter in the cave of Adullam. David's family also fled from their home and joined him in Adullam. Before long others joined him, and what a motley crowd they were – in distress, in debt and discontented. But under David's influence they were moulded into the nucleus of his future chieftains (I Chronicles 11:10-47). David's concern for the safety of his aged parents was a noble trait. It is thought that Psalm 34 is associated with David's cave life. During these trying days, the outlaw constantly waited upon God for direction, as we find reflected in Psalm 27. David felt, the moment he saw Doeg at Nob, that no good would come of it. As the result of his talebearing, the Lord's priests were slain. Our Lord is now the outcast King, being driven without the camp. But as we go to Him bearing His reproach, He seems to say: "Abide with Me, fear not, for he that seeketh thy life shall be as though he sought Mine" (verse 23).

Chapter 23

The goings and doings of David make a fascinating story, reflected in many of the psalms from David's gifted pen. Psalm 31, for example, came out of the days described in this chapter. Conspicuous in the portion dealing with David's desire to smite the Philistines is his dependence upon God for guidance. "David enquired of the Lord yet again" (verse 4). He wanted to be God directed. How futile our journeys, when we go unsent. It is tragic to see how Saul persisted in his resolve to kill David. He knew he was fighting against God's purpose, yet on he went. Unjustly maligned and persecuted, David left his defense with the Lord. Are you suffering from the jealousy of someone who cannot stand your success? Rest in the Lord, and wait patiently for Him to deal with the circumstances.

Chapter 24

Magnanimity is one of the conspicuous traits in David's character. He was never spiteful or revengeful. He did not believe in paying enemies back in their own coin. He left all judgment to God. The incident of the cave reveals the reverence he held for Saul, on whom the anointing oil had been poured. Incited by his men to cut off a fragment of the royal robe, David was inwardly sorry at doing this. But when he was away from the cave, he waved the piece of cloth to Saul as evidence that he bore no malice toward him. Saul, the rejected king, overcome by David's gracious act, repented and confessed that David was more righteous than himself. Many scholars affirm that it was out of these experiences that David, in after life, wrote Psalm 37, the exhortations of which are bathed in new meaning when read in the light of this chapter.

Chapter 25

The death of Samuel, eliciting national sorrow, must have brought deep grief also to both Saul and David. Because of the reverence in which the prophet was held, he received the unusual tribute of being buried within the walls of his own city. David's encounter with Nabal has occasioned unjust criticism. David, however, was right in his treatment of churlish Nabal. Where services were accepted and counted upon, some recompense was due. David, then, was perfectly justified in his request. But Nabal was an unworthy character. Although rich, he was foolish, a man of Belial, rude and uncivil, a drunkard. How different was Abigail his wife! She had brains and beauty, a combination delightful to find! Abigail's tact saved the situation and prevented David from shedding blood. It was better for the Lord to smite Nabal, as He did. One cannot read this chapter without realizing how God uses various ministries to avert tragedy.

Chapter 26

Once again David revealed true kingly restraint. Standing over the prostrate body of Saul, he had a fitting opportunity of doing away with his enemy once and for all, but opportunity for David did not spell permission. Advantage was not taken of the auspicious moment. Knowing the kingdom would be his, David could bide his time. Saul's spear, the badge of his rank, and his cruse of water were carried off as trophies of a daring feat. How humiliated Abner must have been when David taunted him with want of care, and then pleaded with Saul to cease his useless quest! David's self-restraint, loyalty and humility overcame the miserable monarch who, acknowledging his folly and sin, allowed his old chivalrous self to flash forth with an expiring flicker. Read Psalm 54 for David's after reflection of experiences at this time.

Chapter 27

It is somewhat surprising that a man of David's faith and courage should give way to despair. To the fugitive, it seemed hopeless to alter Saul, when such close attendants as Cush, Doeg and Abner were able to instill their poison in Saul's ears. Then, there were increasing difficulties for David in providing for his many men and their families, and faith seemed to fail. To provide for his troops, David fought foes of Israel. Alas, many of his movements at this period were veiled in a tissue of deceit! At your leisure, read Psalms 10, 13, 17, 25, 40, 69 and learn how to kill despair. Other Bible saints, after a display of God's preserving care, have yielded to doubt and discouragement—Elijah and Jonah, for example. From David's lapse of faith we can learn that "when we descend to the lowlands of expedience and worldly policy, a blight comes over the landscape and the song dies into silence."

Chapter 28

David acted wisely among Israel's enemies, augmenting his host until it became like "the host of God" (I Chronicles 12:1-22). While David was confident of victory, Saul, already shaken by mental disease, became unnerved as he saw the vast Philistine host preparing for an onslaught. With heaven shut against him, and prophet and priest denied him, Saul sought help from the black art which he himself had tried to destroy (verse 3). The supposed appearance of Samuel has disturbed many minds. Could this not have been a demon from the spirit-world imitating the prophet who appeared to paralyze despairing, unnerved Saul with fear? One wonders how different Saul's end might have been had he turned, even at the eleventh hour, to God in true repentance!

Chapters 29, 30

We group these two chapters together, seeing that they are taken up with David's deliverance from fighting against Israel, and then his vengeance upon the Amalekites for the destruction of Ziklag. Recovering all and seizing immense booty besides, David was able to send gifts to frontier towns that were friendly to him in his time of need. Standing alone against the trend of his followers, he established a great principle that ruled in after-times. Once again David had power with God, and now with men. With his life endangered, he sprang back to his rest in God. Taken out of the clay of just deceit, a new song was in his

mouth. This is a constant encouragement to all backsliders. From David's treatment of the Egyptian youth we can learn how to be more compassionate over the lost. This Egyptian has many counterparts around us, and if we would take time to tell them the way to be saved, how richly repaid we would be!

Chapter 31

Following Ziklag there came the battle of Gilboa, disastrous to Saul and his sons, as well as for the host of Israel. Panic-stricken, the Israelites forsook many of their towns, and the Philistines took possession. Cruel-like even to a fallen foe, the Philistines severed Saul's head from his body, stripped him of his armor, and sent it to their idol-temple, as a token of their victory over Israel's God. It was, indeed, an ignominious death for a divinely appointed king. It is pitiful to note that out of all Israel there were none to show gratitude to the dead and dishonored Saul who, in the past, had done much for them – save the thoughtful men of Jabesh-gilead who, under cover of night, recovered the bodies of Saul and his sons and gave them a decent burial. Truly, light and shadow chase one another in this chapter so full of human interest! As the world in which we live is full of joys and sorrows, let us learn how to weep with those who weep, and rejoice with those who rejoice.

II SAMUEL

We have already indicated that in the Hebrew Bible the two Books of Samuel form one undivided work, being known as *The Book Of Samuel*. The present division of two books dates only from the 16th century. Largely biographical *II Samuel* covers the 40 years of the reign of David who, without doubt is the hero of the book. Here his triumphs and tragedies are fully reported. As a continuation of *I Samuel*, *II Samuel* abounds in suggestions. Dr. A. T. Pierson reminds us that, *"Poetic retribution* finds examples in Saul's history; also in

David's, whose great sin brought corrective punishment in its own line in the death of the child of his crime, and the incest of Amnon and Absalom. *Implicit obedience* is enforced. David's attempt to bring up the Ark *on a cart* issued in the death of Uzzah; three months later he had it borne *on the shoulders of the Levites*, as God had directed. *Godly repentance is illustrated.* The guilt of adultery, treachery and murder lay heavy on David. Nathan's parable of the ewe-lamb touched the spring of godly sorrow which overflows in Psalm 51. *Grace* finds illustration in David's treatment of Absalom and Mephibosheth, and in the arrested judgment at Araunah's threshing-floor, which became the site of the Temple with its Altar of Atonement." *II Samuel* introduces us to great prosperity and unusual blessings on the one hand, and of severe afflictions and judgments on the other.

Chapter 1

Having twice spared Saul when he was at his mercy, David had no mercy for the Amalekite who came with news of Saul's defeat and death. The king's crown and bracelets were evidence of the veracity of the messenger's sad announcement. To gain favor in the eyes of David, the Amalekite falsely said that he had slain Saul at his own request. To David, the Lord's anointed was ever sacred, and the Amalekite was executed as a regicide. Without doubt, David's lament over the death of Saul and Jonathan is the finest funeral ode in the world. It inspired Handel's "Dead March In Saul." Originally, it was known as "The Song Of The Bow" (18 R.V.) because of its reference to this weapon. David carried no animosity in his heart toward the man who had sought his life. Chivalrous love extolled all that had been brave and noble in Saul's life. Where is there an epitaph comparable to the one David tenderly uttered as he thought of Saul and his son? For Jonathan, a brother-soul, he had a special stanza. Terrible in battle, Jonathan was yet capable of exceeding woman's love.

Chapter 2

With the death of Saul, David knew that the vacant throne would be his, but patiently he waited for the opportune moment. Seeking divine direction, he made Hebron his center, where the elders of Judah placed themselves under his leadership. The leaders of Saul's party, determined to keep David from the throne, proclaimed Ishbosheth, Saul's youngest son, king of Israel. He was a weakling, however, and unable to act apart from forceful Abner. The fierce struggles in the civil war make sad reading. Amid the conflict, Asahel stands out with a glory all his own. He persisted in following a defeated leader, who could only

reward his loyalty by killing him. Abner was rewarded for this cruel death when Joab smote him in exactly the same way as he had killed Asahel his brother (3:27).

Chapter 3

During the two years' truce between Judah and Israel, David's power increased and Ishbosheth's decreased. What an illustration this is of the progressive spiritual life! Is Christ's hold becoming stronger and stronger, and that of self weaker and weaker? The quarrel between the king and Abner brought David to the throne. At last God's purpose was realized. David was king. In verses 17 and 18 we have a double-barreled appeal. Have we, as believers, given Jesus His coronation? For the sinner, we can put it this way: "Ye sought for Jesus to be Saviour; now then do it!" Joab's vengeance of his dead brother grieved the heart of David. His tears moved the whole assembly! Although Abner had been his persistent enemy, David, with a heart of forgiveness, "wove for his grave a chaplet of elegiacs second only to that which he prepared for Saul's."

Chapter 4

Rechab and Baanah, men of Beeroth, enlisted in Ishbosheth's bodyguard for no good purpose. Realizing that Mephibosheth, the lame grandson of Saul, would never succeed to the throne, they thought that the murder of the present king would be the way to assure David's reign. Evidently they reasoned also that a rich reward would be theirs in assisting him to reach such a supreme position. Beheading the helpless monarch, they carried Ishbosheth's head to David, and received from him the reward they deserved for such a dastardly deed. The hands and feet of the murderers, instruments of their guilt and flight, were cut off. Their bodies were publicly exposed, while the remains of the slain king were reverently buried. We cannot but admire David for his devout spirit. Humbly he ascribed his deliverance from all his trials to God, who had redeemed his soul out of all adversity. What else can we do but magnify God for His redeeming mercy?

Chapter 5

At last David comes into his own, just as the Lord Jesus Christ, David's greater Son, will, when the scepter of universal sovereignty rests in his pierced hand. What a great assemblage Hebron witnessed! This was a day of national gladness, with its coronation celebrations "before the Lord." The people, as a whole, had no doubt of the rightness of their act, seeing it had been divinely inspired. Jerusalem became the capital of the united kingdom. The secret of David's illustrious reign is to be found in the words "He went on, and grew great, and the Lord of hosts was with him" (verse 10). David's first task as king was to deal with the Philistines, who, alarmed over his success, endeavored to invade the walls of the new city. Divine guidance and help were sought and given, and the foe was defeated. David's ideal of a king is to be found in Psalm 101. If only he had followed his own ideal, what years of anguish would have been saved! Dying, David compared what was with what might have been (II Samuel 1-5).

Chapter 6

Determined to make his new capital the center of the religious as well as the political life of his people, David arranged for the homecoming of the ark on an imposing scale. The transportation of the ark, even on a new cart drawn by oxen, was contrary to divine instruction. God had decreed that it should be borne by living men (Numbers 4:15; Exodus 25:14). What happened in Nachon's threshing-floor has been connected with Psalm 29. Other illustrations of the house of Obed-edom being blessed for the ark's sake can be found in Laban's experience, and is likewise true of all saints who are forgiven and blessed by God, for Christ's sake. The barrenness overtaking Michal is evidence that God was pleased with David's jubilation over the return of the ark. The king's gladness made him oblivious to what Michal and others might think of his actions. That the Gospel is a savour of life unto life or of death unto death is illustrated in the influence of the ark, which brought life to one and death to another.

Chapter 7

Noble ambitions are not always God-born. David wanted to build a magnificent temple, worthy of God, and received the commendation of a prophet. But the benediction of a good man on our aspirations is not sufficient; we must be certain of God's will. Overnight Nathan had to reverse his sympathy with David's project and dissuade him from building a temple. Of the divine refusal a writer has said: "God's negative was spoken so gently that it is hard to discover the sentence in which it is conveyed. It is hidden in a golden haze of love." In the covenant given to David, we have the promise of the Messiah, who ultimately came as the Son of David. Read slowly the worshipful prayer of David and make much of its sublime language your own. When God seems to say, "No!" to a cherished purpose, even though it was well in that it was in our heart, let us believe that some day we shall understand the reason why. The paradise of Revelation is not far away.

Chapter 8

The succeeding victories of David greatly extended his empire. With the capture of Metheg-ammah, his conquest of the Philistines was complete. The cruel Moabites were likewise subjugated. Complete defeat also overtook the Syrians, with vast spoils of gold and brass falling into David's hands. As the result of his success in battle the king "gat him a name" (verse 13). All the magnificent treasures he gathered from his foes were given to Solomon for the building of the temple. David lived through turbulent days, yet trials and triumphs found him resting in the divine promises. His war years gave birth to some of the grandest Psalms, like 2, 20, 21, 60, 61. Reigning over and executing judgment and justice unto all his people, he supplies us with a type of our coming Hero-King, who, subduing all His foes, will make them His footstool, and will reign without a rival. Presently the heathen rage and the kingdoms are moved, but Christ's coronation day is at hand.

Chapter 9

David proved himself to be every inch a king, when, in true loyalty to a pledge given to Jonathan , he gave Mephibosheth an honored place at the royal table. As a young prince, a boy of five, he was dropped by his nurse, and kept in strict secrecy. David's persistent search, however, discovered him. The lad's spirit must have been broken, for he compared himself to a dead dog and David to God's angel. Graciously, David restored to Mephibosheth the private possessions of his father and treated him as one of the royal family, all of which is a fitting type of grace. Are we not spiritually lame, unable because of inherited and practiced sin to walk in the ways of God? By nature we have neither beauty nor worth to recommend us to the King. Now, however, for the sake of our heavenly Jonathan, we are treated as blood relatives. Accepted in the Beloved, we are welcomed to the table of grace, at the head of which sits the King Himself.

Chapter 10

David proffered kindness to Hanun, king of the Ammonites, and was contemptuously treated. The gross outrage on David's servants left no choice but war. Alarmed over what had happened, Hanun sought the aid of neighboring states, which were marshaled into a strong, menacing confederacy. But Joab, the masterful captain of the Hebrew army, knew how to challenge and use his valiant men for the defeat of the Syrians and Ammonites. Further kingdoms were added to David's dominion, until his sway seems to have extended to the Euphrates, thereby fulfilling God's original promise to Abraham (Genesis 15:18-21). The territory given to the seed of Abraham was now possessed. Alas, these possessions were lost through disobedience, but they are still Israel's in the divine reckoning, and we watch with absorbing interest the establishment of a Jewish State, and of its acquirements by right and gift! (See Jeremiah 31:1-9; 33:14-26.)

Chapter 11

This tragic chapter would never have been written if David had gone with his soldiers to battle. Tarrying at Jerusalem, enervated by luxury, he fell into grievous sin, committed adultery and murder, making Joab a partner in his crime. The only star in the black sky of this record is the loyal, brave conduct of Uriah, who, although not a Jew but a Hittite, a stranger, refused to take comfort at home when he knew his comrades and the ark were out in the open field of battle. It is somewhat striking that while David's victories were magnificent and manifold, less space is given to them than to his terrible fall, with its disastrous results. At this time, David was about fifty years of age and king supreme, yet in an hour he smirched the noble record of a God-honored life. David's deep agony of remorse proves how he felt God-ward. Read Psalm 51, and then Psalm 32, with the background of this and the next chapter in mind.

Chapter 12

A saint's sin and disgrace may cause the enemies of truth to sneer. They always gloss over, however, the self-abhorrence and anguish of a broken and contrite heart, such as David manifested when Nathan brought home to him the enormity of his sin. Although David's sin was forgiven when confessed, David had to face a train of sad consequences. The child of his sin died, and two years later there came Absalom's revolt and also the loss of his trusted counsellor, Ahithophel. That God made crooked things straight is seen in the birth of Solomon, the beloved of the Lord. Fully forgiven, David was again victorious, taking Rabbah, the royal city of Ammon. How strikingly this chapter proves that if we confess our sins, God is faithful and just to forgive them! Nothing can staunch His unceasing love. Is unconfessed sin yours? If so, why not tell the Lord all about it, and seek the restoration of the light of His countenance?

Chapter 13

Amnon's crime and Absalom's revenge present an indictment of the polygamy and the consequent effeminate luxury characteristic of David's family. Amnon, heir to the throne, chose a wrong companion in Jonadab, the king's nephew, who, as an unprincipled man, suggested to Amnon an abominable crime. Tamar's frantic grief and shame aroused the anger of Absalom, her brother, who, for two years nursed the feeling of revenge. Thus, at the annual sheep-shearing feast, Amnon was stabbed. For the next three years Absalom was a fugitive from the royal palace. Yet all the while that Absalom was hiding in his grandfather's kingdom of Geshur, "the soul of David longed to go forth unto Absalom" (verse 39). David could have insisted on his son's surrender for fitting punishment, but he somehow felt that he was only reaping what he had sown. Having treacherously plotted Uriah's death, David could not very well punish the avenger of his sister's wrong.

Chapter 14

Crafty Joab, who wanted Absalom back, knew that the foundation of the kingdom would be shaken if Absalom was recalled without punishment for his crime. Skilfully Joab plotted, and with the aid of the wise woman from Tekoah, David was made to see that as God had forgiven him in the matter of Uriah, he should do as much for his longed-for son, Absalom. The plot succeeded and Joab brought home the repentant son, whose handsomeness, daring and ready affability were to imperil David's throne. After two years of half-hearted forgiveness, Joab forced the king fully to reinstate his son to court life. "Absalom saw not the king's face" (verse 24). God had truly and fully forgiven David for his sin, yet it took David two years to be willing to "kiss Absalom." What a lesson of grace this narrative presents! God devised means whereby sinners should not be expelled, but at what cost! David granted Absalom pardon without sacrifice. The basis of our pardon is Calvary.

Chapter 15

Growing despotism and intrigue among leaders bent on the furtherance of their private ends, helped to bring David's good government into disrepute. Discontent became rife, the people became restless, thus giving Absalom his opportunity to plunge the whole kingdom into anarchy. Under the guise of a reformer, the careless, proud son of David succeeded in raising the standard of revolt in Judah when, at a public feast, he was proclaimed king. Daily the revolt spread, with those out of all the tribes willing to do homage to the new king. What a pathetic figure David is, fleeing from his own son! Hushai was used to turn the counsel of Ahithophel. Give attention to Ittai's noble words as he vowed to be true to David in death or life (verses 19-22). Adversity sifts out our true friends. Of David's attitude during this heartbreaking period, one has written: "Outside the story of Gethsemane, there is no record in Scripture of a nobler spirit than that which animated David when passing through this thicket of thorns."

Chapter 16

Ziba was as false at Ittai was true. Affecting loyalty, Ziba disparaged Mephibosheth and deceived the king. From Shimei David received great insult. Patiently the king accepted his desert, believing that God would vindicate him. Later on, Shimei was paid back in his own coin. To those who met the usurper, it was a surprise to see Hushai, David's trusted counsellor, among those welcoming Absalom, but by God's providence Hushai saved the situation for David. His advice that Absalom should summon all Israel and lead them in person pleased Absalom's vainglory. David came to experience that God's mercies had not gone forever. Shimei cursed, but Ittai swore allegiance. Zadok and Abiathar forgot their ancient rivalry in a common sorrow. Ahithophel pleaded against David. Hushai stood as his friend. Among the psalms colored by these dark days are 3, 5, 26, 27, 28, 62. Read them with these experiences in mind.

Chapter 17

While the people saw in Ahithophel's counsel "the oracle of God," appearances proved to be deceptive. David's men were weak and wearied and could be easily overcome, argued Ahithophel. Hushai, however, sought to prove that such a conquest was not as easy as it sounded. David and his army would fight with vehement fierceness, like a bear robbed of her cubs. The king was no novice in war and would know how to circumvent Absalom and his rebellious host.

Realizing that his counsel had failed, Ahithophel committed suicide. Powerful chiefs and old friends rallied to David's help and, encouraging himself in the Lord, the king calmly awaited the issue. It is not hard to see how Ahithophel typifies Judas in his cruel treachery (Psalm 41:9; Matthew 27:5). Both traitors destroyed themselves when their cause was lost. Both felt they had betrayed innocent blood. The dastardly act of Judas was, of course, the greater sin.

Reflected in Psalms 42 and 43 is David's faith in God during the anguish of these days.

Chapter 18

Forced to fight, David's heart yet bled for his rebellious, misguided son, Absalom. How dramatic was the Battle of the Wood! Absalom's poorly handled men were no match for David's loyal forces, who insisted that the king, as "the Light of Israel" (II Samuel 21:17), must remain out of battle bounds. Valiantly they fought, leaving 20,000 dead on the field. The beautiful wood accounted for the loss of more, for "the wood devoured more people that day than the sword devoured" (verse 8). And how true this is in spiritual experiences! More Christians fall before the seemingly pleasant, lovely things of life than before those that are conspicuously sordid and sinful. Joab, whose darts ended the life of Absalom, knowing how the tidings would break David's heart, contrived to soften the blow. The expression of David's grief, when he ultimately knew that his handsome, attractive son was dead, constitutes one of the most touching in literature. Is there an Absalom in your family, one so wild and godless? May divine comfort be yours!

Chapter 19

The terrible sorrow of David deeply affected his men, who returned to Jerusalem as if they were disgraced. Sensing the situation, Joab acted firmly and aroused the king out of his grief. Once again David was on the throne, with all the tribes eager to renew their homage. Shimei's fear caused him to flee to David and plead for mercy. Abishai would have killed him, but David spared his life. Ziba prejudiced Mephibosheth in the eyes of the king. How often we find ourselves presented in a false light! The men of Israel bitterly resented being excluded from the honor of welcoming the king back. Christ, like David, will return to receive His crown, but what are we doing to bring back the King? Are we "hastening" His return? Do we live and labor as those who believe that our glorious King is coming back? What bliss will be ours, if like Chimham, we are invited to share the King's palace! What will it be when the King comes back?

Chapter 20

David's kingdom was threatened by a greater disaster than that of Absalom's rebellion. A bitter quarrel broke out among the tribes, and Sheba of Benjamin led a revolt against David. Jealousy caused Joab to slay Amasa, proving that such an emotion is as cruel as the grave. Writing of Sheba's revolt, Bishop Hall remarks: "Spiritually this case is ours. Every man's breast is a city enclosed, and every sin is a traitor that lurks within the walls. If we love the head of *one traitor* above the life of our souls, we shall justly perish. We cannot be more willing to part with our sin, than our merciful God is to withdraw His judgments." Alas, how unwilling we are sometimes to cut off the revolting member! We allow the traitor of sin, bent on destroying the reign of the King, to live on unchallenged. Peace can never be ours until we cut off the head of our Sheba.

Chapter 21

Famine, one of the judgments of God, overtook Israel. Saul had shed blood and had broken, thereby, Joshua's solemn oath to the Gibeonites (Joshua 9:3-17). Thus it was with deep regret that David complied with their request and took seven descendants of Saul, and executed them. How touching is the mother love of Rizpah, as she braved the fierce heat of summer protecting the bodies she loved from jackals and vultures! Respecting such grief, David gave the remains an honorable burial in the family tomb of Kish. If, in olden days, men felt that sin could not be condoned but must be atoned for, how grateful we should be for the propitiation God made for our sin in His beloved Son.

Chapter 22

In this Song of Deliverance, found again in Psalm 18, David walks down memory lane, praising God for all His grace and goodness. And, "this invocation touches the high-water mark of the Old Testament devotion, and is conspicuous among its noblest utterances." Reviewing the past with its danger and dread, David knew that God would not fail His child. We may find it hard to agree with David's assertion of integrity. His hands were certainly not clean in the matter of Uriah (verse 21). But then his claim was by God's grace, and not of his own works. In the closing stanzas, David rejoices in the establishment of his kingdom. Can we say that God's gentleness, or condescension, as the margin has it, has made us great? Jesus was meek and lowly in heart, and in His humility, wonderfully great. In a world of hate and war, in which rough dictators trample under foot the finer qualities of life, how deep is the need of divine gentleness!

Chapter 23

This chapter presents us with David's "swan song." In his last words he claims divine inspiration for all his psalms. "The Spirit of the Lord spake by me" (verse 2). Are our lips at God's disposal that He may speak through them? Magnifying the Lord, as David does in the opening part of the chapter, we have the ideal he ever entertained. Somehow the music carried a jar-ring note. Recounting the valiant deeds of his mighty men, he realized that self-mastery, such as David manifested when he refused to drink the sacrificial water, had bound loyal men to him with thews of steel. It ever cheered his heart to know that there were scores of heroes who, animated by his spirit and sharing his faith, were willing to hazard their lives unto death. Thus is it with David's greater Son, the Lord Jesus Christ. His sacrifice has called myriads from the valley of selfish ease, to live daringly, uncompromisingly for the extension of His cause among men.

Chapter 24

The sin in numbering Israel lay in David's reliance on the arm of flesh rather than upon the omnipotence of God. By the census, David expected to know the extent of his resources and thereby to consolidate his position. He came to realize, however, how futile it was to trust in princes, chariots and horses! Rejecting God's defense of the land, David relied upon his 800,000 able-bodied men. But such proud self-sufficiency brought divine chastisement, and the plague carried off 70,000 persons. When David humbly confessed his folly, the plague was stayed. The lesson of this closing chapter is obvious. "It is not by might, nor by power, but by my spirit, saith the Lord" (Zechariah 4:6). We live in an age of statistics. Numbers! Numbers! Why, this is all some preachers live for! Instead of our counting numbers, may God give us numbers that count. When our full reliance is upon the Lord, we come to know that He is able to save by the few, as well as the many.

I KINGS

As with *I and II Samuel*, the two Books of *Kings* were originally one book, but were divided by the Septuagint translators doubtless for convenience of use and reference. The division can be disregarded, however, and the two books treated as having a perfect unity of idea and authorship. The two have a marked internal unity of peculiar style and character. Both the Septuagint and then the Vulgate name *I and II Samuel*. The First and Second Books of *The Kings*, and our Books of the *Kings* are made the Third and Fourth. Some writers even make the whole history from *Judges* to *Kings* one unbroken compilation, in which the present divisions are but accidental. *I and II Kings* have been called the *prophetic record*, and *I and II Chronicles*, the *priestly record* of the time. Taking the Books of *Kings* together we have emphasized the human standard of the Kingdom the people failed to attain. Nine times over in *I Kings* we have the phrase, "As David his father." As for *I Kings*, probably written by Jeremiah while the first temple was standing (Jeremiah 8:8), it presents a history of the kings of Israel and Judah from David to Ahab and Jehoshaphat, covering a period of some 120 years. Within it we have the first recorded instance of kneeling at prayer (8:54) – standing was the earliest posture (I Samuel 1:26). We also have the first recorded instance of the horns of the altar as a refuge – the first claims to the right of sanctuary. Further, the book gives us the only instance of the priests carrying the Ark – work, the Levites were called to and always performed (8:3).

Chapter 1

This book covers a period of over one hundred years. Israel as a kingdom, united and divided, makes up the book. Though the trials of David weighed heavily upon his heart, his mind was alert to the end, and able to deal effectively with the dangerous conspiracy to substitute Adonijah for Solomon. Adonijah, however, a second Absalom in conceit of his beauty and in unfitness to govern, was speedily dealt with. How we have to watch out for the Adonijahs within and around, ever eager to take the King's place in our heart! David had sworn to Bath-sheba that Solomon should succeed him, and renewing his promise with a solemn oath, gave directions, on his death bed, as to the installation of Solomon as king. Vast crowds acclaimed Solomon's enthronement. Solomon acted very kindly toward Adonijah, assuring his half-brother of safety if only loyalty would be his. Does not Solomon's coronation suggest the establishment of a greater than Solomon as King of kings?

Chapter 2

David's deathbed charge to Solomon was full of practical advice. While there may be the aspect of bitterness in dying injunctions, we must remember that here public safety

required drastic action with those who constituted a grave menace to the welfare of others. Reciting his own experience of divine goodness, David urged his son to keep the charge of the Lord. The passing of David, as he went the way of all flesh, is simply told as, "like a tired infant's, those aged eyes closed, and his spirit joined the mighty dead." May ours be the blessedness of those who die in the Lord! Adonijah's effort to use Bath-sheba to further his treasonable design, testifies to the influence of the queen-mother in the eastern court. Adonijah's concealed plot was quickly discerned by Solomon, who ordered his death. The flight and death of Joab make sad reading. For transgressing the limits of a conditional pardon, Shimei died. May the prayers of Psalm 19:13 be ours!

Chapter 3

It might have been the usual policy of an eastern king to strengthen his position by marrying into another royal family, but by his alliance with Pharaoh's daughter, Solomon clearly sinned against light. It was an unequal yoke that boded no good for the young king, who evidently loved his father's God. The public inauguration of Solomon, when he was but 20 years of age, must have been an impressive sight. To his credit, Solomon chose an understanding and discerning heart, graciously granted by God, coupled with unequalled riches and honor. His handling of the problem presented by the two women, and the identification of their babies, gave evidence of his insight into human nature, and of a bestowed wisdom. Are we conscious of our need of wisdom? If so, then God is willing and waiting to give us all we need. First of all, we must know our lack of wisdom; then believingly ask for it, as James enjoins us to do (James 1:5-7).

Chapter 4

Wisdom from above covered administrative matters, and thus Solomon quickly developed his court. The opening verse gives us a vivid description of all appointments, of the division of the land into twelve districts, and of the peace and prosperity the people enjoyed. Truly, it was Israel's summer!

Solomon's high endowments and unusual affluences and influences are summarized for us in verses 20-34. The Book of Proverbs contains many of the three thousand proverbs he gathered. And, in the matchless Song of Solomon, we have one of his thousand and five songs. This chapter presents Solomon in all his glory, but when we turn to the gospels we find Jesus, who became so poor that He had nowhere to lay His head; yet He declared Himself to be greater than Solomon. So He was. In possessions, love and wisdom, Christ is ever the Ideal. The best pale into insignificance beside Him.

Chapter 5

Hiram, ever a lover of David and now a friend of Solomon, greatly aided in the erection of the temple. Hiram agreed to supply all the necessary timber on the understanding that all the laborers, preparing and transporting the wood, be cared for by Solomon. The system of forced, unpaid work, imposed on the Canaanites, was evidently not grudgingly given. Solomon acted in all wisdom, as God had promised him, and his commands were fulfilled. The abiding Temple of God, His Church, is in the process of erection, and all who have a share in the building of it are volunteers. Our heavenly Solomon has no compulsion, no other pressure than that of love. Down the ages, multitudes have been willing to hazard their lives for His dear sake. We cannot but count it a privilege to be builders of a Temple that will never perish with age, and to value our lives as of no account in devotion to the Lord Jesus Christ.

Chapter 6

After three years of laborious preparation, at last the temple went up, as "like some tall palm the noiseless fabric sprung." A striking feature of the building was that "neither hammer nor axe nor any tool of iron (was) heard in the house" (verse 7). All the stones had been prepared in the quarry, and they fitted exactly into one another. No mortar was used. And how silently God works today as He completes His Temple! No noise, no unnecessary show, but in His own wonderful way He brings the living stones together and fits them

into His Church. The last part of the chapter is taken up with the plan of the temple. The symbols of God's presence were conditioned on Israel's obedience. The half-open doors signified that the way into the holiest was not yet open. Now, through the rent veil of the Redeemer's flesh, we have boldness to enter the Holy of holies. Solomon was seven years in building his temple; the Holy Spirit has been some 1900 years at His task, and the Temple is not yet complete.

Chapter 7

The size and splendor of Solomon's palace can be gathered from the fact that it took thirteen years to build. A palatial mansion was also erected for Solomon's Egyptian wife. Seven years building the Lord's house; thirteen years building his own house! Thus Solomon spent almost twice as long on his own abode as he did on God's. What is our proportion? Do we spend more on ourselves, on our own plans, than on the cause of Christ? While much could be written on the magnificence of the temple, there is one small item in the glowing description that we must not overlook: "upon the top of the pillars was lily work" (verse 22) – beautiful handiwork where no one could see it, save the eye of God. The flesh loves prominence. It wants its lily work to be seen and admired by all. Hidden, unnoticed tasks for the Lord may not bring the praise of man, but they do please God. The unknown weight of the precious metal used (verse 47) can suggest the unsearchable riches of Christ.

Chapter 8

The whole of this long chapter, taken up with the dedication of the temple, contains three sections: the solemn *transference of the ark* from Zion to the temple (verses 1-21); *Solomon's dedicatory prayer* (verses 22-61); and the *sacrifice of peace-offering* (verses 62-66). The public consecration of the new edifice must have been a moving sight. The ark, solemnly deposited within the prepared shrine, was the symbol of God's presence. How awesome must have been the moment when the Shekinah-cloud filled the temple, compelling the priests to retire!

Such an overwhelming sense of the august presence of God is all too rare among us today when we gather in His name. Combining priestly with regal functions, Solomon prayed and blessed the people. In this he is a type of Christ, as King-Priest. The colossal sacrifice of 22,000 oxen and 120,000 sheep is hard to realize. Yet the pride and glory of the nation vanished, and now Israel is without her temple.

Chapter 9

"The second time" is a phrase worth tracing through the Word. "The Word of the Lord came to Jonah the second time" (Jonah 3:1). Here Solomon was privileged with a second appearance of God, coming to him on the night following the dedication of the temple. This supernatural vision contained direct answers to Solomon's inaugural prayers. Details of Solomon's commercial enterprises, and his ambition of earth, are before us. Alas, these rapidly corrupted his mind, turning king and people away from God. The temple was high in ideals as well as in elevation, and apostasy was inexcusable. Yet, in spite of warning against disobedience, Solomon turned from God. The remarkable achievement recorded in this chapter resounded through the world, but, turning to Ecclesiastes, we hear the cry of an unsatisfied heart: "All is vanity" (Ecclesiastes 1:1). Earthly glory disappeared as a soap bubble. God has set eternity in the heart of man (Ecclesiastes 3:11, R.V.), and thus no earthly splendor or wealth can ever fully satisfy that heart.

Chapter 10

The visit of the queen of Sheba to Solomon makes a fascinating record. Hearing of Solomon's fame and wisdom, the queen had to come and see for herself the glory and splendor she had heard of. How overwhelmed she was by the pomp of Solomon's court, and the greatness of his wisdom! As she left the palace she gave Solomon a gift amounting to something like three million dollars. The source of Solomon's revenue is staggering. From gold alone he gathered over twenty-five million dollars. Taxes levied on merchants and traders, and the gifts of kings and princes, added considerable wealth to Solomon's treasury. What can be said of his magnificent throne, immense stud of horses and multitude of chariots? Is it not blessed to know that we have a greater than Solomon, who is able to answer all hard questions? How happy we are, as His servants, to stand before Him. When ultimately we see our King in all His glory, we too will confess: "The half was not told me" (verse 7).

Chapter 11

With all his heaven-bestowed wisdom, Solomon was not wise enough to guard himself against grievous apostasy. "Love of the world," says one expositor, "a ceaseless round of pleasure, the adulation of flatterers, a reign of golden splendor, ate out his heart, and left him at fifty, an old and foolish king." Heathen wives turned the king into an idolater and resulted in the division of his kingdom, the major portion of which went to one of his servants, Jeroboam, an active and intelligent superintendent. From Ahijah the prophet, Jeroboam heard a message that revolutionized his life (verses 31-39). What a sad end Solomon experienced! How his glory departed! At his death, unruly passions seethed beneath the external pomp of his reign. A God-given sovereignty was despised, heathen immorality was rampant, and jealousy overtook the tribes. What an eclipse! Yes, Solomon's glorious era failed, just as many other great nations have vanished, but Christ's reign will have no end.

Chapter 12

Rehoboam, Solomon's son, foolishly turned down the advice of older men to mitigate the rigors of his father's reign. The younger men whom he followed had no sympathy with the rights of the common people, and so, in the place of the whip of Solomon's taskmasters, Rehoboam substituted knotted scourges. Revolution broke out, Adoram was stoned to death, Rehoboam was forced to flee, and the work of a generation was shattered. Jeroboam's influence suffered through the erection of the two calves and the appointment of others than Levites as priests, which idolatry led to Israel's undoing. This ruler of the ten tribes built on the sand,

and his portion of the divided kingdom met with disaster. It is sad to read of the tribes parted, but sadder still to witness the lamentable divisions among Christians. Instead of our fighting together against a common foe, the devil has us fighting against each other.

Chapter 13

God's judgment ever falls upon intrusion into holy things. Discarding the functions and authority of the high priest, Jeroboam endeavored to inaugurate a new worship. Judah's unknown prophet appeared, denounced the innovation, and predicted the birth of a prince of David's line who would burn the bones of the wrongly appointed priests. This prophecy was fulfilled by Josiah 360 years later (II Kings 23:15). Judgment fell upon the false altar, and Jeroboam sought the nameless prophet's intercession, who bore a noble title, "the man of God." Yet privileged as he was as a divinely sent one, this prophet fell by the neglect of the details of his mission. If God has given us a task to do, let us never turn aside on the advice of others, no matter how good they and their advice may appear to be. We have our marching orders from God, and we must implicitly obey Him.

Chapter 14

The blind prophet, Ahijah, quickly saw through Jeroboam's ruse, and was ready to greet his wife, much to her chagrin. What heavy tidings she received! The royal house was doomed. Every male belonging to it should die. Abijah escaped by dying before calamities overtook Israel. What a sorrowful journey the wife of Jeroboam had, as she trudged home, and how distressed the parents must have been with the child dying, as mother crossed the threshold! The passing of Jeroboam is briefly stated. How different his twenty-two year reign might have been, had he not caused Israel to sin! Judah's apostasy under Rehoboam reveals how he reaped disaster for having abandoned himself to the idolatry inherited from his father. A necessary lesson to be learned from Jeroboam's wife, feigning herself to be another woman, and Ahijah's exposure of her, is the importance of sincerity. False appearances are

easily discerned by the divine eye. We may be able to cheat man, but all is naked before God.

Chapter 15

This chapter covers varied reigns. Abijam's was a short and troubled one. From such a bad father, however, a good son came. Asa was thorough in his abolition of idolatry and the sinfulness that characterized his father's days. But Asa's alliance with Syria was a fatal blunder, in view of the fact that the introduction of this foreign element interfered with the internal affairs of the two kingdoms. Nadab, who succeeded Asa, was murdered by Baasha after a short reign of two years. Baasha exterminated all the royal family in order to make his position more secure. From Asa we learn several lessons. First, there must be no compromise with evil. Asa removed all idols and so must we. Some idols must be destroyed and others displaced. Asa's early faith was wonderful; yet he failed, and that lamentably, when he called in Ben-hadad. How careful we have to be lest, having commenced in the Spirit, we finish in the flesh!

Chapter 16

Godless Baasha, continuing Jeroboam's idolatrous policy, brought upon his house a fearful curse, pronounced by the fearless prophet Jehu. Like others of his kind, Baasha died without being desired. Elah, his son, was equally worthless. Two years were all too long for such a drunken sot to reign. With his death, the family of Baasha vanished. Zimri, one of the army's commanders and the murderer of Elah, usurped the throne and, after a few days, died a suicide. Anarchy and civil war followed. Ultimately, Omri became the undisputed possessor of the throne, and was worse, if possible, than all that were before him. After six years, Omri was succeeded by his son Ahab, a godless son following a godless father. Jezebel, Ahab's wife, introduced the worst type of nature-worship into Israel. What a danger-signal this chapter is for those who govern nations! When the godless rule, there is bound to be dissolution.

Chapter 17

Elijah's appearance is an oasis in a weary desert. During the prosperous reigns of Omri and Ahab, a vast temple to Baal was built in Samaria, the worship of which was conducted by hundreds of licentious priests. Foremost among the godly prophets to resist the challenge of Baal was Elijah, the Tishbite, mighty in deed and word. Because he stood before God, he was not afraid to stand before Ahab, powerful and cruel though he was. Do we share Elijah's courage, a courage born of faith in God? God's supremacy over all, even the feathered creation, is seen in His command to the ravens to feed Elijah. Have you noticed what a wonderful ministry the widows of the Bible exercised? Look this up. Overwhelmed by Elijah's gaunt figure and commanding personality, the widow of Zarephath gave him lodging, and was amply rewarded with the barrel of meal that never failed. Jewish tradition has it that the son of this widow, who followed Elijah in his journeys, was afterward known as Jonah.

Chapter 18

We cannot review this chapter without thinking of the chorus:

> Elijah's God still lives today
> To take the guilt of sin away;
> And when I pray my heart's desire,
> Upon my soul He sends the fire.

What a contrast there is between Obadiah and Elijah! Obadiah was a good man, but weak. A luxurious court life enervated him. Elijah, a prophet of the desert, was consumed by an overmastering passion for God's glory. How dramatic the meeting of Ahab and Elijah must have been! The prophet was certain God would answer prayers. In spite of the frenzied excitement of the priests, Elijah was calm and confident. The phrase, "the Word of God came," is associated with Elijah on four successive occasions. The God who answered by fire was the true God. How our churches need such a descending flame! Perseverance in prayer, even to seven times, is another essential, if we would see God display His power.

Chapter 19

After a long night journey, Elijah gave way to profound despondency. The terrific strain of Mount Carmel, thought of apparent failure, Jezebel's threat to kill him, and sheer fatigue mastered his courageous spirit for awhile. But how tenderly God cared for His overwrought prophet! Depression sometimes overtakes the finest saints, but thoughtfully God cares for them. At Horeb, Elijah, firmly impressed with the terrible aspects of God's power in nature, came to learn of the gentle Spirit working in the hearts of many. He also came to learn that he was not the only hero of his time. There were seven thousand who refused to bow to Baal. Evidently they were not as bold as Elijah. The anointing of Elisha, Hazael and Jehu relieved the burden of Elijah. It is a greater achievement to set three men to work than to do the work of three men. We learn from this chapter that God's call to service is a supreme one, to which all else must be subordinated.

Chapter 20

Ben-hadad, a most powerful monarch and head of a confederacy of thirty-two petty kings, constituted a menace to Ahab. The king of Israel, however, was divinely assured of victory over the self-confident tyrant who boasted of Samaria's destruction. Drunken Ben-hadad came to experience that boasting leads to humiliation. Self-confidence is the armorbearer of sin. A mere handful of young men was sufficient to turn the tide of battle against the Syrian host. Ben-hadad returned to Damascus, only to ridicule Ahab for his simplicity. Revenge was planned, causing Ahab's family to rue their father's treatment of their crafty foe. How tragic it was for Ahab to make a covenant with Ben-hadad! Evil must never be mercifully dealt with, in heart or in state. Agag must be cut in pieces. What a warning we have in verse 40! Busy with trifles, we sometimes miss the most important issues of life. God save us from frittering away our chances!

Chapter 21

The sin and sorrow of covetousness are written large over this chapter. Naboth refused to sell his vineyard on lawful grounds (Leviticus 25:23). It was a family heritage. Peeved that he could not get what he had set his heart on, Ahab, acting on Jezebel's instigation, committed a dastardly crime in order to possess the vineyard. How terrible to realize that Ahab sold his soul for a piece of ground! Men today sell themselves to the devil for various vineyards. The devil, however, drives a hard bargain, and his price is death. Taking possession of the ill-gotten vineyard, Ahab encountered Elijah and heard from the stern prophet's lips the message of his doom, as well as that of his evil wife's judgment. Because of Ahab's bitter repentance, part of his sentence was delayed; nevertheless the rod of retribution fell upon the godless pair. They reaped what they had sown. We Christians ought so to live as to be, as it were, incarnate consciences to the world's Ahabs and Herods, who live in defiance of God.

Chapter 22

Friendly relations between Jehoshaphat and Ahab could not have been very deep, seeing that they served different masters. Jehoshaphat followed Jehovah, and Ahab worshiped Baal. Can you see a message for your heart in the question: "Know ye that Ramoth in Gilead is ours, and we . . . take it not?" (verse 3). Are you possessing your possessions? Micaiah, the unsparing critic of Ahab, was hated, but he fearlessly revealed the mind of God and predicted Ahab's defeat and death. If only we could have more faithful prophets like Micaiah. How dear to God they are! He sees to it that their words never fall to the ground. Behind the "chance" arrow bringing death to Ahab was the divine hand. But there are no chance arrows. Each are directed to fulfil God's purpose. The ships sent to Ophir for gold were broken at Ezion-geber (verses 47,48). Storms destroyed the fleet. God knew that Ophir's gold would corrupt Jehoshaphat, as it did Solomon. Praise God for His preventive grace!

II KINGS

Noting the perfect order of *I and II Kings* as one book, Dr. E. Bullinger points out that, "They begin with King David and end with the King of Babylon; open with the Temple built and close with the Temple burnt; begin with David's first successor on the throne of his kingdom, and end with David's last successor released from the house of his captivity." A period of some 300 years is covered by *II Kings,* the first half of which is taken up with an account of Elisha's ministry and miracles over 66 years. Elijah is prominent in *I Kings.* Elijah and Elisha can be looked upon as the *Paul* and *Timothy* of the Old Testament. Much prominence is given in this book to the Lord's anger and wrath (13:3; 17:18; 22:13,17; 23:26; 24:20); and also to "the word of the Lord" which, with its equivalent, are mentioned 24 times. The key phrase of the book is, "According to the word of the Lord" (1:17; 10:10; 17:23; 24:2). Wher-

ever found in the Bible, "the word of the Lord" represents divine inspiration and authority. Israel's base treatment of God was responsible for His righteous anger. "Did that which was evil in the sight of the Lord" is found 21 times in the book. The reverse response, "right in the sight of the Lord," occurs but eight times. Taking the two books as one, we have:

1. The Death of King David. I Kings 1, 2
2. The Glory of King Solomon's Reign. I Kings 3-11
3. The Division of the Kingdom. I Kings 12 – II Kings 16
4. The Assyrian Captivity of Israel. II Kings 17
5. The Decline and Babylonian Captivity of Judah. II Kings 18-25.

Chapter 1

This Second Book of Kings, continuing the history of the kingdoms to the captivities, covers a period of over 300 years. Ahaziah, who succeeded to Ahab's throne and to his sins, had a most solemn verdict pronounced upon him (II Chronicles 20:35). For giving himself up to self-indulgence of the worst character, a message of doom reached him from Elijah. How stern the rugged prophet appears to be! Yet he never had any thought of himself. A consuming passion for God's glory bore him along. Fearlessly, Elijah faced the king, and declared his message with boldness. It was thus that Martin Luther entered Worms and Wartburg, rebuking the emperor. Elijah shared the hatred of God toward sin. The divine wrath is a terrible reality (Romans 1:18). True, in the New Testament we see the tenderness, meekness and gentleness of Christ displayed. But let us never forget that when the Lamb comes to manifest His wrath, great will be the anguish of men. Never forget that your life is precious in His sight.

Chapter 2

The original word for "prophet," we are told, means "boiling," or "bubbling over." Thus, "the prediction of future events was not original thought, but the speech of men moved by the Holy Spirit. Elijah realized that his highest duty, and the most permanent result of his life-work, was to train men to speak for God." His school was the missionary seminary of the age. As we read of Elijah's translation, we witness the humility of true greatness. It would have pleased the prophet more if no eye had witnessed his whirlwind ride to heaven. Yes, and from Elijah's experience we learn the folly of dictating to God. The fiery prophet pleaded once that he might die. Better far, to be translated and not taste death. Elijah's translation was convincing evidence to his age of the reality of the unseen, just as our translation will be at the return of our Lord. Elisha's spiritual endeuement as Elijah's successor is conspicuous: the parting of Jordan, the healing waters, and the stroke of God upon irreverence. How different were the ministries of Elijah and Elisha! Yet God needed both.

Chapter 3

Ahab's death was favorable for revolt. Jehoram, although not as wicked as his father, nevertheless clave unto the sins of Jeroboam. Intermarriages and alliances brought about confusion and sorrow. Acting upon a divine suggestion, Elisha saved the day for Israel. A vigorous foe was made to flee. As we think of the necessity of revival among ourselves, how full of import is the command: "Make this valley full of ditches" (verse 16). There must be necessary preparation if God is to travel in the greatness of His strength. Further, the God-given victory over the Moabites teaches us that often God's best gifts overtake us without fanfare of any kind. There was no sound of wind and rain, but the ditches were filled and the Moabites destroyed. God asks of us to dig the ditches of repentance, faith . and prayer. He does the rest.

Chapter 4

Elisha prayed that a double portion of Elijah's spirit must rest upon him. Have you noticed that Elisha performed double the miracles of Elijah? Further, his miracles were akin to his gentle, loving nature. Elijah's miracles were stern and judicial. Elijah's were more the whirlwind type, Elisha's the still, small voice. One illustrates John the Baptist; the other, Christ. So long as we give God capacity, He pours out the oil. It is never a question of how much God can give, but how much we can receive. Note the provision made for Elisha by the woman of Shunem: a bed, symbolic of rest; a table, of fellowship; a stool, of instruction; and a candlestick, of witness. The staff of Elisha was not enough to bring life back to the dead son of the grief-stricken home; flesh had to touch flesh. Dead sticks of religion can never raise the spiritually dead. Our heart must touch hearts. We must learn how to impart ourselves.

Chapter 5

From Naaman we can learn many lessons. First of all, the phrase, "the Lord hath given deliverance," reveals that God was guiding heathen as well as Hebrew history, for Syria, for which Naaman fought, was a heathen nation. How true it is that "God's providence is as long as time and as broad as space." Naaman means, "a good fellow," and he was all that. A valiant, dashing officer, yet a leper. From the little slave girl we learn how to be true to God even amid adverse circumstances. At the opportune moment she testified to the power of God's servant; and her faith, bringing healing to Naaman, has inspired tens of thousands. If compelled to live among strangers, may our light yet shine. The brave soldier was cleansed of his foul disease in a simple way. Humbling to pride though it may be, we must accept God's method of deliverance. Covetous Gehazi teaches us to beware of the hardening effect of hypocrisy.

Chapter 6

The cutting of the stick aroused expectant faith. How striking is the phrase, "the iron did swim" (verse 6). Natural laws are subject to the power of Him who made them. One writer has the comment: "Hearts may be as heavy as iron at the bottom of the stream, but when a splinter of the cross is inserted, they rise to the surface and swim." Have you a sinking heart? Allow God to make it swim. There are those who thought they could take Elisha prisoner. But the angel-host that conveyed Elijah to heaven were on guard for Elisha. The prophet's servant, however, lacked the eye of faith to see the mighty forces on hand to protect Elisha. Do you live in the assurance of verse 16? Fear not, the angel of the Lord still encamps round about His own.

Chapter 7

The taunt of the unknown lord was short-lived. But Elisha knew his God, and "windows in heaven" became a reality. Thus, before night, the famished host feasted on the great store of provisions and enriched themselves with the boundless spoils of the tents that were left behind by the fleeing Syrians. What famine covers the earth today – spiritual famine! Multitudes are dying in their sins, and a Holy Ghost revival is sadly needed. Do we jeer at the possibility of the windows of heaven being opened? May we be among the number who believe that God is able to do great and mighty things! If our prayers and faith are assured in plenteous abundance, let us not keep the wonderful news to ourselves. We are guilty of sinful silence if we hold our peace. The chapter closes with the tragic death of the man who taunted Elisha. Like many another scoffer, this one perished amid abundance.

Chapter 8

Escaping the seven-year famine, the Shunemite sojourned among the Philistines. By a coincidence it would seem, she met Gehazi, and through his good offices her estates were restored. What we sometimes call coincidence is Providence. If we strive to abide in God's will, life will be strewn with divine coincidences. Nothing happens by chance if we are His. What an arrestive verse this is: "He settled his countenance stedfastly until he was ashamed: and the man of God wept" (verse 11). How we need to know how to weep over other men's sins and doom! Our preaching of judgment should ever be accompanied by tears. The rest of the chapter makes sad reading. Joram had a good father, but a bad wife, who led him into gross idolatry. Is it not wonderful how God overrules? Look at Matthew 1, and see how some of the names in this chapter reappear. What matchless grace is God's!

Chapter 9

Widespread idolatry had corrupted the chosen race, and stern measures were necessary to reestablish the worship of God. Elisha rose courageously to his task and executed judgment on Ahab's house. Aided by God, the prophet struck a telling blow for the preservation of divine truth. Tradition has it that the young man commissioned to anoint Jehu was Jonah, but where Scripture is silent, so should we be. Anyhow, we can see from "the young man the prophet," that often the inspiration of a great life may originate in a youth's appeal. All over the world hearts ill at ease are asking, "Is it peace?" But there can be no peace as long as Jezebels are allowed to reign in the heart, the church and nation. Certain retribution overtook the cruel woman with a painted face. Jehu asked: "Who is on my side?" (verse 32). Response came from two or three eunuchs who threw Jezebel to her doom. Are we on the Lord's side, and willing to answer his challenge?

Chapter 10

Jehu was thorough in his destruction of the house of Ahab. The two heaps of heads at the palace gates of Jezreel testified to the end of Ahab's evil dynasty. Ahaziah's kinfolks met a similar end. Although the fate of Ahab had been proclaimed by Elijah at Horeb years before, God had not forgotten His Word. He never does, whether it is promised blessing or destruction (verse 10). What a pointed question Jehu asked of Jehonadab: "Is thine heart right, as my heart is with thy heart?" (verse 15). Jehonadab and his devoted followers were advocates of the pure worship of God, and Jehu found in them kindred spirits. It was by their joint action that Baal-worship was forever rooted out of Israel. Alas, from verse 29 we learn that Jehu did not go all the way. Had he dared act upon Deuteronomy 17:2-5, he might have saved Israel from her ultimate overthrow and captivity. The best of us come far short of complete separation.

Chapter 11

From the time when God declared that the seed of the woman should bruise the head of the serpent, the devil, that old serpent, set out to destroy the seed from which his Bruiser was to spring. The seed royal of Judah was destroyed, with the exception of Joash, who was spared to overthrow and succeed the fiercely cruel and unscrupulous Athaliah. A consuming ambition destroyed any heart this woman had had. Thinking of Joram, hidden in the house of the Lord for six months, we cannot but think also of our blessed Lord, now hidden in the Father's house above, but who will soon appear. Ere long, as the rightful Heir to the throne of the world, He will be manifested to cast out the usurper. There is something beautiful in the alliance formed between young Joash and the aged priest. Then, civil and religious elements were separated, but now, in Christ, priest and king blend, for He is a priest upon the throne (Zechariah 6:13).

Chapter 12

Together the young King Joash (or Jehoash) and Jehoiada the priest, strove to restore divine worship to its former position. However, widespread popularity of evil, of idolatrous rites, proved a formidable barrier. Various methods of paying for the repair of the temple were unsuccessfully tried. Finally, a chest was placed at the temple entrance, the receipts of which were carefully checked and faithfully spent. Many churches have their "Joash Chest," and prove that direct, voluntary offerings are sufficient to meet every obligation. The restored, ancient glory of the temple did not last long. Joash was forced to leave Jerusalem, and captivity overtook great numbers of his people. From Chronicles we learn that, after the death of Jehoiada, the great religious statesman, Joash came under the influence of heathenism and that he reintroduced heathen ways. What a warning is in this chapter for nations today!

Chapter 13

The apostate reign of Jehoahaz over Israel merited divine judgment. Because of the countenance of a licentious form of worship, national chastisements became increasingly severe. Ashtoreth's worshipers were trodden down like dust and the king's military might impoverished. His repentance, it would seem, was unavailing to check national disaster. As Elisha neared his end, he was able to anticipate a brighter day for the kingdom. At his death Joash wept, and confessed that the prophet had been the true defense and glory of his kingdom. Dying, Elisha rebuked the king for his lack of faith. How much each of us misses through unbelief! We go so far, but not far enough. We claim a partial, but alas, not the complete overthrow of Satan. The miracle at Elisha's grave speaks of the influence of the prophet even after his death. Will it be true of us that although dead, we shall yet speak?

Chapter 14

Judah's good king, Amaziah, was true to God. He failed, however, to be wholly the Lord's. At the outset of his reign, Amaziah inflicted death upon those who had murdered his father. Turning to the fuller account of his exploits in II Chronicles 25, we discover something of the terrible punishment meted out to Edom. Amaziah conquered Edom, but adopted Edom's idols. Denunciation of vices in others does not mean that we are personally immune from their snare. The war between Israel and Judah makes sad reading. No strife is so bitter and tragic as that between relations or citizens of the same country. Israel was made very bitter. Yet judgment was mixed with mercy, for God saved the people by the hand of Jeroboam. Restoration of prosperity, however, only produced pride and corruption and further judgment.

Chapter 15

Azariah, known as Uzziah, Isaiah's favorite king, was active and prosperous until he intruded the priest's office. For such offense Uzziah became, and died, a leper. He was excluded by his disease from society, and Jotham, his son, acted as viceroy. Zechariah, the weak and besotted prince, only reigned for six months, being murdered by one of his own generals. In quick succession others reigned over Israel. Evil rulers never make for stability. National sins multiplied. Prophets were raised up to plead with the people to return to God, but their cries were often disregarded. Studying the varying fortunes of Israel, we realize that "there is always the delay of mercy pleading with justice in nations and individuals. True religion is the salt of any nation." When the fear of God decays and the salt becomes savourless, then dissolution is near. It is this fact that guides us in our interpretation of national life today.

Chapter 16

For a graphic description of religious degeneracy in Jerusalem at this time, we have to turn to Isaiah. Under the reign of Uzziah and Jotham, prosperity brought about gross idolatry. God was forsaken. The conspiracy against Ahaz was designed to destroy the family of David, set a puppet on the throne, unite three kingdoms, thwarting, thereby, the Assyrian advance. Against Isaiah's strong remonstrances, Ahaz went to Assyria for help. Such an alliance led to the ultimate captivity of the people, here called "Jews" for the first time (verse 6). In the fashioning of the altar, Ahaz sinned

in that he substituted a heathen pattern for one furnished by divine authority (Exodus 25:40). All life and worship must be shaped according to the pattern God gives us on the mount of vision (Hebrews 8:5). How is your life being shaped – according to the world's pattern or God's?

Chapter 17

We cannot read a chapter like this without realizing what disappointment God's people sometimes occasioned Him. Here we have those who were redeemed and made recipients of divine favor, carried off as slaves. What degradation for those once highly privileged! Uprooted and transplanted, Israel, it was felt, would be less inclined to fight for a lost independence. In new surroundings their unique character would be forgotten. Turning to Hosea, we have only to read the first three chapters of his prophecy to find out the rending of the divine heart as Israel was carried off. That many of the scattered Jews retained their love for, and loyalty to, Jerusalem, is evident from many New Testament Scriptures (Acts 2:9,10; I Peter 1:1). There is a pertinent word in verse 33: "They feared the Lord, and served their own gods." How many there are who profess an outward regard for God, but who worship idols of their own creation! No man can serve two masters.

Chapter 18

With the coming of Hezekiah, the situation changed for those languishing under the Assyrian yoke. Hezekiah means *the strength of God,* and he certainly required all the strength God could give him to grapple with the enormous problems confronting him. Commencing with the destruction of the symbols of idolatry, Hezekiah was not long in shaking off Israel's shackles. With absolute dependence on God, he went on from victory to victory. Knowing God was His defense, Hezekiah knew no fear. If we are loyal to the Lord and His Word, He will be our Defender in the face of opposition. Hezekiah failed in that he tried to bribe Sennacherib, which was a sign of weakness. It never pays to bribe foes, for sooner or later we have to meet them. It is encouraging to read that the threats of Rab-shakeh were received in silence. "The people held their peace, and answered him not a word" (verse 36). Jesus, when threatened, held His peace, and committed His cause to God.

Chapter 19

Hezekiah faced an hour of destiny and agony. Deep sorrow of heart was his. Arrogant foes threatened his people, and in spite of his faith in God, he did not seem strong enough to claim deliverance. His rent clothes expressed horror over the blasphemy of the Assyrians, and the sackcloth spoke of mental distress that the grave crisis caused the king. Isaiah's ministry must have comforted Hezekiah's distressed heart. Sennacherib was threatening the God whom Hezekiah served, but Isaiah assured Hezekiah that God would destroy his foes. The outspread letter, and Hezekiah's noble prayer, are inspiring. What do you do with threatening or disturbing matters? Do you spread them out before the Lord, and let Him deal with them? Isaiah's message that Hezekiah's prayer had been heard cheered the king. With one angel God destroyed 185,000 Assyrians. Then why doubt what He can do?

Chapter 20

All that Hezekiah had endured was enough to produce illness in any man. Such was the nature of his trouble that he should have died. The king craved to live, in order to realize his plans, and because, as yet, he had no heir to the throne. His cry was heard. Fifteen years were added to his life, during which time Manasseh was born. The shadow going back ten degrees on the dial was God's sign of recovery. Can it be that the shadow has gone down on your dial, and spiritual life is waning? Pray that it may be reversed, and that the years, the havoc of the cankerworms of neglect and sin have wasted, may be restored. Imprudently Hezekiah exposed his royal treasures, possibly vast spoils taken from the Assyrians, to the Babylonians. Such thoughtless and vain ostentation merited the rebuke of Isaiah. What are people impressed with when they visit our homes – our prayers or our treasures?

Chapter 21

Manasseh was born three years after his father's recovery. Because he became an abomination in the sight of the Lord, it would have been better for him had he never been born. It is ever a tragedy when an evil-minded son succeeds a good father and tears down the noble structure that prayer and faith built. "He built again the high places which Hezekiah his father had destroyed" (verse 3). Is this your sorrow as a parent? Have you a child that you hoped and prayed for, who is now opposed to your godly ways? If so, you know how hard it is to have that dear one build again the things you once destroyed. But, hope thou in God! He answers prayer. Amon reigned for only two years, and in his brief reign added to the iniquitous influence of his dead father. "He walked not in the way of the Lord" (verse 22). Would that our rulers today knew how to walk with God!

Chapter 22

Good Josiah, godly son of a godless father, restored the worship of God after the dark years of previous reigns. Note that he began to reign when he was eight years old. Verse 1 is a good verse to use in child evangelism. A godly group supported Josiah in his determination to purge the land of idolatry. He was surrounded by prophets like Zephaniah, Nahum, Habakkuk and Jeremiah. God-fearing priests like Shallum, Hilkiah and Maaseiah the governor, also supported Josiah. (Further details of temple repair can be found in II Chronicles 34.) Josiah's enthusiasm for God was shared by his servants. With the discovery of the Law, repentance ensued. How the Scriptures can revolutionize a life or a nation, as for example, Luther's discovery of an old Latin Bible at Erfurt! What a different world this would be if only all churches and nations could rediscover the Word of God, and walk in the light of it.

Chapter 23

How commendable was the action of the king in the public covenant he made to avert the threatened judgment of a broken agreement! If only all of our rulers would make a similar covenant, national idolatry would soon disappear. The reformation of Josiah was thorough. Everything alien to the revealed will of God was stamped out. Idolatrous priests and practices came under the heavy stroke of judgment. After he destroyed every vestige of idolatry in Judah, Josiah toured Samaria carrying the torch of revival as predicted 326 years before his birth. It is sad to relate that, while outwardly purified, many of the people resented these reforms and longed for suppressed idolatries. Thus will it be in the Millennium. Multitudes will render feigned obedience to the King of kings. But with the termination of this blessed era, and the loosing of Satan, universal revolt will come. Hold fast upon the Lord.

Chapter 24

The full report of Nebuchadnezzar's disastrous reign is given by Jeremiah (see chapter 25). Gentile dominion greatly impoverished the people of God. One cannot study the fortunes and misfortunes of Israel without realizing the correspondence between sin and its penalty. Jeremiah is found saying: "The Lord God of recompences shall surely requite" (51:56), and requite with recompence He did! Israel had been guilty of importing the idols of surrounding nations. In turn, she found herself being transported to those lands whose idols she accepted and wor-

shiped. Nebuchadnezzar's conquest was complete. The flower of the Jewish nation was taken to Babylon. Zedekiah endeavored to cast off the Babylonian yoke, but the promise of peace and prosperity gave way to despair. "God is as stern in His judgments as He is forgiving to genuine penitence." Israel was highly privileged, and her penalty corresponded to God-given privileges.

Chapter 25

Zedekiah's revolt, aided somewhat by Pharaoh, was short-lived. Rebelling against a mighty monarch like Nebuchadnezzar was as futile as it was foolish. Jerusalem was seized. Terrible famine prevailed. Brutal atrocities were perpetrated. After eighteen months Nebuchadnezzar destroyed the city, showing no mercy whatever. The inhabitants were taken captive. What a tragic disaster! Yet God did not utterly forsake His people. Through the cleansing fires the impurities of heathenism were burned out, and a distressed people returned to the worship of the true God. In the Books of Ezra and Nehemiah we see how the gold was refined in the fire. A picture of grace can be seen in the king's kind treatment of Jehoiachin, king of Judah. Read verses 28 through 30, and see how you can apply them to all that Christ is willing to do for us who have lived in the bondage of sin. Are you feasting on the King's daily allowance?

I CHRONICLES

While *I* and *II Chronicles* cover the same ground as *Kings* from Saul to Zedekiah, they are not a mere duplication for they include much which does not occur in previous historical books. These last of the books of the Old Testament to come in pairs were given the title by Greek translators, "Things Omitted." God inspired the historian, probably Ezra, seeing *Chronicles* greatly resembles the style and language of *Ezra* and *Nehemiah*, to go over ground previously covered and add details which He considered important. Thus, *Chronicles* is an interpretation of *Kings* which explains the constant reference

in *Kings* to *Chronicles*. The former books give us *man's standpoint* – the latter, *God's standpoint*. In *Kings*, Israel's history is associated with the throne – in *Chronicles*, with the *altar*. While the Books of *Samuel* and of *Kings* deal with both kingdoms of Israel and Judah, *Chronicles* is concerned only with Judah. Breathing an ecclesiastical atmosphere *I Chronicles* emphasizes the Lord's activities on behalf of His people, and the justice of His judgments (See 4: 9,10; 5:20,22,25,26 etc.). Seen from the viewpoint of heaven, Israel's history written during her Babylonian captivity proves that

God reigns over all. This book of Chronicles is occupied all the way through with man's chief end of glorifying God, and of giving Him the right place in heart, home, church and nation.

Chapters 1-4

As the two books of Chronicles cover the same period of history as I and II Kings, and since we dealt fully with such a period when digging for nuggets in those historical books, we group several chapters for daily perusal. The books before us furnish an interesting supplement to the former series of historical books. Many details which they omitted are here stated. The lists in these four chapters are not exhaustive, but indicate the divine choice of channels for the realization of the divine plan. This is clear from the opening verses, where the only son of Adam mentioned is Seth. The story of Jabez deserves special notice. Amid the great procession of history, God ever remembers faithful ones. Prayer saved Jabez. And his is a prayer that we can make our own. God granted his request. He ever does respond to such holy requests. Among these monotonous lists of names we discover precious gems like the one in 4:23. Are we dwelling with our king for His work?

Chapters 5, 6

In these genealogies, heads of certain tribes and high priests are singled out. Chapter 5 cites Reuben, Gad and Manasseh. A key verse to note is verse 2. "Judah prevailed above his brethren, and of him came the chief ruler." Christ came of the tribe of Judah, and His is the advent toward which everything moves. Chapter 6 is the priestly chapter, providing us with a list of high priests. Their ministry of song is emphasized. Verse 31 is suggestive. The service of song came after the ark had rest. A true heart song can only become ours when Christ, our ark, finds a rest within. The chapter concludes with the exact location of cities occupied by the priests and Levites. Chapters like these prove how meticulous the Jews were in the preservation of their records. Great care was exercised in the preservation of genealogies.

Chapters 7-9

These three chapters contain genealogical tables of the tribes of Issachar, Benjamin, Naphthali, Manasseh, Asher, Ephraim and Benjamin. Chapter 9 provides us with lists of those who returned to the land after their release at the close of the seventy years captivity. A gem of truth for our hearts can be found in 9:13. " . . . very able men for the work of the service of the house of God." Are we among the number who love to lodge round about the house of God (verse 27)? The genealogy of Saul is repeated to prepare the way for the reign of David. "It is solemn work to go through these vast cemeteries and to read the names," says one expositor. "Each had a history of tears and smiles, of storm and sin, of success or failure. We, too, shall similarly pass and be forgotten, but let us be sure that our name is chronicled in the Lamb's Book of Life."

Chapters 10 - 12

Saul's defeat and death were covered in our meditations on I Samuel. What the chronicler emphasizes here in chapter 10 is the particular sin for which Saul lost his kingdom, and then his life (verses 13, 14). Chapter 11 omits much that is found in II Samuel. The description of the mighty men who surrounded David in his trials is very graphic. Those who came to him in debt, distress and discontent had been wonderfully transformed. Can you find a parable of grace in verses 22-25? Chapter 12 is supplementary to Samuel. Verses like 18 and 38 anticipate the gathering of the nations to Christ. The day is fast approaching when, at His coming to reign, all peoples will be of one heart to make Him king. Then will be experienced a more lasting joy than the joy in Israel over David's rise to the throne, as Saul's successor.

Chapter 13

The caption that Dr. C. I. Scofield gives this chapter is most expressive. "Doing a right thing in a wrong way." Certainly it was right to bring the ark back, but not in a new cart. God had ordained that the ark should be carried on living shoulders.

The parallel of this chapter can be found in II Samuel 6:1-11. Two additions are here given by Ezra, if he wrote Chronicles: "David and all Israel played before God *with all their might, and with singing*" (verse 8). The death of Uzza, who touched the ark, teaches the necessity of reverence which, in the course of Israel's history, has declined. How richly God blessed the house of Obed-edom for the ark's sake! He is no one's debtor. Any heart entertaining God's beloved Son is favored of Him. And in turn He blesses others for our sakes.

Chapters 14, 15

Chapter 14 is parallel with II Samuel 5:11-25. Confirmation as king gave David influence over the people. Yet, humble as he was, he was dependent upon God. He did not act on his own initiative but inquired of God. The destruction of the idols of Baal-perazim was necessary lest they should be worshiped. Listening for a sound of a going in the tops of the mulberry trees led to expectation of divine reinforcement. Are we ever careful enough to inquire of the Lord before any enterprise? Chapter 15 has been given the caption: "Doing a right thing in a right way." We here find a more elaborate account of the brief summary of the same episode in II Samuel 6:12-16. How imperative it is to worship and serve God in His appointed way! David loved to dance – alone, and before God. Would that modern dancing was of the same order!

Chapters 16, 17

Parallel portions to read, along with chapter 16, are I Samuel 6:17-23, and Psalms 105 and 106. Much can be gathered from David's festival sacrifice, as we think of the blessing and bounty Christ has made possible for His redeemed ones. What a magnificent thanksgiving psalm David composed for the occasion. Every man appointed to sing or serve knew his task and performed it well; so many of us also have the assurance, by the Spirit's gifts or talents bestowed, that we are in the place God would have us be? Coming to chapter 17, the parallel of which is in II Samuel 7:1-3, there is little to add to our previous notes

on David's desire to build a house for the Lord. The commendation of even a good man must not always be taken as a token of divine commendation. Nathan told David it was all right to go forward with his plans, but God said, "No!" How the characteristic humility of David shines forth in his prayer! He knew how to worship and magnify the Lord.

Chapters 18-20

For a fuller treatment of the Davidic kingdom, as given in chapter 18, go back to II Samuel 8. Notice the repeated phrase, "the Lord preserved David whithersoever he went" (verses 6,13). When one's ways please God, He loves to direct and guard his steps. David's first campaign, in chapter 19, can be compared with II Samuel 10. Look at this captain's insistence on the right kind of soldierly behavior in verse thirteen. Reading of how surrounding nations made peace with David (verse 19), one cannot but remember that a greater than David is slowly yet surely reaching the great consummation of Revelation 11:15. A notable feature of chapter 20, as we compare it with II Samuel 11-21, is that the historian omits any reference to David's fall. Such a sin was not to be gloated over or magnified. "Love covereth a multitude of sins." We face many giants today, but in our heavenly David there is one mightier than they.

Chapter 21

Comparing this tragic chapter with its parallel in II Samuel 24, we observe that the cause of David's sin in numbering the people is here attributed to Satan. David, ever humble, yielded to an outbreak of pride and ambition. His exalted position turned his head for a moment, and he sought to depend upon the arm of flesh rather than upon the Lord. His heartfelt confession, however, proved that he was none the less a man after God's own heart, and in his cry and confession knew all about I John 1:7,8 before it was written. What a revelation of David's tender, shepherd-heart we have in the question: "These sheep, what have they done?" (verse 17). Have we been guilty of dependence upon our prestige and possessions, and are we being plagued in some way or another? Well, David's road back is ours. Sincere acknowledgment of our sin, and the recognition of the Lord as one with whom there is forgiveness, result in restored favor.

Chapters 22, 23

The place of deliverance became the place of an altar (21:29), and the site of the temple. May grace be ours to build our worship of God on His deliverances and promises! Although he was denied the privilege of building the temple, David yet prepared abundantly for it. Do we realize that we, too, have been called to the work of temple-building (I Corinthians 3:10-17)? Canaanites and captives were pressed into the preparation for the temple. What treasures David amassed by "the economies of a lifetime and a shearing of superfluities, but there was no self-complacency." And we must exercise a careful concentration on all that is best for the cause of Christ. The closing verses of chapter 22 reveal that the best work is done when God's peace rules the heart. Chapter 23 contains a beautiful addition to David's boundless preparation. He was not so engrossed with a multiplicity of responsibilities as to forget the morning praise and the evening thanksgiving.

Chapters 24-27

In chapter 24, twenty-four classes of priests are enumerated. Then we have the Levites who waited upon them. Each man had his office, just as every believer has his or her sphere in which to serve the Lord. Chapter 25 is taken up with the choristers who, as they sang, revealed divine truth in song.

Harps and lutes, symbaling the tune, give the theme. The next chapter shows us the names of porters, officers and judges. Much of the treasure the Levites guarded dated back to Saul (verse 28). Underline the phrase, in 26:30, where we read that these officers were in "the business of the Lord, and the service of the king." The spiritual and the secular were treated as one. Chapter 27 contains the names of the captains and ministers of the state. What an organization these chapters present! The pattern of it all was of God, who ever supplies men and material for realization.

Chapters 28, 29

We now come to David's final charge. One of the most commendable traits of his character was his absorption in the glory of God. The erection of the temple lay nearest his heart. To have been rejected as its builder was a matter of minor importance, as long as the building was accomplished. David's one anxiety was for Solomon, who was to build the temple, to remain loyal and strong, and to carry the work to completion. David had seen the perfected house so accurately in the Spirit (verse 19) that, when he set out the plan in sketches, all Solomon had to do was to build accordingly. Chapter 29 reminds us that, in addition to immense funds gathered from public sources for the temple-building, David made a further magnificent contribution from his private funds. On the basis of his offering, David appealed to the leaders of the nation, who responded promptly and nobly. The chapter closes with an epilogue on David's reign. Without doubt, he stands out as one of the noblest figures in Hebrew history (see Acts 13:36).

II CHRONICLES

George Goodman in his book of rhyming couplets on the Books of the Bible has the lines –

> In *Chronicles* we have retold the tale of Judah's kings
> The Royal Line of David's Race, and other precious things.

Among the "precious things" of *II Chronicles* are the kingdom under Solomon (1-9) – the kingdom from Rehoboam to Zedekiah (10:36). Compare the remarkable phrase, "The Lord . . . set thee on his throne" (9:8) with I Chronicles 29:23, "Solomon sat on the throne." The frequent phrase, "Seek the Lord" is the key to this book (20:20; 30:19 etc.), and gives us the central message of *II Chronicles*, namely, the secret of a vital religion and a life of victory in a prepared heart to seek and serve the Lord. Another "precious thing" of the book is that of the power of prayer. Through reliance upon God, great and mighty things can be accomplished (13:18; 14:6,11; 15:9; 20:20,27 etc.). The student of *revival* must give consideration to the religious revivals under Asa, Joash, Hezekiah and Josiah. What a mighty spiritual upsurge the nation experienced when, repenting of their sins, the people sought the Lord with all their heart! As we think of the spiritually-decadent condition of our nation today what else can we do but cry, "Wilt thou not revive us again that thy people may rejoice in thee?" (Psalm 85:6).

Chapter 1

The history of First Chronicles is continued in the second book. An announcement of Solomon's establishment commences this opening chapter. The promise given him by his father (I Chronicles 28:20) was being realized to the full. He started out with an altar (verse 6), recognizing God and God alone. How different his end would have been if the altar had never been departed from! (The section dealing with Solomon's vision of God and prayer for wisdom should be compared with I Kings 3:3-15.) He felt his greatest need to be that of wisdom, and God granted this request with the abundant provision of the things Solomon did not ask for. God is saying to each of us: "Ask what I shall give thee." Is our reply the same as Solomon's: "Give me more wisdom and knowledge"? Then look at James 1:5,6. Blessed be God, He never giveth sparingly! Liberally He gave to Solomon, and He waits to do the same for us.

Chapters 2-4

What determination characterized Solomon's preparation to build the temple! Knowing that he had a God-given task to fulfil, he brooked no delay. A great God must have a great house (2:5). Chapters 2 and 4 give us the dimensions and materials of the temple. Solomon built as instructed of his father (3:3). In these modern days, too many sons fail to build as instructed by godly fathers. Our responsibility, as co-builders with the Spirit of a more marvelous temple than the one Solomon built, is to build according to the pattern of the mount. These chapters must be compared with I Kings 6 and 7. With all its glitter and glory the temple that Solomon erected perished with time. But the temple of God, the Church, is indestructible. The gates of hell cannot prevail against her. How privileged we are, if saved by grace, to be counted among the living stones forming the living temple!

Chapter 5

The glory of completion pervades this great chapter, which is an extension of the account given in I Kings 8:1-11. Solomon finished the work entrusted to him by David, and took every care to dedicate the temple as the house of the Lord. All the holy vessels of the old tabernacle, along with the dedicated treasures of David, were solemnly deposited in the house magnifical. God was glorified by the trumpeters and singers, and God Himself set His seal upon the work of Solomon by filling the temple with His Shekinah-glory. It must have been an awesome sight when the glory of the Lord so filled His house that the priests could not minister. How many church congregations could stand an experience like that! If, with such an overwhelming sense of God's presence and glory, the pastor could not preach and the choir was stricken into silence, we wonder how carnally minded church members would react to a glory-filled church.

Chapters 6,7

These two chapters reveal how bountifully God blessed Solomon with wisdom to preach and pray aright, for wisdom covers these realms as well as others. We have already written about his God-honoring, truth-exalting sermon (I Kings 8:12-21). Do you try to find God in the thick darkness of sorrow (6:1)? One prepares, another builds (6:7,10). At the judgment seat of Christ both are to rejoice together. Solomon's prayer of dedication is without doubt the most marvelous petition in the Old Testament. Let us take a sentence or two out of it. "Let thy word be verified" (6:17). God knows how to verify His Word, especially when man denies it. Are we rightly clothed (6:41)? That such a prayer was heard of God is evidenced by the fact that He said, "Amen," by filling the temple again with His glory (7:1). In the divine appearance we have the divine secret of constant revival (7:14). Note the little word "if" in the last part of the chapter.

Chapters 8, 9

How rapidly the fame of Solomon spread! It will be found that the first nine chapters of this second book correspond with I Kings 1-11 and constitute the third part of the whole work. After twenty years, Solomon's greatness was still undimmed. Solomon, in all his glory, became a power among men. There was no end to the increase of his dominion. But a greater than Solomon is coming, whose government will be more glorious and enduring. The queen of Sheba was overwhelmed with the display of the wisdom and wealth of Solomon. Christ's servants, however, are happier than those of Solomon's, as they stand continually before Him to hear his wisdom. Nothing is said in this record of how Solomon came to an ignoble end of a most noble life. Satan is a past-master at bringing down the mighty from their seats. May we give heed to the injunction: "Let him that thinketh he standeth take heed lest he fall" (I Corinthians 10:12).

Chapters 10-12

According to the divine Word, the glorious kingdom was rent in twain. The two tribes of Judah and Benjamin, known as "the House of Judah" thereafter, went with Solomon's son, Rehoboam, while the other ten tribes, generally called "the House of Israel," followed Jeroboam. Refusing the good advice of older men, Rehoboam, headstrong, tried to act like a tyrant, with dire results. Had he followed the mature counsel of the old men, the kingdom would have remained intact. What sorrowful divisions and separations wrong advice can cause!

Chapter 11 makes sad reading. Jeroboam rejected God and became an idolator, and Rehoboam followed the sin of his father in desiring many wives. Further apostasy is then introduced in chapter 12. Rehoboam would not prepare his heart to seek the Lord, and after a reign of seventeen years, died amid national strife and dissension.

Chapters 13, 14

Wars, wars, wars! How different these days are to the peaceful days of Solomon! Because of his eagerness to acquire the sovereignty of the whole country, Jeroboam went to war with Abijah, who succeeded his father, Rehoboam. Abijah, however, threw himself upon God, and Judah was victorious. From his long address, which jeopardized his position for awhile, we can learn that arguing with men is of little avail. The secret of victory is in prayer. When we are threatened, we must rely more absolutely upon the God of our fathers. He cannot fail! Asa was a good man, following in David's steps. He destroyed the idols and restored the worship of God; and the land enjoyed peace. "They sought the Lord . . . and he gave them rest" (verse 7). Heavenly squadrons came to the help of Asa. Along with physical power, spiritual power was added. The Church is slow to learn that spiritual victories can never be won with carnal weapons.

Chapters 15, 16

Azariah the prophet made good use of his opportunity by driving home the moral of Asa's victory. It was due, he insisted, to the alliance between God and the people. And, as Azariah went on to affirm, if only Asa and those he reigned over would pursue the path of obedience and consecration, reward would be vast and permanent. Is it not true with ourselves that the moment of victory is the time in which we most need the warning of the prophet-voice? Asa's remaining years were marked by blessed tranquility. While chapter 16 is parallel with I Kings 15:16-24, verses 7 to 10 of this chapter are peculiar to Chronicles and deserve notice because of Hanani's noble protest, that the prophets were the incarnate conscience of the nation. The strength of any nation depends, not on its armaments but on the recognition of God, the fearlessness of its true prophets, and the sanctity of its homes.

Chapters 17, 18

Chapter 17 is peculiar to Chronicles. To the credit of Jehoshaphat it must be said that he not only sought to eradicate the blight of heathenism but engaged in a system of religious instruction. And is not religious education an absolute necessity of national well-being? A marvelous psalm, like the longest one in the Psalter (119), proves reverence for the pentateuch, which was then the only textbook of the people. Chapter 18 corresponds with I Kings 22. What a wrong alliance the chapter opens with! To be unequally yoked together with unbelievers is ever disastrous. Such an alliance could not pass without an expression of divine judgment. Have you ever thought what momentous deeds were accomplished by unknown persons? It was "a certain man" who drew his bow at a venture and brought about the death of unworthy Ahab.

Chapters 19, 20

The "nevertheless" given to Jehoshaphat suggests a gleam of hope. God is ever looking out for that "nevertheless." Local judges and patriarchal rule, which had existed from Joshua's time but which had fallen out of gear, was now systematized. Ecclesiastical courts, set up in Jerusalem, dealt with such matters as the distinction between murder and manslaughter. This was also a court of appeal. Recognition of God as the judge of all the earth is the foundation of a righteous judicature. Chapter 20 presents us with a great scene. Jehoshaphat is surrounded by all the people as he pleads and, as men ever do when in extremity, as he recites past evidences of God's faithfulness and confesses utter inability to cope with imminent peril. The king's assurance rang out the victory of faith and it was contagious. We have need to give heed to the exhortation: "Deal courageously, and the Lord shall be with the good" (19:11).

Chapters 21, 22

Jehoram got off to a bad start. Married to Jezebel's daughter, Athaliah, he came under her evil influences and became her tool. Murder and the promotion of idolatry were inspired by the demon of a woman. As a king, Jehoram was utterly weak and incapable. But for God's faithfulness to David, the lamp of his house would have burned out. Alas, it is tragic when a servant of God marries a non-Christian! Usually misery follows such a union and alienation from God of the children and household (II Corinthians 6:14). Such was the end of this weak king, that when he died without being desired, he was denied the usual royal funeral. Chapter 22 contains the record of Ahaziah, who followed the wicked counsel of his godless mother. Note the word "counsel" in this chapter. How wonderfully God preserved the "seed royal" from which Jesus was to spring (verses 10-12; Genesis 3:15).

Chapters 23, 24

Place chapter 23 alongside of II Kings 12, and note omissions and any additions. Joash was only a lad when the people anointed him king. Crafty Athaliah died the death she deserved. How terrible is the influence of a bad woman! Godly Jehoiada started a blessed revival. Eagerly and willingly the people cleansed the temple and their lives of all that was unclean. Gladness and tranquility ever follow the slaying of our Athaliahs (verse 21). Although he was only seven, Joash was not too young to reign. If you are interested in Child Evangelism, this is a thought worth remembering (24:24)! From his early days, Joash did that which was right in the sight of the Lord. Faithless priests had to be dealt with. Note the contrast between the death of Jehoiada (verses 15,16) and that of Joash (verses 25,26).

Chapter 25

Amaziah was another good king, of whom Judah might have been proud. Yet the story of his reign begins with the remarkable sentence: "He did right in the sight of the Lord, but not with a perfect heart." He was guilty of a reservation, namely, alliance with Israel. This defection from spiritual perfection grew like the rift within the lute, until he ultimately worshiped Edom's gods. Let each of us be wary of imperfect surrender. Amaziah lingered on for fifteen years, and national misery and resentment resulted in his assassination. He stands as a warning to all that, if one room is occupied by a traitor, ultimately there is surrender to the foe. Let us pray for perfection of surrender. Only thus can we resist the evil, subtle forces waiting either to silence or damage our witness for the Lord.

Chapters 26-28

King Uzziah, a great friend of Isaiah the prophet (6:1), is called Azariah in II Kings 14. Go through chapter 26 and underline choice passages, like verses 5, 7, 10 and 15. Punishment overtook Uzziah when he copied David and Solomon in the combination of the high-priesthood with the throne. He forgot that these kings had acted under exceptional circumstances. Pride attributes success to our own cleverness and dexterity. Unless repentance comes, downfall is inevitable. Jothan was another good king, yet unable to check the increasing corruption of his age. He was a great builder. Have you noticed the connection between "wars" and "ways" (27:7)? Chapter 28 provides additional material to II Kings 16. Luxury and impurity produced national degeneracy. Ahaz was a wicked idolator and "made Judah naked and transgressed sore against the Lord" (verse 19).

Chapters 29-31

Hezekiah, another good king, reversed his evil father's policy. Bravely he fought the bane of idolatry and restored the worship of God. How inspiring it is to read of Hezekiah's purging of the temple and the land, and how the whole congregation joined in the glad and holy acts of national repentance and consecration. Without doubt, Hezekiah's character was largely moulded by his godly mother (Isaiah 8:2). Chapter 30 records the restoration of the passover as a national celebration. Cleansed of all traces of idolatry, the annual feast was again observed in God's way. Further religious reforms make up chapter 31. So deep were

the impressions created by the passover that idolatry was completely overthrown. Hezekiah's work was thorough. What he set his hand to do, he did with all his heart. The principle governing his life is summed up in the phrase "he sought his God."

Chapters 32, 33

Sennacherib, guilty of over-confidence, thought it an easy matter to win the fenced cities of Judah for himself (32:1). Hezekiah, however, had succeeded in uniting the people, and their religious temper laid the foundation of successful resistance. How often God grants us an experience of His gracious presence to prepare us for coming trial! What a wonderful verse is the 8th in chapter 32! Underline it in your Bible. Hezekiah knew the right source to go to for help. One angel was sufficient to slay proud enemies. Look at II Kings 19:35,36, and see how many that angel slew. Chapter 33 covers the same ground as II Kings 21. Manasseh had the longest and worst reign. What a bad son of a good father he was! Yet in his prison, like the prodigal of Luke 15, Manasseh came to himself and, therefore, to God. How immediate was the response of God's forgiving love! It is ever so.

Chapters 34-36

Josiah, as a lad, began to seek after God. He would need all God-given grace and courage to combat the terrible conditions he inherited. But such was his determination and valor that at twenty, without pity he swept the land free of abominations, and at twenty-six set about cleansing the temple. The finding of the law stirred him deeply and made him a great revivalist. To his credit, it is recorded that "all his days the people departed not from following the Lord." Chapter 35, parallel with II Kings 23:21-30, records the keeping of the great passover. The chapter ends with Josiah's lamented death. In chapter 36 we reach the final moments in a downward course. Jerusalem was overthrown. Kings were taken into captivity. Such was the pitiable plight of the people so divinely honored in the past that it is said that the Lord rose up against them till there was no remedy. Yet a bright day awaits the Jews.

EZRA

Because both *Ezra* and *Nehemiah* deal with the nation's return from Babylon and with necessary restoration and reorganization, they are companion books and were regarded as one by ancient Jews. Although presenting a complete picture of post-captivity readjustment in church and state, *Ezra* is taken up with the nation's ecclesiastical history and rebuilding of the temple: and *Nehemiah* with civil history and with the renovation of the walls and gates of the temple. Covering some 80 years, *Ezra*, like *Chronicles*, contains genealogical lists which prove how meticulous the Jews were in recording their pedigree. Ezra himself was both a scribe and an Aaronic priest, and led the Jews – cured of their idolatry while in captivity – in confession and reformation. Mixed marriages were annulled and the knowledge and authority of the ancient law revived. How we should pay tribute to Ezra who was the first to initiate a revival of Bible study, which is God's program for the revival of His people! When we tremble at the words of God, and like Israel give them the place of pre-eminence in our total life – religious, social, business and political (1:2; 9:4; 10:3,5 etc.) – then we, too, experience God's richest blessing. If, as some scholars suggest, Ezra, the great revivalist and reformer, was also the writer of *I* and *II Chronicles*, and of Psalm 119, compiler of the *Psalms*, engaged with others in the settlement of the canon of Old Testament Scriptures, and founder of the Order of the Scribes, then we owe this lover of the Word more than we realize. The fruits of the revival of Bible study and obedience to the revealed Word and will of God under Ezra some 2,500 years ago are with us today. If only we could get back to the Bible, allowing its claims to come to us with the force of a new revelation, what wonders would be wrought in our personal church and national life!

Chapter 1

Ezra was a descendant of the family of Aaron, and a profound student of the law of Moses. This book consists of two parts, separated by many years. The first six chapters contain a record of the return of the first contingent of Jews, under Zerubbabel. The remaining chapters describe an expedition, some sixty years later, led by Ezra himself. The stirring up of Cyrus proves how God can use even a heathen man for the accomplishment of His purpose. He uses the best material at hand. What happiness the Jews must have experienced as they listened to the proclamation of their freedom! Delivered from spiritual captivity, are you helping to build the spiritual house of the Lord? Sheshbazzar, meaning "fire-worshiper," was the name given to Zerubbabel, the recognized hereditary prince of Judah. While in bondage it must have seemed to the Jews that God's promise regarding them would never be realized. But while His purposes may be delayed, they are never abandoned.

Chapter 2

As a ready scribe, Ezra gives us a detailed account of those who formed the returning remnant. A writer of historical research has this considered opinion of Ezra and Nehemiah, with whom Ezra actively cooperated: "The documents preserved in the books of Ezra and Nehemiah are genuine, official documents, and the chronology is correct in every particular." Those who could not prove their pedigree were referred to the high priest for a verdict. How thrilling the spirit of the returning refugees! Viewing the desolation of Jerusalem, the hidden springs of piety and patriotism within them were opened, and they contributed some half a million dollars for the work of restoration. The Israelites were always particular about their genealogy. It is well when men and women today make certain of their relationship to God.

Chapter 3

Six months had passed since the Jews left Babylon, and by now they were settled in Judah. Much hard work had been faced in the clearing away of debris, and the erection of homes. Such was the religious enthusiasm gripping the people that the setting up of the altar on its ancient base stood out as the first and most important task. With what delight the delivered Jews and other settlers must have removed the rubbish and prepared new stones and timber for the temple! Mingled tears and shouts of joy are said to have accompanied the laying of the temple foundations. They knew the new temple would be inferior to the old, but that its glory would be greater, seeing it would receive the Saviour (Haggai 2:9). The temple that God is erecting in our age is indestructible. Things made by human hands have no abiding glory, and are not comparable to the spiritual things (Hebrews 12:27,28).

Chapter 4

This chapter illustrates what Paul felt when he said that a great and effectual door faced him, and there were many adversaries. Denied the opportunity of sharing in the building of the new temple, the Samaritans, who were made up of many races, did their utmost in threatening the workmen and hindering the supply of necessary material. By the *toll*, we understand a *poll tax*. *Tribute* was probably a tax on articles of trade. *Custom* represents a road tax. Because of those who hindered, the building of the temple ceased for fourteen years, being resumed in the reign of Darius (522 B.C.), who proved to be a strong friend of the Jewish cause. It is sad to witness how the moral tone of the new colony was impaired by party conflict. Compromise with worldly ideals can never buy off opposition. Religious circles are suffering the deterioration of ideals through the unwise policy of allowing worldly alliances to dictate their program. In spite of all adversaries, let us arise and build (Daniel 9:25).

Chapter 5

We could give this chapter the title, "Revived Hope." Delay was proving to be dangerous, so Haggai and Zechariah urged the people to respond to the overtures of a friendly monarch, and finish the temple. Through the "good and comfortable words"

of the prophets, work was resumed. Level-headed, fair-minded men, like Tatnai, are of priceless value, and we certainly need more of them in government circles today. What a striking phrase this is: "But the eye of their God was upon the elders of the Jews"! (verse 5). We always work under the eye of God (Psalm 33:18). How different life and labor would be if we would remember that "Thou, God, seest me" (Genesis 16:13). Another lesson to be gleaned from this chapter is that world rulers are, often unknowingly, the instruments of God's far-reaching purposes. Has God not said: "By me kings reign, and princes decree justice" (Proverbs 8:15)? Supreme, He can use whom He pleases.

Chapter 6

The somewhat pure religion of the Persians doubtless prompted Darius to favor the Jews in their strict monotheistic worship and ideals. Behind all the historical records and public documents was the over-ruling providence of God. Is it not blessed to know that all missing records and tangled skeins can be left in His hands? Such was the spirit of the workmen that in four years – twenty-one years after the foundation had been laid – the temple was finished. Opening ceremonials corresponded to the dedication of the tabernacle (Numbers 8:17). Use of the twelve goats symbolized the ideal unity of the nation. The sin-offering for *all* Israel prefigured the day when all the tribes will assemble around the altar. Priests and people alike declared their loyalty to the ancient faith. Separation from all heathen ways was, and is, essential to fellowship with God. And for ourselves, separation from all filthiness of flesh and spirit must precede our feasting upon Christ, our Passover sacrificed for us.

Chapter 7

Between chapters 6 and 7, there was an interval of fifty years. Within this period we can place the happenings recorded in the Book of Esther. Ezra, the priest, is prominent in this chapter. He was consumed with the one passion – to teach the people in the great truths found in the Mosaic law. He likewise prepared his own heart to obey. The only way to understand the Bible is to set our heart *to do* (verse 10). God save us from being sign-posters, pointing the way, but taking no step along it! King Artaxerxes must have been deeply moved to draw on the imperial treasury to the extent of some $100,000 for the maintenance of Jewish worship and the appointment of justices. Ezra's thanksgiving ode is in unison with his whole character. With the hand of the Lord strengthening him, he labored as a copartner of God. May ours be the abiding consciousness of the divine hand upon our shoulder! Whatever need arises, the hand can supply (verse 6).

Chapter 8

Probably a caravan of 6,000, counting men, women and children, accompanied Ezra to Jerusalem. Three days were spent in going over the genealogies of the pilgrims, for none of doubtful blood could be enrolled in such an expedition. Too many around us claim to be pilgrims, bound for the Celestial City, whose names are not in the Lamb's Book of Life. We need constantly to seek divine guidance for ourselves, our little ones, and for all our substance (verse 21). Amid dangers, Ezra sought divine and human protection, and was rewarded. The journey, taking four months, has, because of the perfect safety experienced, been characterized as "one of the most astounding facts on record." How happy Ezra must have been when ultimately his charge was delivered! For ourselves the lesson is obvious. No foes can break through a divine environment. Virtuous and vigilant, let us pursue our journey, and, at last, with joy surrender our charge (Luke 19:16).

Chapter 9

Sorrow was soon to overtake Ezra, who now had a royal mandate appointing him supreme legislator and judge of the law. Mixed marriages and abuses were found in the ranks, and, gathering the sins of the people and making them his own, Ezra confessed and pled for divine forgiveness. And how passionate was his lament! There are one or two striking phrases to underline as you read this chapter. "Everyone that trembled at the words of the God of Israel" (9:4; *cf.* 10:3). Is this our attitude as we approach the Scriptures? "I am ashamed and blush to lift up my face unto thee" (verse 6). Is this our attitude because of sin? Ezra, with all humility, made Israel's sin his own, and acknowledged the gross ingratitude of the people, after such gracious renewing as God had made possible. "We cannot stand before thee because of this" (9:15). No, but in spite of our sin, we can stand before God, providing we are standing in Christ.

Chapter 10

Revered as a priest, and respected as a governor, Ezra's confession created a profound impression, so much so that in true repentance the people gathered for the evening sacrifice. From one of the sons of Elam, the proposal came that they should make a covenant with God in the matter of separation. It was a costly covenant, but the price was paid. On that cold and rainy December day, every case of mixed marriages was carefully dealt with, and necessary separations were enforced. Love may appear stern, but the cutting off of the offending hand or foot is the only way to prevent gangrene. There can be no fellowship apart from separation. Of course, provision had to be made for the women and children put away by the Jews, just as we have to be responsible for those involved in our sin, even though we have been divinely forgiven.

NEHEMIAH

Nehemiah, himself born in exile, who became cup-bearer to the king, was a model organizer who proved the worth of method and system, and whose character appears to be without blot. "He stood like an anvil, till the hammers of opposition wore themselves out vainly beating against him." If Ezra is the representative of priest and scribe – Nehemiah is a noble representative of a dedicated business man. The key word of the book, *so*, occurring 32 times, denotes that Nehemiah was a man of action and of few words who believed that prayer and performance go together (1:4; 6:3). Largely autobiographical *Nehemiah* is a book opening and ending with prayer, and is one with a peculiar and opportune message for all who would serve the Lord. During Nehemiah's administration covering a period of 36 years *the building of the wall in spite of many difficulties was completed* (1-6); *wise organization and preparation were undertaken* (7-12); *necessary reforms were instituted* (13). Both the dedication of the wall, and the energetic administration of necessary reform are vividly described in the first person, indicating that Nehemiah, whose name is given to the book, likely quoted extracts from his personal diary. Prayerful, prudent, pious, unselfish and sagacious, this model worker, in the demands of his divinely-given task, always appealed to the judgment of the merciful God who vindicated the rigorous and vigorous mission of His servant.

Chapter 1

In the ancient Hebrew Scriptures, Ezra and Nehemiah were treated as one book. Some scholars fit Nehemiah into the latter part of Ezra. Ezra rebuilt the temple, while to Nehemiah fell the lot of repairing the walls. It will be found that the book before us is distinctly personal, essentially the book of the worker. Nehemiah knew how to preserve the balance between determination and dependence upon God. Worship and work went together. Nehemiah's position of trust was probably due to Esther and Mordecai. As a man of prayer, Nehemiah knew how to carry his sorrow to God. There is much to learn from this noble man. Although brought up amidst the luxury and temptations of Shushan, he remained untainted. He was in the world, but not of it. Then his unceasing prayers were saturated with his tears. We could not do better than to make Nehemiah's prayer our

daily supplication. "Prosper thy servant" (verse 11).

Chapter 2

The key verse of this book is in verse 17 of this chapter. How could Nehemiah carry his heavy burden for four months and not show it? Yet he knew that no sorrow must be exhibited in the presence of the king (see Esther 4:2). Piety and patriotism, however, could not be hid, and, winning royal favor, Nehemiah obtained remarkable royal concession to fulfil the purpose of his heart. Acquainting himself with the true condition of the ruined walls, he called the leaders together and, outlining his plan of restoration, inspired great hope and confidence. How effective were those secret-hour prayers of his, when emergency arose! Are you surrounded by Sanballats who laugh you to scorn? Take courage, the laugh will be yours some day.

Chapter 3

The builders had a mind to work! Priests, princes and people alike shared a common zeal. Rubbish was removed, foundations strengthened and the gateways fully repaired. Fittingly, the priests rebuilt the gate through which the sheep were led to the temple. Spiritual lessons can be gleaned from all the gates repaired. Restoration commenced at the sheep gate, and ended there. Is this not suggestive of the cross, as the commencement and consummation of the purpose of God? Shame came upon the Tekoite nobles, who built half-heartedly. Do we serve the Lord with all our hearts? Some there were, who built their own walls. How full the world is of broken walls! Family, social, national and international life are in sad need of repair. But restoration begins at home. Are you building your own wall?

Chapter 4

Sanballat was a thorn in Nehemiah's flesh, but the latter took opposition in his stride. Sanballat thought it impossible for the city to emerge from its grave of rubbish in a day. He sadly underrated the determination of Nehemiah. Tobiah, in a sarcastic way, tried to dissuade Nehemiah, but sneers never troubled this prayerful builder. Wise, he kept his powder dry while trusting in God. He not only prayed but took every precaution against the combined attacks of opposers. How contagious was the heroic faith of such a leader! Night and day, ever alert, his trumpet beside him, Nehemiah continued his noble task. Such a chapter is full of spiritual instruction. When those with whom we labor in the cause of Christ seem to weaken, we must cast ourselves more unreservingly upon God. We are builders as well as soldiers, and to some it is given to carry trowels, but no swords.

Chapter 5

The impoverished condition of the Jewish population, and the greed and heartlessness of those who, taking advantage of poverty, drove hard bargains, greatly angered Nehemiah: "I was very angry when I heard their cry and these words" (verse 6). Are we moved with righteous indignation over the injustices of men? Challenged by the stern rebuke of Nehemiah, the money-lenders cancelled bonds and restored what had been taken. Under oath, assurance was given of full cooperation with Nehemiah, who made it clear that if any man went back upon his pledge, God would shake him out as dust. We cannot read of Nehemiah, so distinguished and capable of such princely hospitality, without realizing he shines as one of the finest characters in Scripture. From him we learn how to look into God's face, and how to rebuke fearlessly all crookedness.

Chapter 6

The crafty three, and the rest of the enemies also, gave Nehemiah troubled hours. But their strategems and threats to beguile him from his sacred task and take him prisoner, were successfully resisted. Would that we could have the same wisdom, resolution and singleness of purpose that Nehemiah had! How steadfastly he refused to be drawn from his great task! He knew how to keep one eye upon God, and the other on his enemies. The only thing that mattered was the building of the wall. As for himself, Nehemiah knew he was beyond reproach. He lived so that none could defame him, save in spiritual matters. He believed that no weapon formed against him could prosper. Having made God's business his own, he let God care for his safety.

Chapter 7

The genealogy of this chapter coincides with that of Ezra 3. Nehemiah's commendation of Hananiah reveals how willing he was to recognize the loyalty of friends. Little is known of this God-fearing man. Although not brilliant or gifted, he was no common man, and he stands out in the record of names in this chapter. We are reminded by a writer of note that a double lesson can be gleaned from the portion before us: "First, keep the doors of the inner city, with the same assiduous care. Let them not be opened before you have had time to pray. Second, watch over your own house before meddling with the city's life." A note of triumph can be discerned in the statement: "So the wall was finished." All scoffers were silenced, because "they perceived that his work was wrought of our God" (6:16).

Chapter 8

What a joyful chapter this is! As the result of the reading of the Word of God, and obedience to it, gladness prevailed. It is ever so. Here we have the first mention of a pulpit in the Bible, a piece of furniture that is helpful in giving a preacher a commanding view of his audience. It would be well if all preachers knew how to read distinctly, and cause their hearers to understand what is read. The contrition of the people in this instance, as they discovered how they had drifted from God, was acute. How thrilled loyal preachers would be if only they could witness the same contrition today as the Word is declared! The Jews had not experienced such national joy since the days when Joshua entered Canaan. Our nation sadly needs a revival of Bible reading, which would quickly lead to a desire for Bible exposition. The revival in this chapter proves that contrition must be accompanied by faith.

Chapter 9

Internal arrangements of reformation are still before us. In reading this chapter, mark the various attributes of God mentioned by Nehemiah. How impressive the public confession of sin must have been! After penitence, there came praise and prayer. Here we have one of the memorable prayers of the Bible. Graciously, God had undertaken for His people. With the record of unfailing goodness before them, the people bound themselves in a solemn covenant to serve God more faithfully. Such a covenant was written out and sealed as a permanent witness for future generations. Alas, too often we make a solemn covenant, and then fail to fulfil it! God, however, never turns back. "Faithful is he who promised." As with God's dealings with the Jews, so with our own life history – we are ever conscious of the interweaving of "the gold of God's love and black strands of our ingratitude and sin."

Chapter 10

It was fitting that Nehemiah's name should come first among the covenanters. Priests, princes and people alike took the oath to obey God's law. A pledge to be separated fully from all forbidden alliances was also taken. The people vowed to meet every temple obligation. Giving was not to be spasmodic, but systematic. Attendance at God's house was not to be intermittent, but constant. Churches today would not have to resort to unworthy methods of support, or of attracting people, if only the same spiritual impulse that inspired Israel in Nehemiah's day prevailed among us today. The people brought of the first fruits of their blessings. How do we act if God causes unusual prosperity to come our way? Are we compelled, by love and gratitude, to offer Him a fresh and fuller tribute of our hearts' affection?

Chapter 11

This extract from the national archives appears, in extended form, in I Chronicles 9. Many of these lists of names may appear to us to be unnecessary, yet the Holy Spirit has been careful to incorporate them within the inspired Word. We note that certain families had their particular responsibilities, yet all served the Lord. Whether we are among the great men (verse 14), or the porters (verse 19) makes no difference. At the judgment seat of Christ, fidelity, and not fame is to be rewarded. Further, we learn from this chapter that the men who were willing to sacrifice so much for Jerusalem had every right to dwell therein joyously. There are far too many people today who want to enjoy all the benefits of Christianity without any desire whatever to defend the walls of the city.

Chapter 12

Gems can be found in this priestly chapter. Some of the Levites were in charge of the thanksgiving. Others were responsible for the watches, or were "porters keeping the ward at the thresholds of the gates" (verse 25). At the dedication of the walls, which must have been an imposing ceremony, the joyful gathering was divided into two companies, with Nehemiah leading one company and Ezra the other. The conclusion of the chapter proves how the people fulfilled their vow to care for the temple services. Commenting on the joy found in this chapter, the following constituent elements have been traced by one expositor: "Thankfulness and praise for the past – the recounting of the lovingkindness of the Lord. Purification and consecration – the offering of sacrifices. Fellowship – the rejoicing together, for true joy cannot be solitary."

Chapter 13

Nehemiah could never tolerate half measures; thus he separated from Israel all the mixed multitude. Ammonites and Moabites, who had been encouraged in days of declension, must now be dealt with. What trouble spots so many churches are, all because of a mixed multitude. Persistent in his intense zeal to put away everything alien to the Mosaic law, Nehemiah was thorough in his reformation of the nation. Uncompromisingly he purged the life and ways of the people, earning thereby the favor of God. Note the two "remembers." On those Nehemiah chased from him, there was a "remember" of judgments. Summarizing all his noble tasks, he concludes the book: "Remember me, O my God, for good." And if, like Nehemiah, we are devoted to the divine cause, ours will be an everlasting remembrance.

ESTHER

If Mordecai was the author of *Esther* then he succeeded in giving us a non-re-religious book – a distinction the *Song of Solomon* shares. While the heathen king's name is mentioned 192 times in this book named after a woman, the name of God in every form is entirely absent from the book. His face is hidden. Neither is there any allusion to the Jewish nation as one exiled from their fathers, to that land itself, or to the newly rebuilt temple, or to any Jewish institution whatever. But "if the name of God is not here, His finger is." He is in the shadows keeping watch over His own. Dr. A. T. Pierson calls *Esther*, "The Romance of Providence," and suggests that the key verse of the book is 4:14. *Esther* is "the rose window in the cathedral structure of the Old Testament. If the light it transmits be dim, it reveals exquisite tracery and symbolic design in the framework and colored panes." Yet Martin Luther was hostile to the book and wished it did not exist. All the events of *Esther* which is never quoted in the New Testament center around three Feasts – of Ahasuerus (1, 2); of Esther (3-7); of Purim (8-10). Although apparently destitute of any spiritual teaching, this wonderful story is aglow with the reality of divine providence. To the eye of faith and the attentive observer, "all history is a burning bush aflame with the mysterious presence."

Chapter 1

A sordid story is unfolded in this opening chapter. The great Persian city of Shushan had witnessed a succession of banquets characterized by unparalleled magnificence and prodigality. Vashti, the virtuous, was indeed a queen of queens, and never so queenly as when she refused to expose her form. She thought more of the modesty of her sex and her rank, than the exposure of herself to satisfy a drunken crowd. The wise men, so-called, without whose advice the king would not act (1:14), were too drunk to withstand Memucan's suggested punishment of a queen. Memucan, although a compan-

ion of the king, was a mere parasite. Ahasuerus ruled 127 provinces, but was not able to rule himself. Over the kingdom of his own appetites he had no dominion. The exit of Vashti, however, was overruled for the good of the Jews. Let us never lose sight of her courageous refusal.

Chapter 2

Conscience, it has been said, makes cowards of us all, and the king's conscience was deeply troubled over the queen's deposition. His courtiers also, now sobered up, were convicted and concerned over their own safety, and sought the refuge of unlimited self-indulgence. Esther's Hebrew name, Hadassah, means, "a myrtle." Entering the harem, she became Esther, signifying "a star." Her uncle Mordecai, was employed in the civil service, filling some office at the court. In the choice of Esther as queen, the hidden hand of God is again seen. The conspiracy against the king's life was frustrated by Mordecai, but his noble act, although recorded, was not immediately rewarded. God often uses simple folk for the accomplishment of His purposes. And often, much hinges on little. The Jews, although suffering for their sins, were not forgotten or forsaken. God was silently working on their behalf, as He is on yours.

Chapter 3

Haman, the Jew's enemy, as the prime minister of the kingdom, was a favorite companion of the king. Because of his position, all within the court had to bow to him. This Mordecai refused to do, believing that such prostrations were due to God alone. Mordecai, confessing he was a Jew, gave Haman his opportunity of exterminating all the Jews within this kingdom. Haman's crafty plan is a further evidence of the determined effort of Satan to cut off the royal seed from which Christ was to spring.

The decree was all signed and sealed, and the terrible edict circulated. That night the king and Haman celebrated the event with their revelry, but the city staggered. What a threatened doom awaited multitudes, simply because they were Jews! God, however, was in heaven, waiting to take vengeance upon the king and his prince for taking counsel against His anointed.

Chapter 4

Mordecai, because of his constant court attendance, heard quickly of the royal, bloody edict, and forsaking his official dress, clothed himself in sackcloth as a sign of distress. Through Hatach, Esther was informed of her uncle's public display of sorrow. She was urged to use her utmost influence to reverse the dread decree. Conscious of her perilous position, she never faltered. Her answer was worthy of her race: "If I perish, I perish" (verse 15). After much prayer, the grand venture was made with dramatic results. While it is true that God is well able to carry out His plans, He seldom carries them out alone. He gives us the opportunity of helping Him. Esther held an honored position, which she came to see was a sacred trust for others, and in a crucial moment used it to the full. Perhaps God has placed you in a position of responsibility in Christian service or in the world. Are you using the same for His glory?

Chapter 5

With the preparation of prayer, it was not hard for Esther to be courageous. Careful to attire herself in an appealing way, Esther waited for the king's smile and scepter. At the signal of the extended golden wand, she was promised "half the kingdom" or unlimited favor, by the king. Her request was for a banquet to which Haman was invited, and his cup seemed full. The only fly in the ointment was the obnoxious Jew who had failed to do him obeisance. At Haman's wife's suggestion, gallows were prepared on which to hang Mordecai, which he deemed a happy idea and one in which the king would acquiesce. For our own hearts this chapter is rich in spiritual suggestion. We have not to wait for the waving of our King's scepter. He never keeps us waiting. His ear is ever open to our cry, and our requests are always lovingly dealt with.

Chapter 6

That pride goes before a fall is forcibly illustrated by Haman's sudden change of fortune, and the sleepless night of the king was responsible for it. Restless, the king commanded one of the night watchmen to read him the records of recent happenings, and learning the story of the conspiracy on his life, Ahasuerus wanted to know if Mordecai had been suitably rewarded for his exposure of the conspiracy. Opportunely, Haman came into the court as the king asked: "What shall be done unto the man whom the king delighteth to honour?" (verse 6). How his chest must have swelled, thinking that the king could not possibly mean anybody save himself. It is impossible to measure all that was included in his reply. Alas, however, all the splendor he had actually asked for himself covered Mordecai, and how mortified he must have been as he led the despised Jew through the streets. From this narrative we can learn that sleepless hours can be improved by a rehearsal of God's dealings, and that man's wrath can redound to God's glory.

Chapter 7

What a joyless banquet this must have been for Haman, who read the handwriting on the wall when the king said: "As thou hast said, do ever so to Mordecai the Jew" (6:10). Eloquently, Esther pled for her people. The king, deeply moved by the queen's appeal, demanded to know who had dared to threaten the extermination of Esther's people. How deathly pale Haman must have turned, when the queen replied: "The adversary and enemy is this wicked Haman" (verse 6). What followed sealed his fate, and Haman perished on the gallows he had prepared for Mordecai. Scripture affords several illustrations of enemies of righteousness taken in the net laid for others (Judges 1:7; Psalm 9:15). In Scottish history we read of Ralph the Rover, who was wrecked on the Inchcape Rock, whose warning bell he himself had destroyed. If wicked Haman's escape deserved penalties here, there is eternity beyond where punishment will be exacted.

Chapter 8

How persuasive a woman's tears can be! Tearfully and patriotically Esther pled for the Jews, and Mordecai, now occupying Haman's official position, saw to it that the king's decree regarding the freedom of the Jewish people was circulated far and wide. And, as the Magna Charta of full deliverance reached those who were doomed to perish, it must have brought a great sigh of relief. No wonder we read: "The city of Shushan rejoiced and was glad. The Jews had light, gladness and joy, and honour, . . . And many of the people of the land became Jews, for the fear of the Jews fell upon them" (verses 15-17). All of this is prophetic of a glorious day awaiting God's ancient people, when the Messiah, their heavenly Mordecai, returns for their emancipation in the time of Jacob's trouble. At present, all sinners are under the doom of death, and our solemn task is to go quickly with Calvary's decree of emancipation.

Chapters 9, 10

At last vengeance is executed as the Jews deal with those who have sought their destruction. "The fear of Mordecai fell upon them" (verse 3). Victory over all enemies was celebrated at the Feast of Purim, a feast still celebrated by the Jews, who hold the Book of Esther next in value to the pentateuch. While the name of God is not to be found in the book, yet His divine overruling pervades its pages. And the same overruling providence marks the whole history of Israel. Adolph Hitler, a modern Haman, was indeed the Jew's enemy, and he, too, has perished; but the Jews live on, and are now a recognized nation. Unseen by mortal eye, God is within the shadows. Ere long, the heavenly Mordecai will be "great among the Jews, and accepted of the multitude of his brethren, seeking the wealth of his people, and speaking peace to all his seed" (10:3). Yes, Israel's Messiah is coming.

JOB

Many writers and poets extol *The Book of Job* as the most remarkable book in the Bible. Tennyson spoke of it as "the greatest poem, whether of ancient or modern literature." Martin Luther regarded it as being "more magnificent and sublime than any other book of Scripture." Thomas Carlyle said of it, "I call Job one of the grandest things ever written with pen." This most ancient book known is conspicuous for its revelation of the theological and intellectual culture of the patriarchal age. "Almost every important doctrine is found therein, in addition to scientific truths only fully discovered in our time." Perhaps the principle message of *The Book of Job* is that of the mystery of suffering. While the problem of why the righteous suffer is not fully solved in the book, welcome light is yet given on the permission of pain and suffering. The friends of Job felt that he must have sinned to suffer as he did and in this assumption they were wrong. Perfect and upright, Job's suffering was not sent as a "chastisement but

as a test and revealer of character, and to educate and instruct." Written in prose and poetry *Job* teaches the elect how to die to self. The best man – apart from Christ – who ever lived, responded to the fuller revelation of divine holiness by abhoring himself, and repenting in dust and ashes" (42: 5,6), and became the recipient of a better estate than he had possessed at the beginning.

Chapter 1

In this opening meditation on the literary masterpiece we are to consider, we deem it necessary to say that Scripture speaks of Job as a veritable personage, and not, as modernism asserts, as a mythical character. Who the author of this greatest poem or drama in the world's greatest literature was, we do not know. He is lost in the obscurity of the past (Ezekiel 14:14-20; James 5:11). Job is probably the oldest of the Bible books, being written before the time of

Moses. Yet it "sheds a remarkable light on the philosophic breadth and intellectual culture of the patriarchal age." Its main theme, common to all mankind, and engaging the loftiest intellects is: "The Problem Of Pain," or, "The Mystery Of Suffering." "Why do the righteous suffer and the wicked prosper?" As Job challenges the so-called solutions of his friends, it is inspiring to notice the stages of struggle, doubt, potential innocence and triumphant faith.

What a study in contrasts the Book of Job is! Here, for example, we have prosperity and penury, riches and rags. Job himself is the object of antagonistic attention. Heaven and hell are in the market for the full control of the man of Uz. We are given three cameos of Job. As to his character, he was perfect and upright. Living before the Mosaic era, Job yet knew God. Then, Job was an ideal family man, with a devotion so exemplary toward his own. In respect to his position, his unusual wealth gave him a princely rank among those of his own age. The gathering of all the angel vice-regents in heaven's council-chamber is impressive. It is somewhat surprising to find Satan there, proving that in some mysterious way he had access into God's presence. When he does appear before God, however, it is only as the accuser, as his insinuations of Job's selfishness proves (*cf.* Revelation 12:10). Testing is allowed, but bereft of all, Job clings to the Giver, though all the gifts have been taken. Can you look beyond the sunbeams and say that it is the Lord who has taken away? What He permits is ever best.

Chapter 2

Here we have a further clash, between God and Satan, over Job. As the Advocate of His servant, God affirms Job's sterling character, but the adversary persists in charging Job with having ulterior motives. Permission is given Satan to attack Job's body, and what terrible bodily suffering must have been his! As an outcast smitten with a most loathsome disease, he was forced to remain in the refuse mound of the village. Urged to renounce God, Job rebukes his wife, and declares his unswerving allegiance to God. There thus appear upon the scene the so-called friends of Job, whose arguments and

philosophies form the burden of the book. Eliphaz uses arguments based on oracles and revelations. In his condemnation of Job, Bildad depends on the gathered wisdom of the ancients. Zophar, like the ordinary bigot he was, expresses ideas somewhat harsh and sweeping. How apt people are to form false judgments of God's dealings! Testing times reveal how limited is the help of our supposedly true friends.

Chapter 3

In his first answer, Job curses the day of his birth but not his God. Do not miss some of the beautiful, poetic expressions of this chapter, such as verse 9, where dawn is described as the day opening its eyes. Burdened with physical torment, Job laments the misery of having survived his birth. If only he could have died when born. As it was, he longed to die, seeing that death ends all physical suffering. If there is no worthy end for Job to serve, why should he continue to live? How many other suffering saints have echoed the same sentiment? But no matter what loneliness or pain we may have been born into, entrance into the world is to be coveted because of the privileged opportunity it affords of union with Christ. And at daybreak, one moment with Him will more than compensate for years of pain.

Chapter 4

In this chapter we enter the heart of the poem, which opens with three monologues by Job and his friends. As they speak one by one, Job answers their attacks. The drift of their arguments is that Job has fallen into secret sin and was suffering accordingly. But Job's refusal to admit this irritates his friends, causing them to become harsh and angry. Of Eliphaz, Dr. C. I. Scofield says: "He is a religious dogmatist whose dogmatism rests upon a mysterious and remarkable experience (verses 12-16)." A divine revelation alone, however, can meet and solve Job's problem. Eliphaz argues that Job has been so sympathetic in dealing with the sorrows of others, that it is surprising to find him afflicted as he is. Eliphaz has his creed, but how cold and cruel even a creed can become. While all suffering is the product of sin, there are many who suffer, not for their own, but the sin of others. In Job's case we are to understand that his suffering was not penal, but disciplinary; for his innocence is maintained.

Chapter 5

Continuing his discourse, Eliphaz actually contradicts the divine estimation of Job's character. Who, among the myriads around God's throne, would accept Job's declaration of blamelessness? His plight is an evidence of divine punishment for transgression! Disasters always descend upon the sinful, just as the sparks fly upward, argues Eliphaz; thus Job is only receiving what he deserves. Then, in a passage of acknowledged beauty, pharisaical Eliphaz tells Job what he would do if he were in Job's condition, namely, repent and trust a faithful God to undertake. If only Job would adopt the right attitude of self-examination and faith, then his shadows would vanish, and a serene sunset appear. There is, of course, much we can agree with in the philosophy of Eliphaz. Our journey through life is a divine discipline, with many of our adversities to remain unexplained until we see Him face to face. We can further learn from Job that the way we bear our sorrows proclaims the reality of divine grace. The world is ever watching us as we weep. Let us not sorrow as others who have no hope.

Chapter 6

Job replies and, as in all his answers to arguments, he is calm and humble. He rightly complains of the unjust treatment accorded him. Possibly his words have been vehement, but they were mild in comparison with the deep sorrows that have overtaken him. If only Job's friends had experienced what he was enduring, they would have confessed that his moans were as natural as the braying of hungry beasts. To a distressed soul the advice of non-sufferers is of little value. Then Job compares the proffered help of his friends to deceitful brooks, and the simile is apt. They offer no refreshment for parched lips. In the concluding section of the chapter, Job charges his friends with lack of pity. Why condemn him for his heartfelt cries, if they do not make

clear wherein he has sinned? Let us never rashly condemn our friends. How would we have acted if in their place? Amid all our unexplained sorrows, we can rely upon the abiding companionship of Christ, and He can never be compared to a deceitful brook!

Chapter 7

Job's lamentation becomes more bitter. Vigorously he protests the charge of Eliphaz that he has sinned in making his complaints. Life is indeed a fierce warfare, and death brings a welcome relief. Turning to God, Job begs to be left alone. Note the "I wills," as Job turns God-ward. He wants to be undisturbed as he works out his scheme. But "the Watcher of men" is ever vigilant and knows how to care for His afflicted ones. Subdued, Job pleads for mercy and forgiveness, ere it is too late. We can readily understand why Job questioned the justice of God. Like many of us, he had a "Why?" God, however, was patient with His suffering servant for He knew that behind his reasonable complaints, there was unshaken confidence, and that when all his questionings were answered, and his tears explained, then a clear sky would be his.

Chapter 8

Bildad now enters the verbal onslaught and, in harsh tones, relates the argument of Eliphaz, and takes his stand, not on *revelation*, as Eliphaz has done, but upon tradition (verses 8-10). Addressing himself to the righteousness of God, Bildad asserts that Job is suffering for his sins, and that the death of his children was due to their sins. If only, therefore, Job will repent, then he can expect the night of his sorrow to pass. Let Job seek after the single and obedient heart, then he can expect a life of unclouded joy! With clearer revelation we know that our hope is not as flimsy as the paper plant, the spider's web, or the gourd, withering as rapidly as it grows. God is our unfailing Refuge and where we cannot trace Him, we can trust Him. Dark hours may be ours, but there is an "afterward."

Chapter 9

In this chapter Job begins his answer to Bildad's reasonings. Job's contention is "that if it were true that God punishes sin, *that* would not help him, because, however righteous a man was, his righteousness would not count before the holiness of God." Then he uses a few striking illustrations from the surrounding universe. For a while Job is guilty of uttering some terrible things about God. His suffering turns him into a sceptic, but God understands and does not condemn His tried servant. If God destroys the innocent with the wicked, then the earth is given over to injustice and cruelty! How tragic when doubt hardens into denial. In a somewhat tenderer note Job admits his worthlessness and longs for an umpire who can bring God and himself together. Thank God, we have our Daysman in Jesus, who, as the Mediator, lays a pierced hand on us and on God, and makes us one.

Chapter 10

Continuing his argument with God, Job forgetting his friends and their censure, makes supplication for justice: "Do not condemn me without cause! " He credits God with harsh dealings, as if He could be harsh with any suffering saints! He wants to know if it is right for God, as the Creator, to deal so drastically with the creature He has made. As the Potter, He exercised skill and loving care in fashioning him as an exquisite vase. Can it be that He now has delight in destroying what He has made? In the gathering darkness, Job wonders whether God is not hiding hatred beneath an outward show of love. Why has the previous affection turned to anger? Why is God, as a lion, waiting to devour him. How patient God is! He did not resent the outspoken cries and challenge of Job. Sympathetically, He listened as Job poured out his heart before Him. He knew how the patriarch would rejoice when he saw the end of the Lord's dealings with him. Job came to prove that a weight of glory is ample compensation for the sorrows of earth.

Chapter 11

Zophar now presents his conception of Job's position. Bluntly, he calls him a hypocrite and a liar. Of Zophar, Dr. Scofield says: "He is a religious dogmatist who assumes to know all about God; what God will do in any given case, why He will do it, and all His thoughts about it. Of all forms of dogmatism this is most irreverent, and least open to reason." Zophar feels that Job should have been silenced by the arguments of Eliphaz and Bildad. As it was, Job has become more unreasonable, and so he should listen to some very plain talking. Zophar contends that if Job had only listened to God, he would have found that he really deserved more punishment than he received. What poor comfort! May God help us to be gentle in dealing with our suffering friends!

Chapter 12

In reply to Zophar, Job assails him for useless talk. Zophar's many words have added nothing to the debate. As a professed friend, what he says provides no answer to Job's riddle. Why was he suffering? He makes it clear that their contention that good come to good, and evil to evil, is not true to the mystery of Providence, whereby the innocent are allowed to suffer. Job goes on to argue that we cannot account for God's acquiescence in the prosperity of the wicked on the supposition that He is ignorant of their evil ways. Is He not of purer eyes than to behold iniquity? Enumerating human catastrophes, Job indicates that God's government in life makes no distinction between the good and the bad. Misfortune overtakes the best, and does not always indicate the presence of sin. Reflecting upon this chapter, as well as the book as a whole, we realize that suffering is often the refining crucible in which much dross is lost. Yet it is not easy to glorify God in the fires.

Chapter 13

Continuing his defense, Job with all humility and faith, pathetically blended with courage and fear, is desirous of submitting his whole case before God, and of waiting for the divine verdict. Then, without mercy, Job assails his hollow friends for their empty sophism, fallacious arguments, shallow reasonings, and unworthy contentions. When he cries: "I will take my flesh in my teeth and my life in my hand," he resolves to appeal directly to God. Verse 15 contains one of the great sentences to leave mortal lips. Sure of his innocence, Job has his case ready to present when ushered into the presence of God, feeling that with a fair trial, acquittal would be his. The lesson we gather from this chapter is that although friends misunderstand us and misconstrue our experiences, there is a divine tribunal where the truth is known, and from which we receive all due consideration and justice. Later on, as we shall see, with fuller light Job came to abhor himself as one most vile.

Chapter 14

Job is still speaking and pleading the cause of all men, and not his own alone. The similes he uses of man's lowly estate are most instructive – a flower withering as quickly as it blossoms; a shadow passing over the landscape, but never resting; an unclean thing from which nothing clean can come; an hireling working and paid for his work, then gone; an ebbing tide or drying water course. As the waters of earth fail, so does man. Yet Job does not think of God as a heartless tyrant, playing with His creatures. He knows that God has a day of release for him. This longest of Job's speeches, in the first round, is remarkable for its alternating emotions. Too often adversity throws life out of perspective. But we have no need to wade through Job's "slough of despond." We know what is beyond the grave, for Christ brought life and immortality to light.

Chapter 15

We now come to the second series of speeches, with Eliphaz again leading off in the discussion. In his second speech, however, Eliphaz adopts a different tone. Previously he was courteous and conciliatory, now he is sharp in his accusation. Here he specifically charges Job with sin. Why this changed attitude? Well, Job's three speeches supply the answer. He has rejected with scorn and indignation the doctrines of his friends. He was as wise, or wiser than they. Now his apparent attack upon the righteous government of God is taken up.

Eliphaz regards him as a despiser of religion and a rebel against God. He then goes on to paint a lurid picture of the evil-doer in the hope that Job may be stricken with fear and repent. What Eliphaz forgets is that misfortune and adversity are *not necessarily* evidences of God's displeasure with His people.

Chapter 16

In this, his fourth speech, Job accuses Eliphaz of multiplying words. Hurt, as he has been, by the attitude of his friends, he admits that if he had been in their position he might have acted as they did. But he no longer concerns himself with arguments. Describing the ingredients of his bitter cup, he compares his sudden reverses to the attack of a wild beast. Now his pride is in the dust, and his face covered with tears. Yet he maintains his integrity. His innocent blood, that the ground refuses to cover, cries out to God, and Job feels that the appeal will not be in vain. "Notwithstanding the heavy strokes of the divine *hand,* he is catching sight of the divine *heart,*" and is assured of a Daysman between. Is it not blessed to know that against all accusations of the adversary, we have before the Father's face above, a Mediator who, after the power of an indissoluble life (Hebrews 7:26), pleads so effectively our cause? Never lose sight of the prevailing advocacy of Christ.

Chapter 17

Three signs open this chapter. In ancient times, when a person was accused of crime, or was making a solemn undertaking, his friends would strike hands with his opponent in token of becoming surety for him. Job knows that God is his Witness, but he wants Him to act as his Surety. Will He not openly avouch Job's cause and declare his innocence before accusers? The influence of his sufferings and the contemptuous treatment of his friends, told upon Job's physical condition, reducing him to a shadow. Yet he believes that in spite of losses and lies, he will emerge stronger, and that righteousness will ultimately triumph. With the grave as his cherished hope, Job believes that it will give him rest. The other side of death must have surprised Job!

Chapter 18

From the opening remarks of Bildad's charge, we can detect how hurt he is over Job's scornful treatment of proffered help. The bulk of the chapter is taken up with a minute description of the fate of the wicked. Because of his sin, Job is doomed and, unless he repents, he must perish, root and branch. Such is the contention of Bildad. Much of what he says is true, but mis-applied, for Job is not the sinner Bildad depicts. Let us not minimize the terrible future of those who die lost. May ours be the undying passion of warning sinners to flee from the wrath to come! The "King of Love" has conquered the "king of ter-rors!" With Christ in our hearts, we have no fear as we face the valley of the shadows.

Chapter 19

What an appeal for pity this chapter contains! Weary of trying to answer argu-ments, Job now asks his friends to have pity upon him. Even if God has overthrown him, and taken him in His net, surely they can show mercy and not continue their reproach. Then, rising above all his trials in the energy of faith, Job utters one of the most sublime passages in the Bible (verses 25-27). What he fully meant, when in his prophetic vision he anticipated the Advent of Christ, we cannot say. This we do know, that no matter how dark and mysterious his experiences seemed to be, Job was assured of a Redeemer or Avenger, who would vindi-cate him and appear for his salvation. Further, although his body was corrupted by disease, yet he was to be raised in incorruption, and in his renewed flesh, and see God. So he anticipated I Corinthians 15. Job also knew that there would be a "latter day," when his Redeemer would stand on the earth.

Chapter 20

Zophar, greatly irritated by Job's refusal of his advice of confessing sin and having misery give way to happiness thereby, now insists that Job is not only a sinner, but so in love with his sin as to be unwilling

to let it go. Then he proceeds to enumerate the penalties associated with transgression. For example, the success of a sinner is short-lived. Pleasure and prosperity vanish as a dream. Youthful sins return to avenge them-selves. Using the illustration of an epicure with a dainty morsel in his mouth, enjoy-ing it to the full, Zophar tells Job that sin is his much loved dainty morsel, and that once taken will nauseate. Continuing his condemnation of Job, Zophar compares him to a free-booter, bent on plunder, transfixed by the sword of justice. God save us from bigots who are know-alls! They think they understand the reasons of divine procedure, and all the inner meaning of God's secrets. How happy we are that the bar of Eternal Love is ever just.

Chapter 21

Somewhat weary of all his friends' speak-ing in the same strain, portraying the doom of the sinner, Job now answers them in no uncertain way. He endeavors to look be-yond his own experiences, to moral issues involved. Addressing himself to the vast problems of divine Providence, Job now admits that the wicked do not suffer imme-diate punishment for their sin. Sometimes they evade just penalties. A fact beyond contradiction is that many of the wicked prosper. The middle paragraph of the chap-ter (verses 22-26) recalls the account of Dives and Lazarus (Luke 16:19-31), and the retribution and readjustment in the world beyond. Job wants his friends to know that, although their arguments about the wicked were aimed at him. he refuses their deduc-tion as to his guilt. Job did not have the clearer light of the New Testament as to rewards, yet he suggests that sinners who leave proud monuments behind them, will face a terrible recompense in eternity.

Chapter 22

In this chapter the third cycle of con-troversy begins, with Eliphaz opening as before. Asserting that all God's punishments must be just, he argues that Job must have sinned terribly. Specific crimes are now charged. He suggests that Job's reasoning has been tinged with the thought that God is shut up in heaven and is unconcerned with happenings on the earth. Then Eliphaz gives utterance to a glowing and beautiful description of peace, happiness and power to save, which result from friendship with God. All unconsciously he foreshadows what was to be Job's experience at the end of the great drama, when he is called upon to intercede for his friends. We gather here the lesson that personal acquaintance with God is the heart of religion. In forgiveness, He paves the way for such intimacy. "Forgiveness is only the experience of the portico: it is the entrance to the house, not the house."

Chapter 23

In his opening sentence, Job acknowledges that he has been guilty of speaking against God, but feels he was justified in his action because of the heaviness of his misery. Let it be clearly understood that his language is not that of unbelief, for Job longs to find God. His cry is that of an oppressed soul, who believes that if heard, he will be justified. Job was mystified over the silence of God. And are there not times when we are too? Note two points in Job's longing to appear before God. First, he had never lost faith in God's righteousness. When tried, he knew that he would come forth as gold. In the second place, Job was afraid of God, because of the strangeness of His dealings. Who is there, who has been through deep waters, who cannot sympathize with Job?

Chapter 24

The thought of God's mysterious silence is herewith continued. Why does God not manifest His justice, if He is cognizant of the wrongs and crimes of men? What a pathetic description we have of the condition to which the oppressed may sink! Men suffer from intolerable wrongs, yet God seems to take no action against cruel men. Murderers, adulterers, and thieves appear to be immune from divine justice. Yet Job concludes this graphic chapter by giving an answer to the question of the fitting down of the enemies of light. Five lessons can be gleaned: "First, we cannot judge the character of God by these earthly experiences. Second, it is clear that His final judgments are not passes in the

earth sphere. Third, we must remember that there has been a terrible invasion of God's original plan by the revolt of Satan and his angels. Fourth, the enemy still stands to rebuke Joshua, as in Zechariah 4. Last, this is the reason why we should take refuge under the wings of the Almighty. First the shepherd, then the flock, finally goodness and mercy."

Chapter 25

Bildad, as he reappears, passes from the personal to the universal. He drops his charges against Job, admitting that, though he cannot account for the facts of life, there is evidently a higher Wisdom at work in, and through, them all. God's sovereignty is recognized. All celestial hosts derive their light from Him, and no man can provide a purity, remaining unchallenged in the light of God's burning bliss. Compared with the stellar heavens, man is greater. He is more to God than worlds and worms. We here find the truth of justification. Man can only be justified through the interposition of the Just for the unjust. This is what Christ accomplished by His cross.

Chapter 26

We now enter the portals of those magnificent discourses in which Job reviews and summarizes the whole controversy. At last he is deeply conscious of divine majesty, but he does not quake before it. Ironically, Job affirms that it is easier to see another's failings than to give a helping hand. Maxims may be true and good, but they are useless to relieve. Read this marvelous chapter slowly and mark the following truths: God's majesty extends to every realm; Nature must obey our Lord; and the manifestations of His absolute power is beyond the mind of man to conceive. While the Bible does not exist to teach physical science, it yet carries scientific accuracy. Who can explain the quiver of a leaf or the crash of thunder? To those who know God, not only as Creator but as the God of all grace, there is the realization of the fact that Redemption is His greatest work.

Chapter 27

We now breathe a different atmosphere. Calm succeeds storm, tranquility follows tragedy. Job is reaching the haven of repose. Job knows that, as surely as God lives and he lives, God will never condone sin. As for himself, how can he confess sins of which he is innocent? The arguments and accusations of his friends were not true of himself. He had not sinned in such a way as to merit suffering. Tragedies may pursue the self-confident sinner, even though he tries to create a fortress in which to hide. For ourselves, let us realize that, although we may be free from all *known* sin, there may be that world of undiscovered evil within, which God sees, and that needs the cleansing blood. It is as we walk in the light that the blood keeps on cleansing us from all sin. From verse 10 we learn that persevering prayer in all circumstances is the evidence of reality. No saint has ever called upon God in vain.

Chapter 28

In this somewhat remarkable chapter, Job first of all describes the miner searching for precious metals. What skill and perseverance he exhibits! But a man cannot discover wisdom in this way. God's excellent knowledge comes to him by *revelation,* and not by *searching.* By searching, we cannot find Him out. Hidden wisdom is only revealed to the obedient, trusting heart. Then continuing his discourse on wisdom, Job asks where it can be found. The depth, the sea, riches, death cannot produce it. It can only be found in Christ, who came as the Wisdom of God. To leave Him out of our reasonings, is to fumble in darkness. True wisdom is not of earth. It is "from above" (James 3:17). As God's children, we know by faith those deep things hid from the wise and prudent (Proverbs 8; I Corinthians 2). Holiness of life is the condition of understanding in the deepest sense. To obey is to know. The fear of the Lord is the beginning of wisdom.

Chapter 29

As Job reviews his prosperous past, he reaches the point that a good man remains a good man, though he loses everything. And how many pleasant memories Job had! Young in life, he found the secret of God (verse 4). His early married life was very happy (verse 5). In business, he had been unusually prosperous (verse 6). In civic affairs, he was influential as a judge (verse 7). He had the reverence and respect of all. As a philanthropist he had gathered fame. Apparently settled for life, he anticipated a serene old age, but overnight found himself stripped bare of all his possessions. Pleasant dreams and lovely prospects vanished as the storms fell and destroyed all hopes. Amid the ruins, however, his real treasure was safe, seeing that it consisted not in affluent circumstances, but in his faith in God. Amid all reverses, Job maintained his integrity. Thus, when the Bible extols the virtue of patience, it uses Job as an example (James 5:11). He had wisely built on a rock and storms did not move him.

Chapter 30

Speaking of Job's description of his former position, as found in chapters 29 through 31, a competent writer says that Job's delineation "has never been surpassed for grace and pathos, picturesque narrative and tender emotion." Comparing the former reverence paid him with his treatment by so-called friends, Job condemns their insults in no uncertain language. They resembled a besieging army approaching a walled city. Vividly Job describes his foul, leprous condition, and it is not to be wondered at that his harp yields only mournful notes. (How would we have acted if all of Job's sorrows had been ours?) Man's favor is as fickle as the wind, but God is faithful. Have we discovered how to trust God in the dark? Where we cannot trace Him, we can trust Him.

Chapter 31

What a beautiful chapter this is! For carefully etched pictures of a good man's life, it is outstanding. At the foundation of true holiness is purity of vision. How we have to watch our sight and steps! Job's integrity could be proved in his dealings with his slaves. Made by God, and possessing the same attributes as Job, they deserved to be weighed in an equal balance. As a magistrate, he was careful to observe impartial justice. Without apology, Job confesses that gold has never been his god. False worship he has scorned. Neither has he gloated over the misfortunes of foes, nor refused bountiful hospitality to the needy. So as he lays his case before God, Job pleads perfect sincerity. Let us learn, from this attitude, not to hide ourselves or sins from God, but seek true covering through confession and faith.

Chapter 32

Elihu, the young, scholarly Arab, who has been silent during the debate between Job and his friends, now speaks. Although his speech reveals a clearer spiritual conception of God than the previous arguments, his eloquent discourse is marred by self-assertiveness. He scorns the dogma of the other three friends, that sin and suffering are always bound together. He seeks to prove that both Job and his friends are wrong in that suffering may not be penal, but medicinal in effect. Job was wrong, he contends, in that he justified himself rather than God; and so were Job's friends, in having no answer to Job's problem, yet condemning him. Elihu's question, "Who teacheth like him?" (36:22), carries in itself the answer. For who teaches like God in the size and equipment of His school, in His attention to individuals, in His considerate accommodation to His pupils, in His patience? Elihu may have misinterpreted Job, but he was wise enough to suggest the prayer: "That which I see not teach thou me" (34:32).

Chapter 33

Continuing his eloquent discourse, Elihu turns from the bystanders to address Job directly, advancing several reasons why Job should listen to his speeches. For example, he is anxious for Job to know that his convictions are divinely inspired, even though human lips may utter them. Rehearsing Job's arguments, Elihu first deals with the suggestion that God has been indifferent to his appeals. His silence must not be interpreted as indifference. God is too great to enter into arguments. Yet in many ways He does approach man, and when He does,

and man responds to divine overtures, then he can sing the song of restoration. From this chapter we can learn that calm and kindly reasoning is more helpful than scolding. Bruised hearts need succourers, not scolders. We can further learn that God has a reason for all that He permits, even though He does not give us the reason.

Chapter 34

Elihu turns to the bystanders again, and pleads for cautious judgment on the part of the aged and experienced men among them. He also challenges Job for maintaining that God was not altogether just in His treatment. God would cease to be God if He acted unjustly. Then Elihu appeals to history. Wrong may be on the throne for awhile, and Truth upon the scaffold, but ultimately divine justice overtakes the evildoer, and punishment is sure. Elihu further argues that Job should humble himself under the mighty hand of God, and acknowledge his guilt for sins of ignorance. But Job is silent, and his silence is treated as obstinacy. The message to carry with us is that of God's justice covering all His dealings. Events always prove that God is ever righteous and loving in all He allows.

Chapter 35

The main burden of this speech is that the argument, that the righteous are no better off for their righteousness, as declared by Job, is false. Elihu's contention is that as God dwells above the clouds, the disastrous results of sin cannot reach up to Him, and that human righteousness confers no benefit on Him. God leaves men to reap as they have sown. Using the illustrations of cattle lowing in pain, and young ravens crying in their deserted nests, Elihu contends that when they cry out, their cry is not prayer, but simply the instinctive voice of pain. With Job in mind he affirms that the pain-stricken should look beyond their pain, and trust God – cold advice when it comes from one who has never known pain! The chapter concludes with the assertion that God is never deaf to the cries of sufferers. He reaches down and delivers at the opportune moment. Sometimes it is hard for us to learn that God's delays are not denials, and to sing songs in the night.

Chapter 36

In this, Elihu's last address, he deals with Job's complaint that "God hides Himself from men, so that His providence is impossible to understand or vindicate." He meets this argument by affirming that God's one purpose in all His dealings is to cleanse and teach. With a clearer understanding of the divine character than Job's three friends have, Elihu declares God to be mighty in heart, sympathetic, discerning, and therefore able to judge men mercifully. Take note of the prosperity of those who render obedient service (verse 11). In contrast, we have the despair of those who cleave to their sins (verses 12-14). Tenderly, Elihu answers Job that God's purpose behind his affliction was intelligible and just. Job must not be impatient. Humbling himself before God, he must await the unfolding of His purpose. Nature proclaims that God is not only great, but good, and that His storm-clouds have their rainbow.

Chapter 37

The marvelous description of a storm, as given by Elihu, has never been surpassed. It stands out as a parable of Job's experiences. In the opening verses of the chapter, we have the calamitous storm, then the outbursting radiance of the sun. And, is there not clear shining after rain in individual experiences, as well as in the physical creation? Amid all the thunderous tumult, we have the terrible majesty of God. In fact, the book concludes with the display of God's greatness in creation. The marvels of heaven and earth cause Job to realize his ignorance and nothingness. Would that men would "stand still, and consider the wondrous works of God! How much greater their reverence, and truer their worship would be! Blessed to know that all the excellent powers of God are tempered to our comfort. His light never blinds." True, we cannot find Him out, yet we can trust Him to shelter us beneath His eternal wings.

Chapter 38

The opening phrase can be translated: "The Lord answered for, or on behalf of,

Job." Job did not answer Elihu. He let God do all the talking for him. We are thrice blessed when we know how to cease from self-vindication, and to rest our case and cause with God. Reminding Job of his ignorance, God bids him remember five things: *God's Eternity* – He existed before the morning stars; *God's Power* – whether it be Satan or the sea, He can say: "Hitherto shall thou come, but no further"; *God's Wisdom* - how perfectly He has placed all things; *God's Moral Government* – He justly deals with sinners; and *God's Sovereignty* – He is the Author of life, and Lord of death. The keys of life, death, and hades hang at His girdle. No wonder Job stands in awesome silence. Previously he challenged God; now he adores Him.

Chapter 39

Thomas Carlyle said, of the graphic series of individual portraits carried over into this chapter from the previous one: "Such living likenesses were never since drawn." Here we have the wild rock-goat, the wild ass, the once familiar unicorn, the ostrich, the horse, the eagle, etc., all delineated for our enlightenment. Note how the imposing array opens with the king of beasts and concludes with the king of birds. Inscrutable mysteries are to be found in nature, Providence and Scripture. Clouds and darkness are round about God. Our finite minds cannot fully comprehend the infinite ways and works of the Almighty. But in this truth we rest – that our God is not only the Creator of the ends of the earth, through Christ, but He is also our loving Heavenly Father, and as such will never cause the humblest of His children one unnecessary tear.

Chapter 40

God not only displays His wisdom and majesty in nature, to convince Job that He has the right to deal with His children without explaining His reasons, but He presses upon him the further truth that he cannot save himself (verse 14). "The greatest work of God is not the spreading of the heavens and the shining forth of the light, but the salvation of the sinner, the crowning work of grace through the cross of Calvary." Job has been guilty of condemning God in order to establish his own righteousness. Now, conscious of his sinfulness and folly, he is silenced before God, and at last learns that the God of glory is also the God of all grace. This truth is driven home by the magnificent description of the hippopotamus. For us, the Saviour's broken heart is all we need to convince us of God's willingness to receive and cleanse the sinner. Have you seen yourself as the sinner Christ died to save?

Chapter 41

Is it not somehow unique to find one whole chapter devoted to the crocodile, as many scholars affirm the leviathan to be? Follow the arresting questions as the Lord describes, with graphic eloquence, the features of this powerful creature. A renowned traveler relates: "I saw a crocodile rush from the water. It pulled out its enormous body, and reared its tail in the air. Thick smoke was emitted, with a thundering sound, from its nostrils, and the water boiled beneath it." Superior skill and might are before us as we think of its scales (verses 12-17); its eyes, mouth, and nostrils (verses 18-24); its fearlessness of human attack (verses 25-29);

and its power to lash the sea into a fury, making it boil (verses 30-34). Well, what can we take out of this chapter for our hearts? Is it not the precious truth that if God has spent much thought and power on a crocodile, how much more care will He bestow upon a Christian?

Chapter 42

How true is Solomon's proverb, as we think of Job's experiences! "Better is the end of a thing than the beginning thereof: and the patient in spirit is better than the proud in spirit" (Ecclesiastes 7:8). In strange ways God has sought to teach Job and, confessing that these ways were too wonderful for him, Job repents. At last, his captivity is turned, and his end doubly blessed. Patience has had its perfect work; thus Job is exalted as a model of patience by James (5:11). Satan's challenge has been met. Job did not serve God for what he got, nor did he curse or renounce God during his deep affliction. Faith stood the test. "Though he slay me, yet will I trust him" (13:15). As we close this great drama of Job, we gather the abiding lesson that, while we cannot fully understand the ways of the infinite and holy God, we can trust Him. He ever knows what is best for His own.

PSALMS

The Poetical Books—*Job* to the *Song of Solomon*—are distinctively experimental in character, with each book being taken up with some phase of experimental holiness. In *Job*, we have the holiness through suffering. In the *Psalms*, the devotional religious life. In *Proverbs*, obedience to God in daily life. In *Ecclesiastes*, the vanity of worldliness. In the *Song of Solomon*, the union and communion with the Bridegroom. The *Psalms*, actually means, "Praises" and the 150 psalms forming the Psalter formed the hymnbook of the temple. The majority of the psalms were set to music and accompanied by various instruments were used by the temple choir. This is the favorite part of the Bible, and was greatly loved by our Lord and His

apostles. The *Psalms* record the heart experience of man. Within them "every emotion which ever swept over the keyboard of the human soul" finds a place. Falling into a five-fold division, the *Psalms* have been made to correspond to the Pentateuch—

1. Psalms 1-41—*Genesis*, Generation—Degeneration—Regeneration
2. Psalms 42-72—*Exodus*, Ruin and Redemption
3. Psalms 73-89—*Leviticus*, Saints and the Sanctuary
4. Psalms 90-106—*Numbers*, Peril and Protection
5. Psalms 107-150—*Deuteronomy*, Precepts and Praise.

Here we find that for every sigh God has a psalm.

Psalm 1

The first psalm is a suitable preface to the *Psalms* as a whole. In fact, it has been called, "The Preface of the Holy Ghost." Ancient writers were wont to commence the Psalter with Psalm 2. A study of the psalm reveals the parallel lines running through, not only the *Psalms,* but the entire Bible, namely, *The Blessedness of the Saints* (1-3); and *The Blight of the Sinner* (4-6). The first half of the psalm gives us a description of what the believer will not do, and then what he will do. Saints are like trees planted by a river; sinners are as chaff the wind bloweth away. The all-important question is, "In what part of the psalm do we live?"

Psalm 2

Peter tells us that God spoke by the mouth of David in this Imprecatory Psalm. Applicable to persecutors of any age, especially to the Great Tribulation era, the Early Church could apply its language to godless rulers of their day (Acts 2:24-28). Reviewing the psalm as a whole, we find David declaring man's furious, yet futile, hostility Godward. Four stanzas of three verses each form the psalm: *Rage and Rebellion* (1-3); *Derision and Decision* (4-6); *Jesus and Judgment* (7-9); and *Instruction and Invitation* (10-12). Enthroned in quiet dignity, God is not perturbed over man's rebellion. Some kiss the Son; others kill Him. Which are we doing?

Psalm 3

The title of this psalm tells its own sad story. Says Matthew Henry: "The title of this Psalm and many others is a key hung ready at the door, to open it, and let us into the entertainments of it; when we know upon what occasion a Psalm was penned, we know better how to expound it." We here find David driven from his palace, royal city, and home by Absalom, his rebellious son, who was bent on robbing his father of crown and life. David's confidence in God, however, was unshaken.

The psalmist certainly ran away from Absalom, but he ran into the arms of the Lord. What do we do when Absaloms, within and without, rise up against us?

Psalm 4

The destiny of those freed from sin's guilt and government is that of being set apart by, and for, God. What a position of wondrous grace for all those "who stand in awe, and sin not"! And what a marvelous conception of God, David had! He knew what it was to rest in the joy of what He was. To his heart, God was righteous, prayer-hearing, possessive, full of favor, and the Source of sleep and safety. Do you want His uplifted countenance? Then fulfill the necessary conditions indicated by David in the psalm. Do you want a cure for sleeplessness? Then take verses 4 and 8 to bed with you tonight.

Psalm 5

The keynote of this musical, merciful meditation is indicated by the title, "Nehiloth," meaning *inheritance.* David's central thought is that the righteous are the Lord's inheritance. This is why they ever rejoice in Him, and are increasingly blessed of Him. What an arrestive watchword we have in verse 3: "I will look up"! Which way are we looking? The outlook is altogether gloomy. When we look within and view our failures, we are depressed. But the uplook is ever glorious, so "keep looking up," as my friend, Dr. Wm. Pettingill, always signed his letters. Do not despair. God reigns over all.

Psalm 6

Here we have one of those Penitential Psalms common to the Psalter. It is the pitiful plea of a soul yearning to escape out of "doubting castle." In some "slough of despond" have you been tempted to cry, "O Lord, how long"? Are you weary with your groaning? Then bid despair depart, for the Lord will hear the voice of your weeping. He is never behind His time. He ever remembers His own, and comes down for their deliverance. "Sheminith," meaning *the eighth,* and in music an octave, can represent resurrection, seeing that "eight" is the resurrection number. "Return, O Lord." Here is our hope.

Psalm 7

The sweet psalmist of Israel sang this song of deliverance out of a grateful heart. From the title we learn that the occasion of this psalm was the announcement of Cushi that Absalom was dead and all the king's enemies scattered. Turn to II Samuel 18:3 for one of the most moving expressions of grief in literature, grief occasioned by the tidings Cushi carried. There are at least three glimpses of our Great Deliverer in this Praise Psalm; He is the *Justifier of the justified one* (verse 6); *Judge of the sinning one* (verse 11); and *Joy of the singing one* (verse 17). Can we not trust this "Shield and Defender"?

Psalm 8

This magnificent Messianic Psalm glorifies Christ as Master of ocean, and earth, and sky. (Read the comment in the *Scofield Reference Bible* on this psalm.) The psalmist asks: "What is man?" Well, a mere man is nothing, but the God-Man, who as the last Adam more than regained all the first Adam lost, is excellent in all the earth. Presently crowned with glory and honor, final victory is to be His when all things are put under His feet. Why should we charge our souls with care when we have such a Creator, Conqueror and Companion? Let Him have dominion over our lives.

Psalm 9

This psalm of the "Name" bears an impressive title, "Muthlabben," meaning *death of the son*, and may have a connection with the death of David's son of shame that Bathsheba bore him (II Samuel 12:19,20). The Chaldee Version has it: "Concerning the death of the Champion who went out between the camps," referring to the slaughter of Goliath. Spurgeon suggests that the psalm refers mystically to the victory of Christ over the champion of evil, the devil. The trend of the psalm is that God has an inflexible standard by which He will judge men, namely, His righteousness. In verse

17 we have a most solemn declaration. May it stir us to action!

Psalm 10

This unnamed psalm is reckoned by some writers to be a continuation of the previous one. Here we have a woeful wail. Throughout the psalm we hear the cry of the oppressed. Martin Luther said of this tenth psalm: "There is not a Psalm which describes the mind, manners, works, worth, feelings and the fate of the ungodly with so much propriety, fulness and light as this Psalm." Augustine spoke of it as "The Psalm of Antichrist." As we witness the onward march of wickedness in every form, let us cry out of the intense need of our soul, "Arise, O Lord; O God, lift up thy hand" (verse 12).

Psalm 11

David believed in the sovereignty of God. Even though foundations in appearance were crumbling, the psalmist believed that God had complete control of circumstances at their worst. Possibly when he penned this psalm, David was being hunted by Saul "as a partridge upon the mountains," but strong in faith, David was never timorous. Is ours a full trust in a God who reigns supreme? He has never vacated His throne. Persecution, hostility, and apostasy may be rampant, but a guilty world cannot escape the pronounced judgments of the psalm. Praise God, the portion of our cup is different from that of the wicked!

Psalm 12

We can call this, "The Tongue Psalm." When lawlessness prevails and man becomes haughty, he presumptuously asks: "Our tongues are our own. Who is Lord over us?" Spurgeon entitles the psalm, "Good Thoughts in Bad Times." When spiritual declension overtakes a people, there is a general forsaking of the Word of God. Submission to its teachings is scorned. Human reason is deified. Yet the Scripture stands amid all the change and chance of man's speculation as a lamp amid increasing darkness. If only man would be silent; "hold his tongue," as Job prayed, and listen to the pure and precious words of the Lord.

Psalm 13

Four times over in this short psalm we have the cry, "How long?" betokening great anguish of heart and an intense desire for divine deliverance. Without doubt the psalm provides us with a portrait of our own feelings, when, because of apparent divine indifference, we indulge in murmurings. "How long wilt thou hide thy face from me?" A hidden face, however, is no indication of a forgetful heart, as the Saviour knew when He cried: "My God, my God, why hast thou forsaken me?" David travels from murmuring to merriment in three steps: *The questioning heart* (verses 1,2); *the praying heart* (3,4); and *the singing heart* (5,6). Which are yours, shadows or songs?

Psalms 14, 53

The fools described by David, in this repeated psalm, are not merely those who claim to be atheists, but all who by their rejection say: "No God for me!" And as the Bible and history prove, rejection of the knowledge and claims of God leads to a riot of sin. Further, opposition to God finds expression in active hostility to His people. While definitely related to Israel, Paul indicates that these psalms describe the deplorable state of things in any age when God is cast off (Romans 3:10-12). What is our responsibility in this godless age? The last verse answers the question. We must bestir ourselves to call upon God to make bare His holy arm.

Psalm 15

Here we have a Question-and-Answer Psalm in which David describes himself as a child perfectly at home in the house of the Lord. And yet, no one answers to the man of this psalm as does the Lord Jesus. He fits the description as no other. May we be conformed to His image! One wonders whether some of the language of this psalm was in Shakespeare's mind when he wrote:

His words are bonds, his oaths are oracles;

His love sincere; his thoughts immaculate;
His tears pure messengers sent from his heart;
His heart as far from fraud as Heaven from earth.

Psalm 16

This Golden Psalm has been called "David's Jewel." It bears the title, "Michtam of David," suggesting a prayerful meditation. "Michtam" can mean the revelation of a blessed mystery, and this is what the psalm is, for David is here giving us a prediction of Christ's death and Resurrection (Acts 2:19-31). Paul also used this precious psalm in his synagogue sermon at Antioch (Acts 13:35-38). While we see "Jesus only" in all of the psalm, can we make the last verse our own and declare that we are completely satisfied with the pleasures at His right hand?

Psalm 17

As a man after God's own heart, David was a master in the art of supplication. That he knew how to pray is evident from a study of this psalm, with its appeal to heaven. Such personal intercessions reveal the psalmist's trust in God, and encourage us to call upon the Lord at all times. The spiritual eye can see Jesus here as the prevailing Intercessor, presenting and pleading the needs of His own. David prayed that he might be kept *safe and sheltered* (verse 8); *shielded* (verse 9); *satisfied* (verse 15). Charles Wesley, on his death-bed, shouted: "I shall be satisfied, satisfied, satisfied, when I awake with Thy likeness." Is this our confidence?

Psalm 18

The somewhat full head-note relates the background of this Warrior Psalm. David appears to ransack his vocabulary for fitting terms to describe all God has been to him. Rock – Fortress – Deliverer – Buckler – High Tower! For all crises the psalmist looks for the Lord to intervene, and He does. Then the psalm begins and ends with praise to Him as the mighty Deliverer. From New Testament passages we discover a greater than David is here (Romans 15:9; Hebrews 2:13-18). One of the charms of this repeated psalm (II Samuel 22), apart from its rich poetry, is "the exquisite and subtle alternation of the *I* and the *Thou.*" And yet David has no more monopoly on God than has the humblest believer today.

Psalm 19

David was a man of at least three books. As a youth, near to the heart of nature, he learned many of its secrets. Then, as a student of the first five books of the Bible, the only part he had, David came to love the Law of the Lord. As he journeyed on to maturity, he became a close student of another volume, namely, his own heart. And all three books are found in this delightful poem. We have the *Book of nature* (1:6); the *Book of God* (7:11); the *Book of the Human Heart* (12-14). We here travel from two extremes, "the heavens" above, and the "heart" within. Are you a fellow-student of David, having an ever-expanding knowledge in this three-fold direction?

Psalm 20

"We have before us a *National Anthem,*" says Spurgeon, "fitted to be sung at the outbreak of war, when the monarch was girding on his sword for the fight. If David had not been vexed with wars, we might never have been favored with such psalms as this." We also concur with the above expositor when he suggests that this hymn of pomp is prophetical of Christ, and is the cry of the Church on behalf of her Lord, as she sees Him in vision enduring a great weight of afflictions on her behalf. We are, or should be, a militant people, and with the great Captain of our salvation at hand we must set up our banners, and rest in the saving strength of His right hand.

Psalm 21

There are some scholars who feel that Psalm 20 and the one before us should form one psalm. The preceding psalm, so eloquent with the evidence of answered prayer, is now followed by this one, so naturally full of joy and gladness. Seeing that "the King" is prominent throughout, this triumphant song is directly associated with David's reign as king. All his enemies have been subdued and his throne established. The larger application of this royal triumphal ode, however, is related to David's greater Son, who, when He returns as the King of kings, will judge the world, making His foes as a fiery oven in the day of His anger. Have we given this King a present coronation in our own hearts and lives?

Psalms 22, 23, 24

We group these three Messianic Psalms together, since they form a trinity in unity. Reading them without a break, we have the three-fold view of Christ as *Saviour* (22); *Shepherd* (23); *Sovereign* (24). The *Cross* – the *Crook* – and the *Crown* are combined. What the Lord has done, is doing, and will yet do, are the three glimpses we gather of His work. Again, taken together, these psalms present a progressive experience. We first of all come to know Christ as the Saviour (Psalm 22). Our eyes are open to see Him hanging on a tree for our sins. Receiving Him, we come to know Him as the Shepherd able to meet our every need (Psalm 23). Yielding to His fuller claims, we crown Him as Lord over all, knowing that "if He is not Lord of all, He is not Lord at all" (Psalm 24).

Psalm 25

The petitions of this most personal psalm are expressive and illuminative. David, in various terms, makes a full and unreserved confession of sin. And the very greatness of iniquity but magnifies the grace that puts it away. Further, when fully delivered, the heart cleansed and set free is bound forever to the Lord of the deliverance. Evidently this psalm is a composition of David's later days, for he speaks of the sins of his youth (verse 7). But for these, as well as for all his transgression, the psalmist experienced a bountiful, saving grace. And the deeper we dig into our own hearts, and discover a world of unknown sin, the more we realize the necessity of making the language of this Penitential Psalm our own. Oh, to be more holy in life!

Psalm 26

Protestations and promises go to make up this cry to God. Being redeemed from all iniquity (Psalm 25), separation from sinners becomes the necessary condition of going on with God. And the plea of David is that he has separated himself from evil-doers and that this is the ground of his confidence before God. It is profitable to note the declarations: "I have not sat," "I have hated," "I have walked," and "I have loved." Protesting that he has walked in integrity and in truth, David is confident that God will honor and preserve him. And the consistent truth of Scripture is that if we walk in the light as He is in the light, we have every right to expect the Lord to care for us, and to cause goodness and mercy to follow us all the days of our life.

Psalm 27

If we would have the full enjoyment of freedom from fear, then we must live in the atmosphere of this psalm of assurance. It opens with the joyous strains of confidence. Fear is dismissed as unworthy and impossible. Faith is also here, and out of it courage is born. "A man without hope," Lord Wolseley said, "makes an indifferent soldier; one without cheerfulness is worse than useless." And with no fears to haunt and harass us, we are brave to dare, to suffer and to win. Do we share the calm faith of David, believing that in spite of all opposition, God is our Guide and Guard? Is ours the same consuming passion that kept the psalmist so buoyant and brave! "One thing have I desired of the Lord, that will I seek after" (verse 4).

Psalm 28

Here David gives us another of his "songs in the night." Spurgeon remarks: "The thorn at the breast of the nightingale was said by the old naturalists to make it sing: David's grief made him eloquent in holy psalmody. The main pleading of this Psalm is that the suppliant may not be confounded with the workers of iniquity for whom he expresses the utmost abhorrence; it may suit any slandered saint who, being misunderstood by men, and treated by them as an unworthy character, is anxious to stand aright before the bar of God. The Lord Jesus may be seen here pleading as the representative of His people." May we learn how to make this intense intercession our very own!

Psalm 29

The theme of this striking psalm is "the voice of the Lord." It is also David's "Glory Song." In His temple everything saith: "Glory" (verse 9, R.V.)! From the *Temple of Creation*, the *Temple of His Church* and the *Temple of Heaven*, the music rises, surges and swells. David here reminds us that glory is due the Lord: "Give unto the Lord the glory due to his name" (verse 2). Are we giving Him His due? Or can it be that we seek our own glory. All of nature draws attention to the wisdom and skill of the Creator. The stars, for example, are "forever singing as they shine, the hand that made us is divine." It is man alone who robs God of the glory due Him for His grace and greatness.

Psalm 30

This Dedicatory Psalm was composed for the temple that David was not permitted to see, even though he prepared for it. Any new abode should be dedicated to God. Except He builds the house, and it is built for Him, they labor in vain who build it. One writer suggests that David offered this soulful song at the dedication of the house he built on the threshing floor of Araunah, after the grievous plague bringing so much desolation to his kingdom (II Samuel 24:25; I Chronicles 21:26). Be this as it may, let us ever realize that, apart from God's emancipating and elevating power, we are both helpless and hopeless. Gladness can only be ours as the sadness and sorrow of sin are forever removed by the matchless power of God.

Psalm 31

Passing out of the exhilarating air of gladness, characteristic of the previous psalms, we now hear David singing in the minor key. Strains of grief and woe are before us as the psalmist thinks of the trials and troubles of his life. Some expositors think that this doleful psalm had its birth in the rebellion of Absalom, and when lying lips were spreading malicious rumors against the king. But such is the nature of it that we can make it our own in times of dire affliction. It is sometimes somewhat hard to believe that our times are in His hands, especially when those times are hard and bad. What a ringing challenge the last verse of the psalm presents! Victory waits upon the banners of the brave.

Psalm 32

Paul confirms the given testimony that David wrote this evangelistic psalm (Romans 4:6-8). It bears the title, "Maschil," meaning *instruction,* and is one of "The Instruction Psalms." The experience of one sinning, yet forgiven, saint affords rich instruction to others. In order of history, Psalm 32 follows Psalm 51. Blissful years followed David's repentance over his dark sin and he could do no other than pour out his spirit in the soft music of this "Pauline Psalm," as Martin Luther called it, since it speaks so fully of divine pardon and preservation. My reader, is yours the blessedness of sins forgiven? If not, why not turn to God just now! He stands ready to forgive and forget your transgressions.

Psalm 33

In this anonymous psalm the bells of blessing peal forth their enchanting music. Jubilation and joy are everywhere for God's goodness, providential care, pardoning compassion and pursuing love. The God of creation is also the God of redemption and the God of history. Evident themes are: *The goodness of God is ever new* (verse 5); *the Word of God is ever true* (verse 4); *the work of God is ever perfect* (verse 6); *the counsel of God ever stands* (verse 18); and *the eye of God is ever open* (verse 18). With such a God, what else can we do but rejoice in Him? How we do bless His holy Name for making us the people whom He hath chosen for His own inheritance!

Psalm 34

The *Numerical Bible* gives us the fitting summary of this much blessed psalm of exhortation: "The Thirty-Fourth Psalm, according to its title, was written when David escaped from Gath, from Achish, here called Abimelech, which seems to have been a common title of the Philistine kings. He had failed sadly, as we know, and as on Philistine grounds he always did; and, not knowing Jehovah, had not been honoured by Him. This is itself a general principle of divine government, of which the psalm speaks, and which needs little insisting on." Yet, God is at all times to be blessed, for, whatever the circumstances, He abides the unfailing help and sanctification of His people. Are we living in verse 1?

Psalm 35

The pleading prayer of David before us anticipates our Lord's *Parable of the Unjust Judge:* "Shall not God avenge his own elect, which cry day and night unto him, though he bear long with them? I tell you that he will avenge them speedily" (Luke 18:7,8). Judgment will yet be poured out upon the godless. As for His own, the Lord is able to deliver them out of any pit their foes may dig. "This whole Psalm," says one writer, "is the appeal to heaven of a bold heart and a clear conscience, irritated beyond measure by oppression and malice. Beyond a doubt David's Lord may be seen here by the spiritual eye." Righteousness is exalted throughout the psalm, a righteousness manifested in the doom of the wicked, and in the salvation of believers.

Psalm 36

If we would triumph over the feeling of God's slowness in punishing the workers of iniquity, then we must live in the atmosphere of this "Song of Happy Service." David here calls himself, "the servant of the Lord," and his psalm befits all those who esteem it to be an honor to be known as God's servants. Over against the fatuousness of those who reject the Lord's pleasant service, the psalmist places the blessedness of those who find their salvation and satisfaction in Him. It is a psalm of contrasts. If you want a tonic for your faith, meditate upon God's attributes that David exalts — mercy, faithfulness, righteousness, judgment, lovingkindness, goodness, life, light and justice. What a great God we have! May ours be a great faith!

Psalm 37

There seems to be no prayer in this psalm, written by David in his old age (verse 25). All is certain, predictive, prophetic and ad-monitory. Fretting and murmuring, ever de-structive to the peace of the soul, can be overcome by trusting, delighting and resting in the Lord. The mystery of the prospects of the wicked and the adversity of the right-eous must be looked at in the light of the future, when all men will have their just reward. One old servant of the Lord speaks of the psalm as "the good man's cordial in bad times, a sovereign plaister for the plague of discontent," or "a choice antidote against the poison of impatience." Remem-ber we here have a divine command: "Fret not."

Psalm 38

Here we have another Penitential Psalm, so full of David's self-abasement. Soul-trouble and physical pain produced bitter crying and tears. Life had become burdensome to David, because of his own diseased body and dis-quieted mind, and also on account of the deceitful imaginings of his enemies, but he declares his confidence in God to hear his heartbroken cry. It is classed as a "Remem-brance Psalm," and a reading of it presents David as one forgotten of God. Thus he recounts his sorrows and sufferings, and cries mightily for divine help. Among the wonderful features of this psalm, are the depths of misery David plunges into, and then his grasp of the omnipotent arm of God and the consolation trust produces. Look especially at verse 18!

Psalm 39

What a gloomy theme this psalm contains for Jeduthun, the praise-giver, to whom it is dedicated! While a sense of detachment from the rush and hurry of ordinary life per-vades the psalm, sin is shown as the cause, under divine government, of frailty and vanity of human life. Ewald referred to the psalm as "the most beautiful of all the elegies in the Psalter." "While I was musing the

fire burned" (verse 3), is a most expressive phrase, proving how stirred we become as we meditate upon the promises and prophesies of the Word. What else can we do but speak with our tongue, when our heart is hot within us? Is yours the burning heart?

Psalm 40

That David was inspired to write of One far greater than himself is shown in Hebrews, where Christ is portrayed as coming to do His Father's will (10:5-9). Such an exceed-ingly precious psalm was committed to the most skilled of the temple musicians. A theme so incomparable was deserving of the noblest music. While it is truly a Messianic Psalm, applied to ourselves there are three dominant notes in the new song we can sing and know, namely: *Penitence for Sin, Pardon for Sin* and *Power over Sin.* Have you been delivered out of the horrible pit? Are your feet on the Rock? Have you discovered that you are poor and needy, and that the Lord alone is the Deliverer?

Psalm 41

Whatever bitterness David himself expe-rienced, as he penned this further Messianic Psalm, the betrayal of Christ by Judas is here foreshadowed. And what comfort we can gather from the psalm, if familiar friends have lifted up their hand against us! If you are downcast over the ill treatment of professed friends, and bitterness is begin-ning to grip your mind, read this psalm on bended knee, and, knowing you have the favor of the Lord (verse 11), leave your be-trayers where David and Christ left theirs, in the hand of God. "He preserves His own, and brings their foes to nought: after Passion Week comes Easter."

Psalm 42

With this Instruction Psalm we come to the "Second Book" of the Psalter. And, as indicated by the title, this "Maschil," or instructive ode, was dedicated to that band of choice singers, The Sons of Korah. All who need a cure for despondency can find it here. Are you sailing over rough seas, as David certainly was when fleeing from Absalom, he penned this psalm? Are you struggling with doubts and fears? Then encourage yourself in God. Share the confidence of the psalmist who, although shut out from the long-loved house of God, yet knows that He will cause the clouds to vanish. Let faith banish fear.

Psalm 43

A characteristic feature of the psalm before us is that its last verse is twice repeated in the previous psalm (verses 5,11). And, a three-fold cord is not quickly broken; God is both our "help and health." Do you know Him as your exceeding joy, that is, a joy exceeding all others in its nature, degree and duration? Why not bid your fears cease, and joy in God? Whether in sunshine or shadow, health or sickness, plenty or poverty, life or death, time or eternity, know God as your Anchor. "Hope thou in God." And such a Hope is far better than any present possession. This hope of the soul is the soul of hope.

Psalm 44

The psalmist, in this further Instructive Psalm, is the spokesman for Israel, pleading for power to withstand her enemies. Faith goes back to the victories of the past, and supposes that what God has been, He will be. Traditions of former favor and ancient glory embolden the writer to solicit divine help in present grief. An impressive verse is that one declaring God to be a Searcher of hearts (verse 21). All secret thoughts and intents are open to His all-seeing eye. God is never deceived by our subtlety, nor excluded by our secrecy. The very wounds that shame would hide are known by Him. And blessed be His Name, for what the Light reveals, the Blood can cleanse.

Psalm 45

The various titles of this psalm are worthy of note, and reveal what delight the writer had in its composition. "Shoshannim," meaning "upon lilies," appearing in Spring, Scofield remarks: "The Shoshannim Psalms were probably connected with the Passover season, and hence reminders of redemption out of bondage, and of the origins of Israel." It is also another Maschil Psalm; that is,

a psalm of holy teaching, and not an idle lay. "Song of Love," denotes the theme of the entire psalm. Without doubt, Christ is here as the King in all His beauty (Hebrews 1:8,9). Can we say that our hearts and tongues are in unison, as we meditate upon our King, the God whose throne is forever and ever?

Psalm 46

Calm confidence and triumphant trust breathe in every line of this psalm of experience that Martin Luther used to love to sing, and which gave birth to that stirring battle hymn: "A Mighty Fortress Is Our God." The characteristic Old Testament word, "Selah," occurring three times here, gives us the divisions of the psalm, namely: The *Power of God* (verses 1-3); the *Presence of God* (verses 4-7); and the *Peace of God* (verses 8-11). Do we know what it is to make our very own this psalm so perfectly simple in its meaning, and joyous in expression? Is ours the right conception of God banishing all fear? As thrones, governments and systems change with startling rapidity, may we be still and know that our God reigns.

Psalm 47

While this is another anonymous psalm, "every expert would detect here the autography of the son of Jesse." Our Lord's personal reign on earth is prophesied. All enemies of the Jews are to be subdued, and the Lord is to triumph gloriously. Go through the psalm and note the *personal, powerful* and *praiseworthy reign of Christ*, as He wields the scepter of universal sovereignty and dominion. The question is: Have you made Jesus, King over the empire of your life? Does He reign without a rival? Is He sitting upon the throne of your life? Correct views of His millennial reign will avail little for you, unless He is Lord over all in your little world.

Psalm 48

That choice band of singers, The Sons of Korah, had to use this ode as, "A Song and Psalm." Spurgeon's apt comment is:

"A song for joyfulness and a Psalm for reverence. Alas, every song is not a Psalm, for poets are not all heaven-born, and every Psalm is not a song, for in coming before God we have to utter mournful confessions as well as exulting praises." Relating to event in Jewish history (II Chronicles 20), the psalm is another millennial one. The long night of weeping is over, the morning of joy has come, and there is jubilation in Zion. Is it not blessed to have God as our Guide, not unto death merely, but "over death," as the last verse really means — over death to resurrection.

Psalm 49

In his illuminating volume on "The Psalms," Dr. Alexander Maclaren reminds us that we too often forget that "a psalmist is a poet, and misunderstand his spirit by treating his words as matter of fact prose. His imagination is at work, and our sympathetic imagination must be at work, too, if we would enter into his meaning." Well, with sanctified imagination we can follow the theme of this psalm, which has to do with the mystery: Why the ungodly prosper while the godly suffer. With all his wealth, the rich man cannot buy redemption. A million worlds cannot help those who trust in their possessions. In the end they are no better than the beasts that perish. Is God or gold our trust?

Psalm 50

It is somewhat apt that a warning against sacrificial formalism should be given by a Levite, whose service was to attend to the outward rites of the temple. Asaph the Seer, whose psalms are similar to one another in style, is here emphasizing the folly of trusting in sacraments rather than in the Sacrifice. The continual offerings of the Mosaic economy could not take away sin. They were only efficacious in that they typified the great offering made once and for all by the Saviour at Calvary. "Our hope is built on nothing less than Jesus' blood and righteousness." Summarizing his psalm, Asaph warns all ritualists that they are forgetters of God and in peril of judgment.

Psalm 51

Who among us has not made his own the plaintive wail of this Penitential Psalm? It is stained not only with David's tears of repentance, but with our own. While dispensationally the psalm may trace the road back to God of a returning Israel, yet it indicates, "in its successive steps, the mould of the experience of a sinning saint who comes back to full communion and service." Do we share with David the experienced forgiveness that ever comes through the full confession of sin? Do we see sin in its true light? Are ours the clean hearts, right spirit, restored joy, opened lips, and divine acceptance of a broken and contrite heart?

Psalm 52

If the previous psalm is eloquent with the penitence of the sinner, this one deals with the presumption of the sinner. The title takes us back to the anger and envy of Saul, directed against David (I Samuel 21:22). The case of Saul, the ideal wicked one, against whom this psalm is directed, and David, the mighty hero, illustrates the eternal principle that the triumph of might over wrong is sure. Saul and his sons, "rooted out of the land of the living," typify the doom of the Antichrist. Saul boasted himself in his mighty mischief, but David boasted himself in the Lord, and proved for all time the victory that the trusting soul experiences, when God is one's strength. Over against boastful mischief, deceitful service, and lying speech there is placed the fertility and blessedness of the saint.

Psalm 53

As in the case in Psalm 14, here also the foolish atheist appears in this instructive ode, used by the temple choir. Some scholars interpret "Mahalath" as meaning "sickness," and that it indicates man's spiritual malady, as given in forcible terms within the psalm. But every effort is made to bring the man who does not want God, and whose pestilential presence spreads corruption, to a spiritual understanding. The professed atheist is one with no God before him. David closes the psalm with a fervent prayer for the national and spiritual restoration of Israel. Changing the language a little, we can make the last verse an earnest plea for spiritual conquests by the church militant.

Psalm 54

The title of this short psalm relates its origin. Encircled on every hand by those who sought to betray him into the hands of his enemies, David knew what it was to turn his eyes heavenward, and prove God to be a helper in tight places. What a source of strength and succor he found in the very Name of God! "If temptations round you gather, breathe that holy Name in prayer." Within this song of salvation, we have prayer for deliverance from godless oppressors, the confident anticipation of it, and promised thanksgiving for it. Are you discouraged today because of those oppressors seeking after your soul? Then may the eye of faith be yours to see God advancing as your "Helper."

Psalm 55

Here, again, we see how David's life is reflected in the psalms he wrote. Absalom's rebellious occupation of the city, and Ahithophel's treachery, provide the background of the psalm. Yet in the betrayer depicted in verses 12-14, it is not hard to see Judas. The pathos of this psalm is unparalleled. What a cry of a torn and bleeding heart it contains! In dire distress, the psalmist longs for the wings of a dove, for prayers, like doves speed fast and far. When the soul is in sore straits, there is no solace and cure comparable to prayer. Do you know what it is to fly away and rest in fellowship with your all-sufficient Lord? Whatever your present trial, make the decision of verse 16 yours.

Psalm 56

The somewhat long title, "Jonath-elem-rechokim," can be translated: "a dumb dove among strangers." As the dove represents defenseless innocence, we can understand why David calls himself a dove of dumbness (Psalm 38:13). When in the hands of the Philistines in Gath, he was as a dumb dove (I Samuel 21:13,14). Yet, although so helpless, the psalmist knew that there was a divine force at work on his behalf. What triumph there is amid tears in the declaration: "What time I am afraid, I will trust in thee"! Is this your confidence? Does the thought that God is for you calm your troubled spirit? May David's assurance be yours: "God is for me."

Psalm 57

The superscription of this psalm is most suggestive. "Al-taschith," meaning, "destroy not," reveals the thought uppermost in David's mind as he wrote the psalm as a fugitive in the cave of Adullam. Such a spirit also pervades the psalm. In spite of constant hostility, David was never vindictive. At times, his enemies were in his hands to destroy, but he allowed them to go. "Michtam" or the "secret" of David, indicates that he knew that God would deliver him and deal with his foes. Do we share David's secret? The message of this psalm is summarized in the repeated, unalterable determination, "My heart is fixed." The fixed heart, that is, a heart not torn this way or the other by conflicting interests, but centered and concentrated upon God, is a singing heart. Sobs and sorrows are never able to choke such a song.

Psalm 58

A glance at the title shows that this psalm is connected with the previous one. The predominating theme of the psalm is the desolation and judgment of the wicked. Sinners are "estranged from the womb." Sinners by birth, they become sinners by practice. Infinite love strives to woo transgressors from their evil ways, but if such love is finally rejected, nothing but eternal banishment from God awaits such rejectors. The same inscrutable justice decrees eternal blessing for those clothed in the robe of divine righteousness. Because of the certainty of doom, how eager we ought to be in our efforts to bring the lost to the feet of the Crucified!

Psalm 59

Hunted and harassed, like a beast of prey, David here describes the beginning act in his long wanderings to escape from Saul (I Samuel 19). Within the psalm, we discover *crafty enemies, a cry for deliverance, a compassionate Defender,* and *a continuous song.* "In the morning" is a suggestive phrase. Ere long, such a morning will dawn for every child of God, who is presently surrounded by enemies and encompassed by workers of iniquity. When the shadows are all past, and the trials of earth are over, what a chorus of praise will ascend to Him who has power to make all our enemies and His, His footstool! May grace be ours to live as children of the dawn!

Psalm 60

One of the lessons to be learned from this sister psalm of Psalm 44, is that chastisement is one of the divine methods by which saints are trained and disciplined. "Shushaneduth," signifying "the lily of testimony or speech," is a suggestive title for a National Psalm to be taught to Israel. A lily expresses *loveliness,* and "God's promise of Canaan to Israel is the *lovely testimony* of which assurance was already given in a partial deliverance" (verses 4,5,6). The history of this "Psalm of Confidence" is found in II Samuel 8. An abiding principle of the psalm is that God's holiness demands righteousness, and what His holiness demands, His grace and power supply. Step out today with verses 11, 12 in your heart.

Psalm 61

Amid all his restlessness and change, David knew what it was to have an abiding source of comfort in the heart of God. When overwhelmed by faintness and gloom, he prayed to be led to the Rock that he could not ascend by his own natural powers. If the occasion of the psalm was David's exile beyond Jordan, during Absalom's rebellion, then we can understand how tranquil he must have been with God as his Shelter. And in his distant exile, the psalmist was cheered by the fact that his would be a permanent dwelling in the Lord's tabernacle. *Comfort in God's heart* (verse 2), *shelter under God's wings* (verses 3,4), and *confidence in God's promises* (verses 5-8), are all here for us to feed upon, as we continue our exile from "home."

Psalm 62

We are again in the atmosphere of Absalom's rebellion. David's rebels, hostile to his kingly and spiritual eminence, sought to overthrow him. The psalmist, however, was strong in faith, seeing he was strong in supplication. With God as his salvation, he carried an untroubled heart. Thus, expectance and hope permeate this psalm. As one who had faced all the trials and vicissitudes of life, he offers this practical advice to the saints of all ages: "Trust in him at all times." And *all* means ALL! But how slow we are to learn that "power belongeth unto God," and that such power will ultimately be revealed when He renders to every man according to His work! Despairing heart, find your repose in God.

Psalm 63

In this sweet meditation, David pours out his tender longings for, and his jubilant possession of, God. Written while in exile, the psalm expresses David's intense longing for God. What a stronghold he had on God! "My God." Note, as you read this psalm, the key phrases: *Thy power, Thy glory, Thy lovingkindness, Thy name, Thy wings, Thy right hand.* Away from the quiet of the sanctuary and its holy ordinances, David experienced a soul-thirst for God, and knew that He would ultimately stop the mouths of those who had driven him into the wilderness. Companionship is based upon relationship, so we say: "Thou art *my* God."

Psalm 64

The overall subject of this psalm is that all the schemes of the workers of iniquity, and of Satan himself, will utterly fail, even when they seem to be on the verge of success. "God shall shoot at them with an arrow." And when He shoots, it is a bull's eye every time. His arrows are never amiss. Swift judgment overtakes the wicked. Their secret councils come to nought. Within the psalm we can trace the preservation David enjoyed from the slanders of the tongue in Saul's day, also the protection Christ Himself, and the martyrs all down the ages, have experienced. When malice is heaped upon

you, be glad in the Lord, and trust in Him
who is thy defense.

Psalm 65

A characteristic feature of this Harvest
Psalm is that it begins and ends with praise.
"Praise" and "sing" constitute the first and
last words. It will be noted from the title
that this is both "A Psalm and a Song."
All our songs, however, need not be vocal.
The first phrase can be translated, "For
thee, there is the silence of praise." What
do we know of this "Silence-praise," that
is, the praise producing still repose of the
soul in God? The primary subject of the
psalm is, "God's harvest-blessing, a pledge
of the millennial earth and of God's people."
How good God is, in grace and nature!

Psalm 66

It has been suggested that this song, or
psalm, is a Thanksgiving Ode for the God-
given deliverances from Sennacherib. All
glory is ascribed to God for victory over cruel
foes. Those warriors of old knew how to
trace their conquests back to God. Mark
the three "Selahs" of the psalm. This favorite expression of the psalmist means:
"Think of that!" and usually calls attention
to God's greatness or grace. And through
the psalm there is the manifestation of divine
omnipotence, to which men must submit.
Read verse three and shout, "Selah!" Yes,
and see if you can do the same when you
reach verse eighteen!

Psalm 67

Without doubt, this is a Messianic and
Millennial Psalm. Who is "Thy Way," but
Christ Himself, who could say: "I am the
way." And who is to "govern the nations
upon earth" save the One who, when He
returns, will fashion all the kingdoms of the
earth into His own world-kingdom (Revelation
11:15)? Looking out upon the disordered
condition of things in our broken, blood-
drenched earth, we realize how far removed
it is from the millennial blessedness portrayed in this psalm. Yet, ere long, it will
be relieved of its curse. God's Governor is
on His way to clean up the mess of earth
for which man is responsible.

Psalm 68

An English writer recently said of this
psalm: "Here we have the triumphant march
of a conquering God to His Sanctuary. It
is a hymn unequalled in grandeur, fire and
triumphant praise. It celebrates the victory
of God, who marched in triumph at the head
of His people from Egypt to Canaan, and
established His Sanctuary on Mount Zion."
Christ's ascension-ministry is before us in
verse eighteen (Ephesians 4:7-16). While David consistently uses the name for God that
expresses His supremacy and dominion, see
if you can trace Him in the psalm as a
loving Father, mighty Leader, succoring
Helper, merciful Friend, and a saving
Redeemer.

Psalm 69

Peculiar interest is attached to this further
Messianic Psalm, seeing that it adumbrates
Christ. Psalm 22, and the one before us,
are the two psalms most of all applied to
Him in the New Testament. His humiliation and rejection are clearly written here.
A. R. Fausett remarks that the two characteristics of the psalm, which is "one great
martyr image," are: First, *The fullness of
detail of the judgments on the sufferer's foes;*
second, *the prominence of the fact that he
suffers for the sake of God.* The title "Upon
Shoshannim," that is, "upon the lilies" is
emblematic of His servants (verse 36), and
of the lovely consolation and salvation the
Lord provides for them. Let us live near
this prophetic fingerpost to the One "despised and rejected of men."

Psalms 70, 71

As the latter psalm is without a title, it
is thought probable that both psalms form
a pair with one title. As "Psalms of Remembrance," they are designed to put God
in remembrance of the righteous Sufferer and
His people. When God *seems* to forget us,
we must put Him in remembrance as the
saints of old did. Taking the psalms together, we can trace three thoughts: *a desperate cry for immediate help in time of
distress; a fervent desire for God to exercise
Himself speedily on behalf of His distressed
servants; and the spirit of praise for His*

manifest and manifold deliverances. "Let God be magnified." He truly deserves the highest exaltation.

Psalm 72

While Solomon may be the author of this psalm, and his remarkable reign forms its groundwork, a "greater than Solomon is here." It is Messianic and describes the era when Christ will reign in millennial splendor and glory. As Dr. Scofield puts it: "The Psalm as a whole forms a complete vision of Messiah's kingdom so far as the Old Testament revelation extended. All David's prayers will find their fruition in the kingdom!" And how glorious will Christ's reign be when the knowledge of Him covers the earth as the waters cover the sea! Today He is not recognized among the kings of earth, but as D. L. Moody used to say, "A usurper has the world now, but God's day is coming." Hallelujah!

Psalm 73

Asaph, David's chief musician, faced the same perplexity David speaks of in Psalm 37, namely, the prosperity of the wicked in the providential orderings of life. The difference between these two psalms is the faith we should have, as bad men succeed and good men suffer (Psalm 34), and the conflict raging within, before such a calm faith is attained (Psalm 73). While Asaph does not answer the problem as the New Testament does, he yet shows us that nearness to God is the solution to the above mystery and other riddles of life. The transiency of outward prosperity, and the eternal sufficiency of God, enabled Asaph to climb the heights of confident faith. And so do we need to do.

Psalm 74

The despairing cry, constituting this psalm reminds God, that, as the covenant-keeping One, He must arise for the deliverance of His desolate people. "Have respect unto the covenant." "The strongest plea in prayer is to remind God of *His Covenant* and promises to His people" (Psalm 106:45). The Chaldeans had destroyed the sanctuary and spread ruin all around, but as the sheep of His pasture, the plundered Israelites, desolate and discouraged, turn to the eternal Jehovah. His miraculous interpositions in the past encourage hope as the people turn to Him in prayer. The covenant of God standeth sure, both for the safety of saints and the retribution of sinners.

Psalms 75, 76

We join these psalms together, for the title "Al-taschith," meaning, *destroy not,* covers both. Psalm 75 was written before Sennacherib's overthrow at Jerusalem by God's direct interposition (II Chronicles 20:19-22), and Psalm 76, after such an overthrow of the alien hosts. The striking feature of Psalm 75 is that it is a thanksgiving prayer for a victory *anticipated in faith,* that is, for the victory actually gained in Psalm 76. We must learn how to praise God for answers to prayers, even though such answers are not in sight. "Whatsoever ye shall ask in prayer, believing, ye shall receive." Would that all of us possessed more advance faith!

Psalm 77

The psalmist's grief, so evident in the first half of this psalm, was occasioned by the carrying away of the Ten Tribes, and the prospect of Judah and Benjamin sharing a like fate. Weighed down by national or personal troubles, or both, the author cries out of a stricken heart. Encouraged by the recollection of the past, he reminds God of the wonders of old, and is certain that amid present trials He is still the God who doest wonders (verses 11,14). What He had done, He was still able to do. Thus, the psalm concludes with the triumphant assertion of faith, that the God of the past is the God of the present, and will still function as the Shepherd of His people.

Psalm 78

This further Instruction Psalm by Asaph, the musician contemporary with David, is closely paralleled with the Song of Moses (Deuteronomy 32). The opening sentences of both portions are somewhat similar. Within the psalm, we have the sad story of Israel's waywardness and murmuring. Alongside such a record of rebellion is the wonderful revelation of God's patience and grace. What a mirror this psalm is of our own disobedience! Truly, "it is of the Lord's mercies that we are not consumed" (Lamentations 3:22). Like Israel of old, we sometimes complain because of the hardness of the way, but God is infinitely patient with us, ever bringing us nearer Himself by the skillfulness of His hands.

Psalm 79

The defilement and destruction of the temple during the Babylonian raids are alluded to by the singers of the Asaph school, who look upon themselves as the mouthpiece of Asaph, by which he, though dead, is yet speaking. This is why the Asaph Psalms bear a mutual resemblance. What a dirge of desolation this is! Ruin everywhere! The dead unburied and left in the streets as food for fowls and beasts! Reproach, scorn and derision for those who escaped the sword! Brought low, however, the remnant turn their languid eyes to God for His delivery and sin-purging power. The blood of the dead cries out for revenge, and the sighing of the prisoners for emancipation. What a prayer this is for a blood-soaked earth like ours to offer!

Psalm 80

Reading this Wilderness Psalm, we are impressed with the three-fold: "Turn us again, O God" (verses 3,7,19). Such a fundamental prayer likewise shows a progressive revelation of God: "O God"; "O God of hosts"; "O Lord God of hosts." This ascending climax corresponds to succeeding experiences on the wilderness march from Egypt to Canaan. And these are days when barrenness and blight have overtaken the Church. Would that we could hear the cry arising from multitudes of hearts: "Turn us again, O God"! How we need a divine quickening, so that all of us who profess to be sheep of the Shepherd, may function as fruitful branches of the Vine! May a heaven-sent revival be ours!

Psalm 81

Some scholars suggest that "Gittith" signifies not only an instrument or a tune, but *wine-press*, a song used on occasions of joy, like the vintage. This would account for the joyful nature of the "Gittith Psalms." It may be that this psalm was sung during the Feast of Trumpets (*cf.* verse 3 with Leviticus 23:24; Numbers 29:1). The commanding truth of the psalm is that through the given law, God claims Israel's whole-hearted allegiance, with such a claim resting upon her deliverance from Egypt. We have been saved to serve. God "brought us out," that He might "bring us in" to a land of fuller blessing. When we are among the fully fed, we are satisfied (verse 16).

Psalm 82

This psalm opens with the thought that the psalmist sees what the eye of sense could not see, namely, the God who stands up and comes forward as the righteous Judge. While the silence of God is often a trial of faith, yet the believing soul knows that behind the shadows there is the omnipotent, omniscient One, who is working out His own purposes. In and behind all there stands the eternal, unchanging God, who, when the time is ripe, will dispense justice to the sons of men. Look at verse 6! *"Gods,"* as used of the children of the Most High is a "term not for heathen potentates, but for God's vice-regents in His visible kingdom." God's representatives bear His Name!

Psalm 83

What a precious psalm this is! It reveals God as the protector of His "hidden ones." And because our lives, as Christians, are "hid with Christ in God" (Colossians 3:3), we can lay claim to the protection of Jehovah, who is most high over all the earth. The object of the invaders, referred to by the psalmist, was to root Israel out of her inheritance. Craft was joined with force, and such an evil confederacy was destined to produce panic among the children of God. The "hidden ones," however, had a peace passing all understanding and were confident that their enemies would be confounded. It is a blessed thing to realize that God knows where His "hidden ones" are, and what they are enduring, and in His own time and way, will destroy all conspiracy against them.

Psalm 84

Here is a psalm that is permeated with the soul's intense devotion to God and to the worship of His Name. Beginning with the "longing" and the "fainting" for the courts of the Lord, and pronouncing benedictions on those "that dwell in thy house," it ends with further benedictions upon those who trust in Him. It was this psalm that cheered that saintly Presbyterian minister of the seventeenth century, Samuel Rutherford. Exiled from his parish, he said: "When I think upon the sparrow and swallow that build their nests in the kirk of Anworth, and of my dumb Sabbaths, my sorrowful, blessed eyes look asquint upon Christ, and present Him as angry." It is better to be a doorkeeper in the house of God, surely, than to dwell in the tents of wickedness (verse 10).

Psalm 85

In his most suggestive exposition of this Revival Psalm, Dr. Alexander Maclaren says: "This is a lovely and highly imaginative picture of the reconciliation and reunion of God and man, 'the bridal of the earth sky'." The poet-psalmist, who seems to have belonged to the times immediately after the return from exile, in strong faith sees before him a vision of a perfectly harmonious cooperation and relationship between God and man. He is not prophesying directly of Messianic times. The vision hangs before him, with no definite time upon it. It would be a glorious thing if the Church today, as a whole, would make the prayer of verse 6 her own. Spiritual and material prosperity can only be hers as she turns to God, and forgiven, follows Him fully.

Psalm 86

This meditation of David, born probably at the time of Absalom's revolt, is "a sheaf of prayers." Many of the supplications are quotations from earlier psalms, and so ought our prayers to be saturated with Scripture. And here is a psalm teaching us how to lay hold of God, what to ask for, and how to be sure of answers to our supplications. Further, notice the "fors" in this psalm. They introduce arguments we should use in our prayers, if they would have weight and efficacy with God. When plea is added to plea, what accumulated force our petitions carry! Do you know God well enough to ask Him to show you a token for good? Do you believe He can act in your favor, proving, thereby, that He is for you? Call upon Him in faith, and experience His exceeding abundant answers (*cf.* Ephesians 3:20).

Psalm 87

Twin thoughts predominate within this Patriotic Psalm, namely: *the much loved city of Zion had God as its Founder;* and, *it is conspicuous as the birthplace of nations.* The three-fold repetition of the phrase, "that man was born there," suggests the springs of spiritual life flowing from Zion, the mother city of regenerated mankind. And her chief glory is that she was chosen to be the spiritual birthplace of the world. Each and every one born again derives this spiritual birth from "Jerusalem which is above . . . the mother of us all" (Galatians 3:26). Have you been counted in God's great census? Regeneration is an individual experience. When we have been born again, we shall find our springs in God.

Psalms 88, 89

Whether these psalms are viewed as a song or a psalm, gloom pervades them. As the title of the first apparently covers both, we group them together, for such an agony of affliction is without parallel in the psalms as a whole. The darkest hour is just before the dawn. Psalm 88 presents the darkest hour; Psalm 89, the dawn. The latter is often referred by Jewish teachers to the Messiah.

Such *praise-songs*, for the comfort of the afflicted, urge all who mourn to pour out their grief before God. As the faithfulness of God makes certain all covenanted blessings, trace the word *faithfulness* in this psalm, and then out of a grateful heart sing that heart-stirring hymn, "Great is Thy Faithfulness."

Psalms 90, 91

As some of the older Rabbis ascribed the latter psalm to Moses, we bind them together, for both of them are associated with a pilgrimage. Together, they form "The Traveler's Psalms." Christ, we know, is in Psalm 91, because this psalm was used by Satan in His temptation.

Described as "the man of God," Moses' high character and office are the guarantee of the inspired authority of these psalms. And, coming from Moses, they constitute the oldest, and one of the grandest pieces of religious poetry in the world. The question is: "Is the work of *our* hands being established?" Is the place of the most High our habitation? What a spacious home this is, with all its windows open toward sunrising!

Psalm 92

This is not only a Sabbatic Psalm, a Talmudic reference to which reads, "A psalm-song for the future age, the age of Messiah, all of which will be Sabbath"; but it is a song of joyful praise for every day. Of course, every day should be a Lord's day for the believer. Originally intended for the "holy convocation" or "the Sabbath" (Leviticus 23:3), the psalm directs our attention to Christ's ultimate provision for His own in the coming sabbatical age. "There remaineth therefore a rest (keeping of a sabbath) to the people of God" (Hebrews 4:9). Thankfulness and fruitfulness are scattered throughout the psalm. Those who would like to live long and grow old beautifully will find blessing in reading again verses 13 and 14.

Psalm 93

We can readily understand the magnificent language of this unnamed psalm, if it was written about the time when Assyria threatened Jerusalem. "The arrogant proclamation of the then world-power was, 'the Assyrian reigneth'; the overthrow of him was God's counter-proclamation, 'The Lord reigneth'." Prophetically, the psalm takes us to the proud boast of world-power under the Antichrist (II Thessalonians 2). But the coming of the King of kings will forever terminate the open defiance of godless rulers. Yet, let us not fail to encourage ourselves in the present majesty and might of God. Mark the present tense of the psalm – "Reigneth"; "Is." Amid all disturbing forces in our lives, and among nations, God reigns!

Psalm 94

It would seem as if Psalms 91-100 form a series, and have as their general theme the Lord's care, concern, and comfort for His own, and the ultimate overthrow of their foes. Here the psalmist commences with the expression of confidence. "The God of vengeance shines." The saints of old believed that God's righteousness bound Him to dispense vengeance to those who troubled them. We would do well to emulate them and, rather than to practice self-vengeance, calmly to await divine vengeance. "Vengeance is mine, I will repay, saith the Lord." Therefore, when we are wronged, let us rest our case in the hands of the Judge of all the earth.

Psalm 95

We have New Testament authority for treating this psalm as a Spirit-inspired utterance of David (Hebrews 3:7; 4:7). Twin truths are before us here. First, we have the omnipotence of God. He is sole Lord of nature and men. Then follows a solemn warning against the hardening of the heart against this "great King above all gods." The generation that came out of Egypt did not enter the Canaan-rest because of unbelief. And, for ourselves, lack of faith can rob us of the rest of faith. Here God limits a certain day (Hebrews 4:7). *Today*, not *tomorrow*! Yes, today, this very minute of it, God is calling us to appropriate His promised rest. May grace be ours to cease from sin and self, and find our all in Him!

Psalm 96

This psalm is supposed to be related to the setting up of the ark of God in the tabernacle in Zion (I Chronicles 16:23-33). It is profitable to observe two triads in the psalm. In the first two verses, we have a triplet of "Sings" – Sing! Sing! Sing!; then, in verses seven and eight, three "Gives" – Give! Give! Give! The singing heart is ever the liberal heart toward God. When we know how to praise Him for all He is in Himself, and for all He has accomplished on our behalf, there is never any difficulty about the yielding up of ourselves and our substance to Him, who is worthy of all. Let us sing *and* give, and sing *as* we give.

Psalm 97

Sovereignty and holiness are before us in this psalm, so eloquent with God's judgment upon idolaters. And the day is coming when His righteousness will be displayed before an aroused world. At the sight of His manifested glory, the hills – emblems of duration and strength – melt as wax before Him. How grateful we are that when His judgments fall upon idolatrous nations during the Tribulation, the souls of His saints will be preserved! As the shadows gather around a guilty world, let us be found living in the last three verses of this psalm. We want to excel in the "loving" and "hating" emotions of verse ten: "Ye that love the Lord, hate evil."

Psalm 98

Within this soul-stirring lyric that we can call "A Coronation Psalm," the universal recognition of divine sovereignty is prominent. The whole earth proclaims God as "the Lord, the King." The psalm carried a prophetic vision of Armageddon, when salvation and righteousness will be openly manifested in the sight of hostile nations. Thus, within this noble and lively song, universal jubilation and universal judgment are combined. One old writer suggests that the psalm prefigured Christ's coming into the world. "What is here *foretold* by David is, in the virgin's song, chanted forth as being *accomplished.* David is the *voice*, and Mary is the *echo.*"

Psalm 99

Inherent and governmental holiness are before us in this Sanctus Psalm. Four times the word "holy" occurs, giving us the division of the psalm, and can be placed alongside the three-fold recognition of divine holiness by the Seraphim in Isaiah 6. There are three psalms commencing with "The Lord Reigneth" (93, 97 and 99). Here, in this Psalm of Holiness, the sovereign Lord is found between the Cherubim, implying that God is satisfied in His righteous and holy demands as He gazes upon the blood-sprinkled Mercy-Seat. Divine holiness demanded atonement for sin, and divine love graciously provided the sinner's need of such an atonement. Let us ever worship at His holy hill.

Psalm 100

Among all the psalms forming the Psalter, this is the only one designated "A Psalm of Praise." While originally designed to be sung when the sacrifices of thanksgiving were offered (Leviticus 7:12), it yet reveals the vision of world-wide worship of Jehovah, that the Jewish nation had. Ablaze with grateful adoration, this divine lyric, known as "The Old Hundredth," has been a favorite psalm of the saints in every age. Of the psalm as a whole, it has been written: "This is a bunch of the grapes of Eschol. It is a taste of what is still in the Promised Land. The Jewish church came to its perfection in the reign of Solomon, but a greater than Solomon is here. The perfection of the New Testament is here anticipated." They who enter His gates ought always to do so with thanksgiving.

Psalm 101

Because righteous resolutions are written all over this psalm, which, by the way, no one but a man after God's own heart could write, it is fittingly known as "The Psalm of Pious Resolutions." Holiness of heart and singleness of eye prove how David was determined to practice religion. And what is the use of praise without practice? As we learn from another psalm, our songs must become statutes to live by. Some of the saints of bygone days called this "The Householder's Psalm," affirming that if all homes could be regulated by the rules of the conscientious psalmist, there would be greater domestic happiness. Others have named it, "The Mirror for Magistrates," and political life would be more godlike if all rulers lived this psalm.

Psalm 102

The psalmists were ever patriots, hence the present lament over the nation's distress. We here find the writer making the grief of the country his own. All personal sorrows are eclipsed by the anguish of heart the psalmist experiences as he looks upon the desolation of Zion. But this true patriot does not sorrow as those who have no hope. Through faith he envisions a glorious future for generations unborn. See the expressive title of the psalm. Are you afflicted in some way or another? Then pour out your complaint before the Lord. If overwhelmed, empty your heart before Him. Even the ship with Christ on board was filled with water and began to sink. So ease your burdened heart. Tell it all to Jesus! He is the afflicted One of the psalms.

Psalm 103

Possibly written by David in his failing years, this psalm describes the royal benefactions from the table of Him who daily spreads a glorious feast for the redeemed. Spurgeon says of the psalm: "There is too much in the psalm for a thousand pens to write. It is one of those all-comprehending Scriptures which is a Bible in itself, and it might alone almost suffice for the hymnbook of the church." Within the psalm there is no prayer or supplication. All is purest praise: "His kingdom ruleth over all." *Over all!* Is this so? Over the needs of your body; over all hindrances; over all trials; over all disappointments; over death. Hearken to the victorious organ music of God's *"all"!*

Psalm 104

Beginning and ending in the same way as the previous psalm, this poetical version of *Genesis* is indeed Creation's Chorus. Not blind law, or chance, or fate is behind all natural forces, but God Himself. The panorama of the universe is here viewed by the eye of devotion, and God is praised for what He is in creation and providence. What we love about the psalm is that after describing nature in all the perfection of her beauty, he concludes with his own personal testimony of the Creator: "My meditation of him shall be sweet." And such meditation is sweet both to the Lord and ourselves. The psalmist knew how to magnify God for His works, but his meditation was of *Him* – His person, not His power.

Psalm 105

Turning back to what happened when the ark was brought from the house of Obededom, it would seem as if David was responsible for this Historic Psalm (I Chronicles 16:7), summarizing as it does *Exodus*

and *Numbers*. As the psalm abounds in exhortations to praise God, it is suitable as a triumphal song for any age. God is here exalted as the sovereign Lord. His grace reigns over all. He chooses whom He pleases out of nations and families – individuals for the accomplishment of His purpose. Do we live in the enjoyment of the divine protection of verses 14 and 15? Israel was precious in God's sight, but we are more precious, seeing we have been redeemed by the blood of His Son. And look also at verse 38! Live so near to God as to cause fear to fall upon the surrounding world.

Psalm 106

This "Psalm of Provocation and Preservation" begins and ends with a "Hallelujah"! Between these two hallelujahs we have a record of sin and shame, yet of marvelous grace and patience. What a different nation this would be if only there could rise to God a similar national confession of transgression! The miracle is that He is so patient with this land, as He was with Israel. With all its sin, rebellion and idolatry, why does He not destroy it? What a glimpse we have into the divine heart, in the words: "He regarded their affliction." And, because He has no pleasure in the death of the wicked, may the rulers of this land in which we dwell feel constrained to make the cry of verse 47 their own.

Psalm 107

Isaiah reminds us that salvation and song go together: "I have redeemed thee. Sing!" (Isaiah 44:22,23). And the psalmist agrees with the prophet, for here is a psalm for the redeemed. What a choice song of pilgrimage it is! Before us are outlined all the motives of gratitude. Note how the exclamation of verse 8 is repeated in the psalm (verses 15,21,31). Is yours a singing heart? Or can it be that although saved, you are yet songless? Have you been content to live in "Grumbling Corner"? Then why not move to "Thanksgiving Avenue," where it is just as cheap to live? Further, living as you do in a restless world, do you possess the tranquility of soul referred to in verse 30? If redeemed, learn to repose.

Psalm 108

Here we have the Victor's Song, with God at its outset and conclusion. As a valiant warrior, David knew that his victories did not come merely as the result of his own valor. It was "through God" that he trod down his enemies. An old Prussian officer was wont to invoke the aid of "his Majesty's august ally." And David ever turned to God as his "Ally," and found in Him One stronger than all his foes. Within our own lives we cannot expect to triumph over enemies if we lack the fixed heart of verse 1. When God is our Center, He is able to deal with the circumference. May we be delivered from the wavering, wayward heart! If it is fixed upon the Lord, then we can fight victoriously.

Psalm 109

The string of anathemas forming this Imprecatory Psalm has troubled many minds. It has been called "Iscariot's Psalm," because of Peter's use of it in connection with Judas (Acts 1:20). Certainly the psalm does not breathe the Christian spirit, but then it is not for the Christian age. The Judgment Psalms were conceived and written under the stern dispensation of the Old Covenant. Israel has constant conflict with sword and spear, and they wanted to tread down and crush their enemies. To them it would be righteous triumph to wash their feet in the blood of their foes. But in this Christian age, our struggle is not with carnal weapons. Forgiveness, and not vindictiveness, has come to us from the cross. The Tribulation Period, however, will witness divine judgment.

Psalm 110

In this "Priest-King Psalm" we have come to a most important Messianic Psalm. Christ, in all His glory and power, is the predominant theme of the psalm. For a profitable outline of the psalm, the reader is referred to page 654 in the *Scofield Reference Bible*. This crown of all psalms has been designated in many ways. Martin Luther said it was worthy of being overlaid with precious jewels. Of verse 5 the reformer wrote: "It is a well-spring of joy, a treasury of all

Christian doctrines, understanding, wisdom and comfort, richer and fuller than any other passage of Holy Writ." Take a look at the last verse, and drink deeply of the refreshing brooks God has provided.

Psalms 111, 112, 113

In this trilogy of psalms, each resembles the other in general tone and manner. We group them together, therefore. Each commences: "Praise ye the Lord." Probably these psalms were sung at the eating of the Paschal Lamb, and were among those Christ and His disciples used before they went out into the garden. The intention of this triad of Hallelujah Psalms is to stir up praise to God, for all the reasons stated in them. *Creation and Redemption* (111); *Blessedness of the Righteous* (112); and *Boundless Power and Compassion* (113). True, the Lord's Name is to be praised! Do you glorify Him in this way? Acceptable praise is a sacrifice (Hebrews 13:15). Angels descending are laden with blessings for our needy hearts. But alas, the angels ascending return to our bountiful God so empty-handed!

Psalm 114

True poetry reaches its climax in the grandeur of this Pilgrimage Psalm, wherein the God of Jacob is praised as the Master of ocean, earth and sky. All the forces of nature obey their Lord on behalf of His people during their exodus. Points to observe, looking at the psalm as a whole, are: *Pilgrims* (verses 1,2); *Power* (verses 3-6); *Presence* (verse 7); and *Provision* (verse 8). It is blessed to realize that God is greater than all the powers He created. He is not a prisoner within His own laws. All obey His behest. And, surely, such a fact should encourage our hearts as we continue our journey through the wilderness of this world. Well, God can make any rock that we come up against yield a fountain of water.

Psalm 115

The folly of idolatry is the conspicuous theme of this psalm, commencing with the tribute of the true worshipers of God. What a revelation we have here of the utter and abject helplessness and degrading hopelessness of idol worship! Whether the gods of men are natural objects, riches or worldly pleasures, they have no eyes to pity, no ears to hear, no tongues to counsel and no hands to help. Worshipers become assimilated to the objects of their worship. But the true God is all eyes, ears, hands, feet and heart. And if He is the sole Object of our worship, we become like unto Him. Those who sit in darkness, bowing down to idols, have no song. Only Christianity offers a song. A worshiping people are a singing people. "We will bless the Lord."

Psalm 116

Seeing that this most precious psalm commences with the positive declaration, "I love the Lord," we call it the "Lover's Psalm." "Personal love fostered by a personal experience of redemption is the theme of this Psalm," says one writer, "and in it we see the redeemed answered when they pray, preserved in time of trouble, resting in their God, walking at large, sensible of their obligations, conscious that they are not their own, but bought with a price, and joining with all the ransomed company to sing hallelujahs unto God." The language of the psalm can be fittingly applied to Christ, and also to the believer as he faces his trials. Have you taken the cup of salvation, the Saviour's cup of anguish made possible? If you are saved, surely you are paying your vows unto the Lord!

Psalm 117

Multum in parvo (much in little) is what we can write over this shortest of all psalms, which likewise constitutes the central portion of the whole Bible. Little in letter, it is yet exceedingly large in spirit, seeing that it travels beyond the barriers of race and nationality, and calls upon all mankind to praise the Lord (Romans 15:11). This is a psalm for this Gentile age, and also for the succeeding age, when the knowledge of the Lord is to cover the earth as the waters cover the sea. Being a small portion, made up of only two verses, it suggests that God's worship need not be too long. Few words sometimes say what is sufficient. The shortest text of the Bible is "Jesus wept." And who is there who is able enough to plumb the depth of divine compassion?

Psalm 118

While this psalm was probably associated with the joyful laying of the cornerstone of the temple (Ezra 3:10,11), frequent quotations from it in the New Testament prove that it is another Messianic Psalm (I Peter 2:8). Note the five-fold repetition: "His mercy endureth forever" (verses 1,2,3,4,29). Delitzsch, the German scholar, said of this majestic psalm: "Each verse has of itself its completed sense, its own scent and hue; one thought is joined to another as branch to branch and flower to flower." It was also Martin Luther's favorite psalm, who declared, "I love them all; I love all Holy Scripture, which is my consolation and my life. But this Psalm is nearest my heart, and I have a peculiar right to call it mine." Can you claim it as yours? If today is one of those unwanted days, read verse 24.

Psalm 119

Composed of twenty-two divisions, each beginning with a letter of the Hebrew alphabet in its proper order, this Word-exalting psalm is the longest in the Psalter, just as Psalm 117 is the shortest. The same Holy Spirit, however, is responsible for both. There are times for short hymns and times for long hymns, for short prayers and for long prayers, for short sermons and for long sermons. As far as we can trace, there are only two or three verses out of the 176 in this psalm in which the Word of God is not mentioned in some way or another. And that the psalmist loved what he had of it can be found in the reiterated professions of love for and delight in it. The closing verse presents what we might call a confession. If you, too, have gone astray, the divine Seeker will restore you through the Word.

Psalm 120

The next fifteen psalms bear the same title. "The Songs of Degrees" or "of Ascents." Martin Luther called them: "The Songs on the high key." These psalms were probably chanted by the people as they went up to Jerusalem to the feasts. "The stairs of the city of David at the ascent of the wall." As each Song of Degrees sparkles as a separate star, shining in its own constellation, let us look at them separately. The one before us may contain David's prayer against Doeg. If so, then we can appreciate the psalmist's appeal to "the great Arbiter of right and wrong, before whose Judgment Seat no man shall suffer from slanderous tongues." Sick at heart over sin and strife around, we, who are the Lord's, also long for the peace and quiet of Zion.

Psalm 121

Although it is among the Pilgrim Psalms, this one is more like a soldier's song than a traveler's hymn. God as the Eternal Keeper is before us. Unceasingly He cares for His own. He ever preserves and protects all those who know Him as the Keeper. And, is it not blessed to realize that God's care is not only eternal, but particular and minute? He is your Keeper as if you were alone in all His universe. He knows all about your separate trials, temptations and sorrows. While He has millions to watch over, He never for one moment forgets *you*. Unceasingly and sleeplessly He watches over *you*. Why not, then, live day and night in His thought and love? With verse 1 in mind, we can understand what the natives of India meant, when they said of Sir Henry Lawrence, that when he looked *twice* up to heaven, and then to earth, he knew what to do.

Psalm 122

Jerusalem was dear to the godly Jew, not only because of the beauty of its situation and the stately majesty of its buildings, but because it was the beating and pulsing center of the nations' religious life. This is why David's psalm expresses the delight of returning exiles as they approached the temple in Zion. Matthew Henry says of this psalm: "Observe, first, *the joy with which they were to go up to Jerusalem* (verses 1,2); second, *the great esteem they were to have of Jerusalem* (verses 3,5); and third, *the great concern they were to have for Jerusalem*, and *the prayers they were to offer for its welfare*." And so ought we to pray for the prosperity and increase of the Church of Jesus Christ, the spiritual Jerusalem.

Psalm 123

Ancient writers call this psalm, "The Eye of Hope," or "The Psalm of the Eyes," and the lifted eye indicates the worshiping heart and the waiting spirit. One thought, expressed in an engaging manner, fills this psalm. Whether it was a sigh heard in the days of Nehemiah or no, this short ode, written with singular art, breathes the desire for strength and succor by the saints of every age. Eyes lifted up to the hills, in Psalm 121, are here lifted up to the Lord Himself. Dust looks to Deity for deliverance. The upward glance is the evidence of a believing, humble heart, and is a confident persuasion that God is ready and willing to undertake for us in time of need. The eyes of faith look up. In which direction are you looking?

Psalm 124

Whatever direct application this psalm may have in David's life, it enjoys a delightful universality. The Song is admirably suited as an anthem of the redeemed in every age. As saints, we live in hostile territory with traitors within the camp and unnumbered foes without. But the quick and mighty intervention of God, emphasized in the psalm, can be claimed by the humblest believer. With the psalmist, each of us can rejoice in the fact that God is with us, protecting us on every side. What we sadly need, however, is deliverance from confidence in man and a complete reliance upon our divine Protector. This glorious Lord is our Ally, and well able to overcome all proud, arrogant foes. So, bid your fears depart. Hope thou in God!

Psalm 125

It has been suggested that this psalm, along with the next one, forms a pair, with verse 1 of the psalm before us as an introduction to both. Being a further Pilgrim Psalm, we are presented with a record of the feelings of a pilgrim as he neared Jerusalem. And two peculiar features of the city are used as symbols of spiritual realities; namely, it stood on a mountain, and it was girded by mountains. All who trust in the Lord are set as steadfast as a mountain, and are compassed about by Him. Thus faith gives stability, and likewise secures an encircling defense. Emphasis, of course, is not in the *firmness* of our trust, but in the *object* of our trust, the immovable Lord. How encouraging to realize that all the blessings of this psalm are the birthright of every believer!

Psalm 126

We are still climbing. This further "Song of Ascents" declares that God had worked on behalf of His people. Their sighing for liberty had been answered, and for a while they seemed to be in dreamland. No longer exiles! Why, it seemed too good to be true! And such a psalm is for the comfort and guidance of the saints in every age. Often joyful hopes, raised by deliverances, are threatened with disappointment. But "favours already received are to be the ground of prayer and believing hope that God will crown His goodness by new acts of grace." If you are somewhat discouraged in service, read verses 5 and 6, and know that the seed sown in weakness, and watered with the tears of compassion, will not fail to bring forth an abundant harvest. What a psalm! Laughter and tears (verses 2,5)! Songs and sobs!

Psalm 127

Attributed to Solomon, this psalm differs from the other "Degree Psalms" in that the individual is prominent. John Calvin wrote of it: "The theme suits Solomon, who chiefly occupied the domestic territory." The main thought of the psalm corresponds with the wise monarch's proverb, "The blessing of the Lord, it maketh rich, and he addeth no sorrow with it" (Proverbs 10:22). Except God give His benediction, man's works cannot have a prosperous issue. Temple and home are before us in this psalm, with the Lord as the heavenly Builder of both. God-built churches and God-built homes are the nation's greatest asset. Here is an appeal to every one of us.

Psalm 128

The blessed influence of a sanctified home life, touched upon in the previous psalm, is developed in this one. Walking with God in the quiet of the home enables us to walk with Him and for Him in the busy, hostile world outside. In these days of industrial turmoil, when it is not as common as it used to be to give a fair day's work for a fair day's pay, verse 2 is one that should be reiterated in all labor circles. What a different world this would be, if only it were possible to have the application of the principles of the Bible in every phase of life! Those of us who are grandparents find delight in the last verse of this Pilgrim Psalm. The question is: Am *I* in the enjoyment of the peace that God alone can bestow?

Psalm 129

Experience, both national and individual, is outlined in this psalm, in which the Jews, returning from Babylon, expressed their hope of complete re-establishment in their own land. Many and deep had been their afflictions, but triumph was sure. Amid all declension and tribulation God was on the side of His own, overruling all He permitted, for the people's good. The last verse indicates the custom prevailing in God-fearing Israel. It constitutes the benediction given to the reapers of a harvest (*cf.* Ruth 2:4). Let us take to our hearts this psalm, with its insistence upon the protection and deliverance of our righteous Lord. In spite of each and every difficulty that we may be called upon to face, we have a God who can bring us through.

Psalm 130

In this eleventh step of the spiritual ascent we have the most excellent of the Penitential Psalms, containing, as it does, the most ardent prayer of one overwhelmed by a sense of divine anger against sin. Turning to God in penitence, the psalmist seeks the forgiveness of his iniquities. Bishop James Vaughan says of the psalm that it is marked by its mountain, depth, prayer, conviction, light, hope, waiting, watching, longing, confidence, assurance, universal happiness and joy. Just as the barometer marks the rising of the weather, so does this psalm, sentence by sentence, record the progress of the soul. And you may test yourself by it, as by a rule or measure, and ask yourself at each line, "Have I reached to this? Have I reached to this?" and so take your spiritual gauge.

"Out of the depths have I cried unto thee" (verse 1). We return to this *De Profundis Psalm* in order to trace the psalmist's rapid rise out of the depths of despair to the sunny heights of assurance. Cast into the depths, he came to realize that "pearls lie deep." Depths! What depths man can be cast into! Depths of poverty, stripped bare of all earthly possessions and dear friends. Depths of sorrow, with plans all ripped to pieces by the storms of adversity. Depths of mental darkness, with nothing but surrounding sorrow and despair. Depths of sin – depths to which there seems to be no bottom. What can we do when in such depths? Cry! Cry unto the Lord! It is a blessed "but" that we have in verse 4, that leads us out of the depths.

Psalm 131

David is both the author and subject of this pearl of psalms, "shortest to read, longest to learn." Humility, tranquillity, and simplicity constitute this short ladder rising to great heights. In strong contrast to the preceding psalm, this one is characterized by a sweet and simple guilelessness. Psalm 130 is one of forgiveness; Psalm 131 is a Song of Humility. And the sense of sin and assurance of forgiveness should humble us. With the rags of iniquity stripped from us, we must wrap ourselves with the garment of humility. As children of God, we must be weaned – weaned from self-sufficiency and all worldly entanglements. After being weaned, the child rests quiet and easy in its mother's arms, without the breast. And so, separated from sin and the world, we find our all in God.

Psalm 132

The first verse of this, another Pilgrim Psalm, takes us back to the thrilling hour when David brought the ark of God home to Zion. It is indeed a joyful song, and one all pilgrims can join in. A peculiar feature of the psalm is its division into four stanzas of ten lines, each of which contains the name of David. In the first part, we have David's vow to the Lord; and in the last half, the Lord's promise to David. Trace these points as you read the psalm: (1) *Place for the Lord* (verse 5); (2) *Priests unto the Lord* (verse 9); (3) *Praise to the Lord* (verse 9);

(4) *Peace in the Lord* (verse 14); and (5) *Provision from the Lord* (verse 15). When the ark, symbol of God's presence and favor, is in its rightful place, what else can there be but a joy unspeakable?

Psalm 133

Unity, pleasant in its manifestation, forms the theme of this sparkling sonnet. And none was more fitted than David, who knew by experience the bitterness of division, to pen such a psalm, in which there is no wry word, but is all "sweetness and light." Here we are shown how brotherly kindness and love can span all gulfs and distances. They bind together so many things which seem far apart. Brotherly unity is like the holy anointing oil, the priestly oil of consecration. Poured upon Aaron's head, it flowed down to the lowliest blue fringe of his garments, making both one. And Christ, the Head, and the least of His little ones, are one forever. Such unity is like dawn falling on the mystic hills and lowly slopes alike, making both close of kin. May the Lord enable us to know and guard the unity of the Spirit. For how we need it!

Psalm 134

In this last of the Gradual Psalms, the pilgrims are going home, singing their last song. Such a "Serving and Singing Psalm" teaches us to pray for all those set apart to minister before the Lord. Do we lift up holy hands in prayer as we should? Are we among the night watchers of verse 1? We have come to the world's Saturday night. It is almost the stroke of midnight. Dawn is at hand! Our faces should be turned toward sunrising. Watching, we must not be idle. While others sleep in the night, we watch and pray. Looking at this beautiful small ode, equally full of sublimity and simplicity, we can trace three thoughts in its three verses: (1) *Continual Service;* (2) *Consecrated Supplication;* and (3) *Compassionate Saviour.* Underline the threefold "bless" of this final "Degree Psalm."

Psalm 135

Made up of choice extracts from other Scriptures, this Mosaic Psalm teaches us that the Holy Spirit occasionally repeats Himself, not through lack of material, but to drive truths home to our dull minds. Praise characterizes this glorious psalm. It begins and ends with a "Hallelujah." Praise is commended, and in three aspects: with respect to *God*, for Himself and His works; with respect to *ourselves*; and with respect to *others*. On the psalm as a whole, an old-time expositor wrote: "This is a song of praise to the Lord for His goodness as the Lord of Creation, in seven verses; for His grace as the Deliverer of His people in seven more; and for His unity as the only true and living God in seven more." The psalmist rings the changes on "praise" and "bless." Find out how often these key words occur. *Praise* is for all God's excellencies – *blessing*, for all His benefits.

Psalm 136

The grand peculiarity of this psalm of ecstatic thanksgiving is the regular recurrence of the close of every verse, the reference, "His mercy endureth forever," occuring 26 times in the psalm. "Like a nightingale which, when she is in a pleasant vein, quavers and capers, and trebles upon it, so did David upon His mercy: 'For his mercy endureth forever'." In this psalm, containing nothing but praise, all creation testifies to the majesty and might of God's great power. In the moral and spiritual worlds, as well as in the natural, His power is exhibited. It is both profitable and pleasant to go over this psalm and trace out the various ways in which God is presented. Try the exercise! It is blessed to know that God mingles mercy with His justice. Everlasting mercy! What a theme of everlasting gratitude!

"For His mercy shall endure,
    Ever faithful, ever sure."

Psalm 137

Using our imagination, we can picture a company of sad-visaged men sitting by the riverside, sighing for home, in this plaintive ode, which, for its poetic power, is one of the most charming of compositions. The exiled Jews had seen their temple burned, city ruined, wives ravished and children slain, and could not, therefore, sing the song of the Lord in a strange land. Perowne

says of this psalm, so heavy with complaint: "What a wonderful mixture is the Psalm of soft melancholy and fiery patriotism! The hand which wrote it must have known how to smite sharply with the sword, as well as how to tune the harp. The words are burning words of a heart breathing undying love of his country, undying hate to his foe." The poet is indeed –

    "Dower'd with the hate of hate, the scorn
        of scorn,
    The love of love."

Psalm 138

Many writers connect this psalm with David's thanksgiving in II Samuel 7. Solomon declared that there is a "time to keep silence, and a time to speak." In Psalm 137, there is silence before revilers, but here the whole heart bravely confesses its honor of the Lord. The psalm is eloquent with the kingly fidelity, courage and decision of the "prince of psalmists." God's lovingkindness is the central theme of the psalm. The "Name," David praises, is equivalent of the nature or being of the Lord, His divine, transcendent attributes in all the plenitude of their exceeding greatness. Pressed like a cluster of grapes, praise now produces ripe juice. After mourning, there came music. We pass from captivity to canticles as we consider these psalms. Whether your circumstances are pleasant or painful, the Lord is perfecting that which concerns you.

Psalm 139

This most notable of the psalms could have come from no other than that of the son of Jesse. The psalm, flashing like a sapphire stone, forcibly declares three aspects of God's being, namely: (1) *His Omniscience* (verses 1-6); (2) *His Omnipresence* (verses 7-12); and (3) *His Omnipotence* (verses 14-16). And such a revelation of God is ever an incentive to holy living! He knows all – is everywhere – has all power. And this sublimest composition in the world does not give us an abstract description of the divine attributes. David has a practical purpose in view, and applies them to his heart and life. With such a God, every wicked way in him must be discovered and destroyed. What a precious gem we have in verse 18! When our eyes open in the morning, is God our waking thought? "Still, still with Thee, When purple morning waketh." To go through the day, conscious that God's thoughts are upon us, is to have a day without clouds!

We return to this majestic psalm in order to compare two apparently contradictory phrases: "Thou hast searched me" (verse 1); "Search me" (verse 23). In the first phrase, David asserts that God has searched him, while in the last, he asks Him to do what he declares has been done. The explanation is simple. In the first part of the psalm, David is taken up with his outer life, his downsitting and uprising, and viewing the exterior, feels that he has been searched. But the psalmist journeys on with God, allowing Him to pass from the exterior to the interior, and as David does so, he discovers a world of undiscovered sin within, and cries: "Search me!" From action, he travels into heart and thought, and desires cleansing within, as well as without. The source, stream and issue of life need to be of the same texture.

Psalm 140

This is another psalm related to David's experiences while a fugitive from Saul. It is the cry of a hunted soul. Persecuted and beset by cunning foes, David appeals to God for protection and deliverance. The psalm is divided for us by the use of "Selah"; (1) *the wicked themselves, in all their dark colors* (verses 1-3); (2) *snares spread by the wicked* (verses 4,5); (3) *the attitude of faith* (verses 6-8); and (4) *destruction of foes* (verses 9-13). For ourselves, today, God is our only anchor of hope. Enemies, satanic and human, are ours, and we have no might and wisdom against such foes, but our safety is in God, who ever assures us that no weapon formed against us can prosper. From David we learn not to be revengeful or harbor malice, but to leave vengeance to Him, who said, "Vengeance is mine; I will repay." Undeserved persecution may be yours, it is true; if you are innocent, you can safely leave your reputation in His hands.

Psalm 141

David is still in the realm of conflict. The enemies in this psalm, however, are more or less internal, while those of the preceding psalm were external. Few psalms carry in so small a compass so many gems of precious and holy truth. In God, David has a Sentry for his soul, One who is able to keep the doors of his lips, and sufficient to keep him from snares and nets laid for him. For all of us, verse 3 is an important one to study, seeing that the tongue is the principal instrument in the cause of God, and likewise the chief engine of the devil. A watch over words is better than over wealth. If God keeps the door of the mouth, "it will not move creaking and complaining, as on rusty hinges, for want of the oil and gladness," says old John Trapp. Guarded lips and life! May such double preservation be ours!

Psalm 142

The historical connection of this psalm is indicated by its title. This last of the *Maschil*, or Instruction Psalms, carries the cry of David as he hides from Saul, possibly in the cave of Adullam. "Caves make good closets for prayer"; says Spurgeon, "their gloom and solitude are helpful to the exercises of devotion." And David knew how to pray in a pit as well as in a palace. While the gloom of the cave is over the psalm, David believed that God was able to deliver his imprisoned soul and bring him out into a wealthy place. But as the psalmist was forced to hide in no-man's land, he cried: "No man cared for my soul." No one seemed to concern himself whether the fugitive lived or died. Alas, far too many in this lost world have the same complaint to make against the Church! Souls are not cared for as they should be. Those of us who are saved seem often to be destitute of the passionate love for souls that characterized our Lord and Master, who wept over a lost city.

Psalm 143

Distress, desolation and yet deliverance, are still before us in this Davidic Psalm, more martial than penitential. It will be seen that this outcry of an overwhelmed spirit is divided by its "Selah": *Lamentation over Sorrows* (verses 1-6); and *Supplication for Deliverance* (verses 7-12). Note as you read the psalm, the petitions: Deliver me; Teach me; Lead me; Quicken me. In verse 4, we have a *Desolate Heart;* in verse 9, a *Divine Helper;* and in verse 10, a *Desirable Haven.* As this is an age in which the art of meditation seems to have been lost, it would be well for us to recapture David's desire to meditate on God's works and to stretch out his hands unto Him. Expounding verses 5 and 6, dear old William Gurnall says: "Meditation is as the plough before the sower, to prepare the heart for the duty of prayer; and as the harrow after the sower, to cover the seed when 'tis sown. As the hopper feeds the mill with grist, so does meditation supply the heart with matter for prayer."

Psalm 144

This Warrior Psalm covers the individual, home and nation. Go over the psalm and gather out the designations of the Lord given by David, who is himself, in behalf of his own, a man of war. After six psalms of sorrowful prayer in distress, we have this psalm of praise and thanksgiving to God for His protection and provision. Compare it with David's last song in II Samuel 22. One writer sees in the psalm, "a vision of Christ rejoicing; after His passion, a vision of Glory; and having ascended in triumph, and pleading for us at the right hand of God." The ideal state described in the closing verses will not be realized until Christ returns to earth: "No complainings in our streets." These are days of industrial and national dissatisfaction and riots. Men are fighting for their rights, and the redressing of all wrongs. Such a peaceful and prosperous condition must, however, await the coming of Him whose reign will create complete satisfaction.

Ten strings! We can gather a few spiritual suggestions from the oft-repeated exhortation about praising God on a ten-stringed instrument. Eusebius, in his exposition of this psalm, says of this verse: "The psaltery of ten strings is the worship of the Holy Spirit, performed by means of the five senses of the body and by the five senses of the soul." This he confirms by quoting I Corinthians 14:15: "I will sing with the spirit, and I will sing with the understanding also." We can think of the human frame as an instrument of ten strings: two feet, two hands, two ears, two eyes, one tongue, and one heart; and upon this instrument of ten strings we must sing praises unto God. Can we say that all our powers are combined to bless the Lord? Christ gave His all, in order that there might come the absorption of our whole being for the supreme purpose of glorifying God.

Psalm 145

Here we have another of David's own psalms, and although he ever glorified God in all he wrote, he seems to have reserved his crown jewel of praise for this psalm, without a rival in the realm of literature. "Whoso offereth praise, glorifieth thee," and David certainly knew how to excel in this art, for this whole psalm is taken up with the Lord. He vowed to praise the Lord every day. God's glory is revealed; His greatness magnified; His bounty commended; and His grace extolled. The Jews declared him happy whoever uttered this psalm thrice each day with the heart, mouth and tongue. "Before you pray, repeat or read Psalm 145," was an ancient exhortation. How musical and fragrant the old words are: "The Lord is nigh!" (verse 18). Ring it forth against all fears within and fightings without: "Lo, I am with you alway, even unto the end."

Psalm 146

A peculiar feature of the last five psalms is that each of them commences and concludes with a "Hallelujah." Truly, we are among the Hallelujahs! We are among the delectable mountains. To the close of the book it is all praise. The key is high-pitched, with the music upon high-sounding cymbals. "A sacred censer of holy incense, pouring forth one sweet perfume," the perfume being the possession of the Lord as our happiness. Mark the three-fold "h" in verse 5; happy, help and hope. And the reasons for such sublime happiness are plainly stated in the succeeding verses. As the whole, the psalm gives us the "Gospel of Confidence." It inculcates the elements of faith, hope and thanksgiving. In these days when godless men are causing so much distress in the world, it is encouraging to know that God is able to turn the way of the wicked upside down.

Psalm 147

Divine greatness and goodness are prominent in this remarkable ode, exuberant and enthusiastic with praise to God. He is magnified for what He has done, what He does, and what He can do. In every realm He is able to display His powers. As Creator, Comforter and Consoler, He is incomparable. Such an unfolding of God's supremacy should beget confidence. Edward Taylor, sailor-preacher of Boston, of a past generation, entreated God, on the Sunday before he sailed for Europe, to care well for his church during his absence. All at once he stopped, and ejaculated: "What have I done? Distrust the Providence of heaven! A God that gives a whale a ton of herring for a breakfast, will He not care for His children?" Needless to say, he closed his prayer in a more confident manner. Our God is of great power. Let us therefore, bid our unbelieving anxiety depart.

This "Hallelujah Psalm" will stand another glimpse. Look, will you, at verses 3 and 4, and note their extremes and contrasts. "He healeth the broken in heart . . . He telleth the number of stars." Sorrows and Stars! The Heart and the Heavens. From stars to sighs may be a deep descent, but infinite compassion brings them together. Mercy and Majesty are here combined. God is not so lost in His marvelous creative works as to be ignorant of the trials of the humblest of His creatures. As it has been expressed: "He who acts a surgeon's part with wounded hearts, marshals the heavenly host, and reads the muster-roll of suns and their majestic system. O Lord, it is good to praise Thee as ruling the stars, but it is pleasant to adore Thee as healing the broken in heart!" So we praise Him, the Comforter and the Creator!

Psalm 148

Here we have a song of nature and of grace, sharing with the last psalm in the Psalter the distinction of using "praise" thirteen times. This is another psalm radiant with praise. All creation, animate and inanimate, joins in the great chorus. Bernard, in his sermon on the death of his brother Gerard, relates that in the middle of his last night on earth his brother, to the astonishment of all present, with a voice and countenance of exultation, broke forth in the words of the opening verse of this psalm: "Praise ye the Lord from the heavens, praise him in the heights." How comprehensive verse 12 is: "Both young men, and maidens; old men, and children"! When it comes to praise, there is neither youth nor age. Both sexes and all ages make merry together in it. And so, if God is to have perfect praise, the whole universe must raise its hallelujah. Can it be that He misses our voice in the chorus?

Psalm 149

God, as our Joy and our Judge, is before us in this another psalm devoted to His praise. As a "new song," it is associated with the new creation, and can only be sung by those of a new heart. Both the pleasure and the punishment of the Lord are emphasized here. Notice, please, a most suggestive combination in verse 5. We can expect the saints in glory to be loud in their praises, but joyful upon a bed, especially a sick bed, is another matter. Perhaps these lines are being read by one who, denied health and strength, is forced to spend the days upon a bed! How are you meeting your sickness, or physical disability? Are you joyful, happy in the consciousness that God never makes a mistake? Your bed can contribute to creation's "Hallelujah Chorus." May grace be ours to sing as we suffer!

Psalm 150

Of this last psalm, vibrant as it is with abundant and abounding praise (thirteen times "praise" is used), Spurgeon says: "We have now reached the last summit of the mountain chain of Psalms. It rises high into the clear azure, and its brow is bathed in the sunlight of the eternal world of worship. It is a rapture. The poet-prophet is full of inspiration and enthusiasm. He stays not to argue, to teach, to explain; but cries with burning words, 'Praise him, Praise him, Praise ye the Lord'." It is somewhat interesting to compare the first and last psalms, and note how the last is the echo of the first. The first psalm begins with "Blessed." "Blessed are all they that meditate on God's law and do it" – such is its theme. And now the fruit of that blessedness is shown in this psalm, which begins and ends with "Praise." Both psalms have the same number of verses, although different in scope.

"The Book of Psalms" (Acts 1:20)

Our Lord and the apostles made good use of this favorite book of the Old Testament. Although made up of separate poems from different pens, and belonging to different periods, all the 150 psalms form one priceless volume. And as a book, the psalms have been accepted by both Jewish and Christian teachers as one of the inspired books of Holy Writ. St. Ambrose, of the 4th century wrote: "Although all divine Scripture breathes the grace of God, yet sweet beyond all others is the Book of Psalms. History instructs, law teaches, prophecy announces, rebuke chastens, morality persuades; in the Book of Psalms we have the fruit of all these, and a kind of medicine for the salvation of more." Bless God for causing these precious gems to be gathered into one Book for our edification!

"Sing Unto Him in Psalms" (James 5:13)

A psalm has been spoken of as "a poem to be sung to a stringed instrument." As we have already seen, many of the psalms were set to music and sung by the temple choir. The Psalter, as a whole, was the inspired prayer-and-praise book of Israel. And such songs are so fashioned as to be never exhausted, well-worn, or threadbare. How paltry much of the doggerel in many modern hymns and choruses is alongside the purest spiritual ideas expressed in the language of the most perfect beauty the psalms possess! And one marvel of the psalms is that they can be rendered according to the metre of every language. Anyone who has lived in Scotland, for example, can never get away from the haunting melody of these metrical psalms. Let us store our minds with the psalms and bless God in Spirit-inspired language!

"David . . . in the Psalms" (Luke 20:42)

While David was the principal contributor to the Psalter, it is somewhat misleading to speak of the psalms as a whole as "the

Psalms of David," seeing there were various other psalmists. One cannot read the psalms, however, without realizing how they reflect the life and labors of David. As a man after God's own heart, David relates what passed between God and his own soul, so much so that we find ourselves saying "Amen!" to his prayers and praises. What he learned of the Lord as a Shepherd, as he watched his flocks as a shepherd lad, is given to us in Psalm 23. What he discovered of his own evil heart and of God's forgiving grace, are before us in Psalms 51 and 32. What was revealed to his heart of the crucified, risen Saviour is fully portrayed in Psalm 22. How deep is our debt then, to the sweet psalmist of Israel.

"In the Psalms Concerning Me" (Luke 24:44)

Expounding the Scriptures in the home of Cleopas, Jesus must have had peculiar delight when He came to the psalms, especially the Messianic Psalms. Christ Himself declared that David wrote of Him (Luke 20:41-44). As He came to die, He used the very language of the psalms (Psalms 22:1; 33:5). And it is this Christology that unlocks so many of the psalms, and why, having the key of David, Christ was able to expound in the psalms the things concerning Himself. He is the Crown and Center of their revealed truth. In type and prophecy, His sufferings and the glory to follow are clearly set forth in many of the Royal Psalms, as we have endeavored to indicate. Tracing our Lord's footprints over the highways and byways of Old Testament Scriptures is ever profitable for heart and mind.

"The Holy Spirit by the Mouth of David" (Acts 1:16; II Samuel 23:1-3)

Among David's last words was the confession that as the sweet psalmist the Holy Spirit used his life and pen. Thus, he claimed divine inspiration for his psalms, and Peter confirmed the declaration. More generally, Peter claims inspiration for all Old Testament writers: "Holy men of old wrote as they were borne along by the Holy Spirit" (II Peter 1:21). Possessing native ability as a musician and a poet, David was not left to his own genius or imagination in the composition of his renowned psalms. "The Spirit of the Lord spake by me, and his word was in my tongue" (II Samuel 23:2). This, surely, is a proof of verbal inspiration.

Words, as well as thoughts, were given to David by the Holy Spirit. It is thus that, through the centuries, the psalms have retained their freshness and power.

PROVERBS

George Goodman's simple rhyming couplet on this book is a fitting summary of its contents –

"In *Proverbs*, Wisdom's voice is heard appealing to the young,
To save their feet from many snares and teach them to be strong."

Solomon, who wrote *Proverbs*, and the next two books, was eminently endowed with wisdom, but was not always wise, as his latter years prove. The sacred chronicler tells us that Solomon "spake three thousand proverbs: and his songs were a thousand and five" (I Kings 4:32). A. T. Pierson says of Solomon, "His gift of wisdom finds expression in wise and witty apothegms, that show his intellectual capacity and moral sagacity, his habits of close observation and scientific thought, his common sense and uncommon knowledge of human nature. The subjects treated are such as filial piety, evil company, sensuality and drunkenness, lying and laziness, strife and greed. What the *Psalms* are to devotional life, the *Proverbs* are to practical life." It is said that Solomon "set in order," the proverbs he had composed or gathered. Yet, at first glance, there does not seem to be any order in the book. All of the proverbs seem to hang as separate pearls on the necklace of truth. Yet close examination reveals that there were proverbs by Solomon (10-19:19; 25-26); proverbs for Solomon (1-9, 19:20-24; 27-29); proverbs by Augur (30); proverbs by a mother (31).

Chapter 1

If the psalms were for temple service, the proverbs are for everyday service. The psalms help us to pray and worship; the proverbs tell us how to live wisely when prayers are ended. Practical ethics makes up this book of Solomon, who brought together the condensed wisdom of the ages.

Within the book we have the best of the 3000 proverbs Solomon wrote (I Kings 4:32). The object of Proverbs is to inspire deep reverence for God, a fear of His judgments, and ardent love for wisdom and virtue. A wide range, it will be found, is covered by these terse and perfect sayings. What a difference it would make in the industrial world if only employers and employees could be persuaded to read a chapter of the book every morning before going out to work! Owing to lack of connection between these proverbs, it is not easy to summarize the book by chapters. Key verses of the book are 1:7 and 9:10.

Chapters 2, 3

The constant refrain "my soul," justifies the title sometimes used, "The Young Man's book." Reading chapters 1 to 7, which form the first section of Proverbs, we have two voices – the first, uttering words of wisdom, understanding, knowledge, prudence, instruction and discretion; the other, uttering words of folly, villainy, stupidity, simplicity and ignorance. The two ways our Lord referred to are also here: *the way of wisdom, the narrow way* – "Blessed are all they who keep therein"; *the way of folly, the broad way* – "Whose ways are in the depths of hell." It has been well said that one feature is worthy of note: there is no line from Solomon's pen which palliates Solomon's follies. We cannot read these chapters without realizing that Solomon is the most vehement of sacred moralists against those things by which he, himself, was most easily ensnared. Do you live in verses 5-7 of chapter 3?

Chapters 4-7

These chapters contain Solomon's advice for young men. Yet the wisdom enshrined therein is for all. Filial impiety (7:20,21), evil company (4:14-19), untruthfulness (6:17), sloth (6:6-11), and contention (3:30) are all warned against. Commenting on the results of laziness (6:9-11), Dr. H. A. Ironside has this apt remark: "Sleeping in time of labour is out of place in a scene where man has been commanded to eat his bread by the sweat of his face. No one has the right to count on God to undertake for him in temporal matters, who is not himself characterized by energy and wakefulness." For one who was fabulously wealthy, it is striking to note that Solomon came to realize that there were many things better than gold and jewels. "Wisdom is better than rubies, and all things that may be desired are not to be compared to it" (8:11). Are you rich in such heavenly treasures?

Chapters 8, 9

These two chapters are in praise of wisdom. Without doubt, chapter 8 exhibits our Lord Jesus Christ with unusual clearness, who was made unto us "wisdom." Dr. C. I. Scofield's comment is suggestive: "That wisdom is more than the personification of an attribute of God, or of the will of God as best for man, but is a distinct adumbration of Christ, is sure to the devout mind. Proverbs 8:22-36 with John 1:1-3; Colossians 1:17, can refer to nothing else than the Eternal Son of God." An intimate insight into Christ's happy relationship with the Father can be gleaned from 8:30,31. Are we conscious of our simplicity? Then we are in a fit condition to receive the heavenly wisdom that God offers His own (James 1). Some of us are far too wise for the Lord to help (8:5). Of course, chapter 9 warns us against a wrong kind of simplicity.

Chapter 10

In this beginning of the third section of the book, we have the development of the twin truths of wickedness and righteousness. A marked contrast is maintained. The folly of six and the wisdom of righteousness are clearly set forth. Each verse stands by itself and consists of two portions in which wisdom and folly are emphasized in a striking way. Truly, there is nothing to equal these quick, pithy sentences of sanctified wis-

dom. Take a phrase like this: "Love covereth all sins" (verse 12)! What a vista of truth it presents! The sacrificial love of God, as seen at Calvary, makes possible the covering of our sin. Do you know the blessedness of having your sin covered? Another precious gem is in verse 20. The enriching blessings of the Lord have no sting in them. The addition of sorrows comes when we turn from the Lord and seek for the so-called pleasure and treasure offered by the world.

Chapters 11-13

The contrast between righteousness and wickedness continues. Dr. Ironside, dealing with 11:24,25, asserts that God's plan for increase and enlargement can be found here. If, greedily, we hold what we have, it is not long before our hand is empty.

A man there was, though some did count
     him mad,
The more he cast away, the more he had.
He that bestows his goods upon the poor,
Shall have as much again, and ten times
     more.

The proverb in 12:4 is extended for us in the last chapter of the book. Are we among the number uttering those good words making glad the heavy-hearted (12:25)? In these days of juvenile delinquency, parents should read 13:24. If the rod is spared, the child is spoiled. The old-fashioned, firm handling of children is discounted in these modern days. This is one reason why children grow up to be so wayward.

Chapters 14, 15

Different proverbs can be found relating to the same subject. Link together 13:17, 14:5 and 25, and you will discover a message on faithful witness-bearing. For national life, the wise saying of 14:34 deserves to be published abroad. The word "better," as used by Solomon in this book, is worth tracing, as Dr. R. S. Beal has ingeniously done. "As in the book of Hebrews, 'better things' stand out in marked contrast to the bitter things of the world, the flesh and the devil. Beholding the 'better' things in Proverbs, the Spirit leads us into a deeper and richer understanding of the Christian experience." Here are two "better" things. The fear of the Lord is "better" than great treasure with its trouble (15:16). "Better is a dinner of herbs where love is, than a stalled ox and hatred therewith" (15:17). No matter how poor a family may be, if the atmosphere is saturated with love, frugal meals become a feast.

Chapter 16

From the series of contrasts before us, one or two choice gems can be gathered. Are there times when you want to know how to answer certain people aright? Well, look at verse 1. Pride is one thing God cannot stand (verses 5,18,19). According to verse 7, enemies can be made friends. God is never guilty of giving short weight. His scales are never tinkered with (verse 11). Trust and happiness are twins (verse 20). Note the three-fold influence of pleasant words (verse 24). Are your words always pleasant? What a powerful gospel sermon could be preached from verse 25! The only right way for a man to escape death is to be found in John 14:6. What damage whisperers can cause (verse 28)! Characters are so easily slain by a whisper. Repeating a matter separates friends (17:9). How do your ears react when a whisperer comes your way? Do they close instinctively to anything unsavory?

Chapters 17, 18

An expressive contrast opens chapter 17 – another "better." A loaded table is no guarantee of a tranquil home. Grandfathers and fathers can or should find consolation in 17:6. Two proverbs can be combined in these two chapters, namely 17:17 and 18:24. How true it is that a brother is born for adversity! When trials overtake us and we need the counsel and comfort of a friend, God raises up one who is better than a brother. Our blessed Lord Himself is the friend who sticketh closer than even human friends. The best fail, but Jesus is the friend who loveth at all times. What an impregnable fortress He is (18:10)! James must have had verse 21 of chapter 18 before him when he wrote his discourse on the tongue. Jesus likewise has reminded us that our words either justify or condemn us (Matthew 12:37). Are we being daily saved from lip-sin?

Chapter 19

A saying of vital importance opens this chapter. Separation from the blemish of sin and shame, even although we may be poor, is more to be desired than the wealth of the world. Righteousness is to be desired before riches. Do we emulate the discretion of verse 11? Let us never magnify the faults of others. Nothing can make us as sympathetic over the failures of another as a more thorough knowledge of our own heart. "Let him that is without sin cast the first stone." Jesus was the only one without sin, yet He never threw a stone. The chastisement of verse 18 can be linked to Hebrews 12:3-15. What a blessed proverb and promise is to be found in verse 23! Think of the triad of blessings associated with fear of the Lord – *life, satisfaction* and *immunity from evil.* Certain judgment awaits all scorners and fools (verse 29).

Chapters 20, 21

Multitudes of drink-sodden men and women can tell us that wine is indeed a mocker (20:1). Any person claiming sinlessness is ignorant of verse 9. John agrees with this question (I John 1:10, 2:1). There are some ten proverbs taken up with honesty and fraud. Find others bearing the same sentiment, as 20:10. What priceless gifts sight and hearing are! Do you bless God for hearing ears and seeing eyes (20:12)? Conscience is described for us in 20:27. God's sovereignty is recognized in many proverbs (21:1). Three aspects of sin are mentioned in 21:4. Three benefits accrue from righteousness and mercy (21:21). Sometimes silence is a blessing (21:23). The only way to keep our lips from slips is to keep them closed when speech would be disastrous. Solomon elsewhere has said: "There is a time to keep silence, and a time to speak" (Ecclesiastes 3:7).

Chapter 22

Many words of the wise (verse 17) are to be found in this chapter. Distinctions of earth, for example, vanish in the Lord's presence (verse 2). Would that all parents knew of the proverb on child-training in verse 6! The way every child should go is *in Him who is the way.* Look at the reward of purity in verse 11. In the section commencing with the exhortation to hear the words of the wise (22:17-24), we have practical injunctions, various moral precepts and important cautions. Modernists would do well to read verse 28. How guilty they are of removing ancient landmarks of our faith, set by our forefathers. The infallibility of Scripture, the Virgin Birth of our Lord, Christ's deity, His efficacious death, and His physical Resurrection – these are some of the ancient landmarks that liberals would try to remove, but they cannot. Truth abides.

Chapter 23

What unforgettable proverbs confront us in this chapter renowned for its terrible picture of the physical, mental and moral evil of strong drink. Look at verses 2, 7, 21. Dr. A. T. Pierson speaks of the section 20-35 as "the witness of God's Word against wine," and then quotes fourteen particulars: "Tendency to angry quarrels, inarticulate utterances, physical injury, bleared vision, excess, unhealthy craving, fascination, impure lusts, perversity of feelings, irregularity of walk, unaccountable bruises, unnatural torpor, and despotic appetite." What evils come upon those guilty of indulging in the cursed liquor of hell! Would that we could persuade those who are drink-sodden to read the solemn warnings of this chapter!

Chapter 24

The inequalities of life are hard to understand. Evil men too often succeed (verses 1,19). Within the Bible, sin is described in many ways, but the description given in verse 9 should cause us to take heed to thoughts as well as actions (21:4). As those who know what it is to be strengthened with all might by God's Spirit in the inner man, we should never droop beneath the burden of sorrow. If we faint in the day of adversity, then we fail to impress the Christless with the reality of grace (verse 10). Consideration and compassion for those who fall by the way is taught in verses 17 and 18. How patient God is when we stumble! The closing section of the chapter, verses 27 to the end, is in praise of conscientious work. Altogether, there are some 38 proverbs scattered throughout the book taken up with industry and sloth. God save us from a nettle-covered field (verse 31)!

Chapter 25

Among the proverbs before us, copied out by the king's men, the first is expressive (verse 2). God concealed so many treasures in nature, but man is finding them out. And such treasure-hunts are exciting. Does each day find you rising in the estimation of your heavenly prince (verses 6,7)? Throughout his book, Solomon has a good deal to say about domestic problems, and he was a qualified expert along such lines. One of his "betters" is in verse 24, where he has sharp criticism of the over-powering kind of woman. A nagging husband, who tries to domineer, is likewise guilty of driving a dear one away. Too many men think only of their own comfort and pleasure, and selfishly make a hell out of home. Betrayed confidence is hard to bear (verse 19). Have you an enemy? Look at verses 21 and 22 and see how you can best treat a foe. How descriptive verse 25 is of the glorious Gospel of grace!

Chapter 26

Some of the most expressive moral and religious precepts of the book are in this chapter. Illustrations from nature and life are used with telling effect (verses 1,2). In verse 4 we are reminded of the folly of sinking to the egotistical level of a fool; verse 5 tells us that the shallowness of some fools needs exposure. Note other references to fools in the chapter (verses 7-12). Slothfulness is strongly condemned (verses 13-15). Sluggards, deceivers, talebearers, contentious people and liars are fittingly described in the rest of the chapter. "There are seven abominations in his heart" (verse 25). Have you discovered how desperately wicked and deceitful your heart is? Each of us need to cry with David: "Create in me a clean heart, O Lord."

Chapter 27

Commenting on verses 5 and 6 – look at them – Dr. R. S. Beal reminds us that it is far better to hear the truth than to be lulled to sleep by flattery. "We are given to extolling human merits and praising the deeds of the flesh. Itching ears do not like to be told the truth about sin in the life (I Timothy 5:20; Proverbs 9:8)." How bene-

ficial it would be if only we were as eager
to listen to criticism of ourselves as to commendation! It is only when we see ourselves as God and others see us, that we
can have a true perspective of our lives.
All through Proverbs, Solomon deals with
man's relation to his neighbors. "The tested
sympathy of a neighbour is far better than
the untried affection of a brother that is
afar off" (verse 10). Turn to 11:12 and 14:12,
and see what happens to us when we fail
in our obligation to those around. How expressive is a proverb like verse 15, for *men*
as well as women!

Chapter 28

Those of us who are somewhat timid in
witnessing for Christ should gather courage
from the opening verse of the chapter before
us. The secret of spiritual understanding is
in verse 5. Prayer can become an abomination (verse 9). Open confession is good for
the soul (verse 13). What nation is rightly
characterized by a bear (verse 15)? The salvation of verse 17 is not salvation from the
guilt of sin (verse 18). Many walk uprightly
who are not saved, as we understand salvation. They may experience deliverance
from perverse ways. It always pays to be
industrious. God never places a premium
on laziness (verses 19,20). If we would be
prosperous, let us live in verse 25. There is
a vast difference between trusting in the Lord
and trusting in our own heart. Which are you
doing (verses 25,26)? Combine 19:17 with
28:17, and see what we gain when we share
what we have with those less fortunate than
ourselves.

Chapter 29

This chapter opens with one of the most
solemn warnings to the unsaved to be found
in the Bible. A similar warning can be noted
in 6:15. Such danger signals exclude any
hope beyond the grave–"without remedy."
As we die, so are we when we rise on the
other side. There is no purgatory. If men
die hardened, they remain that way throughout eternity. How apt verse 2 is in these
days of ruthless dictatorship! Multitudes are
mourning because of unrighteous, wicked rulers. It is to be hoped you are not the type
of a fool referred to in verse 11. What a

message for our hearts is in the saying:
"Where there is no vision, the people perish" (verse 18)! Myriads, at home and abroad,
perish in their sins because of our lack of
vision. If only we could be borne along
by Calvary's passion and compassion for
the lost. May it be so!

Chapter 30

Agur, and others mentioned at the outset
of this chapter, are unknown. Many guesses
have been made. While the words forming
the chapter were addressed to Ithiel and
Ucal, the philosophy they contain is for
the hearts of all. Agur's expressive prayer
(verses 7-9) can be prayed by any of us.
A gospel picture can be found in the natural
facts of verses 24-28. "Preparation for future
need speaks of turning to Christ in the
present before the wintry blasts of judgment
fall. Abiding among the rocks suggests finding safety in Christ. Going forth by bands,
without a visible leader, depicts those who
follow Christ, the unseen leader at God's
right hand. The power of faith is illustrated
by the spider taking hold in king's palaces."
If you meet anyone who says he does not
believe a word of the Bible, try wringing
his nose (verse 33)!

Chapter 31

Who King Lemuel, whose name appears
in the opening verse of this last chapter, was,
we are not told. Some scholars say it was
Solomon himself, using an alias. Kitto says:
"If we find any difficulty in identifying
Lemuel with Solomon, the dignity and authority of the book are not in any way
affected. . . . This description here given of
a virtuous woman and a good wife is unequalled in all literature." If only we could
persuade this drunken age to give heed to
the opening admonition of this chapter, we
should have happier homes and a nobler
society. Yes, and if only we had more women
answering to the portrait here given, this
would be a far better nation. No nation can
ever rise above the level of its mothers.
God grant us myriads of mothers whose
price is above rubies because of their faith
in God and their virtuous living.

ECCLESIASTES

The name of this most mournful and perplexing book means "an official speaker in an assembly – the Preacher" (1:1). Largely quoted in the New Testament (7:2 with Matthew 5:3,4 etc.), there is no doubt that it was written by Solomon when in a sad backsliding condition. *Ecclesiastes* is thus "the dramatic autobiography of the King's life and experience when he strayed away from God, and the various methods he tried of securing happiness." Among conspicuous key words and phrases indicating the writer's long search for pleasure and satisfaction we have *under the sun* – 29 times, *vanity* – 37 times, *upon the earth* – seven times. The book begins and ends with the *Law* (1:3 and 12:13), and the statement, "the conclusion of the whole matter" removes all doubt as to the author's design. As the Law was designed to lead men to Christ, so *Ecclesiastes* was written to lead those "under the sun" to the Son above the sun seated in the heavenly places (Hebrews 1:1). The main lesson of the book is indicated by the phrase "Vanity of vanities; all is vanity." Apart from a God-directed life there is nothing save the emptiness of human life, "the unsatisfying character of worldly pleasures; the profitless outcome of worldly pursuits; uncertainty as to whether the best human prudence can secure real and lasting happiness. As to the book as a whole "it is pervaded by belief in the God who rules the world, though it may be in a way incomprehensible to man." Having to live under the sun may be yet be found abiding in God's beloved Son. "This is the whole duty of man" (12:13,14).

Chapter 1

The title of this book denotes, "Preacher," and comes from a Hebrew word meaning, *an assembler or convener.* It occurs seven times in the book (1:1,2,12; 7:27; 12:8,9,10). While there is a division of thought as to the exact authorship, we see no reason to reject Solomon, who was the son of David and king in Jerusalem, as the writer of this somewhat mournful book. The theme developed in the twelve chapters is set forth in this opening one: "All is vanity." This key verse occurs thirty-nine times in the book, and only thirty-three times in the rest of the Bible. The word "vanity," means *emptiness,* and comes from the root, "to exhale or to evaporate." Hence the idea of a vapor is expressed, suggesting something transient and unsubstantial. As used by Solomon, it indicates the unsatisfactoriness of all earthly things apart from Christ.

Chapter 2

Continuing his theme, Solomon depicts the weary round of life. He committed the folly of taking wrong roads to reach the city of heart-satisfaction. As a king, with unlimited means at his disposal, he tried to gratify himself with every kind of luxury, but no satisfaction could be found. He gathers up his experiences into one lament: "All is vanity and vexation of spirit." Can you answer the question why finite man is not satisfied with *temporary joy* (verse 10), *wisdom* (verse 13), and *accomplishment* (verse 24)? "Under the sun" (verse 11), is another key phrase of the book, being used twenty-nine times, and nowhere else in the Bible. It is equivalent to "upon the earth," another phrase often employed by Solomon. The writer does not get "above the sun," where true satisfaction alone can be found, until the end of the book is reached.

Chapter 3

As you read the opening portion of today's chapter, make a list of the things the writer really believed about the nature of God and His activities in connection with man. What a proof of immortality we have in verse eleven: "He hath set eternity (not *world*) in their heart"! Within the breast of savage and saint alike is the belief of an after-life. God's perfect and final accomplishment is emphasized in the declaration: "Whatsoever God doeth, it shall be forever." This is one reason why men should fear Him. It is true that men and beasts alike go to the same place, that is, the grave. Both return to dust. Unlike men, however, beasts are not immortal. In this do we have preeminence over the animal creation.

Chapter 4

Solomon's theme unfolds with a discourse on the oppression and iniquities of life. He observes the wrongs practiced in the world: oppression, the condition of all labor, and the state of solitude and isolation are all reviewed, and upon these the same verdict is pronounced: "Vanity and vexation of spirit." Note the word "better" in this chapter. Solomon, like modern civilization, sought for a remedy for loneliness, but found it not (verses 4-11). In our life and labors, do we experience the strength and blessing of "the three-fold cord"? Who or what can break the power of the Trinity? When it comes to our witness, we can never act as "lone wolves." "Without me," said the Lord Jesus, "ye can do nothing." A good many past kings might have profited by a reading of verse thirteen. Are you walking "under the sun" or living above it?

Chapter 5

We now have practical observations on religion and riches. Solomon had experienced much of both and knew whereof he spoke. Read this chapter slowly and notice some of the sound philosophy it holds. We have, for example, *behavior in church,* which is something many church-goers know little about (verses 1,2); *solemn and sane vows should be kept* (verses 4,5); *the more we have, the more we want* (verse 10); it is folly to allow our possessions to possess us. Wealth cannot buy sleep (verse 12). How differently would the rich use their money if only they remembered verse nineteen: "What thou hast, thou didst receive"! Are we using all that we have as that which is God-given? Apart from divine bounty we are bankrupt. Our money, whether much or little, is a gift of God.

Chapter 6

We here face a continuation of Solomon's dissertation on riches and religion, discussed in view of man's inevitable end. In outlining the evil common among men under the sun, the "preacher" has some true things to say. What is the use of the richest of food if a person has no appetite to enjoy it? This is as bad as a person having a good appetite but no food to satisfy it. Evidently the "preacher" never had the clearer revelation contained in the New Testament, for all men do not go to one place (verse 6). While all are travelers to eternity, there are two stopping places – heaven and hell. The only answer to much of the cynicism of this chapter is faith in Christ. If we are His, then our lives are not vainly spent, and our days are not gone as a shadow. Paul could say: "For me to live is Christ," and such a life never ends in vanity.

Chapter 7

Is it not pitiable that one like Solomon recommends apathy? The righteous and the wicked share alike, he says, so why be concerned? Make the best of things as they are, and without fretfulness or impatience seek to enjoy what is assigned to you. What morbid philosophy! Solomon says: "Sorrow is better than laughter." Paul says: "Rejoice in the Lord alway, and again I say, rejoice." How hollow are the pleasures of the worldling (verse 6)! Which are you, patient in spirit or proud in spirit (verse 8)? Compare verse thirteen with chapter one, verse fifteen. Have you any crooked thing in your life for God to straighten? In how many ways can you apply the phrase: "God also hath set the one over against the other"? Do you believe the "preacher" is right in his affirmation of verse twenty? What do you think of the last verse?

Chapter 8

The theme of the book that "all is vanity" is here unfolded, in view of the mystery of divine providences. Christ is certainly the king, in whose word there is power (verse 4). Think of His miracles! Is the blessing of obedience ours (verse 5)? "No discharge in that war" (verse 8). How true this is of death! All must obey the summons when it comes. Is it not tragic to die wicked, after having come and gone from the place of the holy (verse 10)? Dead and forgotten! Think of the multitudes around who believe that there is nothing better under the sun than to eat, drink and be merry (verse 15)! They live only for the present and the passing. They only live to eat. Is it not better to eat to live? The "preacher" tells us that he applied his heart to know wisdom (verse 16) but it was a one-sided wisdom, resulting in error and pessimism that he gained.

Chapter 9

The "preacher" is still perplexed; all things come alike to all, he says; therefore try to get along the best way possible. Some of the world's wrong standards of values are herewith given. All things do not come alike to all. A living dog is not better than a dead lion. The natural man can see no difference between the two. Happily we are not shut up to human reasonings when we come to the hereafter. With the clearer revelation of the New Testament in hand, we know that Christ has brought life and immortality to light through His Gospel. Verse eight is one that we can apply to ourselves if we desire purity and power. All of us need to obey the injunction of the first part of verse ten. Under the sun, the lame sometimes take the prey (verse 11). One bad apple in a barrel can ruin all the others in time (verse 18).

Chapter 10

A study of the wisdom-maxims, as here set forth, proves the utter futility of wisdom if it is not wisdom from above. Seeking wisdom merely for itself ends in disappointment. It may be that many find little profit in reading this Book of Ecclesiastes. Of course, it was not written to satisfy the Christian. No matter what road he traveled, Solomon fell short of his objective. Restlessness, weariness and monotony make up the book. Vexations will overtake the best of saints but they never disturb the rest of the spirit that Christ imparts. Are there any "dead flies" (verse 1) spoiling your "sweet savour of Christ"? In verses eight and nine, the law of retribution, a manifestation of the relation between cause and effect, works also in the spiritual realm, Paul affirms (Galatians 6: 7,8). It may be that the phrase, "a little

bird told me," had its rise in the last verse of this chapter.

Chapter 11

After passing under review all works done under the sun, the "preacher" reaches the end of his investigation with the reiteration of a cheerless creed and a half-truth: "Vanity of vanities." Apart from God all is vanity; but when He is first and last, so many things that Solomon sought merely for their own sakes, can be rightly used and made to contribute to life's good. In this chapter, revealing the best things possible to the natural man, there are one or two fine truths to underline. If you are discouraged because of the paucity of results in service, cling to verse one. If you are tempted to be somewhat stingy in what you give to God or to others, of your time and treasure, read verse six. If you are young, strong and free, and believe in having your "fling," as you call it, give heed to the warning of verses nine and ten.

Chapter 12

In order to understand the poetry of this chapter, read it aloud two or three times. After his call and challenge to youth, Solomon goes on to describe beautifully the infirmities of old age: sun, moon and stars – earth's comforts; clouds – trials; keepers of the house – arms and hands; strong men, bowing themselves – thighs and legs; grinders cease because they are few – the teeth; those that look out of the windows – the eyes; doors shall be shut – the lips; rise up at the voice of the bird – light sleep or insomnia of old age; the sound of grinding – the digestive organs; the daughters of music – ears; afraid of that which is high – reason; the almond tree shall flourish – the white hairs and gray; the grasshopper shall be a burden – little troubles weigh down; silver cord loosed – spinal cord broken; golden bowl broken – skull emptied; pitcher broken – respiratory organs; and wheel broken at cistern – heart stoppage.

SONG OF SOLOMON

Commenting upon the order and succession of *Ecclesiastes* and the *Song of Solomon,* Dr. A. T. Pierson says that in the former book of Solomon, "man finds his soul too great for this world to feed and fill: all is vanity; there is no profit under the sun. In the latter book, man, looking above the sun, finds in God what not only fills his soul, but cannot be contained. The sea fills the cup, but the cup does not hold the sea. And so from *vanity (Ecclesiastes)* we come to *verity (The Song of Solomon).*" While we have dealt with the book before us by chapters, Pierson suggests that it might be found helpful to disregard the old divisions of chapters, and divide this dialogue into six sections, beginning respectively at chapters 1:2; 2:7; 3:6; 5:2; 6:10 and 8:5, and then follow the outline –

1. The Inscription 1:1
2. The Bride in the King's Chamber; His visit, Her dream, and the Royal Espousals 1:2 – 5:1
3. The King's Wife; Seeking and Finding, The Return Home 5:2 – 8:14.

While there are those who question the inclusion of this oriental poem in the Sacred Canon, the Jews thought of it as "The Holy of Holies of Scripture." To the spiritual mind the dialogue between Bridegroom and Bride typifies the mystery of Christ and His Church (Ephesians 5:25-32. See Psalm 45; Isaiah 62:5; Jeremiah 3).

Chapter 1

King Solomon composed and collected one thousand and five songs (I Kings 4:32), and among them is this one, called "The Song of Songs," seeing it is the chiefest and choicest among the collection. Bernard, the spiritual song-writer of old, commenting on the song said: "It is the Song of Songs because other songs must be learned first – but this is the first of all the rest; grace alone can teach it, experience alone can learn it." Without a spiritual mind it is impossible to enter into the spirit of the Song, illustrating as it does the union and communion existing between Christ as the Bridegroom, and the Church as the Bride. This chapter bubbles over with the deep,

boundless joy the Lord and His saints find in each other. Are we as lost in our contemplation of our loving and lovely Lord, as the Shulamite was in her lover? Let us guard against the folly of trying to keep other vineyards at the expense of neglecting our own.

Chapter 2

Many interpretations have been given of the setting or plot of the renowned song. Solomon, as the shepherd, wooed and won the Shulamite. Knowing nothing of his wealth and honor, she loved him for what he was. She had no idea that her ardent lover was a king in the disguise of a shepherd. Once she became his, then his true station was revealed. Love's charges – "I charge you" – will be noted throughout the song. Are we as quick to recognize the voice of our heavenly Beloved as the Shulamite was able to discover her lover's tones? Trace in the description of spring (verses 11-13), seven signs of a life lived in unbroken fellowship with the Lord. Do we share the bride's privilege of full communion, "the secret of the stairs" (verse 14)? By the foxes and little foxes, we can understand the conspicuous and less conspicuous faults robbing us of fruitfulness. Too many of us are subject to the little hindering things that creep in all unawares to spoil the vine of blessing.

Chapter 3

One has to guard against extremes in the spiritual application of a book like this. There are, however, many precious cameos of Christ and His own in this love-ode. This we know; no soul ever seeks the heavenly Bridegroom in vain. The One our heart loveth is ever near and real. He is the One, so bedecked with fragrant spices, journeying with us through the dreary wilderness of this world. His garments smell of myrrh, aloes and cassia, and as the merchant, He makes us the recipients of all His costly powders. Christ is a mightier King than Solomon; and His valiant ones have greater might and honor. If the scene described in the last half of the chapter is a wedding procession, and the bride is speaking, then what a day it will be for her when the marriage of the Lamb is come. This is why it will be the day of the gladness of His heart; and we, united to Him, shall not only share His joy but assist Him in His governmental control of all things, as He takes over the universal dominion of the earth.

Chapter 4

For language of exquisite beauty this chapter is unequalled. Within it, we have the bridegroom expressing the deep, sincere feelings of his heart, as he dwells upon the unique attractiveness of his bride. How glowingly he describes his loved one's personal features! Prophetically, we have the rejoicing of the Lord over Israel in a coming day. We can also use the chapter to illustrate how precious we are to Christ as His redeemed ones. He has clothed us in spotless righteousness. Our beauty is not of the flesh. We are only perfect and comely in Him, whose beauty is upon us. In ourselves there are plenty of spots, but in Him we are without spot. The chapter concludes with the believer typified as a fruit-bearing garden. Are we bearing much fruit? Can we invite our Beloved to come into the garden of our life and eat His pleasant fruits?

> Like a watered garden,
> Full of fragrance rare,
> Lingering in His presence,
> Let my life appear.

Chapter 5

Heeding the invitation to come into the garden, the bridegroom immediately responds, and eats and drinks abundantly. How the Lord delights to commune with His own! The dream of the Shulamite suggests, does it not, the heavenly Bridegroom outside the door of the Laodicean church? There is also the personal application. Too many of us are occupied with other things. The Lord calls us to sweeter, deeper fellowship with Himself. When we resist His advances He withdraws His overtures. How sensitive true love is! The concluding portion of the chapter (verses 10-16) contains the bride's description of her lovely bridegroom. In her eyes, there is no other so beautiful. She is fascinated by his adorable person.

All of which is wonderfully typical of the believer's estimation of the risen, glorified Lord. How great is His beauty! He is the fairest of all the earth beside! And the wonder is that the humblest believer can say, "This is *my* beloved, and this is my friend."

Chapter 6

Overwhelmed by the Shulamite's description of her beloved, the daughters of Jerusalem want to know where he is, so that they, too, can admire him. Are we so taken up with our lovely Christ, having lives so fragrant with His presence, as to make those around desirous of seeing Him? The Shulamite bears testimony to her loved one's abode, and of their mutual love. "I am my beloved's, and my beloved is mine." But the beloved is not far away, and to him his loved one goes to listen to his praises of her unexcelled loveliness. Would that His own, so precious to His heart of love, were as terrible as an army with banners! If only it could be true of all who are His, "There is not one barren among them!" Four similies of the Church can be found in verse 10. What an arrestive phrase that is, "I went down"! The way *up* is *down*. Our highest place is lying low at our Redeemer's feet. It was the way the Master went. He humbled Himself – God highly exalted Him (Philippians 2:5-11).

Chapter 7

The outline of this chapter, from the helpful notes in *The Pilgrim Bible*, is as follows: *The women of the court describe the Shulamite's beauty* (verses 1-5); *the bridegroom interrupts them with his own praise of her* (verses 6-10); and, *the Shulamite longs for Lebanon* (verses 11-13). Can we say that our stature is like to a palm tree? This particular palm is always straight and upright, never bending or stooping this way or that. It also grows in most unlikely places, thriving in sandy deserts where nothing else would grow. It likewise has a beauty all its own. Thus the application is not far to seek. In the invitation for the beloved to pay her early visit to the vineyards, there is illustrated unbroken fellowship with our Beloved, resulting in genuine soul-worship, the complete yieldedness of all we are and have to Him, and a life of service beneficial to others. May grace be ours to lay up, for Him whom our souls love, "all manner of pleasant fruits, new and old!"

Chapter 8

After the bride's surrender to her bridegroom, as depicted in the last portion of the previous chapter, we would expect an opening such as we have before us. She is "painfully aware of the great gap between her royal Husband and her brothers." He seems to be so far removed from her humble associations. Yet she values fellowship with him above everything else (verse 3). She rests in him, and leans hard upon him (verse 5). Stayed upon Jehovah, we can enjoy rest and safety. Lack of love is often the cause of our departure from Christ. We do not set Him as a seal upon our heart. Love for Him is not as strong as death. Waters of sorrow, adversity, and the world quench our love. The full enjoyment of the Shulamite does not blind her to the need of others. "What shall we do for our sister?" The deeper our love for Christ, the deeper our zeal to reach others for whom He died.

ISAIAH

Approaching the *Prophetic Section* of the Old Testament covering the 17 books from *Isaiah* to *Malachi*, it is necessary to bear in mind that "the key to all prophecy is *The Kingdom of God* – its rise, progress, conflicts and final triumph; from first to last, however various its aspects, in essence and principle it is one and unchangeable." Known as "The Evangelical Prophet," Isaiah gives us prophetic hints of the facts and features of the Messiah, from His cradle to His crown. Chapter 53 – the heart of the Old Testament – anticipates every great truth of the Gospel. The central verse of this central chapter condenses for us the blessed truth of Christ's substitutionary work at Calvary.

> He was wounded for our transgressions; he was bruised for our iniquities; the chastisement of our peace was upon him; and with his stripes we are healed.

For the Bible student there is a rich feast in tracing the *everlastings* in *Isaiah* – constructing from its chapters a life of Christ – noting the prophet's teaching concerning the Holy Spirit, and his thoughts on *Comfort*. As a whole, "The Gospel according to Isaiah," falls into three parts –
1. Denunciatory 1-35, Key verses 1:4; 5:24; 31:1
2. Historical 36-39, Key verse 37:23
3. Consolatory 40-66, Key verses 40:1; 43: 3,14; 49:7; 53:3; 60:17.
With its 66 chapters, Isaiah is a miniature Bible with its 66 Books.

Chapter 1

The opening verse gives us a prologue to the book. Isaiah contains a vision which the Lord gave to the prophet concerning the places and people he mentions in verse 1. The keynote of Isaiah is that God has a remnant, and such a remnant has a glorious future. Keep verse 9 in mind as you endeavor to master the 66 chapters of this book. God's deserved judgment upon Judah and Jerusalem form the burden of this first chapter. All ungrateful children should carefully read verses 2 and 3. Even God knows that a thankless child can be sharper than a serpent's tooth. What a true description of the loathsomeness of sin verse 6 presents! Apart from the balm of Gilead we are hopeless and helpless. There are some things God cannot do. One of them is before us in verses 13-15; He cannot condone mere religious pretense. Religion without regeneration is a stench to His nostrils. Praise God for the glorious Gospel verse 18 proclaims! No wonder Isaiah is spoken of as "the evangelical prophet."

Chapter 2

Again the opening verse is a key to the truth of the chapter. Isaiah was both a *forthteller* and a *foreteller*. As the former, he had a message for his own times; as the latter, he prophesied of an age beyond his own. The first five verses, for example, will never be fulfilled until Christ returns to earth as its rightful Lord and King. In this section Isaiah gives us a vision of the millennial reign of Christ. Not until He comes will the nations learn how to beat their swords into ploughshares. Then, it is interesting to compare the last part of the chapter with the judgment upon Babylon in Revelation 18. Truly prophecy is history written beforehand. The tenor of verses 6-22 is that God abhors pride and idolatry. These are days when arrogant rulers stalk the earth, lauding it over millions of helpless souls. Their lofty looks, however, are to be humbled. They forget they are only men and that their breath is in their nostrils and God can remove it at any given moment. Let us take the chapter as a warning against pride and be found clothed with humility.

Chapter 3

Desolations overtaking Jerusalem and Judah for their sins continue to occupy the mind of Isaiah. How grievously the Jews have had to suffer for their disobedience! During the destruction of Jerusalem in the year A.D. 70, famine was experienced and shameful slavery, when thirty Jews were sold for a penny. Have you ever thought of comparing verses 11 and 12 with Psalm 1 and Matthew 7:13,14? Note the harmony of thought in these three portions. The Jews have suffered much at the hands of Gentiles, but God is to deal with all those who beat His people to pieces (verse 15). Reading of the haughtiness of the daughters of Zion, we realize how God abominates pride in His own people. Fleshly pride of face and of fashion must be scorned. The adornment of a meek and quiet spirit must be sought after if we are not to experience "burning instead of beauty" (verse 24). Says Matthew Henry of the last verse: "If sin be harboured within the walls, lamentation and mourning are near the gates." In these days when there is a tendency to think more of jewelry than of Jesus, and more of clothing than of Christ, it is necessary to live near this chapter.

Chapter 4

Twice over in this short chapter we have the phrase, "in that day," which decides for us the prospective aspect of the chapter. A converted and restored Israel, ready to dwell with the Lord as He returns in glory, is the vision here presented. Providence has wisely ordered it that, on an average of years, there is almost an equality of males and females born into the world. Slaughter and destruction always cut off multitudes of men, leaving a preponderance of women. Jewish women will desire their reproach to be taken away; hence, the seven to one in the opening verse. What great and precious promises will be fulfilled when Israel finally comes into her own! Christ will be seen as the beautiful Branch of the Lord. Thoroughly purged and fully restored, Israel will be holy unto the Lord. No longer "scattered and peeled" (18:2) among the nations and constantly persecuted, but dwelling in Zion in safety, her defense will be the Lord. He will be her tabernacle, place of refuge, and a covert. Presently the Lord Jesus offers Himself as such to all His believing people.

Chapter 5

Two divisions are clearly defined in this judgment chapter. The first seven verses supply us with the beautiful yet pathetic "Song of the Vineyard," which should be read along with the *Parable of the Vineyard* in Matthew 21:33-44. Within this first section we have God's wonderful love for man and man's rebellion against, and rejection of, such amazing love. Israel's tragedy is our own. God has sought to make our lives as fruitful vineyards. Alas, we have produced briers and thorns instead of luscious grapes!

In the last section of the chapter we have the six woes pronounced upon Israel. Among the wild grapes the privileged people had brought forth, love of the world and fleshly indulgences were the two that Isaiah singled out and upon which he uttered his woes. The thirteenth verse reminds us of the bondage of ignorance. God has to say of some of us, as He did of Israel: "My people are gone into captivity, because they have no knowledge." May grace be ours to grow, not only in grace but also in the knowledge of Christ and His Word!

Chapter 6

A fitting caption for this renowned chapter would be, "The Making of a Prophet."

It would seem as if Isaiah, by his vision of the sovereignty and holiness of God, was "set apart for the prophetic office by a more express or explicit commission." In the previous chapter Isaiah had plenty of woes for others; now he has a deep one for his own heart. It is easier to condemn others than oneself. Isaiah's transforming vision falls into three parts. He had *a vision of a throne* (verses 1-4). From a grave of an earthly sovereign his gaze was directed to the throne of an eternal King. He had *a vision of a heart* (verses 5-7). In seeing God, the prophet saw himself. Divine holiness reflected human uncleanness. He had *the vision of a sphere* (verses 8-13). Cleansed, he was commissioned. Purged, he could now proclaim. Note the construction of the commission: "Whom shall I (singular) send, and who will go for us (plural)." Our Lord Himself is the divine speaker (Matthew 28:18-20), but when we go in response to the call we go on behalf of the Trinity. In his obedience Isaiah came to know that God's hard places are difficult to fill, and that only His strength avails.

Chapter 7

This important, prophetic chapter deserves more space than we can devote to it in these comments. Here we have the mixture of judgment and mercy. In the first nine verses "the outcasts of Israel," probably the ten tribes who, under Jeroboam, formed the northern kingdom, are condemned for their evil confederacy. The middle division, verses 10-16, takes us beyond Ahaz to Christ. Here the virgin birth of Christ, as well as the plainness and simplicity of His life on earth, is clearly foretold. That He came as the promised Immanuel is evident from the birth narratives of Matthew and Luke. The concluding section of the chapter contains the prediction of the Assyrian desolation of Judah. How bitterly the people suffered for their departure from God's revealed Word and will! These words were also "written both for our comfort and for our admonition." Judgment is symbolized as God shaving with a razor (verse 20). It is also unique to note that He can whistle, or hiss, as the fly and the bee (verse 18). When we think of the descriptive language Isaiah uses, we can understand his reputation as the chief of the writing prophets.

Chapter 8

While this chapter, and the next four, practically form one discourse, yet we take them separately and indicate their significance. "Signs and wonders" (verse 18) is the key phrase of the chapter before us. Such a key verse, of course, reaches its larger and final reference in Christ and His own people (Hebrews 2:13,14). The destruction of the confederate kingdoms of Syria and Israel by the Assyrians is declared in the first four verses. Then follows a description of the conquest of the proud victorious prince (verses 5-8). Next comes counsel to the true saints of God (verses 9-18). When we find ourselves hemmed in by hostile forces, let us gather comfort from the fact that "God is with us." When John Wesley was dying, he triumphantly declared: "The best of all is, God is with us." The chapter concludes with a strong warning not to seek after familiar spirits. Spiritualism, or spiritism, stands condemned by verse 19. Our only infallible source of light, guidance and comfort is "the law and the testimony." Multitudes are being "driven to darkness" simply because they are rejecting the illuminating Word of God.

Chapter 9

The first part of this great chapter continues the melancholy strain of the previous chapter. But those walking in darkness are to see a great light. A divine Child is the only hope of Israel, as He is also of the world. So the Messiah's government and dominion are given prominent place. In the fullness of time Christ came as Immanuel – God's Son and Mary's Child. As a Son, He was given; as a Child, He was born. The world yet awaits His advent as the Prince of Peace. When He does appear to usher in His reign, then "of the increase of his government and peace there shall be no end." When He ascends "the throne of David," all promises and prophesies related to Israel will be blessedly realized. The threatenings contained in the last section have a double application. They are directly related to Ephraim and Samaria, but look beyond them to all the enemies of the throne and kingdom of Christ, the Son of David. What a terrible day it will be, for all who despise divine rule, when the wrath of the Lord of hosts is manifested.

Chapter 10

We could label this tenth chapter, "Going Home," seeing that it is taken up with the return of the remnant. The key verse is "The remnant shall return, even the remnant of Jacob, unto the mighty God" (verse 21). While God permitted Assyria to punish His disobedient people, Assyria herself will not escape divine vengeance. "The glory of her high looks" must vanish. Having spoiled Samaria, Assyria will come to know complete impoverishment (verses 1-19). God's protection and preservation of His own is full of encouragement for the saints of every age (verses 20-27). Is there not a present application of verse 27: "The yoke shall be destroyed because of the anointing"? Are you under a yoke? Do you find yourself in bondage to some worldly desire or fleshly lust? Well, the Spirit's anointing can quickly destroy the yoke and set you gloriously free. At last all formidable enemies are to be subjugated. Their haughtiness will be humbled. Proud, arrogant rulers are having their day; but when God's Son is set upon His holy hill, then He will break the defiant hordes of earth in pieces (verses 28-34).

Chapter 11

The notes of Dr. C. I. Scofield are worthy of consideration as this messianic chapter is studied: "The order of events in Isaiah 10 and 11 is noteworthy. Isaiah 10 gives the distress of the Remnant in Palestine in the Great Tribulation . . . Isaiah 11 immediately follows with its glorious picture of the kingdom-age . . . Precisely the same order is found in Revelation 19, 20. . . . This (eleventh) chapter is a prophetic picture of the glory of the future kingdom." In verse 1, we have *the King's pedigree;* in verses 2-9, *His power;* and in verses 10-16, *His peace.* What a day it will be for this sin-cursed world when "the earth will be full of the knowledge of the Lord, as the waters cover the sea"! With all His enemies put down, and His kingdom set up, "His rest shall be glorious." Jews and Gentiles alike are to participate in the blessings of His reign. All barriers are to be removed, so

that the peoples can find their way to Him who will stand as their Ensign.

Jesus shall reign wher'er the sun
Does its successive journeys run;
His kingdom spread from shore to shore,
Till moons shall wax and wane no more.

Chapter 12

This is not only the shortest chapter in Isaiah but one of the sweetest. Prophetically, it describes the worship of the millennial host. All those forming the kingdom are to be a singing people. The chapter appears to be in two halves. In the first three verses, the personal note is prominent. The personal pronouns "I" and "my" show that any saint can lay hold of the Lord as the prophet describes. I can make Him "my salvation," "my strength," "my song." As for the many "wells of salvation" from which we can draw refreshing water, what joy they produce! The last half of the chapter is more general, although applying to the same period. Note the repetition of the phrase, "in that day" (verses 1,4).

These are fearful days and many are afraid. This chapter offers men in the world, and a world of men, a cure for despair. "Trust, and not be afraid." Faith and fear can never exist together. The one expels the other. The Holy One in our midst is our salvation; if He be our salvation, He will be our strength; and as we appropriate Him as our strength, we come to know Him as our song.

Chapter 13

One phase of the vision which Isaiah received was that of the burden of Babylon so clearly defined in this chapter. The word "burden" Scofield remarks, "is a heavy, weighty thing . . . concerning Babylon it is heavy because the wrath of God is in it, and grievous for the prophet to declare." We agree that the "Babylon" is used symbolically by the prophet, and that it stands "for the world of corrupt power and corrupted religion." The judgment of the Gentile nations occupies the first sixteen verses. What terror will overtake the godless of earth when "the day of the Lord is at hand"! Isaiah says: "Therefore shall all hands be

faint, and every man's heart shall melt."
Great slaughter will produce a scarcity of
men, so that a man will become more precious than gold. Coming to the description
of the destruction of Babylon, given by the
prophet in verses 17-22, we have New Testament authority for the swiftness and com-
pleteness of judgment: "In one hour has her
judgment come" (Revelation 18:10). It would
seem as if we are fast approaching the final
overthrow of the fancied greatness, pride, and
haughty glory of the world.

Chapter 14

The first eight verses of this revolutionary
chapter serve to prove that the Lord is the
covenant-keeping God. In spite of the unfaithfulness of Israel, covenants made on her
behalf will never be broken. "He will yet
choose Israel, and settle them in their own
land." While a few thousand Jews did return
to Jerusalem in the time of Ezra and Nehemiah, the final fulfilment of God's promise
awaits Christ's return to earth. Divine judgment upon Israel's satanic foe and all foes
is poetically described in verses 9-11. What
joy will be Israel's when her cruel oppressor
is made to endure deserved torments! The
next section (verses 14-17) is important, dealing as it does with the original majesty of
the devil, that is, before he became the
devil. As the highest angelic creature, great
wisdom and beauty were his. But pride of
heart caused him to lose his name as Luci-
fer, "the bright morning star," and become
Satan, the adversary of both God and man.
The doom of Babylon is foretold by Isaiah
(verses 18-27). When God arises against the
godless hordes of earth, how complete will
their destruction be! The last burden (verses
28-32) is related to Palestine. There is the
tendency these days, when we hear a good
deal about the love and goodness of God,
to forget His severity – a severity that will
result in the thorough destruction of evil
forces.

Chapter 15

One cannot do better, in introducing his
comment of this chapter – with its burden,
or heavy message regarding Moab – than to
quote the footnote found in *The Pilgrim
Bible:* "In 705 B.C., Sennacherib laid Moab
waste. This portion not only prophesied this,

but looks ahead to the final world battle."
F. C. Jennings has this fitting summary of
the chapter: "A picture of sorrow that worketh
death. One song amid earth's groans glorifies God who alone gives songs in the night."
The chapter continues the intensely animated
style of the evangelical prophet. One evidence of the integrity of Holy Writ is fulfilled prophecy. Moab, a mighty nation when
Isaiah lived, no longer exists. Its glory
has vanished. Writing of Moab quivering with
sorrow, Jennings remarks: "If that is not a
picture of the effect of a sudden and heavy
calamity on the world, so well symbolized
by Moab, then it would be difficult to find
any. Now suppose that amid all those sounds
of sorrow, one voice should be heard lifted
up in a joyous song, would not that be a
striking testimony to the intervention of
God? Indeed it would. It is easy to praise
in the sunshine, but it takes God Himself
to give us 'songs in the night'."

Chapter 16

Here we have the continuation of the burden of Moab, with Isaiah's trumpet giving
no uncertain sound. Viewing chapters 15
and 16 as a whole, we cannot but be impressed with the prophet's tender sympathy
for Moab in her affliction: "My bowels shall
sound like a harp for Moab." Isaiah mingles
his tears with those whose doom he declares.
A great German writer said: "There is no
prophecy in the book of Isaiah in which
the heart of the prophet is so painfully moved
by what his spirit beholds and his mouth
must prophesy." Two points can be noted.
First, then is *Moab's pathetic appeal for shelter from her foes.* In verse 5, the ground
of appeal is the messianic hope that the
Davidic dynasty will be able to repulse all
foes (see Acts 15:16). Second, *the promise
is made that a small remnant of Moab
will be saved.* "Very small and feeble"
(verse 14). "Wearied of prayer to Chemosh
in his high places, Isaiah predicts that Moab
will seek the living God." Five tragic words
conclude verse 14: "But he shall not prevail." It may be that unprevailing prayer
is ours because of something Moabite-like
within the heart.

Chapter 17

The burden pronounced over Damascus
proves how history repeats itself. To quote

again from F. C. Jennings, whose commentary on Isaiah is one of the best in print: "Once more the rod of the Lord falls, and now it strikes Damascus, the representative city of Syria. But as the ten tribes have joined themselves to Syria, entering into an offensive alliance with it against Judah and the House of David (chapters 7 and 8), they too must share in the implication, for such a communion always means 'a partaking of the evil deeds'; and so necessarily of their punishment (II John 11). In looking back, we are really looking forward at a scene that will be reproduced in the future, for this history will be repeated, only, of course, with different actors, in a day fast approaching. Once more, as Ephraim joined Syria, so shall the mass of the Jewish nation, again restored to its own land, put its confidence in the military resources of the Gentiles (Daniel 11:3,8), with whom a covenant will be made for seven years. This will again bring upon them, both Jews and Gentiles, as here on Damascus and Ephraim, a very heavy burden." Forgetfulness of God ever results in sad desolation (verse 10).

Chapter 18

While chapters 18-20 should be taken together, since they contain three distinct prophecies addressed to Egypt and Ethiopia, let us separate them and look first to this eighteenth chapter. What commotion Isaiah depicts – Ethiopia, excitedly, sending ambassadors hither and thither for help in preparation for war! Fear of invasion created panic. The calmest man on the scene was Isaiah himself, who urged the ambassadors to go home and quietly watch God destroy Assyria's self-confidence. We can learn from this chapter that God cannot condone alliances between His people and unbelievers. Another striking prophecy of Israel's regathering is before us in the closing verse. "Scattered and peeled" among the nations for well nigh 2,000 years, the Jews are returning to their land, withal in unbelief. The day is approaching, however, when in repentance and faith Israel will return to the Lord and herself become "the present" to be offered unto the Lord of hosts. How precious all these Scriptures of Israel's coming glory will be to her when such glory will be an established fact!

Chapter 19

George L. Robinson, in his commentary on Isaiah, says that this "second oracle contains both *a threat* (verses 1-17) and *a promise* (verses 18-25), and is one of Isaiah's most remarkable foreign prophecies . . . (720 B.C.). The prophecy is a marvellous missionary sermon worthy of a place alongside of Paul's sermon on Mars Hill." Past and prospective aspects can be discerned in this chapter. The first seventeen verses have been fulfilled. In expressive symbolic language, so characteristic of Isaiah, the prophet describes what happened to Egypt. The Lord rode upon a swift cloud to her destruction. Such a metaphor portrays the sudden judgment overtaking the Egyptians as Sargon, king of Assyria, came against them. Egypt is a fitting type of the world, and we know from John's Apocalypse that its destruction will be as complete as Egypt's. The remaining section, verses 18-25, is yet to be fulfilled. "In that day" Egypt and Assyria will join with Judah in a triple alliance of common worship of God and of blessing to others. When Christ returns to earth and establishes His reign, then, and not till then, will Egypt be His people, Assyria the work of His hands, and Israel His inheritance.

Chapter 20

This chapter is notable in that Isaiah was commanded to show, in a graphic and appealing way, the fate in store for Egypt. For three years he had to wear the garb of a slave in order to teach Israel the shameful end awaiting the Egyptians, to whom Israel turned for help. Delitzsch says of this action: "With the great importance attached to clothing in the East, where the feelings on this point are peculiarly sensitive and modest, a person was looked upon as stripped and naked if he had only taken off his upper garment. What Isaiah was therefore directed to do, was simply opposed to common custom and not to moral decency. He was to lay aside the dress of a mourner, a preacher of repentance, and to have nothing on but his tunic; and in this, as well as bare-footed, he was to show himself in public." We can imagine how Isaiah's strange attire would arouse attention, and bring the people to a solemn realization. F. C. Jennings' application to the chapter is suggestive: "Just as Assyria (representative of violence) conquers Egypt (representative of corruption), so shall the beast and ten horns destroy the woman" (religion).

Chapter 21

Apart from its direct application, this is a great chapter for preaching texts. Verses 2, 3, 4, 5, 11 and 12 are full of suggestions for pulpit use. An impressive gospel sermon could be preached on verse 4, taking Belshazzar's feast as an illustration of changed fortune. Babylon is described as "the desert of the sea." What a telling type of the world we have in such a double emblem! By the "desert" we understand dryness, despair. "Sea," in Scripture, suggests restlessness, agitation and trouble.

In the fate overtaking Babylon we have another evidence of the divine inspiration of the Bible. Where is the proud Babylon of Isaiah's day? His prophecy was uttered some 200 years before Babylon fell. It was in this way that the prophet functioned as a "foreteller." The burden of Dumah can surely be given a present application. The greatest need of the hour is for watchmen upon the tower to cry: "What of the night? The morning cometh, and also the night." Would that the godless multitudes would enquire after the way of salvation, and return to the Lord!

Chapter 22

The burden of this chapter bears a somewhat cryptic yet suggestive title: "The Valley of Vision." One would have thought that in a valley, with towering hills on either side, a vision would be well-nigh impossible. But being the God of the valleys, as well as the God of the mountains, our God is able to give His servant a vision even in, and of, a valley.

The chapter seems to be made up of two sections. In the first fourteen verses Isaiah rebukes the lack of godliness within the Theocracy. In picturesque language he describes the reckless, God-ignoring citizens of Jerusalem. He turns aside from his warnings for surrounding nations, to rebuke the frivolity, and the gratification of base desires, of the people of God. With the enemy at the gate,

there should be seriousness and spirituality. In verses 15-32 Isaiah addresses himself to Shebna, who had been antagonistic to the high aims of the prophet and the king. Isaiah's prophecy of his degradation was fulfilled, for in 36:3 and 37:2 we have Shebna occupying a much lower position in the royal service. (For an antitype of Shebna, turn to Revelation 19:19-21.)

Chapter 23

"The burden of Tyre," that great merchant city of Isaiah's day, is full of coming prophetic import. Says F. C. Jennings: "The Tyre of this chapter represents the commercial glory of the world, and in the graphic picture given in *her* fall, we may see, as in a mirror, some utter description of the world's commerce in the future" (see Revelation 18). In this last of Isaiah's oracles for foreign nations, there are several aspects of judgment he pronounces upon Tyre: (1) proud and prominent, it shall yet be laid waste; (2) all of her commercial glory is to be taken from her; (3) her beneficial colonies are to become independent; and (4) renowned, she will find herself forgotten for "seventy years."

In grace, however, God was to visit Tyre. After the seventy years in oblivion, trade would revive, prosperity would return, and gathered gains would be dedicated to the Lord (verse 18). How invincible America might be if over all "her merchandise and her hire" could be written, "Holiness to the Lord!"

Chapter 24

Chapters 24 through 27 contain, not only the spiritual message of salvation but the type of prophecy Isaiah seems to revel in, namely, the ability to foretell a definite future which has its foundations in the present. One cannot but be impressed with the prophet's scope of imagination as he lifts the reader out of the sphere of mere history to paint pictures of the far-off future. For a prophetic outline of chapter 24, the divisions given by Dr. C. I. Scofield are suggestive: "*Looking through troubles to the kingdom-age* (verses 1-12); *the Jewish Remnant* (verses 13-15); *the Great Tribulation* (verses 16-20); *destruction of Gentile World-Power* (verse 21); *the First Resurrection* (verses 22,23)."

Comparing this somber chapter with the judgments of John's Apocalypse, we can note many similarities. While the world appears to be going on in its merry way, universal catastrophe may burst like a terrible flood at any moment, overwhelming the mightiest and meanest of earth. Would that the godless multitudes could realize that it is later than they think! "Fear, and the pit, and the snare" are upon them, and they know it not.

Chapter 25

Whatever application there may be to Israel after her deliverance from the Assyrian catastrophe, there is no doubt that Isaiah was inspired by the Spirit to bridge the centuries and express the gratitude of the redeemed of all ages. Not only is the chapter "an enhanced echo of the song on the seashore in Exodus 15," but a prelude of the triumph of the kingdom-age. For beauty of expression this chapter will never be surpassed. Compare verse 8 with I Corinthians 15:54 and Revelation 20:14; 21:4, and see how Paul and John lived in this prophecy. As for verse 9, it has a double application. It will be the voice of joy when the raptured Church gazes upon the Lord, and also the paean of praise when a converted Israel looks upon Him whom she pierced. A useful outline of the chapter is the one suggesting that in verses 1-5 we have a hymn of thanksgiving to God for deliverance, as well as a confession on the part of those conquered. In verses 6-8, we have the Lord's bountiful banquet for all nations! What a feast of fat things that will be! And verses 9-12 unfold in hymn-like language the utmost praise of Israel, also the utter desolation of Moab.

Chapter 26

Here we have another song of the redeemed "sung in the land of Judah." Of its future application to "the worship and testimony of restored and converted Israel," we have no doubt. But who has not hugged to his heart great verses like 3, 4, 12, 13 and 20. While the full realization of such promises may be Israel's, all of us can drink deeply of them. Comparing chapters 25 and 26, F. C. Jennings suggestively comments: "We

have what might be called 'The Tale of Two Cities'; the one representing that proud city, which man is building, contemptuously called 'the city of *tohu*' or confusion (24:10); the other, the building of God. When one is up, the other is down. When Jerusalem is trodden down by the Gentiles then that 'great city' of the nation flourishes. When Jerusalem is lifted up, then *that* falls. This is the burden of the song." Verse 19 gives us the first clear statement of the Resurrection in the Old Testament, which while restricted to Israel's restoration is yet a fitting type of our resurrection at the return of Christ, when He will gather us into His chambers, until His indignation be overpast.

Chapter 27

Actually the last two verses of the previous chapter belong to this one. In the day of God's wrath, while Israel is to be saved, those around are incapable of salvation. "The agents of destruction shall themselves be destroyed: namely, 'the swift serpent,' Assyria; 'the crooked serpent,' Babylon; and the sea 'monster,' Egypt." Prophetically Isaiah describes how these heathen world-powers as ravenous beasts are to be consumed. Israel, however, as God's true vineyard, will gloriously flourish so that the whole earth shall be filled with fruit. Dealing with these divine chastisements, Isaiah makes it plain that Israel's judgment will be light compared with God's judgment of surrounding godless nations. The judgment of the nations was, and will be, punitive. Israel's judgment is always remedial. God sifts Israel but destroys the nations. In one case it is salvation; in the other annihilation. What comfort we can take from the declaration, "He stayeth his rough wind in the day of the east wind!" Burdened soul, ever remember that God will never allow you to carry more than you are able to bear.

Chapter 28

The woe of Ephraim proves how beauty can fade. Ephraim, as we know, was the name of Joseph's son, born while Joseph was in Egypt. Ephraim's seed became one of the tribes of Israel. Ultimately the names of Israel and Ephraim became synonymous.

From the beginning of their sojourn in the Promised Land, the descendants of Ephraim enjoyed a certain prestige. "Geographically, they were at the heart of the nation and provided the setting for national assemblies, as well as a center for worship." God wanted Ephraim to be "a crown of glory and a diadem of beauty." But Ephraim wanted to wear "a crown of pride" of their own making. Thus Isaiah warns them of approaching judgment when their "glorious beauty . . . shall be a fading flower." A study of history proves that national decline is ever tragic. Are America and Britain not weighed in the balances in this respect? Scoffing politicians of today ought to read this great chapter of Isaiah and ponder the fact that God will surely deal with them, as He will with "bibulous priests who stumble in judgment, and the staggering prophets who err in vision" (verses 7,8).

Chapter 29

Approaching the woe on Ariel, it may be fitting to consider the twice repeated name David gave to Jerusalem, where he loved to dwell and which will ever remain dear to the heart of God. Two different renderings are given of "Ariel." The margin reads, "Lion of God." In II Samuel 23:20 we read: "Benaiah . . slew two lion-like (*ariel*) men of Moab." While this is the simplest and most direct meaning of this symbolic name for Jerusalem, in Ezekiel 43:16, as F. C. Jennings points out, "the first part of the compound word, *'ari'* is rendered 'altar'; and the whole may also be translated, 'altar of God,' as the place upon which the *fire* of God will be kindled and maintained." Two sections of this chapter are discernable: first, the prophet's woe to formalists in religion (verses 1-14); second, the woe to those who hide their plans from God (verses 15-24). Note the phrase "upside down" in verse 16 (*cf.* 24:1). Trace this suggestive phrase through the Bible. It occurs some five times. Do we think of ourselves as "the potter's clay"? Are we willing to be moulded by the potter (Jeremiah 18)?

Chapter 30

The woe of verse 1 is capable of many applications. It was originally directed against those who went down to Egypt for help. But God has a good many rebelious children today of whom it can be said that they "take counsel, but not of me." Sometimes it is so hard to believe that our strength is to sit still (verse 7). May ours always be the guidance indicated in verse 21! How solemn is the last verse of the chapter where Tophet is "the dread symbol of the deepest depression in that lake of fire where 'the worm dieth not and the fire is not quenched' . . . When man himself is stripped of all covering and, a naked spirit, departs, then he shares in the uncovered condition of the devil and his angels," and as he has taken the same path of rebellion, he endures the same "fire" as the devil (Matthew 25:41). Within the chapter Israel is urged to repent of her idolatry (verses 18-26). If she will, then copious blessings will be poured out upon her and "the Rock of Israel" will grant her a song in the night (verses 27-29). Is there not a truth for the Church of today in Isaiah's call to separation and repentance? Delivered from all foreign alliances she can become a blessing in the world.

Chapter 31

While Israel had rebelled against God's laws and commandments, originally He meant them to be as fences, restricting only that they might protect against everything outside His will. God's lament was that His people had deeply revolted (verse 6). They had substituted Egypt for Him. God commanded them not to make alliance with surrounding nations, and promised to care for them in every way on the condition they remained true to His Word. But the people jumped the fence and sought material help from Egypt. So in verses 1 to 3 we have the prophet's vehement denunciation of Judah for disregarding the Holy One of Israel by trusting in Egypt's horses and chariots. Judah sought the flesh, forgetting that the arm of flesh ever fails. God promises to deliver His people if only they will turn to Him (verses 4-9). How beautifully Isaiah describes God's protection and provision in verse 5! We do not agree with those who see in this verse a prophecy of the airplane. The chapter ends with the determination of God to deliver Jerusalem and completely vanquish Assyria and her hosts (verses 5-9).

Chapter 32

Here is another chapter containing a near and long view. While its background has to do with Sennacherib's invasion and of God's deliverance of His own, the chapter also carries an inescapable Messianic application. Christ is the King who is to reign in righteousness. He is, and will be, the Man as a hiding place from the wind. During the Millennium His Spirit will be poured upon His heritage, and the earth become a peaceable habitation for His people. Presently we must be active for the Master and sow beside all waters (verse 20). What a transformation awaits this sin-cursed earth of ours, when kings and lords will rule in righteousness, and justice is the coin of the realm! From the top down, society will be regenerated. Moral distinctions will no longer be confused. In Christ's ideal commonwealth of nations, social righteousness, peace and plenty will abound. The sections of the chapter are clear. *The king reigns* (verses 1-8); *tribulation must precede His reign* (verses 9-14); *the latter rain, and the glory of Israel* (verses 15-20). May verse 17 be realized by us all!

Chapter 33

Before indicating the salient features of this chapter, one must pause to point out the preciousness of a verse like the second. Wonderful, is it not, as each new day begins, to have the Lord as our Arm to lean upon? "Who is this that cometh up from the wilderness, leaning upon her beloved?" Lean hard upon Him and acknowledge His might (verse 13). Would that verse 14 were true of the multitudes around!

The historical situation of the chapter can be found in verses 7-12. Notice what happens when a prophet prays (verse 2). God answers by destroying the destroyer's plan. Assyria is vanquished. "With a beautiful picture of the Messianic future, Isaiah's woes find an appropriate conclusion (verses 17-24). The striking feature of the prophecies considered is the constant alternation of threat and promise. Isaiah never pronounced a woe without adding a corresponding promise." Mark verses 16 and 17 in your Bible. Nay, hide them in your heart and drink deeply of them as you wait for your tacklings to

be loosed (verse 23). What blessedness awaits the Church, Israel, and the earth! What will it be when the King comes back?

Chapter 34

"Armageddon," is the title Dr. Scofield gives this chapter, and one cannot read it without realizing that past history cannot exhaust its meaning. The eminent German theologian, Delitzsch, says of the chapter: "We feel that we are carried away from the stage of history, and are transported into the midst of the last things . . . After the fall of Assyria, and when darkness began to gather on the horizon again, Isaiah broke away from his own times – 'the end of all things' became more and more his home . . . It was the revelation of the mystery of the incarnation of God, for which all this was to prepare the way." What anguish will overtake the nations when the sword of the Lord . . . falls upon them (verses 5,6)! Presently, the kings of the earth, and the rulers take counsel together against the Lord; but His day is coming, and when it does, it will be the day of His vengeance (verse 8). All we have to do in these days so heavy with prophetic significance is to seek out the Book of the Lord, and read it (verse 16). The Bible contains God's blueprint of the future. There is no reason, therefore, to flounder in uncertainty as we think of coming events.

Chapter 35

Joy after judgment – song after storm! The crashing finale of divine judgment in chapter 34 is now followed by the sweetest strains of promise. Death and darkness depart and the very desert "laughs with abundance." Delight is everywhere. F. C. Jennings, the gifted expositor whose volume on Isaiah should be in the hands of every Christian, remarks that "the very storm affords a foil that increases the sweetness of that calm. Little do they know of the delights of spring who have never felt the pinch of winter: little do they value the 'time of the singing of birds' who have never lacked their melody; little should we care for the promise, 'God shall wipe away all tears,' had we never wept. So this lovely little chapter is doubly refreshing from its sharp contrast with its predecessor. It has a lilt of joy and is almost metrical in our A.V. without much change." For beauty of expression, the language of this chapter is peerless. The reality of blessedness described will ever be beyond the glowing terms used. A verse like the eighth should have a present realization in the lives of the redeemed.

Chapter 36

We now approach a historical section taking us through chapters 36-39, introduced with the chronological note, "It came to pass in the fourteenth year of king Hezekiah." During this historic interlude, Isaiah himself stands out as a prominent factor in three directions: first, *in the double attempt of Sennacherib to obtain possession of Jerusalem* (chapters 36, 37); second, *in Hezekiah's sickness and recovery* (chapter 38); and third, *in connection with the embassy of Merodach-Baladen"* (chapter 39). Chapter 36:1-3 describes Sennacherib's invasion. Verses 4-21 record the threats of Rabshakeh. How defiant of God and Isaiah he was! Verse 21 reminds one of the silence of the Lord Jesus when He was faced with those who disputed His claims. Verse 22 and on through chapter 37:1-4, speaks of Hezekiah's reaction to the taunts of Rabshakeh. "Let not Hezekiah deceive you; for he shall not be able to deliver you." It must have been hard for a good and godly king like Hezekiah to receive the proud, arrogant threats of the bumptious mouthpiece of "the great king, the king of Assyria," but he was not unduly disturbed. God was on his side.

Chapter 37

Do you not think that the twentieth verse summarizes the dramatic chapter we have reached in these meditations? The burning desire expressed in Hezekiah's prayer has inspired the saints through the ages. No weapons men forge could possibly have the power of such a prayer as the king offered. Hezekiah's heart-cry became a power against the defiant foe. Think of it, a whole army was slain with no casualties to God's people! They had no need to fight in that battle. Hezekiah spread Rabshakeh's threatening letter before the Lord and let Him answer it, which He did in a drastic way.

How do you act when you receive a similar letter? Do you spread it before the Lord for Him to deal with, or do you answer it, giving blow for blow? God is able to deal with all arrogant foes, if only we will let Him. When He acted, one angel was sufficient to destroy 185,000 of Sennacherib's army. One with God is ever in the majority, as Hezekiah proved. Verses to roll under your tongue as sweet morsels are 28 and 31. In these superficial days, we would bear fruit upward without taking root downward.

Chapter 38

This chapter is strictly biographical, being made up of Hezekiah's sickness and recovery. In the fourteenth year of his reign, when he was about 38 years of age, Isaiah was divinely commanded to pronounce the king's death: "Set thine house in order; for thou shalt die and not live." Since the king had no son at the time, Messianic hopes that were centered in the dynasty of David were seriously threatened. Hezekiah, praying earnestly for the king's recovery, had his death sentence revoked, God adding fifteen years to his life, in which time a son was born to him. The poetic song of thanksgiving for recovery fittingly expresses the sentiments and feelings of one who has himself personally been unexpectedly and miraculously delivered from the brink of death. His hopeless melancholy gives way to boundless rapture as he learns of continued life in communion with God in the land of the living. We must remember, as we read of Hezekiah's gloomy view of the future, that he did not have the clear revelation of the New Testament. It was our Lord Jesus who brought life and immortality to light through His Gospel.

Chapter 39

Although this is a short chapter, it is sufficiently long to prove how subtle Satan is. After the deep experiences recorded in the two previous chapters, it was Hezekiah's sincere intention to "walk softly," but he failed to resist flattery, and in a moment of weakness exposed all his royal treasures to the envoys of Merodach-Baladan. He did not realize that he was to undergo a more dangerous trial than the threats of arrogant foes or the suffering from a physical disorder. "What neither of these could effect, Babylon, coming in the guise of friendship, accomplished." Hezekiah committed an inexcusable blunder, for the sight of his precious possessions would only excite his flattering visitors to possess them. As the result of this failure, divine chastisement fell upon the nation. Isaiah, in tones of prophetic authority, rebuked the king for his vanity of heart and lack of faith in God in thus receiving the messengers, and then gave a final prediction of judgment deemed to be the most marvelous of all Isaiah's minatory utterances, forming, as it does, a prophetic basis for chapters 40-46.

Chapter 40

With this chapter we come to the second half of the book. In chapters 1-39, Isaiah looks toward the captivities; now in chapters 40-66, he looks beyond them. Because of the change of style in this latter section, critics affirm that there must have been two Isaiahs. But as another has pointed out, "the change of style is no more remarkable than the change of theme. A prophet, who was also a patriot, would not write of the sins and coming captivity of his people in the same exultant and joyous style which he would use to describe their redemption, blessing and power." John 12:37-44 is our authority for affirming that there was only one Isaiah.

The two opening verses of this chapter provide a prologue and keynote for the entire second section of Isaiah. The basis of Israel's comfort is the infinite, all-wise, all-powerful God, who, in comparison with other gods, is incomparable. Such logic is absolutely unanswerable. The three-fold division of the chapter is as follows: *a comforting God speaks to Israel* (verses 1-11); *the utter futility of idols* (verses 12-26); *divine strength manifested in weakness* (verses 27-31).

Chapter 41

In His challenge to idolatrous Gentiles, God passes from the wonderful works of creation, as evidence of His power, to another proof of His deity, namely, His power to predict. Dumb idols have no power to forecast the future. Two dialogues are before us in this chapter. In verses 1-7, there is *a dialogue between God and the nations;* in verses 21-29, *a dialogue between God and dumb idols.* It would seem as if the world is fast heading up for the climax indicated in verse 1. What F. W. Grant wrote in 1880 is true of today: "Never in the history of man has so terrific a calamity befallen the race as that which all who look may now behold, advancing as a deluge, black with destruction, resistless in might, uprooting our most cherished hope, engulfing in mindless desolation." God has an account to settle with godless nations, and the day is not far distant when they must come together for judgment. See what God can do with worms (verses 14,15).

Chapter 42

This wonderful chapter carries us beyond Cyrus, the temporal agent raised up to mediate Israel's redemption, to Jehovah's "servant," even the Lord Jesus Christ Himself. He is the ideal One who, endued with the Spirit, will restore Israel and rule the world in righteousness. Let us behold God's Servant: *Godward*, the Holy Spirit is to equip Him to execute judgment; *selfward*, He will be self-effacing, scorning all thirst for prominence; and *manward*, He will be gentle in dealing with the feeble, yet brave and determined until His God-given task is finished. Have you ever heard a sermon on "The Undiscouraged Christ" (verse 4)? How easily discouraged we become! Note the precious promises God has for a restored Israel (verses 8-12). Yet He would be a false friend if He did not chasten His own (verses 9-25). Note also the "I wills" in this last section. Verse 19 is likewise suggestive. Christ, as the Servant, was blind and deaf to everything save the will and work of the One who sent Him. Spurgeon used to exhort his students to cultivate "a blind eye and a deaf ear" in their service for the Master.

Chapter 43

The opening "but," connecting the last chapter with this one, brings us to a change of style and substance that is swift and striking. From the outburst of divine fury we immediately come to favor. We pass from chastening to comfort. "The love that has been hidden behind the wrath returns to its prerogative again." After His strange work of punishment, God gladly returns to a far more congenial task. Thus the entire chapter is taken up with Israel redeemed and restored. God's deliverance is all of grace. The people could do nothing worthy of their redemption, as verses 23-25 plainly indicate. "This passage marks the highest point of grace in the Old Testament." For His own sake, and on no other basis, God is to blot out all their transgressions. What jewels of truth flash forth in this great chapter! Are you passing through the waters of trial? Read verses 1-3, and remember that God knows your name, where you live, and all about your adversities. Are you discouraged because evil men seem to prevail? Read verses 11-21. Note the two-fold weariness: Israel weary of God; God weary of Israel's iniquities (verses 22,24).

Chapter 44

Isaiah, knowing that dòom is ahead for Israel if her unrighteous living is continued, pleads with her to return unto the Lord. The message of the entire Bible can be summed up in the words, "Return unto Me, and I will forgive." We have been reminded recently that "Rome lost its glory and France its power because of internal weakness caused by the sins of their people. America is being warned today of a similar destiny if its citizens do not repent and turn to God for guidance." If Israel is to have the power to attract the nations, then she must repent and live obediently. One of the most remorseless exposures in the Bible of the folly of idolatry can be found in verses 9-20. Gods of wood and stone, although dazzling, are dead. In the concluding portion of the chapter, Isaiah bids Israel remember that forgiveness is God's pledge of deliverance (verses 21-23); that as her Maker and Redeemer, He stands ready to confirm His Word on her behalf. Look at verses 22 and 23 and mark how a song follows salvation. Redeemed ones, we can rejoice!

Chapter 45

The last verse of the previous chapter belongs to the prophecy of Cyrus, the divine agent in Israel's deliverance clearly foretold in this chapter. As the Sovereign One, God can use whom and what He deems best. Before he came upon the scene, Cyrus is described in extraordinary and extravagant terms. He was to be God's "shepherd" (44:28). "The name Cyrus in Elamite is said to mean 'shepherd'." Then he is spoken of as God's "anointed," or "messiah" (45:1). This title of transcendent dignity and significance foreshadowed the Messiah, who would make possible a greater deliverance. Cyrus is also named as "the man of my counsel" (46:11); the one whom God called by name and surnamed without his knowing Him (45:3,4); the one "whom God loveth" (48:14); the one whose right hand God upheld (45:1); the one who would perform all God's pleasure (44:28); yet withal "a ravenous bird from the east" (46:11). Josephus, the Jewish historian tells us that when Cyrus found his name written in "the prophesies which Isaiah left behind him two hundred and twenty years before," an earnest desire and ambition seized upon him to fulfil what was written.

Chapter 46

While the name of Cyrus does not occur in this chapter, his destructive overthrow of Babylon is evident. In graphic terms Isaiah depicts the complete collapse of Babylonian idolatry. More concerned with the humiliation of Babylon's idols than the fall of Babylon itself, the prophet thunders forth divine judgment on all false deities. Dr. George Robinson says: "The prophet draws a striking contrast between the ignominious flight of Babylon's idols, borne into exile from the captured city on the backs of wearied beasts, and the matchless power of God, who instead of being borne, is able to bear His people. Even Bel, the chief god of the Babylonian pantheon, and Nebo, the interpreter of the gods, are powerless to help" (verses 1,2). What a comforting promise we have in verse 4! How incomparable God is (verses 5,9)! His superiority and unique deity are seen in His power to predict "the end from the beginning" and bring all His predictions to pass (verses 10,11). May we be delivered from the company of "the stouthearted"! The Lord enable us to be as clay in His hands so that He can mold us after His will.

Chapter 47

A fitting caption for this chapter would be, "Babylon the Great is fallen" (see Revelation 18:2). In fact, the judgment upon Babylon that Isaiah here foretells should be read along with Revelation 17 and 18. As you read, note how Babylon is described: "a tender and delicate queen"; "the mistress of kingdoms"; and, "a lady forever." But because of her boastfulness and cruelty, a humiliating slavery and dethronement await her. What a dirge over the downfall of such an imperial city this chapter contains! And when the stroke of divine judgment falls, "no amount of sorcery or enchantment or science of astrology will suffice to avert the divine desolation which will one day fall upon the haughty capital" (verses 8-15). God save us from dwelling carelessly (verse 8)! Our only confidence is the Lord (verse 9). In these days of astrologers, when even Christians are tempted to find out how their lives are regulated by the stars instead of by the God who made the stars, it is imperative to obey the warning of verse 13. Astrology and star charts are simply a lot of rubbish. Do we hear any amens?

Chapter 48

F. C. Jennings, who, in a very convincing way, proves that the Book of Isaiah as a whole is not only a trilogy but has the number *three* imprinted upon every part of the book, tells us that this chapter is made up of double "three."

"Verses 1, 2, *the call to the man to hear;* verses 12-16, *the call to the remnant to hear;* verses 3-8, *reproach for the neglect of prophecy;* verses 17-21, *tender reproach of the remnant;* verses 9-11, *remnant manifested in chastening;* verse 22, *the apostate mass manifested in penal suffering.*" In the main, Isaiah is here recapitulating all he insisted upon in chapters 40-47. Certain points are touched upon and emphasized for the last time. Verses 20-22 have a double application. Here and now the wicked are without peace. They are like the troubled sea, whose waters cannot rest. In hell, they are to be eternally without peace. What torment awaits all the godless who die without Him who is our peace. Does the peril of the wicked stir us to win them to a peace, unspeakable and full of glory?

Chapter 49

In this second of four "Servant Songs," the first being found in 42:1-9, Isaiah develops the Servant's mission and experience. Within this natural sequel to the first song we can trace the following features: (1) *The Servant's consciousness of his mission* (verses 1-3). May such a description as found in verses 2, 3, be also true of us as servants of the Lord! (2) *The Servant's confession of failure* (verse 4). The best of servants feel at times that their labor is in vain. (3) *The Servant's quickened faith in God* (verses 5,6). He knew he would never fail as a light. Israel is being preserved as a light to the Gentiles. Israel's King and our Saviour also came as a light to banish the world's darkness. In the next lesson, speaking of a restored people (verses 7-21), there are some heart-warming passages. See verse 16, for example. Judgment upon the foes of Israel concludes the chapter (verses 22-26). The mighty One of Jacob will yet deal with all Jew haters.

Chapter 50

In this third "Servant Song," the Servant speaks of himself in monologue, and speaking thus "in the first person describes the prophetic aspect of His own character." Orelli, whom Dr. Robinson quotes, says of this Servant: "He possesses the two fundamental qualifications of an ideal prophet: willingness to listen as often as God speaks, and willingness always to utter without demur whatever God commands" (verses 1-5). The Servant endured the humiliation, yet his patience in trial speaks of His unshaken faith in God (verses 6-9). All who oppose God's Servant must face retribution (verses 10,11). Living as we do on this side of Bethlehem and Calvary, we know that no one fully answers to bitter scorn, hatred and abuse like the Lord Jesus did, who found Himself despised and rejected of men. He it was who gave His back to the smiters and His cheeks to them that plucked off the hair. Read again verses 4 and 5. They were so true of our Lord while He was among men. Can we say they also describe our obedience?

Chapter 51

"The cry from the remnant to the arm of the Lord to awake," says Jennings, "is answered by Jehovah's cry to Jerusalem to awake." Three companies are addressed by the Lord of hosts, the speaker throughout the chapter: (1) *Selfward – Israel must remember her origin* (verses 1-3); (2) *Manward – Israel must function as a light* (verses 4-6); (3) *Godward – Israel must never forget God* (verses 7,8). Underline the three "hearkens" in this opening section. Longing for God can be found in verses 9-11. Ere long our sorrow and mourning will flee away. God's power as the Creator is sufficient ground for faith (verses 13-16). Last of all, we have God's call to His own to arouse themselves (verses 17-23). Verse 20 contains a very expressive symbol – "a wild bull in a net." What strength, vigor, procreative power a wild bull represents, but what a picture of helplessness is suggested by the bull's entanglement in a net! Samson became a bull caught in a net. Do we find ourselves in the net of some unworthy habit? Well, Christ alone can deliver us out of the net.

Chapter 52

Actually, the first twelve verses of this chapter are connected with the previous one, the threefold "Awake, Awake!" (51:9,17; 52:1) making the chapters one stirring call to Zion to shake herself from the dust. The remnant of Israel, preserved by divine grace, has a glorious heritage and she must prepare herself to meet it. Verses 1-6 *promise the deliverance of the Lord's people.* Verses 7-10 *proclaim such a redemption.* Verses 11 and 12 *picture this divine deliverance.* While the entire passage belongs to a renewed Israel in the kingdom-age, yet are we not justified in applying much of it to ourselves, seeing we are the Lord's redeemed ones? Are we not more privileged than Zion? Do not our beautiful garments exceed in splendor those that Zion is exhorted to put on? "Let us, then shake ourselves from the dust of all that is earthly and live as those fully emancipated from all our shackles. Let us also have feet that are swift and beautiful, carrying to multitudes at home and abroad the good tidings of salvation. Let us ever plead that God will make bare His arm in these last days. Yes, and as vessels of the Lord, may we be clean."

Chapter 53

As verses 13-15 of the last chapter belong to this renowned one, it is essential to think of the portion as one, seeing it presents the sorrowing, sacrificial Servant of Jehovah. In this fourth "Servant Song" we approach "the climax of the prophet's inspired symphony and the acme also of Hebrew prophecy." While much discussion has gathered around the true identity of the Servant whom Isaiah depicts, we have no doubt whatever that the perfect fulfillment of all that is prophesied was reached in Christ. From this prophecy, Philip preached Jesus to the Ethiopian. So Christ, the Mediator arising out of Israel, is the suffering Servant whom Isaiah wonderfully portrays. Language fails us as we come to expound this "golden passional of the Old Testament," as Polycarp named it. Every verse seems to drip with the ruby blood of our Redeemer. Said C. H. Spurgeon, preaching on "Christ wounded for our transgressions" (verse 3): "I have lost the power to doubt Him when I see those wounds." Without doubt, "the profoundest thoughts in the Old Testament revelation are to be found in this section." What else can we do but praise this Man of sorrows for bearing the load of our sin?

When Moody was asked to conduct his first mission in London in 1874, union meetings were comparatively new. The committee asked him to explain his methods. Everything went smoothly until one member asked him his creed. Moody calmly replied, "My creed is already in print." A member seized a paper and pencil and asked where it could be found. "In the fifty-third chapter of Isaiah," Moody answered.

Chapter 54

It is significant that this chapter, so full of assurance that the Lord will restore Israel, begins with the word "sing." The previous memorable chapter was equally full of the atoning work of the Saviour. Now, all who rest in His finished work and have had the barrenness of sin taken away, can praise the Lord. Apart from grace we have no song. Heathenism has no hymns. It was

Christianity that gave birth to singing. Verse 2 inspired early missionary pioneers to penetrate the realm of darkness abroad. While the Lord will yet function as husband to Israel, the adulterous wife (verse 5) has brought consolation to many a grief-stricken widow. The prophet's confirmation of Noah as a figure who actually lived, and the flood as a historical fact, destroys the contention of modernists that the story of the flood is simply a myth. If you are up against the animosity, jealousy and ill-will of those who seem to be so un-Christlike in their treatment of you, live in verse 17 and leave your defense to Him who is able to silence any tongue used against you. God has promised to preserve you as the apple of His eye.

Chapter 55

Isaiah here invites his people to turn to God for satisfaction, for He alone can meet their deepest need. Lack of money need be no impediment. All can come into God's market and receive all that He offers, without money and without price. Whether Jews or Gentiles, all can participate in God's bountiful provision of salvation. How many wonderful gospel texts there are in this grand chapter! Verses 6 and 7, for example, have been widely used by preachers to lead souls to Christ; while all who proclaim the Word of life, who are sometimes discouraged over the paucity of results, have found comfort in verses 10 and 11. The last verse will be gloriously realized in the establishment of Israel. But is it not also descriptive of the transformation grace can produce in any barren life? F. C. Jennings suggests that chapters 53-55 form a trilogy: in chapter 53 – the sufferings of the cross; in chapter 54 – the announcement of those sufferings to Israel; in chapter 55 – the worldwide proclamation of these to all men. Notice in verse 5 the three-fold titles that are applicable to Christ. What a different world ours will be when He is its Leader!

Chapter 56

Once Israel is under the new covenant and God's laws are written deep in the hearts of the people, then faithful Sabbath observance, which is the sign that everything is "very good" will add to their glory. In a truer way than under the old covenant, God promises His people a triumphant possession of their own land if they cheerfully and faithfully sanctify the Sabbath. In verses 1-8 we are brought nigh to the millennial reign of Christ. It would seem as if Jerusalem is to have an actual temple (verse 7). Verses 9-12 describe the attack upon Israel by surrounding nations. "Beasts," "dumb," and "greedy dogs" are expressions used to portray these hostile nations. Verse 10 is strikingly true, however, of modernistic preachers today. How "blind," "ignorant" and "dumb" they are! The concluding verse contains an "invitation the god of this world is ever holding out to his votaries, of pleasure unending, only that each day shall give a still greater satisfaction. Alas, to what an awful awakening do such invitations ever lead! 'Vanity of vanity'! is the heart-cry here, and endless weeping beyond."

Chapter 57

Chapters 56-59 are described as containing "ethical instructions." While this may be so, it seems as if the spiritual note is prominent. Here, for example, is a forceful condemnation of idolatry, Israel's constant sin. How guilty she was of inflaming herself with idols under every green tree! This is also a chapter having much to say about "peace" (verses 2,11,19,21). Verse 10 is true of many a Christian walking in Him, who is the Way. Are we not exhorted never to be weary of it? Then what about verse 14? Have we stumbling blocks to blessing in our life? Note God's two dwelling places in verse 15; namely, heaven above, and the heart of the believer. If it is true that He creates the fruit of the lips, then let us have words in our mouths acceptable to Him. What an expressive simile of the sinner the chapter closes with! How restless the wicked are! And tossed about, they cast up mire and dirt. No peace is theirs here or hereafter. But the moment they come to the Lord Jesus they find rest unto their souls.

Chapter 58

In this chapter, in which Isaiah combines true fasting and faithful Sabbath observance, three divisions are discernible. Verses 1-5 hold the rebuke of the people for this utter hollowness of their ritual. The prophet cried aloud and spared not. Verses 6-12 find *the prophet counselling the people* to feed the hungry, house the poor, and clothe the naked. Such alleviation of the need of the distressed would be an evidence of adjustment to the will of God. Verses 13 and 14 are full of *the blessings awaiting the people* if God's holy day is rightly kept. Commentator Robinson says: "All reverence for the seventh day has vanished. Accordingly, the prophet reminds Israel that the Sabbath is holy ground which may not be trodden with irreverent feet: that it is a sanctuary, and 'the holy of Jehovah' – a very remarkable designation for this most ancient of all sacred institutions (Genesis 2:1-3), and that Israel should delight in and honour it" (verses 13-18). Is it not appalling how God's holy day, the first day of the week, is desecrated in our time?

Chapter 59

This is another wonderful chapter, filled with God's eagerness to forgive and bless. Without apology, Isaiah declares that Israel's sins had caused God to hide His face from His people, and had hindered Him from blessing them to the full. The nation had become wholly corrupt. Go over the catalogue of sins in verses 1-9. Like Daniel, however, Isaiah identified himself with the people to whom he preached. "We walk in darkness"; "our transgressions" (verses 9-12). Strong intercession arises for peace and forgiveness. From verses 15-21 we see a God who, although grieved over His people's sin, is yet willing to act on their behalf. Arming Himself as a warrior, He brings salvation to His own. "The scene is an ideal representation of the restoration of the nation from exile (see Romans 11:26). Israel shall be redeemed. With them as the nucleus of a new nation, Jehovah will enter anew into covenant relation, and put His Spirit upon them which shall abide with them henceforth and forever (verses 20,21)." Note the last part of verse 19.

Chapter 60

For continuity of thought, link on to this chapter the last two verses of the previous one, seeing that the entire section is taken up with the Redeemer out of Zion, the One upon whom the Spirit rests (59:21). The long-looked-for "light" (59:9) is about to dawn (60:1). It is impossible to miss the dispensational aspect of the chapter before us. With the completion and rapture of the Church, "the Redeemer shall come to Zion" (Romans 11:23-29; Acts 15:14-17). Going back to chapter 2, we have the Gentiles flocking to Zion (verses 2-4). Here we have them placing their possessions at the disposal of the revived Jewish state (verses 3-5). Those of Israel scattered among the nations are to gather home by land and sea (verses 8,9). The newly formed nation of Israeli offers a partial fulfilment of this prophecy of restoration. Great glory will be Zion's when, as the mistress of the nations, she functions as the spiritual center of the world (verses 10-21). Too few of us realize what a glowing future awaits God's ancient people when they are planted as the work of His hands, as a joy of many generations.

Chapter 61

Dr. Scofield describes this chapter, which Henry Drummond of Scotland called, "the programme of Christianity," as "the two advents in one view." In the first three verses we have the portion the Lord Jesus related to Himself that day when, in the temple, He read from this chapter. Turning to Luke 4:16-21, we find that Jesus omitted the phrase, "the day of vengeance of our Lord." He came as the Spirit-anointed herald of grace. The day of divine vengeance is associated with the Day of the Lord when His righteous judgments are abroad. From verses 3-12 we have the prophecy of Israel's restoration and blessedness. How beautiful she will be when, "as a bride adorned with her jewels," she is in full harmony with her Lord! The prophecy of kingdom peace moves steadily forward toward its goal in Jesus Christ (Luke 4:18-21). How precious that third verse is to the hearts of those who grieve! Who else but God could give us beauty for ashes? Then, in verse 10, we have truths that can be applied to the Church as well as to Israel.

Chapter 62

Actually there is no break between the last chapter and this one. Originally the whole of Isaiah was one continuous scroll, with no divisions into chapters and verses which, although a convenient way of reading the Bible, were not conceived until some centuries later. This chapter, then, continues the kingdom blessings of Israel. At long last the Lord will hold His peace no longer but will go forth as the salvation of His people. In view of the full emancipation awaiting them, they must bestir themselves and undertake all necessary preparation: "Gather out the stones." For her new state, Israel must have a new name which will better symbolize her exalted position. Jerusalem will no more be called "Desolate" but "Hephzibah," meaning, "My delight is in her." A new title expressing a new relationship awaits the people, "beulah," that is, "married," seeing that the Lord will delight in them. In view of our Lord's return for His redeemed ones, have we any need to go through our lives and gather out the stones?

Chapter 63

This "brief poem of peculiar dramatic beauty" has been called "a drama of divine vengeance." The opening six verses portray the Lord as a victorious warrior destroying all those who oppose His own people, and His purpose concerning them. It will be noted that this blood-stained warrior comes from Edom, who had ever been Israel's inveterate foe. So "the prophet represents Jehovah's judgment of the nations as taking place on Edom's unhallowed soil. Jehovah, whose mighty arm has wrought salvation, returns as victor, having slain all of Israel's foes." From verse 7 right through the next chapter, the fear, feelings and thanksgiving of the people are expressed. Mark the references to the Holy Spirit in verses 10, 11 and 14. How tragic to have Him as an enemy! Yet tenderness is His, as well as wrath, for "the Spirit of the Lord caused him to rest." What marvelous truth is wrapped up in verse 9! "In all their affliction he was afflicted." God has a heart that feels for His own!

> "There is no place where earth's sorrows
>   are more felt,
>   Than up in Heaven."

Chapter 64

The progressive and comprehensive prayer stretching from the last half of chapter 63 through the chapter before us, is "one of the most passionate utterances of its kind in the Old Testament." What a passionate cry opens the chapter! Would that the desperate condition of the world and the Church today could compel us to cry out for God to rend the heavens and come down in revival power! Would that the godless nations around us might be made to tremble at His presence! Related, as the chapter is, to the fear and hope of the remnant of Israel, there is much of the chapter we can use. Verse 6 contains a strong declaration of the utter futility of self-righteousness. One reason why we have unanswered prayers can be found in verse 7. When we sing, "Have Thine own way, Lord . . . Thou art the Potter, I am the clay," the message of verse 8 comes to mind. As our Father-Potter, He has a plan for every life. The question is: "Are we the work of His hand?"

Chapter 65

Jehovah, who hears and answers prayer, responds to the supplications of His distressed people. Distinction is drawn between apostates and the true remnant. The persistently rebellious will have to face the destroying sword (verses 7,12). But the faithful remnant, the seed out of Jacob, will inherit the mountains. These loyal servants are to rejoice and sing for joy of heart, and bless themselves in the God of amen, that is, in the God of truth (verses 9,14,16). Remembering all that had happened in the valley of Achor, is verse 10 not suggestive (see Joshua 7:24,26; Hosea 2:15)? Verses 18-25 describe the nature of the kingdom-age, when longevity will be restored and the natural characteristics of beasts will forever be changed. There are those who affirm that we are presently in the Millennium. A strong argument against this teaching is that the wolf and lamb are not able to feed together. Today, the wolf feeds on the lamb. But when Christ sets up His kingdom, all that is cruel and rapacious in the animal world will vanish.

Chapter 66

Now that we have reached the concluding chapter of Isaiah's great book, it is but fitting to state that a mastery of all that the Spirit of God revealed to the prophet's mind regarding the future, means a deep insight into God's blueprint of coming events. No student of prophecy can afford to neglect the extraordinary oracle of Isaiah. Dr. George Robinson summarizes this last chapter thus: "Religion will become spiritual and decentralized, mystic cults will disappear, incredulous scoffers will be silenced. Zion's population will be marvelously multiplied, and the people will be comforted and rejoice (verses 1-14). Furthermore, all nations will flock to Zion to behold Jehovah's glory, and from one new moon to another, and from one Sabbath to another, all flesh will come up to worship in Jerusalem" (verses 15-23). It is striking, is it not, that Isaiah's remarkable vision closes with emphatic proof of God's punitive justice? He had no doubt as to a place of everlasting punishment for those who ultimately reject the message and mercy of God.

JEREMIAH

A reading of this book of such touching beauty from the pen of Jeremiah, the prophet of the broken heart, who met his death by stoning after a rejected ministry of 40 years, forces one to subscribe to the eulogium of Dr. Alexander Whyte that "this book stands to this day second only to *The Psalms* as the most spiritual book in the Old Testament." Of the prophet himself, Dr. W. W. White, the renowned American expositor says, "So far as we have date for judgment, Jeremiah was the healthiest, youngest, bravest, grandest man of Old Testament history." Unlike many of the other prophets, Jeremiah tells us a good deal of his life and labors, hence the autobiographical element in his book. *Backsliding* occurs 13 times, but Jeremiah's harsh message of judgment delivered with tears never won a convert. Such a message was not only unwelcome to the nation whose 70 years' captivity Jeremiah predicted, but totally rejected by a backsliding people. Yet "the grandeur of his character appears in his fearlessness and faithfulness and passion for souls. He faced misrepresentation, persecution, the dungeon and death, rather than keep back one word of truth." *Jeremiah* as a book combines *history, biography, prophecy.*
1. The Call and Commission – 1
2. The Faithful Ministry – 2-51
3. The Captivity of Judah – 52.
Preachers can find in this book, texts suggesting impressive sermons, e.g. 15:9 – *Premature decay.*

Chapters 1, 2

One cannot read of the overwhelming sense of humility that Jeremiah experienced, when the call to divine service reached him – "I cannot speak; for I am a child" – without taking his exercise of soul to one's own heart. A sense of helplessness is of prime importance as a preparation for the service of God. We cannot function properly as God's mouthpieces if we are puffed up with the thought of what we are able to do. His greatest servants are usually those who have been broken under a sense of their utter insufficiency. Read the helpful notes in *The Pilgrim Bible* on Jeremiah's call. Commencing his sermons with chapter 2, Jeremiah speaks of the time when the people would come to rely more on the spiritual presence than the material emblem of the ark. A new covenant would be inaugurated superceding the old. In no uncertain terms the weeping prophet calls on the people to repent and turn wholeheartedly to the God whom they had forsaken.

Chapters 3, 4

The eager pleadings of the young prophet must have created a profound impression.

Passionately Jeremiah protested against the policy of Israel's rulers and the practices of its priests. Perhaps the nation did not realize sufficiently what a new, righteous force had entered its public life in Jeremiah. But from the moment of his call, and through the forty-fours years that followed, this prophet's holy example and heart-pleading words became a potent influence. As we read these chapters, we see power and pathos combined. Dr. F. B. Meyer expresses the appeal of Jeremiah's words thus: "The flame burns higher; the sword has a keener edge; yet the tone is more tremulous and tender. There is more than ever the spirit of Jesus, bewailing the blindness and obstinacy of men, as the vision of impending judgment looms clearer before the soul and the violence done to the redeeming love of God is more clearly apprehended."

Chapters 5, 6

The fiery, fervent words of the young preacher were truly as fire to wood (5:14). How expressive is the call: "If ye can find a man"! The sin of Jerusalem would be pardoned if one righteous man could be found. Alas, we too have to confess that our old nature is as a cage of unclean birds (5:27)! Jeremiah struggles against uttering his message of judgment till he can no longer contain himself and has become weary with holding in (6:11). Think of verse 23, where the prophet addresses Jerusalem as the daughter of his people and bids her gird herself with sackcloth and sit in ashes, mourning as for an only son. The word "backsliding" is characteristic of Jeremiah (2:19; 3:6,8,11,12,22; 5:6; 8:5; etc.). It is thus that he calls a backsliding people to turn to God for the comfort and assurance of abundant pardon.

Chapters 7, 8

For a background of the first twelve chapters of Jeremiah, we must go back to the Books of Kings and Chronicles. King Josiah was an ardent reformer but found himself opposed by those who were fascinated by idol worship. This is why the people felt they could continue such worship and yet look upon the temple of God as a charm to protect them. The temple was the Lord's,

and He could care for it. The people continued in their sinful indulgences, yet pretended to revere God's dwelling place. Religion had degenerated into superstition wherein the people sought the privileges of the temple without the responsibilities involved thereby. One of the charges Jeremiah brought against the nation was that it had lost the power to blush at sin (8:12). The shamefulness of their sin was quite evident in their shamelessness. May we ever retain a tender conscience as far as sin is concerned!

Chapters 9, 10

What grief of heart is expressed in the opening verse of this section! Do we have Calvary's passion and compassion for backsliders, and for the lost? The trouble with the nation was its lack of the knowledge of God. The hearts of the people were not right (9:26). True glory consists not in earthly achievements but in the knowledge of God (9:23,24). It would seem as if Paul had these two verses in mind when he wrote I Corinthians 1:17-31. The tenth chapter makes sad reading. What fellowship could the people have with a lifeless idol (10:3-9)? Then there is the solemn indictment of verse 21. How shepherds of the flock have need to search their hearts by this word of condemnation. Puffed up by what they know and have, so many workers fail to inquire of the Lord (10:21). Self-dependence cripples prayerfulness. The old Latin motto is oft forgotten, that "to pray is to labor."

Chapters 11, 12

There is a message of deep significance in Jeremiah's "Amen" to every soul summoned to stand between God and others. When God recapitulated His promises in the heart of Jeremiah, even though they involved a curse on those who neutralized His words, there arose from it a deep response. He answered and said, "Amen, O Lord!" What an example to follow! Although Jeremiah was called upon to produce the doom of Israel, he is forced to answer and say, "Amen, O Lord!" Chapter 12 opens with a tribute to divine righteousness, even where judgment is concerned. True, Jeremiah reasons with God as to the prosperity of the wicked, but his reasoning commences: "Righteous art Thou, O God!" This is the foundation fact underlying God's throne. We may not be able to understand the significance of all He permits but, as the judge of all the earth, He does right.

Chapter 13

Behind the sign of the linen girdle, making up this chapter, we have the sad disclosure of Israel's refusing to become a people, a name and a glory. Like the spoiled girdle, the nation also had become marred and profitless. Yet God clung to His own. Israel was intimately united to Him as the girdle worn on the prophet's loins. And hope is offered the people. "As the girdle cleaveth . . . so *have I caused to cleave*" (verse 11). Israel, because of her weakness and declension, was not able to cleave. How she had tried, but failed! So encouragement is given. Cause us to cleave, O God. Can we say that we are a name to Him, so that others may understand and revere Him the better because of what we are? Are we a glory to Him? Do we know what it is to be blessedly united to Him as a girdle around His loins?

Chapters 14, 15

The two chapters are taken up with the message of the drought. God was to make one last effort to arouse His people to the awfulness and imminence of their peril. A terrible drought would cast its mantle over the land. Droughts, as we can learn from other Scriptures, came as divine punishment for disobedience. These chapters reveal Jeremiah as a mighty intercessor. How he could pour out his heart before God! The prophet was hated for his preaching, and was forced to face persecution and loneliness. But no one and nothing could close his windows heavenward. It is profitable to think of God's replies. He promised to protect Jeremiah (15:11). He reminded him that something was wrong in his life. We are not told what it was, but he had to lay it aside and be recommissioned for service (15:20). Could you apply verse 19 to your own heart?

Chapters 16, 17

Commenting on these chapters, Dr. C. I. Scofield reminds us that "the sign of the unmarried prophet is interpreted by the context. The whole social life of Judah was about to be disrupted and cease from the land. But note the promises of verses 14-16 and 17:7,8-11." One of the old divines spoke of prayer as "the flight of the lonely man to the only God." Such is the nature of Jeremiah's cry. How lonely he was! Yet think of the way he addressed himself to God: "My strength, my stronghold, and my refuge in the day of affliction"! Do we know the Lord thus? Curse and blessing are before us in chapter 17. Ruin is inevitable if a nation persists in rejecting God (verses 1-4). What is true of a nation is likewise true of an individual (verses 5-8). Read Psalm 1 along with these verses. What a solemn warning verse 16 contains for anyone called to proclaim the message of God! Life and lips must harmonize.

Chapters 18-20

These chapters cover the sign of the potter's house. Our first chapter stands out as one of the most important passages in the Bible. We are here given an insight into God's methods of working and into His reactions to man's response. From the potter, Jeremiah learned what God was about to do with the nation of which he formed a part. God, as the potter, has a plan for every life. Because of her rebellion, Israel became a marred vessel. But God is to remake her. Ere long she is to stand out as a vessel unto honor. Chapter 19 continues the symbol of the potter. Jerusalem was to crumble to pieces as a broken vessel beyond repair. What a true emblem of human life is an earthen vessel – so frail, so brittle! Yet although broken, it can be made whole again (verse 11). Perhaps the most expressive phrase of chapter 20 is the one describing Jeremiah's burdened spirit: "I am weary with forbearing and cannot contain" (verse 9). May this fire of holy impulse be ours!

Chapters 21, 22

During the last extremity of the siege of Jerusalem, Zedekiah sent the message found in these chapters to Jeremiah. King and people alike postponed their compliance with the warnings and invitations of

God's love until the last possible hour. Now they were eager for immunity from the consequences of their sins more than for repentance and a turning to God. Up to the last He pleaded with the people (21:8) but without avail. The denunciation against the king himself was most emphatic: "Woe unto him that buildeth his house by unrighteousness" (22:13). As a godless son of a godly father, Zedekiah turned from the ways of his father, who had judged the cause of the needy, endeavored to know God, and enjoyed His favor. Zedekiah oppressed his laborers, built a palace of unrighteousness, and consequently was destitute of the blessing of God. Those who fatten on the poverty of workers who ought to be more justly treated, should read these two stern chapters.

Chapter 23

The opening verses of this chapter present a true prophecy of the Messiah. Israel's restoration is linked to the coming of the Messiah. The coming of Christ, as the Branch, is the central theme of prophecy, and the Spirit-inspired prophets received such a revelation centuries beforehand. In the closing part of the chapter we have the contrast of false prophets. The name of the coming one was "THE LORD OUR RIGHTEOUSNESS" (verse 6). The lying prophets were guilty of unrighteousness. Much gain was theirs by telling the people things that they wanted to hear, things encouraging them in their wickedness (verse 27). But the pure, unadulterated Word of God burns like fire and falls with hammer-blows on sin (verse 29). Note the phrase, "if they had stood in my council" (verse 22). Here is the cause of much of our failure in Christian work – we do not stand in God's council. We run without being sent. Heaven's signals are ignored and traffic becomes snarled.

Chapter 24

The sign of the figs is related to Judah. In his vision, Jeremiah sees the captives as good figs, and the Jews that remained as bad figs. "Naughty," here means *of naught*, or *worthless*. Blessing is promised for the captives in Babylon but doom is pronounced over those Jews still in Jerusalem. Jehoiachim,

as a good fig, received privileged treatment (II Kings 25:27-30). What a great promise is in verse 7: "an heart to know me!" The goal of all blessing is to know God as He is revealed in His Word, and to be right with Him. If there is within us anything sinful or unloving, then knowledge of God is blurred, as condensed breath on a window will shut out the fairest landscape. If ours is the consciousness that we have strayed from Him, whose love is ever the same, let us return to Him with a whole heart.

Chapter 25

Two general divisions make up this conspicuous chapter. First of all, we have the *prophecy of the seventy years' captivity* (verses 1-14); then there is *the sign of the wine cup of fury* (verses 15-38). Judgment is written all over the chapter. Disasters were to overtake surrounding nations, and are described as a potion presented to each nation for drinking. If any refuse, the answer is given in the words: "Should ye be utterly unpunished?" (verse 29). Judgment was to begin with God's own people, as it ever does (I Peter 4:17). "God always begins with His people, because their sins traduce His character and bring it into contempt; and because sinners might otherwise establish a just charge of favoritism against Him." If the righteous be scarcely saved, where shall the ungodly and the sinner appear? Babylon had done God service as the instrument of chastisement to His own people (see Revelation 3:19).

Chapter 26

Jehoiakim stands out as the most despicable of the kings of Judah. He was neither pious toward God nor just toward men. Godly Jeremiah found himself in constant conflict with this evil-doer. And such an unjust monarch must have hated the prophet, who dared to raise his voice in denunciation of the king's crimes. Naturally, Jeremiah was nervous and sensitive. He spoke of himself as a child, and lamented that he had been born in such troublous times. But God promised to make him as a "defenced city, an iron pillar, and brazen walls . . . against the kings" (1:18,19), and this chapter proves how brazen Jeremiah became in the condemnation of sin. Although his life was in balance, he dared not be silent. Bravely he called upon king and people to amend their ways and their doings (26:12,13). Are you naturally reticent, backward, reserved or timid? Well, take your nature to God and let Him cover it with brass!

Chapters 27, 28

These two chapters can be named, "The Sign of the Yokes." Israel had grossly sinned and violated the bonds of holy fellowship and relationship with God, and He permitted the king of Babylon to invade the land. Thus the people came under the yoke of a Gentile monarch and were made to serve with rigor. There should be only one yoke for the people of God, namely, the one Christ offered His own, which He called, "My yoke" (Matthew 11:28-30). Hananiah's false prophecy and death make up chapter 28. He prophesied of the speedy return of the exiles and the breakup of the power of the king of Babylon, but he spoke out of his own heart. Professing to speak in the name of God, his mind was yet filled with human reasonings. God save us from false prophets who paint their roseate views of the future, being blind to what His infallible Word declares.

Chapter 29

Jeremiah writes to the captives and warns them that their bondage will last for seventy years. It will be useless on their part to plot a speedier return. They must wait out the predicted time, and spend the time quietly waiting for God's deliverance (verses 5-7). All prediction of a quick return made by false prophets had to be spurned (verses 8,9). The people were urged to be ready when the hour struck on God's clock for their return, and to be found seeking Him with all their heart (verses 12,13). Of course, God had a purpose in allowing His people to go into captivity in Babylon. Synagogues were scattered, and the Old Testament, that is, as much as was written to Jeremiah's time, proclaimed throughout the land. It is still true that God permits captivity for the extension of His cause. That thirteenth verse is true of the saints of every age. Our difficulty is that we do not search for Him with all our hearts.

Chapters 30, 31

The prophetic aspect of Israel, during the Great Tribulation, occupies these chapters. It has been pointed out that there is a great difference between the punishment of the ungodly and the chastisement of God's children. In the former case there is destruction; in the latter there will be restoration. "But I will not make a full end of thee" (30:11). When Israel's chastisement is over, the Lord will wash her stripes and restore her joy. Having loved her with an everlasting love, God will bring His own through all chastisement into a large place. As you read the first half of chapter 31, see if you can trace these aspects of God: His *love*, His *fatherhood*, His *redeeming power*, His *goodness*, His *reward* and His *mercy*. Verses 31-33 must be kept in mind as we study the present and future movements of the Jews. What a blessed heritage awaits the sons of Jacob!

Chapter 32

Jeremiah's action, as given in the first part of this chapter, has been called, "the heroic audacity of faith." The Chaldeans had overrun the land, and the prophet knew by the Word of the Lord that they were destined to hold both it and the city. And yet, at the divine command, Jeremiah bought a piece of land which was in the possession of the foe, with as much formality as though he were at once to enter upon its possession. Thus was Israel God's possession, though under the bondage of unbelief. Jeremiah, having obeyed the divine command, poured out his soul in prayer; and what a prayer! Pleading the almightiness of God, Jeremiah knew that the greater included the lesser – that the works of creation proved that God could rid the land of the Chaldeans and cause Israel to repossess what was theirs by divine right and gift.

Chapters 33-36

How much we owe to prison visions and literature! Shut up in the court of the prison, Jeremiah saw God as *the unconfined creator of all things* (33:2), *the unlimited scope of intercession* (verse 3), *the evidences of future blessing* (verses 6-9), *the unbounded joy of the future* (verses 10,11), and *the liberating and righteous Messiah* (verses 14-17). Have you ever proved the promise of verse 3? Chapter 34 contains God's message to King Zedekiah, and Zedekiah's useless decree. Chapters 35 and 36 brings us to Jehoiakim. The first chapter provides us with a "contrast between the strict obedience of the Rechabites to the directions of their ancestors, and the disobedience of Israel to Jehovah." Alas, how this contrast persists! Men are so eager and devoted to the customs and traditions of their families, and so regardless of the yet higher claims of God! In chapter 36 we have a remarkable contrast between Jehoiakim's treatment of the Word of God and the earlier response of King Josiah.

Chapters 37-39

Dr. Scofield names this section: "From the Accession to the Captivity of Zedekiah." What a dramatic account of Jeremiah's arrest and imprisonment as a traitor, when he was trying to visit his home town of Anathoth, chapters 37 and 38 present! Jeremiah, although a true and godly prophet, was not immune from suffering, but, according to promises, he was kept safe to the end. Note 37:21, and see how God cared for His child. In chapter 38 we find the prophet announcing, in graphic words, the doom of the king, and urging upon him the necessity of obeying the voice of the Lord. Jeremiah's advice reminds us of the repeated message of the Lord Jesus about those who keep their lives by losing them, and those who lose their lives in finding them. When Judah's final captivity came, as described in chapter 39, Zedekiah must have remembered Jeremiah's final message: "Thou shalt not escape; but thou shalt be taken by the hand of the king of Babylon" (38:23).

Chapters 40-42

The captain, who acted so grievously toward Jeremiah, has been called a comrade of the centurion of the New Testament. "He seems to have had a remarkable insight into God's dealings with Israel. In verse 3 he speaks

quite prophetically, and in his treatment of the prophet he gives every sign of having been admitted into the secret councils of the Most High." As Elijah was cared for by the ravens, so, through a captain of Nebuchadnezzar's guard, Jeremiah was well cared for. Chapter 41 is full of horrible atrocities. How the decimated remnant of the Jews suffered! Yet God controls all the Nebuchadnezzars and Ishmaels. In chapter 42 Jeremiah is before us again as a man of mighty intercession. For ten days he prayed; then he came forth from God with a message that burned itself into the hearts of the people. The people sent Jeremiah to the Lord – now the Lord sends him back to the people.

Chapters 43, 44

Terrified, the people of Israel fled and settled at Tahpanhes, there to malign and misunderstand the efforts of the one who, for some forty years, had tried to warn them of their peril and recall them to the faith of their fathers. "Almost the last ingredient of bitterness in Jeremiah's cup must have been furnished by their pertinacious obstinacy which would not be controlled by his word, which resisted his entreaties, and suggested that his advice was tinctured by treachery in their best interests." What blessing would have come to the people had they obeyed the voice of God's weeping prophet! Chapter 44 finds the Jews in Egypt, and Jeremiah is discovered warning them of the inevitable fate awaiting them there. Old and gray, his face marred with suffering, Jeremiah did not hesitate to declare that the sorrows of the people were due to their persistence in unholy rites. Think of the heart-appeal of verse 4!

Chapters 45-49

Miscellaneous prophecies make up the rest of the Book of Jeremiah. A brief message to Baruch is in chapter 45. The very association of Baruch with Jeremiah brought forth the mournful exclamation: "Woe is me now! for the Lord hath added grief to my sorrow" (45:3). But out of sorrow and pain, when borne patiently and trustfully, comes the more abundant life. Prophecies against Gentile power commence with chapter 46, within which we have the clash and crash of war. The overwhelming Egyptian invasion is described in the most graphic and stirring of words. Yet amid all the destruction and desolation, God remembers His people, even as they suffer from the results of their sins. Have we need of measured correction (46:28)? Upon the Philistines the sword of the Lord fell. Chapter 47 declares that such an avenging sword could not be quick. And such a sword is two-edged. It either saves or slays. From chapter 48 we learn of Moab's self-complacency. Her vessel was unemptied. In chapter 49 Jeremiah calls upon the people of Edom to seek safe cover – to dwell deep.

Chapters 50, 51

These two chapters contain Jeremiah's prophecies against Babylon and Chaldea. Let us take two suggestive phrases out of chapter 50. In verse 5 we read: "They shall ask the way to Zion with their faces thitherward." The difficulty we confront is the asking of the way to Zion, when our faces are not set that way. People want to make the most of both worlds – feet on the way to Zion, faces set toward the world. Then, in verse 6, there is a warning for our hearts: "They have forgotten their restingplace." Is this true of you? Then return unto thy rest, O soul! In chapter 51 the people are reminded that they have not been forsaken of God. Their transgressions have been the cause of their forsaking Him, but "Israel hath not been forsaken, nor Judah of his God, of the Lord of hosts" (verse 5). There may be times when it seems as if we are forsaken, but we must never mistake feelings for actualities (Hebrews 13:5).

Chapter 52

The first part of this concluding chapter should be compared with chapter 39:1-10. Before us, in retrospect, is the overthrow and captivity of Judah. When led by evil-minded kings, the people were made to suffer. The latter days of Jehoiachin (verses 31-34) offer a parable of grace. The king of Babylon saw to it that the king of Judah was well treated. "Every day a portion until the day of his death, all the days of his life," was his. We live upon the bounty of another. And if a heathen king acted thus for a captive king, what will not God do for His own? Surely He will do no less for prisoners of hope! Ere long He will change the prison garments of our old body and, giving us a body like unto Christ's own, bid us sit at His royal table and eat of His bread through the countless ages of eternity.

LAMENTATIONS

The Septuagint Version of this "funeral dirge," written by Jeremiah, after the third siege and fall of Jerusalem, carries the following preface to *Lamentations*, "And it came to pass, after Israel was taken captive, and Jerusalem made desolate, that Jeremias sat weeping, and lamented with this lamentation over Jerusalem, and said . . . " On the hillside west of Jerusalem is "The Grotto of Jeremiah" where tradition says the prophet stood as he looked down upon the city and wept over it. A Greater than Jeremiah shed tears over the same unholy city. The five chapters of this wail of a broken heart are actually five poems – "five elegiac cantos," with each poem ending with a prayer to the Lord, with the exception of the fourth, but this is made up by the last poem, which is all prayer.

Robert Lee gives us this impressive analysis of the book –

First Poem, Chapter 1 – The City represented as a *Weeping Widow* mourning in solitude

Second Poem, Chapter 2 – The City represented as a *Veiled Woman* now mourning amidst the ruins

Third Poem, Chapter 3 – The City represented as, and by the *Weeping Prophet* mourning before Jehovah the Judge

Fourth Poem, Chapter 4 – The City represented as *Gold*, dimmed, changed, degraded

Fifth Poem, Chapter 5 – The City represented as a *Suppliant* pleading with the Lord.

Chapter 1

The five lamentations forming this book record, on the one hand the faithfulness of God, and on the other the sin and sorrow of the people. In their Hebrew poetical form, all five elegies are acrostic, all but one – the third chapter, wherein are sixty-six verses – consist of twenty-two verses, each verse beginning with a letter of the Hebrew alphabet. In this chapter we have desolation and ruin. Jeremiah laments the fate of Jerusalem. The story of her desolation is mingled with confession of her sin. No sorrow was like unto her sorrow. Yet the sorrow of the city was not in excess of its sin. Sorrow has been called the mother of all joy. Sorrow interprets the true significance of God's dealings, as well as the true nature of our wanderings. What lessons have we learned in the school of sorrow? Has our grief produced self-examination, confession, and the acknowledgment of the righteousness of the divine stroke?

Chapter 2

In Jeremiah's second lamentation, affliction and providence seem to be prominent. Still addressing Jerusalem, the prophet speaks of return from captivity and deliverance from a cruel yoke. Strong, stern words were directed against the false prophets for perpetually seeing visions of deliverance that were never realized. Empty dreams were theirs. They knew, only too well, that captivity could not be turned until sin had been put away. But the unfaithful prophets were unwilling to deal with the iniquity of the people. They promised deliverance from this side and the other. God alone, however, could deliver, and that on the basis of the determination of the people to abandon their wicked ways. Would that we had more

faithful prophet-voices declaring, at any cost, the truth about sin and its consequences!

Chapter 3

Sorrow and consolation make up this third lamentation. A characteristic feature of all five woes is the pouring out of Jeremiah's personal grief. "Mine eye trickleth down, and ceaseth not" (verse 49). Divine grief and national grief can also be traced. Note, as you read this chapter: *the consolation of God's mercy* (verses 22-27); *the consolation of God's righteousness* (verses 28-36); and *the consolation of God's sovereignty* (verses 37-40). Jeremiah's own experience is before us in verse 57. Thrown into the dungeon by malicious foes, he yet proved the goodness and nearness of God. His cry was heard and deliverance came. Can it be that you are in the dark dungeon of sorrow? Despair not; God is near, and He can make your dungeon luminous with the radiance of the Shekinah. Listen for the whisper of His voice. Fear not!

Chapters 4, 5

In Jeremiah's fourth woe we can trace guilt and punishment. How pathetic is the opening phrase: "How is the gold become dim!" Can it be that the gold of our testimony has become dim? Has the brightness gone? Well, visible splendor can be restored. A precious promise is to be found in 4:20. Such a truth will yet be realized by Israel. No matter where the saints are scattered among the nations, God is their protection. The last lamentation is made up of distress and prayer (chapter 5). Weary of chastening, and longing for the return of the pleasures and privileges of the past, the people desired to be right with God. "Renew our days as of old" (verse 21). Have we need of such a divine renewal? Rewards, in the shape of crowns, are offered believers. Let us see to it that our crowns do not fall from our heads (verse 16). May we be saved from the tragedy of a lost crown!

EZEKIEL

Each of the three major prophets emphasized one Person in the blessed Trinity, without neglecting the other two august Persons.

Jeremiah is the prophet of God the Father;
Isaiah, the prophet of God the Son;
Ezekiel, the prophet of God the Spirit.
That the ministry of the Holy Spirit is prominent in *Ezekiel* can be gathered from the twenty-five references to Him. "The glory of the Lord," a conspicuous key phrase of the book can be linked on to "The Spirit of glory." Ezekiel himself an aristocratic priest of Jerusalem (1:1) who, at 25 years of age, was carried captive to Babylon, speaks of Israel in Egypt more than any other prophet. "His pen is more conspicuous than his tongue, and his style is vivid and fervid." How near God was to destroying the whole nation because of its idolatry! The sobs of Jeremiah bore fruit in the success of Ezekiel when the people turned to the Lord. It is in this book alone that we have a glimpse into the past history of our great adversary, the devil (28:11-19); full details of a temple yet to be built, and of the new river (40-42, 47). As to the structure of the book, Lee's analysis is about the best.

1. Preparation and Call of the Prophet, 1-3. The Appearance of the Glory of the Lord.
2. Prophecies of destruction of Jerusalem, 4-24. The Departure of the Glory of the Lord.
3. Prophecies against Seven Nations, 25-32. The Glory of God and surrounding nations.
4. Glorious Prophecies in relation to Israel's Future, 32-48. The Return of the Glory of the Lord.

Chapter 1

Ezekiel was a captive in Babylon when he wrote his highly symbolic prophecy. The world owes a great deal to its captive, exile, and prison literature, as in the writings of Ezekiel; Daniel; John, in the Revelation; and some of the epistles of Paul. There is also the immortal classic, *The Pilgrim's Progress*, which was written by John Bunyan in Bedford Jail. Karle Wilson in her poem, *Prisons*, has this expressive verse:

Masters have wrought in prisons,
At peace in cells of stone;
From their thick walls I fashion
Windows to light my own.

The living creatures, or cherubim, that Ezekiel here writes about represent the entire round of animate existence. By the wheels we can understand the round of Providence, or the circle of nature. It will be noted that there is perfect harmony between the Spirit, creatures and wheels. Conflict is alien to a Spirit-guided life.

Chapters 2, 3

What an authoritative command introduces this section! "Stand upon thy feet!" No timidity must characterize Ezekiel as he delivers a God-given message. The four faces of 1:10 must be his. The prophet must act as the incarnate conscience of the people, reminding them of their evil ways, remonstrating and pleading with them, and leading them back to God. For such a ministry he requires the empowerment of the Spirit. Only thus can he bear the mark of a true prophet. "Eat this roll, and go speak." Ezekiel must make his message part and parcel of himself. Too often, preachers proclaim truth unrelated to their own experience. Unfed themselves, they try to feed others with food they have not tasted. Ezekiel's message is not a pleasant one, yet he sends it forth with a sorrow-laden heart: "I tell you even weeping." The eaten Word produces compassion.

Chapters 4, 5

It is somewhat hard for many readers to understand the striking symbolism of Ezekiel, who was bidden to warn the people in a series of significant actions of their impending fate. The prophet found one of the divine injunctions abhorrent to his soul: "Ah Lord God, spare me from this" (4:14). Graciously God reduced the pressure of the burden laid upon His servant. Does not the counterpart of this happen in our own experience? Note how the prophet had to identify himself with the iniquity of his people. What does this suggest to your mind? The sign of the sharp knife makes up chapter 5. Because of sin, famine and pestilence and sword brought deserved punishment. The people had sinned against conspicuous privilege and opportunity, and were obliged to come under the rod. Punishment for them was infinitely heavier than that inflicted upon others less privileged.

Chapters 6, 7

The mountains of Israel had witnessed the shameless idolatry of God's people, and received the divine condemnation. Judgment upon Israel herself was also pronounced. What heartbreak to God man's sin occasions Him: "I am broken with their whorish heart" (6:9)! Would that our hearts of stone would break as we see the Lord broken by our sin! Our second chapter is full of alarms. Crises face the people: "The time is come; the day is near." What can their silver and gold do for them? Money may be a key unlocking many treasures of life, but what can it do in times when supreme crisis overtakes us? The things of earth, Ezekiel proves, cannot ultimately save or satisfy. They are not able to deliver the soul in the days of remorse and of divine wrath.

Chapters 8, 9

"The combined effect of the four visions of profanation in chapter 8 is idolatry set up in the entire temple," says Dr. C. I. Scofield, "even in the holy of holies" (verses 10,11); women given over to phallic cults (verse 14), and nature worship (verse 16)." God was greatly provoked by the idol-worship of those who bore His name. The elders were guilty of worshiping every form of creeping thing portrayed upon the walls of secret chambers. What else could God do but severely punish those departing from Him in such licentious ways? Chapter 9 depicts God's glory departing from the inner temple. The man with the inkhorn represents the discriminating righteousness of God's judgments. The slaughter weapons fell first upon the sinning elders. Judgment begins with the house of God. Because those who

bear office know better and profess more than others, their judgment is heavier.

Chapter 10

In this dramatic chapter Ezekiel describes, in vivid and terrible minuteness, the gradual withdrawal of God from His house. What a deep and searching lesson the chapter holds for our hearts! "The light of other days fades slowly; the year sinks by almost insensible gradations to the fall of the leaf; gray hairs besprinkle our heads without our knowing it; before we are aware of it, the train has borne us miles off the main line to the wrong station. So gradually our hearts backslide. Satan is too knowing to lead us at a single leap into the precipice, but conducts us by a gradual decline. A little less Bible reading, a slight slackening in watchfulness and prayer, an imperceptible drift worldwards." Later on, as we shall see, the glory of the Lord returned to the renovated temple (43:1-4). Blessed be God, there can be the dawn of a new day for any backslider who repents and returns!

Chapters 11, 12

A vision of divine judgment and the minimizing of the effects of Ezekiel's denunciations of judgment make up chapter 11. As exiles, the people would find themselves removed from all outward obedience and a material temple, yet they would find more than the equivalent in God Himself, who offered Himself "as a little sanctuary" (verse 16). How many there are who, for varied reasons, cannot mingle with God's people in the worship of the sanctuary! Yet, confined to the four walls of their rooms, they can rest beneath the folds of the tabernacle of God's presence. Emphatic is the prophet's declaration: "The word that I shall speak shall be performed, it shall be no more deferred" (12:25,28). The people did not deny that Ezekiel uttered the Word of God, but comforted themselves with the thought that God would be in no hurry to carry out His judgments. What a delusion!

Chapters 13-15

Chapter 13 is full of warning to those who are called to speak for God, to prophesy out of their own heart, and to follow their own reasoning, and who profess to see what they have not seen. It is a temptation to declare, "the Lord saith," when actually no revelation has been received. Lying prophets are by no means extinct. Chapter 14, with its idolatry among holy men and in a holy place, makes sad reading. So heinous was the sin of Jerusalem that God sent upon her His four judgments at once, and together. God save us from idols in the heart! Backsliding commences in the heart. The short vine chapter, chapter 15, is suggestive and should be read alongside of John 15. What is the vine good for? It has only one use – to bear fruit. Israel has failed as a fruit-bearing vine. She became an empty vine. The Lord Jesus appeared as the true vine. Our function, as branches of this vine, is to bear, not produce, fruit.

Chapter 16

Dr. F. B. Meyer suggests that this chapter is rich in spiritual significance. Like the people of whom Ezekiel writes we, too, were born in the land of the Canaanite – our father, the first Adam; our mother, Eve. "There was no beauty in us by nature, but everything to cause abhorrence to the Holy God. And if we are washed and clothed, decked with gold and silver, arrayed in fine linen, silk, and broidered work, eating fine flour, and honey and oil, exceedingly beautiful and arrayed in royal estate, it is all of grace – of the exceeding and eternal grace of God. There is nothing of it at all in which we can boast ourselves." Of Him are we in Christ Jesus, through whom we are what we are. We are perfect only through His comeliness which He has put upon us.

Chapters 17, 18

The parable of the great eagle and the high cedar must have produced deep conviction of sin as "the rebellious house" listened to the prophet unfold the parable. Christ can be likened unto the great cedar tree, and all kinds of people find rest in Him, as birds of every wing. Out of the windy storm and tempest, every soul can make for a roosting place under the shelter of His wing, by faith. The conclusion of chapter 17 teaches us the lesson of humility.

In the ethical instructions following, in chapter 18, Israel is taught that all souls are God's (verse 4). All are His by right of creation, by right of redemption, by right of His own holy and glorious nature. Can we say that we are truly His? What an incentive for soul-winning verse 23 provides!

Chapters 19, 20

Lamentations make up chapter 19. It contains a dirge over two kings of David's house who, like wild beasts, had been carried off; and then over the whole royal family, described under the figure of a wasted vine, humbled and almost destroyed Lamentations were taken up for the kings. Do we lament for the sufferings and sorrows of our heavenly King? Do we weep because our sins nailed Him to His cross? Because the people belonged to God, chastisement overtook them for their disobedience and rebellion. Although His chosen ones, they could not act as they pleased (20:32). Those in covenant relationship with Him could not lightly cast off their sacred bonds. May we ever realize what a solemn thing it is to be God's children. We cannot go our own way. His will must ever be our choice.

Chapters 21, 22

Using two parables, Ezekiel directs his prophecy against Zedekiah and Jerusalem, and predicts the advance of Nebuchadnezzar. Judah's king thought his wit and power would win the day, but God declared His overthrow of man-made schemes. Note the threefold "overturn" (21:27), and its application to Christ's ultimate dominion over all hostile forces. Enumerating the sins of Israel, God punished the people by scattering them among the nations. At long last, however, they are being regathered in the land God gave them. As yet the filthiness has not been consumed, but Israel's day of purification is not far away. The day is fast approaching when, having been refined by fire, God's ancient people will again become a vessel unto honor.

Chapters 23, 24

Another parable occupies chapter 23. Spiritual unfaithfulness is constantly described under metaphors borrowed from the marriage relationship. God is depicted as the husband in whose heart the fire of jealousy burns, while His erring people are compared to a truant wife. Ezekiel clearly shows that it is impossible to be satisfied with self-chosen loves. The prophet was made a sign to the people. A sudden stroke befell his home, yet he was not permitted to mourn. He was called to display in his own silence the solemn, tearless anguish with which Israel would go into captivity. Often in human experience the personal must be subordinated to the spiritual. But it is not easy to choke back our sobs.

Chapter 25

The key phrase, "thus saith the Lord God," divides this chapter (verses 3,8,12,15). Judgment is pronounced upon the Ammonites, Moab, Edom and Philistia. One cannot read a chapter like this without realizing how keen the Hebrew prophets were as politicians, in the best sense of the word. They knew how to watch and interpret the dealings of God in contemporary history. The late saintly Professor Reynolds was in the habit of opening the morning paper by saying: "Let us see what our Heavenly Father is doing in the world." Moab and Seir made the mistake of supposing that God's people were like unto themselves. But God had put a difference between the Jews and surrounding nations. The world may think that our lives, as Christians, are like unto theirs. They cannot see the divine environment within which we live. Note how human vengeance is matched with divine vengeance.

Chapters 26-28

As these three chapters are related to judgment upon Tyre, it is necessary to read them together. At the time of Ezekiel's prediction, Tyre was a preeminent, prosperous and pompous nation. Strong in the sea, the carrying-trade of the world was in her hands. A direct evidence of the divine inspiration of Scriptures is that Ezekiel was able to predict Tyre's approaching fall, and that the site of such a proud and populous city would be sought for in vain. It would seem as if much of the prophet's language was before John knew when he came to describe the fall

of Babylon (Revelation 17:18). In a truly magnificent way, Ezekiel describes Tyre under the image of one of her own merchant vessels. The language of chapter 27 is incomparable. Behind the prince of Tyre we can discern the prince of the power of the air, who was created perfect in his ways until unrighteousness was found in him and he was cast out of heaven.

Chapters 29, 30

For his reward for vanquishing Tyre, the king of Babylon was given the land of Egypt. God's purpose had been wrought even through a heathen nation (29:30). While we do not merit anything from God, He is not unforgetful of services rendered. If He gave Egypt to a heathen king for service in respect to Tyre, what may we not expect from Him if we live and labor for His glory? How striking is the phrase, "when I shall put *my* sword into the hand of the king of Babylon" (30:25). It was God's sword in the hand of Nebuchadnezzar. Thus Babylon became the executor of the divine decree. Natural eyes cannot see certain events carrying the sword of the Lord. Chance, malice of men, and natural and national rivalry are held responsible for international strife. But behind such is the sword of the Lord.

Chapters 31, 32

Prophecy against and lamentations over Pharaoh form the burden of these chapters. The Lord knows how to bring down the mighty from their seats. A blessed application of verse 17 has been made by many a missionary of the cross, who has gone forth to dwell among the heathen. Amid all strange and perilous conditions of heathenism, sacrificial laborers have proved that Christ is there as a shadow of a great rock in a weary land (31:17). The keynote of chapter 32, as of all prophetic Scriptures, is: "The Word of the Lord came unto me" (verses 1,17). Prophets of old claimed divine inspiration for all their utterances. They knew when God spoke to their soul and unhesitatingly declared the God-prompted message. Whether it was a message of blessing or blight was not their responsibility. Their obligation was to function as mouthpieces of God.

Chapter 33

We must go to the last verse of this chapter for a key to its understanding. The people to whom Ezekiel ministered treated him as a delightful diversion. While his ministrations were given expressions of admiration, the true wrath and weight of his words were not realized. Ah, but once his warnings became actualities and his predictions were fulfilled to the letter, they knew that he had been more than a sweet singer. He stood revealed as a prophet of the Lord. There are many solemn truths in this chapter for all those who witness for the Lord, to ponder prayerfully. Whether our sphere is large or small in this present dispensation, may grace be ours to have souls free for the responsibility of bearing witness to all who come our way. The first eight verses should be read on our knees, with the prayer that we may ever manifest a yearning passion for souls.

Chapter 34

Here is another chapter for all who feed the flock of God to study prayerfully. Turning to the faithless shepherds of Israel, Ezekiel has some soul-searching words for them to hear. Whether our flock are children around us in the home or Sunday school, or adults in a meeting place, the shepherd must keep in mind that God will require the flock at his hand (verse 10). Under-shepherds may fail, but the shepherd Himself never will (verses 11-15). Place alongside of this chapter John 10, where the Lord Jesus is the shepherd who brings the sheep into good pasture. Sheep rest when they are satisfied and free from alarm. Christ provides His own with green pastures and still waters. Look at verse 16 and link it on to Luke 15, where the Lord Jesus is portrayed as the shepherd seeking the lost.

Chapters 35, 36

In chapter 35 we find the key in its last words: "They shall know that I am the Lord." A similar thought is in verse 10: "Whereas the Lord was there." (See also 36:38.) Cunningly Mount Seir plotted to possess the land of Israel, seeing that the children of Israel were in captivity in Habor and Gozan, and the children of Judah at Babylon. But while the Lord's people were out of the land, the Lord was not. He was still in possession. What food for comfort this is! Often our foes plot against us, supposing that we constitute easy prey and that spoils can be divided without hindrance. But God is there. In the home beseiged by every kind of misfortune, if only one therein is truly the Lord's, there He is, the stronger than the strong, who is able, therefore, to deal with all calamity.

Chapter 37

A word is necessary regarding the double office of the prophet. He had to prophesy to earth and the heavens: "Prophesy over these bones . . . Prophesy unto the wind" (verses 4,9, R.V.). He was responsible to God and man. We are apt to forget that service fails of its highest result if these two injunctions are not constantly before us. Is it not wonderful that, after some 2,500 years, the prophecy of this chapter may be close to being realized? The Jews are returning to their land. The bones are coming together. Not yet, however, are the four winds blowing upon Israel. She is now a recognized state, but is still in the valley of dry, dead bones. Israel's regeneration is not far distant. God will put His Spirit in the people, and the two sticks, as one mighty weapon in His hand, will accomplish great and mighty things on the earth.

Chapter 38

What a momentous chapter this is in the light of present-day happenings! Meshech and Tubal are doubtless the modern cities of Moscow and Tobolsk. Some 2,500 years ago Ezekiel prophesied of a great northern confederacy, with Russia as the dominating factor, and we have lived to see the day of its formation. Already this evil confederacy, some of its satellite nations even being named by Ezekiel, appears to be on the march. One of these days it will resolve to go up to the land of unwalled villages, such as abound in Palestine, only to be challenged by the merchants of Tarshish in the far West. This opposing force is, we believe, the western confederacy that the recent North Atlantic Pact foreshadows – frequently spoken of, by Bible students, as the revived Roman Empire. How grateful we should be for the sure Word of prophecy, shining as a light in a dark place. God is working out His plan. Christ is at hand. May we live as those who await His appearing!

Chapter 39

This chapter continues the prophecy against Gog. A time of deserved and terrible judgment awaits the brutal forces of the North. Compare the details given of the battle of Armageddon with Isaiah 2:10-22; Revelation 19:11-21; etc. God has not forgotten His promise to restore Israel (verses 25-29). The blindness overtaking the Jew is only till the fullness of the Gentiles is fulfilled. God's covenant cannot be annulled. Already the Jews are being gathered out of their enemies' lands and placed in their own country. As yet, however, God is not being sanctified in them in the sight of many nations. But Israel's conversion is coming. God will not hide His face from her forever but, possessing her by His Spirit, He will make her a praise and glory in the earth. A most glorious future awaits the whole house of Israel. Our present obligation is to win the Jew for Christ.

Chapter 40

The Word came to Ezekiel: "Declare all that thou seest" (verse 4); and his entire prophecy proves the prophet to be a true witness. Visions were his, and courageously he bore testimony to Israel of all he had seen, tasted and handled of the things of God. Ezekiel's visions were not for private advantage and jubilation only. The prophet had to declare all that his eyes had seen. It may well be that the mysterious man with the measuring reed was none other than the Man Christ Jesus, in one of His theophanic appearances. He could not have been a mere man to command Ezekiel, as He did, and to unfold to the mind of the prophet the things pertaining to the future temple. If this chapter refers to Israel during the great kingdom-age, it would surely seem as if she is to have another literal temple, built according to the specifications given to Ezekiel.

Chapter 41

One cannot follow the pattern of the ideal temple without realizing the minute measurements and specifications, even to the ornaments of cherubim and palm trees, that Ezekiel received. Nothing was left to human ingenuity. All had to follow God's pattern, just as Moses was called to follow the divine plan in the erection of the tabernacle. It should be our constant aim to know God's will for our lives. Do we have His plan? Is He working out His purpose? Too often we conceive *our* plan for the temple of our lives and, bringing it to God, ask His approval of our wishes. But He does not work that way. We have been chosen in Christ, and all concerning our lives has been fixed, even down to the details of our pilgrimage. Our responsibility, therefore, is to be submissive to His will in order that He may work out that which is well-pleasing in His sight.

Chapter 42

Continuing the description of the temple, Ezekiel comes to its various chambers and to the ministry of the priests. Note the word, "measure," both here and in surrounding chapters. No mere human guesswork was allowed. The life of every believer is a divinely-measured life. What a truth is wrapped up in verse 13: "The priests that are near unto the Lord shall eat the most holy things." Apart altogether from the question of a restored levitical priesthood, we know that every believer is a priest unto God. Acceptance of Christ as Saviour constitutes priesthood, but whether every believer exercises this privileged priesthood is another matter. Of course, we are not called to offer propitiatory sacrifices, as the priests of old, but to present ourselves as living sacrifices, to offer up a sacrifice of praise to God continually. As priests, we are near unto the Lord. But is ours a realized nearness?

Chapter 43

In chapters 9 and 10 is recorded the departure of the Shekinah cloud from the doomed temple. Now that glory-cloud returns to a new, reconstructed temple. There is a precious promise associated with God's return and indwelling: "I will dwell in the midst of the children of Israel, and they shall no more defile my holy name" (verse 7). The realized presence of God is to make the old sin abhorrent and impossible. Holiness will be manifest on every hand, seeing the Holy One is in full possession of the temple and its worshipers. Applying the narrative to our own hearts, has the glory departed? While we cannot lose the Lord, sin can rob us of the consciousness and manifestation of His presence. Well, the glory can return by the way it went, and life can again be radiant. May His glory fill the inner shrine of our spirits!

Chapter 44

Much can be gathered from the injunctions for the priests and Levites who were given the charge of the sanctuary. Look at verse 5. Ezekiel was exhorted to "mark well" and "behold." Surely this is a command to obey as we endeavor to read the Scriptures. Attention and intention must be combined. Then the priests were commissioned to come near His table, to minister unto Him (verse 16), always remembering the necessary sin-offering whenever God was approached (verse 27). It was only then that He became the inheritance and possession of the true worshiper. Priests we are—to God and the Father. But no matter how holily we may live, as a clearer revelation of God's perfect holiness breaks upon us there is a deeper consciousness of need to shelter beneath the blood of our Sin-Offering.

They who fain would serve Thee best
Are conscious most of sin within.

Let us never fear clearer light. What the holy light reveals, the precious blood can cleanse.

Chapter 45

This chapter contains a very touching provision. It has been expressed thus: "When the services of the newly constituted temple were in full operation, and the priests were performing the usual rites in all the pomp and splendor of their ceremonial on the behalf of the righteous and godly souls, there was to be special thought of the erring

and simple; for these two characters a special offering was made. Perhaps the erring were too hardened and the simple too obtuse to bring an offering for themselves; but they were not forgotten. The blood of the sin-offering was to be placed on the posts of the house and on the posts of the gate of the inner court, each seventh day of the month, on their behalf." Is it not blessed to realize that the blood covers all, that there is room for all erring and simple ones in the Father's house, by faith in Christ, our Sin-Bearer?

Chapter 46

While this chapter covers regulations for ingress and egress in the temple that Ezekiel describes, surely we are warranted in discovering a true and tender thought regarding the relationship between Christ and His own. On the seventh day, which for us is now the Lord's Day, princes and people entered the holy precincts to feast anew upon their offerings. It is thus we turn aside, on the day that reminds us of our own Prince's victory over sin and death, in order to hear His voice, feel the touch of His hand, and feast anew upon the bread of life divine, only to go forth into the valley taking with us the glory of the mount. Within the chapter we read of the prince going forth with the people. Thus is it with our glorious Prince. He never puts His sheep forth alone. When, as redeemed ones, we go forth to witness, our Prince and we go forth together.

Chapters 47, 48

The prophet's vision included the life-giving river reaching even to the Dead Sea, in whose brackish waters no fish can live. Smitten, however, by the crystal tide, a marvelous change takes place—the waters are healed and abound with fish. Everything lives whither the river flows. All of which is a parable of the fertilizing effect of the river of life issuing from the cross. In the abundant life that the Holy Spirit makes possible, there are no dead seas, no marshes, no waste stretches of desert sands. What do we know of the ever deepening river? Son of man, hast thou seen this? Ezekiel concludes his wonderful prophecy with a view of the ideal city, the prominent characteristic of which is the presence of God – "The Lord is there." The tabernacle of God is to be with men, and all are to bask in the sunshine of His realized sovereignty and glory.

DANIEL

We are in hearty agreement with the conclusion Dr. F. A. Tatford reaches in the Introduction to his most enlightening volume, *The Climax Of The Ages*, or *Studies In Daniel's Prophecies*. "Truly, Daniel's was a life rich in historical experience, as well as in earthly honours, although at the same time one of dedication to the service of God and of enrichment by the revelation of the purposes of the Almighty." Carried captive to Babylon when he was but 16 years of age, Daniel was to spend 69 years there (1:21), and in spite of the idolatry of the nation and the vileness of its court he lived a saintly life and exercised tremendous influence in three kingdoms – Babylon, Media and Persia. Ellicott, discussing the aims of the Book of Daniel, says that it has the three-fold object –

"1. To supply a missing link in the chain of the continuity of revelation;
2. To support Israel amidst the doubts and fears occasioned by the Exile;
3. To reveal to a polytheistic nation the eternal power of the One true God."

To our Lord, Daniel was an actual person, and in His quotation from his book set His seal upon it as an integral part of the inspired Word of God (Matthew 24:15). It would seem as if *Daniel* has two main divisions –

1. Historical 1-6, written by the prophet in the third person
2. Prophetical 7-12, written by him in the first person.

In the latter section, nations of the world are judged, and the everlasting Kingdom predicted.

Chapter 1

Revelation, the Bible's last book, is a divine commentary on Daniel. The two books should be studied together. For a brief biographical note, read Dr. Scofield's introduction to Daniel. The modernists reject this book as Daniel's, affirming it to be impossible for the prophet to have lived in the days of Nebuchadnezzar, Darius and Cyrus, and yet to write a book telling of world-empires before they came into existence. The chapter before us is introductory. "It does not have a prophetic character," says Dr. Ironside in his excellent commentary on Daniel, "but it pictures for our instruction, the moral condition suited to enlightenment in regard to the divine ways, and counsels emphasizing the need of holiness as a prerequisite to growth in the truth." Daniel's prophecy is one of the most important books in the Bible to understand.

Chapter 2

This great chapter has been called "The A.B.C. of prophecy." Here we have the most sublime, yet simple, prophetic cameo in the Bible, and here we have also the commencement of the distinctive, designated period, "the times of the Gentiles" (Luke 21:24). Gentile dominion had its rise when the word came to Nebuchadnezzar, "Thou, O king, art a king of kings," and will end when Christ returns as the King of kings to usher in His kingdom (Revelation 11:15; 17:14). The chief thought to bear in mind, while reading this chapter, is that of God-given ability to read the future, that is, "what should come to pass hereafter" (verse 29). The king's wise men failed to interpret his dream and read the future. The Holy Spirit alone can show us "things to come." Daniel, therefore, stands out as a true prophet, Spirit-inspired and taught (4:7; 5:11). We are not shut up to guesses as we face the future (I Peter 1:19).

Chapter 3

This chapter records the pride and punishment of the world emperor, Nebuchadnezzar. The difficulty with this dictator was that, although he could appreciate and reward the wisdom and integrity of Daniel, he had no heart for Daniel's God. We here see how Nebuchadnezzar, instead of being humbled by all that God had revealed to his mind by Daniel, simply used the same to exalt himself and extol his own fancied greatness. So up went the image, with the command for all men to bow before it. But a haughty monarch was brought to realize that there were some consciences that could not be bought. Shadrach, Meshach and Abednego refused to worship the image. Boldly facing the king, they declared their willingness to pay the price of full allegiance to God. Furious, the king ordered the furnace heated seven times more than ordinarily, but from the furnace the noble youths emerged without the smell of fire upon them. That blessed fourth Person in the flames saw to that. He will always come to the aid of His own.

Chapter 4

Dr. Ironside says: "In this stirring chapter, written by Nebuchadnezzar himself, and preserved and incorporated into the volume of inspiration by Daniel, we have the interesting account of the means God used to bring this haughty king to the end of himself, and lead him to abase himself before the Majesty in the heavens." For the third time, God speaks to Nebuchadnezzar. The last two occasions left the king unsubdued. But now this world-ruler is utterly humiliated before his princes. Here we have the monarch's conversion. To quote another: "In all this we see a picture of Gentile power in its alienation from God and bestial character . . . its final subjugation to God in the time of the End, when Christ shall return in Glory, and all nations prostrate themselves before Him." May God save us from all pride of the flesh!

Chapter 5

At the outset of these meditations on Daniel we urged that Daniel and Revelation be read together. It will be found that what is written in this chapter is intimately connected with Revelation 17 and 18. We have here Daniel's association with Belshazzar and Darius, under whose respective reigns the Babylonian Empire crumbled. What drunken orgy the chapter opens with! Holy vessels were desecrated, and God defied. But sud-

den and severe judgment was about to fall. The handwriting on the wall struck fear into the heart of a proud, defiant ruler. Godless astrologers and soothsayers could not interpret a message from another world, just as natural man cannot understand the deep things of God. Amid the horror and consternation of the court, the queen-mother appeared, and, recalling Daniel's Spirit-imparted ability to unravel secrets, urged him to be brought. Belshazzar's doom was declared and delivered. Are we found wanting in anything?

Chapter 6

How wonderfully this chapter illustrates the truth that no weapon, formed against God's own, can prosper! The record of Daniel in the lions' den not only thrills the young, but nerves the brave for conflict. Daniel's flawless character was more than his jealous co-rulers could stand. What a reputation he enjoyed: "He was faithful, neither was there any error or fault found in him . . . . We shall not find any occasion against this Daniel, except we find it against him concerning the law of his God." How do we compare with such a standard? The presidents and princes craftily persuaded Darius to establish a decree, which meant their own doom. These cunning plotters did not reckon on Daniel's determination to keep his window open toward Jerusalem. Of the lions' den much could be written. The God who made the lions was able to close their mouths when Daniel was around, and yet use the same lions for the destruction of Daniel's foes.

Chapter 7

Under different figures, the four great world-empires before us in chapter 2 are here set forth again. Within this chapter the whole course of the times of the Gentiles, beginning with Babylon and ending in the overthrow of all derived authority, under the power of the Son of man, was presented to Daniel. In chapter 2, we see prophetic history from man's standpoint. Here, it is viewed from the divine angle. Man sees the course of world-empires as a stately and noble image; Daniel, God's prophet, views succeeding empires as four ravenous, brutal beasts. We presently live within the fragments of the last world-empire, the fourth beast, dreadful and terrible, and strong exceedingly, namely, the Roman world-empire. The little horn can be identified as the Roman beast of Revelation 17:12,13, the coming supreme arbiter of Europe. Gentile sovereignty will end with Christ's return.

Chapter 8

Attention has been drawn to the fact that chapters 1-2:3 were written in Hebrew for the encouragement of the remnant among the scattered Jews. Chapters 2:4-7 were written in Aramaic, the popular language of the day, so that the Chaldeans could understand their message. From chapter 8 on, we have Hebrew again, seeing that much of this last section is associated with the Jews. After two years, the further vision of this chapter was granted to Daniel. We are not left to our own ingenuity in the identification of the ram. The interpreting angel tells us that it corresponds to the breasts and arms of silver in Nebuchadnezzar's colossal image, and also to the bear in the last vision. Thus, symbol after symbol is used to describe the glory, yet doom, of Gentile dominion, and the necessity of the establishment of Christ's reign and rule. And, praise Him, His day is coming!

Chapter 9

We now come to the vision of the Seventy Weeks, which a renowned student of prophecy has called "The Backbone of Prophecy." A right understanding of these "weeks" will reveal the true interpretation of the prophetic time clock. It is impossible, in the limit of the assigned space of a day's reading, fully to expound "the Seventy Weeks." The reader is referred to the notes in the Scofield Bible, or in The Pilgrim Bible. Studying the Book of Jeremiah, Daniel carefully noted the twofold reference to Jerusalem's seventy years of desolation. Daniel knew that these years were running out and, in simplicity, pleads for the turning away of divine anger from the Jews. Then came the vision of the Seventy Weeks. These seventy "weeks," actually weeks of years, equal 490 years; the first sixty-nine of these "weeks" cover the period from the rebuilding of Jerusalem

and the Babylonian captivity (verse 25), to the cutting off of the Messiah at Calvary. The last "week" covers the Tribulation period. It would seem as if we are near the commencement of Daniel's last week. Are we ready?

Chapter 10

Daniel's last vision covers chapters 10-12, and is the most minute of all his prophecies. There is little need to point out that the Church is not to be found in these prophecies. It is the Jews who are before the prophet here (verse 14). Daniel saw the two massive peaks of the cross and the millennial reign of Christ, but the valley in between – the Church period – seems to have been what troubled his mind (7:28). In the chapter before us, we have an unfolding of angelic agency. The glorified messenger has a description corresponding in many ways to that given of the Lord Jesus in Revelation 1. But he must not be identified as Christ, who needs no angelic help. Beyond any visible conflict there is the invisible. Do you realize sufficiently the power of Satan? As the prince of the power of the air, he surely will endeavor to hinder our prayers from reaching God, and also the answers coming from God. In connection with this chapter, read Ephesians 6:11 and Revelation 12:7-10.

Chapter 11

The record found here, and made in heaven, is one God means us to understand. Wars touched upon by Daniel cover some two centuries, proving that history is "His Story." In verses 21-35, we have the dread person who is called the "Antichrist of the Old Testament," the blasphemous "little horn" of chapter 8. How he hated the Jews, and degraded the priesthood by selling the office of high priest to the vilest man among apostate Jews. The abomination of desolation (verse 31), associated with the pollution of the sanctuary and the taking away of the daily sacrifice, will be repeated by the Antichrist in the last half of the Tribulation. The last part of this chapter minutely describes that impious personage, who is the incarnation of lawlessness and blasphemy, and who, without doubt, prefigures the

Antichrist of whom John speaks. Ere he appears, the Church will be raptured.

Chapter 12

While verses 2 and 3 may not refer to actual physical resurrection, and consequent rewards, but of Israel's moral and national resurrection, and the blessing attending the ministry of the faithful remnant, we can yet apply the verses to two destinies awaiting souls, and the reward of soul-winners. Will there be any stars in our crowns?

How many have you turned to righteousness? Daniel was told to shut up the words and seal the book, even to the time of the end. Thus, the next event in prophetic order is "the time of the end," meaning, the end of the Gentile age. The appendix, verses 5-13, give more light as to times and seasons. The times given by the angel agree with 7:25. (Read also Matthew 24 and Revelation 19 in this connection.) How beautiful and tender is the conclusion of this book! Have you the assurance of eternal rest at the end of your days?

HOSEA

Without doubt Hosea was the Prophet of Restoration, and the book he penned is an exhibition of God's desire for, and method in, the restoration of backsliders. The key word, *Return,* occurring 15 times proves *Hosea* to be a weighty treatise on "Repentance." A striking characteristic of this poetic book is its abundance of arrestive metaphors, offering the preacher a rich field of exposition. Says Eichhorn, "The language of the prophet resembles a garland of divers flowers: images are woven to images, similes strung to similes, metaphors ranged on metaphors," indicating that Hosea was "a man of emotion rather than of logic, a poet rather than a preacher." The pivot of the whole book is that of the unfaithfulness of Hosea's wife (chapters 2, 3). Through this tragic domestic trial God spoke to Israel guilty of spiritual whoredom. As Hosea received back his harlot-wife, so he was commissioned to tell Israel that although she had played the harlot, God yet loved her and waited to restore her to fellowship. Although the book does not appear to have any clear, recognizable outline, the one given by J. Vernon McGee is worthy of expansion –
1. Personal 1-3, The Prophet and His Faithless Wife
2. Prophetic 4-14, The Lord and the Faithless Nation, Israel.
Preachers desiring to warn believers against backsliding could not do better than preach a series of sermons from this conspicuous book for backsliders.

Chapter 1

Hosea was one of the prophets raised up by God to call the people back to Him. "Hosea acted out his message by his life," says *The Pilgrim Bible,* in the most concise summary of the book one could find. "At God's command he married a wife who was unfaithful to him. She loved other men and deliberately left him for all the pleasure and wealth she thought they could give her. Hosea was heartbroken and disowned her. But he still loved her, and finally bought her back and shut her away from everybody, until she would realize her sins and turn back to him again. His very trouble gave him a chance to speak God's message that Israel had treated her Lord in the same way. He has been like a loving husband to Israel, but because she turned away from him, He will disown her. Nevertheless He loves her still, and when her heart turns to Him, He will take her back again." Thus it is that Hosea's message can be summed up in the two descriptive phrases he uses: *Lo-ammi,* "not my people"; and *Ammi,* "my people."

Chapter 2

The chastisement and restoration of Israel, the adulterous wife, make up this chapter. It will be found that "Hosea is remarkable for the frequent use which he makes of events in the former history of his people.

Their past seems to him a mirror in which they may read their future." By "many lovers," we are to understand the gods of surrounding nations, like Baal which Israel followed after. The hedged up way (verse 6) speaks of the suffering the Jews have experienced through the centuries, permitted by God to prove that they can never have peace save in the divinely provided way. When we stray from Him, He knows how to "hedge up our way with thorns." Yet the Valley of Achor, meaning "trouble" can be made a door of hope. Barrenness can be changed into the fruitfulness of vineyards, and sorrows made sources of refreshment. Are you in some Valley of Achor? If so, how are you treating your trouble? Are you making it the avenue by which a happier hope may flow into your life? Trouble that sends us to God always begets a new hope.

Chapter 3

This brief chapter is eloquent with the truth of God's undying love. The book as a whole cannot be outlined, for how can anyone outline the sobbing of a heartbroken person! Here we have Hosea retaining his love for an outcast wife. In spite of her whoredom, or idolatry, she was still loved, and is brought back by Hosea. She sold herself into slavery, and is redeemed by her heart-crushed husband. It is interesting to trace the three-fold reference to the thirty pieces of silver in the Old Testament. In Exodus 21:32, they represent the price paid for a slave gored to death by an ox. In Zechariah 11:12, the same amount stands for the value of a rejected shepherd. Here, in verse 2, Hosea gave fifteen pieces of silver in money, and another fifteen in kind, as the price of his outcast wife. Thus, the thirty pieces of silver are prophetic of Christ's humiliation, who became the slave gored to death, the outcast and the rejected shepherd. Oh, what a Saviour!

Chapter 4

Specific charges are now brought against Israel. The sin of ignorance is still a blight. Many of God's people are still destroyed for lack of knowledge of the deeper things of the Spirit. In spiritual matters, ignorance

is not bliss but a bane (see Matthew 13:19; II Thessalonians 1:8). Does God ever abandon souls? If divine love is trifled with, does it give up the trifler? What is the true significance of "Ephraim is joined to idols: let him alone"? Dr. Alexander Maclaren says that "let him alone" does not mean the same thing as "I will let him alone." Through Hosea, God was doing all He could to bring the nation back to Himself. There are no bounds to God's forbearance and pleading with men in this life. The declaration means that we are to be separated from an idolatrous world. We are to let Ephraim's idols alone. If we mix ourselves up with Ephraim, we shall find ourselves groveling beside him before his idols, ere long. We must not be unequally yoked with those who follow the world.

Chapter 5

That the prophet's style is "abrupt, metaphorical and figurative" is aptly proved by the striking figures of speech in this chapter, in which we have the withdrawn face of God. Dealing with this chapter, a devotional writer asks: "Have you a place, inviolable to God ('framed your doings') in your daily time table (verse 4)?" Make Psalm 90:12 part of your daily prayer. Do you ever get your "fortune" told? He knows all about you; hide nothing from Him, confide completely in Him (verse 9; see Isaiah 42:9; Psalm 62:8). When opportunity offers, ask old Christians if they have ever found blessing through affliction (verse 15). Keep in mind Hebrews 13:5 and Romans 8:28, because of Job 5:7. When God says He was as "a moth unto Ephraim," He meant that He gnawed away his strength. For his sickness, Ephraim went to physicians of no value. Spiritual health can come from God alone. Yet how many there are who spend all their living on physicians and are not better, but rather worse! If only souls in their sin-sickness could turn to the Great Physician, how quickly He would make them whole.

Chapter 6

Prodigal Israel, like the New Testament prodigal son, will return to the Father. The first three verses constitute the repentant action of the remnant, when the Lord goes forth from heaven to descend to earth (Psalm 110:3; Romans 11:26). Note the word "prepared" which indicates that God has set His own time for His Son's return. Surely verse 3 is one we can take for our own hearts today. It contains the true core of our Christian experience (John 17:3). Are you following on to know the Lord in a richer, fuller measure? How blessed will be the response of the Lord to the return of Israel! Mercy, great and free, will be manifested. What God thinks of His Word can be gathered from verse 5. All judgment is according to this illuminative book (see 8:12; 12:10). Do we share God's estimation of His infallible Word? While the harvest of wrath of the Great Tribulation may be the thought in verse 11, is it not likewise true that a glorious harvest of blessing follows upon our full, complete return unto the Lord?

Chapter 7

God's condemnation, yet call, is still before us, and it continues through the rest of this graphic book. That God has a good memory over against the forgetfulness of others is evident from the declaration: "They consider not in their hearts that I remember all their wickedness." What does He remember (Matthew 12.36; Malachi 3:16)? How does He remember (Revelation 21:12)? Does He ever forget (Isaiah 49:15; Hebrews 8:12; 10:17)? What should we forget (Philippians 3:13)? In some things, it is ever pleasant to walk down "Memory Lane." In other things, we do well to practice a good "forgettery." Expressive metaphors abound in this chapter: "Cake not turned" – too much done on one side. "Silly dove, without heart" – fluttering first to one expediency, then to another, forsaking the clear line of the will of God. "Grey hairs are here and there" – unrecognized decay had set in. "Deceitful bow" – an untrustworthy bow, which breaks when stretched and is therefore not a defense, but a danger. We do well to apply such metaphors to ourselves to learn in what state we are, spiritually.

Chapter 8

Acting independently of God is the charge against Israel as this chapter opens: "They have set up kings, but not by me." Do we take God into all our plans and decisions? Is it difficult to reconcile "I knew it not" (verse 4), with God's omniscience? Are we trying to keep anything from God (Proverbs 3:6; Ezekiel 11:5)? The sowing and reaping of verse 7 agree with Paul's word on the same subject (Galatians 6:7-9). Perhaps the most striking expression in the chapter is: "Israel hath forgotten his maker, and buildeth temples" (verse 14). God is left out, but man tries to be tremendously religious. We face the terrible possibility of making carnal substitutes for obedience to God. It is sadly possible to build temples and found societies, and be unceasingly active, yet to forget God. Scripture recognizes a wrong religion (Isaiah 1:11-15; Micah 6:6-8). Prayer can be evil (Proverbs 28:9). The great things of God's Word are counted as a strange thing, even by many so-called religious people today. How blind the unregenerated religionist is!

Chapter 9

Destruction seems to be the keynote of this dark chapter. "The days of visitation are come." It will prove helpful to make a list of these days (see Genesis 6:5-7; 11:6-9; 19:24; Matthew 3:7; 24:37-44; II Peter 3:3-14). Pay no attention to scoffers. You will ever be counted as a fool by those who reject God's Word. Here we have the consequence of rejected law. We speak about "breaking the law," but the law does the breaking. "The wave does not break the rock, but is itself broken upon it." What terrible recompense we have in verse 17! The people had cast God away, now He casts them away. Heredity and environment have much to do with our treatment of God (verse 13). Sin and Satan can be found in all environments. What Satan won in a garden (Genesis 3:1-8), he lost in a wilderness (Matthew 4:1-11). Grace is superior to any kind of heredity or environment. Regeneration provides us with a new heredity and a blessed environment (John 1:12; 3:7).

Chapter 10

Dealing with this chapter under the caption, "Fruit Which Is Death," Dr. Alexander Maclaren says: "Its prophecy has two themes – Israel's sin and its punishment. These recur again and again. Reiteration, not progress of thought, characterizes Hosea's fiery stream of inspired eloquence. Conviction of sin and prediction of judgment are his message. We trace a fourfold repetition of it here. With his love for nature, Hosea draws his similies from it." All that he saw suggested analogies of moral good or ill, as this chapter proves. Praise God, empty vines can be made fruitful (John 15:2-8)! Have you a divided heart? James tells how it will hinder prayer (1:6-8). Chastisement ever overtakes those who have a mixed, rather than a fixed heart. The reason for divine chastisement can be found in Hebrews (12: 6-11). Are you being chastened? Read I Corinthians 11:31, 32, if you would escape it. What a forceful revival message can be found in verse 12! The difficulty is, we are not ready for God's rain. There is not enough "breaking up."

Chapter 11

The opening verse here is used of Israel and Christ (Matthew 2:15). "Oriental prophets used to speak and write thus," says *The Pilgrim Bible.* "They often had at least two meanings to their words. The Holy Spirit used this custom to picture far-off events by speaking of those that were near at hand." As a child of God, are you altogether out of Egypt? How tender God is! He taught His people to walk, as a parent teaches an infant (verse 3). What a glimpse we have into the heart of God in the wail: "How shall I give thee up" (verse 8)! He strives to the limit to restore those who turn from Him. His love is persistent – a love that will not let us go. Have you a bent in the wrong direction (verse 7)? If so, live in I John 1:7 and have a bent in the right direction, where we are told *where* and *how* to walk. Walk after the Lord (verse 10), not away from Him. Power with God ever means loyalty to each other.

Chapter 12

In these days when we are being educated as to the proper vitamins that we should take, in order to have a balanced diet, consideration should be given to the necessity of having the right spiritual diet. Evidently Ephraim fed on the wrong food (verse 1). Trace the word "feed" through the Bible for a study on this eating question (I Peter 2:2; Hebrews 5:12-14). Dealing with verses 7 and 8, a writer remarks: "Sometimes individuals (Luke 12:16-21) and churches (Revelation 3:14-22) become like Ephraim. Agur realized the value of the happy medium (Proverbs 30:7-9)." That God loves to use types or illustrations (verse 10) can be proved by the hundreds of them He employs throughout the Bible. What a wonderful Prophet we have in Christ, who brought us out of the Egypt of this world, and graciously preserves us (verse 13)! Salvation and security we owe to Him. Some, there are, who have the former, but they do not enjoy the latter.

Chapter 13

All through this chapter we can detect "the wail of the parental love of God over the ruin which Israel had brought on itself, and that parental love is setting forth Israel's true condition in the hope that they discern it." God is their help, so that to leave Him spells ruin, and to cling to Him means life. What folly it is to strive against God, the divine helper! Pride is aptly described in verse 3: passing cloud, evaporating dew, light chaff, and smoke out of a chimney. God's swift judgment upon those rejecting His law is expressively set forth in the similies, "as a lion, as a leopard" (verse 7), and "as a bear" (verse 8). Yet mercy is ever mixed with judgment. "In me is thine help" (verse 9). Thus the Holy Spirit, through Hosea, "blends wonderful tenderness with unflinching decision in rebuke, and unwavering certainty in foretelling evil with unfaltering hope in the promise of possible blessing." His words are set in the same key as the still more wonderfully tender one that the Lord Jesus uttered as He looked across the valley from Olivet to Jerusalem, and cried: "O Jerusalem, Jerusalem."

Chapter 14

What a blessed conclusion to a stirring prophecy this chapter affords, proving Hosea to be the preeminent prophet of divine love and human repentance! His ancient sentences have blessed virtue and healing in them.

May grace be mine to appropriate them for my own heart! The chapter is made up of what we are to do, and what God will do. In verses 1 to 3, the very essence of true return to God is set forth in the prayer which Israel is exhorted to offer. Verses 4 to 8 present the forgiving love of God and its blessed results, and are set forth with equal poetical beauty and spiritual power. Verse 9 is a closing epilogue. Note the blessing, growth, stability, beauty and fragrance winsomely portrayed by Hosea, and see how your life measures up to God's provision. Underline the divine "I wills." May ours ever be the joyful privilege of observing Him, as the idol of the heart, and the source of unfailing fruitfulness. With the dew of heaven falling upon us, we can grow as a green fir tree.

JOEL

Made up of only three chapters *Joel* is a literary gem – *multum in parvo,* much in little. Of its style the book is "preeminently pure, and is characterized by smoothness and fluency, strength and tenderness." The key to the understanding and interpretation of the book is the repeated phrase, "The Day of The Lord," which will commence when the Church has been raptured, and will be characterized by divine judgment, and of God's interference once more directly in the course of world politics. Joel himself, of whom so little is known (1:1), is referred to as "The Prophet of Religious Revival," and thus, in some ways his book is one on *Repentance.* Joel knew, and all must know who deal with souls, that genuine repentance is the basis of real revival. When hearts are rent, Pentecostal blessing is experienced. Joel foretells prosperity, on condition of sincere repentance. Would that we had prophets today exhorting the nation to repent of its sins as the essential step in return to, and blessing from, God! Notable features of the book are –

1. The grandest description in all literature of locust devastation, with such an invasion as a type of a more terrible invasion.
2. The prophecy of the Spirit's effusion upon all flesh.
3. Prophecies, remarkable in scope, extending from Joel's day to the end of time.

We have Judgment and Repentance 1-2:17; Promise for the Present and Future 2:18-3:21.

Chapter 1

Of the prophet Joel himself we know very little. Probably he was a contemporary of Elisha. In his brief and pungent prophecy, he makes full use of Judah's afflictions and presses home to conscience divine chastisement, in the devastating plague of locusts. Famine and barrenness overtook the people because of their sin. Joel, however, was a foreteller as well as a forthteller. As the latter, he had a message for his own age and those he was called to minister to. As a foreteller, he was inspired to look down the corridor of time and give his prophecy a far-reaching application. Complete fulfillment of Joel's solemn predictions await the Tribulation era, with its time of Jacob's trouble. Thus Joel uses the desolation of the land by locusts as a type of the day of the Lord. The temporal blight was nothing to be compared to the spiritual dearth of the people. Yet how insensible they were to their needs!

Chapter 2

What a pentecostal prophet Joel was! Peter uses Joel's prophecy of the Spirit as being partially fulfilled at Pentecost. But the advent of the Spirit then by no means exhausts the wondrous manifestations of the Spirit that Israel, as a whole, will experience when the millennial kingdom is established. The use of the trumpet here takes us back to the silver trumpets of Numbers. One blast sounded an alarm; the second blast summoned the people before the Lord. One blow aroused; the other instructed. Thus is it here. The people were warned of the dreadful events ahead; then they were instructed as to what would overtake them when the day of their calamity was past. Joel called upon Judah to repent of sin and to turn to the Lord. Had there been self-judgment and genuine contrition, the avenger would have turned aside, and Jehovah would have been revealed as their deliverer. A time of glorious blessing, however, awaits a truly repentant Israel.

Chapter 3

In this "Valley of Decision" chapter, Joel provides us with more detailed information as to the day of the Lord, which is the period covering the Tribulation, and onward until the ushering in of the day of God. Of this day of the Lord, Dr. H. A. Iron-

side understands "the entire period during which the once-rejected Lord asserts and makes good His title to the earth." Joel's reference to the judgment of the nations agrees with our Lord's teaching in Matthew 25:31-46. The valley of decision is not one in which men are urged to decide for Christ. It represents the great Judge's decisions. The valley will be the threshing floor where the divine winnower will sit to separate all who are to share His kingdom from those who are to go away into everlasting punishment. We who belong to Christ are blessedly aware that ours will be the glorious vision of an up-calling Lord and a Messiah of glory.

AMOS

As a prophet of judgment, Amos, the shepherd of Tekoa, was called from his flocks to proclaim a stern message of punishment upon Israel for her luxurious and self-indulgent ways. As a condemnation upon her sins she would be overthrown by a foreign foe. National sin merits national judgment. Therefore the key verse of the book speaks of punishment (4:12). Although not a graduate of the School of the Prophets, Amos, the gatherer of sycamore fruit (1:1; 7:14,15) believed God to be the Ruler of this world, and that all nations are responsible to Him, and that the measure of their responsibility is determined by the light each nation has. For Israel, this could be no excuse. For surrounding heathen nations (1-2:3), punishment is suited to respective crimes against moral codes, and no final hope is held out for them. But for Israel when truly adjusted to God's will and purpose there is the promise of full deliverance and prosperity under the House of David. The prophecies and promises of *Amos* can be divided thus:

1. Prophecies against surrounding nations 1-2:3
2. Prophecies against Israel and Judah 2:4-6:9
3. Prophecies, consolatory and condemnatory, covering times previous to, and during Messiah's reign 7-9.

Would that more preachers today had a "Thus saith the Lord"!

Chapter 1

Although not of the line of prophets, but simply a herdsman, Amos, of Tekoa, was nevertheless called of God to minister as a prophet of judgment. His name, meaning "burden," is very suggestive, seeing that he was raised up to proclaim the judgments of One burdened with the sins of His people (2:13). The first chapter is taken up with coming judgments upon surrounding nations. As you read this book through, you will be impressed with the style of Amos, "which is in perfect keeping with the simple truthfulness of his character, with his holy awe of his Lord, his tender compassion for the lowly and suffering." The book is likewise characterized by a peculiar rhythm, and is full of beauty and poetry. Certain refrains occur in the rugged sternness used. Amos could combine indignant invective and touching pathos. There is his eight-fold thunderbolt of woe; yet in tender refrain he speaks for God: "Ye have not returned unto me" (4:6-11).

Chapter 2

Charges against Moab, Judah and Israel form the burden of this chapter. Certain refrains occur in the book, like the one in verse 4: "Three transgressions . . . and for four." Another characteristic feature of the prophet's style is his appropriate use of similes from rustic scenes; for example, "as a cart that is full of sheaves presses heavily, so will I press you into your place." As *The Pilgrim Bible* remarks, "God uses men to give forth His Word, but never expects them to speak as other than themselves. . . . All through this book Amos shows his experience of agriculture." Such an illustration as used in verse 13 proves that the long suffering of God is at last wearied out with the obstinacy of sinners. Neither swiftness of foot, nor strength of hand, nor courage of spirit could save the people from the wrath of a righteous God.

Chapter 3

Ponder today the message of this chapter, containing, as it does, God's extraordinary love, repaid by Israel's ingratitude. Then we have the announced necessary judgments because of sin, and the fact that coming oppression will bring ruin to all in Israel, save a small faithful remnant. Tke key verse of the book is found in verse 3: "Can two walk together except they be agreed?" The parable-like questions in this chapter were intended to bring home to the people the solemn truth that their sins had separated them from God, and that heavy judgment must accrue. With each question there is a cause and an effect, leading to the great climax. It is fitting to remember that the One born in Bethlehem came to bridge the terrible chasm between our sin and God. We, being lost, could no longer walk with God. But Christ came to bear our judgment and bring us nigh unto God.

Chapter 4

The prophet forcibly illustrates the degeneracy of Israel's nobles. He calls them "ye kine of Bashan" (verse 1). Other figures for these luxurious yet wanton leaders will be found in chapter 3:9, 10, 12, 15. Calling these rulers, in civil and social life, "cows" was far from complimentary. "Bashan, a region on the east of the Jordan, was renowned for its rich pastures and fine cattle. The bulls of Bashan were fierce in aspect

(Psalm 22:12). The feminine kine or cows, expressed the idea that the luxurious nobles of Israel were more like women than men." God often repays in kind. As Israel's nobles had lived wantonly, the day came when, as eunuchs in the Assyrian palaces and harems, they were made to minister to the wantonness of foreign masters. We further gather from this chapter that Israel had come to look at her standing before God with such satisfaction that there is no mention of a sin-offering among their sacrifices. Note the two famines (4:6; 8:11,12).

Chapter 5

Judgment is mixed with mercy, and thus God calls the people to seek Him and live. Trace the word "seek" in this chapter. Under grace, God is the divine Seeker, and too often seeks in vain. Have you been sought and found? The Name of the Lord, as used by Amos, should be carefully studied. "The Lord is His name" (verse 8; 9:6). Note how these refer to God's creative power in the universe. Other variations of the name should be noted. The sevenfold usage of "the God of Hosts," should be gathered in a group and the connection observed. Another word to watch is "pass." "I will pass through thee," as through Egypt in judgment, taking vengeance this time on His own. The passing by, in chapters 7:8 and 8:2, signifies passing by in the sense of pardoning. Israel maintained the form of Mosaic worship, yet there was the absence of spiritual value; for Israel had turned from God to idols, earning thereby divine judgment. "Little children, keep yourselves from idols."

Chapter 6

The judgment, in this chapter, was pronounced against the nobles and leaders of the people, who had been guilty of reckless ease and carelessness. Men in authority and office, who should have led the people in holy ways, exerted an opposite influence. The indifference of these leaders is summarized for us in the phrase, "they are not grieved for the affliction of Joseph" (verse 6). They satisfied themselves with the fat of lambs and the calves out of the stall, with bowls of wine and the chief ointments. They were given over to the inanities and vulgarities of the world, the follies of fashion, the pride of riches. They had forgotten the sorrows of Joseph. Theirs was not the true aristocracy that it was an honor to be part of. May we be nobles in heaven's peerage, to whom earth's joys and glittering prizes are transient and unreal, and ever desirous of sharing the sorrows of those who are grieved for the afflictions of Joseph.

Chapter 7

Verses like 2 and 5 prove Amos to have been loving and tender-hearted, finding it hard to contemplate the judgments he was divinely commanded to pronounce in such scathing terms. Yet side by side with the prophet's tenderness of heart is his absolute uncompromising faithfulness to his God (verses 12-17). Readers will observe the personal touch in the book: "Amos, what seest thou?" (7:8;8:2). There was a holy familiarity between God and His prophet. Can we not see in Amos a shadow of Christ, the Great Intercessor? Amos interceded for the people (verses 2,5), but with what greater efficacy Christ pleads for His own! This chapter commences the personal revelations of Amos: "Thus hath the Lord God shewed me" (verse 1). The five showings, and their meanings, should be closely studied. Are we in close, unbroken fellowship with the Lord, and able, thereby, to know His mind and will, both for His Church and the world?

Chapter 8

The vision of the basket of summer fruit declares Israel's ripeness for her last punishment, and the end of her existence as a nation. As fruit-gathering closed the whole harvest, so the whole course of God's mercies, chastisements and providential warnings, in the case of Israel, is now completed. "As in holiness, so in sin, there is a sowing, a growth, and a maturity. After the appointed cycle of heavenly influences has acted, in due time, the harvest comes." Amos saw and declared that the long period of God's patience and forbearance had terminated, and that judgment must begin. Thus will it be for multitudes who will realize, when it is too late, that the harvest of grace is past and the summer of salvation is ended, and that for them there is nothing but certain and terrible judgment. For ourselves, the abiding lesson of the book is that our responsibility, like that of Israel's, is measured by our position of privilege.

Chapter 9

How full of import this chapter is, in the light of what is happening in Palestine today. The expression, "they shall no more be pulled up out of the land which I have given them, saith the Lord their God" (verse 15), is no longer future. Israel is back in her land, a State recognized by other nations. The glorious period of which Amos speaks, however, is still future. National peace and prosperity, a time of long and settled habitation, are still to overtake God's chosen people, whom He chose at the beginning because He loved them. What a covenant-keeping God we serve! All He promised through the prophet will yet be realized to the full. Let us bless Him, for not one word of any promise has failed. We deserved nothing but His judgments, yet in mercy He has dealt with us. May His unfailing goodness lead us to repentance!

OBADIAH

This brief, brilliant, prophetic cameo of only 21 verses is a sharp manifesto against Edom whose character and career, doom and downfall, Obadiah presents. The Edomites, or Idumeans, who were the descendants of Esau, were the proud, bitter, resentful neighbors and foes of Jacob. When Babylon assaulted Jerusalem, Edom was only too willing to join the assault (Psalm 137:7). Of Obadiah and his times, Scripture is silent. Pusey says of the prophet, "God has willed that his name alone and his brief prophecy should be known to the world." The two-fold message of the book for our age is evident, namely, a warning against sinful pride and godless defiance, and against cruel treatment of the Jews, whose cause God Himself will undertake, and whose foes He will destroy as the tragic end of Adolph Hitler proves. Ellicott's summary of *Obadiah* is worthy of notice. "Obadiah uses many words or forms of words peculiar to himself, so that even this short writing gives him an individuality. The style is vigorous, and there is one image of almost startling boldness (verse 4), but the parallelism is too defective to allow the work to be classed with the poetical books. As a defect in style, the preponderance of interrogations may be noticed." For the preacher, a serviceable outline is –

1. Edom's Humiliation, 1-9
2. Edom's Crime, 10-14
3. Edom's Doom and Blessing for Zion, 15-21.

Verses 1-9

As a book of only 21 verses, Obadiah's is another *"multo in parvo,"* much in little. The brief vision of the prophet is for our admonition and edification. In the first 9 verses, the humiliation of Edom, against whom Odadiah prophesied, is set forth. Chronologically, he may have been the first of the writing prophets, and the first to use the formula, "thus said the Lord," a phrase claiming divine inspiration for its utterances. Nothing is known of this Obadiah. The most important thing to know is the message and not the messenger who brings it. Edom, exalting itself, is about to be cast down. Everything would be searched out and judged. Complete destruction would overtake Edom. How God abominates pride! When men exalt themselves as eagles, setting their nests among stars, He causes them to lick the dust.

Verses 10-21

From Esau or Edom, the prophet turns to Jacob. Violence against Jacob merited stern dealing. From the day when the king of Edom refused to deal kindly with the Canaan-bound pilgrims, the seed of Esau has been the inveterate enemy of Jehovah's favored people. Edom had forgotten the day when he stood on the other side, when, like Jacob, he too was in bondage. "In the day that thou stoodest on the other side" (verse 11). What a sermon is in this phrase! Let us never forget the pit from which we were digged. It will help us to deal tenderly with sinners, if we remember when we were on "the other side." What a blessed hope this last verse holds for perfect world-government, when all, like Esau, will be righteously dealt with by our Saviour!

JONAH

While those who reject the divine inspiration and infallibility of Scripture, try to laugh this "history of a prophecy," out of the Bible the fact remains that Jonah was a historical person, and was swallowed by the great fish God prepared for the purpose. Jonah was not a myth, for myths cannot restore coasts (II Kings 14:25). The supreme seal of confirmation of Jonah's actuality and experience in the whale's belly is the Lord Jesus Christ Himself (Matthew 12:39-41; Luke 11:30). As *The Truth*, He could not treat a historical person as a myth, or *vice versa*. The one prediction of the book is the overthrow declared in no uncertain way. God is the God of the Gentiles, as well as God of the Jews (Romans 3:29), and it was therefore His purpose that Nineveh should have the opportunity of repenting and turning to Him, which it did. Jonah was an isolationist believing that salvation was of the Jews only, but in the belly of the great fish he learned the lesson of obedience to God and of His pity for all men. This "most beautiful story ever written in so small a compass," as Charles Reade called it, is eloquent with the truth of the futility of man's efforts to frustrate the divine purposes of grace. Further, within the book, the selfish unbelief and vindictiveness of man is contrasted with gracious patience and benevolence of God.

Chapter 1

While the modernist rejects this book, and treats it as a fable, affirming that Jonah never actually lived, to Christ Jonah was a real person who had the experiences described in the book, and we prefer to be on the side of our Lord. In type and picture, Jonah was a figure of Israel, and likewise a preview of Christ's death and Resurrection. In II Kings 14:25, we learn more about Jonah. The first chapter of his book, which can hardly be called a prophetic one, reveals the unwelcome and uncongenial mission Jonah was called to fulfill. His was the task of bearing a message of "judgment to Nineveh, but rather than risk his reputation by going to Gentiles, he fled to Tarshish. In disobedience he ran away, and went down to Joppa. The path of disobedience is ever down." He paid the fare thereof. Yes, there is ever a fare to pay for running away from God. God, however, provided the storm to prevent Jonah's purpose.

Chapter 2

The four chapters of Jonah can be summarized in various ways: chapter 1, *Jonah in a fix;* chapter 2, *Jonah in a fish;* chapter 3, *Jonah in a revival;* chapter 4, *Jonah in a rage:* or, 1, *a man running from God;* 2, *a man running back to God;* 3, *a man running with God;* and 4, *a man running ahead of God.* Here, we see Jonah in a fish, a great fish prepared by the Lord. And since God prepared it, He could make its throat large enough to swallow the disobedient messenger. Expressions like "the Lord prepared," and "God prepared," proclaim the sovereignty of God, which is the glorious theme of the book. (Read Matthew 12:39-41 along with this passage.) Jonah's entombment and deliverance proclaimed to the Ninevites death and resurrection. To them, Jonah was as a man who had passed through death and was alive again. And Christ affirms that this is the only sign now set before men.

Chapter 3

"The Word of the Lord came unto Jonah the second time." Have you failed God? Then He waits to give you a further opportunity of obeying His Word. City and sin go together, and the Ninevites were exceeding sinful. But, as they listened to the shortest revival sermon ever preached, made up of only eight words, all were stirred, from the greatest to the least, and, repenting of their sins, became a type of a great Gentile harvest. Would that all who preach could obey the command: "Preach the preaching I bid thee"! Too many preach their own theories, speculations and philosophies. It filled Jonah with anger to see God merciful to a wicked city. He was willing to pronounce judgment upon it, but his Jewish exclusivism forbade salvation going to any except Jews. A mighty revival swept Nineveh, but Jonah was in no fit condition of soul to rejoice in it.

Chapter 4

Jonah stands out like the elder brother of Luke 15 who, in anger, would not rejoice over the return of the prodigal son, his brother. God turned away from His anger, over Nineveh's sins, but now Jonah was angry over the removal of divine anger. God rebuked his self-occupied servant: "Doest thou well to be angry?" (verse 4). When we lose our tempers, does such a loving question arouse us to our true condition of soul? Going over the chapters again, we have plight, prayer, proclamation and petulance. Wounded vanity took Jonah outside the city to a self-created booth, in which he could see what would overtake Nineveh, as well as his own reputation as a prophet. God prepared a gourd for His agitated servant, which gave Jonah his first touch of joy. Jonah's gladness, however, was short-lived, for God also prepared the worm to destroy the gourd, revealing thereby His sovereignty to spare or to slay. As ever, God had the last word.

MICAH

Nothing is known of this prophet who takes us from Bethlehem to the kingdom reign of Christ, apart from what he tells us of himself in the opening verse of his prophecy so full of poetic beauty. Dr. A. T. Pierson who says that the key word of the book is *Controversy* (6:2), speaks of one portion as, "a little poem of twelve lines in the Hebrew . . . one of the most exquisite things to be found in the entire Old Testament, and would alone be sufficient to prove that this Bible is the Word of God, for there is nothing like it in all the literature of men" (7:18,19). Of another portion (6:6-8), Dean Stanley remarks, "One of the most sublime and impassioned declarations of spiritual religion that the Old Testament contains." The prophet Micah himself, whose name means "Who is like Jehovah?" was raised up to prophesy both to Samaria and Jerusalem, but mainly to Judah; and as in all genuine prophecy, through present judgment future blessing appears. *Micah*, regarded as a summary of the prophecies in *Isaiah*, is similar to *Isaiah* in that the book falls into two general divisions, namely:

1. Denunciatory, 1-3
2. Consolatory, 4-7

How different our lives would be if only God was the Center and Circumference of all things, as He was to Micah to whom God was everything!

Chapters 1, 2

Apart from what this book tells us, we know little of Micah. He prophesied in the days of Jothan, Ahaz and Hezekiah, kings of Judah, and his message concerned Samaria and Jerusalem. Micah was a contemporary of Isaiah, and his book resembles the first of the prophets. Both had been caught up into communion with God, and seeing the actual state of the land, declared their visions. In the chapter before us we have the nation's condemnation. Micah calls upon the world to be witness of what is going on. The condemned nation as a witness to the world of human sin and God's righteousness. Three sins are specified which could not be his: idolatry (1:7); social injustice (2:1-3); and hypocrisy (3:11). Micah denounces the sins of oppression, violence and covetousness, and promises a glorious restoration. Israel will return and will multiply.

Chapter 3

The second section of the book commences with an appeal to hear. First, the princes are charged with violence and oppression, and from such the Lord will hide His face. Then the prophets are called to account. Because they made the people to err, darkness and confusion would cover them. Last of all, the national leaders are shown to be dishonest and mercenary. As it has been stated, "the princes judge for reward, the priests teach for hire, and the prophets divine for money," and disaster overtakes all. Micah declares that he is Spirit-empowered as he witnesses as a prophet of punishment yet of promise: "Truly, I am full of power by the Spirit of the Lord" (verse 8). In the previous chapter he speaks about the Spirit of the Lord being straitened (2:7). Is the Spirit's power operating in our lives, or are we hindering His manifestation?

Chapter 4

This great kingdom chapter deserves our closest study. Note these divisions: *the future kingdom is to be supreme* (verse 1); *universal* (verse 2); *peaceful* (verse 3); *prosperous* (verses 4,5); *reigned over by Christ* (verses 6-8); and *Jewish and Gentile* (verses 9-13). Israel is to be the place of God's habitation (verse 2) in a new sense. The rulers of the earth are to be replaced by one who can rule them righteously. Micah flings out a challenge to faith: "Is there no king in thee? Is thy counsellor perished" (verse 9)? Oh, that one had the trumpet of Gabriel to ring this challenge out through the church today! We, too, have become a spectacle to the world in our denial of the greatness of the salvation of Him by whose name we are called. It will be seen that a portion of this chapter (verses 1-8) is almost identical with Isaiah 2:1-4. Mark the personal pronouns in verses 2, 3, 4 and 7.

Chapter 5

The *center* of the Messianic kingdom is to be the very place of apostasy. Referring to the kingdom of the Messiah which is to be set up, the coming of Christ is identified with that which was seen when He appeared (verse 2). Jerusalem, with its sinfulness and forfeited opportunities, is to be the center of a circle, of which the circumference is the whole world. Bethlehem is to be exalted as the very throne-chamber of the King of kings (verse 2). Christ will be "the peace" (verse 5); there is no clearer foregleam of the Lord as our peace—"the Lord our peace." Ultimate victory is predicted. "The remnant of Jacob . . . shall be as a dew from the Lord." Compare verses two to four with Isaiah 7:14 and 9:6,7, and note a striking familiarity, suggesting that Isaiah and Micah spoke with one mind, using such agreement as might the more convict all rebels.

Chapters 6, 7

Taken together, these concluding chapters proclaim the divine character. What a tender pleading tone Micah uses to persuade the people to remember (verses 3-5)! Then he goes on to remind them that history attests God's righteousness (verses 4,5). The personal significance of this comes home to every believer. Our experience of God's faithfulness forbids us to doubt the steadfastness of His character. Revelation attests God's requirements (verse 8). This verse is matched by only one other in Scripture—Matthew 11:28. We are to do, to love and to walk; to be clean, to be true and to be sincere. God has no pleasure in those who stand still or sit down. Blessing is ours as we progress and grow. Then experience attests God's redemption (7:18-20). We have *lament* (verses 1-6), *intercession* (verses 7-10), and *promise* (verses 11-20). For His ancient people, God is to subdue nations and make her enemies lick the dust.

NAHUM

A native of Galilee, and living at the same time as Hezekiah and Isaiah, Nahum, whose general message was the awful doom of the apostate, was given some 150 years after Jonah's mission and message to Nineveh. The revival under Jonah, while sincere, did not last for Nineveh turned back again to deliberate apostasy from God and Nahum was raised up to proclaim Nineveh's complete destruction which took place 86 years after his prophecy. Nahum's name means *comfort*, and he had "a message of comfort for a harassed and fearful people in peril through the cruel and awful military power of Assyria." Having served God's purpose, Assyria would be destroyed (Isaiah 10:5). The three chapters of "this beautiful, vivid, pictorial poem on the grandeur, power and justice of God, and on the conflict between Jehovah and this cruel and defiant world empire of Nineveh," fall into two general sections—
1. The August Judge, 1:1-7
2. The Awful Judgment, 1:8-3.

A renowned expositor describes the book thus: "None of the minor prophets seem to equal Nahum in boldness, ardour and sublimity. His prophecy forms a regular and perfect poem; the exordium is not merely magnificent, it is truly majestic; the preparation for the destruction of Nineveh and the description of its downfall and desolation, are expressed in most vivid colours, and are bold and luminous in the highest degree."

Chapter 1

The burden of Nahum concerned Nineveh which, under Jonah's preaching, turned to the Lord. Now, some 150 years later, Nahum declares what God's judgment is because of Nineveh's apostasy and sin. The prophecy opens with a vision of the divine character. Who and what God is, forms the basis of all Nahum has to say. The attributes of indignation, anger and jealousy are ascribed to God. Then Nahum passes to divine activities. Under the natural figures of a whirlwind and a tempest, the prophet shows forth the great power of God, held in leash by considerations of love and long-suffering. The entire section dealing with God's power suggests terror to the wicked but comfort for the saints. Divine power, which is for the destruction of God's foes, is employed for the protection of those who are His. The chapter closes with a final note of warning to Judah, Nahum's immediate audience. (Compare verse 15 with Isaiah 52.)

Chapter 2

In chapter 2 we have the voice of divine judgment. The first ten verses are taken up with the vengeance of the Lord. Man can never drive back the tide of divine wrath and judgment. Nahum speaks of God's army under the figure of siege – with His mighty men, chariots and power. Then we understand the irony of the opening sentence: "Do all you can, and still God will punish." But retribution is not retaliation. Because of God's character, He can never retaliate in bitterness and wrath. Nineveh's

judgment is final and irrevocable. Her overthrow is to be complete – "empty, and void and waste." Any nation acting in defiance of God brings about its own destruction. Dr. Campbell Morgan suggests that Nahum's graphic description of Nineveh's overthrow as given in this chapter is in three clearly defined parts – *The Conflict* (3-5); *the Conquest* (6-9); *the Consummation* (10).

Chapter 3

How forcibly this chapter illustrates Paul's declaration that men and nations reap what they sow (Galatians 6:7,8)! God is never mocked by human impunity and perverseness. He may not pay every week, but at last He pays. Thus, the prophet vindicates God's action against sinful Nineveh upon whom vengeance fell because of vice. Having sown to the wind, the city must now reap the whirlwind. Note the seven illustrations Nahum uses to describe God's righteous judgment. A "bloody city," so evil and cruel, is to be paid back in her own coin. Judicial actions taken by God are always in harmony with His own righteous character. He can never act contrary to all He is Himself.

HABAKKUK

This book, with its strongly lyrical character, is preeminent for its literary beauty. The prophet himself, who was one of the Levitical choristers (3:19), had a style nearer *The Psalms* in structure than any of the prophetical writings. Opening in gloom and closing in glory, the best part of the book is made up of a conversation between God and Habakkuk, who has been called *The Prophet of Faith* (2:4 with Romans 1:17; Galatians 3:11; Hebrews 10:38). Yet, somehow Habakkuk could not square his faith in a good and righteous God with the facts of life as he saw them. Hence his *Why?* The outline of the book as given by Dr. Vernon McGee is suggestive –
1. The Perplexity of the Prophet, chapter 1
2. The Perspicuity of the Prophet, chapter 2
3. The Pleasure of the Prophet, chapter 3.
Pierson observes, "Habakkuk's name means

Embrace, and expresses the clinging trust that lays hold on God, and in his poem the central word is 'Faith,' in its vital relation to righteousness and life's trials and triumphs. The prayer with which this book closes touches the summit of the sublime." From perplexity the prophet passes to praise. All mystery vanishes, and the music of a precious confidence in God fills his soul.

Chapter 1

Habakkuk, a contemporary of Jeremiah and very like the weeping prophet in spirituality and personal fellowship with God, has been called "The Questioning Prophet." He cannot understand why God acts as He does, seeing He is what he knows Him to be. Hence he asks God several questions. "Habakkuk is the honest, sincere doubter of the prophets, the Thomas of the twelve prophets." His name means, "one who embraces," and as Martin Luther says, "he caresses the people and takes them in his arms, that is to say, he comforts and cheers them, as one caresses a poor, weeping child." In the chapter before us, the prophet is perplexed by the contradictions between the known character of God and the present experience of His people. Underline these three leading questions: *How long?* (verse 2); *Why?* (verse 3); *Wherefore?* (verse 13). How troubled his mind was as to how the known purpose of God, proclaimed by prophet and priest, could be furthered by such means as the invasion of the Chaldean army? Yet Habakkuk is determined not to let his faith be disturbed by what he does not know (verse 6). Praise God, He can answer all our questions! Our responsibility is to watch and wait.

Chapter 2

Taking the chapter as a whole, we have a five-fold woe pronounced for *rapacity* (verses 6-8); *false confidence* (verses 9-11); *vanity* (verses 12-14); *outrage* (verses 15-17); and *idolatry* (verses 18-20). Have you noticed the words, "watch," "wait," and "write"? The vision had to be so plain and urgent and powerful, that men may run who read it. The prophecy here is built around two contrasting principles. The man whose soul is lifted up with pride is not upright; on the other hand, the righteous man lives by his faithfulness to God, and as he is faithful, life's enigmas are solved. Faith is not

something I hold, but that which holds me. I live by it. The closing verse is so full of comfort for doubting hearts. God is working out His purposes. Nothing happens by chance, nothing is unjust, nothing is unequal. Those who live for iniquity will be filled with shame for glory (verse 16). Those who live by faith, having faith as the self-surrendering union with God, will come to see the earth filled with the glory of the Lord (verse 14). Faith makes eternity's values so real.

Chapter 3

In this prayer song, probably used in public worship, we have one of the most magnificent pieces of poetry in the Bible. It is really a sublime ode, having an exordium, a main subject and a peroration. Having laid hold on the faithfulness of God, the prophet cannot do other than close his prophecy as he does. So he journeys from a quest into a conquest over all doubt, fear and anxiety. From doubt he passes into a determination to rejoice in God although all the evidences are against him, and there is nothing in appearances to justify such a joy. "The man who knows God is content to wait for Him, knowing that He is never late with His mercies, that His clock is never slow." Mark those motto-words: "although – yet" (verses 17,18). If some of your fig trees are not blossoming, and many of your fields are yielding no meat, and there is no herd in your stalls, strike up Habakkuk's tune, "Yet will I rejoice in the Lord."

ZEPHANIAH

Spoken of as "The Compendium of All Prophecy," *Zephaniah*, although addressed to Judah and Jerusalem, is yet a survey of God's universal government. "The whole earth is the theatre where the Judge of all displays the grandeur of Law and the glory of Love. From every quarter, nations are chosen as examples of His just judgment (2:4-15)." The key phrase of the book mentioned 14 times in the first chapter is *The*

Day of Jehovah. Zephaniah, who, from the subscription of his prophecy was a great-great-grandson of King Hezekiah, was one of the earliest to urge a return to the prophetic principles of Isaiah and Micah after the long period of national apostasy brought about by Manasseh's policy. Reading the signs of distress and ruin as the devastating hordes of Scythians began to swarm over Western Asia, Zephaniah struck the note of doom for the invading armies. But for "an afflicted and poor people," a future of great gladness and peace was reserved. Filled with the righteous wrath and judgment of God (1:15; 3:8), yet having an undertone of divine love, *Zephaniah* can be more conveniently divided into three sections—

1. The Judgment of Judah and Jerusalem, 1
2. The Judgment of the Earth and of all Nations 2-3:8
3. The Judgments removed and the Kingdom established 3:9-20.

This last section contains the sweetest love song in the Old Testament. If the first two sections of the book are given over to woe, gloom and sadness, the last chapter ends with a song—a song of the Lord (3:17). When Israel is fully restored, He will sing.

Chapter 1

The prophecy of Zephaniah should be read with prayerful interest by all Christians, seeing that conditions of the prophet's day, and those of today, are largely analogous. Zephaniah had to face the same difficulty all of us need to face now. "His message is identical with the message of the Gospel, and his unfailing inspiration for all his difficulties was identical with ours." His name suggests, "one whom God hides" (see 2:3). Are you one of God's sheltered ones? The key expression of the book is "the day of the Lord," which, to the prophet, was both the day in which he lived, and that which was to come. Judgment is decreed against inferior creation, against man, and against various classes, such as idolators, waverers and apostates. As for the day of the Lord (verses 7-18) Zephaniah declares it to be *imminent* (verses 7-14), *dreadful* (verses 15, 16, *destructive* (verse 17), and *unavoidable* (verse 18). The complete fulfilment of this prediction is reserved for "the great day of the Lord," during the tribulation era. Be doubly grateful for God's salvation.

Chapter 2

In the admonition found in this chapter, the prophet emphasizes the truth that na-

tional repentance alone can save from national ruin. What a message for the nations of today! A call to heart-examination opens the chapter. The people are urged to look within and find out the sins by which God has been provoked, and then repent before Him. Danger is great and imminent. Divine anger is coming; therefore the people must seek the Lord, righteousness and meekness. Encouragement offers a hiding place from universal calamity: "It may be" (verse 3). Here we have a type of Christ as the hiding place to all who trust Him. God's promise, to those who amend their lives at the prophet's warning, is protection. The call comes to young and old alike: "Seek ye the Lord." And the preservation of the faithful is a blessed truth for the Church, as well as for Israel's remnant. The doom of cities teaches us that any city given over to pleasure-seeking and sin cannot expect to escape the sword of the Lord in the great day of His wrath.

Chapter 3

After threatening (chapter 1), and admonition (chapter 2), we now have promise. A serviceable division of this chapter is *denunciation* (verses 1-7), *restoration* (verses 8-13), and *jubilation* (verses 14-20). Note the ascending scale in the crowning passage of restoration, cleansing, victory and joy. No wonder the closing section has been described as the sweetest love song in the Old Testament, an exquisite picture of the motherhood of God. What revelation of the heart of God is more exquisite than this? There is nothing comparable to the picture of God singing for very joy over His people. Yes, we have a God who sobs over sin but sings over those who forsake their sin. The careful reader will note the "He wills"— He will save, rejoice, rest and joy. See too, the "I wills"—I will undo, set, bring and make. The chapter ends showing the place of defeat to be the place of victory (verse 19); also the unlimited influence of those who are fully yielded to the God who loves and cares (verse 20).

HAGGAI

Of the three prophets of the Restoration, Haggai not only preached but practiced for Ezra tells us that Haggai lent a hand in the rebuilding of the temple (5:1,2; 6:14). Although spurred by the prophet's appeals to the conscience of the people, and by his reproaches to work with a will, the community of returned exiles rallied to Haggai's inspired words. All we have of his prophecies is a fragment consisting of 38 verses in all. As a writer, his style is plain, simple and curt. He lacked the brilliance of imagination many of the other prophets possessed. Probably born at Babylon during the Captivity, this Lord's messenger was raised up for a work required at the moment, and that work he accomplished quickly and well. Fours years after his call, the temple was completed and solemnly dedicated. After delivering his first message, Haggai was joined in his ministry by a young prophet named Zechariah. A man of action, Haggai was steadfast, unmoveable, abounding in the work he had to do. Robert Lee says that the key phrase, "The Word of the Lord," occurring five times, marks the division of the book. Perhaps, however, the following analysis is more apt –
1. The Exhortation, chapter 1
2. The Encouragement, chapter 2:1-9
3. The Message to Priests, chapter 2:10-19
4. The Message to Zerubbabel, chapter 2:20-23.

Chapter 1

Haggai opens the last section of the Minor Prophets, and is the first of the three dealing with Jewish history, as the people return from exile. Thus, Haggai, Zechariah and Malachi should be read along with Ezra and Nehemiah. The background of this short book is responsible for the noticeable change of tone, atmosphere and message, as compared with preceding books. Of Haggai himself, we know nothing apart from what the opening verse tells us. This he knew, he was a "sent one," one charged with a divine message, a mouthpiece by whom God's will was to be made known to the people (verse 13). His burden was: "Build the house of God. Cease ministering to yourselves. Put all your redeemed energies into the restoration of the temple." In this first chapter, Haggai rebukes the people for their slackness. They had no time to build God's house, but plenty of time to make themselves snug and comfortable (verse 4). The people must bestir themselves, and place God's interests first. Their hearts were stirred, and they did the work. What a message the chapter contains for our hearts! If we would enjoy God's smile, we must seek first His kingdom.

Chapter 2

Two divine messages make up this chapter. In the first nine verses we have discouragement, yet deliverance. As the people compared their labors with the past, their hearts failed them; but contrasting it with the future, they were heartened. Though they had grieved the Spirit, God was to give them peace. External glory of a temple would give way to One whose coming will fill this house with glory (verse 7). What great advent promises verses 7 and 8 are! Presently, God is shaking all nations, and His Son, as the desire or hope of all nations, is at hand. The final message (verses 10-23) is made up of exhortation and encouragement. Note the contrast between the contagion of ceremonial good and evil – good, *slow* to communicate itself; evil, *swift* to communicate itself. The concluding thought is that God is able to meet all our anxiety regarding foes, by the declaration of His authority. Trace the divine "I" in the closing verses. All enemies are to be destroyed, and the people established and made as a signet, with His sign upon them, and with power to impress it upon others.

ZECHARIAH

Containing more Messianic prophecies than any of the other minor prophets, Zechariah can be termed *The Prophet of the Advent.* "Eight visions in the night unveil God's providence and grace toward the elect nation," says Pierson, "her foes shall be destroyed, her idols removed, her city and Temple restored, and her Messiah revealed." Zechariah saw the promise of a sudden and decisive intervention of God on behalf of His people, and thus painted in glowing colors their blessedness. But the prophet makes it clear that if divine promises are to be enjoyed, divine precepts must be obeyed. As Haggai and Zechariah labored together in the rebuilding of the temple, and if tradition be true were buried in the same grave, the contrast between the two can be noted. Haggai was pragmatic and practical – his feet were on the ground. Zechariah was visionary with his head in the clouds. The one, therefore, was the counterpart of the other, as Elijah and Elisha were. Priest as well as prophet, Zechariah stands out as one of the greatest of ancient inspired seers. His book is in three sections –

1. The Messianic and Millennial Visions, 1-6
2. The Question Concerning Fasting–Obedience turns Fasts into Feasts, 7, 8
3. The Prophetic Prospect reaching to the end of the Kingdom, 9-14.

Chapter 1

Zechariah, like Ezekiel and Jeremiah, was a priest as well as a prophet. He was associated with the restoration period, and his entire activities were confined to less than two years. His name is most suggestive. It means, "remembered of the Lord." His entire prophecy can be read through in thirty minutes. Some forty years ago a renowned expositor wrote: "We read Zechariah to little purpose if we only exercise our ingenuity over his visions and do not bend our spirits in adoration before the holy One, whose coming he announces – the Son of David, the Priest-King, the Shepherd-Saviour – Jesus, who is Christ, the Son of the living God." After introducing his predictions with facts of his genealogy and a statement as to his divine commission, Zechariah gives us the vision of the angel riders – God's messengers, keeping ceaseless vigil, with the vision of the four horns and four smiths, symbolic of Israel's foes.

Chapter 2

The man with his measuring line is "the angel that talked with me," in verse three. Ezekiel uses the measuring-line, or reed, as a symbol of preparation for rebuilding the city and temple in the kingdom-age. The same application can be made in this chapter with its prediction of the glory of the kingdom-age. The lesson for us today is that the Church should look ahead and make provision accordingly. Constantly she is running up walls which cramp and retard extension. We must remember that the message of Zechariah does not exhaust itself in urging on the builders with their work. In it we have the fullest account of the events and transactions connected with the coming of the Lord with His people. A precious message like "he that troubleth you toucheth the apple of his eye" (verse 8), is surely true of the Christian as it is of God's ancient people.

Chapter 3

Those who handle the Word, yet can see nothing but past history fulfilled in the return of a small Jewish remnant from captivity, must suffer from deplorable spiritual blindness. This notable chapter has a twofold implication. His appearance in such unsightly dress showed the sin of Israel and the poverty into which the people had fallen. Joshua, however, as representative of the people, receives a change of raiment, a testimony that the people's sin had been forgiven. This vision, in its sweep, passes on to the day of the Lord when the land shall be under the glorious reign of the one who is called, "my servant the BRANCH." What a parable of grace can be gathered from Joshua's experience! As brands plucked from eternal burning, what a glorious inheritance is ours.

Chapter 4

A word as to the style of Zechariah may be of value. This manner of expression varies according to the nature of his subjects and the way in which they come to his mind. At times he expresses himself in simple, conversational prose; at other times, in poetry. At one time he abounds in symbols; at another time he uses the direct prophetical announcement. As to his symbols, they are enigmatical and require the explanation accompanying them. The vision presented here was probably suggested by the lampstand in the Holy Place. The interpretation of the symbol is easily understood. The people of God derive their power to shine, not by might, nor by power, but by the Spirit of the Lord, who is the golden oil flowing to us through golden pipes of faith and obedience. (See Matthew 5:14-16; Philippians 2:15; John 8:12.)

Chapter 5

We now come to the eighth and ninth visions granted to the prophet. The flying roll speaks of the rebuke of sin by the Word of God. A "roll" is symbolic of the written word, whether of God or of man. This particular roll had the exact dimension of the Holy Place of the tabernacle – twenty cubits long and ten cubits broad. The angel declared the roll to be a curse, containing the declaration of divine wrath against sinners. In the woman in the ephah we see wickedness personified, and a symbol of the removal of the people's sin. "Prophetically, the application to the Babylon of the Revelation is obvious," says Dr. C. I. Scofield. "The professing Gentile church at the time condoning every iniquity of the rich, doctrinally a mere 'confusion,' as the name indicates, and corrupted to the core by commercialism, wealth, and luxury, falls under the judgment of God" (Revelation 18).

Chapter 6

The four chariots are described as going forth from "standing before the Lord of all the earth." The direction of each is mentioned. The going forth of the black horses, and the white after them, into the north country, implies the fall of Babylon, which city was completely destroyed by Darius shortly after this prophecy was given. The four chariots are not to be confused with the four world-empires of Daniel. The authoritative statement of verse five makes it plain that these represent the "four spirits of heaven which go forth standing before the Lord of all the earth." Turn to Revelation 7:1-3; and 9:14,15, for a further reference to these four angels and their judgments and ministry earthward. The chapter concludes with the symbolic crowning of Joshua, the high priest, who as "the branch," typifies Christ, who united in Himself priestly and kingly offices. No high priest of Israel wore a crown. Joshua had this distinction only as a type of Christ.

Chapter 7

This chapter introduces the second part of the book. Chapters seven and eight comprise messages from the Lord through His commissioned servant, Zechariah, and form a four-fold answer to a question by Sherezer in reference to the continued observance of the fast in the fifth month. Taking the two chapters together, we have this division: *obedience rather than fasting is required* (7:1-7); *sin was the cause of the punishment of their fathers* (7:8-14); *favor is promised Jerusalem, and the people exhorted to build the temple and to put away evil* (8:1-17); *and the fast-days shall be turned into feast-days* (8:18-23). What Christian truths can be developed from chapter seven: *prayer* (verse 2), *separation* (verse 3), *fasting* (verse 5), *sobriety* (verse 6), *compassion* (verse 9) and *inspiration* (verse 12)! It is still true that God cries, but men will not hear.

Chapter 8

The dominant theme of the chapter before us is God's unchanging purpose to bless Israel in the coming kingdom, when Jerusalem is the glorious center of the earth. There is a right kind of jealousy, as well as a wrong kind. Which do you think God manifests (verse 2)? Go through the chapter and make a list of the designations of Jerusalem – "a city of truth," "the holy mountain," etc. What a beautiful description of happy social life we have in verse five! Note the repeated phrase: "Let your hands be strong." Strong hands are dependent upon a clean heart. Have we realized that God saved us in order to use us as channels of blessing (verse 13)? Are we speedy about the matter of prayer (verse 21)? Do others want to accompany us on our heavenly pilgrimage because of our experience and expression of God's reality (verse 23)?

Chapter 9

Two general sections characterize Zechariah's prophecy. As the prophet of the Restoration, he discourses on the temple (chapters 1-8), and on the Messiah (chapters 9-14). This ninth chapter commences another subdivision, with a series of prophecies indicated by the phrase, "the burden of the Word of the Lord." Cities surrounding Palestine were to come under judgment. All these strongholds were destroyed as predicted. What a wonderful prediction of Christ we have in verse nine (cf. Matthew 21:11)! Gathering together details of Christ's history, given by Zechariah, we have *His lowliness* (9:9); *His betrayal and suffering* (11:12,13; 13:7); *His wounds* (13:6); and *His glorious return in power* (14). Go through the book and trace the titles symbolic of Christ — branch, king, servant, shepherd, priest, and priest-king. What foregleams Zechariah gives us of our glorious Lord!

Chapter 10

The exhortation to prayer and the promise of redemption and restoration of Israel, making up this chapter, are rich in content. The opening promise carries a physical and spiritual significance. Rain, as of old, has been restored to Palestine, producing marvelous fertility; but a mighty outpouring of the Spirit will be experienced by restored Israel. How many flocks are troubled today, seeing they have no true shepherds (verse 2)! As redeemed ones, what do we know about spiritual increase (verse 8)? How wonderfully the last part of the chapter has been realized in our time! For well-nigh 2,000 years the Jews were dispersed among the nations, but now they are fast gathering in the country which is theirs by divine right and gift, and are recognized, throughout the world, as a nation. Alas, as yet they are not walking up and down in His name!

Chapter 11

We can name this "The Shepherd Chapter." Not only does it set forth Christ as the true Shepherd of Israel, but His imitator in the Great Tribulation, namely, the beast, who is the foolish shepherd (verse 15), the idol shepherd (verse 17). What an idol of a shepherd he will be for the deluded of earth! Zechariah herewith presents the rejection of the Messiah and the overthrow of Jewish power. During the dark days in the year A.D. 70, the predictions of verse six were fulfilled to the very letter. The notes in the *Scofield Reference Bible* are worth following on the entire chapter. Have you responded to the voice of the once rejected, now exalted shepherd: "Give Me My Price"? He has His price, and it never varies. If you want His best you can have it on His unchanging terms. He never has a bargain sale on what He offers.

Chapter 12

In this momentous chapter, judgment on the enemies of Jerusalem is given, and also a description of the conversion of the Jews. The Lord will come in power to destroy all nations that come against the ancient city. This prophecy covers the rest of the book. A five-fold division of the chapter is easily discernable: *the siege of Jerusalem* (verses 1-3); *the battle of Armageddon* (verses 4-9); *the latter rain* (verse 10); *godly sorrow* (verses 11-14); and *the cleansing fountain* (13:1), which rightfully belongs to chapter twelve. Can we not take comfort out of a verse like the eighth? Would that multitudes of Jews, in this day of grace might look upon Him whom they pierced! Thank God for all worthy organizations laboring for the salvation of the Jews. Compare what Paul says about every man bearing his own burden (Galatians 6) with "every family apart."

Chapter 13

Among the most helpful expositions of Zechariah is the one by the late Dr. A. C. Gaebelein, in which he quotes the well-known Jewish commentator, Solomon Ben Jarchi, known as *Rashi:* "The prophecy of Zechariah is very dark, for it contains visions much like dreams, which want interpreting, and we will never succeed in finding the true meaning until the teacher of righteousness arrives." While the full realization of much in the book will not be discerned until Christ does appear, the Spirit is ours to show us things to come. *Uncleanness is to disappear in the fountain* (verse 1), *idolatry is to be banished, along with apostasy* (verses 2-4), *Christ as the crucified is to be worshiped and proclaimed* (verses 5-7), and *alien powers are to be destroyed and truly repentant souls saved, yet as by fire* (verses 8,9). As the time is fast approaching for the fulfilment of much that is here before us, may grace be ours to lift up our heads.

Chapter 14

This closing chapter of Zechariah's prophecy is notable for many reasons. First of all, it is a fitting, condensed epitome, the like of which, as concerning these events of the last days, is not to be found in any other portion of Scripture. Then the whole of this chapter is still future and stretches far beyond our time to that era when favor is to be shown to Israel in the last days. Mark these aspects: *day of Jehovah* (verse 1); *assault on Jerusalem* (verse 2); *manifestation of divine power* (verse 3); *ascent to Mount of Olives* (verse 4); *coming of the Lord with His saints* (verse 5); *disturbances in the heavens* (verses 6,7); *issue of living waters from Jerusalem* (verse 8); *the king and the kingdom* (verse 9); *physical changes* (verses 10,11); *antichrist and his hosts destroyed* (verses 12-15); *worship of the king* (verses 16-19); and *universal holiness* (verses 20,21). What a glorious chapter!

MALACHI

Evidently Malachi was proud of his name, and loved to repeat it. The name of *Malachi,* "the unknown prophet with the angelic name," means "My angel" or "messenger." Levi is referred to as "the *messenger* of the Lord of hosts" (2:7); John the Baptist was to come as God's *messenger;* and our Lord as "the *messenger* of the covenant" (3:1). Thus the name was a description of office. Malachi himself possessed a strong and vigorous personality, and was conscious of a divine call to the work of moral and spiritual reformation. The spiritual life of the people was at a low ebb, and many of the evils against which former prophets had protested were again rampant. Malachi was sent to denounce practices dishonoring to God and His worship, and to strengthen the hands of Nehemiah in deliverance of the people from all abuses. Thus, *robbery of God* is the sad keynote of the book. While idolatry had vanished, the people in their backsliding state were hypercritical and guilty of hollow formalism and complaining scepticism. So we have the eight sarcastic questions addressed to God which make the book notable for its dialogue style. Love and wrath, different attributes of the divine character, are likewise apparent. The book can be divided by its *whereins* or "Ye say," the latter occurring twelve times. A briefer outline can be used –
1. The Message of Love, 1:1-5
2. The Message of Rebuke, 1:6 – 2:17
3. The Message of Hope, 3 – 4.

Chapter 1

Malachi was the last of the prophets, after the captivity to the restored remnant, and the burden of his message had a threefold aspect: the love of God, the sins of priests and people, and the day of the Lord. Malachi's name means, "Jehovah's messenger," and by the Spirit, he was a faithful messenger. At the outset of his message stands the declaration of God's love for Israel, a love widened by His gracious powers. The sting of sin was the thought that any, or all, sin was an offense against this divine love. The people discouraged and sceptical, asked a series of questions, the first being: "Wherein hast thou loved us?" (verse 2). The prophet goes on to prove that the people had grown careless and indifferent in worship, hence their spiritual decline (verses 6-14). How guilty the present day church is of listless and slovenly worship!

Chapter 2

This chapter opens with a stinging rebuke of the priests for their careless and ignorant leadership (verses 1-9). Called to instruct and lead the people in faith and morals, the priests had not taken their high and holy calling seriously. Carelessness, irreverence, and negligence in the study of the law were conspicuous faults, and caused the people to turn aside out of the way. Spiritual leadership must be characterized by spirituality and true spiritual appreciation. Slovenly and ignorant leaders cause many to stumble. Coming to the sins of the people (verses 10-17), Malachi is faithful in his condemnation of marital unfaithfulness and insincerity of a religious profession. The sacrifices of those who offended the law of God could not be accepted by God. Willful sin cripples true worship. Are we guilty of wearying the Lord with words? What He desires is action in putting away of sin.

Chapter 3

The opening section of this chapter (verses 1-6) may be parenthetical, with a double application to John the Baptist and the Lord, who came as messengers of Jehovah.

Is the refiner purifying the silver of your life and mine? Do we allow Him to sit at the crucible and remove all the dross? Amid all change and decay, it is blessed to know God as the unchanging One (verse 6). Spiritual decline produced failure in the stewardship of possessions (verses 7-12). God had been robbed. The tithe acknowledged that God owned all and that all a person has must be administered as in His sight. Restitution and renewal are bound together. When God is fully recognized in tithes and offerings, then the windows of heaven are opened. How beautiful is the description of the faithful remnant (verses 16-18). May we be among His crown jewels!

Chapter 4

God's messenger was not only a forthteller but a foreteller. By the Spirit, Malachi was enabled to look down the corridor of time and prophesy of things to come. The Second Advent of the Lord, especially the judgment aspect of it, forms the burden of this concluding chapter. And how this broken world of ours awaits the coming of the Sun of Righteousness, with healing in His wings! What tribulation will overtake the earth on that great and dreadful day of the Lord! Thrice blessed are those who, through faith in Christ, will never witness the horrors of the Great Tribulation period. Have you noticed that the last word in Malachi, and of the Old Testament, is "curse"? That is the story of the Old Testament – beginning with God and ending with a curse. The New Covenant opens with Christ (Matthew 1:1), who came to remove the curse.

THE

NEW

TESTAMENT

MATTHEW

We find it hard to realize that more than four centuries of silence intervene between *Malachi* and *Matthew*. Yet it would seem as if there were no gap for a remarkable link binds the two books together. The last figures on the inspired page of *Malachi*, and the first on the similarly inspired page of *Matthew*, are the Angel of the Covenant, the Lord Jesus Christ; and His forerunner, John the Baptist. Does this not prove the Bible to be a divine, progressive revelation? As the New Covenant springs from the Old, Matthew commences his *gospel* by tracing the generation of Christ back to David and Abraham. The frequent reference to *prediction* proves that Messianic history fulfills Messianic prophecy. Because Matthew deals upon the Messiahship of Christ, prominence is given to *The Kingdom of Heaven* in announcements and parables. Renan, the renowned French skeptic said of this swinging door between the Old and New Testaments that it was "the most important book in Christendom – the most important book that had ever been written." Preferring to call *Matthew* one of the most important books ever penned, its most characteristic key word is *fulfilled*. There are no less than 60 references to Old Testament writings as being fulfilled in Christ. As the general theme of the book is *The King and The Kingdom*, Vernon McGee's analysis is most suggestive under the caption of "Behold Your King":

1. The Person of the King 1 – 2
2. The Preparation of the King, 3 – 4:16
3. The Propaganda of the King, 4:17 – 9:35
4. The Program of the King, 9:36 – 16:20
5. The Passion of the King, 16:21 – 27
6. The Power of the King, 28.

(Read Matthew 9:4; Mark 2:13-20.) As Levi, the son of Alphaeus, Matthew was associated with the tribe set apart for the worship and service of God. His profession as a tax-gatherer, however, exiled him from his people, seeing that such a vocation was despised by patriotic Jews. Two facts are notable in the life of Matthew. First, Jesus found him at his desk. As Matthew was collecting taxes for the Roman government, the Master passed by and said: "Follow me"; and without a question as to where his future support would come from, Matthew left all and followed Jesus. His surrender was real, for although a publican's business was contemptible, it was very profitable. The second good trait was that, having chosen Christ rather than riches, he gave a party for many publicans. To those whose low standards Matthew had shared, he desired to declare his faith. They might sneer, but in the presence of Jesus he would not care.

Chapter 1

One cannot read the first part of this chapter without realizing how God overruled in the Jewish method of keeping genealogies. Here Joseph's descent is established. Observe that, when it comes to Christ's birth, the word "begat" is not used. Our Lord had no human father. What a stigma Mary had to face as an unmarried woman, but like the One she was about to bear, she, too, was willing to make herself of no reputation. In the wondrous name, Jesus, meaning Saviour, we have the prophecy and plan of God's purpose to deliver from sin. Another name, Emmanuel, offers further revelation. In the Old Testament, God is *for us*. Now, in Christ, He is *with us*, and by His Spirit *in us*. Thus, He came as God in human guise. As Man, He understands our human needs, and as God, He can meet every one of them.

Chapter 2

Bear in mind that the Scripture nowhere says that there were *three* wise men. It is merely assumed that, because of the gifts the Magi presented, there were three. Never lose sight of the fact that Jesus was born as King. He was King before He came. Paul refers to Him as "The King Eternal." When speaking of Herod, the text shows a small "k," but for Christ as King, it is rightfully a capital "K," seeing that He outshines all earthly potentates. In a "dream" and the "angel" we see the combination of the natural and the supernatural. Through common means uncommon messengers often come our way. Innocent babes were the first to die for Christ. The flight to Egypt, and then the return to Nazareth, were all in the divine plan. As a "Nazarene," Christ was a despised One. Good can, however, come out of our Nazareths.

Chapter 3

John the Baptist is the link between the two Testaments. With one hand, he lays hold of the Old Testament; and with the other, the New Testament, and makes them one. What a flaming herald and road-maker he was! His challenging word was "Repent," for he believed repentance to be fundamental, to be demonstrated by conduct and public testimony. Further, his dynamic preaching foreshadowed the non-national character of Christianity (verse 9). The vivid imagery he uses proves him to have been a man of the desert. At Jordan with John, Jesus for the first time identified Himself with sinners that He had come to save. From the benediction of heaven, we glean the thought that, although as Mary's Son, Jesus was not altogether understood, yet as God's Son, He gave nothing but pleasure. May ours ever be the divine approbation! That of earth matters little.

Chapter 4

What a study in contrasts! After the dove, there came the devil; after the benediction of heaven, a battle with hell. The first experience prepared Christ for the second. Ere He could deliver men from Satan's grip, He Himself must realize in His humanity the full strength of the archfoe of God and man. Christ's temptations ranged from appeals to the flesh to the most subtle seduction of the spirit. All were met, as temptation must ever be, by the infallible Word of God, the sword of the Spirit. How comforting verse 11 is! Expect the angels, after you have successfully resisted the devil. In the brief summary of the beginning of Christ's Galilean ministry, several features stand out. As the Fulfiller, He succeeds John the forerunner. Neither books nor colleges make fishers of souls. All are Christ-made. Salvation, submission, service and surrender are all found in the call of the first disciples. Have you left all to follow Him?

Chapter 5

We have not space to dwell upon the separate Beatitudes. Have you ever compared them with the "rosary of graces" in Galatians 5:22? It is only by the Spirit's power that these noble Beatitudes can be realized. The word "blessed" is an attribute of God (I Timothy 1:11). Two similes are given of the believer, namely: salt and light; the one banishes corruption, and the other, darkness. Are we functioning in this two-fold way? Dealing with the law, Christ declares the roots of wickedness to be more significant than crime itself. Sin, as the section from verses 21-30 suggests, is "an attitude of heart, a rebellious spirit, ever likely to issue in acts of open evil, and a seed-bed of temptation." By "perfection" (verse 48) we are not to understand sinless perfection, but a maturity of godliness evident by the godly traits emphasized by our Lord in the narrative. This should be our goal, in the Spirit's power.

Chapter 6

Continuing His memorable Sermon on the Mount, Christ is found condemning mere religious externals. Note the opposite rewards, present and future. Of the so-called Lord's Prayer, much could be written. What a model prayer it is, containing the sections of invocation, petition and doxology. Christ taught His own to approach God, not as beggars, but as worshipers. Of this pearl of prayers one has said: "It forms a rosary of words which can contain and guide all our prayer, a solid way to direct the wandering mind." The part of the sermon dealing with covetousness and unbelieving anxiety should be prayerfully read. How guilty we are of mistaken values! We are prone to imagine vainly that we can have the pleasures of two worlds, and serve two masters. Do you know what it is to be lost in the will of God, and then to leave all else to Him? Why worry about material needs, when God is able to meet them all?

Chapter 7

This chapter continues and concludes the Sermon on the Mount, which is surely for heirs of the kingdom in our age as well as for the Millennium. Christ rightly condemns judgment of others, for none of us is fit to judge others. In the use of the "mote" and the "beam" our Lord shows how petty theft can be castigated, but large-scale commercial dishonesty pass unheeded. Reaching the theme of prayer, God is revealed as a great and ready Giver. He is more eager to give than we are to receive. Compare the two ways of verses 13 and 14 with Psalm 1. John 15 should be studied alongside of verses 15-20. There is such a thing as spurious discipleship (Luke 6:46). Double reactions to the sayings of Christ are before us in the illustration He gives of the two builders. What kind of a builder are you? Is your house stormproof?

Chapter 8

In the first half of this chapter, we have three healings, pertaining to a Jew, a Gentile and a friend. An outcast, an alien and a multitude mirror our Lord's universal appeal. The leper doubted the willingness of Christ to heal. Men are more apt to believe in miraculous power than miraculous love. How delighted our Lord was with the faith of the Centurion! Have we the faith that laughs at impossibilities and cries, "It shall be done"? Would that the multitudes who today are sin-sick could see in Jesus the Healer they need! Matthew's quotation from

Isaiah sets our Lord's healing ministry in its true light, underlining the sympathetic rather than the miraculous. Dealing with the loneliness of Christ, Matthew uses a title appearing thirty-two times in this gospel, "the Son of Man," which is Christ's racial name as the representative Man. The stilling of the waves and the casting out of demons prove Christ to be Lord of every realm. All power is His.

Chapter 9

Returning to Capernaum, Christ continues His healing work. We cannot study the cameo pictures Matthew gives us without seeing our Lord in some new aspects. Ponder the miracles separately, and see how He is revealed. Note that Jesus places spiritual healing first. Matthew's brief autobiographical sketch reminds us of his immediate obedience to Christ's command. The fundamental human sin of jealousy is sternly and ironically rebuked by the Lord Jesus. The sanctimonious reference to fasting by the Pharisees prompted Christ to utter "three pregnant parabolic sayings: bright, genial, felicitous, impromptu." As the cross shadows the path of our Lord, Christian freedom, fellowship, joy and sorrow come in view. The crowd who "marvelled and glorified God," now "laughed him to scorn." Note the varying moods of the crowd in this gospel. This chapter fittingly concludes with the pity of Christ, and the figures of the harvest.

Chapter 10

As we read this account of our Lord's commission and instruction of the Twelve, we observe their various callings and personalities. How destitute of glamor they are! Frederick of Prussia wrote angrily to Voltaire: "If twelve ragamuffins were able to found a religion which exhibited the greatest foolishness, surely it should be easy enough to rid the world of it." But with the power of the Spirit behind them, the Twelve were invincible, and apart from Judas, became the human foundation of the Church. Stirring precepts against undue anxiety, and counsels of common sense, are prominent. But, His chosen ones must go with all urgency, seeing the time is short. Their message must be declared as vital truth, fearlessly and with solemn judgment in view. Persecution will be theirs, but as they war with evil, and suffer thereby, peace of heart will ever prevail. The only way to find one's life is to lose it.

Chapter 11

John's questioning of Christ's authority is quite understandable. Imprisonment and suffering were his and martyrdom was not far away. As the herald of repentance, judgment was the burden of his ministry, and the patience, tolerance, gentleness and sympathy of our Lord were somewhat distant from his conception of the Messiah. Yet the Lord Jesus did not rebuke the prisonbound forerunner, but paid a glowing tribute to him as a man of strength and passion: "There hath not risen a greater than John the Baptist." What judgment Christ pronounced upon the cities! Because of their greater privileges, they deserved more severe judgment, and received it. Note the contrast between the privileged and unprivileged. The religious leaders, custodians of the Word, were blind to the Light, while the untaught rejoiced in it. Have you experienced the double rest in one of the sweetest invitations of the Bible?

Chapter 12

The Lord Jesus showed the Sabbath to be cumbered with tradition and restrictions, robbing it, thereby, of its meaning. The present Lord's Day perpetuates the basic truth that one day in seven is sacred, yet all seven should be sacred. To the believer, every day should be a Lord's Day. The old Sabbath celebrated Creation. The Lord's Day is associated with our Lord's Resurrection.

Many wild things have been said and written on "The Unpardonable Sin," which, by the way, is not a Scriptural term. The blasphemy against the Spirit is the willful, conscious and final rejection of His revelation of Christ. The very fear a person may have of having committed this sin is generally fair evidence that he has not committed it! By the sign of Jonah, some understand that the prophet actually died and rose again. Be that as it may, Jonah's experience in the fish's belly and regurgita-

tion from it was a symbol of our Lord's death and Resurrection after three days. Spiritual relationships are before physical ones, Jesus declares in the closing verse of the chapter.

Chapter 13

The seven parables of this chapter are spoken of as "the mysteries of the kingdom of heaven." Dr. C. I. Scofield remarks: "Taken together, they describe the result of the presence of the Gospel in the world during the present age, that is, the time of seed-sowing which began our Lord's personal ministry, and ends with the 'harvest' (verses 40-43). Briefly, that result is the mingled tares and wheat, good fish and bad, in the sphere of Christian profession. It is Christendom." These parables should be read and understood in their Eastern setting. Parables are earthly stories with a heavenly meaning. Look out for the main lesson in each, but do not stress minor details and thereby extort truth. It is strange, is it not, that *there*, in His own Nazareth home, our Lord could not accomplish mighty works because of unbelief.

Chapter 14

Some promises and oaths should be broken. Herod was afraid to break his immoral vow. C. H. Spurgeon remarks that John was the first preacher to lose his head through dancing! What a confidant is the Lord Jesus! Do we tell Him *everything?* John's disciples, after burying their friend in the heart of the desert, sought out the Lord, and buried their sorrow in His heart. "What a Friend we have in Jesus!" From the palace, we go to the wilderness where under the spell of Christ's preaching the crowd forgot everything. As the shadows of evening fell, hunger was experienced, but for the crisis there was the Christ. He is ever "a very present help in trouble" (Psalm 46:1). He who slept on the water was able to walk on it. Nature obeys her Lord. "The sea is his, he made it." All the time that Peter looked at the Lord Jesus he, too, could walk on the waves; but looking around at the storm, he sank. If only we could have our eyes forever on our omnipotent Lord!

Chapter 15

What varying experiences characterize the pilgrimage of the Master. After the worship, adoration and enthusiasm of the last chapter, we now come to bitterness and hostility. Christ's worst foes were religious men. How they hated His witness! The disciples were condemned by the Pharisees, not for the lack of ordinary cleanliness, but for the violation of many, ridiculously minute, technical rules. In Christ's reply, we have a grave countercharge: a trenchant quotation, and an appeal to the people. With the light of publicity turned on the Pharisees, their anger was roused. The withdrawal of Christ to Tyre and Sidon suggests the need of some rest. His body and mind, as instruments in service, needed refreshment. It may not be possible always to rest from work, but we can learn how to rest in it. Gentiles are as dear to God's heart as Jews. Our Lord commended the faith of the Syrophenician woman, and there is evidence that the needy souls He likewise healed and fed were Gentiles. How sympathetic He is!

Chapter 16

The Pharisees are again rebuked as they look for universal signs. Christ warns the sign-seekers that God does not reveal Himself in spectacular and material ways. There are "signs" all around for the eyes of faith to discern. How remarkable was Peter's declaration of Christ's deity! Of course, such an understanding about our Lord came as a revelation from God. All truth is revelation. Rome's claim that the Church is built on Peter, whom she claims as the first Pope, is entirely false. The Church is built, not on Peter, but on what he said, namely, upon Christ as God. "The Church's one foundation is Jesus Christ her Lord." Peter was certainly called to unlock the door to Jews and Gentiles, but he failed miserably when he tried to interpret God's will to His Lord. How the flesh loves the easy way! It is the way of the cross, however, that leads home.

Chapter 17

The Transfiguration of Christ suggests many truths. First of all, when our Lord turned aside from the "ivory palaces," He did not lose His Glory, but simply unclothed Himself, as it were. Thus, what we have here is the outflashing of His inherent glory. Further, the mount speaks of a great refusal. The Lord Jesus was perfect by creation, perfect through probation, and was now ready to be perfected in glory. Had He wished, He could have gone home from the mount. But down He came and went to the cross in order that multitudes might share heaven with Him. Peter felt it good to be on the mount, and wanted to stay there; but beneath was a valley of need. He was slow to learn, even as we are, that one purpose of mountaintop experiences is to equip disciples to serve the Lord in a world of sin and sorrow. Another lesson Peter learned was the truth that his Master was able to meet any situation. He knows where to find money when it is needed. Can we not learn to trust Him in this matter as in others?

Chapter 18

Calling those who were to serve Him, our Lord instructed them more fully in the matter of eternal realities. As they followed, they were to be fashioned. The first vice to be attacked was pride, the chief cause of misery in home and nation since the beginning. Child-like humility must characterize Christ's followers. Forgetfulness of self and the cultivation of the shepherd-heart must also mark His own. Seeing that the Twelve were to be vitally associated with the Church, our Lord instructed them in necessary church discipline. What constitutes a church? It is the presence of regenerated souls, whether few or many, gathered together in His name. Another necessary lesson the disciples had to learn in the school of Christ was that of forgiveness, Calvary forgiveness! Jesus practiced what He preached. He urged forgiveness from the heart, even as He Himself could forgive on the cross.

Chapter 19

Our Lord's treatment of the marriage question illustrates His relation to the law. In the Pharisaic attitude there is misconception. The Pharisees looked upon Moses as the patron of the divorce law of Judaism, which he was not. In Christ's attitude, the whole question is lifted beyond the reach of quibble. Marriage relationship is a life-long bond. Sad, is it not, that the moral grandeur of the law, unrecognized by the Pharisees was discerned by the multitude? In Christ's treatment of children, we have the Magna Carta of child evangelism. The account of the rich young ruler proved how religious a person may be, and yet fail of the highest. Loved and commended by the Lord, this wealthy young man was unwilling to meet the claims of Him, who, for his sake, had become poor. Away the rich man walked with heavy steps, clinging to his possessions. Gold kept him from a full surrender. Is there a personal application here?

Chapter 20

In His parable of the *Laborers in the Vineyard,* our Lord combats the legalism of His time. The parable was not designed to teach economics, or set forth an ideal of character. Its underlying principle is that "God's will in the matter of remuneration and reward is as absolute as was that of an employer centuries ago." Divine rewards are based, not so much on work done, as on a willing spirit. If we labor merely to fill a contract, then we will get our penny – no more, no less. But if love actuates all our labors, and we serve, not merely for a reward, but because we love the Master, then great gain will be ours. In Christ's third prediction on the cross, He shows how Jews and Gentiles will be responsible for His death. The Jews were to condemn Him; the Gentiles would crucify Him. How indifferent were the disciples when, under the shadow of Calvary, they were so pre-occupied with the old vain question of position and reward! The ordinary matters that the Lord Jesus faced on His way to the cross, proves how ready He was to keep near duty's common path.

Chapter 21

That our Lord had His unknown disciples is evident from the owner of the colt, who was ready to serve Him as need arose. Are we the "colts" He rides upon to a world of need? How commanding Christ must have been, when with whip in hand,

He purged the temple! Can you not imagine the panic He caused? One wonders what He would do if He walked through some churches today, for surely many of them have become dens of thieves. The cursing of the barren fig tree was Christ's only miracle of judgment. A type of Israel's fruitfulness, the barren tree was a living hypocrisy. Its withered condition illustrated that visible ugliness and death which are the final end of fruitlessness. The legalistic questioning of Christ as to His spiritual authority was expertly answered. The parables of the two sons, and the householder, offer further evidence of the barrenness of Israel, and of Christ's condemnation for them.

Chapter 22

The blindness of the Pharisees as to Christ's true identity is before us in the *Parable of the Wedding Feast.* They were unwilling to see in the so-called Carpenter of Nazareth, a worthy Bridegroom, so they spurned the invitation to the feast, and outcasts were called in. It was so in Paul's day, when he turned aside to the Gentiles, causing them to partake of the banquet of God. The religious foes of Christ tried to entangle His speech. Three questions were asked in connection with political and civil duties, natural and physical laws, morals and ethics. Our Lord answered questions by asking questions, and hanged His Hamans on their own gallows. The greatest question facing any soul is: "What think ye of Christ?" Character and destiny depend upon man's answer. If we know Him, owning Him as Lord, we have no questions to ask Him. We know that He is right in all His ways, even though our finite minds cannot understand all.

Chapter 23

What a devastating chapter this is! After routing His foes in argument, Christ pours His woes upon them, leaving them no quarter. No mercy is shown, as He attacks their hypocrisy and ostentation. Profitable points to ponder are: deeds, not profession, matter; true service never courts publicity; spirituality is never self-assertive. Note the significance of the eight woes. Why were they pronounced? May sincerity of heart and life ever be ours! The Lord Jesus commenced His ministry with eight beatitudes, and ended it with eight woes. And truly, the wrath of the Lamb is terrible! Here, His indictment was directed against all pretense in religion. Yet His lament over Jerusalem was pathetic. Indignation melted into love. But the victim of blind leadership, our Lord had to leave the city to travel the road of tragedy. Ever between the Blesser, and any blessing of His, is the unsurrendered will.

Chapters 24, 25

We group these two somewhat long chapters, seeing they both cover the Olivet discourse. From here to the end of the gospel we have the consummation of Christ's work. In the chapters before is "the Vision of the end." This section is made up of questions and answers. In chapter 24, we have the course and consummation of the Gentile age. As the end approaches, diligent service and loving expectancy should characterize the faithful. In "waiting patiently for Him" lies blessing for life and character. Amid gathering shadows, are we resting in *the Lord?* The fact of the Second Advent leads to the three eschatological parables of chapter 25, emphasizing, as they do, the lessons of faithfulness, readiness and diligence. Are we watching for the Bridegroom, and using to the limit every God-given talent, realizing that faithfulness, and not fame, is the basis of final reward?

Chapter 26

Of the first part of this chapter, Dr. W. Graham Scroggie reminds us of the startling contrasts it presents: "A woman, a man; a friend, a foe; giving something, getting something; devotion, deceit; sacrifice, selfishness; buying opportunity, selling opportunity; alone in alliance, a box of ointment, thirty pieces of silver; blessed, cursed. Life is full of such contrasts as these, and they are cheek and jowl all the time." Two feasts are before us, the Passover Feast and the Lord's Supper. Judas was at the first, but not the second. No unsaved person has the right to partake of the Lord's Supper. If he does, it is to his own condemnation. Of the agony in the garden what can one say? Here we stand on holy ground. What

shames us is the failure of the disciples in such a grim hour. The Lord Jesus had a right to expect sympathy when circled with grief, but instead met the sleepiness of His friends.

Chapter 27

As Christ's crucifixion day commences, we have four answers. In his answer, Judas confessed his guilt in selling the innocent Christ. In the answer of the priests, we see how self-deceptions sent the innocent One to death. In Pilate's answer, he is faced by an inevitable choice. Christ was on his hands and he had to do something with Him. In the answer of the crowd, we have a mob choosing a murderer rather than the Master. Alas, the crowd still prefers Barabbas to the Beloved! Are you carrying the cross, not because you are compelled to, but because you love to? The religious leaders wanted a Christ without a cross. "Come down from the cross, and we will believe Him." But Christ, and His cross, are eternally nailed together in their effect on men — although, praise God, He conquered death and the grave — and we cannot have one without the other. If there was a virgin womb for Jesus as He entered the world, there was a virgin tomb for Him as He left it.

Fearing that what Christ had said about rising from the dead might come true, the Pharisees took effective precautions in the sealing and guarding of His tomb. Do you ever wonder where the Holy Spirit was when the body of the Lord Jesus was in the tomb? Well, the Roman government had its seal on the outside, declaring that Jesus would not rise again. It may be God had His seal on the inside, affirming that His Son would rise again; for the Holy Spirit is the Seal, and He it was who assisted in our Lord's Resurrection. Christ was "quickened by the Spirit" (Romans 8:11-13; I Peter 3:18). As the Spirit of Life, He is responsible for all resurrection — spiritual, mental, and physical. Because we are indwelt by the Spirit, we know that resurrection awaits us, seeing we are sealed with the Spirit unto the day of redemption, the redemption of the body.

Chapter 28

Women were the first to receive the great revelation of Christ's dominion over death. What does this suggest? The empty tomb was God's receipt for Calvary. We know the debt was paid, for Christ is alive forevermore. Are you not happy, seeing you serve a risen Saviour? Never forget that the angels did not roll away the stone to let our Lord out of the tomb, but that the disciples might go into the tomb. As easily as He passed through closed doors, our Lord was able to leave a sealed sepulchre. The women, first heralds of the Resurrection, were exhorted to go quickly and tell the disciples what they had seen. Why go *quickly?* Because the enemies of Christ were circulating the lie that His body had been stolen, and truth must get there first. In these days, when Satan is desperately active to flood the earth with lies, are we as speedy as we should be at getting at hearts first with the truth of God?

Reading the chapter as a whole, mark the threefold "Go," and the two-fold "Lo." Matthew closes His gospel with a command and a guarantee. With the "Go" of commission, there is the "Lo" of companionship. Christ is about to leave His own, yet He declares His willingness to remain ever with them until the end of the age. Is it not a privilege beyond price, to have the assurance of the intimate fellowship of our risen Lord as we go forth in His Name? In the last commission, the unity of the Persons of the Godhead is recognized. The Lord Jesus used the single term, "In the *name* (not names) of the Father, and of the Son, and of the Holy Spirit." The question is, "Are we going into the part of the world we represent, preaching the Gospel to every creature crossing our pathway?" This is more a call to personal evangelism even, than missionary enterprise. For each to win another for Christ is His great plan.

MARK

The shortest of the four gospels, *Mark* dwells upon the credentials of Christ as the Servant or Slave. There is no birth-record of Christ here. Who cares, anyhow, about the genealogy of a slave! Mark himself was the nephew of Barnabas. Paul had little confidence in him but later acknowledged his sterling worth (Acts 15:36-41; II Timothy 4:11). Mark wrote for the Romans, whose watchword was *power*. The average, energetic Roman cared little for doctrine. Dynamic, he was for action. Thus, *Mark* is eloquent with, and exhibits the omnipotence of the mighty miracle-worker, and likewise the omnipotence of love is the crowning passion and resurrection of God's Servant. Miracles are prominent rather than parables or discourses. At least 20 of Christ's astonishing miracles are given in detail, and in ten instances Mark adds general statements without going into particulars (1:34). Almost half the book is taken up with some comprehensive summing up of Christ's ministry of power. Crowded with incidents, the book

may be difficult to analyze. Yet we can easily expand the following divisions –
1. The Arrival and Identity of The Servant, 1:1-20
2. The Miraculous Ministry of The Servant, 1:21 – 8
3. The journey of the Servant from Transfiguration to Ascension, 9 – 16.
Christ is indeed the pattern Servant. May our service be more like His!

Chapter 1

The opening phrase of this portion is suggestive: "The beginning of the gospel of Jesus Christ." And the glorious good news of redeeming grace certainly began with, and in Christ. Further, such a *beginning* is now *continuing*. From the time of Christ, each succeeding generation has witnessed a marvelous expansion of the triumphs of the Gospel. This *beginning* will have no *ending*, for through the eternal ages the saints will extol the virtues of Him, who is the Gospel.

Mark introduces us almost immediately to the ministry of Christ, seeing He came as the Servant of Jehovah. This is why this gospel contains no birth record. Who concerns himself with the pedigree of a servant or slave? In Mark, Christ is seen as the Love-Slave of heaven. The key word, *immediately,* is one peculiar to this gospel, being used some 26 times of our Lord, who, as the Servant, moves forward incessantly, yet unhurriedly, to accomplish His Father's business. For His task, He needed helpers, and so chose the twelve. God honors those who leave all to follow Him.

Although He came as a Servant, Christ never lacked authority. Religious leaders were astonished at His authoritative doctrine and miraculous ministry. Demons recognized this divinely sent Servant as the Holy One of God who was able to expel unclean spirits, heal the fever-stricken, cleanse the lepers, and pray and preach effectively. Rising early to commence with God, Christ has left us an example. Alas, we are too fond of sleep to follow Him here! Yet, the solitary place is where power is generated. Thinking of the leper, we can detect three simple stages in his cleansing: *The Urgent Cry:* "Make me clean"; *The Immediate Response:* "Be thou clean"; *The Sure Result:* "He was cleansed." Is it not blessed to know that His blood can make the vilest clean?

Chapter 2

Christian workers can glean many forceful lessons from the miracle of the healing of this palsied man. First of all, is it known that the Lord Jesus is in our house? Because He cannot be hid, He will soon make His presence felt, if there is obedience to His will. Then there is united concern. The four friends were burdened over their sick companion and felt that he and the Master should meet. And it took all four to bring him to Christ. In the conversion of one soul, there are varied factors responsible for a changed life. Nothing daunted these four carriers in their daring resourcefulness, energy and faith. A desperate need required desperate measures. Unconventional! Yes, but most effective; for the man who came in with his back on a bed went out with his bed on his back.

If the method of the four men in claiming Christ's attention was unconventional, so were His methods in attacking all conventionality. For the select circle of the Pharisees, Christ had nothing but contempt. He went to places where sinners could be found. Too many, who name His Name, are sinfully exclusive. Jesus went to the home of Levi, whom we know as Matthew and who became the writer of the first gospel, and won him to Himself. In the *Parable of the Cloth and the Bottle,* as well as in the Sabbath Day episode, Christ is scathingly dealing with a religious life made up of outward disciplines and denials but destitute of inward vigor. Those Pharisees worshiped their ritual and tradition. Jesus came as the Lord of the Sabbath, yet His Lordship passed unrecognized. How tragic it is when any given day or any ritual takes the place of Him who creates all days!

Chapter 3

God-conscious and Spirit-filled, our Lord went about doing good, healing all who were oppressed (Acts 10:38). Think of His works and words in the chapter before us! Any ordinary man would have collapsed under such pressure. Hate and honor came Christ's way. From the leaders of a formal religion there came contempt, enmity, rejection; from the enthusiastic crowds, fame and honor came to cheer Him. But our Lord ever lived for the approbation of heaven. In the choosing of the Twelve, Christ revealed that although He was able to save souls, He was not going to save them alone. He needed others to help Him, and He needs YOU! Of the so-called "Unpardonable Sin," one writes: "From verses 22 and 23 this is quite clearly calling the Holy Spirit a demon. It is the setting of one's heart continuously against God. One thing is certain, that those who are guilty of it are not at all disturbed by it."

Chapter 4

Three parables and a miracle make up this chapter. There is a sense in which parables are miracles, and miracles, parables. From the *Parable of the Sower* we learn that the seed is invariable – not human words, but the Word of God alone. The enemy is persistent, for effective seed must be destroyed.

The fruit is satisfying, bringing delight to God and man. Let us never forget that as sowers we are responsible only for scattering the seed, prayerfully and carefully over the human soil. The harvest is God's responsibility. From the *Parable of the Candle* we gather the lesson of open witness. Coming to the miracle of stilling the storm we see Jesus as One having power, as well as authority. The wind and sea obey Him for He made them both. Nature always obeys her Lord, which is more than man does. Underline these two phrases: "There arose a great storm"; "And he arose." For every crisis, there is the Christ.

Chapter 5

Having met the devil and triumphed gloriously over him, Christ was well able to deal with the denizens of hell. The wonder is that the demons recognized His authority and power. With a word our Lord was able to deliver the hopeless maniac and restore the damage and degradation the demons had caused. What an effective sermon could be preached on "The Unwanted Christ," with verse 17 as the text! How tragic it is when men love their sin so much, that they do not want Christ to trouble their conscience! Are you among the number praying Him not to depart from the edge of your life, but to enter and possess every part of that life? There are those whom Christ wants to stay at home and witness to the wonder of His salvation (verses 18-20). Not *all* are called to go with Him to fields abroad.

Both of the miracles in this section testify to the power of faith. To the woman with an issue of blood, Christ said: "Thy faith hath made thee whole." His word to the ruler was: "Be not afraid, only believe." Is ours the faith that laughs at impossibility and cries, "It must be done"? May our faith venture out upon the declared promises of God. Faith compelled Christ to act for both the woman and the ruler, and act He did, in different ways. True faith will have its genuineness tested, but amid any delay the Lord may permit, we must keep on believing, until faith is rewarded. The raising of the ruler's daughter affords a study in soul-winning. As soon as Christ gave her life, He wanted her fed (verse 43). All who are newly born, need

to be spiritually nourished. Organizations responsible for the salvation of the young must give every attention to the feeding of those who decide for Christ, otherwise they will suffer a terrible backwash. No church should be a nursery with half-starved babes crying for the food.

Chapter 6

To His own family and townspeople, our Lord seemed too ordinary to function as a God-sent messenger. Amazed at His words and works, the Nazareth population yet spurned the Prophet, seeing He was one of themselves. Let us guard ourselves against the folly of thinking that God limits Himself to so-called "special preachers." How sad that sixth verse is! The sending out of the Twelve proves that Christ believed in multiplying His influence. By our prayers and gifts we ought to help to thrust forth more laborers into the harvest field. Of the ministry of John, the forerunner, much could be written. What a fearless, faithful witness he was! He was courageous before royalty, rebuking sin in the palace; consistent before the world, with a life clean and transparent; abiding in influence, for even after his death, his testimony challenged and convicted Herod.

In this portion we have a four-fold portrait of God's Servant. First of all, we see Him as the Rest-Giver. Ever considerate of His own, He called His tired disciples apart from the throngs for relaxation and quietude. In this age of rush and haste we must preserve our seasons of communion. Then, the Master passes before us as the Bountiful Provider. Having compassion for the multitudes, He sought to meet their physical needs. What a prodigality there ever is in His provision! Next, the Lord Jesus is presented as the Triumphant Lord. It must have been awe-inspiring to those one-time fishermen to watch Christ control the elements. No wonder they were amazed beyond measure. It is still true that at His command adverse winds must cease! The last glimpse of the Lord the chapter gives us is that of the Sympathetic Healer. How deeply His loving heart was moved as He encountered the sick and diseased on His journeys! Hands stretched for help received His willing aid. Afflicted as we are with various ills, let us rejoice that His touch has still its ancient power.

Chapter 7

For the Pharisees, with their outward religious show but lack of inner spirituality, the Lord Jesus had nothing but contempt. No language was too strong and stern for these hypocrites, whose talk was very pious, but who neglected the obvious requirements of human society and of God's Word. The Pharisees were concerned about having clean hands, but our Lord made it clear that it is the inner desires and motives about which men must be most careful, seeing that it is these that determine outer actions. There are many today who worship God with their lips, but whose hearts are far from Him. Pious they may appear to be, but they miserably fail in the discharge of elementary, daily duties. There will never be any trouble about outer defilement if our inner life is pure in His sight.

The two miracles recorded in this section demonstrate the value of what we may call "vicarious faith," that is, faith employed on behalf of another. In the healing of the palsied man, we read that when Jesus saw their faith, the faith of the four friends who carried their sick companion to Him, He healed him. Would that we knew how to exercise this vicarious faith! The distressed woman believed for her afflicted daughter and Christ commended her for her audacious faith. Those who brought the deaf and dumb man to Him, came with the faith and conviction that He was able to restore his hearing and speech. There is a noticeable difference, however, in these two miracles. In the first, no means were used. In the second, Christ used His spittal. All healing, of course, is divine. We must be careful not to err in any one direction. God can heal with, or without, means. His will is sovereign, and it is for us to trust Him as the Healer to heal as He sees fit.

Chapter 8

We have here another miracle – feeding. It is profitable to mark the difference between this occasion and the one in chapter 6. Here we have 4000, over against 5000 who were fed before. Here were seven baskets left over, against twelve earlier. Here Christ fed Gentiles over against Jews in chapter 6. No wonder the disciples felt doubtful! They were exclusives, believing that the bounty of heaven was for the Jews, and them alone. Peter suffered from the same narrowness, until the vision of the sheet let down from heaven gave him a large heart. What God has is for all. Look at those nine searching questions Christ pressed upon His own, in which He wanted them to realize the necessity of using all their God-given faculties. To witness miracles and not believe them, to hear Christian teaching and not respond to it, is an inexcusable feature in anyone.

The miracles our Lord wrought established His claims to deity. In the opening of the eyes of the blind man, it is shown that God's power is limited by human faith and response. Christ was able to restore full sight immediately, but the man responded slowly. Full sight came by degrees. In Peter's remarkable confession, we see how revelation transcends reason. Those gathered around saw in Christ one of the prophets; Peter saw in Him, the Son of the living God. As Christ Himself declared, this was a distinct revelation given to Peter from heaven. All Truth is revelation. All who believe Him to be "Very God of Very God" are called upon to meet His demands, namely, the uncompromising denial of self, and the taking up of one's cross. The life of self is death; the death of self is life.

Chapter 9

The Transfiguration served many purposes. First of all, it manifested the inherent glory of Christ. The disciples beheld His glory, and, in the difficult days ahead, found themselves constantly sustained by the fact that they had been eye-witnesses of His majesty. Peter spoke for us all when he asked to stay on the hilltop with the Lord Jesus. It was natural and human to want to remain away from the world below with all its sorrow, hardship and pressure. But he had to learn, as we do, that exalted spiritual experiences are designed to prepare us for the valley with all its need. So leaving the place of spiritual uplift, the three disciples came down to the demon-possessed boy. The other disciples had been so impotent to help: "They could not!" From Christ they learned that power could only come by that fasting that costs time and comfort, and effective prayer.

The disciples wanted a crown without a cross. Christ, however, taught His own that His choicest wreathes are wet with tears. There are no easy roads to the highest places in His Kingdom. What patience the Master had with those nearest Him! The dispute over position makes sad reading. With Christ, human values are reversed; the last is first. Then the lesson of Christian tolerance, so necessary today, is taught by Him in His rebuke of the disciples for their narrow sectarianism. We sadly err, if we feel that spiritual blessing cannot come through any church other than the one with which we are affiliated. God does not empty His fullness into one mould. The solemn warning of hell should stir our hearts to bring the lost to Him, who alone can save. Eternal condemnation was so real to Him. But we cannot rescue the perishing unless we are willing to cut off from our lives, even the most vital and essential things, if they hinder and offend.

Chapter 10

In these days of easy divorces, it is necessary to go back to the fundamental law God laid down when He created our first parents, namely, that it was contrary to nature to sever what God had joined. The abolition of such a plan results in sorrow and tragedy. In His rebuke of the disciples for their misunderstanding of the importance of child-life, we see how necessary it is to win the young. The disciples thought the children incapable of following Christ, and that He was too busy with needy adults to concern Himself about boys and girls. The Child Evangelism Movement of our time deserves the prayerful and practical support of all Christians. Christ's contact with the rich young ruler proves the sadness and selfishness. This otherwise fine young man was chiefly interested in "I"; he used it three times. His money kept him back from Christ's best. With us it may be something else.

Christ's announcement of His death perplexed the minds of His disciples. All their Messianic hopes would be crushed if He went out to die as a felon on a wooden gibbet. But the Master laid down an eternal pattern when He declared Himself a ransom for all. To bless, He must bleed. To deliver, He must die. The cross was the place of death, and our identification with the Crucified One means death to self, to one's own will, to one's own comforts and desires. This gospel of Mark is the one depicting Christ as the True Servant. Here we find Him proclaiming that "the glory of life is to serve, not to be served: to give, not to get: to love, not to be loved." Bartimaeus, the blind beggar, was notable for his determination and earnestness and faith. He obeyed the call of Christ, and found in Him, not only the Restorer of his sight, but the One he should follow and serve.

Chapter 11

Because the humble colt had a share in Christ's so-called triumphal entry into Jerusalem, let us see what we can learn from this privileged creature. It surely teaches us that Christ knows where to find anything, or anyone, He desires to use. He knew where the colt was and said: "Loose him, and bring him." Then the colt was found where two ways met. It is often thus, when Christ calls us to serve Him. We have to choose either the road of self or the road of surrender. How fitting it was that this colt was one "whereon never man sat"! He had been kept for Jesus, and how honored the colt was to carry our Lord through the shouting crowds. As for the populace, how fickle it was! "Hosanna," one day, and ere the week was out they were crying, "Crucify Him!" The Lord Jesus used the barren fig tree to good effect. God save us from the leaves of mere profession! May He grant us the fruit of the Spirit!

As you read about the purification of the temple, do you wonder what Christ would do if He came back to earth and walked through some of our churches? Truly, many of them have become the dens of thieves. Modernism, worldliness, ritualism and dead, barren orthodoxy have robbed them of spiritual power and influence. Some have difficulty about what our Lord said regarding moving mountains. In His day, "removing mountains," was a phrase used of a successful teacher who could remove difficulties, and, as used by Jesus, implies the power of believing prayer to remove obstacles. Maybe your obstacle is the unforgiving spirit. Well, ponder over verses 25 and 26! Because of His claims as the Son of God, Christ was constantly in conflict with religious leaders. With much cunning they tried to trap Him, but He was ever one ahead of His enemies. Knowing their hypocrisy, He forced them back to the evident signs of His authority. But stubbornly they refused the light, and remained blind leaders of the blind.

Chapter 12

The *Parable of the Vineyard* was designed to teach the tragic results of light refused. What a striking figure of speech our Lord used to warn a nation of the inevitable results of the rejection of a God-given revelation! He was forecasting His own death in the heir killed by the husbandman's servant. Christ's enemies did their best to discredit Him. Their subtle planning is seen in the question they asked about paying tribute. They wanted to snare Him into an answer that would bring Him before the Roman authorities on a charge of treason, but Christ could read their crafty minds. With the coin, He showed that there are responsibilities to the State and to God that must be observed. It is only those who put God first, rendering unto Him what is due to Him as Creator and Redeemer that put the very best into the varied relationships of life. Christians should ever make the finest citizens.

The Sadducees, who rejected a resurrection, were the rationalists of Christ's day. No one can be a Christian after the New Testament order who discredits the Resurrection of Christ (Romans 10:9,10). The tricky question about the seven brothers and the one woman gave our Lord opportunity to declare the truth of immortality, and also the perfection of our life in heaven. The discreet scribe, who wanted light upon the commandments, was not far from the Kingdom; but "so near and yet so far." *Almost* will not avail. Although not far, he was not in. We have friends who are near to Christ, as He said the scribe was to the Kingdom, but they are still lost, as lost as the sinner who is far removed from Christ. May the Holy Spirit bring them in!

Chapter 13

The Olivet discourse is worthy of prolonged study. Within it we have a description of the condition of things on the earth during the Tribulation. While characteristic features of the *course* of the Gentile age can be detected, the *consummation* of such an age appears to have been in the mind of the Master. As the present Church age is timeless and signless, we are not to look for signs, but watch for Christ. Amid the clatter of contradictory voices in the world, have we ears tuned to the coming of our Lord? Amid much to discourage us, how we need the grace of endurance!

With the Tribulation in mind, Christ warns against disaster, deception and drowsiness. It is not our belief that the true Church will be on the earth during this period of unparalleled woe and remorse. Tribulation is a judgment period, but for the Church, condemnation is past (Romans 8:1). Ere the vials of wrath are emptied out upon a guilty world, the Church is to be caught up to meet the Lord in the air. Still, coming events cast their shadows before them. As we think of the present world situation, so tense and dangerous, we can see the stage being set for the enactment of the drama of the ages, so graphically given in Revelation 4 - 22. God's prophetic clock seems about to strike. May grace be ours to live as children of the dawn, with our faces toward sunrise!

Chapter 14

In Bethlehem, Mary, like Mary of Bethany, broke her alabaster box in a very real way, giving birth to One, whose spikenard is very precious. This woman had a true insight into the cross, and knew that the One born in the manger, would break His alabaster box of ointment at Calvary. Judas took all he could; Mary gave all she could. And her costly offering must have cheered the heart of the Lord Jesus as He faced the cross. What a worthy commendation she received! Will He say of us at the end of the road: "You have done what you could"? Are you not amazed at the serenity of Christ as He went out to His death? Quietly and carefully He made preparation for the Passover. All had been peacefully planned. Thus may we be restful in every trial or circumstance of life.

Doubtless you have a keepsake, some treasured article a dear one gave upon entering the valley of death. Well, the Lord's Supper is a precious keepsake, something by which to remember Him forever. The broken bread and outpoured wine are lasting memorials to His sacrifice on our behalf. Out into the darkness the Lord Jesus went, singing a hymn. What an example! Can we sing songs in the night? Peter's denial must have added to Christ's anguish. How empty Peter's boast turned out to be! Gethsemane stands out as the sanctuary of sorrow, the place of prayer, the valley of victory. None of the ransomed will ever know the heart anguish of those Gethsemane hours. Judas betrayed our Lord by a kiss – the token of affection! How low Judas fell! May God keep us from betraying our Lord, or following afar.

How full of anguish the final pre-Calvary hours of our Lord were! Indignities and injustice were heaped upon Him by His foes, but the deepest stab came from His own. In the face of danger, they were craven friends. One wonders what would have happened if all of the disciples had stood by Him in a body, and pled His cause before the High Priest, and then Pilate! But they all forsook Him – the One for whom they once forsook all. Think of boastful Peter, who declared his eagerness to go to prison or to death for Christ, but who, when the test came, frankly and fully denied his Lord. The dread of persecution changed the disciples into deserters, leaving the Lord Jesus to go to trial and to death alone. Yet amid His trials, caused by friend and foe alike, the Master stands supreme and undaunted. Alone, He is yet calm and victorious.

Chapter 15

Pilate, and not Christ, was on trial that day when the two faced each other in the palace. Christ was on Pilate's hands, and he had to do something with Him. Against his better judgment, and his wife's intuition, Pilate delivered our Lord to the mob thirsting for His blood. Christ's kingship was ridiculed, but had those Jews, described as wild bulls and mad dogs in the Calvary Psalm

(Psalm 22), known that the One they were reviling was a King with power, who with a word could have destroyed them all, they would have acted differently. Willingly our Lord made Himself of no reputation, in order that He might save even His enemies. His refusal of an opiate, which would have deadened His pain, was also enacted, so that He might feel the full force of the death He was about to taste for every man. Hallelujah, what a Saviour! Do you know Him? Has He claimed your full allegiance? Are you like Simon the Cyrenian, a sharer of His cross?

Here is a portion to be read upon our knees. The bitterest tragedy of the cross was the feeling of desolation. In the depths of His agony, Jesus was alone. Forsaken, not only by His friends, but by His Father! "My God, my God, why hast thou forsaken me?" Ah, we will never know what it meant for this Holy One to bear away our sin! He was forsaken in that lone hour that the joy might be His of saying to every blood-washed child of His: "I will never leave thee, nor forsake thee." Are you presently mystified over the providential dealings of heaven? Are there those experiences you cannot understand? Well, take comfort from the Saviour's "Why?" Our Lord was indebted to two Josephs – one at the beginning of His life, and the other at the end. The one gave Him a shelter, the other, a sepulchre.

Chapter 16

Death could not keep its prey. The king of terrors was no match for Him, who declared Himself, "the resurrection, and the life." The unbelieving disciples were assured by the heavenly guardian of the tomb that the One whom they buried was alive forevermore, and had gone before them unto Galilee. "The resurrection of the Lord Jesus Christ is the best attested fact in all history." Alongside of the resurrection passages we should read I Corinthians 15. Christ was taken down from the cross, but Romanism keeps Him on it and worships a crucifix. Both the cross and the tomb are empty, and, as Dr. E. Schuyler English expresses it in his book on Mark: "The fact of the *empty* tomb is the crown of our faith." Had Jesus remained dead, there would have been no salvation for a sinning race. But

Christ arose, and the Resurrection was God's receipt for Calvary. Our debt was paid by His death, and emerging the Victor o'er the grave, He now offers any sinner a blood-bought cancellation of all transgression.

The psalmist of old declared: "Because they have no changes, they fear not God." Alas, even changes seldom drive men *to* God! Our confidence amid all changes is the fact that Christ is alive forevermore and that

He will be with His own until the end of the age. Girded by the presence and power of the risen Lord, our responsibility is clear. We are to go into all the world, even into our part of it, witnessing unto Him, with accompanying signs. As another day dawns, may ours be the determination to carry out the divine commission to evangelize the world.

LUKE

This "most beautiful book in the world," as Renan called it was written by Paul's fellow-worker (Acts 16:16), the cultured Gentile, Luke the beloved physician (Colossians 4:14). Intended for Greek readers, this third gospel gives us a portrait of Jesus, the perfect Man, who more than meets the highest ideals of the Greek. Writing from the standpoint of our Lord's humanity, Luke, in simple narrative sets forth the events of His life in their chronological order, and discourses, miracles and parables succeed one another, without special emphasis, as in Matthew and Mark. This *gospel* has been fittingly called "The Gospel to the Gentiles." It is because the human birth and genealogy of Jesus are conspicuous, and He is depicted as the One who went about doing good that His genealogy is traced back to Adam. Christ, the second Adam, Son of Man yet Son of God, in His words and works is here identified with our humanity. What tenderness and sympathy He manifested toward the suffering and sinful, the good and the bad. The central chapter, as we shall presently see is the 15th with its trio of parables, marvelously presented. Note –

1. From His Birth to His Public Ministry 1 – 4:13
2. From His Entrance Into His Ministry to the Last Passover 4:14 – 21
3. From the Passover to His Ascension 22 – 24.

(Read Luke 1:1-4; Acts 1:1,2; Colossians 4:14.) As the literary masterpiece we are now to consider has been spoken of as "the most beautiful book in the world," surely we should know something of its

author, who also wrote *The Acts*. Luke, a Greek doctor, was trained to make accurate observations, and is at pains to describe the object and contents of his gospel. On his own confession he tells us that he used both written and oral sources of information. Carefully he sifted all gathered material and, under divine guidance, produced this orderly narrative of Christ's life and labors which he lovingly dedicated to his patron, Theophilus. As a Gentile, and the only one among the apostles, Luke writes for Gentiles; hence the universal appeal of his gospel. Of his accuracy, one has said: "Luke is a historian of the first rank; not merely are his statements of fact trustworthy, he is possessed of true historic sense. . . . In short, this author should be placed along with the very greatest of historians." Paul speaks of him as a constant companion.

Chapter 1

After the preface with its example of unique literary style, Luke takes up his narrative right away. Close contact with the principal characters of his gospel accounts for such an intimate style. In this portion, taken up as it is with the birth of John the Baptist, we have an insight into the purposes of God working out in the lives of the humble few who represented Israel's faithful remnant. In fulfilment of prophecy, John came as a Nazarite (Malachi 4:6). The burning of incense represented the highest privilege of the priest (Deuteronomy 33:10; Psalm 141:2). Incense is a symbol of worship and prayer, and as it was offered twice daily, God was approached morning and evening. Two lessons are before us. First, *God calls His servants as they are busy at their tasks* (verse 9). David was found while tending his father's sheep. The second lesson is that *God demands faith in His power to work in unexpected ways and places* (verse 20).

The intimate facts associated with the conception of John the Baptist and our Lord reveal how Elizabeth and Mary confided in Luke as the trustworthy, beloved physician. How honored and happy Gabriel must have been when chosen as the messenger of salvation! What holy ground we are on in this portion! Note the comparison between verses 18 and 34, and remember that, with God, all things are possible. The two songs preserved for us prove how Elizabeth and Mary had minds stored with the treasures of the Old Testament. Attention has been drawn to the contrast between the loud cry of Elizabeth and the quiet song of Mary (verses 42,46). Then there is the contrast between Elizabeth's leap of faith—"the mother of my Lord"; and Mary's humility as she rejoiced in God's undeserved grace. Note also the phrases: the Son of the Highest, the power of the Highest, and the prophet of the Highest, all speaking of the sovereignty of God.

With lips divinely opened, Zacharias echoes forth the third song of praise to be found in Luke's gospel. Such a song is made up of Old Testament Messianic prophecies. Are we as full of praise over Christ's Second Advent as Zacharias was over the First Advent? A peculiar phase of this song is that Zacharias has the first and greatest praise for Mary's Child, and not his own. He was quite content to be second. John the Baptist came as the prophet of the transition. Born between the Old and New Testaments, he laid one hand on the Old, and the other on the New, thereby making them one. As a preacher, he was trained in the deserts till the day of his shewing to Israel. And, as a preacher, he knew how to gather a congregation in the wilderness. Many a modern preacher turns a congregation into a wilderness. Would that we had more preachers as fearless as John!

Chapter 2

For the fulfilment of Micah's prophecy (verse 52), God overruled in the affairs of men. Thus it came about that Jesus was born in Bethlehem. By "all the world," we are to understand the Roman Empire, the sphere of Gentile world monarchy which is peculiarly the sphere of prophecy (Daniel 2:7). Evidences of Mary's poverty are seen in the fact that there were none to care for her new-born Child. She had to wrap Him in swaddling clothes. Then the place of her confinement was "the inn"—the open courtyard for animals. "Rich, yet for your sakes he became poor" (II Corinthians 8:9). Luke's fourth word is the one of adoring wonder on the part of the angels, and listened to by humble shepherds. How far removed the world is from the content of this heavenly note (verse 14)! Rites attending the birth of a firstborn son were faithfully observed by Mary. Her poverty is seen again in her offering of two pigeons. Have your eyes seen the salvation of the Lord? Simeon held Him! Do we hold Him by faith?

With the return of Jesus to His Nazareth home, the curtain falls upon His life and ways until, at the age of 30, He stood with John at Jordan. It has been pointed out that we can gather from these verses that Christ learned to write and read Hebrew, Greek and Latin, that He never went to rabbinic schools, that He took delight in nature, and that He worked as a carpenter. Both parents and children of today can learn precious lessons from Christ's religious training, and His obedience to Mary and Joseph. The center and circumference of His life can be found in verse 49. Has it ever impressed you that Christ was 30 years preparing for an effective ministry of 3½ years? God is never in a hurry with His choice servants. Does it seem as if, in spite of your desire and determination to enter the service of the Lord, He is very long in opening a door? If so, ask Him for more of the Nazareth-patience that the Lord Jesus manifested.

Chapter 3

Two figures dominate this chapter, namely, John and Jesus, and the two elements, fire and water, describe forerunner and Fulfiller.

Water is negative, and is not sufficient for our natures. Fire is positive, and it is the Lord Jesus alone who can plunge the soul into the fiery baptism (verse 16). In the first twenty verses of this chapter, Luke masterfully describes the ministry of John the Baptist, who came as a roadmaker for the King. Would that multitudes today might repent, seeing the King is at hand! Then, with true historical perspective, Luke traces the genealogy of Christ back to Adam. It was thus He came with a Gospel universal in its scope. Through the redemptive work of the Son of God, there is salvation for all the sinning sons and daughters of Adam's race. At His baptism, Christ received the anointing of the Spirit, and the benediction of His Father. Adam, as the son of God, transgressed, and by his fall, brought sin into the world. Christ, as the Eternal Son, was ever obedient and well-pleasing to God.

Chapter 4

After the baptism, there came the battle. After the dove, the devil. The two are never far apart. Satanic antagonism is a sure sign of heavenly favor. If God is pleased with His Son, such pleasure elicits the devil's displeasure. As Christ was alone in the wilderness, He must have related the grim experience of the temptation to Luke. Our Lord had no doubt regarding the devil's person and power. Conscious of His mission, Christ now sets out to accomplish it. Satan urges easier ways of fulfilling it, by "denying His manhood, replacing human submissiveness with magical power; denying His messiahship, using worldly means to establish His Kingdom; and denying His Sonship, putting His own will in the place of His Father's." As Jesus exercised His Nazareth ministry, the Holy Spirit was upon Him without measure, of course. The same unction is at our disposal, and is to be received by faith.

Chapter 5

Packed into this chapter we have the call of some of the disciples to full-time service, three miracles and a parable. As the disciples forsook all to follow the Lord Jesus, they were reminded that He was able to use their resources, and that surrender to His

will is always rewarded. Have we spiritual reservations, making it impossible for Christ to use us to the full? Christ's compassion is seen in His willingness to touch such an infected man. And touching, He was not contaminated. In the records of the paralytic healed in an unusual fashion, we see the title, "Son of Man," for the first time. This is the designation expressing the humanity of Christ, which is the peculiar feature of Luke's gospel. From Christ's treatment of the Pharisees, and His parable, we learn that Christianity is not a patchwork added to the Old Covenant. Legalism must not be stitched on to grace. False tradition and ritual are dangers the Church must ever guard against.

Chapter 6

As a continuation of the previous chapter, the one before us cites forceful illustrations of the incompatibility of the new wine with the old skins. First of all, we have the Sabbath. Here Christ proves that the beneficial provision of this day was buried in tradition (Deuteronomy 23:25). Then we have the healing power of the new message He taught. In the bringing together of the Twelve, Christ evidenced His courageous love. What differing personalities He gathers around His banner! The Beatitudes emphasize the nature of the new wine in the teaching of the New Covenant. New standards and new commands form the Sermon on the Mount. Here we have four "blesseds," and four "woes." The chapter closes with a reference to the deepest secrets of the new life. A new heart and a new foundation are imperative for its realization. Are you building on a safe foundation?

Chapter 7

The two incidents opening this chapter, illustrating as they do the power of God and the faith of man, offer interesting points of contrast and comparison. In each we have a miracle – one performed while Christ was distant, the other while He was present. In one case it was a servant, in the other it was a son. The first was by request, the second was unasked. One miracle was restoration to health, the other was a resurrection from the dead. Master and mother were blessed. On one it was a Gentile, on the other it was a Jew whom Christ helped. Why did John doubt whether Jesus was the Messiah? Well, we all have our days of doubt. But if John's faith wavered, the Lord Jesus never lost faith in His servant. Tangible evidences of His messiahship were sent to reassure downcast John. The exquisite account of Christ's visit to the Pharisee's home is one that Luke alone has preserved for us. And what literary masterpieces Luke's accounts are!

Chapter 8

In the opening verses of this great chapter, Luke tells us how Christ and His disciples were financially supported, namely, by the free-will offerings of those who valued the Lord's ministry. Parables and miracles make up the chapter. In the *Parable of the Sower*, one of the earliest uttered by Christ, we learn our responsibility. All that the Lord expects of us is the prayerful, careful sowing of the seed. The harvest is His, and He will care for it without fail: "God giveth the increase." From the *Parable of the Lighted Candle* we learn that the candle is the truth – the candlestick is the teacher, who is not the source of light, but only the holder and distributer of it. In what Christ had to say about His relatives, we learn the supremacy of spiritual kinship. Coming to the sudden storm, we are reminded that no boat can sink that has the Lord Jesus on board. The concluding miracles declare Christ's sovereignty in two worlds – satanic and physical. Demon and disease bow before Him.

Chapter 9

After a rapid summary of our Lord's Bethsaida ministry, Luke comes to the return of the apostles and the miracle of the feeding of the five thousand. Christ, as God, knew how to furnish a table in the wilderness. There is a mystical significance to this miracle. A larger crowd was to be fed through the offering of His body. Our Lord prayed much (verse 18). And what great things happened when He prayed! People around were perplexed and divided as to who Christ was. What does He mean to us? Conditions of true discipleship are

easy to trace. Denial of self and daily cross-bearing are the Master's demands. The first points to the exercise of our own will; the second, to submission to the will of Another. "The life of self is death – the death of self is life." If Christ is our greatest gain, then we must talk about Him. If we are ashamed of Him, then we should be thoroughly ashamed of ourselves.

Many truths are associated with our Lord's Transfiguration. The presence of Moses and Elijah on the Mount, long after they left the world, reveals that the saints in the unseen world have lives undiminished by passage from time into eternity. Full consciousness is theirs. They likewise retain their identity. Not knowing what he said, Peter asked that he might stay in the blaze of glory surrounding him. He forgot that the "mount of vision" was necessary equipment for the "valley of need." What follows makes sad reading – the powerlessness, jealousy, pride and sectarianism of the disciples. Then comes the absolute necessity of the cross. Have you ever thought about the loneliness of Jesus? He had nowhere to lay His head. He died, even as He had lived – alone! The test of discipleship is the willingness to put Christ first. Always, everywhere, and in all things His supremacy must be recognized. With Him, the will of God was ever first.

Chapter 10

Taken up with the twelve disciples, we are apt to forget the Seventy whom our Lord commissioned and sent forth, two by two. Tradition has it that Philip, whom Luke knew so well, was one of this honored band. Dr. Graham Scroggie, in writing of the Seventy, remarks: "They who go for Christ go in His strength (verse 3), and at His charges (verse 4), they carry a message of peace (verses 5,6), exhibit a spirit of contentment (verses 7,8), bring blessing to soul and body (verse 9), and become a standard of judgment among the people," (verses 10-12). We must realize that responsibility is measured by privilege (verses 12-15). From His birth on, Christ's gaze was fixed on the cross. He was born to die. Anticipating the cross, He regarded it as an accomplished fact. The superb story of the Good Samaritan, told only by Luke, rebukes the hypocritical legalist, and reveals the powerlessness of the law to save and heal the fallen. The Saviour is our perfect Samaritan.

Chapter 11

Have you graduated from Christ's school of prayer? Approach to God is through Christ (John 14:6). Relationship is based upon regeneration. Unless we have received the Spirit of adoption, we cannot cry: "Abba, Father." Four things have been noted in Christ's teaching about prayer. The *"model prayer"* (verses 1-4); *the need for persistence* (verses 5-9); *the need of faith* (verses 10-12); and *the created gift received by prayer* (verse 13). Is it not blessed to know that Christ is stronger than the strongest (verse 22)? Are you for Christ, or against Him? Nature, we say, abhors a vacuum. And the heart knows no vacuum. Either the Spirit or Satan is within. If the house of our heart is FOR RENT, demons will not be long in taking up their abode.

Chapter 12

Argument gathers a crowd, and in the tense, yet dangerous moment that Luke describes, Christ stands out as Master of the situation. How He could handle a crowd! The sermon on the leaven of the Pharisees proves how our Lord hates all sham, hypocrisy and unreality. Have we forgotten the standard of values set forth in the *Parable of the Rich Fool?* And have we lost sight of the truth that the God who cares for the birds and flowers has promised to meet our every need? Why worry, then, when we have such a God? In His solemn advent warnings, Christ urges upon us the necessity of watchfulness. How different life would be today if we knew Christ would be here tomorrow! The great discourse in this chapter ends with Christ's expressed passion regarding the realization of His redemptive plan. Earnestly He appeals to the crowd to get right with God ere judgment is let loose.

Chapter 13

Still in the presence of the multitude, the Lord Jesus presses upon the consciences of His listeners the need of individual repentance. In His contrasts of the Kingdom,

our Lord cites examples of a woman delivered out of Satan's hand, and of a ruler filled with hatred. In the two parables, we have the growth of the Kingdom, and then its contamination with pharisaical leaven. On His journey to Jerusalem, where the Lord Jesus knew He had to die, He declared that His Kingdom would never lack subjects, and that they would come to Him from the four corners of the earth. What determination was Christ's to fulfil a God-given task! He declared that, in spite of foxy Herod, He was immortal until His work was finished. Do you believe this of yourself, if you have discovered God's plan for your life?

Chapter 14

The five parables of this chapter make profitable reading. Of the Pharisees' criticism of Christ's use of the Sabbath, another has written: "The persons who thought it a sin to heal on the Sabbath day, did not think it a sin to be proud and selfish on that day (verse 7). What an anomaly – a sin to DO GOOD, but not a sin to BE BAD on the Sabbath Day!" Strange, is it not, that with all their religion, the Pharisees were indifferent to human need. As the table-talk continued, the Lord Jesus went in for some fearless speaking. True love, He declared, asks no reward, but gives itself freely and fully. What do we know about "highways and hedges" evangelism? Are we prepared to face the cost of discipleship? Christ's claim takes precedence over every other. And when He has the first place, all other relationships are enriched. Would that we could be more ruthless in the fulfilment of our allegiance!

Chapter 15

In this renowned chapter – "a masterpiece of writing and an inspired revelation of the heart of God," the combined work of the Trinity in redemption is beautifully illustrated in three incomparable stories. In that of the *Lost Sheep*, we have the love of the Son, who gave His life for the sheep. In the *Lost Coin*, "the silver piece, part of the woman's dowry which every married woman wore as a chain across her forehead," we can discern the love of the

Spirit for sinners. In the *Lost Son*, we have a glimpse into the Father-heart of God. Joy is associated over the recovery of the lost sheep, the lost coin and the lost son. Do we share the joy of angels over the return of lost souls to God? In respect to some parables, old expositors used to say that often the key is found at the front door, and that is true here: "This man receiveth sinners."

Chapter 16

The *Parable of the Unjust, Dishonest Steward* proves that we are "to use money and material possessions wisely for eternal purposes, by bringing into the Kingdom souls who will welcome us in heaven." It is a sin to make money an end in itself. How slow we are to believe that we cannot serve God and mammon! We cannot take the joys of the Lord Jesus and the so-called pleasures of the world at the same time. It is Christ or the world, not Christ and the world. The story of the rich man and Lazarus illustrates what our Lord says in verse 6. The rich man might have had Lazarus as a friend to welcome him in heaven, but he loved his money to the losing of his soul. And, in this most impressive story, Christ teaches the utter impossibility of man to alter, after this life on earth ends, his eternal destiny. The torment of the lost is as real and eternal as in the blessedness of the saved. Yes, and the description that Christ offers of the after-life gives the lie to the doctrine of the cessation of consciousness and existence beyond death.

Chapter 17

A striking lesson on the art of forgiveness introduces this chapter. Conscious of the high standards set by the Master, the disciples pray for increased faith. Are we as careful as we should be about causing offence? We are undeserving of thanks for merely doing our duty. Fully obeying the Word and the will of God, do you count yourself an unprofitable servant? The familiar story of the ten lepers needs little comment. Our Lord delights in our thanks for gifts bestowed, but is often disappointed. Only ten per cent of the lepers blessed the Lord for His benefits. Is the grace of gratitude yours? The concluding part of this chapter contains two answers to the question: "When will the Kingdom come?" The first answer, addressed to the Pharisees, was a public one; and the second, a private answer, was reserved for Christ's disciples. The latter is a graphic description of this end-time period of Gentile dominion.

Chapter 18

What a matchless story-teller the Lord Jesus was! There has never been His like. Here we have one parable, illustrating the need of continual dependence upon God, and another related to the conditions of acceptance with God. Prayer characterizes both parables, showing how we should pray, and how we should not pray. Do we realize how dependent we are upon the mercy of God? What a fatal choice the rich young ruler made. He failed to see that the One calling him to a full surrender of his soul and substance was the One, who, although rich, became poor. Is there anything keeping you back from a complete surrender? With the shadow of the cross darkening the path of the Lord Jesus, we find Him solemnly warning His disciples of coming trials. They must expect to share His bitter cup. On the way to die, He yet went on with His task. The call of human need never went unheeded.

Chapter 19

How dramatic is the incident at the sycomore tree? Too many are up a tree, and beyond Christ's touch. Humble they may be, but they must come down. And Christ came to save only one class – sinners. In the *Parable of the Pounds* we can discern three facts: *Christ's departure, His absence* and *His return.* Faithfulness is the basis of reward in eternity. The surrender of the colt proves that our Lord had His loyal friends, who knew His need. And, in these dark days, He has need of you. What passion was Christ's for the souls of men! How He could weep over Jerusalem! And the shedding of tears led to the shedding of blood. We cannot weep over the lost without sacrificial service to rescue them.

Chapter 20

The religious leaders during Christ's earthly ministry were sticklers for the right kind of ordination. Here they practically asked Him where His diploma came from. And because He had not graduated from their "hall of learning," His testimony was spurned. Certainly we are not against acquired knowledge, but with all that can be gathered from a college, university or seminary, let us not neglect the "ordination of the pierced hand." The *Parable of the Vineyard* was directed against the jealous priests and scribes. It is profitable to think of our Lord Jesus as the Stone: the stumbling Stone, on whom the Jews fell; the crushing Stone, grinding Gentiles to powder; and the foundation Stone, on whom the Church is built. How cleverly Christ foiled the deeply laid plot of the priests and scribes to trap Him! What belongs to Caesar, must be given him. What belongs to God, must be surrendered to Him. The Sadducees were rationalists of our Lord's time. Their disbelief in immortality was met with Christ's emphatic teaching (verses 37,38).

Chapter 21

When people talk about giving the widow's mite, they forget that the mite was her all. The rich man had plenty after he cast his offering into the treasury, but the widow had nothing left over. Thus we are judged *not* by what we *give*, but what is left over after we give. Christ's prophetic discourse deserves pages of exposition. Graphically, He describes the course and consummation of the Gentile age. Advent key words are: "Beware!" "Watch!" "Endure!" Our Lord spent His last days on earth in teaching. If these are the last days, and it does seem as if His coming is at hand, how are we spending our time? As the darkness becomes more dense, ours ought to be the determination to shine as lights. "Look up! Lift up!" says the Lord Jesus; and if ours is the advent gaze, then what joy will be ours when we go up. Would that we could see people rising early in our time to drink in the blessed words of the Lord Jesus!

Chapter 22

The dark betrayal by Judas introduces this chapter of Calvary shadows. The choice of Judas will ever remain a mystery. A greater mystery is the Lord's choice of you and me. That the Lord had His secret disciples is evidenced by the fact that someone prepared the Upper Room, and another carried a pitcher of water. While the Lord Jesus had a Judas, He also had some who were faithful in such a dark hour. That pregnant phrase, "the hour was come," speaks of a God-planned life. This was the end for which Christ was born. Note the three actions in the Last Supper; Jesus took, break and gave bread. Too much of our bread is given without being broken. Yet God must have broken saints with which to mend a broken world. It seems almost incredible that the disciples could argue about position and prestige in such a solemn hour. Our Lord met this lust for power with the teaching that he who serves is the only one who is fit to rule. Of Gethsemane, we can say little. Holy is this ground! While the Lord Jesus sweated great drops of blood, the disciples slept. Are not we also guilty of failing our Lord? How low Judas fell, when, with a kiss, the symbol of affection, he betrayed his Master! As to the trial of Christ, five phases are to be noticed: before *Annas*, before *Caiaphas*, before *the Sanhedrin*, before *Herod* and before *Pilate*. The first three were illegal; and the last two unjust. Peter's backsliding, as given in this chapter, should serve as a warning to us all. "Let him that thinketh he standeth, take heed lest he fall" (I Corinthians 10:12). While Christ's own claim to deity was treated as criminal by the chief priests and elders, yet in the face of fanatical opposition, He asserted His Godhead. Amid Jewish and Gentile mockery our Lord was not ashamed to confess who and what He was. What shame He willingly endured for our sakes! How utterly unworthy we are of the buffeting and bleeding He suffered!

Chapter 23

The Lord Jesus was made to stand before Pilate and Herod. But *He* was not on trial. The *rulers* were, and their contact with Him revealed what they really were. Religious and political charges were brought against Him. It was affirmed that He had perverted the people, forbade His followers to pay tribute or taxes, claimed to be a King, and all three charges were lies. Even His judges were forced to recognize His innocency and sinlessness. Pilate had Jesus on his hands and had to do something with Him, so he sent Him to Herod. But no one can shirk his own responsibility. Christ is in the hands of every man, as it were, and a decision regarding Him is ever a personal matter. The alternative before Pilate is the one that is before the world today – Jesus or Barabbas. It is striking to observe that only women cared for Christ's comfort as He went out to die. The men forsook Him. Oh, let all our glory be in the cross on which the Saviour died.

Chapter 24

What a victorious chapter this is! Death could not keep its prey. Jesus was taken down from the cross; thus a Crucifix is foreign to the New Testament. Then, the grave was emptied. Hallelujah, Christ arose! His Resurrection was God's receipt for Calvary. "They remembered his words." The empty tomb explained so many things! Within this chapter we have a series of openings: opened *grave*, opened *eyes*, opened *Scrip-*

tures, opened *understandings*, and opened *heaven*. What a privilege, if we could have Him expound the Scriptures to us, as He did that day on the Emmaus road! Yet, ours can be the burning heart, and the fully recognized Christ, if only we will trust the Holy Spirit to lead and guide us into all truth! May ours be the constant prayer: "Open my eyes that I may see, glimpses of truth Thou hast for me."

Is there not something tender in Christ's dealing with His frightened disciples? How willing He was to share what they had! Are we giving Him to eat? Fish and honeycomb He no longer needs. Now He feeds upon our love, trust and surrender. The reason for His death and Resurrection is given in verse 47, namely, repentance and remission. We must be true witnesses of the redemptive Gospel. For such a plan there is power. Pentecost released the power from on high for evangelism. How fruitless our witness if it lacks the enduement of the Spirit! Christ's triumphal entrance into heaven radically transformed the disciples. They knew how invincible they would be, now that their risen Lord had ascended on high, there to carry on His advocacy on their behalf. And because all power is His in heaven and on earth, let us continually worship Him, and constantly work and witness in His Name.

JOHN

This "spiritual Gospel," as the early church Fathers named it, contains no parables, and only eight miracles, six of which are omitted by the other evangelists. A fisherman who evidently belonged to a family of means and influence, John, probably the youngest member of *The Twelve*, records for Christians of all time, his own personal recollections, with peculiar emphasis on the life and labors of Christ as the God-Man, and in doing so, "excels in the depths of divine mysteries." He wrote as he did that men might believe that Jesus is the Christ, the Son of God (20:31). Leaning on the bosom of Him who loved him, John unveils many secrets of his Lord. *Life, Light* and *Love*

can summarize the teaching of the "apostle of love" whose *gospel* has been called "The Heart of Christ." Origen, one of the early Fathers, said of it, "The gospel of John is the consummation of the gospels as the gospels are of the Scriptures." It would seem as if every expositor has his own outline of the great truths enshrined in this fourth gospel. Dr. Pierson's is here given –
   1. The Prologue, 1:1-18
   2. Successive Manifestations to Jews, Samaritans and Galileans, 1:19 – 12
   3. Christ's Passion and Death, 13 – 19
   4. Resurrection and Epilogue, 20 – 21.
John also wrote the three *epistles* bearing his name, and the *Book of Revelation*.

(Read Mark 3:17; Luke 5:10,11.) As we come to John's gospel and epistles, let us take a brief look at the writer himself. He was the younger son of Zebedee and Salome. His father owned a vessel and had hired servants (Mark 1:20), while his mother was one of the women who ministered unto Jesus, was present at the cross, and anointed His body with spices. A native of Bethsaida in Galilee, and, by profession a fisherman, he was called to apostleship while plying his nets (Mark 1:19,20). Chosen as one of the Twelve, he was yet the youngest of the apostolic band. As we know, he formed one of the select triumvirate. He was surnamed by Christ, Boanerges, "Son of Thunder" (Mark 3:17). With prophetic zeal and firm resolution he bore unfailing testimony to Christ and His Word. His is a life to be emulated by us all.

(Read John 13:23; 19:26; 20:2; 21:7,20.) The original of John's name is suggestive. It means, "whom Jehovah loved," and is a name corresponding to experience, for he was loved of the Lord, and loved the Lord. Five times over, this disciple who leaned on Jesus' bosom is spoken of as the one whom He loved. Jesus and John were bosom friends. And such holy intimacy adds significant value to John's Christ-honoring work. He was treated by our Lord with greater familiarity than the other disciples. Evidently he shared his Master's secrets; thus he gives us a series of pictures of marvelous beauty in which Christ is the central figure. John's gospel is characterized by Christlike spirituality, heavenliness and love, surpassing all other inspired writings. It is also marked by historical truth, and glory such as, perhaps, no other gospel possesses. As we are to see in our meditations, the result of this David-and-Jonathan-like love is a divine picture gallery of Christ.

(Read John 1:11; 13:1.) The gospel of John falls into two general sections, marked by the repeated phrase, "his own." In the first twelve chapters, Christ is seen coming unto His own – His own things, possessions and people; but He was not received. This first section contains His public manifestation, and covers the first three years of His ministry. He is here presented to sinners in a needy world, hence, twelve glimpses of sinners. From chapter 13 through 21, Christ is related to His own – His own in reality, namely, those given Him by the Father, bought by His blood, and His through the surrender of their own will. The last section is His private manifestation, and covers the last 24 hours of our Lord's life and part of His post-resurrection ministry on earth. As He is presented to His very own, whom He ever loves, we are given nine glimpses of saints in the nine chapters. Thus, all the portraits of Christ are related to sinners and saints. And so, He is offered to every possible character.

Chapter 1

While the division of books into chapters is of human origin, and often tantalizing, yet it will be found that John's gospel gives us a striking portrayal of Christ in each chapter. Foremost among these cameos of our Lord, are those found in this opening chapter. He is here presented as the Son of God, and the Lamb of God. Genesis commences with man made in the image of God; John begins with God made in the image of man, for "the Word became flesh." The first five verses present a most solid epitome of Christ's history; we are indeed blessed. John's is "The Gospel of Glory," and, in verses 1-14, we behold Christ's glory. The next part of the chapter (verses 15-34) is taken up with the witness of John the Baptist, whose ministry brought the Old Testament and the New together. In him, we have the burial of the Old and the birth of the New. Trace "walk" and "talk," "Follow" and "find," and "search" and "see" in verses 35-51.

Chapter 2

In this "Cana" chapter, the Lord Jesus is before us as the Son of Man, a title He bears some eighty times. As the Son of Man, He knew what was in man. Here we have His racial name as the representative Man. It must be declared, however, that although He is the Son of Man, He was never the Son of a man. The initial miracle performed at the wedding feast portrays Christ as the Wine, the joy of life. He came to sanctify our joys, as well as our sorrows. Can you invite Him to participate in your social intercourse? As well as the *first sign*, we have the *first judgment* in this chapter.

Christ is ever against a privileged class in His house making merchandise of His people, and lording it over His heritage. The cleansing of the temple proves that He is against secularism and vested interests being mixed with religion. In the turning of the water into wine, He revealed His glory; in the turning out of profiteers from the temple, He manifested His zeal.

Chapter 3

We here see Christ as the divine Teacher. Man is sometimes a religious sinner. Trace how Christ instructed Nicodemus in the necessity, nature, secret and results of regeneration. Then see if you can outline twin truths in verses 1-21, commencing with two teachers. Have you ever noticed the middle word of that marvelous sixteenth verse? Are you certain that you have been born again? Born in sin, we need to be re-born; hence, the work of the Spirit. What noble magnanimity the Baptist reveals! Jesus and he were not rivals. One was the forerunner – the Other, the Fulfiller (verses 22-30). Performing his service, John the Baptist departs from the scene, that Christ might have all the glory. Ultimately, John the Baptist was murdered to satisfy the revenge of a hateful woman. The chapter concludes with the writer's acknowledgment of the deity of Christ (verses 31-36).

Chapter 4

Within this conspicuous chapter we have several portraits of Christ. Here we see Him as Lord, Man, Jew, Prophet, Messiah, Healer, Master, Saviour and Satisfier. Certainly there is no better chapter in the study of personal evangelism. Christ is the perfect example in the art of going from the material to the spiritual, using the material as the vehicle of the spiritual. One of the predominant themes of the chapter is the gift of the Spirit. Outlining the chapter we have the *Saviour and the Sinner* (verses 1-30); the *Saviour and the Sower* (verses 31-38); the *Saviour and the Samaritans* (verses 39-42); and the *Saviour and the Sick* (verses 43-54). This last portion, containing our Lord's second Galilean act of healing, is precious to study. We have the *Request of Faith* (verses 43-47); the *Repose of Faith*

(verses 48-50); and the *Reward of Faith* (verses 51-53). Faith was crowned with sight. The urgency of faith was turned to the joy of faith.

Chapter 5

The opening phrase "After these things," suggests that Christ acted according to plan. And what a plan we here observe! He went to the place where the neediest were in the habit of gathering. Are we going out to some pool of Bethesda, where the most helpless and abandoned sinners are to be found? Viewing the chapter as a whole we have *impotence and omnipotence* (verses 1-16); and *Father and Son* (verses 17-47). In this concluding section there is a four-fold proof of the deity of Christ. Under Mosaic law, two or three witnesses were required to establish a matter. Christ went beyond the requirements of the law and cited four witnesses to His prerogatives as the Son sent by the Father – *proof from John* (verses 32-35); *proof from His works* (verse 36); *proof from the Father* (verse 37); and *proof from Scriptures* (verses 39,40,46,47). And every believer has the privilege of adding his personal witness. Are we witnessing for Christ as the Source of Life – physical, spiritual and eternal?

Chapter 6

In this longest and most instructive chapter in John's gospel we see the Lord Jesus as the Bread of Life. Every miracle is a parable of spiritual truth, just as every parable is a miracle of grace. Christ's reference to the manna (Exodus 16:4) shows how effectively He could use and apply Old Testament Scriptures. Seven sections can be traced: *a crowd and its hunger* (verses 1-7); *a lad and his loaves* (verses 8-11); *a basket and its fragments* (verses 12-14); *a storm and its sequel* (verses 15-21); *a desert and its manna* (verses 22-31); *a heaven and its bread* (verses 32-59); and *a challenge and its results* (verses 60-71). In Christ, as the Bread of God, we have One who satisfies both God and man. Think of Him as He passes before us in this chapter as Prophet, Lord, Master, Bread of God, True Bread, Bread of Life, Living Bread, Bread from Heaven, the Son, the Son of Joseph, the

Christ, and the Son of the living God. Truly, this "running over Saviour" is able to meet our every need.

Chapter 7

God has promised that our bread and water shall be sure. In the previous chapter, we have our Bread; here, we have our Water. Is ours the experience of verses 37 to 39? If bread and water are essential to our physical life, we must have Christ as both for meeting our spiritual needs. And we have Him as our Manna, and the Giver of the Spirit. The chapter introduces us to His *unbelieving relatives* (verses 1-10). Those, bound to Him, more or less by human ties, did not understand Him. Then we have the *unbelieving Jews* (verses 11-36), who fought against His set and continuous teachings. In turn, we have the *blessing of faith* (verses 37-39), and the *bone of faction* (verses 40-53). As Christ ever divides (verse 43), it is important whose side we take. Are we for or against Him? Neutrality is impossible where He is concerned. The Spirit-filled life (verse 38) means true identification with Him as the Sent One of God. Nicodemus was not afraid to speak a good word for Christ (verses 50,51). Are we?

Chapter 8

Our Lord was an early riser (verse 2). As the Sinless One (verses 7,46) He was the gallant Defender of the fallen (verses 3-11). The only One without sin never threw a stone. In verses 1-11, we see the Lord *Jesus and a fallen woman;* in verses 12-59, *Jesus and a faithful witness.* Have you noticed how John extols the Lord as Light (verse 12), Truth (verse 32), Emancipator (verse 36), and Pre-existent One (verses 56-58)? He is *Light for all* (verses 12-18), *Life for all* (verses 19-30), and *Liberty for all* (verses 31-59). There is no contradiction between verses 32 and 36. The liberating Truth is Christ Himself (14:6). Pilate asked the question: "What is truth?" not knowing that it stood before him personified in Christ. As the Truth, and through the truth, He ever emancipates.

> He is the freeman whom the Truth sets free,
> And all are slaves besides.

Chapter 9

Coming as the Light of the World, Christ demonstrates His right to such a position and title by giving sight to the man born blind. Our Lord's glory shone through the darkened lids and lighted them forever. Morally, we have been blinded by the god of this world, but Jesus can give us sight. The whole chapter lends itself to a serviceable outline: *the Manifest Deity of Christ* (verses 1-7); *the Questions of Curious Neighbors* (verses 8-12); *the Inquisition of Prejudiced Pharisees* (verses 13-17); *the Desertion of Cowardly Parents* (verses 18-23); *the Taunts of Bullying Foes* (verses 24-33), *the Worship of a Healed Man* (verses 34-38); and *the Spiritual Blindness of Rulers* (verses 39-41). How true it is that none are so blind as those who will not see (verse 39). Do you know the Lord Jesus Christ as the Light-Giver? If not, He waits for you to say, "Lord that I may receive my sight!"

Chapter 10

Christ is before us in this "Good Shepherd" chapter, as the Giver of His life for His own. He is also portrayed as the Door, as the Christ, and as the Son of God. Sheep are peculiar among animals in that they quickly hear and detect the voice of the shepherd, and follow no one else. In redemption, Christ is the Good Shepherd; in resurrection, the Great Shepherd; in return, the Chief Shepherd. Christ assures His own of infinite care and unfailing protection. Outlining the chapter we have: *the Parable of the Shepherd* (verses 1-18); *the Partition among the Jews* (verses 19-21); and *the Proof of Deity* (verses 22-42). What do you know of the double grip emphasized in verses 28, 29? "None shall be able to pluck them out of my hand . . . out of my Father's hand." While we may not be able to perform miracles, we may yet have grace to speak of the Lord Jesus Christ in such a way as to help men believe on Him (verse 41).

Chapter 11

As the Resurrection and the Life, Christ proves His right to such a title in the raising of Lazarus. Christ and death cannot exist together. Have you noticed that while Lazarus received life, he yet needed Liberty? "Loose him and let him go." Some believers today have life but lack liberty. Born again, are you yet bound? If so, let the Son set you free. This chapter presents a four-fold revelation of Christ: At Peraea, *to his disciples* (verses 1-16); at Bethany, *to the mourners* (verses 17-37); at the Tomb, *to all* (verses 38-44); and *to the Pharisees* (verses 45-47). The sorrowing sisters offer a study in character. Martha was true to the energy and activity of her nature, and Mary, true to her placid frame of mind. Martha loved to work; Mary loved to worship. The ideal combination is that of Martha and Mary. Such is the balance that all of us need. Verse 35 is the shortest verse in the Bible. What a sublime spectacle – the Son of God in tears!

Chapter 12

In this "Palm Sunday" chapter, in which Christ is portrayed as the King of Israel, the Son of Man, the Arm of the Lord, and as a Light, the world around was blind to His kingly glory (verses 40,41). One devout soul recognized His royalty (verse 3). His cross was the way to His Crown (verses 32,33). Looking at the chapter as a whole we have: *honor from Mary* (verses 1-9); *honor from the Multitude* (verses 10-19); *honor from Gentiles* (verses 20-34); and *honor from the Rejected* (verses 35-50). Like some of the chief rulers who believed, are we afraid to confess Him? Loving the praise of men more than the praise of God, are your lips sometimes silent? Note the importance of Christ's words, His Word, in verse 47. At the Great White Throne it is to be the basis of judgment. Coming as the culmination of the revelation of the Father, our Lord's utterances have behind them the authority of the Father. We ought both to live, and love to obey, His Word.

Chapter 13

Entering this second section of John's gospel, our Lord Himself is revealed, rather than what He was able to do. Undertaking the task given to a slave, Christ assumed a lowly place. Washing the feet of His own, He left them an example of true humility.

He wanted His disciples to learn that pride ruins power (verses 4,5). The basis of effective service is love (verses 34-38). Love is the only badge the Lord Jesus asks us to wear. We can trace a four-fold warning: *against pride* (verses 1-17); *against greed* (verses 18-20); *against hate* (verses 31-35); and *against desertion* (verses 36-38). "Shalt follow me," was a prophecy of Peter's crucifixion. Legend has it that when Peter came to die, he begged his crucifiers to hang him upside down, since he felt that he was not worthy to die in the same way as his Lord. Learning the lesson of humility from the Master, the apostle, in after years, urged the saints to wear the apron of humility (I Peter 5:5,6).

Chapter 14

Walter Scott, the famous novelist, found great consolation in this chapter. On his deathbed it was read to him by his son-in-law. In the first three verses, upon which millions have pillowed their heads, we have a trinity in unity: *Faith in Christ, faith in heaven,* and *faith in Christ's Return.* Under the shadow of the cross, carrying, as He was, a broken heart, Christ was not unmindful of the anguish of His own. The only bequest the poverty-stricken Master had to leave was the legacy of Peace (verse 27). Are we truly living on this legacy? As the Way, Truth and Life, Christ meets the three-fold need of man, who is lost, in error and dead. It will be seen that this is a God-glorifying chapter: *the way to God* (verses 1-6); *the personification of God* (verses 7-14); *the gift of God* (verses 15-20); *the love of God* (verses 21-26); and *the greatness of God* (verses 27-31). Go over the chapter and underline the five-fold "also" of the Lord Jesus. Have you found your way to God through Christ?

Chapter 15

Abiding saints are represented in a four-fold way: *as branches, in relationship to Christ* (verses 1-8); *as friends, in relationship to each other* (verses 9-17); *as sufferers, in relationship to the world* (verses 18-25); and *witnesses, in relationship to the Spirit and the Word* (verses 26, 27). In contrast to Christ, the True Vine, Israel was an empty vine (Hosea 10:1; 14:8). There is a difference between work and fruit. It is sadly possible to serve the Lord, and yet be fruitless. Our responsibility is not to *produce* fruit, but only to *bear* it. Apart from Christ, we are helpless and hopeless (verse 5). The Master was hated without cause (verse 25). Our philosophy is, "Where there is smoke, there is fire." But this was not the philosophy of the Lord. We ought to be fruit-bearing branches. And of the three degrees of fruit, we ought to come to the "much more fruit" (verses 2,5).

Chapter 16

As the Giver of the Holy Spirit, the Lord Jesus offers us valuable teaching on the Spirit's ministry in chapters 14 – 16. Here we see *the need of the Spirit* (verses 1-4); *the promise of the Spirit* (verses 5-7); and *the work of the Spirit* (verses 8-33) in conviction, revelation, transmutation, intercession and tribulation. As the result of the Spirit's advent, we have teaching far beyond the express words of the Master Himself (verse 12). Christ could not say much regarding the significance of His death, since He could not get His disciples to believe that He was going to die. As Dr. Dale once expressed it: "Christ did not come to preach the Gospel: He came that there might be a Gospel to preach." Are we appropriating the promises of answered prayer (verse 23) and of a deep settled peace (verse 33)? May ours be tranquility *amid* tribulation!

Chapter 17

Many a saint, like John Knox the Scottish Reformer, has cast his anchor in this "Holy of holies" chapter, affording, as it does, a study of Christ at prayer. As we read the chapter, we can hear the deep breathings of the soul of the Son of God. This "high-priestly prayer" reveals the necessity of method as we approach the "throne of grace." It is in three discernible sections: *prayer for Himself* (verses 1-8); *prayer for His own* (verses 9-19); and *prayer for the world* (verses 20-26). Go over the chapter and mark the "I haves" of the Lord Jesus, as well as His gifts to His own. This is a prayer that truly teaches us to pray! Christ's prayers, we are reminded, were ever accompa-

nied by "strong crying and tears." Alas, so few of our prayers are drenched with tears! We have dry eyes and cold hearts. This is why we fail to prevail in prayer. Ceasing to travail, we fail to bring forth.

Chapter 18

What a model sufferer our Lord was! Complaint was never His. Think of the many ingredients in the bitter cup He submissively drank: the sin of the world, betrayed by Judas, Peter's denial, rejection by His own – enough, surely, to break any sensitive soul. Within the chapter we have Christ presented as Jesus of Nazareth, a malefactor, and the King of the Jews. For a division, we have the sections: *Jesus and Judas* (verses 1-9); *Jesus and the High Priest* (verses 10-14); *Jesus and Peter* (verses 15-27); *Jesus and Pilate* (verses 28-40). Contact with Him tests and sifts all characters. What a testimony to His sinlessness Pilate gave: "No fault in Him"! He is also holy, harmless, undefiled, and separate from sinners. Notice the effect of His deity upon those who came to take Him to the high priest (verse 6). Link verse 9 to chapters 14:12 and 10:28. There need be no lack of the assurance of the eternal security of the child of God.

Chapter 19

In both this chapter and the previous one, Christ is revealed as the whole Burnt Offering. Here we have Him lifted up from the earth. Have you thought of the three crosses in verse 18 – rejection, redemption and reception? We now see the Lord Jesus *crowned* (verses 1-3); *judged* (verses 4-12); *rejected* (verses 13-15); *crucified* (verses 16-37); and *buried* (verses 38-42). It is interesting to note that our Lord was associated with two Josephs – one at His birth, and the other at His burial. The garden, in which He was buried, carried the promise of resurrection. Mark the "beholds" in the chapter. Titles to meditate upon are: the King of the Jews, the Man, the Son of God, your King, and Jesus of Nazareth. Have you ever stopped to think of Christ's answer to Pilate: "Thou couldest have no power at all against me, except it were given thee from above"? What a theme of utmost importance is *the will of God.* Is it directive or permissive? – we ought always to ask ourselves.

Chapter 20

In this "resurrection" chapter, the Lord Jesus Christ is before us as the gathering Center of the saints – "Jesus stood in the midst." Here we have *wonder* (verses 1-10); *worship* (verses 11-18); *wounds* (verses 19-29); and *writing* (verses 30,31). As the Victor over death, Christ met and vanquished the king of terrors in a four-fold way: *at the bedside of the little maid* (Matthew 9:24); *at the bier of the widow's son* (Luke 7:11-15); *at the tomb of Lazarus* (John 11:43); *at His own burial,* when He entered the citadel of the grim destroyer and emerged as Conqueror. He is alive forevermore (Romans 1:4; Hebrews 2:14; Revelation 1:18)! Would that the Church as a whole would realize this! By a crucifix, attention is focused upon a dead Christ. But both the cross and the tomb are empty. He lives! Is He real to us – as the *living* One? This is important.

Chapter 21

Coming to the end of John's portrait gallery of the Master he dearly loved, we have to confess: "The half hath not been told me." John certainly wrote well of Him, but our blessed Lord exceeds the best men could pen. Here Jesus and Peter are together again. Look at these aspects: *fishing,* without, and then with, Christ (verses 1-11); *fellowship* (verses 12-14); *feeding* (verses 15-17; and *following* (verses 18-25). The only creed Christ desired His own to subscribe to was the "creed of love." Loving Him, as we should, we shall manifest loyalty to Him and His Word. In verse 24, John tells us that he is the author of this great gospel, and in chapter 20:30,31, he tells why he wrote the book. It was written to extol the deity of Christ. Do you believe that Jesus is the Christ, the Son of God? Have you experienced life through His Name? If not, dear friend, believe now on the Lord Jesus Christ, "and thou shalt be saved" (Acts 16:31).

ACTS

This "fifth gospel," as it has been styled, is the sequel in time and history to the preceding four gospels. Beginning with the Ascension of Christ and the historical foundation of the Church and ending with the imprisonment of Paul, about A.D. 60, *The Acts* witnesses to the Gospel having been planted in all the great capitals of the then known world. Luke, the historian, covers the first thirty years of church history, and tells us in his book of witness that the things Jesus "began to do and teach" in the *gospels* is here, through the Holy Spirit, continued in *The Acts* which is "the *sequel* to the *gospels,* and the *basis* of the *epistles.*" The Bantu title for this book is *Words Concerning Deeds,* which has also been described as *The Acts Of The Holy Spirit* and *The Gospel Of Resurrection.* "The door of Faith is opened successively to Hebrew, Roman and Greek, as in the order of the *gospels.* Pentecost links Old Testament

prophecy to New Testament *history.*" With its abrupt conclusion, *The Acts* is the only unfinished book in the Bible, and can be divided in this three-fold way –
1. The Lord at work in Jerusalem, 1 – 7
2. The Lord at work in Judea and Samaria, 8, 9
3. The Lord at work even unto the uttermost parts of the Earth, 10 – 28.

These widening circles of witness are the extension of the Master's commission (1:8).

Chapter 1

It is fitting that The Acts has been called "The Fifth Gospel," and "The Gospel of the Spirit," seeing that it contains the ministry of the Lord Jesus, *after* His Ascension. Behind the ministry of the apostle "stands the unseen figure of the living Christ directing and empowering them through the Spirit." Thus, as Dr. A. T. Pierson suggests, we can rename the book, "The Acts of the Holy Spirit Through the Apostles." Within this first chapter we have the promise of the risen Lord, and also His program. Then we have the preparation of the disciples. Prayerful preparation did not bring the Spirit. He came as the promised Gift of the Father and the Son. It is said of John Wesley that he lived much in the "upper room." Do we? With a plan we must have the power of execution, and for this the Spirit is ours to accomplish God-given tasks.

Chapter 2

Upon that memorable Pentecost Day, the Holy Spirit was represented in a three-fold way. He came as wind, fire, and speech, and how we need His dynamic ministry in these ways! We are so listless, lukewarm and indolent. May the wind of God blow away all our indifference and lethargy! Then there are those sins, imperfect motives and inconsistencies requiring the purging fire. As such we need the infusion of the new warmth and glow He alone can produce. As the tongue, we must have the utterance He imparts. Our lips must be Spirit-touched to witness boldly to the saving grace of Christ. It is blessed to know that, as the Holy Spirit came upon young and old alike, transfiguring them completely, the same energizer is at our disposal.

Chapter 3

Of the first apostolic miracle much could be written. Peter told the lame man to attempt the seemingly impossible, namely, to rise up and walk. But assured of Christ's ability, the lame man took the step of faith. Divinely healed, he crystallized his faith by his clear testimony. There are cripples among us still – cripples in morals, in will-power, and also, alas, cripples through their own sins or through sins of others. How full the world is of poor, disabled souls, so spiritually impotent! They lie at the doors of the Church, but are not cured. As Peter became the medium of healing, so only as the love of God flows through us can the dying spiritual cripples of our times be blessed.

Chapter 4

The first persecution of the Early Church brought out irrepressible boldness on the part of the apostles. Although imprisoned for his preaching, Peter was the means of leading thousands to Christ. In his third speech since Pentecost, Spirit-inspired Peter bore vital testimony before the Sanhedrin of the all-sufficing grace of Christ. Man may turn to other refuges, and, impatient with the old-fashioned Gospel, create saviours of his own, but apart from Christ he is helpless and hopeless. The Puritans were wont to say that the Lord Jesus had 108 names, and in every one of them there is salvation, free and full, present and eternal. We cannot read this great chapter without being impressed by the unity of the early Christians. They prayed, served and suffered together.

Chapter 5

The Holy Spirit so filled the fellowship of the Early Church that a sin against it was a sin against the Spirit Himself. Note the declaration of the deity of the Spirit (verses 3,4). Those who do not realize the exceeding sinfulness of sin may be shocked by the account of the seemingly unchristian treatment of Ananias and Sapphira. An expositor writes: "So familiar are we with spots and wrinkles in the Church that we can with difficulty realize the significance of this, the first sin in and against the community. It corresponds to the entrance of the serpent into Eden, and the first fall from the ideal must have staggered the apostles and the multitude." Who can estimate the power of a holy Church? Advance was made in spite of opposition. From the warning of Gamaliel we learn that truth conquers all.

Chapter 6

With the appointment of the first deacons we learn that all service for God, no matter how practical it may be, requires the infilling of the Spirit. We are apt to separate our tasks, referring to them as sacred and secular. To the believer, however, nothing should be secular. A further lesson to be gleaned from the narrative is that our ministry, irrespective of its nature, can only be effective as we give ourselves to prayer, Bible study and Spirit-inspired testimony. Stephen had a radiancy of faith and face none could gainsay. Meditate upon verses 8, 10, 15, and ask yourself whether you are dominated by the Spirit as Stephen was. The Holy Spirit is the same today and waits to accomplish spiritual wonders through fully surrendered lives.

Chapter 7

Stephen, the first Christian martyr, was possibly the first to realize that "the Gospel would overreach all racial prejudices and national frontiers." In his address before the Council, he affirmed that the Gospel was for all. A cruel death was Stephen's reward for a powerful witness. Stoning was an agonizing death, but God kept His courageous servant calm, so much so that in the spirit he manifested and the prayer he offered, Stephen reflected the spirit of Calvary. Why did the Lord Jesus stand, when He is pictured, in Hebrews 1:3, as being seated? Was it the Master's way of honoring and welcoming this hero-saint to heaven? Dying, Stephen saw Jesus. "His eyes were beautiful, because you saw that they saw Jesus." God grant that when our last hour comes, our gaze may pass beyond this world into another, where Christ waits to welcome us!

Chapter 8

The untimely death of Stephen must have seemed like a disaster to Peter and the rest. But they came to learn that the blood of the martyrs is the seed of the Church. Stephen dies; Saul is born again. Scattered abroad by persecution, the Church increased. From Simon, we learn that it is tragic to seek God's gifts for self-advancement. Coming to Philip's ministry, we discover that cooperation with God produces great results. It might have seemed unwise to Philip to be taken from the midst of a city revival and placed in a desert to win one soul for Christ. Immediate and unquestioning obedience, however, made Philip the soul-winner he was. And, from the Old Testament he knew how to preach Christ. Yes, and how full of the Gospel his sermon is!

Chapter 9

Looking down from the heavenly heights (granting such a thing is possible), Stephen must have seen that it was well worth his death to bring about the conversion of Saul the persecutor, who became Paul the apostle. As a passionate Pharisee, Saul violently hated Christianity, but three years after Pentecost, the miracle happened, and Saul's surrender to Christ was "one of the most far-reaching events in the history of the world." How useless it is to stifle any "pricks" of conscience! Let us learn from Ananias how to care for converts. From a spiritual miracle, we pass to two physical miracles. Peter's word to Aeneas is full of import. The poet speaks of "jewels five words long," and such is Peter's note of melody: "Jesus Christ maketh thee whole." And what a mighty Saviour He is!

Chapter 10

Like Jonah, Peter too had to be saved from racial prejudice. So we come to the formal admission of the first Gentile convert into the Christian Church. Looking upon Cornelius, and understanding the significance of his vision, Peter came to realize that God is no respecter of persons. Grace breaks down all barriers. No longer a bigoted, orthodox Jew, Peter is blessed as he gives the Gospel to the Gentiles. This chapter brings us to the first recorded sermon preached to Gentiles. What a powerful sermon it was, with emphasis upon the life, death, resurrection and return of Christ! No wonder the Holy Spirit fell on those who heard, and the Gentiles knew what it was to have their Pentecost. Would that all present-day preaching was as powerful!

Chapter 11

As the Gentiles began to form a definite part of the Church, strict Jews stirred up a good deal of controversy over their inclusion. Do we always rejoice to witness the fruit of the Spirit in denominations or groups other than our own? Ultimately the Church acknowledged the circumference of the Gospel, and welcomed the Gentiles. Often we hinder God's work because of our unwillingness to accept a new thing from

His Hand. The first use of the title, "Christian," was at Antioch. Given as a "nickname," it yet described the disciples as those who were true followers of Christ. Commendable Christian charity was manifested by the Church as word came through as to the plight of fellow-Christians in the famine area. So ought we to give to the extent of our ability to help those in need.

Chapter 12

"The whole of this chapter provides an illuminating study in the ways of Providence," says a gifted expositor, "being chiefly concerned with the details of Peter's deliverance. James was not delivered, and his martyrdom is dismissed in one sentence. Are we therefore to conclude that there was no Providence watching over James? Read Hebrews 11:32-39, where we learn how God was glorified by the death of some of His servants just as by the life of others." Peter's appearance as the saints were praying for his deliverance proves that interruption may be an answer to prayer. Of Rhoda, an old servant of the Lord has said: "She has an Oriental fragrance about her." Only a slave-girl, yet she has everlasting remembrance!

Chapter 13

Hitherto Peter has been prominent; now Paul becomes the leading figure, as he sets out on his missionary journeys. Having given proof of their calling, Paul and Barnabas are set apart for special service. Would that church councils could be as certain of the seal of the Spirit as was the Early Church, when men are selected for the ministry! What misfits it would be spared! Paul's masterly sermon at Antioch reveals how deeply versed he was in Old Testament Scriptures, and in their application to Christ. Though Paul went first to the Jews, he knew how the Gentiles hungered for the Gospel. Many Jewish leaders, deeming themselves superior, objected to Paul's wider ministry, but on he went declaring the glorious message that whosoever will may come.

Chapter 14

Dreaming of Rome, the then "mistress of the world," Paul came to Iconium and Ly-stra, which were on "the great Roman highroad running east and west, filled with a stream of life flowing towards the heart of the Empire." Have you ever tried to imagine the feelings of Paul as he was stoned? He must have thought of Stephen's anguish, which he himself had been witness to (7:58; 8:1). Division and dissension follow the triumphs of the Gospel. Opposition is ever to be expected when the stern demands of Christ are preached. But despite all adversity and tribulation, the number of disciples increased. In days like our own we have need to confirm the disciples, exhorting them to continue in the faith. The ministry of encouragement, of exhortation, can be exercised by every one of us.

Chapter 15

The problem before the council at Jerusalem was whether the Gentile converts were to be part of a Jewish sect, or was Paul right in his emphasis regarding the liberty of the Gospel? Peter, Paul and Barnabas gave their views, while James summed up the situation. The letter dispatched to the Gentiles was "a model of tact and courtesy, and a triumph for Christianity as a world-wide missionary faith." Good men like Paul and Barnabas clashed over the fitness of Mark and had to separate from each other, even though they had been designated as co-workers by the Spirit. After events seem to prove that Paul was right, for Barnabas vanishes from the scene. Ultimately Mark made good and became profitable to Paul (II Timothy 4:11), which should encourage some who once failed in service. It may be that God will restore your witness to His Son.

Chapter 16

How this chapter extols the grace of God! Salvation is for all classes and conditions of people. Think of the four trophies of Christ's power to save that we have in this remarkable portion. There is young Timothy, whom Paul led to Christ, and who had a life to dedicate to the Lord. Then we have Lydia, the wealthy, influential business woman, who, finding Christ, placed her home and possessions at the disposal of missionaries. She represents culture and refinement captured by Christ. Coming to the demon-possessed young woman, who was akin to a spiritualistic medium, we have an illustration of Christ's ability to save the most depraved. The conversion of the jailor proves that Christ can likewise transform the hard-hearted and rebellious.

Chapter 17

Without doubt Paul was a noble witness. Working hard at tent-making to support himself, he yet gave himself to aggressive evangelism, and stands out as the greatest church-builder of all time. But many difficulties and hindrances came his way, especially from religious quarters. Undaunted, Paul sought other fields. Compelled to leave Berea, he left behind him many young disciples who knew how to search the Scriptures. Digging deep, do you touch gold as you daily meditate upon the Word? Reaching Athens, "the cultural, artistic and philosophical center of the world," Paul knew how to appeal to the Athenians. What a masterpiece his sermon on Mar's Hill is! Beginning with the truths of natural religion, he led his hearers on to the Lord Jesus Christ and His Resurrection.

Chapter 18

How good God is when He brings across our pathway like-minded souls! What fellowship Paul must have found in the home of Aquila and Priscilla! At Corinth, the apostle came to experience that God was able to give to His beloved in sleep. In the night, by a vision, the Lord revealed His will to His servant (verses 9,10). The dreams of the saints are watched over and made sweet by their Lord, the Lord who neither slumbers nor sleeps. The leading of Apollos into a deeper life proves that Paul's association with Aquila and Priscilla bore fruit. Well trained, in turn they are found equipping another for more effective service. "He helped them much." Are you a helper or a hinderer?

Chapter 19

Paul found the work of establishing the Church a glorious task, but what opposition he encountered! Yet, despite hostility, he was continually on the offensive. That public dedication in Ephesus must have been an impressive sight as curious arts and evil books were burned up, witnessing, thereby, to new life in Christ. Many of us have some worldly rubbish that ought to go on the bonfire. The uproar of those silversmiths proves how disturbed men can become if Christianity touches the pocket. Christ, as the Way (verse 23), caused no small stir. Is our witness aggressive enough to excite wonder, and awaken the dislike of godless men? A courageous Christian warrior once remarked that we should make ourselves a nuisance until every evil nuisance is put down.

Chapter 20

Added to Paul's evangelistic labors was the care of the churches he founded. His return to old battlegrounds reveals that Paul did not forget his converts. He never felt that, once saved, Christians would develop without further help. At Troas, his long sermon was too much for a young man, who fell asleep with tragic consequences. But the apostle was ready for any emergency. What a touching charge that was to the Ephesian elders! In all things Paul was an example to those whom he led to Christ. He practiced what he preached. There is preserved for us (verse 35), a flower of the Master's speech which is not enshrined in the gospels. There must be many of the priceless sayings of our Lord that are unrecorded; but may we believe and obey those that we have!

Chapter 21

This important chapter in the life and labors of the Apostle Paul reveals how the Holy Spirit seeks to control the Lord's own. Some have considered Paul's determination to go to Rome a parallel to our Lord's set purpose to go to Jerusalem. The apostle was warned against visiting Rome, but on he pressed, believing, surely, that God was leading. At whatever cost, may we ever desire and do the will of God. The advice of godly friends is ever valuable, but above all, obviously, must be the assurance of the Spirit's leading through God's Holy Word.

Chapter 22

How courageous Paul was in his witness! Seizing upon every opportunity of recounting his conversion, he constantly brought conviction to many of his hearers. Uniting within himself "the three great nations of the Mediterranean world, Jews, Greeks and Romans, Paul made an effective missionary. Although he possessed a master-intellect, Paul was always teachable." "What shall I do, Lord?" Are we so conceited as to think that we are sufficiently wise that further light, even from humble sources, is impossible? It is interesting to compare our Lord's behavior at His trial with that of Paul's trial here. Courage, forgiveness, magnanimity are exhibited as virtues for all of us to emulate.

Chapter 23

Before the Jewish Sanhedrin, Paul manifested great tact. This august assembly was made up of Sadducees and Pharisees, who were resurrectionists and anti-resurrectionists respectively, and cleverly Paul brought the one section against the other. The escape of Paul, as the result of his nephew's prompt action, shows how God, in wonderful ways, preserves and protects His own. He knows how to circumvent the evil schemes of Satan and men. Of the letter Felix wrote, a Bible expositor remarks: "In your own letter writing do you ever sacrifice strict truth in the interests of 'diplomacy or business'?" Letter writing can be a gracious task, fragrant with the perfume of heaven.

Chapter 24

One evident lesson that we learn from this chapter is that whenever the work and truth of God make progress, Satan, as the prince of lies, will endeavor to wreck the testimony of the Lord's witnesses by circulating untruths. Paul's conscience was clear, and thus with boldness he defended himself against all attacks. Charges against him, political, religious and legal, were convincingly refuted. From Felix we learn the foolishness of waiting for "a more convenient season." Felix listened, and even trembled, but never yielded. How fatal was his indecision! He did not buy up his opportunity.

"There are two sworn enemies of my soul. Their names are Yesterday and Tomorrow," says Dr. Alexander Smellie. "Yesterday slays his thousands—Tomorrow slays his tens of thousands."

Chapter 25

After two years as a prisoner at Caesarea, Paul was brought before Festus, who tried hard to "conciliate the Jews while preserving the Roman reputation for justice." Paul's appeal to Caesar, however, changed the entire position. Wrongfully imprisoned, Paul carried his case to the highest court. Festus acknowledged his dilemma. He realized the injustice of Paul's imprisonment, and knew he had no charge against him. With public opinion against him, Festus stands out as having been a coward. Compare his contemptuous reference to our Lord, and his respect to Caesar. Put this question to your heart: "Does Christ mean more to me than anyone else in the world?" Festus uttered the right word in the wrong tone. "One Jesus," he said with contempt in his voice. To humble saints, such a Name is ever used with deep reverence and feeling.

Chapter 26

Adhering strictly to the facts of his own Christian experience, Paul knew he was on safe ground. As a true soul-winner, after presenting undeniable facts and evidences, Paul urged Agrippa, who was well-versed in the customs and law of the Jews, to decide for Christ. The convincing testimony of the apostle, in which he revealed that through the passage of years Christ had become more precious to his heart, must have made a profound impression, not only on Agrippa but upon all within the Court. Paul declared his right to wear a two-fold title: "a minister and a witness." There are no names so much to be desired. Servants and spokesmen we are to be—servants, yielding absolute obedience to the Master; spokesmen, telling forth what great things He hath done.

Chapter 27

At last, Paul began to achieve his ambition to be on his way to Rome. This chapter has been eulogized as the most accurate account of ancient navigation in ancient literature. When the apostle wrote to the Romans, "having a great desire these many years to come unto you" (Romans 15:23,24), he little dreamed that he would travel to Rome as a prisoner, with condemned criminals as his fellow passengers. But, when the storm arose, "the prisoner became the preacher, the captive is the captain of the laboring ship. It is a picture of how the child of God is kept in perfect peace when the rains descend and the fierce winds blow." How do we stand the test of the storms? Is panic or peace ours? Adversity provides a real test of our faith in God's providential power.

Chapter 28

Forced to spend the winter months on the island of Malta, Paul made the most of his opportunity. He was the center and life of the shipwrecked party, as well as a blessing to the islanders, who, like ourselves, jumped to hasty conclusions as the viper coiled around Paul's hand. The chapter ends with Paul in the imperial city, preaching and teaching the Word. At last he was in Rome, but not in the way he desired. Let us not be disappointed if our prayers are not answered in the way we expect. The Acts presents an unfinished story, for the complete story of the apostle's abiding influence is still unwritten. New chapters are being added every day. The story of grace cannot end until the last soul has been added to the Church.

ROMANS

As our meditations have brought us to the *epistles*, both Pauline and general, it is essential to bear in mind that all 21 of them amplify and apply for our fuller instruction, solution of practical problems, and exposure of errors, the germs of doctrine found in the *gospels*. *Romans* is not only first in order, but easily foremost in the rank of the doctrinal *epistles* because with it nearly every great doctrine of the Christian Faith is touched upon. William Tyndale said of •*Romans* that it is, "A light and way into the whole Scriptures." Without doubt, the outstanding, fundamental truth Paul deals with in this his *Magnum Opus* is "Justification by Faith." Three points can summarize the apostle's argument in his letter to Rome, namely, Salvation *needed* by all; Salvation *provided* for all; Salvation *free* to all, Jew and Gentile, on the one condition of faith in Jesus Christ. This "Cathedral of the Christian faith," as Godet describes *Romans*, has two outstanding sections –
1. How bad men can be made good, 1 – 11
2. How good men can be made better, 12 – 16.
The first section is *doctrinal;* the second, *practical.* Wise preachers who desire to

exercise an effective ministry, must emulate the apostolic method of first preaching doctrine, then making the application.

Chapter 1

Having a deep desire to visit Rome, Paul announced beforehand the distinctive, Christian truths he would proclaim, once he was within the metropolis of the world. Dr. Leon Tucker remarks: "Romans begins with the Apostle desiring to go to Rome. When the Book of Acts closed he is there, but in chains. God has a way" (16:22; Acts 28: 17-31). There is no contradiction in both Paul and Tertius being named as writers of this matchless epistle. Tertius, as Paul's amanuensis, adds his own name to the salutation. The epistle should be read at one sitting, as a preparation for these daily chapter meditations.

As Romans holds the passkey to the rest of Paul's epistles, it is essential fully to grasp the elementary and fundamental truths of this Roman letter, which opens with the note of great joy. In the opening verses we have the promise, person and purpose of the Gospel emphasized by Paul. An important section of chapter 1 can be found in verses 14-17. Verses 14-16 present Paul's three "I ams." Here we have *obligation, preparation, declaration* – trinity in unity. Then, in verses 16 and 17, we have the foundational thesis of the epistle. Bishop Moule says: "These words give out the great theme of the epistle." Examining this brief summary of the book, we find that its language permeates all that follows. It has been pointed out that the eleven leading words in these two pivotal verses occur 462 times in the epistle. As to the chapter as a whole, it is a tragic record of sin, Gentile sin. Man's ruin is beyond repair. The picture given is not merely Roman, although Rome was the cesspool of iniquity, but of the race as a whole.

Chapter 2

From the Gentiles Paul passes to the Jews and proves that there is an indictment against them. The expressed sentiment of a Latin writer covers this chapter: "I see the good and approve of it, and I follow the evil." With those more highly privileged than the poor besotted heathen, it should have been different. The Jews could boast of the law, yet they constantly dishonored God by breaking it. So Godet puts it: "Paul is about to drag to God's tribunal the nation which thinks itself at liberty to cite all others to its bar. It is a bold enterprise." The basis of God's judgment of the Jew is of a four-fold nature: *according to the truth* (verse 2); *according to deeds* (verse 6); *without respect of persons* (verse 11); and *according to my gospel* (verse 16). Bishop Moule, reviewing the chapter, says: "The undertone of the whole passage is a warning that the brighter the light will prove the greater ruin."

Chapter 3

Paul is here found proclaiming the universality of sin. "All have sinned," whether Jew or Gentile. In his terrible indictment, Paul proves from seven Old Testament quotations that all within the human race stand condemned before the judgment bar. The phrase, "but now the righteousness of God," is a pivotal point of this epistle. For the crisis of sin, there is the Christ, who came as the personification of divine righteousness.

All are under sin (verse 9), but God gets under the sin, makes it His own, and provides salvation for the sinner. As he lay dying, Adolph Monod, the saintly French scholar, said of Romans 3:10-18: "I am sure that when this vail of flesh shall fall, I shall recognize in this passage the truest portrait ever painted of my own natural heart." What a mirror it is of your heart and mine! The last part of this chapter has been called, "The Brazen Altar of Romans," for here we see expiation being made for man's guilt.

Chapter 4

We can rightly name this, "The Faith Chapter," for sinners can only be justified by faith, apart from works. "Grace is the principle on which God acts in reckoning a sinner righteous, and now faith, as opposed to merit or works, (is that) by which the sinner receives it." As we know, it was this truth of justification by faith, and faith alone, that aroused Martin Luther to sense his need and, in turn, to produce the Reformation. Here Paul illustrates the living, active, saving faith, by reminding his readers of Abraham's willingness to believe God. The apostle then defines justifying faith, showing it to be apart from any or all ordinances, and also apart from the law. Christ is able fully to meet our need, seeing He fully met God's righteous claims. What a Gospel to proclaim! Our character and works are of no avail. Moral, as well as immoral, are lost and need to be saved in the only way of salvation, namely through the Blood.

Chapter 5

We now enter into peace. What a blessed "therefore" begins this chapter! The first two verses give us another summary of Romans. Justification, sanctification and glorification are all here. Can you trace, in the first eleven verses, the seven results of justification? Let us never tell a sinner to make his peace with God. Peace was made at Calvary. It was there that righteousness and peace kissed each other. All the believing sinner can do is to accept the proffered peace Christ has provided. Peace becomes ours through faith. Later we are to have glory as the result of hope. Note the two-fold salvation in verse 10: salvation from the penalty of sin through the death of Christ – this is past; salvation from the power of sin through the life of Christ in His present, exalted throne-life – this is present. Is a present salvation yours? Then, saved from the guilt of sin, are we being saved from its government?

Chapter 6

This chapter and the next should be taken together, seeing that both describe the struggle that went on between Paul the believer, and the old Saul of Tarsus: "When I (new Paul) would do good, evil (old Saul) is present with me." Drawing the distinction between sin, the root; and sins, the fruit, Paul tells us what we are to do with both the root and the fruit, namely, to reckon ourselves dead to such. Sin does not die, but we die to it. And if all that belongs to the old nature is reckoned dead, no provision will be made to gratify the flesh. We have not to crucify the flesh. Paul says this was done at the cross: "Our old man is crucified with him" (verse 6). This is God's viewpoint and it must be ours. Faith reckons that the old man died in Christ. When it makes its appeal, faith says: "You are dead to me, and I am dead to you." Dead yet alive! What a paradox of faith!

Chapter 7

Continuing the truth of the previous chapter, Paul uses the illustration of a woman held under the law of marriage to a man as long as he lives. If death removes him, then she is free to marry another. In Christ, we are dead to sin and the law, and are now married to another, even to Christ Himself. The conflict of the two natures, so vividly described by Paul, is one we all experience. The old nature and the new nature subsist together in the believer. When God saved us, He did not take away our old nature. He made us the recipients of the new nature; hence, the unceasing struggle. Paul's failure at first was in the thought that the new nature was able to keep the old nature in the place of daily death, but it did not work. Not one reference to the

Holy Spirit can be found in chapters 6 and 7. Paul learned, as we shall in the next chapter, that victory could only be his as the Spirit, controlling the new nature, kept the old nature daily dead.

Chapter 8

Martin Luther called this Spirit-saturated chapter, "The Masterpiece of the New Testament." One could multiply the glowing expressions of praise on this remarkable chapter which one saint has described as "the song of songs in which we hear the man of faith sing." Commencing with "no condemnation," Paul ends with, "no separation." Is yours the blessed assurance that all condemnation is past? Have you realized that when Christ died, He died for you, and that if we are in Him, *all* present and future condemnation has been removed? Then Paul goes on to show that a new work within means a new walk without. Because of the indwelling Spirit, there comes the outer manifestation of His presence. Where the likeness of sinful flesh was seen, now a new likeness prevails. By the grace of the Spirit we walk well-pleasing unto God.

Chapter 9

Several scholars treat chapters 9, 10 and 11 as a parenthetical portion. A subject not hitherto mentioned is now introduced. The main argument of Romans would be complete without this parenthesis, yet how grateful we are for this qualifying portion, dealing as it does with the *past unconditional election, the present rejection,* and *the future re-gathering of Israel.* Here Paul is addressing himself specifically to the Jews, as God's chosen people. If this is borne in mind, many of the seemingly perplexing matters in the epistle will be clearly understood. In the chapter before us, the apostle sets forth the sevenfold privilege of Israel, namely: adoption, glory, the covenants, the law, service, the promises, the fathers (verses 4,5). "These distinguishing principles belong wholly to Israel, and any attempt at interpretation which fails to recognize this unchangeable principle leads to much dismay and failure." Let us not steal for the Church what belongs to the Jew.

Chapter 10

No one knew the Jews better than Paul did. As a Pharisee, none could instruct him in the law. Once regenerated and enlightened by the Spirit, the apostle came to understand the threefold rejection of his nation. Israel had rejected their Jehovah, the Christ of God who came as Messiah, and the Holy Spirit's offer of the Kingdom at Pentecost. Yet, amid all this denunciation of the Jewish people, there was his burning passion to see them saved. Great heaviness of heart was Paul's as he thought of the gross blindness of Israel. Alas, it is not Jews only who have a zeal for God that is not according to knowledge! We should memorize verses 6-17, if it is our heart's desire to see lost men and women saved. How many have taken verse 13 at its face value, and, calling upon the Lord, have found in Him their Saviour from a guilty past! As a believer, are you a confessor (verses 9,10)?

Chapter 11

Paul's convincing argument is that God has not cast away His people whom He foreknew. Amid declension, there was always the remnant, and in Paul's day such a godly remnant was embraced within the Church. In this chapter Paul achieves a double purpose. First of all, he deals with Israel; then he solemnly warns the Gentiles. The temporary setting aside of the Jew has brought spiritual enrichment to the Gentile, but God will not depart from His original purpose to bless the nations of the earth through the house of Abraham. Let not the Gentiles be guilty of the same folly as the Jews. If wise in their own conceit, they, too, will find themselves set aside. What a marvelous doxology concludes the chapter!

Chapter 12

We now enter the last section of Romans. Exhortation covers the remaining five chapters of the book. This chapter tells those who form the body of Christ how they should live, labor and love. It will be noted that for any exhortation there is a doctrinal foundation. Going back over the first eleven chapters of this epistle, in which Paul has a great deal to say about divine righteousness, we are surprised to discover that "the mercies of God," which, of course, include His righteousness, are singled out as the apostle's basis of appeal. Would that the presentation and transformation of the opening verses could be ours in greater degree! Have you discovered what your regeneration-gift is, and are you using it to the limit for the Giver? Note the blessed triads in verses 11 and 12! And do we treat our enemies in the apostolic way, as taught in verses 19 to 21?

Chapter 13

From Christian character in chapter 12, Paul passes to Christian conduct. Our duties to the powers that be form the present appeal. Subjection to authorities is a most practical aspect of life in Christ. It is somewhat hard to realize that it makes no difference what kind of government we are under, or what laws may be made; whether we like them or not, we have to be subject to them. At present, there is no Christian form of government. National life is satanically controlled yet divinely overruled. In the world, yet not of it, we are commanded to obey our rulers, no matter how godless their rule. Of course, we must *never* deny God or His Word. The aspect of salvation that Paul touches on, in verse 11, is salvation from the presence of sin, within and around us, as we look for the return of Christ. The last verse contains the message that turned Augustine from his evil ways, and made him the saint that he became.

Chapter 14

We cannot improve on Dr. C. I. Scofield's caption for this chapter: "The law of love concerning doubtful things." If, as some suggest, the chapter should commence with "but," then we can see how Paul, on the basis of the former chapter, makes such a strong appeal for Christian considerations. Here we are invited to strip ourselves of self, and although we have liberty to act as we deem right, we are not to use our liberty as a means of detriment to a weaker brother. Our good, says Paul, is not to be evil spoken of. Christian testimony can be marred by censoriousness. Who are we that we should constitute ourselves judges of others? Each of us must keep the judgment seat of Christ before our minds, and live as unto that day. Selfishness must not spoil our witness. What may be harmless for us may be dangerous for others. So we must crucify our desires. Amid all personal problems, the last verse is ever a safe guide.

Chapter 15

Paul not only exhorted the saints to exhibit self-abnegation, he daily practiced it. Through his many years of consecrated service he was dead to all self-pleasing. With the Master's example ever before him, Paul experienced that "the life of self is death, but the death of self is life." Have you noticed the cameos of God in this chapter? He is *the God of patience* (verse 5); *the God of consolation* (verse 5); *the God of hope* (verse 13); and *the God of peace* (verse 33). Then we have the glory of God, the truth of God, the Gospel of God, the Spirit of God, and the will of God, all emphasized by the apostle. Go over the chapter again and underline references to the Holy Spirit, to hope, to Christ, and to the many things with which we can be filled. As members of one body, note that we are to help, please, receive, admonish, minister and pray for one another. Have you thought of the ever widening circles of verse 29: Christ; Gospel of Christ; blessing of the Gospel of Christ; and fullness of the blessing of the Gospel of Christ?

Chapter 16

Ever a friendly soul, Paul was rich in friendships. This is why he remembers so many believers, even if only by name in a few cases. Men and women alike ministered to him of their substance and earned the apostle's gratitude. Where praise was due, Paul never failed to express his heartfelt thanks. He believed in people enjoying the fragrance of flowers while they lived. So Phebe was commended for being a succourer; Priscilla and Aquila for being sacrificial helpers; Mary, because she bestowed much labor on Paul and his co-workers; Apollos as approved in Christ; and other noble souls. Praises for faithful were also combined with anathemas for the faithless and apostate. The latter were to be avoided, as one would turn aside from a foul object, in order to prevent contagion. Today we are too tolerant toward those who cause divisions and offenses contrary to the doctrine we have learned. May grace be ours to live in the closing doxology of the chapter (verses 25-27)!

I CORINTHIANS

Paul, knowing that Corinth was the greatest and most profligate city of Greece — "The Vanity Fair of the Ancient World" — prepared his two epistles to the Corinthians not only to meet the Greek mind, as he does in renouncing *wisdom,* as to the Romans he renounced *power,* but also to meet grave questions affecting the life of the Church in Corinth. Judaizing teachers had come from Jerusalem and divided the Church. Matters relative to Christian living, Church administration and doctrine had split the Corinthian Church into factions which were warring against one another. Thus Paul wrote this first epistle to answer, in no uncertain way, certain questions which had arisen.

Is it not interesting to observe that the lordship of Christ is the conspicuous message of this epistle? The designation *Lord* is prominent throughout the book, occurring six times in its first ten verses. "There is deep significance in this, for all the disorders that had crept into their lives had arisen through failure to recognize Jesus Christ as Lord." The book falls naturally into two principal sections, after the introduction 1:1-9.
1. Reported to Paul, 1:10 – 6:8
   (Church Disorders 1:10 – 4:21, Social Irregularities 5 – 6:8.)
2. Answered by Paul, 6:9 – 16
   (Social Irregularities 6:9 – 10, Church Disorders 11 – 16.)

(Read Acts 18:1-18; 19:23; 20:1-3.) As we approach the epistles to the Corinthians we group these passages together, seeing that they provide us with the background of these two remarkable letters. The carnality of the restless Corinthians caused Paul a good deal of heartache; hence his grief and holy indignation of the first epistle, which, although it deals with various themes, has the underlying emphasis on Christian conduct. It is amazing to find that some of the deepest spiritual truths Paul wrote were sent to the Church in Corinth, outstanding for its low spiritual life. As their father in Christ, the apostle was faithful in his rebuke of the factions and minor disorders among the believers. They attempted to ignore his authority, and so Paul defended his claim to apostleship as he addressed them.

Chapter 1

Paul gives us a two-fold description of the Church. It is made up of those who are *sanctified* in Christ, and *called* into fellowship with Him (verses 2-9). The Corinthians excelled in spiritual gifts (verses 5-7), but these had the tendency to create jealousy, contention and division. The magnificent partnership they had been called into meant fellow-sharing. Unity is, therefore, stressed by the apostle. In his rebuke of the pride of human wisdom, Paul glories in what appears to have been a paradox to Jewish religiousness and to Greek wisdom, namely, the mystery of the cross displaying God's power. God, of course, is never foolish, but what He does appears foolish to man's fancied pride.

Chapter 2

Passing from his condemnation of the utter futility of human wisdom, which reached its climax in the rejection of the Lord of Glory, Paul comes to the necessity of possessing spiritual understanding. There is a wisdom the believer must have—"the wisdom of God." What cannot be discerned by our own imagination, investigation or ingenuity, can be revealed by the Spirit. He is our Teacher. Spirit-taught, we become the recipients of a discernment that acquired wisdom cannot produce. All truth is revelation. The pressing question is: Are we progressive scholars in the school of the Spirit? Do we revel in the understanding of divine mysteries?

Chapter 3

In this chapter Paul brings the light of the judgment seat of Christ to bear upon all phases of Christian service. Blind devotion to a particular minister is an evidence of spiritual babyhood. As builders, we have to guard against three mistakes: first, *the laying of a wrong foundation;* second, *we may build unworthily upon a right foundation;* and third, *if we are not careful, we can damage what has been built* (verses 11-17). For those who are ministers of the Word, Paul has some sound counsel. They must realize that they belong to the whole Church of Christ; that they are simply servants, being put in touch with the Gospel; that they must be faithful in their calling, pleasing God at all times, not men; and that they should live and labor with eternity's values in view.

Chapter 4

Apostolic exhortation, humility, patience and authority are before us in this portion for today. Note the three judgments: *man's judgment; self judgment; divine judgment* (verses 1-8). Paul does not hesitate to contrast the deception and deceit of the carnally minded Corinthians with his own experiences. To be "puffed up" (verses 6, 18,19) means, "inflated with success." Do we need such a rebuke? Are we conceited because of attainments? Paul looked upon himself as dung, the off-scouring of the earth. True humility was his. He had much to make him justly proud, but all his glory was in the Lord. In order to convince the high-minded Corinthians, Paul sent Timothy to show them the true way of life.

Chapter 5

From Paul's insistence upon the excommunication of a church member, guilty of a most heinous sin, we can learn many lessons. We should learn how to walk circumspectly, lest we should bring reproach upon the name of Christ. Then, we are sadly in need of some sort of restoration of godly discipline in church-life today, and ought to give heed to Paul's instruction as to the responsibility of a local assembly in dealing with members guilty of glaring sin. Says Matthew Henry: "Church-censures are Christ's ordinances and should be dispensed in His name. . . These censures on notorious and incorrigible sinners should be passed with great solemnity." (See Matthew 18:15-20 in this connection.)

Chapter 6

The key phrase of this chapter, "Know ye not?" occurs six times, and indicates Paul's frankness in dealing with the low, spiritual condition of the church. As believers, washed, sanctified and justified, the Corinthians should have acted differently. Destined to assist Christ in His coming rule and reign, they should also know how to exercise wise judgment in settling disputes among themselves. As Christians, they should not appeal for justice from the "unjust," but "unto the church." Controversies with one another should be determined by church counsel and advice. Paul has some solemn things to say about the believer's body. Seeing Christ died for it, and indwells it, and one day is to raise it, it must be kept for Him. Would that our bodies were more fully yielded!

Chapter 7

In these days when the marriage tie counts for little, it is imperative to give heed to Paul's counsel and directions about marriage. Excess should be avoided, and priority given to prayer and worship. Discussing verses 6-12, one writer comments: "It is important to distinguish between what is *commanded* by the Lord and so obligation for all, and what is *permitted* to or preferred by some (e.g., Paul) in certain circumstances." The apostle is not trying to force celibacy upon the Corinthians. He desires them to serve the Lord without distraction. For each of us, whether single or married, life's dominant passion should be to please the Lord. He must ever have the first place, and all relationship must be subject to His control.

Chapter 8

The portion dealing with Christian conduct and liberty, beginning here, ends with chapter 11:1. For the sake of weaker brethren, self-abnegation must be practiced. If what we surrender produces no spiritual loss to ourselves, but encourages others to believe in the reality of the sufficiency and satisfaction of Christ, then by our denial of even lawful things we glorify Him. To persist in doing things that cause spiritual damage to others is to sin against Christ. Are we willing to give up some dispensable habit for another's good? Christ was willing to give up all, even His life's blood, that we might be saved. Surely, then, we shall not continue in those things which, although they may not harm us, do cause others who are weaker to stumble. While liberty is valuable, there are times we must waive it.

Chapter 9

There is something magnificent about this challenging vindication of Paul's apostolic authority. He had to face opposition without and discouragement within, but Paul knew how to meet all cavils. With all humility he presents himself as an example of the self-denial that he recommends for others in the previous chapter. He had liberty to marry and to claim maintenance from the church, but Paul refrained from using his own rights for three compelling reasons: *the Gospel's sake, the sake of others,* and *his own sake.* May we be delivered from the fatal silence Paul hints at in verse 16! If we fail to preach the Gospel to those God brings our way, our reticence may cause them to perish in their sins. If we are silent, their blood will be on our heads.

Chapter 10

In his endeavor to dissuade the Corinthians from participation in unworthy fellowships, Paul cites Israel of old, who, while enjoying glorious privileges, yet failed to please God. Lust and idolatry robbed the people of further blessings, and resulted in grievous punishment. That the best of us are subject to enticement is emphasized in verse 12. The most holy must take heed. Paul urges abstinence for the glory of God and the spiritual good of others. He himself did not live an impoverished life, even though he perpetually denied himself for the sake of others. His was an abundant life. And we never regret the sacrifice of our desires, even lawful ones, for the well-being of others. By such surrender we gain "life in its fire and force and fullness."

Chapter 11

We now approach the section of this first epistle dealing with congregational worship. Various questions are handled from this point on through to chapter 14. For their common good, God has ordained that women must be subordinate to men. The wearing of a veil was the sign of this subordination. Among the Corinthians, shaved hair was punishment for adultery, and any woman appearing thus was disgraced. From the latter part of the chapter we learn that church attendance at Corinth was far from the ideal. There was, for example, the abuse of the Lord's Supper. Its solemn significance had been lost sight of. Alas, how many there are today who eat and drink condemnation to themselves! Participation should ever help faith to appropriate the fruits of Christ's death.

Chapter 12

In this section of the epistle we come to those spiritual gifts abounding, yet abused, in the Corinthian Church. Many extraordinary powers were bestowed upon the apostles for the conviction of the lost, and also for the establishment of the Church as a divine institution, just as the miracles of Christ confirmed His deity. But with the establishment of the Church unique gifts were withdrawn: "whether there by tongues, they shall cease" (13:8). Looking at the chapter as a whole we realize that every believer has a divinely appointed place in which to exercise his own divinely-bestowed gift for the glory of God and the benefit of men. As with the members of the body, so we are dependent upon each other. I need your gift, and you need mine. Our gifts, of course, differ, but there is unity in diversity, because God is one.

Chapter 13

Paul's *Hymn of Love* is illuminated if *Christ* is substituted for *charity*, or *love*. Try it, and see how it reads. Many there are who have gifts, but they lack grace. The exercise of their talents is spoiled by the absence of the lovelike spirit. This gift of love is one that should permanently abide among believers. Paul makes it clear that the most glorious gifts are nothing, of no account to us, of no esteem in the sight of God, unless accompanied with the properties and effects of love. Dare we measure our lives against the test of verses 4-7? Love is, indeed, the greatest of gifts. Faith is the eye by which we see the loveliness of Christ; but, when we see Him, faith will not be necessary any longer. Hope is necessary, enabling us to look beyond the present. But once with Christ, hope will be dispensed with. Love, however, will abide throughout eternity, becoming more intense as glories unfold.

Chapter 14

The theme is still that of gifts. Here Paul declares how any gift had to be regulated in the primitive, apostolic assembly of saints. In the gift of prophecy or preaching, there must be the intelligent presentation of the message, so that the hearers can easily understand what is being proclaimed. Empty heads, like drums, can make a good deal of noise. But whether we pray, preach or praise, all ministry must be in the Spirit and with the understanding. Women are not to distract attention by chattering. Orderly and seemly conduct must characterize the gathering of saints and, at all times, instruction and edification must be the goal before those who have gifts to use. Decency and order are certainly lacking in some highly emotional centers today.

Chapter 15

It would take pages fully to expound this great resurrection chapter. First of all, Paul states the sum and substance of the sublime yet simple Gospel with which he accomplished mighty victories. Christ died for our sins, was buried, was raised, and appeared to His saints. If, as one early leader wrote, there are shallows in this very full and potent Gospel where a little lamb may wade, there are depths where an elephant must swim. The "if" Paul uses is a baseless dread. If Christ did not rise again, then the progress of our lives will never be finished, the work of our hands will never be completed, the friendships of our hearts will be shattered, and the God of our trust will have played us false. But away with such a cheerless supposition! Christ is alive forevermore, and is with us, and will be, through the everlasting years.

Chapter 16

Paul closes his long epistle with a few final instructions and greetings. For long,

he had had a desire to help poverty-stricken Christians of Judea (Galatians 2:9,10) and so encourage the Gentile churches to send a generous contribution as an evidence of their oneness with less privileged saints. Instruction is also given as to the regular surrender, and proper administration of the fruits of our income. Other servants of the Lord are to be treated with due respect, and their ministry rightly acknowledged and supported. Further, among those who are Christ's there should always be the expression of mutual love and prayerful concern for one another. All that is associated with such a privileged relationship must be undertaken in the light of Christ's return: "Maranatha," our Lord will come.

II CORINTHIANS

This second epistle to the Church at Corinth was occasioned by the report of Titus that while the Apostle's first epistle had served its purpose, and that wrongs had been righted (II Corinthians 7:7-16), yet a fresh peril had arisen demanding immediate attention. Judaizing teachers, bearing letters of introduction from the Jerusalem Church were in Corinth, preaching a different Gospel from that of Paul's, and denouncing the apostleship of Paul. The results of the efforts of these false teachers was the rapid growth of a party hostile to Paul (3:1-3; 4:2; 10:10; 11:1-13). Quickly Paul acted and sent this letter warning the Church against heresies (11:3,4,13), and vindicating his own true apostleship – which is why the letter contains more of Paul's personal history than any other of his epistles. What a moving narrative he gives us of his sufferings, sorrows and secrets (1:8-10; 5:4; 12). Here abound the contrast of sorrow and joy; humiliation and exaltation. "Comfort" is the key word of the epistle (7:6,7). Because of the depth and strength of his love (5:14), Paul was grieved by the sins of the Corinthians, but comforted by their repentance (1:3,4; 2:4; 7:6,7). The preacher will find ample sermonic material in the many glowing and brilliant metaphors Paul uses. Sec-

tions to develop are –
    1. Explanation, 1 – 7
    2. Exhortation, 8 – 9
    3. Exoneration, 10 – 13.

Chapter 1

Written about a year after the former epistle, this second epistle to the Corinthians is most touching in that it reveals the spiritual and physical burdens Paul was enduring. Again, we find him having to prove the reality of his apostleship and authority, as he encounters the legalizers and their cold doctrine. The paragraph on Separation (6: 14 – 7:1) divides the epistle. Is there not something pathetic in "the sentence of death" Paul received from God? Yet he looked beyond death to resurrection. For our own hearts, Dr. F. C. Atkinson tells us that there are these lessons to be learned: *the peace of God* (verse 2), *comfort in suffering* (verses 3-7), *experience for the sake of others* (verses 6,7), and *simplicity and sincerity* (verse 12). Paul certainly knew how to exercise the ministry of a bleeding heart! Do we? It is only as we bleed, that we can bless.

Chapter 2

Here Paul is found giving directions about the restoration, and reception again into communion, of the censured, incestuous person mentioned in the previous epistle. As the culprit was overwhelmed with contrition, Paul forgives him and urges the Corinthian Church to do likewise. That they did is evident from chapter 7, where Paul declares his satisfaction on receiving the report of their good behavior in the affair. As to Paul's triumphant ministry, he rejoices that the apostles led in the train of Christ's triumph, "like captives in the triumphal procession of a Roman General, thus contributing to the glory of Christ." How solemn the declaration of the double effect of the Gospel we preach (verses 15,16)! The sun that melts the wax likewise hardens the clay. As a two-edged sword, the Word either saves or slays.

Chapter 3

Apologizing for seeming to commend himself, Paul protests his sincerity and absence of vainglory as he faces those who sought to ruin his reputation. The Corinthian Church itself was his real commendation of his pure purpose. Thus, the chapter has two divisions: *The Corinthians themselves are sufficient proof of Paul's apostleship* (verses 1-3); and *the Gospel Paul preached was superior to the Law* (verses 4-18). Note references to the Holy Spirit; as a *Letter-Writer* (verse 3); as a *Life-Giver* (verse 6); *as a Liberator* (verse 17); and as a *Transformer* (verse 18). We are being changed from glory to glory. If we are rejoicing and resting in the freedom of the Spirit, the things of earth ought surely to become more dim in the light of His glory and grace. Link on to this last verse what Paul says in Romans 12:2.

Chapter 4

As a faithful minister of the Word, Paul's words to fellow ministers carry much weight. Truth taught is commended by life. Not self, but Christ as Lord, must be preached. Power in, and for, service is of God alone. Suffering accompanies a sincere witness. Amid all trials, the minister is sustained by the hope of glory to come. Paul and his fellow-sufferers knew how to put all their tribulation on one side of the scale and heavenly glory on the other, and found their afflictions to be light and short, and out-weighed by the glory to come. Would that all who stand to declare the Gospel, had lives corresponding to the ideal set forth in this pastoral chapter! How necessary it is, both by lip and life, to magnify our office!

Chapter 5

The opening verses of this chapter seem to suggest that believers, dying before the Lord's return, do not have a disembodied state. While they must await the resurrection morn for a glorified body, at present they are provided with a temporary covering. In verses 9 and 10, Paul returns to the judgment seat of Christ and is "ambitious," which is the word for "labor," to receive a full reward at the hand of the Master. How tragic it will be, if we appear before Him at that day with a saved soul but a lost life! Paul's own sincerity in motive and object, as he served the Lord, convinced the apostle that his devoted, diligent service would be rewarded. Would that we were under the constraining love of Christ that Paul experienced in his ministry!

Chapter 6

In the first half of this chapter, the Apostle Paul rehearses the circumstances and manner of his ministry. Unswervingly, he seeks to approve himself as a true minister in the ways indicated in verses 4-10. Then he comes to a personal appeal for separation from all that is false and unclean. While the direct interpretation of verse 6:11–7:1 admittedly has to do with idols and idolatry, the passage assuredly embraces separation from *all* that defiles. Severance from error and evil doctrine must therefore be included in the commands here written. Let those closely tied to modernism in denominations or local churches take heed, therefore. All separation should be based on Scripture. The precious promise contained in 6:16-18 forms the impelling motive in the call to holiness of life.

Chapter 7

All due regard must be shown to true ministers of the Gospel. They are not to be flattered, but highly esteemed *for the truth's sake.* How comforting to Paul was the coming of Titus! Is there some weary worker you could cheer today? Of the chapter as a whole, another has said that we should "meditate on the *Apostle's love for his converts* (verse 3); *the conflicts that his work brought him* (verse 5); *godly sorrow* (verses 10,11); and *the interplay of personalities and human affection that runs throughout the passage,* all taken up and used by the Holy Spirit in the ministry of the Gospel." Paul's admonitions had good effect upon the Corinthians, and he rejoiced over their repentance and good behavior. At last, they were a credit to the Gospel.

Chapter 8

Paul approaches financial matters with delicacy and sympathetic understanding. He certainly knew how to "get a collection." A noble rule is enunciated: "Provide for honest things, not only in the sight of the Lord, but also in the sight of men." This was the way of Christ, who told men to render unto Caesar the things which are Caesar's, and unto God the things which are His. True giving, divinely directed, consists of thank-offerings, and must ever be voluntary, and has, as its object, God's glory in the salvation and relief of the needy. The apostle makes it clear that God does not want our silver without ourselves. We must first give ourselves to the Lord, then dedicate our substance, for God will never recognize the surrender of our wealth unless, with it, there is the worship of the heart.

Chapter 9

Continuing his exhortation regarding financial aid for the needy, Paul was anxious that the Macedonians should not be disappointed. He had boasted of the ability and readiness of the Corinthians to help, and did not want to be let down. They are reminded that God, because of His sufficiency and bounty, loves cheerful giving. Some there are who give merely to satisfy the importunity of those who seek their aid. What they give is forced from them, and this unwillingness spoils all that they do. May we never be guilty of giving

with a grudge! There is some doubt as to whether Paul meant, by the "unspeakable gift," the gift of grace bestowed on the saints, making them able and willing to give, or Jesus Christ, God's gift to the World. Well, Calvary should color all our giving!

Chapter 10

Paul gets back to the main theme of this epistle, namely, the vindication of his apostleship. His warfare had not been carnal, but spiritual. He had been Christ's love-slave, and was proud of it. When he met his critics, he would be as bold in rebuking them face to face as he was in his letters. The practical results of his work attested to its purity. Yes, and he wanted those who challenged him to know that his only ultimate Judge was the Lord. How important it is to understand the spiritual conflict in verses 3-5! Satanic warfare with the saints is little understood. As to victory, our powerful weapons are written in Ephesians 6:13-17; the channel of victory, in Revelation 12:11; and the spoils of victory in Revelation 21:24.

Chapter 11

This is a most enlightening chapter in that it reveals the power and devices of Satan, which are ever the same. One of his diabolical methods is the sowing of the seeds of doubt and disunity. He was behind the deceivers appearing among the Corinthians, teaching error. He was the instigator of the contempt and prejudice Paul had to face. No matter how plausible false teachers may be, even if they are "ordained" ministers, *all* of them are satanically inspired. They are not included among those so delicately and beautifully described as "a chaste virgin" (verse 2). Paul found his boasting distasteful, yet necessary. His sufferings, his devotions to his converts, and his manifold dangers all alike proved his genuineness as an apostle. How he shames us all by his absolute devotion to the Master!

Chapter 12

Much has been written about the supernatural experiences of Paul, as well as his physical weakness. Introduced, as he was, in some miraculous fashion to the other world, there to see things human language could not describe, he was yet made painfully conscious of the fact that he was still in the flesh. Three times over he prayed for the removal of his thorn, whatever it was, but it was not removed. God, however, gave him grace to bear it. Many of us find it hard to be brought back to earth after ecstatic, spiritual experiences. When on the mount, we say with Peter: "Lord, it is good for us to be here," and we should like to stay. But there must also be the vexations of life, so that we might glory in our infirmities; as well as glory in heaven.

Chapter 13

Paul minces no words when, in concluding his vindication of authority, he tells the Corinthians how severe he will be when he visits them and deals with wrongdoers. He trusts, however, that they will right all wrongs, so that he can use all his time for their edification. The word "reprobate," used twice in the chapter, means "discarded,"

or "put on the shelf." Paul tells the Corinthians to test themselves to find out whether they were "on the shelf." How many there are who have need to examine themselves! Alas, it is sadly possible to work *for* the faith, yet not be *in* the faith! Too many are religious, but not regenerated; they have been baptized, yet never washed in the blood of the Lamb.

The last verse in this epistle has become one of the most renowned in church worship, for such an apostolic benediction usually closes all our services. It contains a threefold cord. It is a trinity in unity. It is an evidence of the Oneness of the Godhead. This solemn, renowned benediction places God in the center, and this is as it should be, for His love is the source and foundation of all His gifts. Because of His love, grace was manifested in Christ. Because of Christ's finished work, we have all the blessings of the Holy Spirit. As sinners we need grace; as saints we need all the Spirit can bestow. How rich we are with God's twin love-gifts – Christ and the Spirit!

GALATIANS

Next to *Romans*, the epistle before us is Paul's strongest doctrinal book. In fact, "*Galatians* takes up controversially what *Romans* puts systematically." By nature and training, Paul was a controversialist, and the fire of controversy flames forth from this "Magna Charta of the Early Church" in which Paul, for the second time, declares the great center of the doctrinal system he stoutly defended, namely, "The just shall live by faith." Adroit and plausible Jews were instructing Paul's converts in Galatia that the law and ritual of Moses were still binding upon them, that circumcision had not been abrogated, and that the righteousness which is of the law was not to be displaced by that which comes of faith in Christ. Consequently, many turned away from the great Pauline doctrine of justification, and lapsed into sensualism and license, under the guise of Christian liberty. But in his declaration of emancipation from legalism of any type, Paul gives us a series

of contrasts – *grace* in contrast to *law; faith* in contrast to *works; liberty* in contrast to *license*. In *Galatians* more than in any other of his epistles, the human yearning of Paul finds pathetic expression. The six chapters can be divided in this three-fold way –

1. The Doctrine of Salvation by Grace, 1, 2
2. The Bondage of the Law, 3, 4
3. The Liberty of Sons, 5, 6.

Chapter 1

This epistle, the key text of which – "the just shall live by faith" – brought Martin Luther to a realization of salvation by grace, is taken up with a mutilated Gospel and a compromising ministry. "Another gospel" and "false brethren" are also too common today. God's ideal and Satan's counterfeit stand side by side. Where you have an Eden, you have a serpent; where there is a Joshua, an Achan; and where Jesus, Judas. In this chapter, Paul begins to counteract a perverted Gospel. He rebukes those who begin in grace and go back to the law – beginning in the Spirit, going back to the flesh; beginning in Christ, going back to self; justified by faith, yet sanctified by works. And these mixed and debased gospels are still with us. A divine work in the soul excludes all legalism.

Chapter 2

In the key verse of this chapter (verse 20), we note two inescapable truths. First, the cross is the judgment-seat of sin. "I am crucified with Christ." Through this epistle, which is so full of the cross, Paul proves that the doctrine of the cross excludes all legalism. By His death, Christ disposed of all legality, because in the cross the law is fulfilled and the crucified One is the law fulfillment. He bore our guilt and curse, and died our death. Thus, in Him as our Substitute all claims are cancelled. Second, the cross is the coronation stone where self is deposed, and Christ enthroned. "I live; yet not I." At Calvary, Christ died for sin and self, thus the big "I" is blotted out. This does not mean the destruction of our individuality, but it teaches the magnifying of His.

Chapter 3

Arrested spiritual progress, a prominent theme of this epistle, is emphasized in this chapter, in which Paul shows that the purpose of the New Covenant is to sum up, fulfil, and supersede the Old. How absurd it is to think of the flesh as the finishing school of faith (verse 3)! How monstrous it is to come to Christ for salvation, then go back to the law for righteousness of life (verse 21)! A peculiar feature of this chapter is the first mention of the Holy Spirit in the epistle (verses 2,3,5). The Person, power, and presidency of the Spirit form a distinctive mark of the New Covenant. Righteousness that the law failed to produce is the product of the Spirit alone, the blessed Spirit liberated for us by the cross. And, where the Spirit is Lord, there is ever liberty.

Chapter 4

This chapter revolves around the cross and adoption into sonship. Because of a filial relationship, we must cast off the slavish spirit of the law. Four truths can be noted: (1) *our relationship to God is filial* (verse 6); being saved, we are sons. (2) *Our devotion must be spontaneous and ungrudging* (verse 15). While the law demanded a tenth, Christ demands all. (3) *Our spiritual education is no longer ceremonial and delegated, but direct and personal* (verse 19). As sons, we must bear the family likeness. And (4) *our spiritual liberty is the Gospel's dowry* (verse 26). Such "liberty is the sign of life, the seal of emancipation – it promotes loyalty, is essential to growth and is twin sister to love and holiness."

Chapter 5

Keeping near the cross, Paul here speaks of it as "the divine laboratory where the flesh is cauterized and put to death." As the flesh was as truly nailed to the cross in God's sight as Christ was, how can redeemed ones take up the flesh-life again? We have been "cauterized" all over, so that we ought to find ourselves dead to our former selves and circumstances, and wide awake and alive to the new "divine" self *in Christ*. The apostle pictures two antagonistic forces as in continual conflict; namely, the flesh and the Spirit. We are not to stand undecided between these two opposing currents, but go over completely to the Spirit. Carried away by the divine current, we shall become fruit-bearing branches (verse 22). Note the Contrast between "works" and "fruit."

Chapter 6

Last of all, Paul declares the cross to be the terminus, or boundary-line, between us and the world. Trace the references to the cross in this chapter, and pause to consider the three crosses in verse 14. Many there are who believe in a "crucified Christ," but who know so little of a "crucified life." At Calvary, the world was crucified unto me; now that must be carried out in my life, experimentally. And, being sharers of the cross, we become not only burden-bearing (verse 2); seed-bearing, Christians (verse 8), but cross-bearing ones (17). We bear branded in our body, the slave marks, the Calvary marks, of the Lord Jesus. These slave marks are stigmatized by the world, but rejoiced in by every freed sin-slave.

EPHESIANS

Passing from *Galatians* to *Ephesians* – the Epic of the New Testament – we breathe a different atmosphere. The sword of controversy is in its sheath, and Paul, the lofty teacher, is now meditative rather than controversial. Essentially Gentile in scope and spirit, *Ephesians*, called "the Alps of the New Testament, for here we are bidden by God to mount, step by step, until we reach the highest possible point where man can stand, even in the presence of God Himself," stresses the great truth of Christian unity. *First, there is unity with the divine nature of God through Christ; Second, there is the unity of all Christians one with another in purity of doctrine and holiness of living.* In Christ we *are* and *have* all. Dr. Pierson speaks of *Ephesians* as "Paul's *third heaven* epistle. In it he soars from the depths of ruin to the heights of redemption" (1:3). Profitable Bible readings can be gathered from key words and phrases like – "In Christ Jesus" – "Walk" – "Together" – "Therefore" – "Wherefore" – "According to" – "In heavenly places" – "Riches" – "Love." The three figures of the Church – *building* (2:21,22), *body* (1:22,23; 4:15), *bride* (5:25-32) can likewise be used with effect. Two general sections are apparent –
1. Doctrinal – The Heavenly Calling of the Church, 1 – 3
2. Practical – The Earthly Conduct of the Church, 4 – 6.

Position and *practice* should never be parted.

Chapter 1

The title of the late Ruth Paxson's helpful studies fittingly summarizes the contents of this priceless epistle: *The Wealth, Walk and Warfare of the Christian.* Untold wealth is before us in this chapter. The phrase, "in the heavenlies" (verse 3), occurring three times in the epistle, is the master key to the storehouse of our spiritual riches. We can translate "spiritual blessings" as "bless-ings of the Spirit," and in this chapter alone we have a remarkable list of them. Holiness, adoption, acceptance, redemption, grace, enlightenment, revelation, fellowship, and sealing are a few of the treasures Paul exposes to our gaze. Read the chapter through and note that God is the Author of all these blessings; Christ is the Medium of them; and Spirit is the One who makes all the blessings our very own. How rich and increased with spiritual goods we are! Yet too often we live like spiritual paupers.

Chapter 2

Expositors have given us some excellent divisions of Ephesians, the spiritual alps of the New Testament. In these meditations we prefer chapter study, and it is not hard to name each chapter. We can call this "The Body Chapter," for within it Paul upholds the mystery hid from the ages, namely, the making of Jew and Gentile into "one new man." Dr. Norman B. Harrison, in his rich study of Ephesians, *His Very Own*, divides the chapter thus: "The Three-fold Work of the Triune God (verses 1-22) – *His body quickened by the grace of God the Father* (verses 1-10); *His body formed by the blood of Christ the Son* (verses 11-17). *Formed thus into one body, we become a building* (verses 19-22); looking back to the pit from which we have been digged, we too were Christless – *without Christ;* homeless – *alienated;* messageless – *strangers from the covenants of promise;* hopeless – *no hope;* Godless – *without God in the world.*" But all has been changed. Through grace we are new creations.

Chapter 3

In this mystery chapter, Paul develops the truth that the previous chapter concludes with, namely, the Church as a building, or habitation, of God. There are those who disagree that the Church can be a bride, body and building at the same time. But why not? It is surely no more difficult to believe that the Church is both the bride and the body, than it is to believe that Christ is both the Lamb and the Priest. Throughout the chapter, Paul thinks of himself as the divinely-appointed minister of the New Covenant temple. The word, *"mystery,"* used three times here, does not mean something mysterious, but truth "hidden until the appropriate and appointed time for revealing it." The particular mystery Paul speaks of is not that the Gentiles should be saved, but that, along with the saved Jews, they should form part of the body of Christ. Gentiles are now ço-heirs of God, co-members of the body, co-sharers of the promise of the Spirit.

Chapter 4

We now pass from doctrine to duty, but withal a duty motivated by doctrine. This is "The Walk Chapter," or as Norman Harrison styles it: "The Most Wonderful Walk Ever Undertaken." Then Dr. Harrison divides the chapter: "We are to walk worthily, in *inward* realization of Christ (verses 1-16); we are to walk differently, in *outward* manifestation of the Spirit (verses 17-32)." In the ministry gifts of Christ to His body, there is a truth lost sight of by many members of the body. He gave gifts unto men, thus to *every* one of us is given grace (or gift) according to the measure of the gift of Christ. Does this not imply that in regeneration every believer receives not only the Holy Spirit as a gift from God, but likewise a gift from the Spirit to use in the service of Christ? No member of the body is without a gift of some sort. Some have more than one gift. The question is: Have you discovered your particular gift and are you using it to the full?

Chapter 5

The seed, nature, and results of the Spirit-filled life make up this great chapter. If we are to walk in love and holiness, the Spirit alone can make such a walk possible. You will find it profitable to go through the epistle and gather out the cameos of the Spirit. As the Spirit of light, He must deal with the works of darkness. As the Spirit of gladness, He it is who imparts the melodious heart and grateful mind. As the Spirit of Pentecost who came as the Promise of the Father and the Son, He helped to produce the mystic fabric, the Church, and alone can make Church-truth real. Intimate ties are used to illustrate the blessed union existing between Christ and His own. Here is the Church that He said He would build (Matthew 16:18). Are you a member of His body? Your name may be on a church roll, but it is without avail unless you are united to Christ by faith.

Chapter 6

From our walk we come to warfare, for this is a militant chapter. From the high spiritual blessings we pass to a battlefield. After dealing with the domestic life of Spirit-filled believers, Paul takes up their conflict against mighty, unseen foes. Our exalted life in Christ and the Spirit is the signal for satanic hostility, for the devil is bent on recapturing all the territory that the Lord has taken. The deeper our spirituality, the more intense the onslaught of the foe is. We wrestle – of course, we do – but not against flesh and blood, that is, visible foes. Too often we want to fight the flesh and blood which are antagonistic to our spiritual position. We must, however, go behind these things to those wicked forces that inspire them, as Christ Himself did, when in rebuking Peter, He addressed Himself to Satan, responsible for Peter's utterance. Are you a happy, victorious warrior? Look well to your armor!

PHILIPPIANS

Like *Philemon, Philippians* reveals the human side and grateful heart of Paul. Both are personal rather than doctrinal. Paul is now a prisoner at Rome, and dependent upon the kindly offerings of his friends, foremost of which were those in Philippi who commissioned Epaphroditus to carry their liberal gift to their imprisoned father in Christ. Deeply moved by the kindly thought of the Philippians, Paul sent this letter of gratitude which is in gentle contrast to his incisive logic and bold aggressiveness elsewhere. Dr. F. B. Meyer in his devotional exposition of this epistle says of it that it is, "the tenderest Epistle Paul ever wrote." Bishop Handley Moule in his volume on *Philippians* calls it, "One of the fairest and dearest regions of the Book of God." This love letter to the church at Philippi is most practical and has as its key word, *Joy,* which occurs in some form or another 19 times in the epistle. When Paul wrote "Rejoice in the Lord alway," he was not sitting in comfort in pleasant surroundings but languishing in the Roman Mamertine Prison. As for an outline, we cite the following comprehensive one by Vernon McGee—

1. The Philosophy for Christian Living, Chapter 1 (Key verse 21).
2. The Pattern for Christian Living, Chapter 2 (Key verses 5-11).
3. The Prize for Christian Living, Chapter 3 (Key verses 10-14).
4. The Power for Christian Living, Chapter 4 (Key verse 13).

Chapter 1

About ten years after Paul founded the church at Philippi, he sent this love letter, expressing his peculiar and tender regard for the saints there. Spontaneously and lavishly, he expresses his warm affection for his readers. The opening verses carry three sets of twins: *a twin description of believers* – servants and saints; *twin environment of those to whom Paul was writing* – in Christ Jesus and in Philippi; and *a twin blessing for all* – grace and peace, the root and fruit of all Christian experiences. Retrospect and prospect are before us in verses 3-6. Love will perfect what it begins. Paul's secret of success as an evangelist and teacher shines forth in the heart of this chapter – his burning heart, his passion for souls and his mighty love for men. How homesick he was as he thought of Philippi! Examine Paul's love-prayer, and check whether your prayers are the criterion of love. Go through this chapter and make a list of the cameos of Christ that it contains. It is indeed a Christ-honoring chapter.

Chapter 2

The divisions of this great chapter, as given by Dr. Scofield, form a serviceable outline: *exhortation to unity and meekness* (verses 1-4); *seven-fold humbling of Christ* (verses 5-8); *exaltation of Jesus* (verses 9-11); *outworking of the inworked salvation* (verses 12-16); and *the apostolic example* (verses 17-30). Temptations to rivalry and discord were working at his beloved Philippi, and Paul set his heart to expel this evil, by expounding the mind of Christ. Motives that compelled Christ to serve and surrender as He did, and which likewise actuated the apostle himself, were the only effective bulwark against the pride and strife Paul hints at in the previous chapter. Those Philippians knew how Paul had at heart their true spiritual welfare and Christian dignity, and they were eager to gladden his heart; hence the appeal: "Fulfil ye my joy." Do we aim to please Christ and satisfy that loving heart of His?

Chapter 3

Of this chapter Dr. Robert Rainy says: "Paul here gives us one of his most remarkable expositions of true Christian religion as he knew it, and as he maintains it must essentially exist for others also. He does this in a burst of thought and feeling expressed together: so that, if we are to take his meaning, the fire and light must both alike do their work upon us; we must feel and see both at once." This is one of those pages to which a Bible reader turns again and again, a passage that has special power to find and to stir believing men. The key words of the chapter are contained in the compelling phrase: "Have no confidence in the flesh." All trust in human morality and in the holiest Christian rites is condemned as being destitute of intrinsic value. Nothing and nobody must be allowed to substitute for Christ or to detract from His glory. All must be counted loss for Him.

Chapter 4

It will be noted how joy abounds in this epistle. Trace the references to joy and rejoicing, and as you do so remember that when Paul wrote, "Rejoice in the Lord alway,"

he was languishing in a dank prison cell. His was a joy triumphant over all adversity and suffering. The apostle was ever mindful of the ministry of warm-hearted Christian women. He likewise knew how to rebuke them lovingly. In connection with the secret of peace that Paul deals with in verses 5-7, it is encouraging to know that the peace of God can pass all misunderstanding, as well as all understanding. What great assurances verses 13 and 19 give! Do you believe both of them? "All things" – "all your need"! Blessed it is to realize that, while there is every need for grace, there is always grace for every need. And, the divine supply is inexhaustible, seeing it is according to His riches in glory.

COLOSSIANS

In the church at Colosse, the deity and headship of Christ had been assailed, and information of the abominable combination of Judaism, gnosticism and asceticism was brought to Paul in prison by Epaphras. To assert the supreme glory, supremacy and dignity of Christ, and to combat the heretical teaching regarding the worship of angels, Paul wrote this strong doctrinal epistle. The heresies being taught "cast a cloud over the glory of Jesus Christ by putting Him into the background." *Colossians*, however, extols the pre-eminence of Christ and exalts the true *pleroma*, or plentitude of being – a *pleroma* all in Christ share. A profitable way of studying *Colossians* is to trace the portrait of the church it sketches. Here the headship of Christ is affirmed (1:18; 2:10,19); the position and privilege of believers are stated (1:13,14 etc.), the characteristic features of the Christian worker are given (4:7-13 etc.). The main section of the epistle is from 1:15 – 2:3 in which the unapproachable pre-eminence of Christ is viewed from every standpoint – in deity, in creation, in providence, in the Church, in redemption, in gospel mystery. For a general analysis of the epistle we have the two main divisions –

1. The Doctrinal Section, 1 – 2:3
2. The Practical Section, 2:4 – 4.

Chapter 1

It is in the second chapter that we come upon the keynote of this epistle: "Beware lest any man make a spoil of you through philosophy and vain deceit" (2:8). Throughout the letter Paul maintains and proves the independence and superiority of the Church over all conflicting philosophies of the world, whether ancient or modern. Philosophers known as gnostics, concerned about angels and the person of Christ, creep into the Church with false doctrines: hence this Christ-exalting epistle. In chapter 1 we have one of the greatest prayers ever prayed. Christ, as the one supreme transcendant personality, with His unspeakable majesty, stands out vividly before us (verses 15-23). So we have not only "the kingdom of the Son of His love," but also a full-length portrait of the King Himself. Oh, to know more of the secret of the indwelling of Christ (verse 27)!

Chapter 2

Here the Colossians are warned against worldly philosophy, by being reminded of what God had done for them in and through Christ. Old world philosophies are powerless, imperfect and unholy. The Gospel crushes to pieces all human ideals and brain-spun sophistries, all man-made systems, theosophies and philosophies, whether gnostic or agnostic. Reading the chapter we note also that *thanksgiving marks all true Christian conduct* (verse 7); *Christ completely satisfies and provides for His people's every need* (verses 9,10); *the old nature and its ways must be renounced* (verses 11,12); *death is replaced by life* (verse 13); *sin can be forgiven* (verses 13,14); and *Satan was conquered by the cross* (verse 15). The cross is the cancelled record-office of heaven's "court of justice."

Chapter 3

What ascension heights are before us in this chapter, with its sweeping condemnation of ritualism! Christianity is Christ, and Christ is within the hearts of His own. Mark as you read: *the abhorrence of all evil* (verses 5-9); *union in Christ* (verses 12-17); *instructions for Christian family-life* (verses 18-22); and *God-glorifying service and its reward* (verses 23-25). Attention should be drawn to a divine order in our risen life in Christ: "put off"; "put on" (verses 9,10); "putting away" (Ephesians 4:25). Here we have strip-

ping, strengthening and severing. The first two are definite and decisive acts to be done, once and for all, at some supreme moment of crisis. "Putting away" is equally definite and decisive, but implies a continuous habit of action by which we sever ourselves from all that is alien to God's will.

Chapter 4

By "servants" we are to understand "slaves." Thus, all relationship must be permeated with the love of God. Christian masters and Christian slaves were to be viewed as brothers in Christ. If we would win some we must be winsome (verses 2-6). Personal and fraternal greetings occupy the rest of the chapter. Paul was a prisoner in Rome when he wrote this matchless letter, yet how filled with works he was. He knew how to buy up every opportunity. Do we lay out carefully all our time, so that its opportunities for witness, both to the saved and to the unsaved, are used to the full? We might accomplish mighty things for God if only we knew how to practice a strict economy of our time, with the Spirit's help. The Scotch have a proverb: "Time taken can never be over-taken."

I THESSALONIANS

The two Thessalonian epistles mark the beginning of Paul's writings. During his mission in Thessalonica, Paul instructed his converts in all the fundamentals of the faith, including the Second Advent of Christ. Later on, when away in Athens, Paul received a report from Timothy regarding the vigorous and healthy state of the church at Thessalonica. But he reported to Paul that some of the believers were concerned about their dear ones who had died in Christ. Would they have no part in the glory of Christ's return? Paul assured them in this ·letter to those troubled saints that *all* the saints are to share in the Rapture. Then there were others who, thinking Christ's coming was imminent ceased to work – which fault was lovingly corrected (4:11-18). The student will observe what is said about

other doctrines, such as, the Holy Spirit, the Trinity, election, holiness. Made up of five chapters, this first epistle from Paul's gifted pen, can be divided into five sections, with each ending with a reference to the Second Advent.

1. The Return and Salvation, 1:3,9,10
2. The Return and Service, 2:19,20
3. The Return and Stability, 3:12,13
4. The Return and Separation, 4:13-18
5. The Return and Sanctification, 5:23,24.

Chapter 1

In this, the earliest of Paul's letters, the apostle set out to encourage the Thessalonian saints. Much persecution had been theirs, and it was to their spiritual father that they turned for comfort and guidance concerning

some questions troubling them. A characteristic feature of Paul's writings is his unceasing intercession for his converts. Have
you noticed how the trinity of verse 3 answers
to the trinity of verses 9 and 10? Other
aspects to meditate upon are the evidence
of election (verse 4), the believer's witness
(verse 8), and deliverance from wrath (verse
10). What remarkable advent Christians the
saints in Thessalonica became! Although
newly saved from heathenism, they manifested marvelous growth in spiritual matters,
and readily understood the return of Christ
and His glory.

Chapter 2

The model soul-winner is one who labors
in the light of Christ's coming. Such a hope
did not make the apostle careless or inert.
Read this great chapter carefully and mark
Paul's solicitude, devotion and tenderness as
he cared for his converts *as a nurse* (verse
7), *as a father* (verse 11), *as a lover* (verse
17), and *as a soul-artist* (verses 19,20). All
who contemplate missionary work can here
find those requisites making effective such
a calling: *conflict* (verse 2), *unselfishness*
(verse 8), *hard toil* (verse 9), *blamelessness*
(verse 10), *loving exhortations* (verse 11)
and *satanic hindrances* (verse 18). We ought
to share Paul's intense passion for souls.
Are there those we have won for Jesus who
will be woven into a crown we can wear
at "that day"? May grace be ours to labor
for the soul-winners' reward!

Chapter 3

In this chapter, Paul effectively proves
that expectation of the Second Advent of
Christ ought to affect the unity of the saints.
Frost-bitten brethren, who cannot shake
hands with one another, would quickly thaw
if they took this chapter to heart. In three
ways Paul proves his great love for the
Church: first, *by sending them Timothy*
(verse 2), as we send out missionaries today;
second, *by rejoicing with sympathetic joy*

over the good report of spiritual progress;
third, *by unceasing prayer.* Abounding in
love, and blameless in holiness, Paul makes
the one to be the equivalent of the other.
Do not miss the precious truth of verse 3.
How do we meet divinely appointed applications? The sweetest scents are only obtained by tremendous pressure.

Chapter 4

Here Paul shows how expectation of the
Second Advent affects the bereavements and
separations of life. As vacancies come in
your life and mine, how comforting are the
words of this chapter! Three worlds await
Christ's return – *heaven,* where all the redeemed and the angelic host await the hour
when Jesus will take to Himself His great
power, and reign; *earth,* where His Church
eagerly sighs for His speedy coming; and
the grave, where the dead, the sleeping dust
of the dead in Christ, await redemption.
Meantime, as we linger amid the shadows,
we are to walk: *pleasing to God* (verse 1),
in purity (verse 3), *in quiet activity* (verse
11), and *in moderated grief* (verses 13,18).
What blissful reunion awaits the saints of
God!

Chapter 5

This final chapter is made up of five sections: *The suddenness of the Lord's coming*
(verses 1-11); *exhortations to respect leaders
and behave consistently to all, to watch, to
pray and to strive for perfect holiness* (verses
12-24); *request for prayer* (verse 25); *personal
conclusion* (verses 26,27); and *salutation*
(verse 28). From the opening chapter, we
learn how sinners are saved by grace through
the Word. From this concluding chapter,
we learn how saints, saved by grace, are to
be sanctified. Verses 23 and 24 carry Christ's
calling, His consecrating, His keeping, His
coming, and His covenanting – all assured
and guaranteed to us. Go over the closing
watchwords Paul has for all advent watchers
and see if your life is fulfilling them all.

II THESSALONIANS

It has been pointed out that in the two epistles to the Thessalonians there are twenty distinct references to the Second Coming which together are used as a comfort in bereavement, a motive to patience, an inspiration to hope, a security in temptation, a help to purity, a ground of rejoicing, a sanctifying power. While there is only the one Advent, there are two stages of it to be distinguished, namely, Christ's return *for* His saints – the teaching of *First Thessalonians* – and His return *with* His saints accompanied by His mighty angels, taking vengeance on His foes – the aspect before us in *Second Thessalonians*. In the first epistle, we have *The Day of Christ* – in the second, *The Day of The Lord*. Paul was the first to teach *The Rapture,* or Christ's return for His true Church. Between the two aspects or stages of the Second Advent, there is the period known as *The Great Tribulation,* covering a period of some seven years (Daniel 9; Revelation 7). How different our lives would be if only we could live with our faces toward dawn! For an analysis the preacher could expand –

1. Consolation under Persecution, chapter 1
2. Consummation of Evil, chapter 2:1-12
3. Closing Exhortations and Instructions, 2:13 – 3.

May we not be a shame to Christ now, and ashamed before Him when He returns!

Chapter 1

The purpose of this second epistle was to correct misapprehension that had arisen over Paul's first epistle, and restore the balance of truth which had in part been disturbed. Excitement prevailed, seeing some of the Thessalonians thought Christ was so near that they should give up their work. After his usual salutation, Paul encourages endurance during persecution, and exhorts the saints to consistency of life. As with the first epistle, so with this second, Paul presents in each chapter some special and further aspect of advent truth. Here he is taken up with retributive judgment at the Lord's coming. What unutterable doom awaits all those who are unsaved when He returns! Would that they could be stirred by verses 8 and 9!

Chapter 2

In this great chapter, Paul shows how the Second Advent of Christ affects the approaching consummation of evil. As you read the chapter, mark (1) the final battle between the champion personalities of the universe and their host. The struggle is between *The Sinless Man* and *The Man of Sin.* (2) Observe the battle of principles. It is "the mystery of godliness" over against "the mystery of iniquity," with no doubt whatever of the glorious outcome. Mark (3) the rival comings. The very same word is used of the "coming" of Christ and of the Antichrist. There is to be a hellish imitation of the true by the false. But the epiphany of Christ is to destroy the coming of the lawless one as he comes as the messiah of darkness. Observe (4) there is a progressive satanic development. Trace Satan's names.

Chapter 3

In conclusion, Paul brings the light of advent truth to bear upon our home-life and duties. Surely, there is nothing that can affect our everyday life like hope in the return of Christ. Here we see *a promise to encourage us* (verse 3); *a prayer to constrain us* (verse 5); *a precept to obedience* (verses 6,11,12); and *a benediction,* personal, permanent and providential, *to consecrate us* (verse 16). Expectation should lead to, and result in, consecration. If we believe that Christ is coming again, how can we live unbalanced lives and neglect the ordinary occupations of life? The "blessed hope" should make us practical, as well as spiritual. God forbid that we should become so heavenly-minded as to be of no earthly use!

I TIMOTHY

Because of all the practical advice they contain for all who labor in the vineyard of the Lord, *I and II Timothy* and *Titus*, are known as "The Pastoral Epistles," and bring to us the mellow wisdom of Paul's old age. These three epistles addressed to individuals and not to congregations have as their central theme, effectiveness in the Christian ministry. Timothy was Paul's son in the faith and between the two there was that beautiful friendship, so helpful to both (Philippians 2:22). Commenting upon the peculiar relations between Paul the aged and Timothy the young evangelist, Dr. A. T. Pierson says that, "Paul, like his Master, bore the burden of loneliness and consciousness of approaching martyrdom, but like his Master he forgot himself and urged Timothy to the diligent use of the gift of God. He forsaw coming apostasy and false teachers; but he encouraged him by *four* grand motives –
1. The verity and certainty of sound doctrine
2. The mutual testimony of Christ and the Scriptures
3. The approval of the Master
4. The coming Epiphany of Christ and the day of Award."

As to a division of this epistle, Robert Lee's Outline is one of the best –
1. The Imperative Need of Sound Doctrine, 1
2. The Nature and Order of Prayer, 2:1-8
3. The Qualifications Necessary for Spiritual Oversight, 2:9 – 3
4. The Christian's and Worker's Spiritual Duties, 4 – 6.

Chapter 1

The two epistles to Timothy, and the one to Titus, are known as "The Pastoral Epistles," seeing that they are taken up with the Christian ministry and church government. If any distinction can be drawn between the letters to Timothy, in the first we have the ideal church every pastor ought to have; and in the second, the ideal pastor every church ought to have. Alas, the two seldom go together! In this first chapter, legalism and apostate teaching are sternly rebuked by Paul. Without vainglory, he refers to his own faithful ministry, and charges his young, spiritual son to hold the faith as tenaciously as he himself has held it. It is a sad reflection upon some of our centers of learning, where men are prepared for the minsitry, that they teach that many of the authentic records in the Bible are fables, myths, mere imaginings of the human intellect. What shipwrecks we have today in the guise of educated ministers!

Chapter 2

Instructions as to Christian worship, and the duty of intercessory prayer and thanksgiving, introduce this chapter. Our Lord told us that worship is only acceptable to God if it is in Spirit and in truth, which means according to truth. Of the two grand doxologies in this epistle, the one here in verse 17 is a fitting climax to this remarkable chapter. Laying down principles to guide us in the subject matter of prayers and thanksgivings, Paul passes on to press a few directions respecting our behavior when we meet together for common worship – attitudes of body and mind. Women's attire and ornament are associated with effective worship. Unseemly dress is not compatible with reverent worship. Of course, we are to be free from all meretricious decoration. We reverence God by reverencing ourselves. When body and soul are clothed in fitting attire, then worship is pleasing to God.

Chapter 3

It is well, in these days of ecclesiastical trappings, to go back to the origin of the Christian ministry and find out how the Church was organized. Here we have the origin and qualifications of elders and deacons, that is, the sanction of those who, although of the congregation, were yet elected to rule over its affairs. What a difference there would be in church life and witness today, if all office-bearers and their wives answered to the qualifications here set forth by Paul. "Behave thyself in the house of God" (verse 15). What an exhortation for all churchgoers to obey! Often the behavior of some, a few minutes before worship begins, suggests the rabble of a market rather than the solemnity of the house of God, where He waits to meet His own. In this last part of the chapter we may have the fragment of a primitive hymn. Six balanced clauses emphasize the mystery of godliness. In contrast, the mystery of lawlessness is written in II Thessalonians 2:7.

Chapter 4

Commencing with an evidence of the Spirit's personality—for He is able to speak—Paul goes on to describe the characteristic features of the latter times which, surely, are our own. Then, in discoursing upon the value of godliness, the apostle proves that discipline of the body, by means of a severe rule of life, is profitable for something, but in not everything. The chief purpose in life is godliness. Bodily exercise has its limits, but to godliness there are no limits. Athletes exercise in order to be as physically fit as possible. As Christians, we are to exercise ourselves unto godliness of life. Seeing that we wrestle with the powers of evil, as Christian athletes we must be trained for such grim contest. Godliness, says Paul, is profitable for all things. It influences every part of our lives. Whether it be business, amusement, social intercourse, or private meditation, the godly person is ever the best and happiest.

Chapter 5

The best part of this chapter is taken up with pastoral behavior toward women. Although only a youth, Timothy is not to allow lack of experience to deter him from giving guidance regarding the women of the flock. The Early Church never neglected its widows. Do you realize what a part widows played in the lives of many Bible saints? Do you know any poor widow needing material and spiritual help? Well, in the light of this chapter, your immediate duty is clear. The last part of the chapter is taken up with the pastor's responsibilities in ordaining and judging elders. Wisdom and circumspection are needed in dealing with widows and elders alike. It is an oft misunderstood verse that enjoins Timothy to take a little wine. Alas, frequently those who do take a little wine do not have Timothy's weak stomach and oft infirmities. The last two verses can be read in the light of the judgment seat of Christ.

Chapter 6

Paul's attitude toward Roman slavery, so common in his day, is here set forth. In three other passages, the apostle deals with slaves and masters (Ephesians 6:5-9; Colossians 3:22; 4:1; Philemon 21). Here he looks at the question from the slave's point of view; in Philemon, from the master's viewpoint. In both Ephesians and Colossians Paul addresses masters and slaves. Paul seems to have accepted it as a necessary fact, and urged the slaves not to rebel or escape, but to be obedient to their masters. Paul inspired Christian masters and slaves to realize that the relation between them should be carried on in a brotherly way, insofar as possible. In the last half of this stirring chapter, we can trace the gain of a love of godliness and the ungodliness of love of gain. Underline these three key words—flee, follow and fight. Are we keeping all that has been committed to our trust? Can we say that we are "rich in good works"?

II TIMOTHY

If any distinction can be drawn between the previous epistle and the one before us, we can say that in *I Timothy* we have the *ideal church* every pastor ought to have; while in *II Timothy*, we have the *ideal* *pastor* every church ought to have. Alas, the two are seldom paired! As this second epistle was the last letter Paul wrote—his swan song—as such it possesses a pathetic interest for all lovers of the Word. Writing from his prison cell, with death imminent, Paul writes to the young man who had been converted as a boy through his witness, and quite naturally pours out his fatherly love upon his beloved Timothy. The old preacher exhorts the young evangelist to "stir up the gift that is in him"; and the old soldier admonishes his successor that he has "fought a good fight," and has "kept the faith." The key word of the epistle is *ashamed* (1:8,12,16; 2:15 etc.). A serviceable outline of this book, Dr. Handley Moule says he "found it difficult deliberately to read without finding something like a mist gathering in the eyes," is the following –

1. The Christian Minister and His Mission, chapter 1, (see verse 9)
2. The Christian Minister and His Master, chapter 2, (see verse 1)
3. The Christian Minister and His Message, chapter 3, (see verse 16)
4. The Christian Minister and His Motive, chapter 4, (see verse 8).

In chapter 4:6-8, Paul writes his own epitaph. May it be ours!

Chapter 1

Death throws its dark shadow over the pages of this epistle, a letter which we may call "The Swan Song of Paul." It is his last will and testament. Shortly after penning these last known words of his, Paul went out and faced martyrdom for the Lord that he so dearly loved. This is why we here have a striking but thoroughly natural mixture of gloom and glory. Writing with full consciousness that his end is near, the apostle issues his last instructions to his favorite disciple and, through him, to us all. It will be found that this epistle is more personal than I Timothy and Titus. The aged, veteran preacher is counseling a young man as he faces his evangelistic career; hence the fact that almost one-third of this letter is taken up with the young man himself. Have you noticed the two committals, in verses 12 through 14? What we commit to God is ever secure. What He commits to us we are to keep. Learn to seek out needy saints and refresh them with kindness.

Chapter 2

In a personal, rather than in an official way, Paul urges Timothy to secure the establishment of apostolic doctrine. The chapter, as a whole, revolves around Christ, who is the unfailing source of strength to enable Timothy to carry out these last instructions. Several metaphors are used to describe Timothy's relationship to the Lord. Christ is the captain; Timothy is a soldier. Christ is the umpire; Timothy the athlete. Christ is the master, Timothy the slave. In verse 19, we have a two-sided seal – on one side, known of the Lord; on the other, the negative and positive side of holiness. We are to flee, then follow (verse 22). Some try to flee, but forget to follow. Can we say that we are vessels unto honor? Are we fit to be used? How does the exhortation of verse 24 fit you?

Chapter 3

Generally speaking, in chapter 1, Paul looks back over the past; in chapter 2, he gives direction about the present; and in chapter 3, he looks forward to the future. And what a great chapter this is! The last days, heresy and magic, divine inspiration of Scriptures are all expertly handled. In Paul's description of the last days is written an ancient record of modern times. We have lived to see the perilous times of which he wrote. Paul was certainly no believer in a "golden-age-around-the-corner" gospel. "Worse and worse" is his description of the end-time period of the age of grace. Have your children been familiar with the Scriptures from infancy? Paul believed in the infallibility of Holy Writ – not of some Scripture, but *all* of it. Amid gathering apostasy the Spirit-breathed Word is our unfailing source of courage and strength.

Chapter 4

If Timothy is to make full proof of his ministry, then he must live and labor with eternity's value in view. Such is Paul's final word to his son in the faith. Through a long and faithful ministry, the judgment seat has been the apostle's constant incentive. Now, as he is about to die, he knows the righteous Judge will richly reward his tears, trials and toils. He is not afraid to be offered as a sacrifice. John Wesley used to say that all his preachers died well, and Paul could die well, seeing that he had lived well. Think of his three "I haves," in verse 7! Then underline the two loves – love of His appearing; love of this present world. The one love blasts the other. If you love Christ's appearing, you will not love the world. It is pathetic also to see how Paul, like his Master before him, was deserted by so-called friends as death drew near.

TITUS

Another of Paul's converts (1:4), Titus was most valuable to Paul as a "partner and fellowhelper." Older than Timothy in years and grace, Titus was also stronger, physically and morally. Thus Paul was less anxious about the conduct of Titus, and the way others might treat him than he was about Timothy. It was "the fidelity and sagacity of Titus that led Paul to trust him with special missions, and to leave him in Crete as his own representative, to complete the organization of churches." Short and practical, *Titus* is mainly occupied with church "*order, ordination* and *organization.*" Pierson calls the passage (2:11-14) "one of the *loca classica* of Scripture. It covers past redemption, present duty and future glory. It is a table of contents of the entire New Testament; the Epiphany of Grace well describes the *gospels* and *Acts;* the instructions in holy living, the *epistles;* and the expectation of the coming of the Lord, *The Apocalypse.*" The general theme of *Titus* is that sound belief should be sustained by sound behavior. For an outline and key verses, this simple outline could be profitably expanded –
1. The Importance of Sound Doctrine – An orderly Church, chapter 1, (see verse 9)
2. The Dynamic of Divine Grace – A sound Church, chapter 2, (see verses 11-14)
3. The Transformation of God's Children – A practical Church, chapter 3, (see verses 3-8).
God's ideal for the Church is – orderly organization, soundness in faith and morals, and practical works of piety and philanthropy.

Chapter 1

The epistle to Titus, written at about the same time as I Timothy, carries the same pastoral emphasis. Both epistles are taken up with church doctrine and government. Paul, in his official character as an apostle, is found counseling his son in the faith as to how to institute divine order in the churches. Subjects treated by Paul follow in natural order. "Persons with their hearts and heads full of things which they wish to say to a friend, do not sit down with an analysis before them to secure an orderly arrangement of what they wish to write. They start with one of the main topics, and then the treatment of this suggests something else, and they are not distressed if they repeat themselves, or if they have to return to a subject which has been touched upon before, then dropped. This is just the kind of writing in this epistle." Christian congregations, large and scattered flocks, needed supervision. For the most part they were without shepherds; thus Titus was sent to inaugurate a properly organized ministry throughout Crete.

Chapter 2

Several classes are named by the apostle in this section of his pastoral letter – aged men, aged women, young men, young women and slaves. Titus also is addressed, and is exhorted to preach by his life as well as his lips. Note the "sound" things in the chapter – sound doctrine, sound faith and sound speech. Then observe the "good" things – good things, good mothers, good works and good fidelity. "Sober," too, is a word used in various ways. We also have two "offerings," one past and the other future. In between, there is the present, in which we are to live soberly (life within), righteously (life without), and godly (life upward). By "peculiar people," we are not to understand a people somewhat queer, eccentric in habits, but a people for God's own possession, "a special people unto himself, above all people that are upon the face of the earth" (Deuteronomy 7:6). Paul reminds Titus that Christ died to make us God's very own.

Chapter 3

Having sketched the special duties different classes of Christians must face, Paul now passes on to indicate what must be impressed upon all Christians alike, especially as regards their conduct toward those who are in authority, and who are not

Christians. Paul is aware that he is on delicate ground, trying to shape the turbulent Cretans thus. This is why he warns Titus against "unruly" men, even in some of the churches. His instructions about being subject to rulers and authorities would be unwelcome to many, but Paul does not argue the case. Loyal Christians must subject themselves to those over them, and render obedience to the powers that be, whether the powers be godly or godless. Then Paul goes on to magnify the matchless grace of God. What a peerless evangelist he was! See how he extols the love of God, the finished work of Christ, and the ministry of the Spirit (verses 4-8).

PHILEMON

The backgound of this "Idyl of the New Testament," combining beauty with brevity, as Pierson puts it, is clearly apparent. Onesimus was a slave, the property of Philemon, who stole from his master and ran away to Rome and there came under the preaching of Paul in "his own hired house." Possibly he had heard Paul before in the home of his master, Philemon. Brought to Christ by Paul, this runaway slave was given transportation back to his far-away home, bearing this pleading epistle to Philemon to receive Onesimus not as a slave but as a brother begotten, as Philemon himself, of Paul's gospel. This private, tender little epistle known as *The Courteous Epistle*, is a revelation of Paul's character as a lovable, humble, holy and unselfish man. It also provides us with an example of the apostle's tact and wisdom. In the realm of literature, *Philemon* is a masterpiece of expression, a model of graceful, tactful and delicate pleading. How could Philemon resist such a letter, especially when Paul said he was willing to reimburse him for what Onesimus had taken! Here, the practice of Christian forgiveness is enforced and illustrated. While it may be true that a love letter like this cannot be outlined without doing violence to its message, these four divisions can be used –

1. The Greeting 1-3
2. The Character of Philemon Commended 4-7
3. The Intercessor for Onesimus 8-21
4. The Salutation or Epilogue 22-25.

Philemon

Onesimus, the subject of this epistle, is spoken of by Paul as "faithful and beloved brother" (Colossians 4:9), indicating how this slave had become valuable to the apostle. Dr. Frank E. Gaebelein writes of Philemon as *The Gospel of Emancipation*. This personal letter is a standing example, as Dr. C. I. Scofied reminds us, of practical righteousness, Christian brotherhood and Christian courtesy – the law of love. In this story of a runaway slave, Paul plays upon the name of Onesimus, which means "profitable." He had proved himself to be "unprofitable," but was now "profitable" (verse 11). God's overruling of all circumstances is behind verse 15. How able He is to cause all things to work together for our good! We cannot but be impressed with Paul's delicacy, tact and the expression of the love and sympathy of his heart as we read this priceless gem.

HEBREWS

While this epistle stands unaddressed in the original, there can be little doubt that its present title, *To the Hebrews*, is its true one because every line of its argument suggests that it was designed for the instruction and admonition of those who were Hebrew in blood and Christian in faith, many of whom were in danger of going back to Judaism. Those addressed had not made spiritual progress – had not striven after a deeper spiritual experience. They were content to remain as babes (5:12-14), and were also in danger of being carried away by erroneous doctrines (13:9), and were thus urged to go on unto perfection. The recurring phrase "Let us go on," makes *Hebrews* the epistle of Christian progress. Volumes have been written over the authorship of the epistle. From early church days, however, its Pauline authority has been accepted. It is essentially Pauline in style, in logical argument, in the characteristic temper of the apostle, and even in the terms of language Paul uses elsewhere in his writings. It cannot be denied that *Hebrews* breathes Paul's spirit. The epistle's main theme is the superiority of Christ, and an outline can be worked out around the thirteen references to the key word *better*.
1. Doctrinal 1 – 10, Christ is Better than Old Testament Economy
2. Practical 11 – 13, Christ Brings Better Benefits and Duties.

Coleridge said that if *Romans* reveals the *necessity* of the Christian faith – *Hebrews* reveals the *superiority* of the Christian faith.

Chapter 1

As we commence this marvelous epistle, we may be allowed to point out that in every book of the Bible there is a key word that summarizes its teaching. For Hebrews, the key word is "better," which occurs thirteen times in the thirteen chapters. It is used by the writer to analyze the contents of his epistle, the purpose of which is to prove that Christ is better in every way than all that is offered in the old dispensation. In this first chapter, Christ is proved to be better than the prophets and angels. Think of all the marvelous truths of the Lord Jesus that are packed in the third verse! Read it slowly. Deity, sovereignty, redemption and majesty are all there. The phrase, "sat down," can be translated, "sat Himself down." Christ had power to lay down His life, and to take it up again. "Sat down"! Surely this attitude speaks of a completed task. Angels at best are only ministering spirits. Christ is better than the most exalted angelic being. He is the Lord of glory whom all in glory worship. He is above all, eternally supreme.

Chapter 2

The warning opening this chapter tells us that men are to be judged by how they hear, as well as by what they hear. Here we have the thought of a better dispensation. If punishment overtook those who disobeyed the Word brought them through the medium of angels, how can we escape final condemnation if we neglect and reject the Gospel brought us in the person of Christ? What a paradise this sin-cursed earth will become when all things are in subjection under His feet! As yet, Christ is not crowned with glory and honor by the nations, but universal dominion will be His with His return to the earth. Christ's humiliation was the basis of His honor, and the guarantee of ours. Made lower than angels to die for our sins, Christ now, in virtue of His death and Resurrection, raises us to a position above angels. Of the angels, He can never say: "Behold I and the children which God hath given me."

Chapter 3

Christ, the apostle and high priest, is better in so many ways than Moses. For one thing, Moses lost his temper; the Lord Jesus never did. Moses, speaking unadvisedly with his lips, forfeited the privilege of leading the hosts, whom he had governed for forty years, into Canaan. Christ, however, leads all His own into the Promised Land. How miserably Israel failed to enter their Canaan-rest! Unbelief caused so many of them to perish in the wilderness. Remember that, for the believer, this Canaan-rest is not the prospect of heaven. It is the present rest of faith. And how many are robbed of this through unbelief! It is to the Lord's people the Holy Spirit speaks: "Today, if ye will hear his voice, harden not your hearts." Are lack of faith in God, and obedience to His will, robbing you of heart rest? Do you give way to worry, despair, unbelieving anxiety? Why not seek the rest of faith? This is the rest we take (Matthew 11:28-30).

Chapter 4

God's creation-rest is a type of the rest we can appropriate. Such a rest does not mean inactivity or indolence. Amid all spiritual activities, and surrounded by foes of all kinds, we are never agitated. We rest in the Lord. We need to learn to sing:

My Saviour, Thou hast offered rest,
    Oh, give it now to me!
The rest of ceasing from myself,
    To find my all in Thee.

The description of the Bible is most expressive (verse 12). It is a sword and a critic. The word "discerner," is, in the original, equivalent to our English word "critic." We call the modernist a "destructive critic," because of his adverse criticism of the Word. But here we learn that the Bible does the criticising. And what a faithful critic it is!

Chapter 5

Christ's high-priestly ministry occupies this chapter. In the first four verses, the office of the high priest is dealt with. Christ is better than the best high priest of old, seeing that all priests had to offer sacrifices for their own sins, as well as for the people; but Christ had no sin of His own to atone for. He knew no sin. The order of Melchisedec takes us back to Genesis 14:18-24. This Old Testament king-priest is a fitting type of Christ. He was not appointed by man. He had no recorded beginning of days or end of life. His name means, "my king is righteous." Linger over the tear-saturated prayers of the Lord Jesus (verse 7). How

many of our supplications are accompanied with sobs? Perhaps too many of our prayers are too dry. In the parenthetical portion, with its appeal and warning, we have a tribute to the Word of God. It can suit all ages.

Chapter 6

We are still in the parenthetical portion, which concludes at verse 12. These verses have caused much concern, and one would not minimize the solemn warning they carry. Much has been written on the picture of apostates as found here. It must be borne in mind that the portion was addressed to Hebrews who professed to acknowledge Christ's messiahship, but who gave up their messianic confession and returned to Judaism. Such people failed to make a clean break with Judaism and to go on to the perfection of Christianity. For those who are saved, the writer has this exhortation: "We are persuaded better things concerning you, and things accompanying salvation" (verse 9). Resuming the theme of the high priest, the writer speaks of Christ as the High Priest, entering the veil on our behalf. He has entered the Holiest of all as our representative. Ere long, we are to join Him.

Chapter 7

The reader will do well to follow the outline that Dr. Scofield gives of this chapter, proving as it does that Melchisedec was superior to the Aaronic priesthood. All we know of the royal priest, who reigned in Salem, is in Genesis 14:18-20; and Psalm 110. Christ is saluted as a priest after the order of Melchisedec. He is to come forth from the new Jerusalem, after the Armageddon conflict, as a royal priest to bless His delivered people. The Levitical priesthood failed to reach perfection; hence the appearance of another priest after a better order. Christ's priesthood resembled that of Aaron's. But Christ, like Melchisedec, was king and priest by divine choice, and not human succession. Death took its toll of priests of old, but Christ has an unchangeable and eternal priesthood. He lives for us up there, that we might live for Him down here. As we plead His cause before men, He pleads our cause before the Father's face.

Chapter 8

After summarizing all the privileges and blessings accruing from the heavenly priesthood of our Lord, the writer of this epistle comes to the matter of covenants, and shows how the new is better than the old. In the opening verse, Christ is seen again on the right hand of the Majesty in the heavens (1:3). In Him, shadow gave way to substance. His priesthood, heavenly in character, is exercised on our behalf. The Old Covenant was related to an earthly people. The New Covenant, a blood covenant, (I Corinthians 11:25), covers a heavenly people. This more glorious covenant secures the personal revelation of the Lord to every believer (verses 10,11). The Old Covenant served its purpose up to the cross, but through the cross is now null and void. The Old Covenant decayed and vanished away. Now, through grace, we can sing, "Free from the law! O happy condition!" Are you free? Has Christ dealt with your sins and iniquities? If not, do accept the sin-bearer now, this very moment.

Chapter 9

Entering the heart of this great epistle, the writer commences his discourse on the perfection of Christ's work. A key passage to have before you is, "The Holy Spirit thus signifying" (verse 8), that is *signifying*, meaning that the ordinances and sanctuary of the Old Covenant were simply signs or types. The first sanctuary was "worldly" or "earthy," of the earth in contrast to the heavenly sanctuary that Christ is responsible for. Under the old dispensation no priests had access into the Holy of holies. The high priest alone enjoyed this privilege, and he, only once a year. But through the cross, all veils are taken away, and all the saved have the joy of entering the Holiest of all, even into the immediate presence of the Lord. In verse 14 we see how Father, the Son, and the Spirit were related to redemption. Note the three appearings of Christ — *past* (verse 26), *present* (verse 24), and *prospective* (verse 28). Thus, atonement, advocacy, and advent are all bound together. Verse 27 is a solemn fact for both saint and sinner to contemplate.

Chapter 10

In the first eighteen verses of this chapter, contrasts between law-sacrifices and Christ's supreme and solitary sacrifice are clearly defined. The Levitical order was but a shadow of better things to come. Jewish sacrifices could not atone for sin, but were accepted in virtue of the offering up of God's holy Lamb.

Not all the blood of beasts, on Jewish altars slain,
Could give the guilty conscience peace, or wash away the stain.
But Christ, the heavenly Lamb, takes all our sins away;
A sacrifice of nobler name, and richer blood than they.

The warning against apostasy is fitting for our day, when so many are wavering. Note the persuasive expressions: "Let us draw near" (verse 22); "Let us hold fast" (verse 23); "And let us consider one another" (verse 24). Amid gathering darkness cling to the advent hope of verse 37.

Chapter 11

This renowned chapter, called, "The Westminster Abbey of the Bible," or "God's Honor Roll," is a remarkable record of the triumphs of faith in all past ages. What an illustrious roll! Faith, not human wisdom or sagacity, as the basis of spiritual understanding, opens the chapter. Then follow instances of faith. Conspicuous saints are mentioned, and in each case faith was the controlling power in their exploits. There is a somewhat neglected evidence of grace between verses 29 and 30. Verse 29 ends with the Jews leaving the land of Egypt. Verse 30 opens with the Jews in the land of promise. Not a word is said about the forty years of wandering between Egypt and Canaan. How like God! "Their sins and iniquities will I remember no more" (8:12). He forgets as well as forgives. Have you the assurance that your sins have been blotted out?

Chapter 12

"Let us" is one of the favorite phrases of the book. "Let us go on" makes the epistle one of Christian progress. Surrounded by a great cloud of faith-heroes, as listed in the previous chapter, we are exhorted to cast off all entanglements. All sins are weights, but weights are not necessarily sins. The emphasis seems to be on the article – *the* sin that easily besets each of us. "The sin which clingeth closely round us," that is, as a garment fitting well all around. What is your besetting sin? Well, look away to Jesus, or look away from all else to Him, who alone can deliver. He is ever the soul's delight and deliverer. Alas, we sadly lack the blood-resistance urged upon us! The portion dealing with the Father's chastening has brought sweet consolation to multitudes of tested saints. Vivid contrasts of the old and new covenants close the chapter. Are you not grateful to be under grace, and able to serve God acceptably?

Chapter 13

After doctrine there comes duty; thus, this last chapter is taken up with Christian behavior. Sundry exhortations are addressed to those who are the Lord's: brotherly love; hospitality to strangers; courtesy to all men, slaves included; preservation of the marriage covenant; holy life without covetousness. The fifth verse offers a trinity in unity – a life with covetousness; contentment amid all circumstances; and the abiding companionship of Christ. Have you noticed that the royal promise (verse 5) is about the only verse in Scripture you can read backwards, to find that it means the same thing: "Thee forsake, nor thee leave never will I." Unfailing loyalty of leaders must be imitated. Christ must be trusted as the unchanging One. Perverse teaching must be rejected. Christian separation and worship occupy verses 10-14. Then come the believer-priest's sacrifice and his obedience. What a blessed, beautiful benediction closes the epistle!

JAMES

Written by a Jew to Jewish Christians and having much that is distinctively Jewish in style and spirit, *James* is reckoned to be the *first* of the New Testament to be written. Although Martin Luther had little use for it, calling it, "a right strawy epistle," yet it is most valuable as a manual on holy living. Exceedingly practical, James, the Lord's brother, is short on *doctrine*, but long on practice and morals. Here we are presented with a vindication of Christian works, not as a ground of salvation, but as the test of the genuine Christian. Paul stresses *faith* – James emphasizes *works*, and the one is complement to the other for James simply gives us the morality side of justification by faith Paul preached. There is no conflict between the two. Paul and James stood back to back, beating off common foes. Somewhat stern and severe, akin to some of the Old Testament prophets, and with a style curt and bold, James seems to have a love of metaphors (1:6,10,17,18, ·21,23; 5:5). Apparently fragmentary and disconnected like *Proverbs*, this epistle yet develops in an orderly fashion the theme of Christian Living which must ever spring from regeneration (1:18).

1. Christian Living Is the Subject of Scripture, chapter 1 (see verses 22-25)
2. Christian Living Demonstrates its Faith by its Works, chapter 2 (see verse 22)
3. Christian Living Provides a Corrective for the Evil of the Tongue, chapter 3 (see verses 6,17,18)
4. Christian Living Secures a Victory Over Satan, chapter 4 (see verses 4-8)
5. Christian Living Is Sustained by the Lord's Return, chapter 5 (see verse 8).

Chapter 1

The writer of this epistle, which we may group with the wisdom literature of the Bible, was known as "James the Just," because of his unusual piety. He was a striking example of the graces that he presses upon others in his letter. He wore "the white flower of a blameless life" that he urges the saints to exhibit (verse 27). In the verses before us, the theme is temptation. Follow the connecting words of James. "Lacking," for example (verse 4), leads to the new paragraph (verses 5-7). "Lacking nothing" –"lack wisdom." We are sometimes too proud to confess our lack of wisdom and humbly to ask God to meet such a need in His liberal way. Coming to the subject of temptation, James makes it clear that God permits it but never sends it. There is no sin in being tempted. Christ was tempted. Sin comes when we yield to temptation.

How worthless orthodoxy of belief is, unless it is combined with orthodoxy of life! So James exhorts those who are Christ's to have a quick ear, cautious tongue, calm temper and a pure heart. How do we measure up to the standard of this portion? Our words and works must be in harmony. James illustrates his point by the use of two men who react in different ways as they look in the "mirror of truth." The one forgets what he saw. The other remembers, and is blessed. Then false and true ritualism are mentioned (verses 26,27). Negative and positive are here. James does not teach that works form the *way* of salvation, but are simply the evidence of it. We do not work to be saved; we work because we are saved.

Chapter 2

In this section, taken up with the respect of persons, James makes it clear that saintliness and snobbishness cannot exist together. The world's children vie with each other in luxury and display. The Spirit of Christ, on the other hand, chooses lowliness and humility, virtues compelling simpler faith in God. Respect of persons in churches is abominable. Yet is it not true that, in many cases, the person with the fattest purse, independent of his spirituality, is bowed to, and rules matters? Riches come before religion, clothes before character, and position before piety. Alas, too many religious centers stink with the worship of mammon! The poor must never be despised. So many

of them are "rich in faith," and are "close relatives" of Him, who had nowhere to lay His head!

James is nothing if not practical. In this forceful portion, he emphasizes the fruit of works. There is no contradiction between Paul, who preaches faith, and James, who proclaims works. They form the two sides of the shield. Works cannot save, but they are evidence of our salvation. Note three sections: (1) *the worthlessness of an unproductive faith* (verses 14-17). If our faith is not practical, it is not evangelical; (2) *the necessity that genuine faith gives evidence of its existence* (verses 18,19). Faith must be experimental, as well as intellectual; and (3) *the proof that justification is only by the faith that works* (verses 20-26). Abraham and Rahab are quoted as illustrations of faith. It is a vital, potent faith that is so needed today.

Chapter 3

Have you ever come across that practical prayer in the Book of Job – "Teach me, and I will hold my tongue" (6:24)? Here James discourses on the sins of speech. How innumerable are the sins of uncontrolled tongues! There are sins of speech about ourselves – our tongues boast great things. There are sins of speech about others – our tongues utter harsh words or flatter unduly. There are sins of speech in connection with Christ's cause – our tongues disparage other workers, criticize when they should be silent. Three graphic illustrations are used to prove the power of the tongue: the horse-bridle, the ship's rudder and the tiny spark. We need to pray much about our tongues. The Christian's speech ought always to be seasoned with grace.

Chapter 4

Evidently worldliness was rife among the believers to whom James wrote. Seeking the friendship of the world, they became unfaithful to their divine Lover. Christ and the world are opposites, and the saint cannot have both. It is not Christ *and* the world, but Christ *or* the world. If the Holy Spirit fully controls us, He dethrones all that is opposed to our life in Christ. *Submission to the will of God* (verses 7-10), *the sin of detraction* (verses 11,12), and *life as a plan of God* (verses 13-17) are other aspects of this chapter that we must pause over. Are we seeking the will of God in *all* things? Too often, alas, we glibly talk about the will of God, at the same time projecting our own wills into His.

Chapter 5

How different labor relationships would be if only the truth of this chapter could be blazed abroad. The first section is taken up with the wicked rich (verses 1-6). While many rich are wicked, it is not wicked to be rich. When wealth is wrongly amassed and selfishly used, then it is poor wealth indeed. All who have ill-gotten gains should carefully consider their future miseries. James has some wise things to say about the grace of patience also (verses 7-11). When persecuted by the ungodly, or up against the collision of feeling among ourselves, we have need of patience. Encouragements to patience are before us in Christ's return, as well as in the example of the saints of old.

In closing his epistle, James briefly mentions several themes. Profanity, for example, comes within notice. Is it not sad to realize that the chief swear-words are the Names of God and Christ? Then the apostle tells us how to meet various experiences, such as, depression and sickness. Songs should be mingled with our sobs. The subject of prayer is not forgotten. What a great passage on intercession is found here (verses 13-18). The prayer of faith is that which is so sure of the divine answer that it knows that it has received it, even though the eyes cannot see it. The last word of James deals with soul-winning. Have you experienced lately, or ever, the thrill of converting a sinner from his evil ways?

I PETER

Addressed to both Jews (1:1, R.V.) and Gentiles (2:9,10), spoken of as "the strangers scattered" abroad after the destruction of Jerusalem, this epistle was written by Peter almost at the end of his pilgrimage while he was staying in Babylon (5:13). These scattered saints endured severe trials because of their faith, and the plain intent of Peter's letter was to minister comfort and encouragement to his persecuted brethren. At the junction in the history of the Early Church, when the world was fast breaking up, evil rulers abounded, and the fires of persecution were being kindled, Peter strengthened his brethren by holding up before them as their great example, Christ in His suffering and exaltation. "The joy of reward in prospect for the faithful is set vividly in contrast with their present affliction. Peter is thus before us as *The Apostle of Hope*, as Paul is *The Apostle of Faith;* John, *The Apostle of Love*, and James, *The Apostle of Action.*" Key words of the epistle are *hope, suffering* (21 times) and *precious*. Trace the seven precious things in Peter's two epistles. As *suffering* is mentioned in every chapter, the epistle can be made to revolve around this conspicuous key word.

1. Suffering and Salvation 1:1-13 (Key verse, 6)
2. Suffering and Holiness 1:14-3 (Key verses 2:12,19,20; 3:1,17 with 4:15,16)
3. Suffering and Fellowship 4 (Key verse 13)
4. Suffering and Glory 5:1-5 (Key verses 1,10 see 1:11,13)
5. Suffering and Humanity 5:5-26 (Key verse 9).

Chapter 1

In his most helpful commentary on this epistle, *Tried by Fire*, Dr. F. B. Meyer remarks: "This epistle was the child of many tears and of much sorrow." Much physical persecution was the lot of Christians when Peter wrote his epistles, hence, his reference in this chapter to "the trial of your faith." Are you assured of the fact that you are included with that mystic circle which Peter calls the elect? Of our inheritance, Dr. Howard Ferrin says: "It is incorruptible as to its substance – undefiled as to its purity – unfacing as to its beauty." What a pregnant phrase that is – "whom having not seen, ye love"! Our eyes have never seen that radiant form of His, but precious is He to our heart. It is one of the paradoxes of our faith that we endure as seeing Him who is invisible. Read the chapter carefully for aspects of grace and the Spirit. Ours may be the unspeakable joy that suffering can never quench.

Chapter 2

Admonitions addressed to members of the heavenly family, presented in the previous chapter, are continued in this one. Glean the chapter for expressive emblems of believers. Note also the negatives and positives of the children of God. All that is expected of us can be summarized in the phrase, "follow his steps," which implies far more than imitation. Christ has left us an example, or a writing copy, such as set by masters for their pupils. But outward imitations of a Christ-like life would be fruit without root. We must follow Him, not only in His outward conduct, but in His inner life of self-renunciation and trust in His Father's Word. We must be carried along by the same inner principles that prompted Him in all His ways. Christ is not only the sign-post pointing the way; He is also the power to bear us over every God-directed road. A Christ-like life is only possible as the life of Christ possesses us.

Chapter 3

Peter, a married man himself (Matthew 8:14, etc.) is here found counseling wives and husbands on matters relating to marital obligations. The subjection that Peter urges wives to manifest does not imply the unwholesome yielding of their rights and privileges, or any feeling of inferiority. The apostle is simply enforcing the recognition of man's authority as taught by Paul (I Corinthians 11:3). Mutual yieldedness is the Christian attitude. From Christian home-life, Peter passes to Christian nobility. He shows us how we can all belong to heaven's aristocracy. Five beautiful Christian virtues are conspicuous in Peter's language. The counsel regarding giving an answer to every man

is striking, coming, as it does, from the man who was afraid of the taunt of a servant girl and failed to answer for his Lord. The portion dealing with preaching to the spirits in prison has occasioned much discussion. Dr. Scofield's heading on the subject satisfies the writer's mind; or see the footnote in *The Pilgrim Bible*.

Chapter 4

The key word of this epistle is "suffer," used some 15 times in all. In this chapter we are told how to suffer, and how not to suffer. What an arresting phrase that is – "the rest of his time"! Do we ever stop and consider: "The rest of my time! How much more time have I"? How should we spend the rest of our time? Well, Peter tells us. The end of all things is at hand. Live as advent-watchers. Scanning the chapter as a whole, we have several advent-attitudes, characteristic of all those who live as children of the dawn – sobriety, prayerfulness, fervent love, ungrudging hospitality, full use of talents, suffering with Christ, judgment of the Church, committal of the entire life to God, who, as the faithful Creator, will undertake for His own until traveling days are o'er. What a way to spend the rest of our time!

Chapter 5

Peter now comes to view the Christian ministry in the light of our Lord's return, when, as the Chief Shepherd, He is coming to reward His undershepherds. Would that all who believe Peter to be the first pope, which he was not, could take these pastoral injunctions to heart! Thrice over Peter had heard the Master say: "Feed my Sheep!" Now, in turn, he exhorts all undershepherds to feed the flock. And there will never be wanting a flock, if the right kind of food is provided. In pride, Peter had once said: "I am ready." Unconscious of his own weakness, however, he had denied his Lord. Now he urges the saints to be clothed with humility. He knew from experience that "self-confidence is the armor-bearer of sin," as Spurgeon expresses it. Is yours the life without care, as taught in verse 7? Can you sing: "I have no cares, O blessed Will, for all my cares are Thine"?

II PETER

Although the style and language of this epistle is different from *I Peter*, this is no reason to doubt Peter's authorship of it, as some critics do. The apostle now writes with a different purpose in mind. If his first epistle was for the encouragement of the faithful, this second epistle was meant as a sharp rebuke of the unfaithful among the professing disciples of Christ. The same atmosphere of unrest, suffering and persecution pervades the two epistles. Now, Emperor Nero is about to undertake his fierce persecution of Christians throughout the Roman Empire, and heresies, false teachers and apostates abound. So Peter utters his last warning before his own martyrdom at Rome. Tradition says that at his own request Peter was crucified with head downward. He didn't deem himself worthy to die in the same way as his Lord. Sketching the *iniquity* of the last days, as Jude does the *apostasy*, Peter utters his swan song which is similar, in some ways, to that of Paul's swan song in *II Timothy*. The characteristic word of *II Peter* is *knowledge* which with its cognates, is used 16 times. Saints are to grow not only in *grace* but in *knowledge* as well (3:18). Surveying the three chapters as a whole we have –
1. Moral Corruption 1:1-14 – Safeguard, *remembrance* 1:12,13
2. Doctrinal Corruption 1:15 – 2 – Safeguard, *remembrance* 1:1,15
3. Victory Over Corruption 3 – Safeguard, *remembrance* 3:1,12.

Chapter 1

The apostle, realizing that his own martyrdom was near, and that apostasy would characterize the professing church from his time onward, wrote this challenging epistle. While much controversy has raged around its authorship, we see no reason why we cannot accept the opening statement of this chapter. What a wonderful lesson in Christian arithmetic Peter gives us! Are you good at addition? If so, live in verses 5 to 9. How stirring Peter's ministry must have been (verse 13)! Aware of his approaching death, the apostle exercised a God-honoring,

Scripture-exalting ministry. Would it make a difference in our lives and labors if we knew that shortly we must put off this tabernacle? As an eyewitness of Christ's majesty, Peter had in mind the overwhelming vision on the Mount of Transfiguration. Let us be grateful to have the Spirit-inspired Scriptures as a light shining amid the world's gathering darkness.

Chapter 2

One cannot read this chapter without recalling the priceless epistle of Jude. The two have much in common. Peter and Jude are in full agreement as to the cause, curse and condemnation of apostasy. Peter places those who spurn the blood of Christ foremost in his warning against apostate teachers. Alas, it is all too common these days, in theological circles, to deny the efficacious work of the cross. A recent press report quotes a representative of a once fundamental publishing firm as saying that, in a new hymnbook about to be printed, all "blood and wounds stuff" will be eliminated. Other marks of apostate teachers are given by Peter, which aptly describe many in the so-called Christian ministry today. Ours is an apostate age, and we certainly need spiritual enlightenment to detect any and all shades of apostasy. Our duty is clear. At all costs we must declare and defend the faith.

Chapter 3

Peter has no hesitation in claiming divine inspiration for Old Testament writers (1: 20,21; 3:2,3). Prophets and apostles alike confirm Christ's coming in power and glory. Sad to say, we have many ministerial scoffers, who are ignorant of the promise of His coming again. But the Lord is not slack concerning His promise to return. His apparent delay is an evidence, says Peter, of His long-suffering. Eager for multitudes more to repent, the Lord lengthens the day of grace. The question is: Are we living in the light of our Lord's sure return? What manner of persons ought we to be, as the hour is about to strike on God's clock for

His Son to return! We should be growing in grace. Observe that we do not grow *into* grace, but once in grace through faith in Christ, we grow *within* it.

I JOHN

What a precious trio John gives us in his three epistles! This first epistle is general, that is, for all saints and not addressed to persons as the other two are. Pierson says that the tone of this first epistle is *"paternal,* both in authority and affection; and *prophetic,* having an air of final decision and declaration. Its thoughts cluster about three grand centers – *Light, Love, Life." Know,* and its equivalent occurs 32 times in the epistle, the main object of which is that all believers may "know that they have eternal life, and so their joy may be full" (1:4; 5:13). John, who outlived all the other apostles, lived to see grave heresies creep into the Church, the most dangerous of which was *gnosticism,* which held that sin was in matter and not in spirit. This heresy led to two things in practice – *asceticism,* or the punishment of the body as the supposed seat of sin; and *licentiousness,* on the ground that nothing the body could do would taint the spirit. So John writes to all believers stating the true doctrine of Sin, rebuking the dangerous heresy of *gnosticism* and declaring the grounds of Christian assurance as obedience, brotherly love and the indwelling Holy Spirit. Expand –
1. The Message of the *Logos,* 1:1-4
2. The Message of the *Light,* 1:5 – 2:11
3. The Message of *Love,* 2:12 – 5:3
4. The Message of *Life,* 5:4-21.

Chapter 1

Life and *light* are the twin truths developed by John in his first epistle which, along with the Song of Solomon, can be ranked as the most intimate of the inspired writings. At the outset, the apostle takes us back to "the beginning" of his gospel (1:1). As a whole, the epistle is a family letter from the Father to His "little children." In his gospel, John leads us across the threshold of the Father's house; in this, his first epistle, he wants us to be at home

there, to walk in the light of our eternal home, and to emit something of its fragrance. The first three chapters show the family with the Father, and the remaining chapters, the family and the world. To walk in the *light* implies unbroken fellowship with the Father and the Son. Indeed, the *light* whereof John speaks throws light into the darkened cells; but we need not fear, for what the *light* reveals, the *blood* can cleanse (verse 7).

Chapter 2

While John contemplates the possibility of a Christian's sinning, he yet makes it clear that it is not necessary for him to sin. With the Spirit dwelling within the believer, and also, on account of Christ's advocacy above, there is abundant power for each of us against the commission of sin. Before us are the tests of true fellowship, namely: obedience to God and His Word; love one for another; separation from the world; rejection of all that is apostate; and a life lived in the light of Christ's return. Have you noticed the *advocacy* and *anointing* of this chapter (verses 1,20,27)? One is above, the other within. The tender term "little children" (verses 1,28) deserves attention. It is *teknia,* meaning "born ones," or the expressive Scottish designation, "bairns." As children of God, through faith in Christ we must abide in Him (verse 28), and we shall bear the family likeness (verses 6,15).

Chapter 3

Living in fellowship with God and with each other, as children in the same divine family, are the truths before us in this great chapter. Note the purifying influence of the blessed hope (verses 2,3). John's reference to sinlessness (verses 6,9) has troubled many saints. One who habitually practices sin is the person the apostle describes. He makes it clear that "if we say we have no sin, we deceive ourselves, and the truth is not in us" (1:8). Love for other believers, no matter whether they are loving or not, is one evidence of the assurance of salvation: "We know . . . because" (verse 14). The indwelling Spirit is also linked to assurance (verse 24). What a chapter this is for a loveless age like ours! What bitter feuds and estrangements characterize so many professing Christians today! We have need to pray: "O God, give us love."

Chapter 4

Loyalty to the Lord and His Word, and the love life of the believer, are the twin themes expounded in this chapter. In the first six verses, John tells us how to discern false teachers. He tells us to try, or to test, the spirits (verse 1). A crucial test is the deity of Christ (verses 2,3). No matter how religious and educated a person may be, he is not a Christian, after the New Testament order, if he denies that Christ was God manifest in the flesh. Such a one is a forerunner of the Antichrist (verse 3). Coming to the believer's life of love, the "apostle of love," as John is called, stresses the point that love and fear are antagonistic one to another. If we are saved, then we have no dread of meeting God, as the God of Judgment. Covered by the blood, boldness is ours, to come into His presence at any time.

Chapter 5

John closes his first epistle with a practical word for all those blessed with the gift of eternal life. Saved, we are yet as weak and helpless as ever; but in Christ is fulness and victory perfectly available for all the saints. How slow we are to appropriate all that we have in Him! Would that faith was ours to mount up to that pure and blessed place in which all fullness is found! With shame we must confess how far short we come of attainment. We are not as obedient and victorious as John urges. One striking feature of this chapter is that eternal life is not "something," but "Someone." Eternal life is the life of the Eternal One. "This life is in his Son" (verses 11,20), and this Life is His Son. Do you share the confidence of verses 14 and 15? Do you believe that God hears and answers prayers? It is not difficult, surely, to solve the problem of *some* unanswered prayers – they are not "according to his will."

II JOHN

This brief epistle of a single chapter was addressed to one of John's disciples – an unknown Christian lady and her family – and by authority of the Early Church was placed among the *catholic* epistles, as designed for the churches generally. Written from the same place as *I John*, it carries the same rebuke of the rising heresies of the times. *For the truth's sake,* is the theme of the letter. Truth is worth contending for, not only because it is wrong to receive false teachers, but because truth is TRUTH. How grateful we ought to be to John for providing us with this precious homily on truth, giving us its nature, test, fruit, character and defense. In this, the only book in the New Testament to be addressed exclusively to a lady, *truth* occurs five times, verses 1, 2, 3, 4. Pierson suggests that *II John* is "a tribute to the dignity of womanhood, wifehood and motherhood. It sets a high value on the piety of a mother and her household; and warns against the abuse of hospitality by those who undermine holy living and propagate error."

1. Love Expressed Is the Boundary of Truth 1-6
2. Life Is an Expression of the Doctrine of Christ 7-11
3. Light is to the Reception of True and False Teachers 12, 13.

True to his nature as the "apostle of love," John stresses different aspects of Love (1,2,3,5,6).

II John

This epistle, an appendix of the first, emphasizes the same truth, namely, that love must be in the truth – not love without truth, or truth without love, but a blending of both. Here John addresses himself to a woman, the only time in Scripture that a book is thus sent. Some have thought that this lady is a local church. Two thoughts are dwelt upon as John reminds "the elect lady and her children" of their responsibilities; namely, that truth and love are inseparable in the Christian life, and that doctrine is ever the final test of reality. John writes of those who, by their apostasy, were already casting the shadow of the future over his day. What strong language he uses about those who have departed from the faith! Why, he urges that such apostates be denied a common greeting, which is the force of "neither bid him God speed." And this is the intolerance of love. Today, those who abide not in the doctrine of Christ are often not only tolerated but are sometimes given the chief place. How sad is such disobedience to God's Word!

III JOHN

Here again, is a personal letter written in the form of an apostolic commendation of a Christian gentleman. He had extended warm-hearted Christian hospitality to certain missionaries who had been treated inhospitably by an office-bearer of the local church, Diotrephes by name. Such old-fashioned hospitality, especially to messengers of Christ, is a grace worthy of apostolic praise in any age of the Church. In the previous epistle, the Elect Lady was warned not to be partaker of the evil deeds of propagators of error – here Gaius, Paul's convert and host (Romans 16:23; I Corinthians 1:14), is praised as a fellow-helper to the truth. The preacher has ample material here for a biographical sermon on the three different characters John portrays, namely, Gaius 1-8, Diotrephes 9-11, and Demetrius 12-14. The first is commended for his *soul-health* – the second is condemned for his *ambition and arrogance* – the third is praised as a *witness to the Truth* which is the source of love (verse 1), and our weapon in work and warfare (verse 8). Every believer should be a "fellow-helper to the truth" (verse 1). We do not know if Demetrius is the same one Luke mentions as the silversmith who made the small silver shrines for Diana (Acts 19:24). If so, what a mighty change had taken place in his life. Bless God, grace can transform the most unlikely!

III John

This epistle of John is a personal one, being sent to Gaius, a much loved friend. Three individuals are named in this brief letter, beloved Gaius (verses 1-8); domineering Diotrephes (verses 9-11), and faithful Demetrius (verses 12-14). The key word is *truth* which occurs six times. Dr. Scofield remarks that II John "conditions the personal walk of a Christian in a day of apostasy; III John, the personal responsibility in such a day of the believer as a member of the local church." Diotrephes, who rejected apostolic letters and authority, was proud of his own position and ability to teach. He wanted to keep the assembly to himself. How different was Demetrius, whose useful service was known to all. The word "pre-eminence" occurs twice in the New Testament: in Colossians 1:18: "that in all things he might have the pre-eminence"; and here: "Diotrephes, who loveth to have the pre-eminence" (verse 9). And the one form blasts the other, for we cannot, at the same time, give the pre-eminence to Christ and to ourselves.

JUDE

Written for believers of every age, this last epistle was written, not by an apostle, but an ordinary disciple–"a plain man, of fiery spirit, and filled with prophetic zeal." The Hebrew converts who first received this most solemn epistle would be familiar with Jude's references to Old Testament figures and incidents–unbelieving Israel, disobedient angels, lustful Sodomites, self-righteous Cain, greedy Balaam, presumptuous Korah and blasphemous mockers. The epistles of Peter and of Jude have much in common. Both are conspicuous for a bold denunciation of a condition of apostasy and corruption. If there is a difference, Peter writes of an impending apostasy– Jude writes of it as at hand. This is the only book in the Bible recording strife over the body of Moses, and also Enoch's remarkable prophecy (9,14,15). Dr. C. J. Rolls says that "the entire body of teaching of preceding books is recognized, and the bold testimony they contain is ratified. The climax of all truth is reached, and a practical appeal and application of it is made to the believer . . . . We find packed into one page an amazing abridgement of Biblical history and a short summary of the essential verities and cardinal facts of salvation." Dr. Rolls divides the book thus–

1. Illustrations of Apostasy
2. Instructions for Loyalty
3. Instruments of Fidelity.

Verses 1-7

Constrained by the Spirit to pen this brief epistle, Jude vividly describes the cause, course and condemnation of apostasy. The salutation is made up of two triads. After introducing himself in a delightfully delicate way, proving that spiritual relationships are before family relationships, Jude describes those to whom he writes as sanctified, preserved and called. "Preserved for Jesus Christ" can be translated "kept for Jesus Christ." This word "kept" is a suitable keynote for the epistle. Trace its uses. Then we have a triad of graces: mercy, peace and love, which are not ours in any scanty measure, but multiplied. By the

"common salvation," we are to understand a salvation for all. Jude goes on to make it clear that we must contend for the faith without being contentious. Apostate men, angels and cities are "kept" for final judgment, just as saints are kept for final bliss.

Verses 8-19

After citing examples of past apostates, Jude goes on to describe in dramatic fashion apostate teachers of his and our age. They are as "sunken rocks," "waterless clouds," "fruitless trees" and "wandering stars." While in the flesh, they lived in the limelight of men's praise; now they are plunged into the eternal, impenetrable "outer darkness." Their progressive apostasy is illustrated in a three-fold way: "gone in the way of Cain," meaning attempting an approach to God apart from sacrificial blood; "run greedily after the error of Balaam," signifying a voracious grasping for material reward; and "perished in the gainsaying of Korah," implying the direct and immediate usurpation of spiritual privileges. The three-fold character of all apostates may be found in verse 19.

Verses 20-25

These stirring verses present an impressive contrast. Over against wreckers of the faith, we have builders of the faith. The constructive activity of the builders is given in a four-fold way: building, praying, keeping and looking. We are to build, not on our emotions or on personal conceptions of right or wrong, or on experiences, but on the glorious faith once delivered to the saints. Our prayer life must neither be jointless nor promiscuous, but powerful. To pray in the Holy Spirit is to allow the Holy Spirit to pray in us. The expression, "keeping ourselves in the love of God," does not contemplate the possibility of drifting outside the sphere of that love, but the loss of the enjoyment of that love by waywardness and worldliness. Another safeguard against apostasy is the uplook of love. As God delights to keep the best until the last, Jude closes with the benediction of eternal security.

REVELATION

Although this last book of the Bible is neglected by the majority of religious people as being too mysterious or difficult to understand, the fact remains that it was written to be read and understood and that a special blessing is promised to all who are willing to read it (1:3). As it is the book recording the downfall and doom of the devil, we can understand why he strives to keep people from a study of it. *Revelation* means an unveiling, which this book is of the Lord Jesus Christ. The scope of *The Book Of Revelation* covers the progress of Christianity from the first century to the end of time. Here is unfolded the "drama of the ages." Of course, the book is highly symbolic for the simple reason that, "apocalyptic prophecy is *essentially prophetic.* Mysteries, having no analogy in earthly things or past events, demand images for their expression." A simple fact to bear in mind is that there is no symbol in *Revelation* that is not explained for us in some other part of the Bible. There are various features of the book we could dwell upon such as the use of a numerical system in which numbers express ideas – the Law of Recurrence – the contrast between *Genesis* – the commencement, and *Revelation* – the consummation. The simplest outline of the book is that suggested by Dr. G. Campbell Morgan –

1. The Glory of Christ, chapter 1
2. The Grace of Christ, chapters 2, 3
3. The Government of Christ, chapters 4 – 22.

Chapter 1 CHRIST GLORIFIED

The opening phrase of this chapter describes the character of the entire book. It is a "revelation," or an unveiling of Christ in His high priestly and kingly glory, and also of those events preceding and accompanying His return to earth. The book is not a curiosity shop of symbols, or a patchwork of Jewish and heathen folklore, as modernists suggest, but a prophetic book unfolding in dramatic form the climax of all things. Here we have the authentic and accurate account of present and future things – a Spirit-inspired book, not meant to confuse the mind, but an intelligible, unsealed volume, to which is attached a special blessing for its readers and hearers alike. Are you a servant of the Lord? Then this is God's *Revelation* to you, a marvelous book you dare not neglect in these momentous days. God grant us insight into its truths!

Chapter 2:1-7 BACKSLIDING EPHESUS

As backsliding begins in the heart (Proverbs 14:14) the church at Ephesus commenced to backslide when it left, not lost, its first love. It is significant to note that the name "Ephesus" means: *to relax,* or *let go,* and aptly describes the character of the church so soon after the warning of Paul (Acts 20:29,30). Christ found much to commend in Ephesus. To many, at that time, it would stand out as an almost perfect church. Yet it is called by Christ, a fallen assembly. With its orthodoxy, fervor and activity, the forfeiture of its first intense love for Him is tantamount to a fallen condition requiring deep repentance of heart. Our personal devotion for the Bridegroom needs to be as passionate as it used to be. Of course, we are still fundamental, and are eager to serve the Lord. But has the old time flame gone? Remember – Repent!

Chapter 2:8-11 PERSECUTED SMYRNA

The duration of "ten days" suffering may be a prophetic reference to the "Ten Great Persecutions" under the old Roman emperors, seven of which occurred during the "Smyrna Period" of Church History. "Smyrna" itself means *bitterness,* or *myrrh,* and is symbolic of the terrible experiences overtaking its members. Faithfulness was urged as bitter martyrdom approached, with the promise of a crown of life from Him who is alive forevermore. How encouraging the Master's "Fear not" must have been! It may be that we are not called upon to die as martyrs, yet we must adorn the martyr spirit. Amid all apostasy, hostility and godlessness we must be found faithful, knowing that it is faithfulness, and not fame, that the Lord Jesus emphasizes as being the basis of reward.

Chapter 2:12-17 Compromising Pergamos

We now reach the period of the circle of church history when Constantine embraced Christianity in A.D. 313. By this time the Church had settled down in the world, and the enemy had planned to favor the faith he had fought, and defile what he could not destroy. Christ is here pictured as fighting against those holding false doctrines, with "the sword of my mouth," the sword being His Word in its judgment character. As a two-edged sword, it destroys all that is sinful in the life of the believer, and metes out stern judgment upon the apostate and Christless. Amid gathering darkness Antipas stood out like a beacon light. "My faithful witness, My faithful one." What Christ was to God (Revelation 1:5), Antipas was to Christ. So in faithfulness may we qualify for the hidden manna, and the white stone with its new name.

Chapter 2:18-29 Papal Thyatira

A peculiar feature of this church is that it is the only one out of the seven mentioning a woman's name, Jezebel, the crafty, cruel murderess. The earlier mention of Thyatira is associated with a woman, but one of different character altogether (Acts 16). This fourth letter is the longest of the seven sent to the churches, and contains the first direct reference to the Second Advent. What Pergamos tolerated, Thyatira taught, becoming, in turn, the mother of similar evil systems. Jezebel, the prophetess, not only was the forerunner of the papal system with its worship of a woman, but also of many false cults, like Christian Science, having as their founders women. All Jezebel systems of religion, with their deluded adherents, are to be punished. My soul, come not nigh their dwelling!

Chapter 3:1-6 Protestant Sardis

What a condemnation was heaped upon this church by the Lord! Ritualistic and formal, having a name to live, He spoke of it as *dead*. If the Sardis period covers Protestantism during the Reformation era, then the description is apt of the ignorance prevalent at that time. But there is the wider application to the Church of today, for with all its denominations, ornate churches, machinery and amenities, it has a name that it lives, but is dead. There is the appearance of life, but He whose eyes search all things, pierces the outward trappings, and discerns that which is spiritual death. In all of these churches there can be found the personal appeal. "If any man." Deadness prevails on every hand. The energy of life, and the expression of life, are the proper characteristics of the faithful Christian.

Chapter 3:7-13 Fundamental Philadelphia

Following the "dead" Sardis church, we come in church history to the famous revivals from 1750 through 1900, with their evangelistic and missionary movements. "Philadelphia," meaning *brotherly love*, describes devotion to Christ and His Word and Work, and the consequent love for one another that should characterize the Church in any age. Of this church, it is said that it had "little strength." Full energy was lacking. It was spiritually feeble. It faced "an open door," however. And from William Carey's day in 1793, the Church has stood before open doors, but never one as widely open as today. Next, the Church was to be kept from "the hour of temptation" or tribulation, a prediction of God's care of His own, and that they will not pass through the Great Tribulation. Nothing can touch you, O child of God, apart from His permissive will.

Chapter 3:14-22 Apostate Laodicea

We now come to the last phase of the professing church. The church leaving its first love, is now left by the Lord. Of course, the professing church is in view, for no true believer will be "spued out" of the Lord's mouth. For the other churches there was commendation—here, no praise whatever. Church life today is largely mechanical. Societies, clubs, social functions, and organizations dominate. There is little warmhearted spirituality. Laodicea was guilty of self-deception. The church thought it had everything, but knew not that it was destitute of Christ. It is almost unthinkable to imagine Christ excluded from a church bearing His Name. Yet it was to such a church that He said: "Behold, I stand at the door and knock!'' A Christless church! God forbid that any who read this should have a Christless heart!

Chapter 4 GLORIOUS THRONE

The opening words of this chapter mark a new commencement. Church history has been written. The Lord's own have been translated, and mere religious professors spued out. And so with the removal of the true Church, the subjects of prophecy take their allotted place. This is why prophetic scenes and visions now occupy the attention of John, and why this chapter and the next describe heavenly ascents of incomparable majesty. The throne of God now comes into view, and from this point on *Revelation* becomes, *"The Book of the Throne."* Now we approach the throne of grace, but the throne of heaven that John saw is the sign and symbol of God's universal government. The stage is now being set for His governmental control of all things. And this eternal throne is in sharp contrast to the tottering thrones of earth. True worship, such as we ought to give, is found in verses 9-11.

Chapter 5 SEALED BOOK

This great chapter is really a continuation of the previous one, with the two prominent additional features of the sealed book, and a slain Lamb. Reading the chapter, we realize that the Lion-Lamb is alone worthy to receive honor and glory. There are the glories of His wounds, His royalty, His guardianship and His triumph. How glorious to be able to sing the new song of verse 9! Of the seven-sealed books, Walter Scott says: "The 'seven seals' expresses the perfection with which the hidden counsels of God are securely wrapped up in the divine mind till their open disclosure by the Lamb. . . . For as the seven-sealed book, with its full and minute disclosure of the future, is no longer a hidden mystery, prophecy, once a secret, is no longer a secret." The royal dignity and priestly nearness of verse 10 are the gracious privilege of every child of God.

Chapter 6 OPENED SEALS

As we now approach the strictly prophetic part of *Revelation*, we will encounter three different series of judgments: seals, trumpets and vials. "The judgments under the seals and trumpets are not contemporaneous, but successive. . . . The Lamb is connected with the seals, angels with the trumpets, and God with the vials." The six seals can be indicated in order: antichrist, war, famine, deathly pestilence, martyrdom, and physical changes. The scene described under the sixth seal is both tragic and sublime. Chaos is everywhere. Disorder reigns. There is the total collapse of all governing authority. Through a revolutionary crisis the multitudes of earth are in abject terror. What a fearful world to contemplate! And as we think of the present distress among nations, it would seem as if we are fast heading up for the coming crash that John depicts.

Chapter 7 TRIBULATION SALVATION

During the respite in the breaking of the seals, we have a season of salvation and sealing. Three sections of this chapter are easily traced. First, we have the restraining angels, holding back the direct judgments of heaven. Angelic activity in the *Revelation* forms a fascinating study. Then we have the sealing of the 144,000 of Israel, who, in spite of the terrible tribulation surrounding them, refuse to bow the knee to the Antichrist. Last of all, the blood-washed multitude, gathered out from all the nations, come before us. And this last section is one of the most striking in the book. Yes, souls will be saved during the tribulation, but they will not form part of the Church, seeing the Church, which is Christ's body, will be complete and gathered out before this tribulation revival takes place. The preciousness of God's handkerchief (verse 17) has been of comfort and cheer to countless numbers of His saints.

Chapters 8, 9 TRUMPET JUDGMENTS

The seventh seal gives birth to the seven trumpets, six of which are before us in these two chapters. The silence of the opening verse is ominous. It indicates a lull before the storm, the stillness in nature preceding a tempest. Others interpret the silence as the forbearance of God. "His steps from mercy to judgment are always slow, reluctant, and measured." As trumpets were used to arouse and warn the people of God against their enemies, so here, the angels, sounding the trumpets, declare and dispense divine judgment. There is an inescapable comparison between these judgments and the plagues that fell upon Egypt. And viewing the judgments as a whole, we note a progressive degree of displeasure and disaster. To read of the horrible days awaiting the godless of earth, as well as the earth of the godless, is to lead us to bless God for our salvation. For us, as Christians, judgment is past!

Chapter 10   Rainbow Angel

Here the public intervention of God is witnessed in symbol and word. The vision of this chapter is one of the most profound in the book. With the descent of the mighty angel to earth is announced the close of providential dealing. Crowned with a rainbow, this angel is a reminder of God's constant, unfailing mercy amid apocalyptic scenes of judgment. The little book open, in the angel's hand, is in contrast to the sealed book of chapter 5. This open book, eaten by John, was both bitter and sweet. So prophecy both gladdens and saddens. It is sweet to know that God, as the Sovereign, will conquer all His foes, but what bitterness will be the portion of the godless. This chapter closes with John's call to a prophetic ministry. And as we have God's blueprint for the future, we dare not be silent. Regardless of how men react, we must proclaim our bitter-sweet message.

Chapter 11:1-12   Prophetic Witnesses

The whole of this chapter is anticipative in character, and presents the initial stages in the development of God's glorious earthly purpose for the Jews. Time measures require a note. The 42 months of trial for Jerusalem, months of 30 days each, correspond to the 1,260 days of sackcloth borne by the two witnesses. As to the identity of the two witnesses called to accomplish the most astonishing task ever committed to men, conjectures have been innumerable. Some identify them as Moses and Elijah. The presence of these last witnesses, before the earth is given over to Satan and his masterpiece, the Antichrist, indicates a full and adequate testimony. Under Jewish law, two witnesses were required to give competent evidence (Deuteronomy 17:6; 19:15; see John 20:12; Acts 1:10). Amid the godlessness of our day, we are only *true* witnesses as we bear testimony to Christ in *life* as well as in word.

Chapter 11:13-19   God Glorified

How dramatic is this portion, with its divine vindication of the two witnesses! Like their Master in suffering and death, they are now like Him in resurrection and exaltation. At last, they have strength and stability death could not touch. In this portion, we find ourselves on the eve of events concluding the last prophetic week. The seventh trumpet, with its third woe, includes all that transpires down to chapter 20, verse 3. "God is about to act openly and inflict a series of short, sharp and decisive judgments on the vast consolidated and apostate power then dominating the earth. This concluding series of divine chastisements is seen to issue from God Himself." What a glorious day it will be for this blood-soaked earth when Christ returns to it and fashions the kingdoms of the world into His own world-kingdom!

Chapter 12:1-6   Sun-Clothed Woman

Coming to prophetic events as God sees them, we have the portrayal of seven personages, three of whom are before us in this section, namely, the woman, who is Israel; Satan; the Child, who can be no other than Christ Himself, who was of the tribe of Judah. Chapters 12, 13 and 14, it will be found, form one connected prophecy, and should be of great interest to all students of the Word. While it is true that Israel has endured terrible tribulation through the centuries, here is an unprecedented sorrow of God's ancient people, and His gracious deliverance of them during the time of Jacob's trouble. Satan is before us in his worst character. But One is able to deliver and preserve the woman. The despotism of the devil is destroyed, and Israel escapes. Praise God for our St. George, who can deal with the dragon!

Chapter 12:7-17   HEAVEN'S WAR

As Satan is the prince of the power of the air, he has his abode in the stellar heavenlies, and the conflict herewith described centers around his expulsion from his abode. And when cast down to earth, what wrath will be his! What a scene! Heavenly and hellish powers meet, and heaven prevails. Michael and the dragon, with their respective forces, join battle, with the outcome never in doubt. Satan and his sinful angelic forces suffer an ignominious defeat. Cast out, and down from heaven, the devil exerts all his energy to scatter ruin and destruction all around. No longer the accuser, he becomes the adversary. As the dreadful dragon, he strives to engulf the Jews, but God providentially frustrates all his diabolical schemes of destruction. Here and now, the Lord's people share His conquest of the devil. Are you resting in His victory?

Chapter 13:1-10   SEA BEAST

In this chapter we reach the form and activities of the principal agents of Satan, as he battles against divine counsels. Three great empires are here portrayed in the culmination of Gentile dominion: the lion of Babylon, the bear of Persia, and the leopard of Greece. World dominion, offered to Christ by Satan, is his gift to his imperial agent, the beast out of the sea. "When this revived imperial power rises out of the turmoil and confusion of a troubled world," says Dr. F. Tatford, "men will probably be longing for strong and settled rule and stable government. The Roman Empire will provide the answer to their yearnings, and they will voluntarily, and gladly, yield their allegiance to its iron strength." But what cruel bondage will overtake the deceived earth dwellers paying homage to this supreme monarch, "the little horn"! The characteristics of the saints of verse 10 are the same as the Lord Jesus gives to His own today: patience and faith – double grace.

Chapter 13:11-18   EARTH BEAST

The first beast rose out of the sea, that is, the restless nations. This second beast rises out of the earth, probably the land of Israel, implying that this false imitator of Christ may be a Jew. Diverse in their features and characteristics, both beasts are alike in their nature. The second beast is the vicar of the first beast; and the power delegated to him is used primarily for the glorification of his master. He is the religious head, just as the first beast is the political head of the revived empire. Countless attempts have been made to identify the number, 666. Whoever the individual may be, it is certain that he will not be fully known until he appears. "The clue given by the Apocalypse will probably then be adequate for the godly of that day to realize the identity of their foe and act accordingly." How much better it is to bear the brands of Christ (Galatians 6:17), because of faithfulness to Him!

Chapter 14   SONG AND SICKLE

The scene before us is sublime: heaven and earth join in a glad hymn of praise. It will be noted that none could sing the new song save those who had been purchased out of the earth. Have you learned the new song? Close upon the heels of rapturous joy comes righteous judgment. Conscious and eternal punishment is to be the plight of Babylon and her beast-worshipers. The One, despised and rejected, rides upon a white cloud and, thrusting in His sickle, reaps the over-ripe harvest of earth's judgment. Joined by an angel, who also has a sharp sickle, the corruption of earth is quickly removed by direct judicial acts. Unsparing and unmitigated wrath will overtake the godless horde of earth. Bless God, we will in the day of grace and mercy! God grant us a deeper passion to save the lost!

Chapter 15   SALVATION'S SONG

While this chapter opens with the subject of the seven vials of wrath, we quickly meet the interjection of the vision of the sea of glass mingled with fire: "a mighty reservoir of just judgments about to be precipitated upon the world below." In the "song of the overcomers," material and spiritual salvation are combined. The last half of the chapter is taken up with the preparation of the ministers of God's wrath. Being clothed in pure and bright linen suggests the righteous character of the judgment these angels are to dispense. Would that we could persuade the multitudes of earth to realize that the Eternal God, the God of judgment, is about to plague the earth and visit it with His fury! May He manifest Himself in revival blessing as this age closes, so that a still greater host will be found singing the song of grace and glory.

Chapter 16 WRATHFUL VIALS

No act of judicial judgment can be taken until God authoritatively gives the command. Thus, the golden bowls of fury of the previous chapter are withheld until this chapter. Truly, the ways of God in judgment are calm and measured. It is interesting to compare the seven vials with the Egyptian plagues. Boils, blood-colored sea and rivers, great heat, darkness, Euphrates dried up, and great hail, describe the intense suffering and desolation awaiting all beast-worshipers. The whole of the guilty scene feels the vengeance of an angry God – "awful visitations of divine wrath successively inflicted out of the sanctuary, and from the bowls, hallowed by temple use and service, now diverted to purposes of judgment." In this present age we cry: "Kiss the Son, lest He be angry!"

Chapter 17 HARLOT CHURCH

Throughout Scripture, Babylon stands as the figure of false worship and idolatry, and upon it God's sternest judgment is to fall. In this chapter, Babylon is before us as a woman. In chapter 18, it is a city. Dr. C. I. Scofield comments that chapter 17 is the divine view of Babylon, and chapter 18, the human and angelic views. Dr. F. Tatford remarks: "The great harlot of Revelation 17 is in contrast to the spotless Bride of Revelation 19, and the idolatrous city of chapter 18 is in contrast with the holy city of chapter 21. Since the Bride of the Lamb is not an actual woman and the New Jerusalem not an actual city, there is no ground for assuming that Babylon is anything but symbolical. . . . Here we have an apostate religious system, which is clearly identifiable with Papal Rome, although possibly covering far more than Rome."

Chapter 18 CONDEMNED BABYLON

Divine judgment overtakes the guilty city because of its boasted greatness, bewitching sorcery and martyrdom of the saints. The Babylon before us is the social and commercial one. This political and economic city, holding complete dominion and control over the financial and commercial affairs of the nations, is brought to nought in one hour. The description of the irremediable catastrophe, resulting in universal lamentation, is unmatched in the realm of literature. Monarchs, merchants, and mariners are caught up in the holocaust of destruction, while over such divine vengeance saints, apostles and prophets rejoice. Babylonian organization is rapidly developing today. Ruthless dictatorship and soulless political systems are with us, but God's day is coming, when He will suddenly destroy Babylon and its hordes.

Chapter 19 ALLELUIAS

What a marvelous doxology this chapter contains! Rejoicing ascends to God over the doom of guilty Babylon. It has been pointed out that "Hallelujah" occurs four times here, in reference to the victory of God over the earth, the signature of which is four. The marriage of the Lamb claims our attention. Among ourselves we speak of the marriage of the bride, but here it is the marriage of the Lamb. Why? Well, the chief joy is to be His! This is the blissful hour He awaits. When all the redeemed are around Him, then, and not till then, will He see of the travail of His soul and be satisfied.. From this bridal banquet, the Church goes forward to assist the Lamb in His governmental control of all things, as He returns to dispense wrath upon the unregenerate, and upon satanic forces.

Chapter 20 DOOMED DEVIL

The Apocalypse given to John is made up of sevens, among which we have seven dooms, four of which are in the previous chapter, and three here. The binding, loosing, and ultimate doom of the devil are herewith declared. And this is one reason why Satan endeavors to keep us from reading this book. He wants to keep us in ignorance of his real nature and deserved retribution. It is sad to realize that, after 1,000 years of Christ's beneficent rule, the earth will revolt. In spite of the blessings of the millennial Kingdom, human nature remains unchanged, and because of innate hatred of divine things, is easily deceived by Satan. The final doom of the Christless is a theme of most solemn import. Saved by grace, how grateful we ought to be that we shall not appear at the Great White Throne.

Chapter 21 NEW THINGS

At last, we are on the threshold of the "eternal day." The long anticipated "new heaven and new earth wherein dwells righteousness" come into view. Tears are all wiped away, and God is all in all to the glorified saints. By contrast, nothing but eternal desolation awaits the unregenerate, who are described in an eight-fold way. What hopelessness is wrapped up in "the second death," overtaking the godless! It implies eternal separation from God. Have you the assurance that your name is written in the Lamb's Book of Life? Do not be content just because it is inscribed on some church scroll. How dreadful it will be if, with all your religious associations, you are among those denied entrance into the Eternal City, seeing that Christ was not your personal Saviour! "Is your name written there?"

Chapter 22:1-7 PARADISE REGAINED

The last prophetic picture, that of the eternal joy of the millennial day, virtually concludes the book. What follows is an epilogue. What a sense of bliss and glory

are here unfolded! Paradise "lost" in Genesis is now "regained." The new paradise is to be "lighted directly by the presence and effulgence of God." Pre-eminent among the pleasures and privileges of His servants is the vision of the Lamb's face. Our eyes are to see the King in His beauty. "Face to face with Christ my Saviour, Face to face what will it be?" The glorious City, with its fruit-laden garden, will be wonderful to behold, but the sight of the Glorified One will eclipse all else. What unrestrained love and life await us! Encourage your heart with the blessed realization that earth's shadows will soon disappear. Glory is ahead!

Chapter 22:8-21 FAREWELL PROMISE

Within this epilogue of the most remarkable book in the Bible, we have a *last message*, a *last promise* and a *last prayer*. Three times over within the chapter, Christ declares that He is coming quickly, and in verse 17 we see the Holy Spirit and the Bride combined in their desire for Him to return. "The Spirit and the bride say, Come," which is not an appeal to the unsaved, but to Christ. The last word Christ uttered from glory was an advent one, proving how uppermost in His thoughts His coming was, as the Revelation closes, and still is. And John replied with the prayer echoing the desire of the Church all down the ages: "Even so, come, Lord Jesus." Then divine revelation closes with a benediction, in contrast to the old dispensation ending with a curse (Malachi 4). Dear Christian friend, are you ready for His coming?

Bibliography

Atkinson, Dr. F. C., *Exposition of Romans.*

Bunyan, John, *Pilgrim's Progress,* Zondervan Publishing House, Grand Rapids, n.d.

Calvin, John, *Commentary on the Psalms,* Eerdman's, Grand Rapids, n.d.

Darby, J. N., *Synopsis of the Books of the Bible,* Loizeaux, Neptune, New Jersey, n.d.

Eichhorn, *Studies of the Prophets.*

Ellicott, Charles J., *Commentary on the Whole Bible,* Zondervan Publishing House, Grand Rapids, 1959.

English, E. Schuyler, *Studies in the Gospel According to Mark,* Loizeaux, Neptune, New Jersey, 1943.

Gaebelien, Arno C., *Annotated Bible, Vol. V,* Loizeaux, Neptune, New Jersey, n.d.

Godet, Frederick L., *Commentary on the Epistle to the Romans,* Zondervan Publishing House, Grand Rapids, 1957.

Goodman, George, *Brief Bible Notes,* Pickering and Inglis, London, n.d.

Grant, Frederick, *Numerical Bible, Vol. III,* Loizeaux, Neptune, New Jersey, 1944-1953.

Gurnall, Wm., *The Christian's Armour.*

Harrison, Dr. Norman B., *His Very Own,* Moody Press, Chicago, n.d.

Henry, Matthew, *Commentary on the Whole Bible,* Zondervan Publishing House, Grand Rapids, 1961.

Ironside, H. A., *Daniel the Prophet,* Loizeaux, Neptune, New Jersey, 1953.

––––. *Proverbs,* Loizeaux, Neptune, New Jersey, 1952.

Jennings, F. C., *Studies in Isaiah,* Loizeaux, Neptune, New Jersey, n.d.

Keil, Carl F. and Delitzsch, Franz, *Commentary on the Psalms,* Eerdman's, Grand Rapids, n.d.

Kellogg, Wm., *Leviticus,* (Expositor's Series), T. and T. Clarke, Edinburgh, n.d.

Kitto, *Hours With the Bible,* Hodder, Stoughton, London, n.d.

––––. *The Pilgrim Bible,* Oxford University Press, New York, 1948.

Luther, Martin, *Psalms,* Concordia, St. Louis, Mo., 1955.

Maclaren, Alexander, *Expositions of Holy Scriptures,* Eerdman's, Grand Rapids, 1959.

––––. *The Psalms.*

McGee, J. Vernon, *Briefing the Bible,* Zondervan Publishing House, Grand Rapids, 1964.

––––. *Ruth, the Romance of Redemption,* Dunham, Grand Rapids, 1963.

Meyer, F. B., *Jeremiah,* Marshall, Morgan and Scott, London, 1960.

––––. *Our Daily Homily,* Zondervan Publishing House, Grand Rapids, n.d.

––––. *Philippians,* Zondervan Publishing House, Grand Rapids, n.d.

––––. *Tried By Fire,* Christian Literature Crusade, Fort Washington, Pa., 1962.

Morgan, G. Campbell, *Expositions of Holy Scriptures,* Revell, Westwood, New Jersey, 1959.

––––. *Great Chapters of the Bible,* Revell, Westwood, New Jersey, 1935.

Moule, H. C. G., *Epistle to the Romans,* Zondervan Publishing House, Grand Rapids, n.d.

––––. *Philippian Studies,* Zondervan Publishing House, Grand Rapids, n.d.

––––. *I, II Timothy,* (Cambridge Series), Cambridge University Press, Cambridge, n.d.

Paxson, Ruth, *The Wealth, Walk and Warfare of the Christian,* Revell, Westwood, New Jersey, 1939.

Pierson, A. T., *Keys to the Bible,* Hodder, Stoughton, London, n.d.

Perowne, J. Stewart, *The Psalms,* George Bell and Sons, London, 1879.

Pink, Arthur W., *Gleanings in Genesis,* Moody Press, Chicago, n.d.

Pusey, E. B., *Minor Prophets,* Baker Book House, Grand Rapids, n.d.

Rainey, Dr. Robert, *Romans,* (Expositor's Series), T. and T. Clarke, Edinburgh, n.d.

Robinson, George L., *Book of Isaiah,* Baker Book House, Grand Rapids, n.d.

Rolls, Dr. C. J., *Study of Jude,* Bell and Co., Sydney, n.d.

Scofield, C. I., *The Scofield Reference Bible,* Oxford University Press, New York, 1945.

Scott, Walter, *Exposition of the Revelation of Jesus Christ,* Revell, Westwood, New Jersey, n.d.

Scroggie, Dr. W. Graham, *Guide to the Gospels,* Revell, Westwood, New Jersey, n.d.

Simeon, Charles J., *Expository Outlines on the Whole Bible,* Zondervan Publishing House, Grand Rapids, 1955.

Spurgeon, Charles H., *The Treasury of David,* Zondervan Publishing House, Grand Rapids, 1955.

Tatford, F. A., *The Climax of the Ages,*

Zondervan Publishing House, Grand Rapids, 1953.

Thomas, W. Griffith, *Genesis – A Devotional Commentary*, Eerdman's, Grand Rapids, 1946.

Trapp, John, *The Sermons of John Trapp.*

Tucker, Leon, *The Wonderful Word.*

White, W. W., *Old Testament Studies*, International Committee of Y.M.C.A., New York, 1902.

Whyte, Alexander, *Whyte's Bible Characters*, Zondervan Publishing House, Grand Rapids, 1952.

THE BOOKS OF THE BIBLE OUTLINED

THE BOOKS OF THE BIBLE OUTLINED

GENESIS
Key Word – "beginning"
Primeval History   1-11
Patriarchal History   12-50

EXODUS
Key Word – "redemption"
The Exodus   1-18
The Law   19-24
The Tabernacle   25-40

LEVITICUS
Key Word – "holiness"
The Way of Approach to God   1-16
The Way of Abiding With God   17-27

NUMBERS
Key Word – "journeys"
The Old Generation   1-14
The Transition Era   15-20
The New Generation   21-36

DEUTERONOMY
Key Word – "remember"
Looking Backward   1-11
Looking Forward   12-36

JOSHUA
Key Word – "possession"
Entering the Land   1-5
Overcoming the Land   6-12
Occupying the Land   13-24

JUDGES
Key Word   –   "sin,   sorrow,   salvation,
  suffering"
Introduction   1:1-2:10
Cycle of Judges   2:11-16:31
Life in Israel in Days of Judges   17-21

RUTH
Key Word – "rest"
The Choice of Love   1-2
The Reward of Love   3-4

I SAMUEL
Key Word – "prayed"
Shiloh and Samuel   1:1-7:1
Samuel and Saul   7:2-15:35
Saul and David   16-31

II SAMUEL
Key Word – "sin and grace"
David as King of Judah   1-4
David as King of all Israel   5-24

I KINGS
Key Word – "glory"
Death of King David   1-2
Glory of King Solomon's Reign   3-11
Division of the Kingdom   12-22

II KINGS
Key Word – "word of the Lord"
Division of the Kingdom   1-16
Assyrian Captivity of Israel   17
Decline and Babylonian Captivity of Judah
  18-25

I CHRONICLES
Key Word – "temple"
Israel's Genealogies   1-9
David's Reign at Jerusalem   10-29

II CHRONICLES
Key Word – "revival"
Solomon's Reign   1-9
Judah's History to Exile   10-36

EZRA
Key Word – "rebuild"
Return Under Zerubbabel   1-6
Return Under Ezra   7-10

NEHEMIAH
Key Word – "so"
Building of Wall in Spite of Many Diffi-
  culties Was Completed   1-6
Wise Organization and Preparation Was
  Undertaken   7-12
Necessary Reforms Instituted   13

ESTHER
Key Word – "providence"
Feast of Ahasuerus   1-2
Feast of Esther   3-7
Feast of Purim   8-10

JOB
Key Word – "suffering"
Prologue   1-2
Dialogue   3-42:6
Epilogue   42:7-17

PSALMS
Key Word – "praise"
1-41 – *Genesis*, Generation-Degeneration-Regeneration
42-72 – *Exodus*, Ruin and Redemption
73-89 – *Leviticus*, Saints and the Sanctuary
90-106 – *Numbers*, Peril and Protection
107-150 – *Deuteronomy*, Precepts and Praise

PROVERBS
Key Word – "conduct"
Wisdom   1-9
Conduct   10-31

ECCLESIASTES
Key Word – "vanity"
The Theme   1:1-1:3
The Theme Proved   1:4-3:22
The Theme Unfolded   4:1-10:20
The Best Thing Possible for Man   11-12

SONG OF SOLOMON
Key Word – "verity"
The Inscription   1:1
The Bride in the King's Chamber   1:2-5:1
The King's Wife   5:2-8:14

ISAIAH
Key Word – "salvation"
Denunciatory   1-35
Historical   36-39
Consolatory   40-66

JEREMIAH
Key Word – "backsliding"
Call and Commission   1
Faithful Ministry   2-51
Captivity of Judah   52

LAMENTATIONS
Key Word – "destruction"
City as Weeping Widow   1
City as Veiled Woman   2

City as Weeping Prophet   3
City as Gold   4
City as Suppliant   5

EZEKIEL
Key Word – "Spirit of glory"
Preparation and Call of the Prophet, 1-3. The Appearance of the Glory of the Lord.
Prophecies of Destruction of Jerusalem, 4-24. The Departure of the Glory of the Lord.
Prophecies Against Seven Nations, 25-32. The Glory of God and Surrounding Nations.
Glorious Prophecies in Relation to Israel's Future, 32-48. The Return of the Glory of the Lord.

DANIEL
Key Word – "prophecy"
Historical   1-6, written by Prophet in Third Person.
Prophetical   7-12, written by Prophet in First Person.

HOSEA
Key Word – "return"
Personal 1-3. The Prophet and His Faithless Wife.
Prophetic 4-14. The Lord and the Faithless Nation, Israel.

JOEL
Key Word – "repentance"
Judgment and Repentance   1-2:17
Promise for Present and Future   2:18-3:21

AMOS
Key Word – "punishment"
Prophecies Against Surrounding Nations 1-2:3
Prophecies Against Israel and Judah   2:4-6:9
Prophecies Governing Times Previous to and During Messiah's Reign   7-9

OBADIAH
Key Word – "pride"
Edom's Humiliation   1-9
Edom's Crime   10-14
Edom's Doom and Blessing for Zion   15-21

JONAH
Key Word – "go"
A Man Running From God   1
A Man Running Back to God   2

EPHESIANS
  Key Word – "church"
  Doctrinal – The Heavenly Calling of the Church 1-3
  Practical – The Earthly Conduct of the Church 4-6

PHILIPPIANS
  Key Word – "joy"
  The Philosophy for Christian Living 1
  The Pattern for Christian Living 2
  The Prize for Christian Living 3
  The Power for Christian Living 4

COLOSSIANS
  Key Word – "pre-eminence"
  The Doctrinal Section 1-2:3
  The Practical Section 2:4-4

I THESSALONIANS
  Key Word – "second coming"
  The Return and Salvation 1
  The Return and Service 2
  The Return and Stability 3
  The Return and Separation 4
  The Return and Sanctification 5

II THESSALONIANS
  Key Word – "second coming"
  Consolation Under Persecution 1
  Consummation of Evil 2:1-12
  Closing Exhortations and Instructions 2:13-3

I TIMOTHY
  Key Word – "government"
  The Imperative Need of Sound Doctrine 1
  The Nature and Order of Prayer 2:1-8
  The Qualifications Necessary for Spiritual Oversight 2:9-3
  The Christian's and Worker's Spiritual Duties 4-6

II TIMOTHY
  Key Word – "ashamed"
  The Christian Minister and His Mission 1
  The Christian Minister and His Master 2
  The Christian Minister and His Message 3
  The Christian Minister and His Motive 4

TITUS
  Key Word – "behavior"
  The Importance of Sound Doctrine – An Orderly Church 1

The Dynamic of Divine Grace – A Sound Church 2
The Transformation of God's Children – A Practical Church 3

PHILEMON
  Key Word – "forgiveness"
  The Greeting 1-3
  The Character of Philemon Commended 4-7
  The Intercessor for Onesimus 8-21
  The Salutation or Epilogue 22-25

HEBREWS
  Key Word – "better"
  Doctrinal 1-10, Christ Is Better than Old Testament Economy
  Practical 11-13, Christ Brings Better Benefits and Duties

JAMES
  Key Word – "works"
  Christian Living Is the Subject of Scripture 1
  Christian Living Demonstrates its Faith by Its Works 2
  Christian Living Provides a Corrective for the Evil of the Tongue 3
  Christian Living Secures a Victory Over Satan 4
  Christian Living Is Sustained by the Lord's Return 5

I PETER
  Key Word – "hope, suffering, patience"
  Suffering and Salvation 1:1-13
  Suffering and Holiness 1:14-3
  Suffering and Fellowship 4
  Suffering and Glory 5:1-5
  Suffering and Humanity 5:5-26

II PETER
  Key Word – "knowledge"
  Moral Corruption 1:1-14
  Doctrinal Corruption 1:15-2
  Victory Over Corruption 3

I JOHN
  Key Word – "know"
  The Message of the *Logos* 1:1-4
  The Message of the *Light* 1:5-2:11
  The Message of *Love* 2:12-5:3
  The Message of *Life* 5:4-21

INDEX

INDEX